Baby Names around the World

Bruce Lansky

 **Meadowbrook Press**

Distributed by Simon & Schuster
New York

Acknowledgments

The lists of the 100 most popular girls' and boys' names in the U.S. were compiled by Michael Shackleford at the Social Security Administration. The lists are based on a 100 percent sample of births through the first nine months of 1998. The names are not grouped by variant spellings. (For example, Hannah and Hanna are treated as two separate names and ranked based on their individual popularity.)

The lists of the 10 most popular names from 1880 to 1990 are based on data compiled by the Social Security Administration and made available by Michael Shackleford. Thank you, Michael, for all your help.

Library of Congress Cataloging-in-Publication Data

Lansky, Bruce.
    Baby names around the world/Bruce Lansky.
       p. cm.
    ISBN 0-88166-329-8 (Meadowbrook). — ISBN 0-671-31658-3 (Simon & Schuster)
    1. Names, Personal—Dictionaries. I. Title.
  CS2377.L355   1999
  929.4'403—dc21   98-55766
                                      CIP

Editor: Liya Lev Oertel
Production Manager: Joe Gagne
Production Assistant: Danielle White
Cover Art: Amanda Haley

© 1999 by Bruce Lansky

All rights reserved. No part of this book may be reproduced or transmitted in any form or by any means, electronic or mechanical, including photocopying, recording, or using any information storage and retrieval system without written permission from the publisher, except in the case of brief quotations embodied in critical articles and reviews.

Published by Meadowbrook Press, 5451 Smetana Drive, Minnetonka, Minnesota 55343

BOOK TRADE DISTRIBUTION by Simon & Schuster, a division of Simon and Schuster, Inc., 1230 Avenue of the Americas, New York, NY 10020

03 02 01 00   10 9 8 7 6 5 4 3 2

Printed in the United States of America

CONTENTS

15 THINGS TO CONSIDER WHEN NAMING YOUR BABY

1. Namesakes

Exact reproductions of a person's name, even if it is followed by Jr. or II, are often confusing to everyone involved. Parents frequently vary the middle name of a son who carries his father's first and last names, and then call the son by his middle name to distinguish him from his father; but the potential for confusion still exists. What's worse, the child never gets the satisfaction of having a name and a clear identity of his own.

Namesakes can also lead to unfortunate name choices. Somehow the name Mildred just doesn't seem to fit a little girl comfortably, even though it fits eighty-year-old Aunt Mildred perfectly. Generally, make sure that a namesake's name is one you'd choose on its own merits, quite apart from the good feelings you have for the person you're complimenting this way.

2. Nationality

If you choose a "foreign-sounding" name, be sure it's not unpronounceable or unspellable, or the name will be a burden to your child. Combinations of names from different countries, like Francois Finklebaum or Marco Mazarowski, may provoke smiles. So if you want to combine names with different ethnic roots, try them out on lots of people before making a final decision.

3. Religion

To some parents it is important to follow religious traditions in naming a baby. Roman Catholics have traditionally chosen saints' names, sometimes using Mary as a first name for each daughter and pairing it with different middle names: Mary Rose, Mary Margaret, and so on. Jews traditionally choose Old Testament names, often the name of a deceased relative, while Protestants choose both Old and New Testament names. Muslims turn to the Koran and the names of Mohammed and his family as traditional sources of names.

4. Gender

There are two opposing lines of thought on names that can be given to boys and girls alike, whether they are changeable ones like Carol/Carroll, Leslie/Lesley, and Claire/Clair or the truly unisex names like Robin, Chris, and Terry. Some parents feel that a unisex name allows them to pick a name with certainty before the baby's sex is known and that such names "type" children in sexual roles and expectations less than traditional boy-girl names do. Others argue that it's unfair and psychologically harmful to require a child to explain which sex he or she is (remember the song "A Boy Named Sue"?). Finally, boys feel more threatened or insulted when they are presumed to be girls than girls do when they're taken to be boys.

5. Number of Names

No law requires a person to have three names, though most forms provide spaces for a first name, middle initial or name, and surname. When choosing a name for your child, you have several options: a first and last name; a first and last name and only a middle initial (Harry S Truman's S is just an S); initials for both first and middle names; or several middle names. Keep your child's lifelong use of the name in mind when you do something unusual—four middle names are going to cause space problems for your child every time he or she fills out a form!

6. Sounds

The combination of letters in a person's name can make saying the name easier or harder. Alliteration, as in Tina Turner or Pat Paulsen, is fine, but such rhymes as Tyrone Cohn or Alice Palace invite teasing. Joke names, punning names, and other displays of your wit may sound funny, but living with such a name is no laughing matter.

7. Rhythms

Most naming specialists agree that unequal numbers of syllables create pleasing rhythms. Such names as Dwight David Eisenhower or Molly Melinda Grooms fit this pattern. When first and last names have equal numbers of syllables, a middle name with a different number creates a nice effect, as in Albert Anthony Cleveland or Gail Canova Pons. Single-syllable names can be especially forceful if each name has a rather long sound, as in Mark Twain or Charles Rath.

8. Pronunciation

Nobody likes having their name constantly mispronounced. If you pick an unusual name, such as Jésus or Genviève (Hay-soos and Zhan-vee-ev), don't expect people to pronounce them correctly. Other names with high mispronunciation potential are names that have more than one common pronunciation, as in Alicia (does the second syllable rhyme with fish or leash?) or Shana (does the name rhyme with Anna or Dana?). And if you choose a unique pronunciation of a name (for example, pronouncing Nina like Dinah), don't expect many people to get it right.

9. Spelling

In his poem *Don Juan,* Byron writes, "Thrice happy he whose name has been well spelt," and it's true that you feel a special kind of irritation when your name gets misspelled.

Ordinary spellings have the force of common sense behind them. On the other hand, a new or unusual spelling can revitalize an old name. If the name Ethel only reminds you of Ethel Mertz in the old *I Love Lucy* show, but your mate is crazy about having a daughter with that name, perhaps Ethelle will be a happy substitute. However, some people think it's silly to vary from "traditional" spelling of names and are prejudiced against any Thom, Dik, or Hari.

10. Popularity

Some names are so popular you shouldn't be surprised to find more than one child with that name in your child's classroom. A child with a very popular name may feel that he or she must "share" it with others, while a child with a very uncommon name is likely to feel that it is uniquely his or hers. However, a child with a popular name may be accepted by peers more easily than a child with a very uncommon name, which may be perceived as weird.

11. Uniqueness

Did you ever try to look in the phone book for the telephone number of someone called John Smith? You wouldn't be able to find it without also knowing the address. To avoid confusion, many people with common last names choose distinctive first and/or middle names for their children. However, a highly unusual name, such as Teague or Hestia, could be an even greater disservice to your child than Michael or Emily.

12. Stereotypes

Most names call to mind physical or personality traits that often stem from a well-known namesake, real or fictional. Some names—Adolph and Judas, for instance—may never outlive the terrible associations they receive from a single person who bore them. Because the image of a name will affect its owner's self-image, as well as the way he or she is perceived by others, consider what associations come to mind as you make your selections.

13. Initials

Folk wisdom has it that a person whose initials spell a word—any word—is destined to be successful in life. But it can be irksome, even embarrassing, to have DUD or HAG stamped on your suitcases and jewelry. So be sure your child's initials spell "happy" words—or none at all—to avoid these problems.

14. Nicknames

Most names have shortened or familiar forms that are used during childhood or at different stages of life. For example, Michael might be called Mikey as a child, Mike as a teenager, and Michael on his college application. So, if you don't want your daughter to be called Sam, don't name her Samantha.

If you are thinking of giving your child a nickname as a legal name, remember that Trisha may grow weary of explaining that her full name is not Patricia. And consider the fact that names that sound cute for a child, as in Missy and Timmy, could prove embarrassing later in life. Can you picture Grandma Missy and Grandpa Timmy?

15. Meanings

Most people don't know the meanings of their names—first, middle, or last. But most names do have meanings, and you should at least find out what your favorite choices mean before giving them to your child. A name that means something funny or embarrassing probably won't overshadow your child's life, but if you have to choose between two names that are equally attractive to you, meanings may help tip the balance.

THE 100 MOST POPULAR GiRLS' NAMES iN 1998

1. Emily
2. Hannah
3. Samantha
4. Ashley
5. Sarah
6. Alexis
7. Taylor
8. Jessica
9. Madison
10. Elizabeth
11. Alyssa
12. Megan
13. Kayla
14. Lauren
15. Rachel
16. Victoria
17. Brianna
18. Amanda
19. Abigail
20. Jennifer
21. Emma
22. Olivia
23. Morgan
24. Nicole
25. Brittany

26. Jasmine
27. Stephanie
28. Alexandra
29. Sydney
30. Rebecca
31. Julia
32. Anna
33. Katherine
34. Allison
35. Amber
36. Kaitlyn
37. Haley
38. Destiny
39. Courtney
40. Danielle
41. Natalie
42. Jordan
43. Maria
44. Brooke
45. Savannah
46. Mary
47. Gabrielle
48. Sara
49. Madeline
50. Shelby

51. Kimberly
52. Vanessa
53. Sierra
54. Kelsey
55. Michelle
56. Erin
57. Grace
58. Melissa
59. Katelyn
60. Bailey
61. Andrea
62. Mariah
63. Paige
64. Jenna
65. Mackenzie
66. Marissa
67. Sabrina
68. Tiffany
69. Hailey
70. Christina
71. Laura
72. Makayla
73. Caroline
74. Sophia
75. Cheyenne

76. Caitlin
77. Breanna
78. Briana
79. Miranda
80. Alexandria
81. Autumn
82. Diana
83. Mikayla
84. Cassandra
85. Kaylee
86. Kelly
87. Chloe
88. Isabella
89. Katie
90. Kathryn
91. Erica
92. Alexa
93. Claire
94. Chelsea
95. Lindsey
96. Amy
97. Monica
98. Jacqueline
99. Alicia
100. Michaela

Sophie   Zoe   Ainsley

Callie   Carrie

THE 100 MOST POPULAR BOYS' NAMES IN 1998

1. Michael	26. Dylan	51. Sean	76. Luke
2. Jacob	27. Jordan	52. Juan	77. Jesus
3. Matthew	28. Samuel	53. Jared	78. Cole
4. Joshua	29. Jose	54. Gabriel	79. Stephen
5. Christopher	30. Kevin	55. Alex	80. Antonio
6. Nicholas	31. Noah	56. Richard	81. Garrett
7. Brandon	32. Benjamin	57. Patrick	82. Tanner
8. Tyler	33. Thomas	58. Trevor	83. Blake
9. Andrew	34. Nathan	59. Nathaniel	84. Kenneth
10. Austin	35. Hunter	60. Isaiah	85. Spencer
11. Daniel	36. Cameron	61. Jack	86. Mason
12. Joseph	37. Aaron	62. Carlos	87. Miguel
13. William	38. Ethan	63. Devin	88. Dalton
14. Zachary	39. Eric	64. Evan	89. Seth
15. John	40. Jason	65. Bryan	90. Paul
16. David	41. Brian	66. Mark	91. Victor
17. Ryan	42. Caleb	67. Isaac	92. Tristan
18. Anthony	43. Cody	68. Jeremy	93. Jeffrey
19. James	44. Logan	69. Chase	94. Alejandro
20. Justin	45. Luis	70. Angel	95. Bryce
21. Jonathan	46. Adam	71. Elijah	96. Lucas
22. Alexander	47. Steven	72. Ian	97. Brendan
23. Kyle	48. Connor	73. Adrian	98. Travis
24. Robert	49. Timothy	74. Jesse	99. Marcus
25. Christian	50. Charles	75. Dakota	100. Jake

Aidan

Avery

Clayton

Davis

Kellen Cooper Antione

MOST POPULAR NAMES FROM 1880 TO 1990

1880

Boys	Girls
John	Mary
William	Anna
Charles	Elizabeth
George	Margaret
James	Minnie
Joseph	Emma
Frank	Martha
Henry	Alice
Thomas	Marie
Harry	Annie, Sarah (tie)

1890

Boys	Girls
John	Mary
William	Anna
James	Elizabeth
George	Emma
Charles	Margaret
Joseph	Rose
Frank	Ethel
Harry	Florence
Henry	Ida
Edward	Bertha, Helen (tie)

1900

Boys	Girls
John	Mary
William	Helen
James	Anna
George	Margaret
Charles	Ruth
Joseph	Elizabeth
Frank	Marie
Henry	Rose
Robert	Florence
Harry	Bertha

1910

Boys	Girls
John	Mary
William	Helen
James	Margaret
Robert	Dorothy
Joseph	Ruth
Charles	Anna
George	Mildred
Edward	Elizabeth
Frank	Alice
Henry	Ethel

1920

Boys	Girls
John	Mary
William	Dorothy
James	Helen
Robert	Margaret
Joseph	Ruth
Charles	Virginia
George	Elizabeth
Edward	Anna
Thomas	Mildred
Frank	Betty

1930

Boys	Girls
Robert	Mary
James	Betty
John	Dorothy
William	Helen
Richard	Barbara
Charles	Margaret
Donald	Maria
George	Patricia
Joseph	Doris
Edward	Joan, Ruth (tie)

1940

Boys	Girls
James	Mary
Robert	Barbara
John	Patricia
William	Carol
Richard	Judith
Charles	Betty
David	Nancy
Thomas	Maria
Donald	Margaret
Ronald	Linda

1950

Boys	Girls
John	Linda
James	Mary
Robert	Patricia
William	Barbara
Michael	Susan
David	Maria
Richard	Sandra
Thomas	Nancy
Charles	Deborah
Gary	Kathleen

1960

Boys	Girls
David	Mary
Michael	Susan
John	Maria
James	Karen
Robert	Lisa
Mark	Linda
William	Donna
Richard	Patricia
Thomas	Debra
Steven	Deborah

1970

Boys	Girls
Michael	Jennifer
David	Lisa
John	Kimberly
James	Michelle
Robert	Angela
Christopher	Maria
William	Amy
Mark	Melissa
Richard	Mary
Brian	Tracy

1980

Boys	Girls
Michael	Jennifer
Jason	Jessica
Christopher	Amanda
David	Melissa
James	Sarah
Matthew	Nicole
John	Heather
Joshua	Amy
Robert	Mishelle
Daniel	Elizabeth

1990

Boys	Girls
Michael	Jessica
Christopher	Ashley
Joshua	Brittany
Matthew	Amanda
David	Stephanie
Daniel	Jennifer
Andrew	Samantha
Joseph	Sarah
Justin	Megan
James	Lauren

GENDER-NEUTRAL NAMES

In the past few years, the naming trends have been heading in less traditional directions. One of such trends is using gender-neutral names for both boys and girls. Below is a list of such popular cross-gender names. While **all** the names below are given to both boys and girls, some names are used **equally** by both genders, some are used **more for girls,** and some are used **more for boys.**

USED EQUALLY

Avery	Carey	Gurpreet	Kayle	Kirby	Mandeep
Britt	Casey	Harpreet	Kendal	Kristian	Regan
Brook	Channing	Jean	Kerry	Loren	Sandeep

MORE FOR GIRLS

Alexis	Aubrey	Jaime	Kelly	Mackenzie	Shannon
Ali	Carmen	Jamie	Kelsey	Madison	Shelby
Amandeep	Courtney	Jayme	Kim	Michele	Stacey
Andrea	Dana	Jessie	Leigh	Morgan	Stacy
Angel	Dominique	Jody	Leslie	Nicola	Stevie
Ariel	Elisha	Justine	Lindsay	Paris	Tracy
Ashley	Erin	Kacey	Lindsey	Robin	Whitney
Ashton	Jackie	Kasey	Lynn	Sandy	

MORE FOR BOYS

Aaron	Christian	Daryl	Frankie	Logan	Shawn
Adrian	Corey	Devan	Jan	Micah	Shea
Alex	Cory	Devin	Jesse	Michael	Taylor
Austin	Dakota	Devon	Joel	Noel	Terry
Blair	Dale	Drew	Jordan	Quinn	Tory
Bobby	Dallas	Dusty	Kendal	Randall	Tristan
Cameron	Daniel	Evan	Kyle	Riley	
Charlie	Darcy	Francis	Lee	Ryan	

In addition, various spellings of the same name influence how that name is perceived. Below are some examples of how a slightly different spelling determines whether that name is used for girls or boys.

GIRLS	BOYS
Adrienne	Adrien
Billie	Billy
Bobbie, Bobbi	Bobby
Carlyn	Carlin
Casie, Casy	Casey
Codi, Cody	Codey
Cori, Corie, Corrie	Corey, Cory
Dani	Danny
Darci, Darcie	Darcy
Dionne	Dion
Frances	Francis
Gabriell, Gabrielle	Gabriel
Geri	Gerry
Jacey	Jace
Jerri	Jerry
Jo	Joe
Juliann	Julian
Kalyn	Kalin
Kellyn	Kellen
Kori	Korey, Kory
Lani	Lanny
Loni	Lonni
Michell, Michelle	Michel
Randi	Randy
Ricki, Rikki	Rickey, Rickie, Ricky
Toni	Tony
Terri	Terry
Tori, Torrie	Torrey

HOW TO CREATE A UNIQUE NAME

Many parents believe that if they give their baby a unique name, their child will grow into a unique person. Of course, every child is born unique, but I don't doubt that a unique name can make a child feel special and proud of his or her name; or special and unhappy with his or her name.

As long as you understand that a unique name can have positive and negative consequences for the child, let's review some ways to create one:

1. Spell a traditional name in a unique way, but retain the pronunciation. For example you might want to use a phonetic spelling:

Britnee or Britni instead of Brittany
Dwain or Dwane instead of Dwayne
Jesica or Jessika instead of Jessica
Mikul or Mikl instead of Michael

2. Add a prefix, such as Da, De, Ja, Je, La, Le, Na, Ne, Sha, She, Ta, Ti, Tra, Tri, or Wa, to the beginning of a name. For example:

Leron instead of Ron
Deandre instead of Andre
Shakara instead of Kara
Shalena instead of Lena
Taleah instead of Leah
Wanita instead of Nita

3. Change the last syllable of the name or add a syllable to the end, such as al, do, el, elle, ika, ique, ita, etta, kita, on, na, nita, rita, shay, von, vonna, vonne, or yell. For example:

Davon instead Dave
Donaldo or Donyell instead of Donald
Erique instead of Erik
Sharika or Sharita instead of Shari
Wondetta or Wondelle instead of Wanda

4. Change the first letter or letters of a name. For example:

Devin instead of Kevin
Jarryl instead of Darryl
Maura or Naura instead of Laura
Nolly instead of Molly or Polly
Shavonne instead of Yvonne

5. Choose a word that describes a personal characteristic or trait you admire. For example:

Faith	Pride
Hope	Tuff

6. Choose a river, mountain, city, state, or country you like as a name. For example:

Capri	Montana
China	Nevada
Dakota	Rio

7. Choose an occupation or hobby as a name. For example:

Chantal	Rider
Fisher	Skipper
Hunter	Solo

8. Choose a weather term as a name. For example:

Aurora	Starr
Breezy	Stormi
Dawn	Sunny
Rainy	Windy

9. Choose some aspect of nature as a name. For example:

Fawn	Buck
Forest	Robin
Brooke	Skye

10. Choose the name—first or last—of an author, artist, musician, politician, or character in a book, play, or movie you admire. For example:

Celine	Prince
Kennedy	Ringo
Matisse	Shania
Monet	Sting

11. Choose the name of a product you like:

Chanel	Nike
Cheer	Starbuck
Hershey	Tide

12. Combine the names of the two parents into a name. For example:

Jamal or Jamali is a combination of James and Ali

Mardon is a combination of Mary and Don

Ronell is a combination of Ron and Ellen

After you've had your fun creating a unique name for your child, think again about the fact that your child will have to live with this name for a lifetime. And during that lifetime, tens of thousands of people will form an opinion about your child after seeing the name in print or hearing it. Think carefully about whether this name will give off positive or negative vibes—whether it will be a help or nuisance to your child when he or she is introduced to classmates on the first day of kindergarten or when he or she applies to college or for a job.

Remember, names don't make children unique; biology, parenting, and life experience do. So, pick a name that will present your child to the world in the best possible way.

BiRTHSTONES AND FLOWERS

JANUARY
Birthstone: garnet
Flower: carnation

FEBRUARY
Birthstone: amethyst
Flower: violet

MARCH
Birthstone: aquamarine
Flower: jonquil

APRIL
Birthstone: diamond
Flower: sweet pea

MAY
Birthstone: emerald
Flower: lily of the valley

JUNE
Birthstone: pearl
Flower: rose

JULY
Birthstone: ruby
Flower: larkspur

AUGUST
Birthstone: peridot
Flower: gladiolus

SEPTEMBER
Birthstone: sapphire
Flower: aster

OCTOBER
Birthstone: opal
Flower: calendula

NOVEMBER
Birthstone: topaz
Flower: chrysanthemum

DECEMBER
Birthstone: turquoise
Flower: narcissus

COUNTRIES/LANGUAGES REPRESENTED IN THIS BOOK

African

Abaluhya
Afrikaans
Akan
Ashanti
Ateso
Bambara
Benin
Dutooro
Egyptian
Ethiopian
  (Amharic,
  Tigrinya)
Ewe
Fante
Ga
Ghanian
Hausa
Ibo
Kakwa
Kikuyu
Kiswahili
Lomwe
Luganda
Lunyole
Luo
Muganda
Musoga
Mwera
Ngoni
Nigerian
North African
Nyakusa
Ochi
Rhodesian
Rukigo
Runyankore
Runyoro
Rutooro
Shona
Somali
South African
Swahili
Tanzanian
Tiv
Tswana
Twi
Ugandan
Umbundu
Uset
Xhosa
Yao
Yoruba
Zimbabwean
Zulu

Native American

Algonquin
Apache
Arapaho
Blackfoot
Carrier
Cherokee
Cheyenne
Chippewa
Choctaw
Comanche
Coos
Dakota
Dene
Eskimo
Fox
Hopi
Iroquois
Kiowa
Lakota
Lenape
Mahona
Mohawk
Moquelumnan
Navajo
Omaha
Osage
Pawnee
Pomo
Ponca
Quiché
Sauk
Shoshone
Sioux
Taos
Tupi-Guarani
Ute
Watamare
Winnebago
Zuni

East Asian & Pacific

Australian
Burmese
Cambodian
Chinese
Filipino
Fijian
Hawaiian
Japanese
Korean
Malayan
Maori
Polynesian
Samoan
Tai
Tibetan
Vietnamese
West
Australian
Aboriginal

Eastern European & Northern Asian

Armenian
Basque
Bulgarian
Czech
Estonian
Hungarian
Latvian
Lithuanian
Mongolian
Polish
Romanian
Russian
Slavic
Turkish
Ukranian

Western European

Cornish
Danish
Dutch
English
Finnish
French
German
Gypsy
Icelandic
Irish
Italian
Norwegian
Portugese
Scandinavian
Scottish
Spanish
Swedish
Swiss
Welsh
Yiddish

Middle & Near Eastern

Afghani
Arabic
Hebrew
Hindi
Pakistani
Pashto
Persian
Punjabi
Tamil
Todas
Urdu

South & North American

American
Peruvian

Historical Languages

Aramaic
Assyrian
Babylonian
Greek
Latin
Phoenician
Sanskrit
Syrian
Teutonic

NAME INDEX BY COUNTRY/LANGUAGE

Abaluhya

Boys
Jimiyu
Nangila

Afghani

Girls
Seema
Shahla
Yashira

Boys
Iskander
Matteen
Mirwais
Nadir
Yasir
Zalmai
Zelgai
Zemar

African

Girls
Afi
Ama
Baba
Halla
Imena
Kia
Pita
Poni
Reta
Sharik
Siko
Tawia
Thema
Winna
Zina

Boys
Afram
Bello
Kosey
Liu
Moswen
Ohin

Paki
Senwe
Ulan
Zareb

Afrikaans

Boys
Bron
Kerel

Akan

Girls
Morowa

Boys
Adom
Bodua
Donkor
Gyasi
Kojo
Kontar
Kwabena
Kwako
Kwame
Kwasi
Minkah
Msrah
Nsoah
Sono
Yawo
Yoofi

Algonquin

Girls
Odina

American

Girls
Abelina
Abianne
Abinaya
Adaya
Adriyanna
Ajanae
Akayla

Akeisha
Akeria
Akia
Akira
Alaysha
Albreanna
Alexanne
Alora
Amberly
Amberlyn
Ambria
Andee
Anetra
Annjanette
Areli
Arlynn
Babe
Babs
Baby
Barbie
Barbra
Becky
Betsy
Bettina
Beverlyann
Billie-Jean
Billie-Jo
Blinda
Blondie
Bobbette
Bobbi
Bobbi-Ann
Bobbi-Jo
Bobbi-Lee
Bonnie-Bell
Braelyn
Brandy-Lynn
Brenda-Lee
Brieana
Brooklyn
Brylie
Buffy
Caeley
Caelin
Cailin

Caleigh
Camara
Camberly
Camisha
Camri
Camryn
Candi
Carlisa
Carlissa
Carolane
Caylee
Chalonna
Chanise
Charnette
Charnika
Charyanna
Chavonne
Chesarey
Chessa
Cheyla
Cheyna
Cissy
Corabelle
Coralee
Coralie
Cordasha
Coriann
Corianne
Crisbell
Crystalin
Daelynn
Daeshawna
Dafny
Daisha
Dakayla
Dakira
Dalisha
Damonica
Danalyn
Danella
Danesha
Danessa
Danessia
Danette
Danice

Danille
Danyel
Darilynn
Darnesha
Dashawna
Dashonda
Davalinda
Davalynda
Davalynn
Davisha
Dawnisha
Daysha
Deandra
Debra
Dedra
Dedriana
Deena
Delacy
Denisha
Deshawna
Dolly
Dondi
Doneshia
Doniella
Doretta
Dori
Dyshawna
Eddy
Elnora
Elodie
Elora
Emilyann
Emmalee
Emmalynn
Emmylou
Fannie
Flo
Frankie
Geena
Genell
Genice
Genita
Gennifer
Geralyn
Geri

Glennesha
Glorianne
Ideashia
Iesha
Isha
Jacalyn
Jacelyn
Jackalyn
Jackeline
Jacki
Jacklyn
Jaclyn
Jacqulin
Jadelyn
Jaelyn
Jailyn
Jakelin
Jakki
Jaleesa
Jalena
Jalesa
Jalia
Jalisa
Jalyn
Jalysa
Jamani
Jamaria
Jamesha
Jammie
Jamonica
Jamylin
Janae
Janai
Janalynn
Janesha
Janessa
Janita
Jaquana
Jaquelen
Jarian
Jas
Jasmarie
Jatara
Jaycee
Jaydee

13

(American girls continued)

Jayla	Judyann	Keandra	Laneisha	Maitlyn	Quaneisha
Jalene	Jumaris	Keesha	Laporsha	Makaela	Quanesha
Jaylin	Kacey	Keisha	Laqueena	Makayla	Quanika
Jaylyn	Kaci	Keneisha	Laquinta	Makell	Quanisha
Jazlyn	Kadedra	Kenisha	Laquisha	Makenna	Queisha
Jelisa	Kadelyn	Kenyatta	Laquita	Malley	Quenisha
Jenelle	Kadesha	Keosha	Lashae	Mamie	Quiana
Jenessa	Kadisha	Kesha	Lashana	Marciann	Quinesha
Jenilee	Kaelee	Keshia	Lashanda	Marcilynn	Quinshawna
Jenisa	Kaelin	Keyana	Lashawna	Marieve	Quintrell
Jennilee	Kaelyn	Keyona	Lashonda	Marilee	Qwanisha
Jennilyn	Kailee	Keysha	Latanya	Marilou	Raeann
Jeri	Kailyn	Khrissa	Latara	Markayla	Raelene
Jerica	Kaishawn	Kiana	Latasha	Marquisha	Raelyn
Jerilyn	Kalee	Kianna	Latavia	Marybeth	Rashawna
Jerrica	Kalisa	Kineisha	Latesha	Maryellen	Rashel
Jessa	Kalisha	Kinsley	Latia	Maryjane	Rayanne
Jessalyn	Kalyn	Kiyana	Latisha	Marykate	Raylene
Jesslyn	Kameron	Kizzy	Latonya	Marylou	Reanna
Jetta	Kamri	Klaudia	Latoria	Maylyn	Reanne
Jevette	Kamryn	Kloe	Latosha	Mckayla	Reshawna
Jimi	Kandace	Kodi	Latoya	Mckell	Rexanne
Jimisha	Kandi	Kolby	Latrice	Mckenna	Rickelle
Jin	Kandra	Koral	Latricia	Mekayla	Ricki
Jinny	Kaneisha	Kori	Lavonna	Melly	Ricquel
Jizelle	Kapri	Kourtney	Lawanda	Melonie	Roanna
Jo	Karelle	Kris	Layce	Micki	Rodneisha
Jocacia	Kariane	Krissy	Lekasha	Mikayla	Rohana
Jodi	Karilynn	Kristy	Leneisha	Mikhaela	Roneisha
Jodiann	Karlee	Krystal	Lindsi	Minnie	Ronisha
Johnna	Karlene	Krystalee	Lissie	Moesha	Ronni
Johnnessa	Karley	Krystalynn	Liza	Monisha	Roshawna
Jolisa	Karli	Krystle	Lizzy	Myesha	Ruthann
Jolynn	Karlotte	Kyana	Loni	Mykaela	Sadella
Jonelle	Karolane	Lachandra	Lora	Myriam	Saralyn
Jonesha	Karolyn	Ladasha	Lorelle	Nakeisha	Satara
Joni	Karri	Ladeidra	Loren	Nakeita	Shaday
Jonika	Karyn	Ladonna	Lori	Nakita	Shadrika
Jonni	Kasey	Lajuana	Lorin	Nashawna	Shajuana
Jontel	Kashawna	Lakayla	Lou	Nekeisha	Shakarah
Joriann	Kassi	Lakeisha	Luann	Nichelle	Shakeena
Jorja	Kassidy	Laken	Lynda	Niesha	Shakeita
Josee	Kaycee	Lakendra	Lyndsay	Nikayla	Shakia
Josiane	Kaydee	Lakenya	Lyndsey	Nikki	Shalana
Joyanne	Kaylee	Lakesha	Lynsey	Nisha	Shaleah
Joycelyn	Kayleigh	Laketa	Lysanne	Nitasha	Shaleisha
Joylyn	Kayley	Lakresha	Macayla	Nyesha	Shalena
	Kaylin	Lamesha	Mackenna	Onesha	Shalisa
	Kaylyn	Lamonica	Mahalia	Quadeisha	Shalita

Shalona	Shug	Tina	Ceejay	Dewayne	Jayde
Shalonda	Sienna	Tinesha	Chuck	Dionte	Jayden
Shalyn	Sindy	Tinisha	Daequan	Diquan	Jaylee
Shameka	Sissy	Tiona	Daeshawn	Dontae	Jaylin
Shamika	Sueann	Tocarra	Daevon	Dontrell	Jaylon
Shamiya	Sueanna	Tonesha	Daiquan	Draven	Jayquan
Shanda	Sugar	Tonisha	Daivon	Dreshawn	Jayvon
Shandra	Sumaya	Tranesha	Dajuan	Drevon	Jazz
Shaneisha	Susie	Trashawn	Damarcus	Dushawn	Jequan
Shaneka	Sylvianne	Trixie	Damario	Dwaun	Jerrick
Shanel	Taesha	Tyanna	Dannon	Gabby	Jevonte
Shaneta	Takayla	Tyeisha	Dantrell	Gabino	Jimbo
Shania	Takeisha	Tyesha	Daquan	Hank	Jock
Shanice	Takenya	Tyfany	Dashawn	J	Jomar
Shanida	Takeria	Tykeisha	Davante	Jacari	Jontay
Shanika	Takila	Tykera	Davaris	Jace	Jorell
Shaniqua	Takira	Tynesha	Davion	Jack	Juwan
Shanise	Taleah	Tynisha	Davon	Jackie	Kacey
Shanita	Taleisha	Tyshanna	Davonte	Jacorey	Kadarius
Shantal	Talena	Unika	Dawan	Jadrien	Kaiven
Shantana	Talesha	Vantrice	Daylon	Jaelen	Kashawn
Shantara	Talina	Veanna	Dayquan	Jahmar	KC
Shanteca	Tamesha	Vianey	Dayshawn	Jailen	Keandre
Shantel	Tamila	Vianna	Dayvon	Jajuan	Kendarius
Shanteria	Taneisha	Voneisha	Dejuan	Jakari	Kenyatta
Shantesa	Tangia	Vontricia	Delon	Jakeem	Keonte
Shantia	Taniel	Wakeisha	Delshawn	Jalan	Keshawn
Shantille	Tanika	Waynesha	Demarcus	Jalen	Keyshawn
Shantina	Tanisha	Yaletha	Demarius	Jalin	Kishan
Shantora	Tanissa	Yamary	Demarquis	Jalon	Kyven
Shantrice	Tanita	Yamelia	Demichael	Jam	Labaron
Shaquanda	Tarissa	Yaneli	Demorris	Jamar	Ladarian
Shaqueita	Tashana	Yanet	Deontae	Jamarcus	Ladarius
Shaquila	Tashara	Yareli	Deonte	Jamari	Ladarrius
Shaquira	Tashawna	Yaritza	Deontre	Jamario	Laderrick
Sharissa	Tasheena	Yomara	Dequan	Jamarquis	Lanny
Sharita	Tashelle	Ysanne	Deron	Jamond	Laquan
Sharlotte	Tawanna	Zabrina	Desean	Jamor	Laquintin
Sharma	Tawnya	**Boys**	Deshane	Janeil	Larnell
Sharmaine	Teanna	Adarius	Deshaun	Jaquan	Lashawn
Shatara	Telisha	Ajay	Deshawn	Jaquarius	Lashon
Shatoria	Tenesha	Akshay	Deshea	Jaquavius	Lathan
Shavon	Tennille	Bubba	Deshon	Jaquon	Latravis
Shavonne	Teralyn	Buddy	Destry	Jareth	Latrell
Shawanna	Terriann	Buster	Devante	Jashawn	Lavaughan
Shelsea	Terrianna	Butch	Devaughn	Javante	Lavon
Sherylyn	Terrica	Caden	Devayne	Javonte	Ledarius
Shevonne	Terry-Lynn	Cayden	Devonta	Jawaun	Lequinton
Shiquita	Tichina	Cazzie	Devonte	Jayce	Leron

(American boys continued)

Leshawn
Levon
Lucky
Marquan
Marquel
Marquice
Marquon
Marshawn
Maverick
Montel
Mychal
Mykal
Naquan
OJ
Okie
Philly
Pinky
Quadarius
Quamaine
Quandre
Quantavius
Quashawn
Quindarius
Quintavius
Raekwon
Raequan
Raeshawn
Raishawn
Rangle
Raquar
Rashaan
Rashard
Rashaun
Rashawn
Rashean
Rashon
Rayshawn
Rayshod
Rayvon
Rebel
Red
Reno
Reshad
Reshawn
Reshean
Rishad
Rishawn
Rocky

Ronel
Ronté
Roshad
Roshean
Ryker
Sambo
Sanjay
Saquan
Savon
Shaheem
Shaquan
Shaquell
Shaquon
Shavon
Shawnta
Shiquan
Shon
Tadarius
Taishawn
Tajuan
Taquan
Taren
Taron
Taryn
Tashawn
Tavon
Tayshawn
Tayvon
Tedrick
Telvin
Tequan
Terrick
Terron
Teshawn
Tevan
Tevin
Tevon
Tex
Tiger
Tiquan
Tishawn
TJ
Traquan
Trashawn
Traven
Travion
Travon
Trayvon
Treavon
Trequan

Treshawn
Trevaughn
Trevin
Trevion
Trevon
Treyvon
Tyquan
Tyran
Tyrees
Tyrel
Tyrick
Tyrin
Tyron
Tyshawn
Tyvon
Vashawn
Woody
Wrangle
Zaquan
Zeshawn
Ziggy

Apache

Boys
Cochise
Nantan

Arabic

Girls
Abia
Abida
Adara
Adila
Adra
Afra
Aiesha
Aisha
Akilah
Alea
Alima
Aliye
Alma
Almeda
Almira
Amal
Aman
Amina
Amira
Anisa

Ara
Arin
Asha
Ashia
Aza
Bibi
Cala
Callie
Cantara
Elmira
Emani
Faizah
Fatima
Ghada
Guadalupe
Habiba
Halimah
Hana
Hayfa
Iman
Imani
Jalila
Jamila
Janan
Janna
Jarita
Jena
Jenna
Jesenia
Kadejah
Kadijah
Kaela
Kala
Kalila
Karida
Karimah
Kayla
Kaylah
Keila
Khadijah
Khalida
Laela
Laila
Lakia
Lamis
Lamya
Lateefah
Layla
Leila
Lila

Lilith
Lily
Lina
Lisha
Lucine
Lulu
Lydia
Mahala
Maja
Majidah
Manar
Maritza
Mariyan
Martiza
Marya
May
Maysa
Medina
Mina
Mocha
Mouna
Mumtaz
Muriel
Muslimah
Nabila
Nadda
Nadira
Naila
Najam
Najila
Nakia
Natara
Nekia
Nima
Nisa
Oma
Omaira
Polla
Qadira
Qamra
Qitarah
Qubilah
Rabi
Radeyah
Radwa
Rafa
Ráidah
Raja
Rana
Raniyah

Rasha
Rashieka
Rayya
Rida
Rihana
Rima
Rukan
Saarah
Saba
Sabi
Sabiya
Sadira
Sadiya
Safiya
Sahara
Saida
Salima
Sameh
Sami
Samira
Sana
Saree
Selma
Shahar
Shahina
Shakayla
Shakera
Shakila
Shakira
Shakyra
Shamara
Shardae
Shatara
Sherika
Shula
Skye
Sommer
Syreeta
Tabina
Tahira
Takia
Talitha
Tara
Thana
Ulima
Vega
Wadd
Waheeda
Walad
Xaviera

Yamila	Antwan	Hamza	Kalen	Mohammed	Rakin
Yaminah	Antwon	Hanbal	Kali	Mohamud	Ramadan
Yashira	Anwar	Hanif	Kalil	Mouhamed	Rashaad
Yecenia	Arif	Harb	Kaliq	Mousa	Rashad
Yemena	Asád	Harith	Kamal	Muhammad	Rashaud
Yesenia	Asadel	Haroun	Kamil	Muhannad	Rasheed
Yessenia	Aswad	Hasan	Kardal	Muhsin	Rashid
Yiesha	Atif	Hashim	Kareem	Muhtadi	Rashod
Zada	Azeem	Hassan	Karif	Mujahid	Rayhan
Zafina	Azim	Hatim	Karim	Mukhtar	Reda
Zafirah	Aziz	Hibah	Kaseem	Munir	Reyhan
Zahra	Bahir	Hilel	Kasib	Musád	Rida
Zakia	Basam	Hud	Kasim	Mustafa	Rigel
Zakiya	Bilal	Husam	Kasimir	Mustapha	Riyad
Zarifa	Borak	Hussain	Kateb	Muti	Saddam
Zaynah	Boutros	Hussein	Kayden	Nabiha	Sa'id
Zia	Cairo	Hussien	Kayle	Nabil	Salam
Zita	Caleb	Ibrahim	Khaldun	Nada	Sálih
Zuleika	Cemal	Imad	Khälid	Nadidah	Salím
Zulima	Coman	Imran	Khalíl	Nadim	Sameer
Zurafa	Dabir	Isa	Khaliq	Nadir	Samír
Boys	Daoud	Isam	Khayru	Naeem	Samman
Aaron	Dekel	Ishaq	Khoury	Nailah	Saqr
Abbud	Fadi	Ismael	Labib	Najee	Sariyah
Abdirahman	Fadil	Ismail	Lais	Naji	Sayyid
Abdul	Fahd	Jabir	Lateef	Najib	Seif
Abdulaziz	Faisal	Jabril	Lukman	Nakia	Shadi
Abdullah	Fakhir	Jamaal	Lutfi	Nasser	Shahid
Abdulrahman	Fakih	Jamaine	Mahammed	Nazih	Shakeel
Aden	Farid	Jamal	Mahdi	Nibal	Shakir
Adham	Faris	Jamel	Mahir	Nizam	Shakur
Adil	Faruq	Jamil	Mahmoud	Numa	Shaquille
Adnan	Fath	Japheth	Mahmúd	Numair	Sharíf
Ahmad	Fatin	Jawhar	Mahomet	Nuri	Shihab
Ahsan	Ferran	Jemal	Maimun	Nuriel	Shunnar
Akbar	Firas	Jemel	Majid	Nusair	Siraj
Akil	Gadi	Jericho	Makin	Omar	Sofian
Akmal	Gamal	Jermal	Malcolm	Omer	Subhi
Aladdin	Ghazi	Jibril	Malek	Qabil	Sued
Alam	Gilad	Jimell	Málik	Qadim	Suhail
Alem	Guadalupe	Jumah	Mansür	Qadir	Sulaiman
Ali	Habib	Kadar	Marid	Qamar	Syed
Alim	Haddad	Kadeem	Marr	Qasim	Tabari
Altair	Hadi	Kaden	Marwan	Qudamah	Tahír
Amal	Haidar	Kadin	Masud	Rabi	Talib
Amani	Hakeem	Kadir	Mazin	Rafiq	Tamir
Amar	Hakim	Kaeden	Mohamad	Raghib	Tarek
Amin	Halim	Kahlil	Mohamed	Rahul	Tarif
Amir	Hamal	Kairo	Mohamet	Raíd	Tarik
Amit	Hamid	Kale	Mohammad	Rakim	Táriq

(Arabic boys continued)

Taz
Thabit
Timin
Tut
Ubadah
Umar
Usamah
Uthman
Wahid
Waleed
Wali
Wasim
Wazir
Witha
Xavier
Yahya
Yardan
Yasin
Yasir
Yazid
Yusuf
Zafir
Zahid
Zahir
Zaid
Zaim
Zakariyya
Zaki
Zavier
Zero
Zimraan
Ziyad
Zuhayr

Aramaic

Girls
Beth
Bethani
Bethany
Mardi
Maren
Marit
Martha
Noor
Nura
Nuria
Razi

Samantha
Shera
Tabatha
Tabetha
Tabitha
Tabytha
Tameka
Tara

Boys
Barnabas
Og
Razi
Talmai
Talman
Tavares
Tavaris
Tavi
Tavor
Thomas

Arapaho

Girls
Natane

Boys
Hosa
Nakos

Armenian

Girls
Nairi
Seda

Boys
Dickran
Jirair
Kaloosh
Khachig
Krikor
Magar
Nishan
Shabouh
Vartan
Yervant
Zeroun

Ashanti

Girls
Kessie

Boys
Kesse

Assyrian

Boys
Abel

Ateso

Boys
Ejau
Opio

Australian

Girls
Narelle

Aztec

Girls
Xochitl

Babylonian

Girls
Eden

Boys
Shadrach
Shedrick

Bambara

Girls
Pemba

Basque

Girls
Floria
Julene
Kalare
Kesare
Landa
Leire
Lide
Lore
Lucine
Mendi
Molara
Ula
Xaviera
Yera

Yordana
Yulene
Zelizi
Zuri

Boys
Balasi
Dabi
Dunixi
Edorta
Edur
Errando
Erroman
Estebe
Exavier
Gilamu
Gilen
Iban
Ibon
Iker
Ilan
Ilari
Illan
Inigo
Jakome
Jerolin
Jokin
Kasen
Kelmen
Kemen
Kerbasi
Kerman
Kindin
Kuiril
Lander
Luken
Luki
Maren
Matai
Mikel
Ortzi
Palben
Patxi
Peli
Pello
Sabin
Sein
Todor
Txomin
Ugutz

Unai
Urtzi
Xabat
Xaiver
Xarles
Xavier
Xzavier
Yuli
Zadornin
Zigor
Zorion

Benin

Girls
Isoka
Oseye

Boys
Ode
Odion
Omolara
Osahar
Osayaba
Osaze

Blackfoot

Girls
Peta

Bulgarian

Boys
Andrei
Foma
Gedeon
Grigori
Ioan
Iustin
Kir
Matai
Mihail
Petr
Piotr
Veniamin

Burmese

Girls
Chun
Meit
Mima

Mya
Nu
Yon

Boys
Lin
Min
Myo
On
Saw
Tan
Than

Cambodian

Girls
Chan
Chantrea
Kalliyan
Kannitha
Tevy
Vanna

Boys
Arun
Bourey
Chankrisna
Dara
Kiri
Munny
Nhean
Phirun
Rangsey
Rithisak
Sovann
Veasna
Win
Yo

Carrier

Girls
Peni
Sadzi

Boys
Kuzih
Tadzi
Yakez

Cherokee

Girls
Ayita
Salali
Sequoia

Boys
Adahy
Cherokee
Tennessee
Tooantuh

Cheyenne

Girls
Cheyanne
Cheyenne
Chyanne
Shaianne
Sheyenne
Shianne
Shyann

Boys
Cheyenne
Hiamovi
Shayan
Viho

Chinese

Girls
An
Bo
China
Chu Hua
Chyna
Ciana
Hua
Jun
Lee
Lian
Lien
Lin
Ling
Mani
Marrim
Mei
Meiying
Nuwa
Ping
Shina

Shu
Syà
Sying
Tao
Tu
Ushi
Xiang
Xiu Mei
Yáng
Yen
Yín
Zhen

Boys
An
Chen
Cheung
Chi
Chun
Chung
De
Délì
Déshì
Dewei
Dingbang
Fai
Gan
Guotin
Ho
Hop
Howin
Hu
Jin
Jing-Quo
Joss
Jun
Kanoa
Keung
Kong
Kueng
Lei
Lí
Liang
Liko
Lok
Long
Manchu
On
Park
Po Sin

Quon
Shaiming
Shen
Shǐlín
Shing
Sying
Taiwan
Tywan
Wang
Wei-Quo
Wing
Yong
Yu
Zhìxin
Zhuàng

Chippewa

Boys
Namid
Ogima
Waban

Choctaw

Girls
Nita
Opa
Poloma
Tallulah

Boys
Koi
Nashoba

Comanche

Boys
Quan
Quanah

Coos

Girls
Yoomee

Cornish

Girls
Kerensa

Boys
Denzel
Denzil
Donzell

Czech

Girls
Anezka
Anica
Anna
Bela
Fiala
Gizela
Jenka
Jirina
Juliana
Katarina
Krista
Krystin
Magda
Markita
Milada
Milka
Ondrea
Otilie
Pavla
Reza
Rusalka
Ruza
Ryba
Teodora
Trava
Tyna
Vondra
Zusa

Boys
Adamec
Arno
Bela
Bobek
Brandeis
Cestmir
Dano
Durko
Edo
Eman
Erich
Ezven
Frantisek
Hanus
Holic
Honza
Ianos
Imrich

Izak
Janco
Jaroslav
Jindra
Jiri
Josef
Jur
Karel
Karol
Klement
Kuba
Ladislav
Lukas
Matus
Maxi
Milko
Miloslav
Miroslav
Noe
Ondro
Ota
Pepa
Rostislav
Rubert
Ruda
Salman
Samo
Slane
Tonda
Tynek
Vaclav
Viliam
Waltr
Zdenek
Zenda
Zlatan

Dakota

Girls
Kenda
Lakota
Macawi
Nahimana
Nokomis
Wakanda
Weeko

Boys
Ciqala
Dakoda

Dakota
Dakotah
Dekota
Hinto
Lakota
Tasunke
Tokala
Wicasa

Danish

Girls
Caryn
Helsa
Kara
Karah
Kari
Ovia

Boys
Anker
Aren
Argus
Espen
Gert
Ib
Jens
Jorgen
Kaj
Loritz
Lucas
Mette
Niels
Perben
Poul
Rasmus
Sakeri
Sören
Steen
Stetson
Tage
Torquil

Dene

Boys
Enli
Nalren
Yakecen

Dutch

Girls
Aleena
Aleene
Brandee
Brandi
Brandy
Hester
Lia
Loris
Mariel
Mariela
Marika
Mena
Sanne
Schyler
Skye
Skylar
Skyler
Trudel
Tryne

Boys
Brandy
Deman
Dutch
Gerrit
Govert
Haven
Hendrick
Henrick
Jaap
Jan
Jilt
Joop
Joost
Joris
Jurrien
Kees
Kerstan
Kleef
Kort
Laurens
Loris
Lucas
Marten
Mogens
Narve
Pieter
Ramone
Rip
Roosevelt
Schuyler
Schyler
Skelton
Skye
Skylar
Skyler
Skylor
Van
Vandyke
Zeeman

Dutooro

Boys
Kiho
Kugonza

Egyptian

Girls
Icess
Isis
Nenet

Boys
Ammon
Keb
Moses
Nen
Pinchas
Sef
Shen

English

Girls
Ada
Addison
Adela
Adele
Adelina
Adeline
Adelle
Adilene
Adison
Adria
Adriane
Adrien
Adrina
Afton
Agate
Aida
Airiana
Alden
Alfie
Alfreda
Alicia
Alina
Alisha
Alishia
Alison
Allysha
Allyson
Alonza
Alvina
Alycia
Anabel
Analisa
Anamaria
Anice
Anissa
Anka
Annabel
Annabelle
Annalisa
Annamarie
Annelisa
Annie
Anona
Anyssa
Arden
Arianne
Arleigh
Arlette
Artis
Ashely
Ashlee
Ashleigh
Ashley
Ashlin
Ashlyn
Ashten
Ashton
Ashtyn
Asia
Aspen
Aster
Aubriana
Audey
Audreanne
Audree
Audrey
Audriana
Avery
Bailee
Baileigh
Bailey
Baylee
Bayley
Berkley
Berlynn
Bernadine
Berni
Berti
Bertina
Bethann
Betty
Bev
Beverly
Billi
Binney
Birdie
Blake
Blakely
Bliss
Blossom
Blythe
Bonnie
Bradley
Braeden
Branden
Braxton
Bree
Brenda
Brennan
Brita
Britaney
Britani
Britany
Britin
Britney
Britni
Briton
Britteny
Brittini
Brittnee
Brook
Bryttani
Bunny
Cady
Caralyn
Carla
Carlee
Carleen
Carli
Carly
Carol
Carole
Carolyn
Carrie
Carson
Carter
Catherine
Chancey
Chanel
Chanell
Charla
Charlaine
Charlee
Charlene
Charlie
Chelci
Chelsea
Chelsee
Chelsey
Chelsie
Chenelle
Cher
Cherilyn
Cherish
Chrissy
Christine
Christy
Chrys
Cicely
Cinderella
Clare
Codi
Colby
Corliss
Cortney
Courtenay
Courtnee
Courtney
Cristy
Dae
Daisy
Dale
Dana
Daniella
Darla
Darnelle
Daryl
Davonna
Dawn
Dawna
Dayle
Daysi
Dayton
Deana
Deisy
Delaney
Delicia
Della
Delsie
Dena
Deonna
Devon
Devonna
Dixie
Domino
Dona
Doralynn
Dusti
Dustine
Earlene
Eartha
Easter
Eda
Edeline
Edie
Edith
Edwina
Effie
Elberta
Elisa
Elise
Elissa
Elizaveta
Ella
Ellen
Ellice
Ellie
Elva
Elvina
Emilee
Eppie
Erica
Erna
Ernestine

Essie	Hailey	Jaymee	Laurie	Madison	Nan
Estee	Haili	Jayne	Laury	Madisyn	Nanci
Ethel	Halee	Jaynie	Lauryn	Madyson	Nancy
Etta	Haleigh	Jemma	Lean	Mae	Nara
Evelin	Hali	Jeraldine	Leanna	Maggie	Natie
Evelyn	Halley	Jetta	Leanore	Maggy	Nedda
Evline	Halsey	Jill	Lee	Maia	Nellie
Faith	Happy	Joana	Leeann	Maida	Neva
Fancy	Harlee	Joanne	Leeza	Malina	Nollie
Farah	Harley	Jobeth	Leigh	Malva	Odella
Faren	Harleyann	Joby	Letty	Marabel	Olivia
Faye	Harriet	Joleen	Liana	Marcelen	Ollie
Felicity	Hattie	Jolene	Liane	Marci	Ona
Fern	Haven	Jonquil	Lilibeth	Marcy	Ora
Flair	Hayden	Juliann	Lillyann	Maretta	Orva
Florie	Haylee	Julie	Lin	Marge	Osma
Floris	Hayley	Kadie	Lindsay	Margery	Paige
Flossie	Hazel	Kady	Linsey	Margie	Paiton
Frannie	Heather	Kaltha	Lisa	Marian	Parker
Freddi	Heaven	Karalynn	Lisbeth	Mariane	Patia
Gail	Henna	Karsen	Lisette	Maribel	Patience
Gardenia	Henrietta	Kate	Liz	Maridel	Patty
Garnet	Hertha	Katee	Lizabeth	Marigold	Payge
Garyn	Hetta	Kathi	Lizbeth	Markeisha	Peace
Gayle	Holley	Kathryn	Lolly	Marla	Pierce
Gayna	Hollis	Katie	Lona	Marlana	Piper
Genna	Holly	Katy	London	Marlee	Pippa
Georgeanna	Hollyann	Kelsey	Lorena	Marley	Pollyanna
Georgeanne	Hollyn	Kenda	Loretta	Marlis	Presley
Georgene	Honey	Kendal	Louisa	Marlo	Primrose
Georgianna	Hope	Kendall	Love	Marsha	Princess
Georgie	Hunter	Kendra	Lucetta	Marta	Purity
Georgina	Ida	Kenenza	Lucille	Marti	Queen
Gerardo	Idalina	Kennice	Luella	Maryann	Queenie
Gilda	Idalis	Kim	Lulu	Mattie	Quenna
Ginette	Ilisa	Kimber	Luvena	Maud	Quinn
Ginnifer	Iolanthe	Kimberlee	Lyla	Maxie	Quintana
Ginny	Ivy	Kimberlyn	Lyndell	May	Rae
Giorgianna	Jamey	Kinsey	Lyndsey	Meg	Raeven
Golda	Jami	Kirby	Lynelle	Mercia	Ragine
Goldie	Jamia	Kortney	Lynette	Mercy	Raina
Graceanne	Jamilynn	Kymberly	Lynn	Merilyn	Rainbow
Gracie	Jan	Kyndal	Lynnell	Merry	Ramsey
Grant	Janet	Lallie	Mada	Mildred	Randall
Grayson	Janeth	Landon	Madaline	Millicent	Randi
Gypsy	Janice	Lane	Maddie	Millie	Raven
Hadley	Janie	Laney	Maddison	Minta	Ravin
Haeley	Janis	Lark	Madelina	Missy	Ravyn
Haiden	Jannie	Lauren	Madeline	Misty	Rayna
Hailee	Jayme	Laurianna	Madisen	Myla	Rayven

(English girls continued)

Reanna
Reggie
Regina
Remington
Rennie
Reyna
Rhona
Rina
Robbi
Roberta
Robin
Robinette
Robyn
Rodnae
Romy
Ros
Rosalie
Rosanna
Rosanne
Rosemarie
Rosemary
Rosie
Rosina
Rowan
Rowena
Royale
Royanna
Rue
Rula
Rusti
Sable
Sabreena
Sabrina
Sabryna
Sada
Saffron
Sage
Saige
Salliann
Sally
Saundra
Sawyer
Scarlett
Sebrina
Seelia
Sela
Shandi
Sharee

Shelbi
Shelby
Sheldon
Shelee
Shelley
Sherleen
Shirlene
Shirley
Shyla
Sibley
Sigourney
Sommer
Spencer
Spring
Stacia
Starla
Starleen
Starley
Starling
Starr
Sterling
Stockard
Stormie
Stormy
Summer
Sunny
Sunshine
Suzanne
Sybella
Tabby
Tacey
Taci
Taelor
Tailor
Taite
Talisa
Tallis
Tammi
Tammy
Tandy
Tanner
Tate
Tatum
Tauri
Tawni
Tawny
Taya
Tayla
Taylar
Tayler

Taylor
Teal
Tetty
Teylor
Timi
Timothea
Tinble
Topsy
Tori
Toria
Toriana
Torie
Torilyn
Torri
Tory
Tottie
Trilby
Tuesday
Twyla
Tyler
Tyne
Udele
Unice
Unity
Vail
Vanetta
Vanity
Velvet
Vina
Walker
Wallis
Wanetta
Waverly
Waynette
Wendelle
Weslee
Whitley
Whitney
Whitnie
Whittney
Whoopi
Wilda
Wileen
Willette
Willie
Willow
Wilona
Windy
Winnie
Winter

Wren
Wynter
Yetta
Yudelle
Zanna
Zelene
Zeta
Zina

Boys

Ackerley
Acton
Addison
Adney
Afton
Ahearn
Aiken
Alcott
Aldair
Alden
Alder
Aldred
Aldrich
Aldwin
Alfie
Alford
Alfred
Alger
Algernon
Algie
Alistair
Allard
Alston
Alton
Alvar
Amicus
Archer
Archie
Arledge
Arley
Arlo
Armstrong
Arnette
Art
Arthur
Artie
Arundel
Ascot
Ashford
Ashley

Ashton
Aspen
Aston
Atherton
Atley
Atwater
Atwell
Atwood
Atworth
Auden
Audie
Audrey
Audric
Averill
Avery
Ayers
Aylmer
Baker
Bancroft
Banner
Barclay
Barker
Barlow
Barnaby
Barnard
Barnes
Barnett
Barney
Barnum
Baron
Barric
Barrington
Bartlet
Barton
Bartram
Bassett
Bat
Baxter
Bay
Bayard
Beacher
Beaman
Beamer
Beasley
Beaver
Beck
Bede
Belden
Bell
Benoit

Bentley
Benton
Ber
Berkeley
Berry
Bert
Bertie
Berton
Bertram
Berwyn
Beverly
Bickford
Binky
Birch
Birkey
Birkitt
Birley
Birney
Birtle
Bishop
Blade
Blaine
Blake
Blakely
Blaze
Bliss
Blythe
Bo
Bob
Bobby
Bond
Booker
Booth
Borden
Bosley
Bourne
Brad
Bradburn
Braden
Bradford
Bradlee
Bradley
Bradly
Bradon
Bradshaw
Brady
Bradyn
Braeden
Braedon
Brainard

Bramwell	Byford	Clint	Darnell	Dwight	Emerson
Brand	Byram	Clinton	Darren	Dyer	Emmett
Branden	Byrd	Clive	Darton	Dyke	Emmitt
Brandon	Byrne	Codey	Darwin	Dyson	Eric
Brandt	Byron	Codi	Daulton	Ean	Erick
Brandyn	Cable	Cody	Dawson	Earl	Erickson
Branson	Cadby	Colbert	Dax	Earnest	Erland
Brant	Calder	Colby	Dayton	Easton	Erling
Brantley	Caldwell	Cole	Dean	Eaton	Ernest
Brawley	Calvert	Coleman	Dearborn	Ebner	Ernie
Braxton	Carl	Colley	Deems	Ed	Errol
Brayden	Carlisle	Collier	Del	Edbert	Erskine
Braydon	Carlton	Colson	Delbert	Eddie	Ervin
Brendan	Carnell	Colt	Dell	Eddy	Ervine
Brendon	Carson	Colten	Delton	Edgar	Esmond
Brennan	Carter	Colter	Delvin	Edison	Evan
Brent	Cartwright	Colton	Delwin	Edmond	Evelyn
Brenton	Carvell	Connie	Dempster	Edmund	Everett
Brewster	Carver	Cook	Denham	Edric	Everley
Brick	Case	Cooper	Denley	Edsel	Everton
Bridger	Cater	Cornwallis	Denman	Edson	Ewert
Brigham	Cedric	Corwin	Dennison	Edward	Ewing
Brighton	Cedrick	Courtland	Denton	Edwin	Fairfax
Brock	Chad	Courtney	Denver	Egbert	Falkner
Brod	Chadwick	Coy	Dermot	Egerton	Fane
Brodrick	Chance	Crandall	Derward	Elbert	Farley
Bromley	Chancellor	Crawford	Derwin	Elden	Farnell
Bronson	Chandler	Creighton	Deverell	Elder	Farnham
Brook	Channing	Cromwell	Dexter	Eldon	Farnley
Brooks	Chanse	Crosley	Diamond	Eldred	Farold
Brown	Chapman	Crowther	Dickson	Eldridge	Farr
Bryon	Charles	Culver	Dixon	Eldwin	Farrow
Bryton	Charlie	Cuthbert	Doane	Elgin	Felton
Buck	Charlton	Cutler	Dob	Elian	Fenton
Buckley	Chauncey	Daegel	Drake	Ellery	Field
Buckminster	Chaz	Daelen	Draper	Elliot	Fielding
Bud	Chester	Dagwood	Drew	Ellis	Filbert
Buell	Chet	Dalbert	Dru	Ellison	Filmore
Buford	Chick	Dale	Dryden	Ellsworth	Firth
Burgess	Chilton	Dalen	Dudd	Elmer	Fiske
Burke	Chip	Daley	Dudley	Elmo	Fitch
Burl	Churchill	Dallan	Dunley	Elmore	Fitz
Burleigh	Clay	Dallin	Dunstan	Elsdon	Fitzgerald
Burne	Clayborne	Dalston	Dunton	Elston	Fitzhugh
Burney	Clayton	Dalton	Durell	Elsworth	Fitzpatrick
Burr	Cleavon	Dalvin	Durward	Elton	Fleming
Burris	Cleveland	Dane	Durwin	Elvin	Fletcher
Burt	Cliff	Danforth	Dustin	Elvy	Flint
Burton	Clifford	Darby	Dusty	Elwell	Floyd
Butcher	Clifton	Darell	Dustyn	Elwood	Flurry

(English boys
continued)
Ford
Forester
Fowler
Frank
Frankie
Franklin
Franklyn
Fraser
Frayne
Freeborn
Freeman
Frewin
Frey
Frick
Fridolf
Fuller
Fulton
Galton
Gar
Gardner
Garen
Garfield
Garland
Garman
Garnett
Garrad
Garrick
Garren
Garroway
Garry
Garson
Garvin
Garwood
Gary
Geary
Geffrey
Gent
Genty
Geoff
Geoffery
Geoffrey
Geraint
Gerard
Germain
Gerome
Gerry
Gerson
Gib

Gibson
Gifford
Gig
Gil
Gilbert
Gilmer
Gipsy
Gladwin
Glanville
Glentworth
Godwin
Goldwin
Gomer
Gordon
Gordy
Gore
Graham
Grant
Grantland
Gray
Grayden
Graydon
Grayson
Greeley
Greenwood
Gresham
Greyson
Grimshaw
Grover
Guilford
Hadden
Haden
Hadley
Hadwin
Hagley
Haiden
Haig
Hal
Halbert
Hale
Halford
Hall
Hallam
Hallan
Halley
Halliwell
Hallward
Halsey
Halstead
Halton

Hamill
Hamilton
Hammet
Hammond
Hampton
Handel
Hanford
Hanley
Harden
Harding
Hardwin
Harford
Hargrove
Harlan
Harland
Harley
Harlow
Harman
Harper
Harris
Harrison
Harry
Hart
Hartley
Hartwell
Hartwood
Haslett
Hassel
Haven
Hawk
Hawley
Hawthorne
Hayden
Hayes
Hayward
Haywood
Hearn
Heath
Heathcliff
Heaton
Hedley
Henderson
Henley
Hewson
Hilton
Hobson
Hodgson
Holbrook
Holden
Hollis

Holmes
Holt
Horton
Houghton
Houston
Howard
Howie
Howland
Hubie
Hudson
Huey
Hugh
Hunt
Hunter
Huntington
Huntley
Hurst
Hutchinson
Hutton
Huxley
Hyatt
Hyde
Hyder
Hyman
Ingram
Iram
Irv
Irvin
Irving
Irwin
Isham
Ives
Jackson
Jacobson
Jagger
Jago
James
Jameson
Jamie
Jamison
Jarett
Jarrell
Jarrett
Jasper
Javaris
Jaxon
Jay
Jayme
Jaymes
Jeff

Jefferson
Jeffery
Jefford
Jeffrey
Jeffry
Jem
Jerald
Jerall
Jerel
Jeremy
Jermey
Jeron
Jervis
Jim
Jimmie
Jimmy
Johnson
Judson
Kane
Karson
Keane
Keaton
Kedrick
Keene
Kelton
Kelvin
Kemp
Kempton
Kendal
Kendall
Kendell
Kenley
Kenneth
Kenrick
Kent
Kenton
Kentrell
Kenward
Kerrick
Kerwin
Kester
Kestrel
Key
Kidd
Kim
Kimball
King
Kingsley
Kingston
Kingswell

Kinsey
Kipp
Kirby
Kirkland
Kirkley
Kirklin
Kirkwell
Kirkwood
Kirton
Klay
Knight
Knowles
Knox
Kodi
Kody
Kolby
Kole
Koleman
Kolin
Kolton
Korbin
Kordell
Kortney
Kourtland
Kyler
Kyndall
Kyne
Ladd
Laine
Lake
Landen
Lander
Landon
Landry
Lane
Langdon
Langford
Langley
Langston
Latham
Lathrop
Latimer
Laurie
Lave
Lawford
Lawson
Lawton
Layne
Layton
Lee

Leigh	Mansel	Moe	Orrin	Piers	Raymond
Leighton	Mansfield	Montgomery	Orton	Pierson	Rayne
Leland	Manton	Monty	Orval	Pitney	Read
Leonel	Manville	Moreland	Orvin	Pitt	Reading
Les	March	Moris	Osbert	Pollock	Redford
Lester	Markham	Morley	Osborn	Powell	Redley
Lew	Marland	Morse	Osgood	Prentice	Redpath
Lewin	Marley	Mort	Osman	Prescott	Reed
Lewis	Marlin	Morton	Osmar	Presley	Reeve
Lex	Marlow	Moss	Osmond	Preston	Reg
Lin	Marsden	Myer	Osric	Princeton	Reggie
Linc	Marsh	Nat	Oswald	Purvis	Reginal
Lincoln	Marston	Nayland	Oswin	Putnam	Reginald
Lindell	Martell	Ned	Oxford	Quentin	Reid
Linden	Marv	Nellie	Ozzie	Race	Remington
Lindley	Marvin	Nelson	Pace	Rad	Renfred
Lindon	Marwood	Nesbit	Paden	Radbert	Renshaw
Lindsay	Massey	Nevin	Padget	Radburn	Renton
Lindsey	Mather	Newbold	Paige	Radcliff	Rexford
Linford	Maxfield	Newell	Palmer	Radford	Rexton
Linley	Maxwell	Newland	Park	Radley	Reyes
Linton	Maxy	Newman	Parker	Radnor	Reymond
Linwood	Mayes	Newton	Parkin	Rafe	Reynold
Lister	Mayhew	Nichols	Parr	Raine	Rice
Litton	Maynard	Nick	Parrish	Raleigh	Rich
Livingston	Mayo	Niles	Pat	Ralph	Richard
Locke	Mead	Nixon	Patton	Ralphie	Richie
London	Mel	Norris	Payden	Ralston	Richman
Lord	Melbourne	Northcliff	Payton	Ram	Ricker
Lorry	Meldon	Northrop	Pearce	Ramsden	Rickey
Louvain	Melvin	Norton	Pearson	Ramsey	Rickie
Lovell	Mendel	Norville	Peers	Rance	Rickward
Loyal	Mercer	Norvin	Peirce	Rand	Ricky
Ludlow	Merlin	Norward	Pelham	Randal	Rider
Lyman	Merrick	Norwood	Pell	Randall	Ridge
Lyndal	Merton	Nowles	Pelton	Randolph	Ridgeley
Lyndon	Mick	Nye	Pembroke	Randy	Ridgeway
Lynn	Mickael	Nyle	Penley	Rankin	Ridley
Mace	Milborough	Oakes	Penn	Ransford	Rigby
Macon	Miles	Oakley	Perkin	Ransley	Rigg
Maddox	Milford	Obed	Perry	Ransom	Ring
Madison	Miller	Obie	Pete	Raven	Ringo
Maitland	Mills	Ode	Peterson	Ravenel	Rip
Malden	Milt	Odell	Peyton	Ravon	Ripley
Malin	Milton	Ogden	Phelps	Rawdon	Risley
Malvin	Miner	Olin	Philbert	Rawleigh	Riston
Manford	Mister	Ollie	Phineas	Ray	Ritchard
Manfred	Mitch	Onslow	Pickford	Rayburn	Ritchie
Manley	Mitchel	Ormond	Pickworth	Rayce	River
Manning	Mitchell	Orrick	Pierce	Raymon	Roan

(English boys continued)

Rob
Robbie
Robby
Robert
Roberts
Robin
Robinson
Robyn
Rochester
Rock
Rockford
Rockland
Rockledge
Rockley
Rockwell
Rod
Roddy
Roden
Rodney
Roe
Rollie
Rollin
Rollo
Roper
Rosswell
Roswald
Rover
Rowan
Rowell
Rowland
Rowley
Rowson
Roxbury
Royce
Royden
Rudd
Rudy
Rudyard
Ruford
Rugby
Rumford
Rush
Rushford
Rutherford
Rutledge
Rutley
Rycroft
Ryder

Rye
Ryerson
Ryese
Rylan
Ryland
Ryle
Ryman
Sadler
Safford
Sage
Salton
Sanborn
Sander
Sanders
Sandy
Sanford
Santon
Sawyer
Sax
Saxon
Scott
Scottie
Scotty
Seabert
Seabrook
Searle
Seaton
Sedgely
Seeley
Sefton
Seger
Seibert
Selby
Seldon
Selwyn
Severn
Seward
Sexton
Shadwell
Shandy
Shap
Shattuck
Shaw
Sheffield
Shel
Shelby
Sheldon
Shelley
Shelton
Shem

Shep
Shepherd
Shepley
Sherborn
Sherill
Sherlock
Sherman
Sherrod
Sherwin
Sherwood
Shipton
Siddel
Sidwell
Sinjon
Skeeter
Slade
Slater
Smedley
Smith
Snowden
Somerset
Somerville
Son
Sonny
Southwell
Spalding
Spark
Spear
Spence
Spencer
Spenser
Spike
Spoor
Sproule
Spurgeon
Squire
Stacey
Stafford
Stamford
Stan
Stanbury
Stancliff
Standish
Stanfield
Stanford
Stanley
Stanmore
Stannard
Stanton
Stanway

Stanwick
Stanwood
Starbuck
Starling
Starr
Steadman
Steel
Steph
Sterling
Sterne
Stevie
Stewart
Stillman
Sting
Stockman
Stockton
Stockwell
Stoddard
Stoker
Stone
Storm
Stover
Stowe
Stratford
Strong
Stroud
Stu
Stuart
Studs
Styles
Suffield
Sugden
Sully
Summit
Sumner
Sunny
Sutcliff
Sutton
Swaggart
Swain
Swaley
Swinbourne
Swindel
Swinfen
Swinton
Symington
Tab
Taffy
Taft
Talcott

Talen
Talmadge
Talon
Talor
Tam
Tammy
Taner
Tanner
Tannin
Tanny
Tanton
Tarleton
Tarver
Tate
Tatum
Tayler
Taylor
Tearle
Teasdale
Ted
Teddy
Tedmund
Teller
Telmo
Templeton
Tennant
Tennyson
Terry
Thane
Thatcher
Thaw
Thel
Theo
Thom
Thompson
Thorgood
Thorley
Thorndike
Thorne
Thornley
Thornton
Thorpe
Thurlow
Thurmond
Tieler
Tige
Tilden
Tilford
Tilton
Tinsley

Todd
Toft
Toland
Tolbert
Toller
Tom
Tomlin
Tony
Topper
Torr
Torrey
Townley
Townsend
Trader
Trae
Travell
Travis
Tray
Trayton
Tredway
Trevelyan
Trevis
Trey
Trip
Trot
Trowbridge
Troy
True
Truesdale
Truitt
Truman
Trumble
Trustin
Tucker
Tupper
Turk
Twain
Twitchell
Twyford
Ty
Tyger
Tylar
Tyler
Tylor
Tymothy
Tyrus
Udell
Udolf
Ulmer
Unwin

Upshaw
Upton
Upwood
Urbane
Vail
Vance
Vian
Vince
Vinny
Vinson
Wade
Wadley
Wadsworth
Wain
Wainwright
Waite
Wakefield
Wakely
Wakeman
Walcott
Walden
Waldron
Wales
Walford
Walker
Wallace
Waller
Wally
Walsh
Walt
Walter
Walton
Walworth
Walwyn
Warburton
Ward
Wardell
Wardley
Ware
Warfield
Warford
Warley
Warton
Warwick
Washburn
Washington
Watford
Watkins
Watson

Waverly
Wayland
Waylon
Wayman
Wayne
Webb
Webley
Webster
Weddel
Welborne
Weldon
Welford
Wells
Welsh
Welton
Wendell
Wenford
Wentworth
Werner
Wes
Wesley
West
Westbrook
Westby
Westcott
Westley
Weston
Wetherby
Wetherell
Wetherly
Weylin
Whalley
Wharton
Wheatley
Wheaton
Wheeler
Whistler
Whit
Whitby
Whitcomb
Whitelaw
Whitey
Whitfield
Whitford
Whitley
Whitman
Whitmore
Whitney
Whittaker

Wickham
Wickley
Wid
Wilbur
Wilder
Wildon
Wiley
Wilford
Wilkie
Wilkins
Wilkinson
Will
William
Willoughby
Wills
Wilson
Wilt
Wilton
Win
Winchell
Windsor
Winfield
Wingate
Winslow
Winston
Winter
Winthrop
Winton
Winward
Wit
Witter
Witton
Wolcott
Wolf
Wolfe
Wood
Woodfield
Woodford
Woodrow
Woodruff
Woodson
Woodward
Woodville
Woolsey
Worcester
Wordsworth
Worth
Worton
Wray

Wren
Wright
Wrisley
Wriston
Wybert
Wycliff
Wylie
Wyman
Wymer
Wyn
Wythe
Yale
Yardley
Yates
Yeoman
York
Young
Yudell
Yule
Zain
Zane
Zayne

Eskimo

Girls
Hiti
Kirima
Sedna

Estonian

Girls
Kati
Leena
Reet

Boys
Jaan
Juku
Leks
Nikolai
Peeter
Riki
Toomas

Ethiopian (Amharic, Tigrinya)

Girls
Desta
Louam
Maharene
Melesse
Seble
Selam
Zena

Boys
Beniam
Dawit
Hagos
Hakim
Kelile
Lebna
Mengesha
Ogbay
Semer
Tefere
Tekle

Ewe

Girls
Quaashie

Boys
Coffie
Lumo
Mawuli
Mensah
Quaashie
Tse
Yao

Fante

Girls
Panyin

Boys
Ata
Ebo
Fifi
Jojo
Kesse
Lado
Osei

Sisi
Twia
Yooku
Yorkoo

Fijian

Girls
Levani

Filipino

Girls
Mahal
Malaya
Rosario

Boys
Bienvenido
Honesto
Lauro
Matalino
Pacifico
Rosito

Finnish

Girls
Aili
Annalie
Kalle
Lusa
Maija
Marja
Meri
Mielikki
Valma

Boys
Antti
Eikki
Hannes
Janne
Juhana
Kalevi
Kelevi
Kosti
Lasse
Mikko
Nilo
Paavo
Reku
Risto

Taaveti
Taneli
Tapani
Tauno
Timo
Viljo
Yrjo

Flemish

Boys
DeWitt
Jenkin

Fox

Boys
Nashashuk

French

Girls
Abrial
Abrielle
Abril
Aimee
Alair
Alberta
Ambar
Amber
Ami
Angelique
Annette
Antionette
Antoinette
Ariane
Arielle
Armine
Auberte
Aubree
Aubrey
Aubrie
Audra
Avril
Babette
Belle
Bernadette
Berneta
Bertille
Bette
Billie
Blaise

Blanche
Blondelle
Briar
Brie
Brielle
Brienne
Brigette
Brigitte
Burgundy
Cachet
Cami
Camille
Camylle
Cantrelle
Caressa
Carol
Caroline
Cera
Cerise
Chablis
Chadee
Chalice
Chambray
Chandelle
Chantal
Chante
Chantel
Chantilly
Chantrice
Chardae
Chardonnay
Charla
Charlotte
Charmaine
Chauntel
Cher
Cherelle
Cheri
Cherise
Cherry
Cheryl
Christabel
Christelle
Christine
Cidney
Cinderella
Claire
Claudette
Colette
Cosette

Cydney
Daeja
Daija
Daja
Damica
Danielle
Danielle
Darcelle
Darci
Darielle
Darlene
Darselle
Daryl
Déja
Dejanae
Dejon
Demi
Denise
Denisse
Desarae
Deserae
Desi
Desiree
Dessa
Desta
Destany
Destinee
Destiney
Destiny
Destynee
Dezarae
Dior
Dixie
Dominique
Doreen
Elaina
Elaine
Elayna
Elise
Elita
Eloise
Ember
Emerald
Emmaline
Esmé
Estelle
Estrella
Étoile
Evaline
Eve

Evette
Evonne
Fancy
Fawn
Faye
Femi
Fifi
Fleur
Fontanna
Francine
Françoise
Frederique
Gabriel
Gabrielle
Gaby
Garland
Gay
Gena
Geneva
Genevieve
Genevra
Genovieve
Georgette
Germaine
Gervaise
Gigi
Guinevere
Harriet
Helene
Heloise
Isabeau
Isabelle
Ivette
Ivonne
Jackquel
Jacquelin
Jacqueline
Jacquelyn
Jacqui
Jae
Jaime
Jaimee
Jaimie
Jamee
Janel
Janelle
Janette
Janine
Jaquelin
Jaquelyn

Jardena
Jeanette
Jermaine
Jessamine
Jewel
Jolie
Josephine
Josette
Juliet
Karessa
Laine
Lainey
Laverne
Leala
Liana
Linette
Lisette
Lizet
Lori
Lorraine
Lourdes
Lucie
Lyla
Madelaine
Madeleine
Mallorie
Mallory
Manette
Manka
Manon
Mardi
Margaux
Margo
Marguerite
Maribel
Marie
Marion
Marjolaine
Marquise
Marvella
Maureen
Maurelle
Maurise
Mauve
Mavis
Melisande
Mérane
Merle
Michelle
Miette

Mignon
Mimi
Minette
Monet
Monique
Moriah
Moselle
Musetta
Nadette
Nadia
Nadine
Naeva
Nanette
Natalle
Nettie
Nichole
Nicki
Nickole
Nicole
Nicolette
Nicoline
Nicolle
Nikole
Ninon
Noelle
Nycole
Odelia
Odetta
Oralia
Orva
Padget
Page
Pansy
Paris
Parris
Pascale
Patrice
Pernella
Perri
Pier
Pippi
Pleasance
Precious
Questa
Quiterie
Rachelle
Racquel
Raphaelle
Raquel
Raula

Rayna
Remi
Renae
Renata
Renée
Renita
Richelle
Riva
River
Rochelle
Romaine
Romy
Rondelle
Rosabel
Rubi
Ruby
Rue
Russhell
Salena
Salina
Sarotte
Satin
Sebastiane
Shanta
Shari
Sharice
Sharita
Sharla
Sharlene
Shelley
Sheree
Sherelle
Sheri
Sherice
Sherissa
Sherita
Sherleen
Sherry
Sheryl
Sidney
Sidonie
Simone
Sinclaire
Solange
Solenne
Sorrel
Stella
Susammi
Susette
Suzette

Sydnee
Sydney
Sydni
Talia
Talley
Tallis
Tempest
Toinette
Turquoise
Vedette
Verna
Veronique
Vi
Vilette
Violet
Violeta
Virginie
Vonna
Vonny
Yvette
Yvonne

Boys
Adrien
Aimon
Alain
Alaire
Albert
Alexandre
Amando
Amato
Ames
Andre
Ansel
Antione
Antoine
Aramis
Arnaud
Aubrey
Audon
Avent
Averill
Aymon
Bailey
Bay
Bayley
Beale
Beau
Beaufort
Beaumont

Beauregard
Belden
Bell
Bellamy
Benoit
Berger
Bevis
Blaise
Boden
Boone
Borden
Bourne
Boyce
Briar
Brigham
Bruce
Byron
Cable
Camille
Campbell
Canaan
Cannon
Carvell
Cassius
Chace
Chaise
Chaney
Channing
Chante
Chase
Chayse
Chevalier
Chevy
Christophe
Clark
Claude
Coco
Colar
Cordell
Cornell
Cory
Coty
Coyne
Crepin
Curtis
Dandré
Darcy
Darrell
Darryl
Daryl

Dax
Dean
Deandre
Delano
Delroy
Demont
Deondre
Derrell
Derryl
Destin
Didier
Dominique
Donatien
Dondre
Drury
Duke
Duval
Edouard
Elroy
Émile
Étienne
Fabron
Fermin
Ferrand
Firman
Florent
Fontaine
Forest
Forrest
Fortune
Franchot
François
Fraser
Frayne
Frederique
Gage
Gaige
Garland
Garner
Garrison
Gaspar
Gaston
Gautier
Gaylord
Gedeon
Georges
Géraud
Germain
Gervaise
Ghislain

Giles
Gillett
Granger
Granville
Griswold
Grosvener
Guillaume
Guy
Hackett
Hackman
Hamlet
Hamlin
Harbin
Harcourt
Henri
Hervé
Hewitt
Holland
Hyacinthe
Jacque
Jacques
Jacquez
Jasper
Jay
Jean
Jehan
Jemond
Jerard
Jermaine
Jocquez
Jontae
Jules
Justis
Kristophe
Kurt
Kurtis
Lafayette
Lamar
Lamond
Lancelot
Landry
Laramie
Laron
Larrimore
LaSalle
Laurent
LaValle
Lavell
Leggett
Lemar

Leron
Leroy
Leverett
Lionel
Lourdes
Lowell
Luc
Lucien
Lyle
Mace
Macy
Mallory
Manger
Manville
Marc
Marcel
Marin
Marion
Markese
Markis
Marlon
Marmion
Marquis
Marsh
Marshal
Marshall
Martial
Martin
Maslin
Mason
Mathieu
Maxime
Melville
Merle
Merrill
Merville
Michel
Montague
Montre
Montreal
Montrell
Moore
Morel
Morell
Mort
Mortimer
Narcisse
Neville
Noe
Noël

29

(French boys continued)
Norman
Norris
Norville
Olivier
Orville
Page
Parnell
Pascal
Patrice
Pembroke
Percival
Percy
Pernell
Peverell
Philippe
Pierre
Pierre-Luc
Platt
Pomeroy
Prewitt
Purvis
Quennell
Quincy
Ranger
Raoul
Rapier
Raul
Rawlins
Ray
Raynard
Remi
Remy
Renard
Renaud
René
Renny
Reynard
Roi
Romain
Rondel
Ross
Roy
Royal
Ruff
Rush
Ruskin
Russ
Russel

Russell
Rusty
Saber
Salaun
Sargent
Satchel
Satordi
Saville
Scoville
Searlas
Sebastien
Senior
Sennett
Séverin
Seymour
Shantae
Sid
Sidney
Simeon
Sinclair
Sorrel
Stéphane
Sully
Sydney
Sylvain
Talbot
Talon
Tanguy
Telford
Tempest
Teppo
Thayer
Thibault
Thierry
Tiennot
Travaris
Travers
Trent
Troy
Tyson
Urson
Vachel
Vallis
Vardon
Vere
Verney
Verrill
Victoir
Warner
Wyatt

Yves
Yvon

Ga
Boys
Oko

German
Girls
Ada
Adalia
Addie
Adelaide
Adelle
Alberta
Alda
Alice
Alisha
Aloisa
Amalia
Amalie
Amelia
Amelie
Amilia
Amorie
Anna
Aria
Armine
Arnelle
Aubrey
Audris
Axelle
Babette
Barrett
Berit
Bernadine
Bertha
Berti
Billie
Birdie
Bruna
Brunhilda
Carla
Carol
Catarina
Charlee
Charlie
Christa
Clotilda

Dagmar
Delana
Delia
Derika
Dustine
Edda
Elfrida
Elga
Elke
Elsa
Elsbeth
Elsie
Elvira
Emery
Emily
Emma
Emmy
Etta
Everett
Fern
Fernanda
Freda
Frederica
Frederike
Fritzi
Genevieve
Geraldine
Gerda
Gertie
Gertrude
Gilberte
Gill
Gisela
Giselle
Gissel
Greta
Gretchen
Gricelda
Grisel
Griselda
Hedda
Hedy
Heidi
Helga
Helma
Hermina
Hetta
Hettie
Hilda
Hildegarde

Hydi
Ida
Ilise
Ilse
Ima
Imelda
Johana
Karla
Katrina
Keana
Klarise
Klarissa
Lamia
Landra
Lene
Lenia
Lenore
Leona
Leonie
Liese
Liesel
Lise
Lois
Lona
Lorelei
Lotte
Louise
Lovisa
Luann
Luanna
Ludovica
Luella
Lulu
Lurleen
Mallory
Malorie
Marelda
Margret
Mariel
Mariela
Marilla
Marlena
Mathilde
Matilda
Melia
Mena
Meryl
Meta
Mileta
Milia

Mina
Minna
Mitzi
Monika
Nan
Nixie
Odetta
Oma
Orlanda
Ormanda
Porscha
Quinn
Radella
Raena
Raina
Raymonde
Reanna
Resi
Reynalda
Richelle
Rilla
Roderica
Rolanda
Rolene
Rosamond
Rudee
Rue
Selda
Selma
Sigreda
Sigmunda
Stina
Tilda
Tillie
Trudy
Ulla
Ulrica
Ulva
Unna
Uta
Vala
Valda
Vanda
Velda
Velma
Vilhelmina
Vilma
Walda
Wanda
Wandie

Warda
Wilda
Wilhelmina
Willa
Wilma
Win
Winifred
Winola
Yseult
Zelda
Zelma

Boys
Abel
Abelard
Addy
Adelard
Adler
Adolf
Adolph
Aimery
Alaric
Albern
Albert
Aldair
Alder
Aldous
Aleric
Alger
Algis
Alois
Aloysius
Alphonse
Altman
Alvan
Alvin
Alwin
Amory
Anno
Anselm
Anson
Archibald
Archie
Aric
Arlo
Armand
Arne
Arnie
Arno
Arnold

Arnulfo
Arvin
Auberon
Aubrey
Audie
Aurick
Axel
Baden
Baldemar
Baldric
Baldwin
Ballard
Bardolf
Barnum
Baron
Barrett
Bastien
Benedikt
Berg
Bergen
Berl
Berlyn
Bern
Bernal
Bernard
Bernie
Bert
Berthold
Bertram
Bertrand
Bill
Billy
Bing
Bogart
Bruno
Bryon
Buck
Buell
Burke
Burl
Carl
Carroll
Casper
Chadrick
Charles
Charlie
Claus
Clovis
Conrad
Cort

Darick
Dedrick
Dereck
Derek
Deric
Derrek
Derrick
Detrick
Dick
Diedrich
Dietbald
Dieter
Dino
Dirk
Dolf
Dustin
Eberhard
Edel
Eginhard
Egon
Ehren
Elger
Ellard
Elman
Emerson
Emery
Emil
Emmett
Emmitt
Emory
Emrick
Engelbert
Erbert
Erhard
Eric
Erich
Ernst
Eugen
Everardo
Ewald
Faber
Faxon
Ferdinand
Finn
Folke
Fonso
Fonzie
Franz
Fred
Freddie

Freddy
Frederic
Frederick
Frederik
Fredrick
Fremont
Friedrich
Fritz
Fulbright
Gary
Gerald
Gerhard
Gert
Gilen
Goddard
Godfrey
Gottfried
Gotzon
Griswold
Guthrie
Guy
Hackett
Hackman
Hagan
Hamlet
Hamlin
Handel
Hanno
Harbin
Hardy
Hartman
Hartwig
Harvey
Hassel
Heinrich
Heinz
Helmer
Helmut
Henning
Henry
Herb
Herbert
Herman
Hernan
Herrick
Hewitt
Hildebrand
Hilliard
Hobart
Hobert

Horst
Howe
Hubbard
Hubert
Hulbert
Humbert
Humphrey
Ingelbert
Ivo
Jaegar
Jarman
Jarvis
Jerry
Johan
Johannes
Jupp
Kai
Kaiser
Karl
Kasper
Kass
Kay
Keane
Keene
Keiffer
Kelby
Kiefer
Klaus
Konrad
Konstantin
Korb
Kort
Krischan
Kurt
Lamar
Lambert
Lance
Len
Lenard
Lenny
Leo
Leon
Leonard
Leonhard
Leopold
Lindberg
Linfred
Lonnie
Lonzo
Loring

Lothar
Lou
Loudon
Louie
Louis
Lucas
Ludovic
Ludwig
Luther
Macon
Mallory
Mandel
Manheim
Mann
Manny
Mathe
Matheu
Mathias
Mauritz
Medgar
Medwin
Meinhard
Meinrad
Menz
Meyer
Miles
Milko
Milo
Moritz
Myles
Nando
Nardo
Oberon
Obert
Odolf
Onofrio
Orlando
Orman
Othman
Otis
Otto
Ottokar
Paulin
Penn
Penrod
Pepin
Philipp
Pippin
Poldi
Pollard

(German boys continued)

Raimund
Rainer
Rainey
Redmond
Reinhart
Richart
Richmond
Rick
Rigoberto
Ritter
Roderich
Roderick
Rodger
Rodman
Rodrick
Rodrik
Roger
Roland
Rolf
Rory
Roth
Rowland
Rudolf
Rudolph
Ruland
Rune
Rupert
Ruprecht
Schafer
Schmidt
Schneider
Schön
Seifert
Selig
Sepp
Shon
Siegfried
Sig
Sigifredo
Siggy
Sigmund
Sigurd
Sigwald
Spangler
Stark
Steen
Stefan
Stein

Stern
Stoffel
Strom
Tab
Talbert
Tarell
Terell
Terrell
Terrill
Tewdor
Theobald
Theodoric
Thoma
Till
Tomas
Toni
Traugott
Udo
Ulbrecht
Ulf
Ulfred
Ulger
Ullock
Ulmo
Ulric
Ulrich
Uwe
Varick
Vasyl
Vernados
Verner
Verrill
Viktor
Vilhelm
Volker
Volney
Von
Wagner
Waldemar
Waldo
Walfred
Wallach
Waller
Walmond
Walter
Walther
Warner
Warren
Weber
Welby

Wendell
Wies
Wilbert
Wilfred
Wilhelm
Willard
Willem
Williams
Willie
Willis
Wilmer
Winfried
Wolf
Wolfgang
Wouter
Yale
Yoan
Yohan
Zacharias
Zamiel

Ghanian

Girls
Effia

Boys
Fynn
Manu
Odom
Tano
Tuaco

Gothic

Boys
Attila

Greek

Girls
Aalisha
Acacia
Adair
Adara
Addie
Adrienne
Afrodite
Agatha
Agathe
Aggie
Agnes

Alcina
Aleasha
Alecia
Aleisha
Aleksandra
Alesia
Alessa
Aleta
Alethea
Alex
Alexa
Alexandra
Alexandrea
Alexandria
Alexandrine
Alexas
Alexi
Alexia
Alexis
Alexius
Alexsandra
Alexzandra
Alexsis
Alexys
Ali
Alice
Alie
Aliesha
Alisa
Alise
Alisha
Alix
Alixandra
Alli
Allise
Allissa
Allysa
Alpha
Althea
Alysa
Alysha
Alyssa
Alysse
Alyx
Alyxandra
Amairani
Amara
Amari
Amaryllis
Anastacia

Anastasia
Anatola
Andrea
Andreana
Andreane
Andria
Andriana
Aneesa
Anessa
Angel
Angela
Angelia
Angelica
Angie
Anjelica
Anthea
Antonia
Aretha
Ariadne
Ariana
Arista
Asia
Astra
Atalanta
Athena
Aundrea
Aura
Ava
Belen
Berenice
Bernice
Beryl
Bunny
Calandra
Cali
Callie
Callista
Calypso
Candace
Candice
Carina
Carisa
Carissa
Casandra
Casey
Cass
Cassandra
Cassaundra
Cassia
Cassie

Cassiopeia
Cassondra
Catharine
Catherine
Cathi
Cathrine
Cathryn
Celena
Celene
Celina
Celine
Charis
Charissa
Cherese
Chloe
Chloris
Chris
Chrissa
Christain
Christen
Christena
Christi
Christian
Christin
Christina
Christophe
Christyn
Cindy
Cinthia
Clairissa
Clarisa
Clarissa
Clea
Cleo
Cleone
Cleopatra
Cleta
Clio
Cloe
Colette
Cora
Coretta
Corey
Corina
Corinne
Corissa
Corrina
Cristina
Crystina
Cybele

Cyndi	Elissa	Kandace	Lexis	Melissa	Panthea
Cynthia	Ella	Kara	Lexus	Melita	Parthenia
Cyrilla	Esmeralda	Karah	Lia	Melody	Pasha
Dacey	Eudora	Karen	Licia	Melyssa	Patra
Damaris	Eugenia	Kari	Lida	Mena	Peggy
Damiana	Eugenie	Karis	Lidia	Milena	Pelagia
Danae	Eulalia	Karissa	Lina	Milissa	Penelope
Daphne	Eunice	Kasandra	Lissa	Millicent	Penny
Daphnee	Euphemia	Kassandra	Loris	Mindy	Peony
Daria	Eurydice	Kate	Lotus	Mona	Peri
Darian	Eustacia	Katharine	Lycoris	Monica	Pernella
Darien	Eva	Katherine	Lyda	Mylene	Perri
Daryn	Evangelina	Kathrine	Lydia	Myrtle	Persephone
Deitra	Evania	Katlyn	Lyra	Naida	Petra
Delfina	Fantasia	Kay	Lysandra	Naiya	Petronella
Delia	Feodora	Kearsten	Madalyn	Nani	Phaedra
Delphine	Gaea	Kineta	Madeline	Nara	Phebe
Delta	Galen	Kirsten	Madelyn	Narcissa	Pheodora
Demetria	Galena	Kirstyn	Madge	Nastasia	Philana
Demi	Gemini	Kitty	Madilyn	Nelle	Philantha
Dessa	Georgia	Kora	Madolyn	Neola	Philippa
Diantha	Hadriane	Korina	Magan	Neona	Philomena
Dionna	Haidee	Korine	Magdalen	Nereida	Phoebe
Dionne	Hedy	Kosma	Magdalena	Nerine	Phylicia
Dodie	Helen	Kristan	Maggie	Nerissa	Phyllida
Dora	Helena	Kristen	Maia	Nessa	Phyllis
Doreen	Hera	Kristian	Maida	Nike	Psyche
Doria	Hermia	Kristina	Maiya	Nitsa	Pyralis
Dorian	Hermione	Kristyn	Mala	Nora	Rasia
Doris	Hilary	Krysten	Malinda	Nyssa	Rea
Dorothea	Hyacinth	Krystian	Malissa	Obelia	Reena
Dorothy	Ianthe	Krystina	Mara	Oceana	Rene
Dorrit	Ilena	Kynthia	Margaret	Odele	Reyna
Dottie	Iliana	Kyra	Margarit	Odelia	Rhea
Drew	Iola	Lacey	Maris	Odessa	Rheanna
Ebone	Iona	Lalita	Marjorie	Ofelia	Rhoda
Eboni	Iphigenia	Lara	Marlene	Ola	Rissa
Ebony	Irene	Larina	Marmara	Olesia	Rita
Echo	Iris	Larisa	Maya	Olinda	Ritsa
Edrianna	Jacey	Larissa	Mead	Olympia	Riza
Effie	Jaci	Leanore	Medea	Omega	Ronaele
Elana	Jacinda	Leda	Medora	Ophelia	Saba
Eleanor	Jolanda	Lelia	Megan	Ora	Sandi
Eleanora	Kacia	Lena	Megara	Orea	Sandra
Electra	Kaia	Leonore	Melanie	Oretha	Sandrea
Elena	Kairos	Leora	Melantha	Orsa	Sandrica
Eleni	Kalli	Leta	Melba	Pallas	Sandrine
Elexis	Kalliope	Lexandra	Melina	Pamela	Sandy
Elexus	Kallista	Lexi	Melinda	Pandora	Sapphire
Elisha	Kalyca	Lexia	Melisa	Pansy	Sebastiane

(Greek girls continued)

Seema
Selena
Selene
Selina
Serilda
Sibley
Sirena
Sofia
Sondra
Sonya
Sophia
Sophie
Sophronia
Stacey
Staci
Stasya
Stefani
Stefanie
Stefany
Steffi
Stephani
Stephanie
Stephany
Stephene
Stephenie
Stephney
Stevie
Sula
Sybil
Symphony
Tabatha
Tabetha
Tabitha
Tabytha
Tahlia
Talia
Taliyah
Tansy
Tasha
Tassos
Tecla
Teddi
Tedra
Teona
Teresa
Terese
Teri
Terrelle

Terri
Terry
Tess
Tessa
Tessie
Thaddea
Thalassa
Thalia
Thea
Thelma
Theodora
Theone
Theophania
Theophila
Theresa
Therese
Theta
Thetis
Tia
Tiana
Tiauna
Tiffany
Tita
Titania
Titiana
Tiyana
Toni
Tracey
Tracy
Tresha
Tressa
Triana
Trice
Trina
Trini
Tryna
Tytiana
Urania
Ursa
Ursula
Vanesa
Vanessa
Vanna
Vannesa
Vorsila
Xandra
Xanthe
Xanthippe
Xena
Xenia

Xylia
Yalanda
Yalena
Yolanda
Yolie
Zandra
Zanthe
Zena
Zenaide
Zenobia
Zephania
Zephyr
Zina
Zoe
Zoey
Zondra

Boys

Achilles
Adon
Adonis
Adrian
Aeneas
Agamemnon
Alcandor
Alec
Aleksandar
Alekzander
Alex
Alexander
Alexandro
Alexi
Alexis
Alic
Alisander
Alixander
Altair
Ambrose
Anastasius
Anatole
Andonios
Andrea
Andreas
Andrew
Andy
Anfernee
Angel
Annas
Antares
Anthany

Anthonie
Anthony
Apollo
Aretino
Ari
Arian
Aries
Arion
Aristides
Arsenio
Artemus
Athan
Atlas
Aundre
Avel
Aymil
Baltazar
Balthasar
Barnabas
Basil
Belen
Binkentios
Bishop
Cadmus
Carey
Cornelius
Carsten
Castor
Cerek
Chris
Christain
Christian
Christien
Christofer
Christopher
Christophoros
Christos
Cleon
Cletus
Cole
Colin
Collins
Colson
Cornelius
Corydon
Cosmo
Costa
Cristian
Cristobal
Cristopher

Cyrano
Cyril
Daemon
Daimian
Daimon
Dametrius
Damian
Damien
Damion
Damon
Darius
Darrick
Darrius
Daymian
Deacon
Deion
Demetri
Demetris
Demetrius
Demos
Denis
Dennis
Denny
Deon
Dimitrios
Dimitrius
Dinos
Diogenes
Dion
Dionysus
Doran
Dorian
Elias
Elmo
Eneas
Ennis
Enrikos
Erasmus
Erastus
Euclid
Eugene
Eustace
Evagelos
Feoras
Filip
Gale
Galen
Gaylen
Gene
George

Georgios
Georgy
Geronimo
Gil
Gino
Giorgos
Hali
Hector
Hercules
Hermes
Hesperos
Hieremias
Hieronymos
Hippolyte
Homer
Iakobos
Ilias
Iorgos
Iosif
Isidore
Isidro
Jacen
Jaison
Jason
Jasson
Jayson
Jörg
Jörn
Josef
Julian
Julius
Karey
Karsten
Kay
Khristian
Khristopher
Khristos
Kimball
Kit
Korudon
Kosmo
Kostas
Kris
Kristian
Kristo
Kristoff
Kristopher
Kyros
Lazarus
Leander

Leon
Leonidas
Leopold
Lexus
Lidio
Linus
Lukas
Lysander
Makarios
Makis
Maximos
Mette
Mihail
Mikhail
Mikolas
Miles
Milos
Mimis
Mitsos
Morey
Moris
Myron
Napoleon
Narcissus
Nectarios
Nemo
Nestor
Nicholas
Nicholaus
Nickalus
Nicklaus
Nickolas
Nicky
Nico
Nicodemus
Nike
Nikola
Nikolas
Nikolaus
Nikolos
Odell
Odysseus
Orestes
Orion
Otis
Panayiotis
Panos
Paris
Parthenios
Pello

Perben
Pericles
Petar
Peter
Petros
Phil
Philander
Philemon
Philip
Phillip
Phillipos
Philo
Pirro
Plato
Pollux
Polo
Porfirio
Prokopios
Quant
Rasmus
Rhodes
Rodas
Romanos
Sabastian
Sandro
Sebastian
Sebastion
Semon
Socrates
Solon
Soterios
Spiro
Spyros
Stamos
Stavros
Steeve
Steeven
Stefanos
Stephan
Stephen
Stephon
Stevan
Steve
Steven
Stevens
Stevin
Strephon
Strom
Symon
Tad

Taddeus
Takis
Tanek
Telly
Thad
Thaddeus
Thanos
Theodore
Theophilus
Theron
Thomas
Tim
Timmothy
Timmy
Timon
Timothy
Tino
Titus
Toni
Tony
Topher
Tracy
Tyrone
Urian
Vasilis
Venedictos
Xan
Xander
Xenophon
Xenos
Xylon
Yanni
Yoni
Yorgos
Ysidro
Zale
Zander
Zeno
Zephyr
Zeus
Zorba
Zotikos

Gypsy

Girls
Chavi
Miri
Patia
Rawnie

Tasarla
Tawny

Boys
Baul
Bavol
Bersh
Cam
Cappi
Chal
Chik
Danior
Dukker
Durriken
Durril
Fordel
Jal
Jibben
Kerey
Kistur
Lash
Lel
Lennor
Lutherum
Mander
Nav
Nicabar
Patrin
Pattin
Pias
Pov
Rye
Stiggur
Tas
Tawno
Tem
Tobar
Wen
Wesh
Yarb

Hausa

Girls
Tashi

Boys
Danladi
Daren
Ibrahim
Rago
Taliki

Yohance
Zaki

Hawaiian

Girls
Ailani
Akela
Alamea
Alana
Alani
Aleka
Alika
Aloha
Amaui
Ana
Anela
Ani
Anouhea
Aolani
'Aulani
Halia
Ikia
Ilima
Inoa
Iolana
Kai
Kalama
Kalani
Kalea
Kalei
Kalena
Kali
Kalia
Kalina
Kamea
Kamiya
Kanani
Kani
Kanoa
Kapua
Kaulana
Kawena
Keala
Keiki
Keilani
Kekona
Kiele
Kina
Kini

Kona
Lahela
Laka
Lana
Lani
Lea
Lei
Leilani
Luann
Makala
Makana
Makani
Malana
Malia
Mamo
Mana
Mei
Mele
Miliani
Mililani
Moana
Mohala
Nalani
Nana
Nani
Noelani
Noma
Okalani
Olina
Peke
Pua
Pualani
Rapa
Roselani
Suke
Sukey
Suse
Ululani
Wainani
Wanika
Wilikinia

Boys
Aukai
Bane
Ekewaka
Elika
Hanale
Haoa
Havika
Hiu

(Hawaiian boys continued)	Lei	Abagail	Aviva	Elicia	Jem
Iokepa	Lekeke	Abbagail	Aya	Elisabeth	Jemima
Ionakana	Liban	Abbey	Ayla	Elisha	Jemma
Iukini	Likeke	Abbygail	Basia	Eliza	Jerusha
Ka'eo	Liko	Abegail	Bathsheba	Elizabet	Jesica
Kahale	Lio	Abigail	Becca	Elizabeth	Jesse
Kaholo	Loe	Abira	Bess	Elsa	Jesseca
Kai	Lokela	Abra	Beth	Emanuelle	Jessica
Kaili	Lono	Abria	Betty	Emmanuelle	Jessie
Kainoa	Lopaka	Abygail	Betula	Ethana	Jessika
Kaipo	Lui	Adah	Bina	Eva	Jessyca
Kala	Lukela	Adama	Boacha	Eve	Jésusa
Kalama	Lulani	Adena	Branda	Ezri	Jezebel
Kalani	Mahi'ai	Adina	Carmela	Gada	Jimi
Kale	Makaio	Adira	Cayla	Gail	Joan
Kali	Makani	Adleigh	Chai	Gali	Joanie
Kamaka	Maleko	Adrielle	Chana	Ganya	Joanny
Kamakani	Mamo	Aerial	Chava	Gavriella	Joaquina
Kamuela	Mano	Afra	Chavon	Geela	Joby
Kanaiela	Manu	Ahava	Chavonne	Geva	Joelle
Kane	Mauli	Ahliya	Chaya	Gilana	Johanie
Kanoa	Meka	Ailya	Dalia	Gisa	Johnnie
Kapono	Mikáele	Airiél	Daneil	Gurit	Jolene
Kawika	Mililani	Aldine	Danelle	Hadara	Jonatha
Keahi	Nahele	Aleeya	Dani	Hadassah	Jonina
Keaka	Namaka	Aleeza	Dania	Hagar	Jonita
Kealoha	Nohea	Aleya	Danica	Hania	Jora
Keawe	Oke	Alia	Danielle	Hanna	Jordan
Kekapa	Oliwa	Aliya	Danit	Hannah	Jordana
Kekipi	Onaona	Aliza	Danna	Hanni	Jorden
Kekoa	Pakelika	Alizabeth	Dannielle	Hava	Jordyn
Kele	Palaina	Allia	Dara	Haviva	Jori
Keli	Palani	Alliyah	Davida	Hinda	Josey
Keli'i	Paulo	Alyah	Debbie	Ian	Joshlyn
Keoki	Pekelo	Amaris	Deborah	Ikia	Jourdan
Keola	Peleke	Amira	Delilah	Ilana	Jozie
Keoni	Peniamina	Amissa	Dena	Ileana	Judith
Kiele	Pilipo	Amita	Denae	Ilisha	Judy
Kika	Uku	Anais	Devora	Itamar	Kaela
Kimo	Wene	Aphra	Dina	Ivria	Kaila
Kimokeo	Wikoli	Ardi	Dinah	Iyana	Karmel
Kini	Wile	Ardice	Diza	Jacobi	Katriel
Koi	Wiliama	Ardith	Dodie	Jael	Kayla
Koka		Arella	Dorrit	Jaffa	Kaylah
Kona	**Hebrew**	Ari	Eden	Jami	Kaylan
Konane	**Girls**	Ariel	Edna	Jane	Kayleen
Koukalaka	Aaleyah	Arin	Eleora	Janice	Keila
Laban	Aaliah	Aryn	Elia	Janna	Kelila
Lani	Aaliyah	Atara	Eliana	Jardena	Kenia
		Atira	Eliane	Jayna	Kenya

Keren
Keziah
Kitra
Laela
Lateefah
Layla
Leah
Leeza
Leila
Lena
Leora
Levana
Levia
Levona
Lewana
Lia
Liana
Liane
Libby
Liora
Lirit
Liron
Lisa
Lisha
Livana
Livia
Liviya
Livona
Luann
Machaela
Magali
Mahira
Maika
Malha
Malina
Mangena
Maraya
Maria
Mariah
Mariam
Marilla
Marily
Marlyn
Marni
Marnie
Marnina
Mary
Maryam
Matana
Mathena

Mattea
Mazel
Mehira
Mehitabel
Meira
Meka
Micaela
Micah
Micayla
Michaela
Michala
Mika
Mikaela
Mikala
Milena
Mireille
Mireya
Miriam
Moriah
Moselle
Nagida
Naomi
Naomie
Nasya
Natania
Nava
Neta
Nili
Nima
Nina
Nirel
Nissa
Nita
Nitza
Nizana
Noemi
Noemie
Noemy
Noga
Nurita
Nyomi
Odeda
Odelia
Odera
Ofira
Ofra
Ohanna
Oma
Oprah
Oralee

Orinda
Orli
Ornice
Orpah
Oz
Ozara
Pazia
Peninah
Perah
Pora
Rabecca
Rachael
Racheal
Rachel
Rae
Raechel
Rafaela
Rama
Rani
Ranita
Raphaela
Raya
Raychel
Reba
Rebeca
Rebecca
Rebekah
Rebi
Rena
Reubena
Reva
Rimona
Rinah
Rishona
Riva
Rivka
Rochelle
Ronli
Rubena
Ruth
Ruthie
Sabra
Sabrina
Sade
Sadie
Saida
Saira
Salome
Samala
Samantha

Samatha
Sameh
Sami
Samone
Samuela
Samuelle
Sanne
Sapphira
Sara
Sarah
Sarai
Saree
Sariah
Sarina
Sarrah
Sayde
Sayra
Selima
Serafina
Shamira
Shana
Shara
Sharai
Sharna
Sharon
Sharonda
Sharrona
Shauna
Shawna
Shayna
Sheba
Sheena
Shifra
Shilo
Shira
Shoshana
Shulamith
Shyra
Sidonia
Simcha
Simone
Sue
Sula
Susan
Susana
Suzanna
Symone
Tahlia
Takenya
Talia

Tamar
Tamara
Tamassa
Tamera
Tamira
Tammy
Tamra
Temira
Thirza
Thomasina
Tirza
Tivona
Tobi
Tommie
Tovah
Urit
Varda
Vida
Vina
Yachne
Yadira
Yael
Yaffa
Yahaira
Yajaira
Yakira
Yarkona
Yehudit
Yeira
Yesica
Yessica
Yoanna
Yonina
Yonita
Yosepha
Yovela
Zacharie
Zachary
Zahar
Zahavah
Zaira
Zakira
Zara
Zayit
Zemirah
Zera
Zilla
Zilpah
Zimra
Zipporah

Ziva
Zohar
Zohra

Boys
Aaron
Abbey
Abbott
Abe
Abel
Abiah
Abie
Abiel
Abir
Abisha
Abner
Abraham
Abrahan
Abram
Absalom
Adam
Adamson
Adar
Addy
Adin
Adir
Adiv
Adlai
Admon
Adon
Adriel
Ahab
Akeem
Akiva
Almon
Alon
Alva
Amal
Ameer
Amiel
Amin
Amir
Amon
Amos
Amram
Ardon
Ari
Ariel
Armani
Armon

(Hebrew boys continued)

Arnon
Aron
Arran
Arvid
Aryeh
Asa
Ash
Ashby
Asher
Asiel
Avi
Aviv
Avner
Avram
Avshalom
Azriel
Azuriah
Barak
Barnabas
Bart
Bartholomew
Baruch
Ben
Ben-ami
Benjamen
Benjamin
Benjiman
Benny
Beno
Benoni
Benson
Benzi
Ben Zion
Binah
Boaz
Bram
Cain
Cale
Caleb
Carmel
Chaim
Chanan
Chiram
Chuco
Coby
Dagan
Dan
Danial

Daniel
Daniele
Danno
Danny
Danyel
Dar
Dave
Davey
David
Dekel
Dermot
Deron
Deror
Didi
Dor
Doran
Dotan
Dov
Dovev
Dur
Eb
Eben
Ebenezer
Eden
Eder
Efrain
Efrat
Efrem
Efren
Eitan
Elam
Elan
Elchanan
Eleazar
Eli
Eliazar
Elie
Elihu
Elijah
Eliseo
Elisha
Eliyahu
Elkan
Elrad
Ely
Emanuel
Emmanuel
Enoch
Enos
Ephraim

Esau
Esequiel
Eshkol
Ethan
Ezekiel
Ezequiel
Ezer
Ezra
Gabe
Gabrial
Gabriel
Gavriel
Geremia
Gershom
Gibor
Gideon
Gidon
Gil
Gilon
Givon
Goel
Goliath
Gomer
Gozol
Gurion
Guy
Hadar
Ham
Hanan
Harel
Harrod
Haskel
Heber
Heman
Herschel
Hersh
Hershel
Hezekiah
Hillel
Hiram
Hod
Honi
Hosea
Ichabod
Ike
Ilan
Iman
Immanuel
Ira
Isaac

Isaak
Isaiah
Isaias
Ishmael
Israel
Isreal
Issac
Issiah
Itzak
Izzy
Jabez
Jabin
Jacan
Jacob
Jacobi
Jacobo
Jaden
Jadon
Jadyn
Jael
Jahvon
Jaiden
Jaivon
Jake
Jakob
James
Jamin
Jamon
Japheth
Jarad
Jarah
Jardan
Jareb
Jared
Jaren
Jarod
Jaron
Jarred
Jarren
Jarrod
Jarryd
Jaryn
Javan
Javon
Jaycob
Jeb
Jebediah
Jed
Jediah
Jedidiah

Jehu
Jerad
Jerahmy
Jeramie
Jere
Jered
Jereme
Jeremiah
Jeremie
Jeriah
Jermiah
Jerod
Jerrett
Jeshua
Jess
Jesse
Jessy
Jesus
Jethro
Jett
Jevan
Jevon
Jim
Jo
Joab
Joachim
Job
Joby
Jodan
Jody
Joe
Joel
Joeseph
Joey
John
Johnathan
Johnathon
Johnnie
Johnny
Jon
Jonah
Jonas
Jonatan
Jonathan
Jonathon
Jonny
Jora
Joram
Jordan
Jorden

Jordon
Jordy
Jordyn
Jory
Joseph
Josh
Joshua
Josiah
Josue
Jotham
Jourdan
Jubal
Judah
Judd
Kaeleb
Kaleb
Kaniel
Karmel
Kayle
Kayleb
Kayne
Kedem
Kenaz
Kenya
Kiva
Lapidos
Lavan
Lavi
Lemuel
Leor
Lev
Levi
Levin
Liron
Lot
Lyron
Magen
Mahir
Malachi
Manuel
Marnin
Mathew
Matson
Matt
Matthew
Matty
Mayer
Mehetabel
Meir
Melchior

Menachem	Palti	Sivan	Yisrael	Zephaniah	Kerani
Menassah	Pesach	Sol	Yitro	Zev	Kiran
Mered	Pinchas	Solly	Yitzchak	Zevi	Kirsi
Meshach	Raanan	Solomon	Yoav	Zia	Kona
Meyer	Racham	Tal	Yochanan	Zimra	Kusa
Micah	Rafi	Tam	Yoel	Zion	Lajila
Micha	Rani	Tamar	Yonah	Ziv	Lakya
Michael	Raphael	Telem	Yonatan	Zohar	Lalasa
Mika	Rapheal	Teman	Yoram	Zollie	Latika
Mikal	Ravid	Teva	Yosef	Zubin	Lila
Mike	Raviv	Thaniel	Yoshiyahu	Zuriel	Mahesa
Misael	Rayi	Timur	Yosu		Makara
Mordecai	Reuben	Tivon	Yoyi	**Hindi**	Malini
Mose	Reuven	Tobias	Yuri		Mandara
Moses	Ron	Tobin	Yuval	**Girls**	Matrika
Moshe	Roni	Tommie	Zac	Aditi	Maya
Naaman	Ruben	Tommy	Zacary	Adya	Medora
Nachman	Ruby	Tovi	Zaccary	Aiyanna	Mehadi
Nadav	Rueben	Tuvya	Zaccheus	Aja	Mela
Naftali	Salomon	Tzadok	Zach	Ajia	Mesha
Nagid	Sam	Tzion	Zachari	Amlika	Mina
Namir	Sami	Tzuriel	Zacharia	Amma	Minda
Natanael	Sammy	Tzvi	Zachariah	Anala	Mitra
Nate	Samson	Uri	Zacharie	Ananda	Narmada
Nathan	Samual	Uriah	Zachary	Anila	Natesa
Nathanael	Samuel	Uriel	Zachery	Artha	Nirveli
Nathanial	Sasson	Uzi	Zachry	Ayanna	Nitara
Nathanie	Saul	Uziel	Zack	Baka	Opal
Nathaniel	Sean	Vered	Zackary	Bakula	Padma
Nathen	Seraphim	Yadid	Zackery	Bel	Pandita
Nazareth	Seth	Yadon	Zackory	Chandler	Pausha
Nehemiah	Shai	Yael	Zadok	Channa	Pinga
Nemo	Shalom	Yagil	Zaide	Daru	Pollyam
Nethaniel	Shamar	Yair	Zakaria	Deva	Priya
Nimrod	Shamir	Yanton	Zakary	Devi	Rama
Nissan	Sharron	Yaphet	Zakery	Ganesa	Ratri
Noach	Shavar	Yarden	Zakkary	Hara	Rekha
Noah	Shayne	Yarom	Zamir	India	Risha
Noam	Shem	Yaron	Zanvil	Indira	Rohana
Noé	Shiloh	Yavin	Zared	Jaya	Rohini
Nuri	Shimon	Yechiel	Zayit	Jayne	Ruana
Nuriel	Shimshon	Yedidya	Zeb	Jibon	Ruchi
Obadiah	Shlomo	Yehoshua	Zebediah	Kalinda	Rudra
Oded	Shmuel	Yehoyakem	Zebedee	Kamala	Sadhana
Ofer	Si	Yehudi	Zebulon	Kanya	Sagara
Ophir	Simcha	Yeshaya	Zechariah	Karma	Sakari
Oren	Simms	Yeshurun	Zed	Karuna	Sakti
Ori	Simmy	Yigal	Zedekiah	Kasi	Sala
Oved	Simon	Yirmaya	Zedidiah	Kaveri	Saura
Oz	Simpson	Yishai	Zeév	Kavindra	Shaka

39

(Hindi girls continued)

Shakti
Sharan
Shatara
Shivani
Sita
Soma
Sumati
Syreeta
Taja
Tira
Tirtha
Trina
Tula
Tulsi
Uma
Usha
Vina
Yamuna

Boys
Aakash
Adri
Agni
Akash
Amin
Amol
Anand
Anil
Arjun
Arun
Ashwani
Ashwin
Balin
Balraj
Bhagwandas
Braham
Chander
Daksh
Dandin
Darshan
Deven
Hansh
Hara
Hari
Hasin
Hastin
Inay
Inder

Indiana
Ishan
Jahlil
Jaleel
Jalil
Jatinra
Jivin
Josha
Kabir
Kakar
Kala
Kalkin
Kamal
Kami
Kannan
Kantu
Kapila
Karu
Kavi
Kedar
Kesin
Kinton
Kiritan
Kistna
Krishna
Lal
Linu
Lusila
Madhar
Mahesa
Manu
Marut
Mayon
Mohan
Murali
Nadisu
Nandin
Narain
Natesh
Navin
Nehru
Nila
Onkar
Palash
Paramesh
Pavit
Pramad
Prem
Purdy

Qimat
Rajah
Rajak
Rajan
Raktim
Ram
Ramanan
Ranjan
Ravi
Rishi
Rohan
Rohin
Rohit
Sahir
Sajag
Salmalin
Sanat
Sani
Sanjiv
Sankar
Santosh
Sarad
Sarngin
Sarojin
Shalya
Shiva
Siddhartha
Singh
Siva
Sunreep
Tayib
Thaman
Ultman
Vadin
Valin
Varun
Vasin
Venkat
Vidur
Vijay
Vikas
Vikram
Vikrant
Vimal
Vinay
Vinod
Vipul
Viraj
Virat

Vishal
Vishnu
Vivek
Yash
Yashwant
Yatin
Yogesh

Hispanic

Boys
Chavez
Jesús
Julio

Hopi

Girls
Hola
Kai
Kasa
Kaya
Mansi
Nova
Sunki
Takala
Talasi
Toski
Totsi
Una
Yamka
Yoki
Zihna

Boys
Makyah

Hungarian

Girls
Anci
Bela
Evie
Franci
Ila
Ilka
Ilona
Juci
Juliana
Klara
Lenci
Mali

Malika
Margit
Neci
Nusi
Onella
Réz
Sarolta
Sasa
Shari
Teca
Tsigana
Vianca
Zigana
Zizi
Zsa Zsa
Zsofia
Zsuzsanna

Boys
Andor
András
Antal
Bandi
Bela
Csaba
Domokos
Elek
Endre
Erno
Ferenc
Gábor
Gellert
Gyula
Imre
Ince
István
János
Jenö
Kelemen
Lajos
László
Loránd
Lóránt
Maco
Maks
Marcilka
Maxi
Micu
Miksa
Miska

Natan
Niki
Nikko
Ödön
Orbán
Pál
Pista
Rendor
Réz
Sándor
Szygfrid
Tabor
Tass
Tibor
Tomi
Vencel
Vidor
Viktor
Vili
Vinci
Zako
Zoltán
Zsigmond

Ibo

Girls
Adamma
Chinue
Olisa

Boys
Agu
Chike
Chinua
Chioke
Chuma
Dumaka
Ilom
Iniko
Jaja
Madu
Mazi
Ngozi
N'nambi
Ogbonna
Okechuku
Okeke
Okorie
Okpara
Orji

Uche
Worie
Yafeu

Icelandic

Girls
Artis
Falda
Sula

Boys
Arthur
Erikur

Indonesian

Boys
Kersen

Indo-Pakistani

Boys
Adri

Irish

Girls
Africa
Afrika
Aileen
Ailis
Aislinn
Alaina
Alana
Alanna
Allana
Allena
Alonna
Arlene
Artis
Ashlyn
Barrie
Bedelia
Berget
Biddy
Blaine
Brady
Brea
Breana
Breann
Breauna

Breck
Bree
Breeana
Breena
Breiana
Brenda
Brenna
Breona
Brett
Breyana
Breyona
Briana
Brianne
Bridey
Bridget
Bridgett
Brienna
Brina
Briona
Brita
Briyana
Brodie
Bryana
Bryna
Bryona
Caitlan
Caitlin
Caitlyn
Cara
Caralee
Carlin
Carlyn
Carra
Casey
Casidy
Casie
Cassady
Cassidy
Catelyn
Cathleen
Ceara
Ceira
Ciara
Ciera
Colleen
Collina
Connor
Corey
Cori
Cristen

Curran
Cyerra
Dacey
Dacia
Dallas
Darby
Darci
Darion
Darnee
Daron
Daryn
Deidra
Deirdre
Delainey
Delaney
Delanie
Derry
Devan
Devin
Devyn
Diedra
Dillan
Doreen
Earlene
Eda
Edana
Eileen
Ena
Erin
Erinn
Eryn
Evania
Fallon
Fiona
Fionnula
Flannery
Gitta
Gladis
Gladys
Glenna
Ilene
Ina
Ita
Jilleen
Kacey
Kaetlyn
Kaitlin
Kaitlyn
Karah
Kasey

Kassidy
Katalina
Katelin
Katelyn
Kathleen
Katilvn
Katlin
Katlyn
Kaytlin
Keaira
Keana
Keara
Keeley
Keelyn
Keena
Keiana
Keira
Kelley
Kelli
Kelly
Kellyanne
Kellyn
Kenna
Kennedy
Kenzie
Keona
Keri
Kerry
Kevyn
Keyara
Kiara
Kiera
Kiley
Kyara
Kyla
Kyle
Kylee
Kyleigh
Kylene
Kylie
Lana
Lee
Logan
Mab
Mackenzie
Maegan
Maeve
Maira
Makenzie
Mare

Maura
Maureen
Maygan
Mckinley
Mckinzie
Meagan
Meara
Megan
Megane
Melvina
Meri
Meriel
Meryl
Moira
Mollie
Mona
Morena
Muriel
Myrna
Nayely
Neala
Neely
Neila
Nessie
Nevina
Nia
Nila
Niya
Nokomis
Nola
Noreen
Nuala
Nya
Nyla
Ona
Oona
Oriana
Orinda
Orla
Ornice
Payton
Peyton
Phallon
Quincy
Raegan
Ragan
Raleigh
Ranait
Reagan
Regan

Reganne
Reilly
Riana
Richael
Rilee
Riley
Riona
Rori
Ryan
Rylee
Ryleigh
Ryley
Sass
Seana
Seirra
Selma
Shae
Shaelee
Shaelyn
Shana
Shanae
Shane
Shanley
Shanna
Shannen
Shannon
Shauna
Shaunda
Shaunta
Shawna
Shawnda
Shawnee
Shawnta
Shay
Shayla
Shaylee
Shaylyn
Shea
Sheena
Sheila
Shena
Sheridan
Shona
Shonda
Shonta
Shunta
Siara
Sianna
Siera
Sierra

(Irish girls continued)

Sina
Sinead
Siobhan
Sloane
Tara
Tari
Tarra
Taryn
Tierney
Tipper
Trevina
Trevona
Troya
Tullia
Ula
Una
Yseult

Boys
Adan
Aden
Aiden
Aimon
Aindrea
Al
Alan
Allan
Allen
Alpin
Ardal
Arlen
Arthur
Bain
Bainbridge
Baird
Banning
Bard
Barry
Beacan
Beagan
Blaine
Blair
Blane
Blayne
Bogart
Bowie
Brady
Brannon

Brayan
Breck
Brendan
Brenden
Brennan
Breyon
Brian
Brion
Brodie
Brody
Bryan
Bryant
Caley
Calhoun
Callahan
Callum
Car
Carlin
Carney
Carrick
Carroll
Case
Casey
Cass
Cassidy
Cassie
Cavan
Cian
Clancy
Cleary
Cluny
Colin
Collins
Coman
Conall
Conan
Conary
Conlan
Conner
Connie
Connor
Conor
Conroy
Conway
Corcoran
Corey
Cormac
Corrigan
Corrin
Cosgrove

Cowan
Coyle
Craig
Crofton
Cullen
Culley
Cunningham
Curran
Cyle
Dacey
Daley
Daran
Darby
Darcy
Daren
Darian
Darien
Darin
Darion
Daron
Darren
Darrin
Darrion
Darron
Declan
Delaney
Delano
Demond
Dempsey
Dermot
Derren
Derry
Desmond
Devan
Deven
Devin
Devine
Devlin
Devon
Devyn
Dewayne
Dezmon
Digby
Dillan
Dillon
Dinsmore
Doherty
Dolan
Donahue
Donal

Donavan
Donnell
Donnelly
Donnie
Donovan
Dooley
Dow
Doyle
Duane
Dugan
Dwayne
Ea
Eachan
Eagan
Eamon
Earl
Egan
Eion
Erin
Eron
Evan
Evin
Fagan
Farrell
Fergus
Ferrell
Ferris
Fineas
Finian
Finlay
Finn
Finnegan
Fitzroy
Flann
Flynn
Forbes
Gair
Galbraith
Galen
Gallagher
Galloway
Galvin
Gannon
Garett
Garret
Garrett
Garvey
Gaynor
Genty
Ghilchrist

Gilby
Gilchrist
Gillean
Gillespie
Gilmore
Gilroy
Girvin
Glen
Glenn
Glenville
Godfrey
Gorman
Grady
Guthrie
Hagen
Hailey
Haley
Harkin
Hogan
Hoyt
Hurley
Innis
Irv
Irvin
Irving
Kacey
Kaelan
Kaenan
Kagan
Kailen
Kain
Kalan
Kallen
Kalon
Kane
Karney
Kasey
Kassidy
Kavan
Kavin
Kaylen
Keagan
Keanan
Keane
Keanu
Kearn
Kearney
Keary
Keaven
Keefe

Keegan
Keelan
Keeley
Keenan
Keenen
Keevon
Kegan
Keigan
Keivan
Kellan
Kellen
Keller
Kelly
Kelvin
Kenan
Kendrick
Kennard
Kennedy
Kenneth
Kenyon
Keon
Kermit
Kern
Kerry
Kerwin
Kevan
Keven
Kevin
Kevon
Kevyn
Keyon
Kiel
Kieran
Kiernan
Kile
Killian
Kinnard
Kion
Konner
Konnor
Korey
Korrigan
Kory
Kraig
Kyele
Kylan
Kyle
Larkin
Laughlin
Lawler

Lennon
Liam
Lochlain
Logan
Lomán
Lorcan
Lucas
Lunn
Lynch
Macallister
Macarthur
Maccoy
Maccrea
Mackenzie
Mackinnley
Macklain
Maclean
Macmahon
Macmurray
Magee
Maguire
Mahon
Mairtin
Maitias
Maitiú
Makenzie
Mal
Malachy
Maloney
Malvin
Mannix
Mayo
McKenzie
Mckinley
Mel
Melrone
Melvin
Merrill
Merritt
Merv
Mervin
Micheal
Mickenzie
Mickey
Mikeal
Monahan
Monroe
Moss
Mundy
Murphy

Murtagh
Neal
Neil
Nevan
Nevin
Niall
Nolan
Nyle
Ode
Odell
Odran
Oistin
O'neil
Oran
Oren
O'Shea
Owen
Owney
Paddy
Padraic
Parth
Parthalán
Patterson
Phelan
Phinean
Piran
Quigley
Quillan
Quinlan
Quinn
Rafer
Rafferty
Raghnall
Rayan
Reagan
Regan
Reilly
Renny
Rhyan
Rian
Riddock
Riley
Riordan
Roarke
Rogan
Ronán
Rooney
Rory
Ryan
Ryen

Rylee
Ryley
Ryne
Ryon
Scanlon
Scully
Seamus
Sean
Searlas
Sedric
Shaine
Shamus
Shan
Shanahan
Shane
Shanley
Shannon
Shaun
Shawn
Shay
Shea
Sheehan
Sheridan
Sierra
Siseal
Skelly
Slevin
Sloan
Strahan
Struthers
Sullivan
Sully
Sweeney
Taggart
Teagan
Teague
Tegan
Thady
Tiernan
Tierney
Tomás
Tomey
Torian
Torin
Tormey
Torn
Torrance
Torren
Torrence
Trace

Tracey
Tracy
Trev
Trevor
Troy
Tully
Tynan
Tyrone
Uaine
Uilliam
Uinseann
Uistean

Iroquois

Girls
Onatah
Orenda
Seneca

Italian

Girls
Abriana
Adriana
Adrienna
Alessandra
Anna
Aryana
Bambi
Bianca
Bianka
Bionca
Blanca
Camellia
Camila
Capri
Caprice
Carina
Carine
Carlotta
Carolina
Chiara
Ciana
Clarice
Clarissa
Concetta
Crista
Daniela
Deangela
Dona

Doña
Donna
Elena
Elisa
Emilia
Filippa
Filomena
Francesca
Franchesca
Francisca
Gabriela
Gaetana
Gema
Gessica
Ghita
Gianna
Gina
Giordana
Giovanna
Giulia
Isabella
Italia
Jianna
Jina
Jovanna
Jovannie
Justina
Kami
Karah
Klarissa
Lia
Lucia
Lucrezia
Margarita
Maria
Marice
Marietta
Marsala
Mia
Michele
Mila
Milana
Nicola
Ortensia
Paola
Pia
Primavera
Rosa
Rosetta
Ruffina

Speranza
Vedette
Venecia
Zola

Boys
Adriano
Aldo
Alessandro
Alfonso
Alfredo
Alphonso
Amadeo
Angelo
Antonio
Aretino
Arrigo
Arturo
Benito
Beppe
Bonaro
Bonaventure
Braulio
Bruno
Carlo
Carmine
Cirillo
Claudio
Clemente
Cola
Corrado
Cristoforo
Deangelo
Deanthony
Demarco
Demario
Dino
Domenico
Donato
Drago
Edoardo
Elmo
Emiliano
Emilio
Enrico
Ercole
Eriberto
Ermanno
Este
Ettore

43

(Italian boys continued)

Fabiano
Fabrizio
Falito
Faustino
Fausto
Federico
Felippo
Fiorello
Flavio
Florencio
Fonso
Fortino
Francesco
Gabrielli
Gaetan
Geno
Genovese
Georgio
Geovanni
Geraldo
Geremia
Geremiah
Geronimo
Giacomo
Gian
Giancarlo
Gianluca
Gianni
Gianpaolo
Gino
Giona
Giordano
Giorgio
Giosia
Giotto
Giovani
Giovanni
Giovanny
Giuliano
Giulio
Giuseppe
Giustino
Gregorio
Gualtiero
Guglielmo
Guido
Gustavo
Innocenzio

Jeovanni
Jiovanni
Lanz
Larenzo
Lave
Lazaro
Leobardo
Leonardo
Leopoldo
Lorenzo
Loretto
Luca
Luciano
Lucio
Luigi
Marcelino
Marcelo
Marciano
Marco
Mariano
Marino
Mario
Markanthony
Marsalis
Martino
Masaccio
Massimo
Maurizio
Maximiliano
Michelangelo
Michele
Milan
Napoleon
Nicola
Nicolas
Nicolo
Nuncio
Olindo
Orsino
Otello
Paco
Paolo
Pasquale
Peppe
Piero
Pietro
Pino
Primo
Rafaele
Raimondo

Ranieri
Renardo
Renato
Ric
Rico
Rinaldo
Rocco
Rodrigo
Romario
Romello
Romeo
Romy
Rudolpho
Ruggerio
Ruperto
Sal
Salvatore
Samuele
Sandro
Santo
Saverio
Sergio
Severiano
Silvano
Silvestro
Silvio
Stefano
Taddeo
Tazio
Teobaldo
Teodoro
Tiberio
Tino
Tito
Tomasso
Tonio
Tristano
Tulio
Uberto
Ugo
Umberto
Urbano
Valentino
Vicenzo
Vincenzo
Vinci
Vittorio
Zan

Japanese

Girls

Aiko
Aki
Akiko
Akina
Amaya
Aneko
Asa
Chika
Chiyo
Dai
Gen
Gin
Hachi
Hama
Hana
Hanako
Haru
Hisa
Hoshi
Ima
Ishi
Jin
Kaedé
Kagami
Kaiya
Kameko
Kami
Kane
Kaya
Kei
Keiko
Kiaria
Kiku
Kimi
Kioko
Kishi
Kita
Kiwa
Koko
Koto
Kuma
Kumiko
Kuniko
Kuri
Kyoko
Leiko
Machiko

Maeko
Mai
Mari
Mariko
Masago
Matsuko
Michi
Midori
Mieko
Mika
Miki
Mina
Miné
Mio
Miwa
Miya
Miyo
Miyuki
Morie
Mura
Nami
Nara
Nari
Nishi
Nori
Nyoko
Oki
Orino
Osen
Raeden
Raku
Ran
Rei
Ren
Rin
Rui
Ruri
Ryo
Sachi
Sada
Sai
Sakaē
Saki
Sakura
Sasa
Sato
Sawa
Sayo
Seki
Sen

Shika
Shina
Shino
Shizu
Sugi
Suki
Sumi
Suzu
Suzuki
Taka
Takara
Taki
Tama
Tamaka
Tamika
Tamiko
Tani
Taree
Tazu
Tera
Tetsu
Toki
Tomi
Tomo
Tora
Tori
Toshi
Umeko
Uta
Wakana
Washi
Wattan
Yasu
Yei
Yoi
Yoko
Yoné
Yori
Yoshi
Yuki
Yuri

Boys

Akemi
Akira
Benjiro
Botan
Chiko
Dai
Danno

Goro
Hideaki
Hiromasa
Hiroshi
Hisoka
Isas
Jiro
Jo
Joben
Joji
Jomei
Jun
Juro
Kado
Kaemon
Kana
Kane
Kaori
Kazuo
Keitaro
Ken
Kentaro
Kin
Kioshi
Kiyoshi
Makoto
Manzo
Mareo
Maro
Masahiro
Masao
Masato
Michio
Miki
Minoru
Montaro
Morio
Naoko
Raiden
Rayden
Rei
Renjiro
Ringo
Saburo
Samuru
Sen
Shiro
Takeo
Tani
Taro

Tomi
Toshi-Shita
Udo
Yasashiku
Yasuo
Yōshi
Yuki
Zen
Zinan

Kakwa

Boys
Tombe

Kikuyu

Boys
Barasa
Kamau

Kiowa

Boys
Apiatan
Gomda
Täpko
Zotom

Kiswahili

Boys
Rehema

Korean

Girls
Cho
Eun
Hye
Ki
Sook
Sun
Sun-Hi
U
Yeo
Yon

Boys
Chul
Gi
Hyun-Ki
Hyun-Shik
Ja

Jae-Hwa
Kwan
Man-Shik
Man-Young
Mun-Hee
Myung-Dae
Suck Chin
Yon-Sun
Young-Jae
Young-Soo

Lakota

Girls
Chumani
Winona
Wynonna

Boys
Chayton
Hotah
Kange
Kohana
Lootah
Mahkah
Mahpee
Matoskah
Napayshni
Odakota
Ogaleesha
Ohanzee
Ohitekah
Otaktay
Paytah
Skah
Takoda
Teetonka
Wahkan
Wahkoowah
Wamblee
Wanikiya
Yahto

Latin

Girls
Adora
Adreana
Adrienne
Aida
Aidan
Aimee

Alba
Alette
Alida
Alivia
Allegra
Alma
Aloma
Alta
Alva
Amabel
Amanada
Amanda
Amelia
Amilia
Amity
Amy
Andrea
Antonia
Antonice
April
Apryl
Arabella
Araceli
Ardelle
Armine
Augusta
Augustine
Aura
Aurelia
Aurelie
Aurora
Austin
Autumn
Avalon
Avis
Axelle
Babe
Baptista
Barbara
Beata
Beatrice
Beatriz
Bella
Belva
Benecia
Benedicta
Benedicte
Bennett
Benni
Bente

Bibi
Bibiana
Bina
Brina
Britt
Bryn
Bryna
Cadence
Calvina
Cambria
Cameo
Candida
Candra
Cara
Carita
Carla
Carlin
Carmen
Caryl
Cecelia
Cecilia
Cecily
Ceil
Celeste
Celia
Cerella
Cesilia
Charity
Chasidy
Chasity
Chastity
Cherry
Christabel
Christal
Chrystal
Cindy
Clara
Clarabelle
Clarie
Claudia
Claudie
Clementine
Concordia
Connie
Constance
Coral
Corbin
Cordelia
Cornelia
Cristal

Crystal
Dayana
Deana
Deanna
Deanne
Dextra
Di
Dia
Diamond
Diana
Diane
Dianna
Divinia
Dominica
Donata
Drew
Drusi
Drusilla
Dulce
Dyamond
Dyana
Dynasty
Elida
Elita
Elvira
Elyse
Elysia
Elyssa
Emalee
Emelia
Emely
Emily
Erma
Ermine
Essence
Eustacia
Fabia
Fabiana
Fabiola
Faline
Felecia
Felice
Felicia
Felisha
Fidelia
Fidelity
Flavia
Flavie
Flora
Florence

45

(Latin girls continued)

Fonda	Josselyn	Liana	May	Olivia	Procopia
Fortuna	Jovana	Liberty	Maya	Olyvia	Promise
Fran	Jovanna	Lida	Maybeline	Ona	Pru
Frances	Jovita	Lide	Medea	Ondine	Prudence
Francis	Joy	Lilian	Melba	Onora	Prudy
Gema	Joyce	Lillian	Melina	Oona	Prunella
Genesis	Julia	Lily	Meliora	Ora	Quartilla
Gill	Julisa	Lillyann	Meranda	Orabella	Quinella
Gillian	June	Lina	Mercedes	Orela	Quinetta
Ginger	Juno	Lita	Merissa	Oriana	Quintana
Ginia	Justice	Liv	Merle	Oriole	Quintessa
Gladys	Justine	Lona	Minerva	Ormanda	Quiterie
Gloria	Kalare	Lora	Mira	Orsa	Raine
Glory	Kambria	Lore	Mirabel	Osanna	Regina
Grace	Karley	Lorenza	Miracle	Ovia	Regine
Grazia	Karmen	Lori	Miranda	Palma	Reva
Grecia	Kesare	Loris	Mireille	Passion	Réz
Gusta	Kira	Lorna	Modesty	Pat	Risa
Hadriane	Konstance	Lorraine	Monica	Patia	River
Harmony	Kornelia	Lucerne	Morrisa	Patra	Roma
Hermina	Kosta	Lucero	Myra	Patricia	Rosalba
Honey	Kristal	Lucinda	Myranda	Patsy	Rose
Honora	Krystel	Lucretia	Nata	Paula	Rula
Hortense	Laci	Lucy	Natalee	Paulette	Sabina
Ignacia	Lacrecia	Luna	Natalie	Pauline	Sabrina
Imogene	Lana	Lupe	Nataline	Paxton	Salvia
Indigo	Lara	Lupita	Nataly	Pearl	Samara
Irma	Laraine	Luvena	Nathalie	Pepper	Sebastiane
Isadora	Latisha	Mabel	Nelia	Perdita	Secilia
Ivory	Latona	Madonna	Nidia	Perla	Secunda
Jae	Latonya	Magnolia	Nige	Perlie	Selia
Jasleen	Laura	Manda	Nila	Pernella	Septima
Jaye	Laurel	Mandy	Noel	Perri	Serena
Jillaine	Laurence	Maranda	Nohely	Persis	Serenity
Jillian	Laveda	Marcela	Nokomis	Petra	Serina
Jocelin	Lavelle	Marcella	Nola	Petronella	Shaila
Jocelyn	Lavena	Marcena	Noleta	Petula	Sheila
Jocelyne	Laverne	Marcia	Nona	Philicia	Sidra
Joi	Lavina	Maren	Noreen	Phylicia	Signe
Jonquil	Leandra	Maresa	Norma	Placidia	Silvia
Josalyn	Lecia	Maricela	Nova	Polly	Stella
Joscelin	Lena	Marina	Novella	Pomona	Sulia
Joselin	Lenita	Maris	Nunciata	Poppy	Sylvana
Joselyn	Leontine	Marisa	Nydia	Porcha	Sylvia
Joshlyn	Leta	Marisela	Octavia	Porsha	Sylvie
Josilin	Leticia	Marissa	Oksana	Portia	Tacita
Jossalin	Levana	Martina	Olethea	Prima	Taesha
	Levina	Maryssa	Olinda	Priscilla	Talia
	Lian	Maxine	Olive	Prissy	Tansy

		Boys	Cornelius	Errol	Julius
Taura	Valeria	Ace	Cash	Eulises	Junior
Tavia	Valerie	Adrian	Cassius	Eustace	Justen
Teaira	Valery	Agustin	Castle	Fabian	Justice
Tera	Valli	Alban	Cato	Fabio	Justin
Terrene	Valonia	Albin	Ceasar	Falco	Justyn
Tertia	Valora	Albion	Cecil	Faroh	Juvenal
Thaddea	Valorie	Aleron	Cephas	Faust	Kalvin
Tiara	Varvara	Alvern	Cicero	Favian	Kornel
Tiarra	Venessa	Alvin	Clare	Felix	Kornelius
Tiberia	Venus	Amadeus	Clarence	Fidel	Krispin
Tiera	Vera	Amicus	Claude	Flavian	Kurt
Tiff	Verbena	Angel	Clem	Florian	Kurtis
Tiffani	Verda	Anthany	Clement	**Foster**	Larry
Tiffany	Verena	Anthonie	Cole	**Fran**	Laurence
Tiffy	Verenice	Anthony	Coleman	Francis	Lawerence
Tiphanie	Verity	Antony	Columba	Franco	Lawrence
Tish	Verlene	Aquila	Constant	Gaius	Leo
Tisha	Verna	Ardell	Constantine	Garnett	Lester
Toni	Vernice	Arden	Corbett	Genaro	Lombard
Tonia	Veronica	Armand	Corbin	Greg	Loren
Topaz	Veronika	Auburn	Cornelius	Greggory	Lorimer
Tory	Vespera	Augie	Corry	Gregory	Loritz
Tracey	Vesta	August	Cory	Griffin	Lorne
Traci	Vi	Augustine	Creed	Hadrian	Lucian
Tracy	Vicki	Augustus	Crispin	Hastings	Lucius
Tralena	Vicky	Aurelio	Curt	Herman	Luke
Treasure	Victoria	Aurelius	Curtis	Hilary	Magnus
Triana	Vienna	Austen	Cyprian	Honoré	Major
Tricia	Viktoria	Austin	Dacey	Horace	Marcellus
Trinity	Vincentia	Axel	Daimon	Horacio	Marcus
Trish	Viola	Balbo	Damon	Horatio	Marius
Trisha	Virgilia	Barnabas	Dante	Hugo	Mark
Trissa	Virginia	Basil	Deante	Iggy	Markel
Trista	Viridiana	Beattie	Decimus	Ignacio	Marko
Tristan	Viridis	Benedict	Delfino	Ignatius	Markus
Tristen	Virtue	Bennett	Delmar	Illan	Mars
Tristin	Vita	Blaze	Devine	Janus	Martin
Triston	Viv	Boniface	Dexter	Jarlath	Martinus
Trycia	Viva	Boone	Dom	Jerolin	Marty
Ulla	Viveca	Bourne	Domenic	Jerome	Maurice
Ultima	Vivian	Branch	Dominic	Jeromy	Maurizio
Una	Viviana	Caesar	Dominick	Jovan	Maury
Undine	Yocelin	Cal	Dominik	Jovani	Max
Unique	Yoselin	Calvin	Durand	Jovanny	Maximilian
Urbana	Zea	Camilo	Durant	Jr	Maximillian
Ursa	Zerlina	Campbell	Eloy	Judas	Mayer
Val	Zia	Candide	Elvern	Jude	Merritt
Valerie	Zinnia	Canute	Emil	Julian	Miles
Valene	Zona	Carmine	Emilien	Julien	Millard
Valentina					

(Latin boys continued)

Minor
Modesto
Mordred
Morey
Morrie
Morris
Myles
Mynor
Neci
Nelius
Neptune
Nero
Nigel
Noble
Nollie
Octavio
Octavious
Oliver
Oral
Oratio
Ordell
Orien
Orleans
Orono
Orris
Orry
Orson
Ostin
Pastor
Patric
Patrick
Patryk
Paul
Pauli
Pax
Paxton
Payne
Pelí
Penn
Peregrine
Perine
Pervis
Peter
Pharaoh
Phelix
Phoenix
Pio
Porter

Prince
Proctor
Prosper
Pryor
Quade
Quenten
Quentin
Quenton
Quinten
Quintin
Quinton
Quitin
Ransom
Regis
Remus
Renzo
Rex
Roman
Romel
Romero
Romulus
Ross
Rufus
Sanchez
Sancho
Scorpio
Seasar
Sebastian
Septimus
Sereno
Sextus
Silas
Silvan
Silvester
Stan
Stanislaus
Sy
Sylas
Sylvester
Tad
Taddeus
Tatius
Taurean
Taurus
Tavey
Tavian
Tearance
Temple
Terance
Terence

Terran
Terrance
Terrence
Terrin
Terris
Tertius
Thad
Thaddeus
Titus
Tony
Torrence
Tracy
Trent
Trenton
Trini
Trinity
Tullis
Tully
Turner
Ulises
Ulyses
Ulysses
Unique
Urban
Val
Valentin
Valerian
Varian
Vedie
Vere
Vergil
Vernon
Vic
Victor
Vin
Vincent
Virgil
Vitas
Vito
Xanthus

Latvian

Girls
Lizina

Boys
Ansis
Brencis
Janis
Karlen

Martins
Mikelis
Mychajlo
Niklas
Oleg
Zanis
Zigfrid

Lenape

Boys
Talli

Lithuanian

Boys
Antavas
Jonas
Jurgis
Moze
Petras
Raulas
Raulo
Valter
Vanda

Lomwe

Boys
Unika

Luganda

Girls
Masani
Nafuna
Sanyu

Boys
Dembe
Kamoga
Kamya
Kibuuka
Kizza
Lutalo
Madongo
Magomu
Mayonga
Mpoza
Mukasa
Mwaka
Mwanje
Sanyu

Semanda
Sempala
Setimba
Zesiro
Zilaba

Luo

Boys
Kifeda
Ocan
Okuth
Otem

Mahona

Girls
Kamali

Malayan

Girls
Javana
Javona

Maori

Girls
Nyree

Mongolian

Boys
Yul

Moquelum-nan

Girls
Hateya
Hausa
Heltu
Kaliska
Kamata
Litonya
Lusela
Luyu
Mituna
Oya
Pakuna
Papina
Pati
Sanuye

Sawa
Sibeta
Suki
Suletu
Taipa
Takenya
Wauna
Winema

Boys
Elki
Helki
Hesutu
Honon
Howi
Kono
Kosumi
Lanu
Leyati
Lise
Liwanu
Lokni
Luyu
Metikla
Misu
Molimo
Momuso
Muata
Notaku
Oya
Patakusu
Sewati
Sipatu
Telutci
Tiimu
Tiktu
Tuketu
Tukuli
Tumu
Tupi
Utatci
Uzumati
Wilanu
Wilu
Wuyi
Yelutci
Yoskolo
Yotimo
Yutu

Muganda

Boys
Najji

Musoga

Girls
Wesisa

Boys
Mulogo

Mwera

Girls
Kanika

Boys
Beno
Makalani
Nangwaya
Tumaini
Tuwile

Native American

Girls
Aiyana
Anaba
Angeni
Aquene
Bena
Chenoa
Cherokee
Cholena
Dakota
Dena
Dyana
Halona
Helki
Heta
Imala
Izusa
Kachina
Kahsha
Kanda
Kiona
Leotie
Lomasi
Lulu
Magena

Mahala
Malina
Mausi
Mika
Minal
Minowa
Nashota
Nata
Netis
Nina
Nituna
Nuna
Ogin
Olathe
Onawa
Oneida
Petunia
Rozene
Sakuna
Satinka
Shada
Shappa
Sihu
Sisika
Sora
Soso
Taima
Tala
Tiponya
Utina
Waneta
Wyanet
Wyoming
Yenene
Yepa
Yoluta
Zaltana

Boys
Ahanu
Ahdik
Akule
Anoki
Awan
Bly
Chesmu
Delsin
Demothi
Dyami
Elan

Elsu
Enyeto
Etu
Eyota
Gosheven
Guyapi
Hahnee
Hakan
Helaku
Hinun
Honovi
Hototo
Huslu
Hute
Igashu
Inteus
Isekemu
Istu
Iye
Jolon
Kaga
Kijika
Knoton
Langundo
Lenno
Lonato
Manipi
Maska
Masou
Mato
Melvern
Milap
Mingan
Mojag
Motega
Muraco
Nahma
Nawat
Nayati
Neka
Nibaw
Nigan
Nikiti
Nitis
Nodin
Nokonyu
Ohanko
Otadan
Otu

Paco
Palladin
Pat
Patamon
Patwin
Payat
Pillan
Powa
Sahale
Sahil
Sakima
Siwili
Son
Songan
Tadan
Taima
Tate
Tohon
Tyee
Wakiza
Wapi
Wemilat
Wemilo
Wenutu
Wichado
Wilny
Wingi
Wuliton
Wunand
Wynono
Yana
Yancy
Yottoko
Yuma

Navajo

Girls
Kai
Mai
Yanaba

Boys
Nantai
Sani

Ngoni

Boys
Dulani
Funsoni
Kafele

Kamuzu
Kasiya
Kwacha
Kwayera
Kwende
Mpasa
Mtima
Ndale
Sabola
Tsalani
Zikomo

Nigerian

Girls
Adanna
Fayola
Femi

Boys
Azi
Ekon
Kayin
Nwa
Nwake
Ogun
Ottah
Uzoma

North African

Girls
Kami
Kamilah

Norwegian

Girls
Elga
Gala
Gunda
Haldana
Lena
Runa
Unn

Boys
Aksel
Arkin
Arve
Arvid
Birger

Bodil
Dreng
Dyre
Egil
Eskil
Faste
Finn
Frode
Galt
Gaute
Halvor
Hauk
Havelock
Kare
Kleng
Magnar
Mikkel
Morten
Nicolai
Odd
Odo
Ottar
Oystein
Petter
Ragnar
Reidar
Roald
Roar
Skule
Stefen
Steinar
Stian
Storr
Tor
Trygve
Vegard
Vidar

Nyakusa

Boys
Ipyana
Mposi
Mwamba
Watende

Ochi

Boys
Essien

Omaha

Girls
Migina
Nida
Tadita
Urika

Boys
Mikasi
Tadi

Osage

Girls
Minya
Niabi

Pakistani

Girls
Surata
Surya

Boys
Sharad
Sharod

Pashto

Girls
Mallalai

Pawnee

Boys
Kuruk
Lesharo
Sakuruta
Skiriki

Persian

Girls
Alea
Anahita
Armani
Ayesha
Esther
Hestia
Jasmain
Jasmin
Jasmine
Jasmyn
Jazmin

Jazmyn
Jazzmin
Kira
Laleh
Lila
Lilia
Marjan
Mehri
Mina
Mitra
Nahid
Pari
Parveneh
Peri
Roxana
Roxann
Roxy
Sadira
Soraya
Souzan
Taraneh
Vashti
Yasmeen
Yasmin
Yazmin
Zena
Zenda
Zohreh

Boys
Aban
Arman
Arsha
Bahram
Bijan
Casper
Cass
Cy
Cyrus
Dareh
Feroz
Jamsheed
Jasmin
Kasper
Kaveh
Mehrdad
Nard
Nasim
Shah
Sohrab

Soroush
Tabor
Xerxes

Peruvian

Boys
Manco

Phoenician

Girls
Adama
Tanith

Boys
Adam
Anibal
Hannibal
Ib

Polish

Girls
Ania
Anka
Bryga
Ela
Elizaveta
Elka
Gita
Jasia
Jula
Kasia
Krysta
Macey
Macia
Magda
Manka
Marjan
Mela
Minka
Morela
Nata
Pela
Tawia
Tola
Tosha
Waleria
Wera
Weronika
Wicktoria

Wira
Wisia
Zocha
Zusa
Zytka

Boys
Andros
Atek
Aurek
Bronislaw
Cerek
Crystek
Danek
Dobry
Fil
Garek
Genek
Gerek
Gerik
Gwidon
Heniek
Holleb
Honok
Iwan
Janek
Jas
Jedrek
Jerzy
Karol
Kazio
Koby
Krystian
Liuz
Lubomir
Luboslaw
Machas
Maksym
Mandek
Marcin
Marian
Marke
Mateusz
Matyas
Michal
Mikolaj
Milek
Miron
Moshe
Natan

Nelek
Olés
Onufry
Otek
Patek
Paulin
Pawel
Radoslaw
Rafal
Rufin
Slawek
Stasio
Stefan
Stefon
Szczepan
Szymon
Tadzio
Tedorik
Telek
Tymon
Tytus
Walerian
Wicent
Wiktor
Wincent
Wit
Witek
Wladislav
Zarek
Zygmunt

Polynesian

Girls
Lulani
Oliana
Palila
Ulani

Boys
Kannon

Pomo

Boys
Dasan

Ponca

Girls
Pazi

Boys
Mika

Portuguese

Girls
Mel
Vidonia
Xuxa
Zetta

Boys
Belmiro
Cruz
Duarte
Francisco
Giacinto
Gregorio
Guilherme
Henrique
Humberto
Jacinto
Jaco
João
Joaquim
Josef
Lando
Laudalino
Liberio
Lidio
Markes
Marques
Marquez
Martinho
Miguel
Moises
Paulo
Raimundo
Ramiro
Ricardo
Roberto
Rogerio
Rolando
Ronaldo
Rosario
Serafino
Simão
Timoteo
Tonio
Zacarias
Zeusef

Punjabi

Girls
Amandeep
Bandi
Chardae
Gurpreet
Harpreet
Jaspreet
Mandeep
Manpreet
Raheem
Sandeep
Shardae
Sherika
Thanh
Tosha

Boys
Ajay
Amandeep
Amar
Amir
Amit
Gurpreet
Hardeep
Harpreet
Jaspal
Maalik
Málik
Mandeep
Raheem
Rakeem
Sandeep
Shad
Sundeep

Quiché

Girls
Xela

Rhodesian

Boys
Kaseko
Matope
Mundan

Romanian

Girls
Ioana
Jenica

Boys
Andrei
Enric
Ioan
Iosua
Mihail
Petru
Toma

Rukigo

Boys
Ruhakana

Runyankore

Boys
Kabonero
Kamuhanda
Kamukama
Kariisa
Karutunda
Kato
Katungi
Kayonga
Nkunda

Runyoro

Boys
Kaikara
Mugamba

Russian

Girls
Alena
Angelina
Annik
Anya
Breasha
Dasha
Duscha
Ekaterina
Galina
Gasha
Gelya
Halina
Irina
Jelena
Jereni
Karina
Karine
Katia
Khristina
Kisa
Lada
Lelya
Lenore
Lera
Liolya
Lizabeta
Lubov
Magda
Manka
Manya
Marisha
Masha
Melana
Mika
Milena
Misha
Nata
Natacha
Natalia
Natasha
Natosha
Neva
Nika
Niki
Nikita
Nyusha
Olena
Orina
Orlenda
Panya
Pavla
Pheodora
Raisa
Rusalka
Sacha
Sasha
Shura
Sonia
Sonya
Stasya
Stepania
Svetlana
Tamar
Taneya
Tania
Tanya
Tasha
Tata
Tosha
Valera
Vania
Yalena
Yekaterina
Yelena
Yelisabeta
Yudita
Yulia
Zasha
Zilya

Boys
Adrik
Aizik
Aleksei
Andrei
Arkady
Baran
Beredei
Bladimir
Borka
Christoff
Dima
Dimitri
Dmitri
Egor
Evgeny
Feliks
Fillipp
Filya
Foma
Fyodor
Gavril
Gena
Grisha
Gyorgy
Helge
Igor
Ioakim
Iosif
Iustin
Ivan
Jasha
Karlen
Kenya
Kesar
Khaim
Kharald
Kolya
Konstantin
Labrentsis
Lavrenti
Leonid
Lev
Maksim
Matvey
Maxim
Michail
Mika
Mikhail
Misha
Natan
Nicolai
Nikita
Nikolai
Nil
Oleg
Oleksandr
Osip
Osya
Panas
Pasha
Pavel
Pyotr
Sacha
Sachar
Sasha
Sergei
Slava
Stasik
Stepan
Tano
Timofey
Tisha
Todor
Ustin
Valerii
Vanya
Vasily
Venya
Viktor
Vitya
Vladimir
Vlas
Vova
Vyacheslav
Wanya
Wasili
Yakov
Yan
Yanick
Yanka
Yasha
Yegor
Yeremey
Yeska
Yevgenyi
Youri
Yov
Yuri
Yusif
Yustyn
Zhek
Zhora
Zigfrid

Rutooro

Boys
Gonza
Irumba
Kabiito
Kabonesa
Karwana
Mugisa
Sabiti

Sanskrit

Girls
Amrit
Chaka
Chakra
Chanda
Chandra
Kali
Kama
Kashmir
Kumuda
Lalita
Lilac
Mahila
Nata

(Sanskrit girls continued)

Rana
Rani
Rita
Roshan
Rupinder
Sanya
Veda
Vida
Zudora

Boys
Ajit
Akshat
Alok
Ambar
Amish
Amrit
Bal
Chan
Dalal
Ja'far
Javas
Kiran
Kumar
Kyran
Malajitm
Manoj
Mehtar
Mukul
Poshita
Pumeet
Shaman
Tanmay
Tapan
Tarak
Taran
Tarun
Tej
Tejas
Tungar
Uday
Udit
Uja
Umang
Uttam
Vasant
Vasu

Ved
Veer

Sauk

Boys
Nashashuk

Scandi-navian

Girls
Arica
Astrid
Dagny
Dahlia
Darby
Dayna
Erica
Ericka
Freja
Gudrun
Haley
Hallie
Helga
Inga
Ingrid
Karena
Karin
Kelsey
Kerstin
Khristina
Kiersten
Kirby
Kirsta
Kirsten
Kirstin
Kirstie
Kristen
Kristi
Kristin
Kristina
Kristine
Linnea
Lurleen
Nessa
Niesha
Nissa
Norell
Ola
Oletha

Olga
Quenby
Quinby
Ragnild
Ran
Rane
Rayna
Rona
Selma
Signe
Sigrid
Sonja
Thora
Tyra
Ula
Yvonne

Boys
Alvis
Asgard
Ashby
Audun
Balder
Beck
Bengt
Bergen
Bergren
Bjorn
Boden
Bodie
Booth
Borg
Bragi
Brede
Canute
Carr
Cort
Crosby
Dag
Dana
Davin
Dayne
Delling
Denby
Einar
Elvis
Erek
Eric
Erik
Frey

Gamble
Garth
Georg
Gilby
Gunnar
Gunther
Gus
Gustave
Hakon
Halden
Hamar
Hammet
Hans
Hansel
Hansen
Hanson
Harald
Harold
Ing
Inger
Ingmar
Ingvar
Ivar
Ivor
Janson
Jantzen
Jarell
Jarl
Josef
Kalle
Karr
Kell
Kelsey
Kerr
Kirby
Kirk
Knute
Lamont
Lang
Lars
Latham
Leif
Matteus
Nels
Nollie
Norbert
Odin
Olaf
Olav
Ole

Oliver
Orman
Osborn
Oscar
Oskar
Peder
Quenby
Quimby
Raynor
Rikard
Roscoe
Rothwell
Rutger
Rutland
Skee
Skerry
Skip
Skipper
Sutherland
Sven
Tait
Tamson
Tate
Thor
Thorald
Thorbert
Thorbjorn
Thorleif
Thorwald
Thurston
Trigg
Tug
Turpin
Wray
Wyborn
Wyck

Scottish

Girls
Aileen
Aili
Ailsa
Ainsley
Alina
Aline
Ansley
Artis
Berkley
Blair

Blaire
Bonnie
Cameron
Christal
Connor
Davina
Davonna
Elspeth
Geneen
Greer
Ilisa
Isela
Isla
Jean
Jeana
Jeanie
Jeanine
Jinny
Keita
Kelcey
Kelsea
Kelsey
Kelsi
Kenzie
Lesley
Leslie
Lesly
Maisie
Malvina
Marjie
Marjorie
Mckenzie
Mhairie
Paisley
Rhona
Roslyn
Rossalyn
Scotti
Tavie

Boys
Adair
Ahearn
Ainsley
Alastair
Angus
Annan
Ansley
Arran
Arthur

Balfour
Banner
Barclay
Blackburn
Boyd
Brayan
Bret
Breyon
Brian
Brion
Brit
Britton
Busby
Buzz
Caelan
Calen
Calhoun
Cam
Camaron
Camden
Cameron
Campbell
Camron
Carmichael
Carney
Caylan
Chalmers
Clyde
Collin
Conan
Connor
Craig
Dallas
Dalziel
Denholm
Don
Donald
Dorrell
Doug
Dougal
Douglas
Drummond
Duer
Duff
Duncan
Dunham
Dunlop
Dunmore
Dunn

Durell
Edan
Ennis
Erskine
Ewan
Farquhar
Fife
Fyfe
Geordan
Geordie
Glendon
Graeme
Gregor
Hamish
Hearn
Henderson
Iain
Ian
Kade
Kamden
Kameron
Kamran
Keddy
Keith
Kendrew
Kendrick
Kenn
Kennan
Kenny
Kenzie
Kincaid
Kraig
Lachlan
Laird
Leith
Lennox
Les
Leslie
Lochlain
Lundy
Lyall
Mac
Macadam
Macaulay
Macbride
Macdonald
Macdougal
Macgregor
Mack

Macnair
Malcolm
Malcom
Manius
McGeorge
Mckade
Mckay
Morgan
Morven
Muir
Mungo
Murdock
Murray
Nairn
Parlan
Perth
Pony
Ronald
Ronnie
Ronny
Ronson
Ross
Seumas
Stratton
Tavish
Tearlach
Tevis
Tormod
Tramaine
Tremaine
Tyree
Wyndham

Shona

Boys
Dakarai
Hondo
Jabulani
Kokayi
Mashama
Petiri
Rudo
Runako
Sekaye
Tichawanna
Zuka

Shoshone

Girls
Kimana

Sikh

Girls
Gagandeep
Gurleen
Ramandeep
Simran
Sukhdeep

Boys
Gurvir
Harjot
Harvir
Jaskaran
Navdeep
Pardeep

Sioux

Boys
Akecheta
Chaska
Enapay

Slavic

Girls
Alina
Catrina
Chesna
Danica
Denica
Hana
Iva
Ivana
Jana
Janika
Kalina
Kallan
Kamila
Karla
Karolina
Karoll
Katerina
Lala
Lida
Ludmilla
Mara

Marika
Marlene
Mila
Mrena
Nadia
Nadine
Neda
Neza
Paulina
Radinka
Radmilla
Reveca
Roza
Sonia
Sonya
Tana
Taneya
Tani
Tania
Tanis
Tanya
Tashi
Tasia
Tatiana
Tatianna
Tatiyana
Tatyana
Tonia
Tonya
Valeska
Velika
Vera
Veta
Wava
Yana
Yarina
Yarmilla
Yvanna
Zhana
Zofia
Zora
Zorina
Zoya

Boys
Anton
Benedikt
Boris
Cash
Casimir

Cezar
Damek
Danick
Danilo
Feodor
Jan
Jarek
Jerney
Jovan
Kasimir
Kiril
Lomán
Marek
Milos
Rad
Radman
Radomil
Stane
Stanislav
Taman
Tavo
Toni
Vasyl
Vladislav
Wenceslaus
Yoakim
Yovani
Zelimir
Ziven
Zorya

Somali

Girls
Deka
Kalifa

Spanish

Girls
Adalene
Adalia
Adana
Adonia
Alameda
Alandra
Alanza
Alegria
Alejandra
Alida
Alita

(Spanish girls continued)

Almira
Alondra
Alva
Amada
Amaranta
Amparo
Ana
Anita
Bebe
Belicia
Belinda
Benita
Bibi
Bonita
Bonnie
Brisa
Cailida
Calida
Camden
Catalina
Chalina
Charo
Chavella
Chiquita
Cira
Clarita
Coco
Conchita
Constanza
Consuelo
Corazon
Damita
Danielan
Delores
Dita
Dolores
Dorinda
Drinka
Dulcinea
Eldora
Elisa
Elmira
Elvira
Enrica
Esmeralda
Esperanza
Estefani
Estephanie

Evita
Felica
Florida
Fonda
Gitana
Gracia
Guillerma
Hermosa
Ines
Isabel
Isobel
Issie
Itzel
Izabella
Jacinda
Jacinthe
Jacynthe
Jada
Jade
Jaden
Jadyn
Jaida
Jaiden
Jaira
Jamaica
Jamecia
Jameika
Jamica
Jardena
Javiera
Jayda
Jayde
Jayden
Josefina
Juana
Juandalyn
Juanita
Juliana
Julita
Kiki
Lali
Landra
Leya
Linda
Lindy
Lola
Lolita
Lorinda
Lucia
Lucita

Luisa
Lupe
Luz
Lynda
Lyndi
Madrona
Mahogony
Maita
Malia
Manda
Manuela
Margarita
Mari
Maria
Mariana
Marisol
Marita
Marquita
Maruca
Matusha
Mel
Melita
Melosa
Mercedes
Miguela
Milagros
Mira
Montana
Mora
Necha
Neena
Nelia
Neva
Nevada
Nina
Nita
Novia
Nuela
Oleda
Olinda
Ora
Orquidea
Paca
Palmira
Paloma
Pancha
Paquita
Patia
Paz
Pepita

Perfecta
Pilar
Primavera
Querida
Queta
Raman
Ramona
Reina
Remedios
Reseda
Ria
Rica
Ricarda
Rocio
Rosa
Rosalind
Rosalinda
Rosalyn
Rosario
Roselyn
Rosita
Ruperta
Salvadora
Salvia
Sancia
Santana
Santina
Savana
Savanah
Savannah
Senalda
Sevilla
Shaba
Sierra
Socorro
Solana
Soledad
Suela
Tequila
Tia
Tijuana
Tina
Tita
Toya
Trella
Ula
Valencia
Verdad
Vianca
Vina

Viñita
Vitoria
Xandra
Ynez
Ysabel
Yuana
Yuliana
Zaneta
Zanna
Zarita
Zaviera
Zelia
Zerlina
Zita

Boys
Adolfo
Alejándro
Alfonso
Alfredo
Aloisio
Alonso
Alroy
Alvaro
Andres
Antjuan
Aquila
Araldo
Armando
Arrio
Barto
Bebe
Bernardo
Bertín
Berto
Blanco
Bonaro
Carlito
Carlos
Cesar
Chago
Chan
Charro
Ché
Checha
Cheche
Chencho
Chepe
Chico
Chilo

Chuminga
Chumo
Cid
Cisco
Clemente
Cordaro
Cordero
Cortez
Currito
Dario
Decarlos
Desiderio
Diego
Domingo
Edgardo
Edmundo
Eduardo
Elonzo
Elvio
Emilio
Enrick
Enrique
Ermano
Ernesto
Estéban
Estevan
Estevao
Eugenio
Farruco
Federico
Felipe
Fermin
Fernando
Fico
Filberto
Flaminio
Flip
Francisco
Frederico
Fredo
Frisco
Galeno
Garcia
Geraldo
Gerardo
Giacinto
Gilberto
Gitano
Gonzalo
Gualberto

Guillermo	Mateo	Peyo	Santino	Ashanti	Tabia
Gustavo	Matías	Phelipe	Santo	Asia	Tisa
Gutierre	Mauricio	Pilar	Santonio	Aziza	Winda
Heraldo	Maxi	Pirro	Santos	Batini	Yiesha
Heriberto	Máximo	Piti	Sarito	Bina	Zahra
Hernando	Menico	Pitin	Savon	Chiku	Zakia
Hilario	Miguel	Placido	Segundo	Chinira	Zalika
Honorato	Miquelangel	Ponce	Senon	Dalila	Zawati
Huberto	Mincho	Porifirio	Servando	Dashiki	Zuri
Iago	Minel	Quico	Sidonio	Dinka	Zuwena
Jacinto	Mingo	Quiqui	Sierra	Eshe	**Boys**
Jade	Mique	Quito	Stancio	Goma	Abasi
Jaguar	Moises	Rafael	Tabo	Hadiya	Ahmed
Jaime	Montana	Raimundo	Tadzio	Hasana	Ali
Jairo	Monte	Rami	Tajo	Hasina	Annan
Jando	Montez	Ramiro	Tano	Jaha	Ashanti
Javier	Mundo	Ramón	Teb	Jina	Ashon
Joaquín	Naldo	Raymundo	Teobaldo	Jokla	Ashur
Jobo	Napier	Raynaldo	Teodoro	Kalere	Azizi
Joquin	Nardo	Reinaldo	Terencio	Kaluwa	Bakari
Jorge	Natal	Renaldo	Tiago	Kamaria	Chane
Jorrín	Natan	Rey	Ticho	Kameke	Chui
José	Navarro	Reymundo	Timoteo	Kanene	Dauid
Joseluis	Nelo	Reynaldo	Tino	Kapuki	Enzi
Juan	Nemesio	Ric	Tobal	Kesi	Faraji
Juancarlos	Nero	Ricardo	Tomás	Koffi	Haji
Juaquin	Neto	Rico	Topo	Kolina	Hamisi
Kiki	Nevada	Riel	Tulio	Kudio	Hasani
Kruz	Nicho	Rio	Turi	Kwashi	Idi
Lando	Niño	Riqui	Tutu	Kwau	Issa
Lao	Noé	Roberto	Vicente	Leta	Jaali
Larenzo	Norberto	Rodas	Victorio	Malena	Jabari
Laurencio	Oalo	Rodolfo	Vidal	Marini	Jahi
Leandro	Olo	Rodrigo	Vincente	Mashika	Jelani
Lencho	Orlando	Rodriguez	Virgilio	Mosi	Jimoh
Lobo	Oro	Rodriquez	Waterio	Neema	Joshi
Lon	Osvaldo	Rogelio	Wilfredo	Nuru	Jumaane
Lonnie	Oswaldo	Rogerio	Ximenes	Paka	Jumah
Lonzo	Othello	Roja	Yago	Panya	Kanu
Lorenzo	Pablo	Rolando	Zacarias	Pasua	Khalfani
Luis	Paco	Rolon		Penda	Khamisi
Macario	Pancho	Rosalio	**Swahili**	Ramla	Kito
Mango	Paquito	Rudi	**Girls**	Rashida	Kitwana
Manny	Pascual	Rusk	Adia	Raziya	Kondo
Mano	Patricio	Ruy	Aiesha	Rika	Kwasi
Marcos	Paulino	Salamon	Aisha	Sanura	Mansa
Marr	Paz	Salvador	Aleela	Shafira	Masud
Martez	Pedro	Sansón	Alika	Shani	Mbita
Marti	Pepe	Santana	Asha	Shany	Mbwana
Martinez	Perico	Santiago		Siti	Mhina

(Swahili boys continued)
Mosi
Musa
Mwinyi
Mwita
Mzuzi
Nuru
Okapi
Omari
Pili
Rajabu
Rashida
Rashidi
Sadiki
Safari
Saka
Salim
Sefu
Simba
Siwatu
Sudi
Suhuba
Sultan
Tambo
Tembo
Vuai
Yusuf
Zahur
Zakia
Zuberi

Swedish

Girls
Anna
Anneka
Birgitte
Carina
Ulla

Boys
Adrian
Alvar
Anders
Anderson
Burr
Frans
Gustaf
Hadrian
Halen

Hilmar
Kjell
Krister
Kristofer
Lauris
Lennart
Lukas
Lunt
Mathias
Mats
Mikael
Nansen
Niklas
Nils
Pal
Paulo
Per
Pol
Reinhold
Rickard
Rolle
Rune
Stefan
Steffan
Stig
Torkel
Valborg
Valdemar
Valfrid
Valter
Ville
Yngve

Swiss

Girls
Leli
Sefa

Syrian

Boys
Adar
Aram

Tai

Girls
Jai
Kanya
Lawan
Mali

Mayoree
Mayra
Ratana
Solada
Suchin
Sumalee
Sunee
Tida

Boys
Aran
Aroon
Atid
Decha
Jai
Kasem
Kiet
Kovit
Lek
Niran
Pravat
Pricha
Runrot
Sum
Virote

Tamil

Girls
Leya

Tanzanian

Girls
Akili

Taos

Boys
Anchali

Teutonic

Girls
America
Kay
Xiomara

Boys
Amerigo
Bardrick
Patxi
Wilmot

Tibetan

Boys
Polo

Tiv

Girls
Iverem
Limber

Boys
Bem
Boseda
Gowon
Teremun
Tor

Todas

Girls
Suri

Boys
Kers

Tswana

Girls
Moswen

Boys
Montsho
Tale
Tau

Tupi-Guarani

Boys
Jacy
Piñon
Raini

Turkish

Girls
Elma
Neylan
Rashida
Reyhan
Sarila
Sema
Umay
Zerdali
Zerrin

Boys
Abi
Acar
Adli
Ahir
Akar
Anka
Asker
Aydin
Azad
Baris
Basir
Berk
Cahil
Duman
Emre
Enver
Erol
Halil
Hasad
Husamettin
Ihsan
Kabil
Kahil
Kahraman
Kemal
Kerem
Khan
Kiral
Mesut
Murat
Ohannes
Onan
Onur
Osman
Ottmar
Ozturk
Sener
Sevilen
Sukru
Tabib
Umit
Uner
Yunus
Yurcel
Zeki

Twi

Girls
Kunto

Boys
Kofi

Ugandan

Girls
Kissa

Ukrainian

Girls
Yeva

Boys
Bohdan
Burian
Fadey
Osip
Yuri

Umbundu

Girls
Kasinda

Urdu

Boys
Taj

Uset

Boys
Kibo

Ute

Boys
Ouray

Vietnamese

Girls
Am
Bian
Cai
Cam
Hoa
Hong
Huong
Kim
Lan
Le
Mai
Nu

Ping
Tam
Thanh
Thao
Thi
Thuy
Tuyen
Tuyet
Xuan

Boys
An
Anh
Antoan
Bay
Binh
Cadao
Cham
Chim
Dinh
Dong
Duc
Gia
Hai
Hieu
Hoang
Hoc
Hung
Huy
Hy
Lap
Long
Minh
Nam
Ngai
Nghia
Ngu
Nien
Phuok
Pin
Son
Tai
Tam
Tan
Teo
Thai
Thang
Thanh
Thian
Thuc

Tin
Tong
Tu
Tuan
Tung
Tuyen

Watamare

Boys
Marar

Welsh

Girls
Bevanne
Blodwyn
Bronnie
Bronwyn
Bryce
Bryn
Carey
Cari
Caron
Carys
Cordelia
Cordi
Dee
Delia
Deryn
Dilys
Dylan
Dyllis
Enid
Genevra
Ginnifer
Gladys
Glenda
Glynnis
Guinevere
Gwen
Gwenda
Gwendolyn
Gwyn
Gwyneth
Idelle
Iola
Isolde
Jenifer
Jenna
Jenni

Jennifer
Jenny
Jennyfer
Linette
Lynette
Mab
Meaghan
Meghan
Meredith
Morgan
Morghan
Olwen
Owena
Perri
Rhian
Rhiannon
Rhonda
Ronda
Ronelle
Ronette
Rowan
Rowena
Sulwen
Taffy
Teagan
Tegan
Trevina
Vanora
Wenda
Wendi
Wendy
Winifred
Wynne
Yenifer
Yseult

Boys
Aneurin
Arvel
Barry
Bevan
Blair
Bogart
Bowen
Brice
Broderick
Brodrick
Bryce
Bryson
Caddock

Cade
Cadell
Cai
Cairn
Calder
Carey
Carrington
Cary
Cerdic
Clyde
Colwyn
Craddock
Cruz
Dafydd
Davis
Dewey
Dilwyn
Drew
Dylan
Dylon
Emlyn
Eoin
Gareth
Garnock
Garth
Gavin
Gawain
Gerwin
Gethin
Glendower
Glyn
Gower
Griffith
Gwayne
Gwilym
Gwyn
Hew
Howell
Iago
Idris
Iestyn
Inek
Iolo
Irv
Irvin
Irving
Ithel
Jestin
Jones

Kai
Kain
Kane
Keith
Kent
Kynan
Lewis
Llewellyn
Lloyd
Maddock
Maddox
Malvern
Meredith
Merion
Meurig
Newlin
Parry
Pembroke
Price
Reece
Reese
Renfrew
Rhett
Rhys
Rice
Romney
Sayer
Taffy
Taliesin
Tarrant
Trahern
Treston
Trev
Trevor
Tristan
Tristen
Tristin
Triston
Tristram
Tristyn
Trystan
Tudor
Vaughn
Wren
Wyn
Yestin

West Australian Aboriginal

Girls
Kylie

Winnebago

Boys
Maona
Nawkaw

Xhosa

Girls
Mandisa

Yao

Boys
Ligongo
Lisimba
Mandala
Mapira
Masamba
Simba
Thenga
Umi
Useni
Usi

Yiddish

Girls
Blum
Chava
Gita
Kyla
Raizel
Rayna
Selda
Shaina
Zelda

Boys
Ber
Feivel
Fischel
Gershom
Henoch
Hertz

(Yiddish boys continued)

Kuper
Leben
Leib
Moishe
Shneur
Tevel
Velvel
Welfel
Yousef
Youssel
Zalman
Zelig
Zindel
Ziskind

Yoruba

Girls

Bayo
Fola
Iyabo
Monifa
Oba
Oni
Shardae

Boys

Ade
Ajala
Akins
Asa
Ayinde
Ayo
Dada
Foluke
Iyapo
Jibade
Jumoke
Kayin
Kayode
Kehind
Kunle
Mongo
Nika
Oba
Obadele
Ojo
Oko
Ola
Olajuwon
Olamina
Olatunji
Olubayo
Olufemi
Olujimi
Olushola
Orunjan
Segun
Shangobunni
Soja
Sowande
Taiwo
Tobi

Zimbabwean

Girls

Jendaya

Zulu

Boys

Ganya
Shaka
Sipho

Zuni

Girls

Kwanita
Lolly
Malia
Pelipa
Suni
Taci
Tiwa
Tusa

Boys

Elia
Halian
Kwam
Lonan
Lusio

GiRLS' NAMES

AALEYAH (Hebrew) an alternate form of Aliya.
Aalayah, Aalayaha, Aalea, Aaleah, Aaleaha, Aaleeyah, Aaleyiah, Aaleyyah

AALIAH (Hebrew) an alternate form of Aliya.
Aaliaya, Aaliayah

AALISHA (Greek) an alternate form of Alisha.
Aaleasha, Aaliesha

AALIYAH (Hebrew) an alternate form of Aliya.
Aahliyah, Aailiyah, Aailyah, Aalaiya Aaleah, Aalia, Aalieyha, Aaliya, Aaliyaha, Aaliyha, Aalliah, Aalliyah, Aalyah, Aalyiah

ABAGAIL (Hebrew) an alternate form of Abigale.
Abagael, Abagaile, Abagale, Abagayle, Abageal, Abagil, Abaigael, Abaigeal

ABBAGAIL (Hebrew) an alternate form of Abigale.
Abbagale, Abbagayle, Abbegail, Abbegale, Abbegayle

ABBEY, Abbie, Abby (Hebrew) familiar forms of Abigail.
Aabbee, Abbe, Abbea, Abbeigh, Abbi, Abbye, Abeey, Abey, Abi, Abia, Abie, Aby

ABBYGAIL (Hebrew) an alternate form of Abigale.

Abbeygale, Abbygale, Abbygayl, Abbygayle

ABEGAIL (Hebrew) an alternate form of Abigale.
Abegale, Abegaile, Abegayle

ABELINA (American) a combination of Abbey + Lina.
Abilana, Abilene

ABIA (Arabic) great.
Abbia, Abbiah, Abiah, Abya

ABIANNE (American) a combination of Abbie + Anne.
Abena, Abeni, Abian, Abinaya

ABIDA (Arabic) worshiper.
Abedah, Abidah

ABIGAIL (Hebrew) father's joy. Bible: one of the wives of King David. See also Gail.
Abagail, Abbagail, Abbey, Abbiegail, Abbiegayle, Abbigael, Abbigail, Abbigal, Abbigale, Abbigayl, Abbigayle, Abbygail, Abegail, Abgail, Abgale, Abgayle, Abigael, Abigaile, Abigaill, Abigal, Abigale, Abigayil, Abigayl, Abigayle, Abigel, Abigial, Abugail, Abygail, Avigail

ABINAYA (American) an alternate form of Abianne.
Abenaa, Abenaya, Abinaa, Abinaiya, Abinayan

ABIRA (Hebrew) my strength.
Abbira, Abeer, Abeerah, Abeir, Abera, Aberah, Abhira, Abiir, Abir

ABRA (Hebrew) mother of many nations. A feminine form of Abraham.
Abree, Abri, Abria

ABRIA (Hebrew) an alternate form of Abra.
Abréa, Abrea, Abreia, Abriah, Abriéa, Abrya

ABRIAL (French) open; secure, protected.
Abrail, Abreal, Abreale, Abriale, Abrielle

ABRIANA (Italian) a form of Abra.
Abbrienna, Abbryana, Abreana, Abreanna, Abreanne, Abreeana, Abreona, Abreonia, Abriann, Abrianna, Abriannah, Abrieana, Abrien, Abrienna, Abrienne, Abrietta, Abrion, Abrionée, Abrionne, Abriunna, Abryann, Abryanna, Abryona

ABRIELLE (French) an alternate form of Abrial.
Aabriella, Abriel, Abriell, Abryell

ABRIL (French) an alternate form of Abrial.
Abrilla, Abrille

ABYGAIL (Hebrew) an alternate form of Abigail.
Abygael, Abygale, Abygayle

ACACIA (Greek) thorny. Mythology: the acacia tree symbolizes immortality and resurrection. See also Casey.
Acasha, Acatia, Accassia, Acey, Acie, Akacia, Cacia, Casia, Kasia

ADA (German) a short form of Adelaide. (English) prosperous; happy.
Adabelle, Adah, Adan, Adaya, Adda, Auda

ADAH (Hebrew) ornament.
Ada, Addah

ADAIR (Greek) an alternate form of Adara.
Adaire

ADALENE (Spanish) an alternate form of Adalia.

Adalene *(cont.)*
Adalane, Adalena, Adalin, Adalina, Adaline, Adalinn, Adalyn, Adalynn, Adalynne, Addalyn, Addalynn

ADALIA (German, Spanish) noble.
Adal, Adala, Adalea, Adaleah, Adalee, Adalene, Adali, Adalie, Adaly, Addal, Addala, Addaly

ADAMA (Phoenician) woman, humankind. (Hebrew) earth; a woman of the red earth. A feminine form of Adam.

ADAMMA (Ibo) child of beauty.

ADANA (Spanish) a form of Adama.

ADANNA (Nigerian) her father's daughter.
Adanya

ADARA (Greek) beauty. (Arabic) virgin.
Adair, Adaira, Adaora, Adar, Adarah, Adare, Adaria, Adarra, Adasha, Adauré, Adra

ADAYA (American) a form of Ada.
Adaija, Adaijah, Adaja, Adajah, Adayja, Adayjah, Adejah

ADDIE (Greek, German) a familiar form of Adelaide, Adrienne.
Aday, Adde, Addee, Addey, Addi, Addia, Addy, Ade, Adee, Adei, Adey, Adeye, Adi, Adie, Ady, Atti, Attie, Atty

ADDISON, Addyson (English) daughter of Adam.
Addis, Addisen, Addisson, Adison

ADELA (English) a short form of Adelaide.
Adelae, Adelia, Adelista, Adella

ADELAIDE (German) noble and serene. See also Ada, Adela, Adeline, Adelle, Ailis, Delia, Della, Ela, Elke, Heidi.
Adelade, Adelaid, Adelaida, Adelei, Adelheid, Adeliade, Adelka, Aley, Laidey, Laidy

ADELE (English) an alternate form of Adelle.
Adel, Adelie, Adile

ADELINA (English) an alternate form of Adeline.
Adalina, Adeleana, Adelena, Adellyna, Adeliana, Adellena, Adileena, Adlena

ADELINE (English) a form of Adelaide.
Adaline, Adelaine, Adelin, Adelina, Adelind, Adelita, Adeliya, Adelle, Adelyn, Adelynn, Adelynne, Adilene, Adlin, Adline, Adlyn, Adlynn, Aline

ADELLE (German, English) a short form of Adelaide, Adeline.
Adele, Adell

ADENA (Hebrew) noble; adorned.
Adeana, Adeen, Adeena, Aden, Adene, Adenia, Adenna, Adina

ADIA (Swahili) gift.
Addia, Adéa, Adea, Adiah

ADILA (Arabic) equal.
Adeala, Adeela, Adela, Adelah, Adeola, Adilah, Adileh, Adilia, Adyla

ADILENE (English) an alternate form of Adeline.
Adilen, Adileni, Adilenne, Adlen, Adlene

ADINA (Hebrew) an alternate form of Adena. See also Dina.
Adeana, Adiana, Adiena, Adinah, Adine, Adinna, Adyna

ADIRA (Hebrew) strong.
Ader, Adera, Aderah, Aderra, Adhira, Adirah, Adirana

ADISON, Adyson (English) alternate forms of Addison, Addyson.
Adis, Adisa, Adisen, Adisynne, Adysen

ADITI (Hindi) unbound. Religion: the mother of the Hindu gods.
Adithi, Aditti

ADLEIGH (Hebrew) my ornament. A feminine form of Adlai.
Adla, Adleni

ADONIA (Spanish) beautiful. A feminine form of Adonis.
Adonica, Adonis, Adonna, Adonnica, Adonya

ADORA (Latin) beloved. See also Dora.
Adore, Adoree, Adoria

ADRA (Arabic) virgin.
Adara

ADREANA, Adreanna (Latin) alternate forms of Adrienne.
Adrean, Adreanne, Adreauna, Adreeanna, Adreen, Adreena, Adreeyana, Adrena, Adrene, Adrenea, Adréona, Adreonia, Adreonna

ADRIA (English) a short form of Adriana, Adriene.
Adrea, Adriani, Adrya

ADRIANA, Adrianna (Italian) forms of Adrienne.

Addrianna, Addriyanna,
Adreiana, Adreinna, Adria,
Adriannea, Adriannia, Adrionna

ADRIANE, Adrianne (English)
forms of Adrienne.
Addrian, Adranne, Adria, Adrian,
Adreinne, Adriann, Adriayon,
Adrion

ADRIELLE (Hebrew) member of
God's flock.
Adriel, Adrielli, Adryelle

ADRIEN, Adriene (English)
alternate forms of Adrienne.

ADRIENNA (Italian) a form of
Adrienne. See also Edrianna.
Adreana, Adrieanna,
Adrieaunna, Adriena, Adrienia,
Adriennah, Adrieunna

ADRIENNE (Greek) rich. (Latin)
dark. A feminine form of
Adrian. See also Hadriane.
Addie, Adrien, Adriana, Adriane,
Adrianna, Adrianne, Adrie,
Adrieanne, Adrien, Adrienna,
Adriyanna

ADRINA (English) a short form
of Adriana, Adrianna.
Adrinah, Adrinne

ADRIYANNA (American) a form
of Adrienne.
Adrieyana, Adriyana, Adryan,
Adryana, Adryane, Adryanna,
Adryanne

ADYA (Hindi) Sunday.
Adia

AERIAL, Aeriel (Hebrew) alter-
nate forms of Ariel.
Aeriale, Aeriela, Aerielle, Aeril,
Aerile, Aeryal

AFI (African) born on Friday.
Affi, Afia, Efi, Efia

AFRA (Hebrew) young doe.
(Arabic) earth color. See also
Aphra.
Affery, Affrey, Affrie, Afraa

AFRICA (Irish) pleasant. History:
a twelfth-century queen of the
Isle of Man. Geography: one
of the seven continents.
Affrica, Afric, Africah, Africaya,
Africia, Africiana, Afrika, Aifric

AFRIKA (Irish) an alternate
form of Africa.
Afrikah

AFRODITE, Aphrodite (Greek)
Mythology: the goddess of
love and beauty.
Afrodita

AFTON (English) from Afton,
England.
Aftan, Aftine, Aftinn, Aftyn

AGATE (English) a semiprecious
stone.
Aggie

AGATHA (Greek) good, kind.
Literature: Agatha Christie
was a British writer of more
than seventy detective nov-
els. See also Gasha.
Agace, Agaisha, Agasha, Agata,
Agatah, Agathe, Agathi, Agatka,
Agetha, Aggie, Ágota, Ágotha,
Agueda, Atka

AGATHE (Greek) an alternate
form of Agatha.

AGGIE (Greek) a short form of
Agatha, Agnes.
Ag, Aggy, Agi

AGNES (Greek) pure. See also
Aneesa, Anessa, Anice,
Anisha, Ina, Inez, Necha,
Nessa, Nessie, Neza,
Nyusha, Una, Ynez.

Aganetha, Aggie, Agna, Agne,
Agneis, Agnelia, Agnella, Agnés,
Agnesa, Agnesca, Agnese,
Agnesina, Agness, Agnessa,
Agnesse, Agneta, Agneti,
Agnetta, Agnies, Agnieszka,
Agniya, Agnola, Agnus, Aignéis,
Aneska, Anka

AHAVA (Hebrew) beloved.
Ahivia

AHLIYA (Hebrew) an alternate
form of Aliya.
Ahlai, Ahlaia, Ahlaya, Ahleah,
Ahleeyah, Ahley, Ahleya, Ahlia,
Ahliah, Ahliyah

AIDA (Latin) helpful. (English)
an alternate form of Ada.
Aidah, Aidan, Aide, Aidee

AIDAN, Aiden (Latin) alternate
forms of Aida.

AIESHA (Swahili, Arabic) an
alternate form of Aisha.
Aeisha, Aeshia, Aieshia,
Aieysha, Aiiesha

AIKO (Japanese) beloved.

AILANI (Hawaiian) chief.
Aelani, Ailana

AILEEN (Scottish) light bearer.
(Irish) a form of Helen. See
also Eileen.
Ailean, Aileena, Ailen, Ailene,
Aili, Ailina, Ailinn, Aillen

AILI (Scottish) a form of Alice.
(Finnish) a form of Helen.
Aila, Ailee, Ailey, Ailie, Aily

AILIS (Irish) a form of Adelaide.
Ailesh, Ailish, Ailyse, Eilis

AILSA (Scottish) island dweller.
Geography: Ailsa Craig is an
island in Scotland.
Ailsha

AILYA (Hebrew) an alternate form of Aliya.
Ailiyah

AIMEE (Latin) an alternate form of Amy. (French) loved.
Aime, Aimée, Aimey, Aimi, Aimia, Aimie, Aimy

AINSLEY (Scottish) my own meadow.
Ainslee, Ainsleigh, Ainslie, Ainsly, Ansley, Aynslee, Aynsley, Aynslie

AIRIÉL (Hebrew) an alternate form of Ariel.
Aieral, Aierel, Aiiryel, Aire, Aireal, Aireale, Aireel, Airel, Airele, Airelle, Airi, Airial, Airiale, Airrel

AIRIANA (English) an alternate form of Ariana, Arianna.
Airana, Airanna, Aireana, Aireanah, Aireanna, Aireona, Aireonna, Aireyonna, Airianna, Airianne, Airiona, Airriana, Airrion, Airryon, Airyana, Airyanna

AISHA (Swahili) life. (Arabic) woman. See also Asha, Asia, Iesha, Isha, Keisha, Yiesha.
Aaisha, Aaishah, Aesha, Aeshah, Aheesha, Aiasha, Aiesha, Aieshah, Aisa, Aischa, Aish, Aishah, Aisheh, Aishia, Aishiah, Aiysha, Aiyesha, Ayesha, Aysa, Ayse, Aytza

AISLINN, Aislynn (Irish) alternate forms of Ashlyn, Ashlynn.
Aishellyn, Aishlinn, Aislee, Aisley, Aislin, Aisling, Aislyn, Aislynne

AIYANNA (Hindi) an alternate form of Ayanna.
Aianna, Aiyannah, Aiyonna, Aiyunna

AIYANA (Native American) forever flowering.
Aiyhana, Aiyona, Aiyonia, Ayana

AJA (Hindi) goat.
Ahjah, Aija, Aijah, Ajá, Ajada, Ajah, Ajara, Ajaran, Ajare, Ajaree, Ajha, Ajia

AJANAE (American) a combination of the letter A + Janae.
Ajahnae, Ajahne, Ajana, Ajanaé, Ajane, Ajané, Ajanee, Ajanique, Ajena, Ajenae, Ajené

AJIA (Hindi) an alternate form of Aja.
Aijia, Ajhia, Aji, Ajjia

AKAYLA (American) a combination of the letter A + Kayla.
Akaela, Akaelia, Akaila, Akailah, Akala, Akaylah, Akaylia

AKEISHA (American) a combination of the letter A + Keisha.
Akaesha, Akaisha, Akasha, Akasia, Akeecia, Akeesha, Akeishia, Akeshia, Akisha

AKELA (Hawaiian) noble.
Ahkayla, Ahkeelah, Akelah, Akelia, Akeliah, Akeya, Akeyla, Akeylah

AKERIA (American) an alternate form of Akira.
Akera, Akerah, Akeri, Akerra, Akerra

AKI (Japanese) born in autumn.
Akeeye

AKIA (American) a combination of the letter A + Kia.
Akaja, Akeia, Akeya, Akiá, Akiah, Akiane, Akiaya, Akiea, Akiya, Akiyah, Akya, Akyan, Akyia, Akyiah

AKIKO (Japanese) bright light.

AKILAH (Arabic) intelligent.
Aikiela, Aikilah, Akeela, Akeelah, Akeila, Akeilah, Akeiyla, Akiela,

Akielah, Akila, Akilaih, Akilia, Akilka, Akillah, Akkila, Akyla, Akylah

AKILI (Tanzanian) wisdom.

AKINA (Japanese) spring flower.

AKIRA (American) a combination of the letter A + Kira.
Akeria, Akiera, Akierra, Akirah, Akire, Akiria, Akirrah, Akyra

ALAINA, Alayna (Irish) alternate forms of Alana.
Aalaina, Alainah, Alaine, Alainna, Alainnah, Alane, Alaynah, Alayne, Alaynna, Aleine, Alleyna, Alleynah, Alleyne

ALAIR (French) a form of Hilary, Hillary.
Alaira, Ali, Allaire

ALAMEA (Hawaiian) ripe; precious.

ALAMEDA (Spanish) poplar tree.

ALANA (Irish) attractive; peaceful. (Hawaiian) offering. A feminine form of Alan. See also Lana.
Alaana, Alaina, Alanae, Alanah, Alane, Alanea, Alani, Alania, Alanis, Alanna, Alawna, Alayna, Allana, Allanah, Allyn, Alonna

ALANDRA, Alandria (Spanish) forms of Alexandra, Alexandria.
Alandrea, Alantra, Aleandra, Aleandrea

ALANI (Hawaiian) orange tree.
Alaini, Alainie, Alania, Alanie, Alaney, Alannie

ALANNA (Irish) an alternate form of Alana.
Alannah

ALANZA (Spanish) noble and eager. A feminine form of Alphonse.

ALAYSHA, Alaysia (American) forms of Alicia.
Alaysh, Alayshia

ALBA (Latin) from Alba, Italy, a city on a white hill. A feminine form of Alban.
Albana, Albani, Albanie, Albany, Albeni, Albina, Albine, Albinia, Albinka, Elba

ALBERTA (German, French) noble and bright. A feminine form of Albert. See also Auberte, Bertha, Elberta.
Albertina, Albertine, Albertyna, Albertyne, Alverta

ALBREANNA (American) a combination of Alberta + Breanna.
Albré, Albrea, Albreona, Albreonna, Albreyon

ALCINA (Greek) strong minded.
Alceena, Alcine, Alcinia, Alseena, Alsinia, Alsyna, Alzina

ALDA (German) old; elder. A feminine form of Aldo.
Aldina, Aldine

ALDEN (English) old; wise protector.
Aldan, Aldon, Aldyn

ALDINA, Aldine (Hebrew) forms of Alda.
Aldeana, Aldene, Aldona, Aldyna, Aldyne

ALEA, Aleah (Arabic) high, exalted. (Persian) God's being.
Aileah, Aleea, Aleeah, Aleia, Aleiah, Allea, Alleah, Alleea, Alleeah

ALEASHA, Aleesha (Greek) alternate forms of Alisha.
Aleashae, Aleashea, Aleashia, Aleassa, Aleeshia

ALECIA (Greek) a form of Alicia.
Aalecia, Ahlasia, Aleacia, Aleacya, Aleasia, Alecea, Aleceea, Aleceia, Aleciya, Aleciyah, Alecy, Alecya, Aleeceia, Aleecia, Aleesia, Aleesiya, Aleicia, Alesha, Alesia, Allecia, Alleecia

ALEELA (Swahili) she cries.
Aleelah, Alila, Alile

ALEENA (Dutch) an alternate form of Aleene.
Ahleena, Aleana, Aleeanna

ALEENE (Dutch) alone.
Aleen, Aleena, Alene, Alleen

ALEEYA (Hebrew) an alternate form of Aliya.
Alee, Aleea, Aleeyah, Aleiya, Aleiyah

ALEEZA (Hebrew) a form of Aliza. See also Leeza.
Aleiza

ALEGRIA (Spanish) cheerful.
Aleggra, Alegra, Allegra, Allegria

ALEISHA, Alesha (Greek) alternate forms of Alecia, Alisha.
Aleasha, Aleashea, Aleasia, Aleesha, Aleeshah, Aleeshia, Aleeshya, Aleisa, Alesa, Alesah, Aleisha, Aleshia, Aleshya, Alesia, Alessia

ALEJANDRA (Spanish) a form of Alexandra.
Aleiandra, Alejanda, Alejandr, Alejandrea, Alejandria, Alejandrina, Alejandro

ALEKA (Hawaiian) a form of Alice.
Aleeka, Alekah

ALEKSANDRA (Greek) an alternate form of Alexandra.
Alecsandra, Aleksasha, Aleksandrija, Aleksandriya

ALENA (Russian) a form of Helen.
Alenah, Alene, Alenea, Aleni, Alenia, Alenka, Alenna, Alennah, Alenya, Alyna

ALESIA, Alessia (Greek) alternate forms of Alice.
Alessea, Alesya, Allesia

ALESSA (Greek) an alternate form of Alice.
Alessi, Allessa

ALESSANDRA (Italian) a form of Alexandra.
Alesandra, Alesandrea, Alissandra, Alissondra, Allesand, Allessandra

ALETA (Greek) a form of Alida. See also Leta.
Aletta, Alletta

ALETHEA (Greek) truth.
Alathea, Alathia, Aletea, Aletha, Aletheia, Alethia, Aletia, Alithea, Alithia

ALETTE (Latin) wing.

ALEX (Greek) a short form of Alexandra.
Aleix, Aleks, Alexe, Alexx, Allex, Allexx

ALEXA (Greek) a short form of Alexandra.
Aleixa, Alekia, Aleksa, Aleksha, Aleksi, Alexah, Alexsa, Alexssa, Alexxa, Allexa, Alyxa

ALEXANDRA (Greek) defender of mankind. A feminine form of Alexander. History: the last czarina of Russia. See also Lexia, Lexie, Olesia,

Alexandra *(cont.)*
Ritsa, Sandra, Sandrine, Sasha, Shura, Sondra, Xandra, Zandra.
Alandra, Alaxandra, Aleczandra, Alejandra, Aleksandra, Alessandra, Alex, Alexa, Alexande, Alexandera, Alexandre, Alexas, Alexi, Alexina, Alexine, Alexis, Alexsandra, Alexius, Alexsis, Alexus, Alexxandra, Alexys, Alexzandra, Alix, Alixandra, Aljexi, Alla, Alyx, Alyxandra, Lexandra

ALEXANDREA (Greek) an alternate form of Alexandria.
Alexandreana, Alexandreia, Alexandriea, Alexandrieah, Alexanndrea

ALEXANDRIA (Greek) an alternate form of Alexandra. See also Drinka, Xandra, Zandra.
Alaxandria, Alecsandria, Aleczandria, Alexanderia, Alexanderine, Alexandrea, Alexandrena, Alexandrie, Alexandrina, Alexandrine, Alexanndria, Alexandrya, Alexendria, Alexendrine, Alexia, Alixandrea, Alyxandria

ALEXANDRINE (Greek) an alternate form of Alexandra.
Alexandrina

ALEXANNE (American) a combination of Alex + Anne.
Alexan, Alexanna, Alexane, Alexann, Alexanna, Alexian, Alexiana

ALEXAS, Alexes (Greek) short forms of Alexandra.
Alexess

ALEXI, Alexie (Greek) short forms of Alexandra.
Aleksey, Aleksi, Alexey, Alexy

ALEXIA (Greek) a short form of Alexandria. See also Lexia.
Aleksia, Aleska, Alexcia, Alexea, Alexsia, Alexsiya, Allexia, Alyxia

ALEXIS (Greek) a short form of Alexandra.
Aalexis, Ahlexis, Alaxis, Alecsis, Alecxis, Aleexis, Aleksis, Alexcis, Alexias, Alexiou, Alexiss, Alexiz, Alexxis, Alixis, Allexis, Elexis, Lexis

ALEXIUS, Alexus (Greek) short forms of Alexandra.
Aalexus, Aalexxus, Aelexus, Ahlexus, Alecsus, Alexsus, Alexuss, Alexxus, Alixus, Allexius, Allexus, Elexus, Lexus

ALEXSANDRA (Greek) an alternate form of Alexandra.
Alexsandria, Alexsandro, Alixsandra

ALEXSIS, Alexxis (Greek) short forms of Alexandra.
Alexxiz

ALEXYS (Greek) a short form of Alexandra.
Alexsys, Alexyes, Alexyis, Alexyss, Allexys

ALEXZANDRA, Alexzandra (Greek) alternate forms of Alexandra.
Alexzand, Alexzandrea, Alexzandriah, Alexzandrya, Alixzandria

ALEYA, Aleyah (Hebrew) alternate forms of Aliya.
Alayah, Aleayah, Aleeya, Aléyah, Aleyia, Aleyiah

ALFIE (English) a familiar form of Alfreda.
Alfi, Alfy

ALFREDA (English) elf counselor; wise counselor. A feminine form of Alfred. See also Effie, Elfrida, Freda, Frederica.
Alfie, Alfredda, Alfredia, Alfreeda, Alfreida, Alfrieda

ALI, Aly (Greek) familiar forms of Alicia, Alisha, Alison.
Allea, Alli, Allie, Ally

ALIA, Aliah (Hebrew) alternate forms of Aliya. See also Aaliyah, Alea.
Aelia, Allia, Alya

ALICE (Greek) truthful. (German) noble. See also Aili, Aleka, Alie, Alisa, Alison, Alli, Alysa, Alyssa, Alysse, Elke.
Adelice, Alecia, Aleece, Alesia, Alicie, Aliece, Alise, Alix, Alize, Alla, Alleece, Allice, Allis, Allise, Allix

ALICIA (English) an alternate form of Alice. See also Elicia, Licia.
Aelicia, Alaysha, Alecea, Alecia, Aleecia, Ali, Alicea, Alicha, Alichia, Aliciah, Alician, Alicja, Alicya, Aliecia, Alisha, Allicea, Allicia, Alycia, Ilysa

ALIDA (Latin) small and winged. (Spanish) noble. See also Aleta, Lida, Oleda.
Aleda, Aleida, Alidia, Alita, Alleda, Allida, Allidah, Alyda, Alydia, Elida, Elidia

ALIE, Allie (Greek) familiar forms of Alice.

ALIESHA (Greek) an alternate form of Alisha.
Alieshai, Alieshia, Alliesha

ALIKA (Hawaiian) truthful. (Swahili) most beautiful.
Aleka, Alica, Alikah, Alike, Alikee, Aliki

ALIMA (Arabic) sea maiden; musical.

ALINA, Alyna (Slavic) bright. (Scottish) fair. (English) a short form of Adeline. See also Alena.
Aliana, Alianna, Alinah, Aline, Alinna, Allyna, Alynna, Alyona

ALINE (Scottish) an alternate form of Alina.
Alianne, Allene, Alline, Allyn, Allyne, Alyne, Alynne

ALISA, Alissa (Greek) an alternate form of Alice. See also Elisa, Ilisa.
Aalissah, Aaliysah, Aleessa, Alisah, Alisea, Alisia, Alisza, Alisza, Aliysa, Allissa, Alyssa

ALISE, Allise (Greek) alternate forms of Alice.
Alics, Aliese, Alis, Aliss, Alisse, Alisse, Alles, Allesse, Allis, Allisse

ALISHA (Greek) truthful. (German) noble. (English) an alternate form of Alicia. See also Elisha, Ilisha, Lisha.
Aalisha, Aleasha, Aleesha, Aleisha, Alesha, Ali, Aliesha, Aliscia, Alishah, Alishay, Alishaye, Alishia, Alishya, Alitsha, Allisha, Allysha, Alysha

ALISHIA, Alisia, Alissia (English) alternate forms of Alisha.
Alishea, Alisheia, Alishiana, Alyssaya, Alisea, Alissya, Alisyia, Allissia

ALISON, Allison (English) forms of Alice. See also Lissie.
Ali, Alicen, Alicyn, Alisan, Alisann, Alisanne, Alisen, Alisenne, Alisin, Alision, Alisonn, Alisson, Alisun, Alles, Allesse, Alleyson, Allie, Allisson, Allisyn, Allix, Allsun

ALITA (Spanish) a form of Alida.
Allita

ALIVIA (Latin) an alternate form of Olivia.
Alivah

ALIX (Greek) a short form of Alexandra, Alice.
Alixe, Alixia, Allix, Alyx

ALIXANDRA, Alixandria (Greek) alternate forms of Alexandra, Alexandria.
Alixandriya, Allixandra, Allixandria, Allixandrya

ALIYA (Hebrew) ascender.
Aaleyah, Aaliyah, Aeliyah, Ahliya, Ailya, Alea, Aleya, Alia, Alieya, Alieyah, Aliyah, Aliyiah, Aliyyah, Allia, Alliyah, Aly, Alyah

ALIYE (Arabic) noble.
Aliyeh

ALIZA (Hebrew) joyful. See also Aleeza, Eliza.
Alieza, Aliezah, Alitza, Aliz, Alizah, Alize, Alizee

ALIZABETH (Hebrew) an alternate form of Elizabeth.
Alyzabeth

ALLANA, Allanah (Irish) alternate forms of Alana.
Allanie, Allanna, Allauna

ALLEGRA (Latin) cheerful.
Legra

ALLENA (Irish) an alternate form of Alana.
Alleen, Alleyna, Alleynah

ALLI, Ally (Greek) familiar forms of Alice.
Ali, Alley

ALLIA, Alliah (Hebrew) alternate forms of Aliya.

ALLISSA (Greek) an alternate form of Alyssa.
Allisa

ALLIYAH (Hebrew) an alternate form of Aliya.
Alliya, Alliyha, Alliyia, Alliyyah, Allya, Allyah

ALLYSA, Allyssa (Greek) an alternate form of Alyssa.
Allissa, Allyisa, Allysa, Allysah, Allyssah

ALLYSHA (English) an alternate form of Alisha.
Alishia, Allysia

ALLYSON, Alyson (English) alternate forms of Alison, Allison.
Allysen, Allyson, Allysonn, Allysson, Allysun, Alyson

ALMA (Arabic) learned. (Latin) soul.
Almah

ALMEDA (Arabic) ambitious.
Allmeda, Allmedah, Allmeta, Allmita, Almea, Almedah, Almeta, Almida, Almita

ALMIRA (Arabic) aristocratic, princess; exalted. (Spanish) from Almeîra, Spain. See also Elmira, Mira.
Allmeera, Allmeria, Allmira, Almeera, Almeeria, Almeira, Almeria, Almire

ALOHA (Hawaiian) loving, kind hearted, charitable.
Alohi

ALOISA (German) famous warrior.
Aloisia, Aloysia

ALOMA (Latin) a short form of Paloma.

ALONDRA (Spanish) a form of Alexandra.
Allandra, Alonda

ALONNA (Irish) an alternate form of Alana.
Alona, Alonnah, Alonya, Alonyah

ALONZA (English) noble and eager. A feminine form of Alonzo.

ALORA (American) a combination of the letter A + Lora.
Alorah, Alorha, Alorie, Aloura, Alouria

ALPHA (Greek) first-born. Linguistics: the first letter of the Greek alphabet.
Alphia

ALTA (Latin) high; tall.
Allta, Altah, Altana, Altanna, Altea, Alto

ALTHEA (Greek) wholesome; healer. History: Althea Gibson was the first African American to win a major tennis title. See also Thea.
Altha, Altheda, Altheya, Althia, Elthea, Eltheya, Elthia

ALVA (Latin, Spanish) white; light skinned. See also Elva.
Alvana, Alvanna, Alvannah

ALVINA (English) friend to all; noble friend; friend to elves. A feminine form of Alvin. See also Elva, Vina.
Alveanea, Alveen, Alveena, Alveenia, Alvenea, Alvie, Alvinae, Alvincia, Alvine, Alvinea, Alvinesha, Alvinia, Alvinna, Alvita, Alvona, Alvyna, Alwin, Alwina, Alwyn

ALYAH, Alyiah (Hebrew) alternate forms of Aliya.
Aly, Alya, Aleah, Alyia

ALYCIA, Alyssia (English) alternate forms of Alicia.
Allyce, Alycea, Alyciah, Alyse, Lycia

ALYSA, Alyse, Alysse (Greek) alternate forms of Alice.
Allys, Allyse, Allyss, Alys, Alyss

ALYSHA, Alysia (Greek) alternate forms of Alisha.
Allysea, Allyscia, Alysea, Alyshia, Alyssha, Alyssia

ALYSSA (Greek) rational. Botany: alyssum is a flowering herb. See also Alice, Elissa.
Ahlyssa, Alissa, Allissa, Allyssa, Alyesa, Alyessa, Alyissa, Alysah, Ilyssa, Lyssa, Lyssah

ALYSSE (Greek) an alternate form of Alice.
Allyce, Allys, Allyse, Allyss, Alys, Alyss

ALYX, Alyxis (Greek) short forms of Alexandra.

ALYXANDRA, Alyxandria (Greek) alternate forms of Alexandra, Alexandria.
Alyxandrea, Alyxzandrya

AM (Vietnamese) lunar; female.

AMA (African) born on Saturday.

AMABEL (Latin) lovable. See also Bel, Mabel.

AMADA (Spanish) beloved.
Amadea, Amadi, Amadia, Amadita

AMAIRANI (Greek) an alternate form of Amara.
Amairaine, Amairane, Amairanie, Amairany

AMAL (Arabic) hopeful.
Amala

AMALIA (German) an alternate form of Amelia.
Ahmalia, Amalea, Amaleah, Amaleta, Amalija, Amalina, Amalisa, Amalita, Amaliya, Amalya, Amalyn

AMALIE (German) an alternate form of Amelia.
Amalee, Amali, Amaly

AMAN, Amani (Arabic) alternate forms of Imani.
Aamani, Ahmani, Amane, Amanee, Amaney, Amanie, Ammanu

AMANADA (Latin) an alternate form of Amanda.

AMANDA (Latin) lovable. See also Manda.
Amada, Amanada, Amandah, Amandalee, Amandalyn, Amandi, Amandie, Amandine, Amandy

AMANDEEP (Punjabi) peaceful light.

AMARA (Greek) eternally beautiful. See also Mara.
Amar, Amaira, Amairani, Amarah, Amari, Amaria, Amariah

AMARANTA (Spanish) a flower that never fades.

AMARI (Greek) an alternate form of Amara.
Amaree, Amarie, Amarii, Amarri

AMARIS (Hebrew) promised by God.
Amarissa, Amarys, Maris

AMARYLLIS (Greek) fresh; flower.
Amarillis, Amarylis

AMAUI (Hawaiian) thrush.

AMAYA (Japanese) night rain.

AMBAR (French) an alternate form of Amber.

AMBER (French) amber.
Aamber, Ahmber, Ambar, Amberia, Amberise, Amberly, Ambria, Ambur, Ambyr, Ambyre, Ammber, Ember

AMBERLY (American) a familiar form of Amber.
Amberle, Amberlea, Amberlee, Amberleigh, Amberley, Amberli, Amberlie, Amberlly, Amberlye

AMBERLYN, Amberlynn (American) combinations of Amber + Lynn.
Amberlin, Amberlina, Amberlyne, Amberlynne

AMBRIA (American) a form of Amber.
Ambrea, Ambra, Ambriah

AMELIA (Latin) an alternate form of Emily. (German) hardworking. History: Amelia Earhart, an American aviator, was the first woman to fly solo across the Atlantic Ocean. See also Ima, Melia, Millie, Nuela, Yamelia.
Aemilia, Aimilia, Amalia, Amalie, Amaliya, Ameila, Ameilia, Amelie, Amelina, Ameline, Amelisa, Amelita, Amella, Amilia, Amilina, Amilisa, Amilita, Amilyn, Amylia

AMELIE (German) a familiar form of Amelia.
Amaley, Amalie, Amelee, Ameleigh, Ameley, Amélie, Amely, Amilie

AMERICA (Teutonic) industrius. A feminine form of Amerigo.
Americana, Amerika

AMI, Amie (French) forms of Amy.
Aami, Amiee, Amii, Amiiee, Ammee, Ammie, Ammiee

AMILIA, Amilie (Latin, German) alternate forms of Amelia.
Amilee, Amili, Amillia, Amily, Amilya

AMINA (Arabic) trustworthy, faithful. History: the mother of the prophet Mohammed.
Aamena, Aamina, Aaminah, Ameena, Ameenah, Aminah, Aminda, Amindah, Aminta, Amintah

AMIRA (Hebrew) speech; utterance. (Arabic) princess. See also Mira.
Ameera, Ameerah, Amirah

AMISSA (Hebrew) truth.
Amissah

AMITA (Hebrew) truth.
Amitha

AMITY (Latin) friendship.
Amitie

AMLIKA (Hindi) mother.
Amlikah

AMMA (Hindi) god, godlike. Religion: another name for the Hindu goddess Shakti.

AMORIE (German) industrious leader. A feminine form of Emory.

AMPARO (Spanish) protected.

AMRIT (Sanskrit) nectar.
Amrita

AMY (Latin) beloved. See also Aimee, Emma, Esmé.
Amata, Ame, Amey, Ami, Amia, Amie, Amio, Ammy, Amye, Amylyn

AN (Chinese) peaceful.

ANA (Hawaiian, Spanish) a form of Hannah.
Anai, Anaia

ANABA (Native American) she returns from battle.

ANABEL, Anabelle (English) alternate forms of Annabel.
Anabela, Anabele, Anabell, Anabella

ANAHITA (Persian) a river and water goddess.
Anahai, Anahi, Anahit, Anahy

ANAIS (Hebrew) gracious.
Anaise, Anaïse

ANALA (Hindi) fine.

ANALISA, Analise (English) combinations of Ana + Lisa.
Analice, Analicia, Analis, Analisha, Analisia, Analissa

ANAMARIA (English) a combination of Ana + Maria.
Anamarie, Anamary

ANANDA (Hindi) blissful.

ANASTACIA (Greek) an alternate form of Anastasia.
Anastace, Anastacie

ANASTASIA (Greek) resurrection. See also Nastasia, Stacey, Stacia, Stasya.
Anastacia, Anastase, Anastascia, Anastasha, Anastashia, Anastasie, Anastasija, Anastassia, Anastassya, Anastasya, Anastatia, Anastaysia,

***Anastasia** (cont.)*
Anastazia, Anastice, Annastasia, Annastasija, Annastaysia, Annastazia, Annstås

ANATOLA (Greek) from the east.

ANCI (Hungarian) a form of Hannah.
Annus, Annushka

ANDEE, Andi, Andie (American) short forms of Andrea, Fernanda.
Ande, Andea, Andy

ANDREA (Greek) strong; courageous. (Latin) feminine. A feminine form of Andrew. See also Ondrea.
Aindrea, Andee, Andera, Anderea, Andra, Andrah, Andraia, Andraya, Andreah, Andreaka, Andreana, Andreane, Andree, Andrée, Andreea, Andreia, Andreja, Andreka, Andrel, Andrell, Andrelle, Andreo, Andressa, Andrette, Andreya, Andria, Andriana, Andrieka, Andrietta, Andris, Aundrea

ANDREANA, Andreanna (Greek) alternate forms of Andrea.
Ahndrianna, Andreina, Andrena, Andreyana, Andreyonna, Andrina, Andriona, Andrionna

ANDREANE, Andreanne (Greek) alternate forms of Andrea.
Andrean, Andreeanne, Andree Anne, Andrene, Andrian, Andrienne

ANDRIA (Greek) an alternate form of Andrea.
Andri, Andriea

ANDRIANA, Andrianna (Greek) alternate forms of Andrea.

ANEESA, Aneesha (Greek) alternate forms of Agnes.
Ahnesha, Ahnesia, Ahnesshia, Anee, Aneesah, Aneese, Aneeshah, Aneesia, Aneisa, Aneisha, Anessa, Anessia

ANEKO (Japanese) older sister.

ANELA (Hawaiian) angel.
Anel, Anelle

ANESSA (Greek) an alternate form of Agnes.
Anesha, Aneshia, Anesia, Anessia, Annessa

ANETRA (American) a form of Annette.
Anitra

ANEZKA (Czech) a form of Hannah.

ANGEL (Greek) a short form of Angela.
Angele, Angéle, Angell, Angelle, Angil, Anjel

ANGELA (Greek) angel; messenger.
Angala, Anganita, Angel, Angelanell, Angelanette, Angelee, Angeleigh, Angeles, Angeli, Angelia, Angelica, Angelina, Angelique, Angelita, Angella, Angellita, Angie, Anglea, Anjela, Anjelica

ANGELIA (Greek) an alternate form of Angela.
Angelea, Angeleah, Angelie

ANGELICA, Angelika (Greek) alternate forms of Angela.
Angalic, Angelic, Angelici, Angelicia, Angelike, Angeliki, Angellica, Angilica

ANGELINA, Angeline (Russian) forms of Angela.
Angalena, Angalina, Angeleen, Angelena, Angelene, Angeliana, Angeleana, Angellina, Angelyn, Angelyna, Angelyne, Angelynn, Angelynne, Anhelina, Anjelina

ANGELIQUE (French) a form of Angela.
Angeliqua, Angélique, Angilique, Anjelique

ANGENI (Native American) spirit.

ANGIE (Greek) a familiar form of Angela.
Ange, Angee, Angey, Angi, Angy

ANI (Hawaiian) beautiful.
Aany, Aanye

ANIA (Polish) a form of Hannah.
Ahnia, Anaya, Aniah

ANICA, Anika (Czech) familiar forms of Anna.
Aanika, Anaka, Aneeky, Aneka, Anekah, Anicka, Anik, Anikah, Anike, Anikka, Anikke, Aniko, Anneka, Annik, Annika, Anouska, Anuska

ANICE (English) an alternate form of Agnes.
Anesse, Anis, Anise, Annes, Annice, Annis, Annus

ANILA (Hindi) Religion: a Hindu wind god.
Anilla

ANISA, Anisah (Arabic) friendly.
Annissah

ANISSA, Anisha (English) forms of Agnes, Ann.
Aanisha, Aeniesha, Anis, Anisa, Anissah, Anise, Annisa, Annisha, Annissa, Anyssa

ANITA (Spanish) a form of Ann, Anna. See also Nita.
Aneeta, Aneetah, Aneethah, Anetha, Anitha, Anithah, Anitia, Anitra, Anitte

ANJELICA (Greek) an alternate form of Angela.
Anjelika

ANKA (Polish) a familiar form of Hannah.
Anke

ANN, Anne (English) gracious. Forms of Hannah.
Anissa, Anita, Annchen, Annette, Annie, Annik, Annika, Annze, Anouche

ANNA (German, Italian, Czech, Swedish) gracious. A form of Hannah. Culture: Anna Pavlova was a famous Russian ballerina. See also Anica, Anissa, Nina.
Ahnna, Ana, Anah, Anica, Anita, Annah, Annina, Annora, Anona, Anya, Anyu, Aska

ANNABEL (English) a combination of Anna + Bel.
Amabel, Anabel, Annabal, Annabelle

ANNABELLE (English) an alternate form of Annabel.
Anabelle, Annabell, Annabella

ANNALIE (Finnish) a form of Hannah.
Analee, Annalea, Annaleah, Annalee, Annaleigh, Annaleigha, Annali, Anneli, Annelie

ANNALISA, Annalise (English) combinations of Anna + Lisa.
Analisa, Analise, Annaliesa, Annaliese, Annalissa, Annalisse

ANNAMARIE, Annemarie, Annmarie, Anne-Marie (English) combinations of Anne + Marie.
Annamaria, Anna-Maria, Anna-Marie, Annmaria

ANNEKA (Swedish) a form of Hannah.
Annaka, Anneke, Annika, Anniki, Annikki

ANNELISA (English) a combination of Anne + Lisa.
Analiese, Anelisa, Anelise, Anneliese, Annelise

ANNETTE (French) a form of Ann. See also Anetra, Nettie.
Anet, Aneta, Anetra, Anett, Anetta, Anette, Anneth, Annett, Annetta

ANNIE (English) a familiar form of Ann.
Anni, Anny

ANNIK, Annika (Russian) forms of Ann.
Aneka, Anekah, Annick, Annicka, Annike, Annikka, Anninka, Anouk

ANNJANETTE (American) a combination of Ann + Janette.
Angen, Angenett, Angenette, Anjane, Anjanetta, Anjani

ANONA (English) pineapple.

ANOUHEA (Hawaiian) cool, soft fragrance.

ANSLEY (Scottish) an alternate form of Ainsley.
Anslea, Anslee, Ansleigh, Anslie

ANTHEA (Greek) flower.
Antha, Anthe, Anthia, Thia

ANTIONETTE (French) a form of Antonia.
Antionet, Antionett, Anntionett

ANTOINETTE (French) a form of Antonia. See also Netti, Toinette, Toni.
Anta, Antanette, Antoinella, Antoinet, Antonella, Antonetta, Antonette, Antonice, Antonieta, Antonietta, Antonique

ANTONIA (Greek) flourishing. (Latin) praiseworthy. A feminine form of Anthony. See also Toni, Tonya, Tosha.
Ansonia, Ansonya, Antania, Antinia, Antionette, Antoinette, Antona, Antoñia, Antonice, Antonie, Antonina, Antonine, Antoniya, Antonnea, Antonnia, Antonya

ANTONICE (Latin) an alternate form of Antonia.
Antanise, Antanisha, Antonesha, Antoneshia, Antonise, Antonisha

ANYA (Russian) a form of Anna.
Aaniyah, Aniya, Aniyah, Anja

ANYSSA (English) an alternate form of Anissa.
Anysa, Anysha

'AOLANI (Hawaiian) heavenly cloud.

APHRA (Hebrew) young doe. See also Afra.

APRIL (Latin) opening. See also Avril.
Aprele, Aprelle, Apriell, Aprielle, Aprila, Aprile, Aprilette, Aprili, Aprill, Apryl

APRYL (Latin) an alternate form of April.
Apryle

AQUENE (Native American) peaceful.

ARA (Arabic) opinionated.
Ahraya, Aira, Arae, Arah, Araya, Arayah

ARABELLA (Latin) beautiful altar. See also Belle, Orabella.
Arabela, Arabele, Arabelle

ARACELI, Aracely (Latin) heavenly altar.
Aracele, Aracelia, Aracelli, Araseli, Arasely, Arcelia, Arceli

ARDELLE (Latin) warm; enthusiastic.
Ardelia, Ardelis, Ardella

ARDEN (English) valley of the eagle. Literature: in Shakespeare, a romantic place of refuge.
Ardeen, Ardeena, Ardena, Ardene, Ardenia, Ardi, Ardin, Ardina, Ardine

ARDI (Hebrew) a short form of Arden, Ardice, Ardith.
Ardie, Arti, Artie

ARDICE (Hebrew) an alternate form of Ardith.
Ardis, Artis, Ardiss, Ardyce, Ardys

ARDITH (Hebrew) flowering field.
Ardath, Ardi, Ardice, Ardyth

ARELI, Arely (American) forms of Oralee.
Areil, Areile, Arelee, Areli, Arelis, Arelli, Arellia, Arelly

ARELLA (Hebrew) angel; messenger.
Arela, Arelle, Orella, Orelle

ARETHA (Greek) virtuous. See also Oretha.
Areatha, Areetha, Areta, Aretina, Aretta, Arette, Arita, Aritha, Retha, Ritha

ARI, Aria, Arie (Hebrew) short forms of Ariel.
Ariah, Ariea, Aryia

ARIADNE (Greek) holy. Mythology: the daughter of King Minos of Crete.

ARIANA, Arianna (Greek) holy.
Aeriana, Aerianna, Aerionna, Ahreanna, Ahriana, Ahrianna, Airiana, Arieana, Ariona, Arionna, Aryonna

ARIANE (French), Arianne (English) forms of Ariana, Arianna.
Aerian, Aeriann, Aerion, Aerionne, Airiann, Ari, Arianie, Ariann, Ariannie, Arieann, Arien, Ariene, Arienne, Arieon, Arionne, Aryane, Aryann, Aryanne

ARICA (Scandinavian) an alternate form of Erica.
Aerica, Aericka, Aeryka, Aricca, Aricka, Arika, Arike, Arikka

ARIEL (Hebrew) lioness of God.
Aerial, Aeriale, Aeriel, Aeriela, Aeryal, Ahriel, Aire, Aireal, Airial, Ari, Aria, Arial, Ariale, Arieal, Ariela, Arielle, Arrieal, Arriel, Aryel, Auriel

ARIELLE (French) a form of Ariel.
Aeriell, Ariella, Arriele, Arriell, Arrielle, Aryelle, Aurielle

ARIN (Hebrew) enlightened. (Arabic) messenger. A feminine form of Aaron. See also Erin.
Aaren, Aerin, Aieron, Aieren, Arinn, Aryn

ARISTA (Greek) best.
Aris, Arissa, Aristana, Aristen

ARLA (German) an alternate form of Carla.

ARLEIGH (English) an alternate form of Harley.
Arlea, Arlee, Arley, Arlie, Arly

ARLENE (Irish) pledge. A feminine form of Arlen. See also Lena, Lina.

Airlen, Arlana, Arleen, Arleene, Arlen, Arlena, Arlenis, Arlette, Arleyne, Arliene, Arlina, Arlinda, Arline, Arlis

ARLETTE (English) a form of Arlene.
Arleta, Arletta, Arletty

ARLYNN (American) a combination of Arlene + Lynn.
Arlyn, Arlyne, Arlynne

ARMANI (Persian) desire, goal. A feminine form of Arman.
Armahni, Arman, Armanee, Armanii

ARMINE (Latin) noble. (German) soldier. (French) a feminine form of Herman.
Armina

ARNELLE (German) eagle. A feminine form of Arne.
Arnell, Arnella

ARTHA (Hindi) wealthy, prosperous.
Arthi, Arti, Artie

ARTIS (Irish) noble; lofty hill. (Scottish) bear. (English) rock. (Icelandic) follower of Thor. A feminine form of Arthur.
Arthea, Arthelia, Arthene, Arthette, Arthurette, Arthurina, Arthurine, Artina, Artice

ARYANA, Aryanna (Italian) forms of Ariana, Arianna.
Aryan, Aryanah, Aryannah

ARYN (Hebrew) an alternate form of Arin.
Aerryn, Aeryn, Airyn, Aryne, Arynn, Arynne

ASA (Japanese) born in the morning.

ASHA (Arabic, Swahili) an alternate form of Aisha, Ashia.

ASHANTI (Swahili) from a tribe in West Africa.
Achante, Achanti, Asante, Ashanta, Ashantae, Ashante, Ashanté, Ashantee, Ashantie, Ashaunta, Ashauntae, Ashauntee, Ashaunti, Ashonti, Ashuntae, Ashunti

ASHELY (English) an alternate form of Ashley.
Ashelee, Ashelei, Asheley, Ashelie, Ashelley, Ashelly

ASHIA (Arabic) life.
Asha, Ashya, Ashyah, Ashyia, Ayshia

ASHLEE, Ashli, Ashlie, Ashly (English) alternate forms of Ashley.
Ashle, Ashlea, Ashleah, Ashleeh, Ashliee

ASHLEIGH (English) an alternate form of Ashley.
Ahsleigh, Asheleigh, Ashlei, Ashliegh

ASHLEY (English) ash tree meadow. See also Lee.
Ahslee, Aishlee, Ashala, Ashalee, Ashalei, Ashaley, Ashely, Ashla, Ashlay, Ashleay, Ashlee, Ashleigh, Ashleye, Ashli, Ashlie, Ashly, Ashlye

ASHLIN (English) an alternate form of Ashlyn.
Ashlean, Ashliann, Ashlianne, Ashline

ASHLYN, Ashlynn (English) ash tree pool. (Irish) vision, dream.
Ashlan, Ashleann, Ashleen, Ashleene, Ashlen, Ashlene, Ashlin, Ashling, Ashlyne, Ashlynne

ASHTEN, Ashtin (English) alternate forms of Ashton.
Ashtine

ASHTON (English) ash-tree settlement.
Ashten, Ashtyn

ASHTYN (English) an alternate form of Ashton.
Ashtynne

ASIA (Greek) resurrection. (English) eastern sunrise. (Swahili) an alternate form of Aisha.
Ahsia, Aisia, Aisian, Asiah, Asian, Asianae, Asya, Aysia, Aysiah, Aysian, Ayzia

ASPEN (English) aspen tree.
Aspin, Aspyn

ASTER (English) a form of Astra.
Astera, Asteria, Astyr

ASTRA (Greek) star.
Asta, Astara, Aster, Astraea, Astrea

ASTRID (Scandinavian) divine strength.
Astri, Astrida, Astrik, Astrud, Atti, Estrid

ATALANTA (Greek) mighty huntress. Mythology: an athletic young woman who refused to marry any man who could not outrun her in a footrace. See also Lani.
Atalaya, Atlanta, Atlante, Atlee

ATARA (Hebrew) crown.
Atarah, Ataree

ATHENA (Greek) wise. Mythology: the goddess of wisdom.
Athenea, Athene, Athina, Atina

ATIRA (Hebrew) prayer.

AUBERTE (French) a form of Alberta.
Auberta, Aubertha, Auberthe, Aubine

AUBREE, Aubrie (French) alternate forms of Aubrey.
Auberi, Aubre, Aubrei, Aubreigh, Aubri, Aubrielle

AUBREY (German) noble; bearlike. (French) blond ruler; elf ruler.
Aubary, Aubery, Aubray, Aubrea, Aubreah, Aubree, Aubrette, Aubria, Aubrie, Aubry, Aubury, Avery

AUBRIANA, Aubrianna (English) combinations of Aubrey + Anna.
Aubreyana, Aubreyanna, Aubreyanne, Aubreyena, Aubrianne

AUDEY (English) a familiar form of Audrey.
Aude, Audi, Audie

AUDRA (French) a form of Audrey
Audria, Audriea

AUDREANNE (English) a combination of Audrey + Anne.
Audrea, Audreen, Audrianne, Audrienne

AUDREE, Audrie (English) alternate forms of Audrey.
Audre, Audri

AUDREY (English) noble strength.
Adrey, Audey, Audra, Audray, Audree, Audrie, Audrin, Audriya, Audry, Audrye

AUDRIANA, Audrianna (English) a combination of Audrey + Anna.
Audreanna, Audrienna, Audrina

AUDRIS (German) fortunate, wealthy.
Audrys

AUGUSTA (Latin) a short form of Augustine. See also Gusta.
Agusta, August, Auguste, Augustia, Augustus, Austina

AUGUSTINE (Latin) majestic. Religion: Saint Augustine was the first Archbishop of Canterbury. See also Tina.
Agustina, Augusta, Augustina, Augustyna, Augustyne, Austin

'AULANI (Hawaiian) royal messenger.
Lani, Lanie

AUNDREA (Greek) an alternate form of Andrea.
Aundreah

AURA (Greek) soft breeze. (Latin) golden. See also Ora.

AURELIA (Latin) golden. Mythology: the goddess of dawn. See also Oralia.
Auralea, Auralia, Aurea, Aureal, Aurel, Aurele, Aurelea, Aureliana, Aurelie, Auria, Aurie, Aurilia, Aurita

AURELIE (Latin) an alternate form of Aurelia.
Auralee, Auralei, Aurelee, Aurelei, Aurelle

AURORA (Latin) dawn.
Aurore, Ora, Ori, Orie, Rora

AUSTIN (Latin) a short form of Augustine.
Austen, Austin, Austyn, Austynn

AUTUMN (Latin) autumn.
Autum

AVA (Greek) an alternate form of Eva.
Avada, Avae, Ave, Aveen

AVALON (Latin) island.
Avallon

AVERY (English) a form of Aubrey.
Aivree, Averi, Averie, Avry

AVIS (Latin) bird.
Avais, Avi, Avia, Aviana, Avianca, Aviance, Avianna

AVIVA (Hebrew) springtime. See also Viva.
Aviv, Avivah, Avivi, Avivice, Avni, Avnit, Avri, Avrit, Avy

AVRIL (French) a form of April.
Averil, Averyl, Avra, Avri, Avrilia, Avrill, Avrille, Avrillia, Avy

AXELLE (Latin) axe. (German) small oak tree; source of life. A feminine form of Axel.
Aixa

AYA (Hebrew) bird; fly swiftly.
Aia, Aiah, Aiya, Aiyah

AYANNA (Hindi) innocent.
Ahyana, Aiyanna, Ayan, Ayana, Ayania, Ayannica, Ayna

AYESHA (Persian) a form of Aisha.
Ayasha, Ayeshah, Ayessa, Ayisha, Ayishah, Aysha, Ayshah, Ayshe, Ayshea, Aysia

AYITA (Cherokee) first in the dance.

AYLA (Hebrew) oak tree.
Aylana, Aylee, Ayleen, Aylene, Aylie, Aylin

AZA (Arabic) comfort.
Aiza, Aizha, Aizia, Azia

AZIZA (Swahili) precious.
Azize

BABA (African) born on Thursday.
Aba

BABE (Latin) a familiar form of Barbara. (American) an alternate form of Baby.
Babby

BABETTE (French, German) a familiar form of Barbara.
Babita, Barbette

BABS (American) a familiar form of Barbara.
Bab

BABY (American) baby.
Babby, Babe, Bebe

BAILEE, Bailie (English) alternate forms of Bailey.
Baelee, Baeli, Bailea, Bailei, Baillee, Baillie, Bailli

BAILEIGH, Baleigh (English) alternate forms of Bailey.
Baeleigh

BAILEY (English) bailiff.
Baeley, Bailee, Baileigh, Bailley, Bailly, Baily, Bali, Balley, Baylee, Bayley

BAKA (Hindi) crane.

BAKULA (Hindi) flower.

BAMBI (Italian) child.
Bambee, Bambie, Bamby

BANDI (Punjabi) prisoner.
Banda, Bandy

BAPTISTA (Latin) baptizer.
Baptiste, Batista, Battista, Bautista

BARA, Barra (Hebrew) chosen.
Bára, Bari

BARB (Latin) a short form of Barbara.
Barba, Barbe

BARBARA (Latin) stranger, foreigner. See also Bebe, Varvara, Wava.
Babara, Babb, Babbie, Babe, Babette, Babina, Babs, Barb, Barbara-Ann, Barbarit, Barbarita, Barbary, Barbeeleen, Barbera, Barbie, Barbora, Barborah, Barborka, Barbra, Barbraann, Barbro, Barùska, Basha, Bebe, Bobbi, Bobbie

BARBIE (American) a familiar form of Barbara.
Barbee, Barbey, Barbi, Barby, Baubie

BARBRA (American) a form of Barbara.
Barbro

BARRETT (German) strong as a bear.

BARRIE (Irish) spear; markswoman. A feminine form of Barry.
Bari, Barri, Berri, Berrie, Berry

BASIA (Hebrew) daughter of God.
Basya, Bathia, Batia, Batya, Bitya, Bithia

BATHSHEBA (Hebrew) daughter of the oath; seventh daughter. Bible: a wife of King David. See also Sheba.
Bathshua, Batsheva, Bersaba, Bethsabee, Bethsheba

BATINI (Swahili) inner thoughts.

BAYLEE, Bayleigh, Baylie (English) alternate forms of Bailey.
Bayla, Bayle, Baylea, Bayleah, Baylei, Bayli, Bayliee, Bayliegh

BAYLEY (English) an alternate form of Bailey.
Bayly

BAYO (Yoruba) joy is found.

BEA, Bee (American) short forms of Beatrice.

BEATA (Latin) a short form of Beatrice.
Beatta

BEATRICE (Latin) blessed; happy; bringer of joy. See also Trish, Trixie.
Bea, Beata, Beatrica, Béatrice, Beatricia, Beatriks, Beatrisa, Beatrise, Beatrissa, Beatriz, Beattie, Beatty, Bebe, Bee, Trice

BEATRIZ (Latin) an alternate form of Beatrice.
Beatris, Beatriss, Beatrix, Beitris

BEBE (Spanish) a form of Barbara, Beatrice.
BB, Beebee, Bibi

BECCA (Hebrew) a short form of Rebecca.
Beca, Becka, Bekah, Bekka

BECKY (American) a familiar form of Rebecca.
Beckey, Becki, Beckie

BEDELIA (Irish) an alternate form of Bridget.
Bedeelia, Biddy, Bidelia

BEL (Hindi) sacred wood of apple trees. A short form of Amabel, Belinda, Isabel.

BELA (Czech) white. (Hungarian) bright.
Belah, Biela

BELEN (Greek) arrow.
Belina

BELICIA (Spanish) dedicated to God.
Beli, Belia, Belica

BELINDA (Spanish) beautiful. Literature: a name coined by English poet Alexander Pope in *The Rape of the Lock*. See also Blinda, Linda.
Bel, Belindra, Belle, Belynda

BELLA (Latin) beautiful.
Bellah

BELLE (French) beautiful. A short form of Arabella, Belinda, Isabel. See also Billie.
Belita, Bell, Belli, Bellina

BELVA (Latin) beautiful view.
Belvia

BENA (Native American) pheasant. See also Bina.
Benea

BENECIA (Latin) a short form of Benedicta.
Beneisha, Benicia, Benish, Benisha, Benishia, Bennicia

BENEDICTA (Latin) blessed. A feminine form of Benedict.
Bendite, Benecia, Benedetta, Benedicte, Benedikta, Bengta, Benita, Benna, Benni, Bennicia, Benoîte, Binney

BENEDICTE (Latin) an alternate form of Benedicta.

BENITA (Spanish) a form of Benedicta.
Beneta, Benetta, Benitta, Bennita, Neeta

BENNETT (Latin) little blessed one.
Bennet, Bennetta

BENNI (Latin) a familiar form of Benedicta.
Bennie, Binni, Binnie, Binny

BENTE (Latin) blessed.

BERENICE (Greek) an alternate form of Bernice.
Berenise, Berenisse, Bereniz, Berenize

BERGET (Irish) an alternate form of Bridget.
Bergette, Bergit

BERIT (German) glorious.
Beret, Berette, Berta

BERKLEY (Scottish, English) birch tree meadow. A feminine form of Barclay.
Berkeley, Berkly

BERLYNN (English) a combination of Bertha + Lynn.
Berla, Berlin, Berlinda, Berline, Berling, Berlyn, Berlyne, Berlynne

BERNADETTE (French) a form of Bernadine. See also Nadette.
Bera, Beradette, Berna, Bernadet, Bernadete, Bernadett, Bernadetta, Bernarda, Bernardette, Bernedet, Bernedette, Bernessa, Berneta

BERNADINE (German) brave as a bear. (English) a feminine form of Bernard.

Bernadene, Bernadette, Bernadin, Bernadina, Bernardina, Bernardine, Berni

BERNETA (French) a short form of Bernadette.
Bernatta, Bernetta, Bernette, Bernita

BERNI (English) a familiar form of Bernadine, Bernice.
Bernie, Berny

BERNICE (Greek) bringer of victory. See also Bunny, Vernice.
Berenice, Berenike, Bernessa, Berni, Bernicia, Bernise, Nixie

BERTHA (German) bright; illustrious; brilliant ruler. A short form of Alberta. A feminine form of Berthold. See also Birdie, Peke.
Barta, Bartha, Berta, Berthe, Bertille, Bertita, Bertrona, Bertus, Birtha

BERTI (German, English) a familiar form of Gilberte, Bertina.
Berte, Bertie, Berty

BERTILLE (French) a form of Bertha.

BERTINA (English) bright, shining. A feminine form of Bert.
Bertine

BERYL (Greek) sea green jewel.
Beryle

BESS, Bessie (Hebrew) familiar forms of Elizabeth.
Bessi, Bessy

BETH (Hebrew, Aramaic) house of God. A short form of Bethany, Elizabeth.
Betha, Bethe, Bethia

BETHANI, Bethanie (Aramaic) alternate forms of Bethany.
Bethanee, Bethania, Bethannie, Bethni, Bethnie

BETHANN (English) a combination of Beth + Ann.
Beth-Ann, Bethan, Bethane, Bethanne, Beth-Anne

BETHANY (Aramaic) house of figs. Bible: a village near Jerusalem where Lazarus lived.
Beth, Bethaney, Bethani, Bethanney, Bethanny, Bethena, Betheny, Bethia, Bethina, Bethney, Bethny, Betthany

BETSY (American) a familiar form of Elizabeth.
Betsey, Betsi, Betsie

BETTE (French) a form of Betty.
Beta, Beti, Betka, Bett, Betta

BETTINA (American) a combination of Beth + Tina.
Betina, Betine, Betti, Bettine

BETTY (Hebrew) consecrated to God. (English) a familiar form of Elizabeth.
Bette, Bettey, Betti, Bettie, Bettye, Bettyjean, Betty-Jean, Bettyjo, Betty-Jo, Bettylou, Betty-Lou, Bety, Boski, Bözsi

BETULA (Hebrew) girl, maiden.

BEULAH (Hebrew) married. Bible: the Land of Beulah is a name for Israel.
Beula, Beulla, Beullah

BEV (English) a short form of Beverly.

BEVANNE (Welsh) daughter of Evan. A feminine form of Bevan.
Bevan, Bevann, Bevany

BEVERLY (English) beaver field. See also Buffy.
Bev, Bevalee, Beverle, Beverlee, Beverley, Beverlie, Beverlly, Bevlyn, Bevlynn, Bevlynne, Bevvy, Verly

BEVERLYANN (American) a combination of Beverly + Ann.
Beverliann, Beverlianne, Beverlyanne

BIAN (Vietnamese) hidden; secretive.

BIANCA (Italian) white. See also Blanca, Vianca.
Biancca, Biancha, Biancia, Bianco, Bianey, Bianica, Bianka, Biannca, Binney, Bionca, Blanca, Blanche, Byanca

BIANKA (Italian) an alternate form of Bianca.
Beyanka, Biannka

BIBI (Latin) a short form of Bibiana. (Arabic) lady. (Spanish) an alternate form of Bebe.

BIBIANA (Latin) lively.
Bibi

BIDDY (Irish) a familiar form of Bedelia.
Biddie

BILLI, Billy (English) alternate forms of Billie.
Billye

BILLIE (German, French) a familiar form of Belle, Wilhelmina. (English) strong willed.
Bilee, Bileigh, Bili, Bilie, Billee, Billi, Billy, Billye

BILLIE-JEAN (American) a combination of Billie + Jean.
Billiejean, Billyjean, Billy-Jean

BILLIE-JO (American) a combination of Billie + Jo.
Billiejo, Billyjo, Billy-Jo

BINA (Hebrew) wise; understanding. (Latin) a short form of Sabina. (Swahili) dancer. See also Bena.
Binah, Binney, Binta, Bintah

BINNEY (English) a familiar form of Benedicta, Bianca, Bina.
Binnee, Binni, Binnie, Binny

BIONCA (Italian) an alternate form of Bianca.
Beonca, Beyonca, Beyonka, Bioncha, Bionica, Bionka, Bionnca

BIRDIE (German) a familiar form of Bertha. (English) bird.
Bird, Birdee, Birdella, Birdena, Birdey, Birdi, Birdy, Byrd, Byrdey, Byrdie, Byrdy

BIRGITTE (Swedish) a form of Bridget.
Birgit, Birgita, Birgitta

BLAINE (Irish) thin.
Blane, Blayne

BLAIR (Scottish) plains dweller.
Blaire

BLAIRE (Scottish) an alternate form of Blair.
Blare, Blayre

BLAISE (French) one who stammers.
Blaize, Blasha, Blasia, Blaza, Blaze, Blazena

BLAKE (English) dark.
Blaque, Blayke

BLAKELY (English) dark meadow.
Blakelea, Blakelee, Blakeleigh, Blakeley, Blakeli, Blakelyn, Blakelynn, Blakesley, Blakley, Blakli

BLANCA (Italian) an alternate form of Bianca.
Bellanca, Blancka, Blanka

BLANCHE (French) a form of Bianca.
Blanch, Blancha, Blinney

BLINDA (American) a short form of Belinda.
Blynda

BLISS (English) blissful, joyful.
Blisse, Blyss, Blysse

BLODWYN (Welsh) flower. See also Wynne.
Blodwen, Blodwynne, Blodyn

BLONDELLE (French) blond, fair haired.
Blondell, Blondie

BLONDIE (American) a familiar form of Blondell.
Blondee, Blondey, Blondy

BLOSSOM (English) flower.

BLUM (Yiddish) flower.
Bluma

BLYTHE (English) happy, cheerful.
Blithe, Blyss, Blyth

BO (Chinese) precious.

BOACHA (Hebrew) blessed. A feminine form of Baruch.

BOBBETTE (American) a familiar form of Roberta.
Bobbet, Bobbetta

BOBBI, Bobbie (American) familiar forms of Barbara, Roberta.

Bobbi, Bobbie *(cont.)*
Baubie, Bobbe, Bobbey, Bobbisue, Bobby, Bobbye, Bobi, Bobie, Bobina, Bobbie-Jean, Bobbie-Lynn, Bobbie-Sue

BOBBI-ANN, Bobbie-Ann (American) combinations of Bobbi + Ann, Bobbie + Ann.
Bobbiann, Bobbi-Anne, Bobbianne, Bobbie-Anne, Bobby-Ann, Bobbyann, Bobby-Anne, Bobbyanne

BOBBI-JO (American) a combination of Bobbi + Jo.
Bobbiejo, Bobbie-Jo, Bobbijo, Bobby-Jo, Bobijo

BOBBI-LEE (American) a combination of Bobbi + Lee.
Bobbie-Lee, Bobbilee, Bobbylee, Bobby-Leigh, Bobile

BONITA (Spanish) pretty.
Bonesha, Bonetta, Bonnetta, Bonnie, Bonny

BONNIE, Bonny (English, Scottish) beautiful, pretty. (Spanish) familiar forms of Bonita.
Boni, Bonie, Bonne, Bonnee, Bonnell, Bonney, Bonni, Bonnin

BONNIE-BELL (American) a combination of Bonnie + Belle.
Bonnebell, Bonnebelle, Bonnibell, Bonnibelle, Bonniebell, Bonniebelle, Bonnybell, Bonnybelle

BRADLEY (English) broad meadow.
Bradlee, Bradleigh, Bradlie

BRADY (Irish) spirited.
Bradee, Bradey, Bradi, Bradie, Braedi, Braidee, Braidi, Braidie, Braidey, Braidy, Braydee

BRAEDEN (English) broad hill.
Bradyn, Bradynn, Braedan, Braedean, Braedyn, Braidan, Braiden, Braidyn, Brayden, Braydn, Braydon

BRAELYN (American) a combination of Braeden + Lynn.
Braelee, Braeleigh, Braelin, Braelle, Braelon, Braelynn, Braelynne, Brailee, Brailenn, Brailey, Braili, Brailyn, Braylee, Brayley, Braylin, Braylon, Braylyn, Braylynn

BRANDA (Hebrew) blessing.

BRANDEE (Dutch) an alternate form of Brandy.
Brande, Brandea, Brendee

BRANDEN (English) beacon valley.
Brandan, Brandon, Brendan, Brandyn, Brennan

BRANDI, Brandie (Dutch) alternate forms of Brandy.
Brandei, Brandice, Brandiee, Brandii, Brandily, Brandin, Brandis, Brandise, Brani, Branndie, Brendi

BRANDY (Dutch) an after-dinner drink made from distilled wine.
Brand, Brandace, Brandaise, Brandala, Brandee, Brandeli, Brandell, Brandi, Brandye, Brandylee, Brandy-Lee, Brandy-Leigh, Brann, Brantley, Branyell, Brendy

BRANDY-LYNN (American) a combination of Brandy + Lynn.
Brandalyn, Brandalynn, Brandelyn, Brandelynn, Brandelynne, Brandilyn, Brandilynn, Brandilynne, Brandlin, Brandlyn, Brandlynn, Brandlynne, Brandolyn,

Brandolynn, Brandolynne, Brandylyn, Brandy-Lyn, Brandylynne, Brandy-Lynne

BRAXTON (English) Brock's town.
Braxten, Braxtyn

BREA, Bria (Irish) short forms of Breana, Briana.
Breah, Breea, Briah, Brya

BREANA, Breanna (Irish) alternate forms of Briana.
Brea, Breanah, Breanda, Bre-Anna, Breannah, Breannea, Breannia, Breasha, Breawna, Breeanna, Breila

BREANN, Breanne (Irish) alternate forms of Briana.
Breane, Bre-Ann, Bre-Anne, Breaunne, Bree, Breean, Breeann, Breeanne, Breelyn, Breeon, Breiann, Breighann, Breyenne, Brieann, Brieon

BREASHA (Russian) a familiar form of Breana.

BREAUNA, Breunna, Briauna (Irish) alternate forms of Briana.
Breaunna, Breeauna, Breuna, Breuna, Briaunna

BRECK (Irish) freckled.
Brecken

BREE (Irish) a short form of Breann. (English) broth. See also Brie.
Breay, Brei, Breigh

BREEANA, Breeanna (Irish) alternate forms of Briana.
Breeanah, Breeannah

BREENA (Irish) fairy palace.
Breenea, Breene, Breina, Brina

BREIANA, Breianna (Irish) alternate forms of Briana.
Breiane, Breiann, Breianne

BRENDA (Irish) little raven. (English) sword. A feminine form of Brendan.
Brendell, Brendelle, Brendette, Brendie, Brendyl, Brenna

BRENDA-LEE (American) a combination of Brenda + Lee.
Brendalee, Brendaleigh, Brendali, Brendaly, Brendalys, Brenlee, Brenley

BRENNA (Irish) an alternate form of Brenda.
Bren, Brenie, Brenin, Brenn, Brennah, Brennaugh, Brenne

BRENNAN (English) an alternate form of Brenden.
Brennea, Brennen, Brennon, Brennyn

BREONA, Breonna (Irish) alternate forms of Briana.
Breeona, Breiona, Breionna, Breonah, Breonia, Breonie, Breonne

BRETT (Irish) a short form of Brittany. See also Brita.
Bret, Brette, Brettin, Bretton

BREYANA, Breyann, Breyanna (Irish) alternate forms of Briana.
Breyan, Breyane, Breyannah, Breyanne

BREYONA, Breyonna (Irish) alternate forms of Briana.
Breyonia

BRIANA, Brianna (Irish) strong; virtuous, honorable. Feminine forms of Brian.
Bhrianna, Brana, Brea, Breana, Breann, Breauna, Breeana, Breiana, Breona, Breyana,

Breyona, Bria, Briahna, Brianah, Briand, Brianda, Briannah, Brianne, Brianni, Briannon, Brienna, Brina, Briona, Briyana, Bryanna, Bryona

BRIANNE (Irish) an alternate form of Briana.
Briane, Briann, Brienne, Bryanne

BRIAR (French) heather.
Brear, Brier, Bryar

BRIDEY (Irish) a familiar form of Bridget.
Bridi, Bridie, Brydie

BRIDGET (Irish) strong. See also Bedelia, Bryga, Gitta.
Berget, Birgitte, Bride, Bridey, Bridger, Bridgete, Bridgett, Bridgette, Bridgid, Bridgot, Brietta, Brigada, Briget, Brigid, Brigida, Brigitte, Brita

BRIDGETT, Bridgette (Irish) alternate forms of Bridget.
Bridgitte, Brigette, Bridggett, Briggitte, Bridgitt, Brigitta

BRIE (French) a type of cheese. Geography: a region in France known for its cheese. See also Bree.
Briea, Brielle, Briena, Brieon, Brietta, Briette

BRIEANA, Brieanna (American) combinations of Brie + Anna.
Brieannah

BRIEANN, Brieanne (American) combinations of Brie + Ann. See also Briana.
Brie-Ann, Brie-Anne

BRIELLE (French) a form of Brie.
Briel, Briele, Briell, Briella

BRIENNA, Brienne (Irish) alternate forms of Briana.

Briene, Brieon, Brieona, Brieonna

BRIENNE (French) a form of Briana.
Brienn

BRIGETTE (French) an alternate form of Bridget.
Briget, Brigett, Brigetta, Brigettee, Brigget

BRIGITTE (French) a form of Bridget.
Briggitte, Brigit, Brigita

BRINA (Latin) a short form of Sabrina. (Irish) a familiar form of Briana.
Brin, Brinan, Brinda, Brindi, Brindy, Briney, Brinia, Brinlee, Brinly, Brinn, Brinna, Brinnan, Briona, Bryn, Bryna

BRIONA (Irish) an alternate form of Briana.
Brione, Brionna, Brionne, Briony, Briunna, Bryony

BRISA (Spanish) beloved. Mythology: Briseis was the Greek name of Achilles's beloved.
Breezy, Breza, Brisha, Brishia, Brissa, Bryssa

BRITA (Irish) an alternate form of Bridget. (English) a short form of Brittany.
Bretta, Brieta, Brietta, Brit, Britta

BRITANEY, Brittaney (English) alternate forms of Britany, Brittany.
Britanee, Britanny, Britenee, Briteny, Britianey, British, Britkney, Britley, Britlyn, Britney, Briton

BRITANI, Brittani, Brittanie (English) alternate forms of Britany, Brittany.

Britani, Brittani, Brittanie (cont.)
Brit, Britania, Britanica, Britanie, Britanii, Britanni, Britannia, Britatani, Britia, Britini, Brittane, Brittanee, Brittanni, Brittannia, Brittannie, Brittenie, Brittiani, Brittianni

BRITANY, Brittany (English) from Britain. See also Brett.
Brita, Britana, Britaney, Britani, Britanna, Britlyn, Britney, Britt, Brittainny, Brittainy, Brittamy, Brittana, Brittaney, Brittani, Brittania, Brittanica, Brittanny, Brittany-Ann, Brittanyne, Brittell, Britteny, Brittiany, Brittini, Brittlin, Brittlynn, Brittnee, Brittony, Bryttany

BRITIN, Brittin (English) from Britain.
Britann, Brittan, Brittin, Brittina, Brittine, Brittini, Brittiny

BRITNEY, Brittney, Brittny (English) alternate forms of Britany, Brittany.
Bittney, Bridnee, Bridney, Britnay, Britne, Britnee, Britnei, Britni, Britny, Britnye, Brittnay, Brittnaye, Brytnea, Brytni

BRITNI, Brittni, Brittnie (English) alternate forms of Britney, Britney.
Britnie

BRITON, Brittin (English) alternate forms of Britin, Brittin.
Britton

BRITT, Britta (Latin) short forms of Britany, Brittany. (Swedish) strong.
Brett, Briet, Brit, Brita, Britte

BRITTENY (English) an alternate form of Britany, Brittany.
Britten, Brittenay, Brittenee, Britteney, Brittenie

BRITTINI, Brittiny (English) alternate forms of Britany, Brittany.
Brittinee, Brittiney, Brittinie, Brittiny

BRITTNEE (English) an alternate form of Britany, Brittany.
Brittne, Brittnea, Brittnei, Brittneigh

BRIYANA, Briyanna (Irish) alternate forms of Briana.

BRODIE (Irish) ditch; canal builder.
Brodee, Brodi, Brody

BRONNIE (Welsh) a familiar form of Bronwyn.
Bron, Bronia, Bronney, Bronny, Bronya

BRONWYN (Welsh) white breasted.
Bronnie, Bronwen, Bronwin, Bronwynn, Bronwynne

BROOK, Brooke (English) brook, stream.
Bhrooke, Brookelle, Brookie, Brooks, Brooky

BROOKLYN, Brooklynn (American) combinations of Brooke + Lynn.
Brookellen, Brookelyn, Brookelyne, Brookelynn, Brooklen, Brooklin, Brooklyne, Brooklynne

BRUNA (German) a short form of Brunhilda.
Brona

BRUNHILDA (German) armored warrior.
Brinhilda, Brinhilde, Bruna, Brunhilde, Brünnhilde, Brynhild, Brynhilda, Brynhilde, Hilda

BRYANA, Bryanna, Bryanne (Irish) alternate forms of Briana.
Bryann, Bryanni

BRYCE (Welsh) alert; ambitious.

BRYGA (Polish) a form of Bridget.
Brygid, Brygida, Brygitka

BRYLIE (American) a combination of the letter B + Riley.
Brylee, Brylei, Bryley, Bryli

BRYN, Brynn (Latin) from the boundary line. (Welsh) mound.
Brinn, Brynee, Brynne

BRYNA (Latin, Irish) an alternate form of Brina.
Brynan, Brynna, Brynnan

BRYONA, Bryonna (Irish) alternate forms of Briana.
Bryonia, Bryony

BRYTTANI, Bryttany, Bryttni (English) an alternate form of Britany, Brittany.
Brytani, Brytanie, Brytanny, Brytany, Brytnee, Brytnie, Bryton, Bryttanee, Bryttanie, Bryttine, Bryttney, Bryttnie, Brytton

BUFFY (American) buffalo; from the plains.
Buffee, Buffey, Buffie, Buffye

BUNNY (Greek) a familiar form of Bernice. (English) little rabbit. See also Bonnie.
Bunni, Bunnie

BURGUNDY (French) Geography: a region of France known for its burgundy wine.
Burgandi, Burgandie, Burgandy, Burgunde

CACHET (French) prestigious; desirous.
Cachae, Cache, Cachea, Cachee, Cachée

CADENCE (Latin) rhythm.
Cadena, Cadenza, Kadena

CADY (English) an alternate form of Kady.
Cade, Cadee, Cadey, Cadi, Cadie, Cadine, Cadye

CAELEY, Cailey, Cayley (American) alternate forms of Kaylee, Kelly.
Caela, Caelee, Caeleigh, Caeley, Caeli, Caelie, Caelly, Caely, Cailee, Caileigh, Caili, Cailie, Cailley, Caillie, Caily, Caylee

CAELIN, Caelyn (American) alternate forms of Kaelyn.
Caelan, Caelinn, Caelynn, Cailan, Caylan

CAI (Vietnamese) feminine.
Cae, Cay, Caye

CAILIDA (Spanish) adoring.
Kailida

CAILIN, Cailyn (American) forms of Caitlin.
Caileen, Cailene, Cailine, Cailynn, Cailynne, Calen, Cayleen, Caylen, Caylene, Caylin, Cayline, Caylyn, Caylyne, Caylynne

CAITLAN (Irish) an alternate form of Caitlin.
Caitland, Caitlandt

CAITLIN (Irish) pure. An alternate form of Cathleen. See also Kaitlin, Katalina, Katelin, Katelyn, Kaytlyn.
Caetlin, Cailin, Caitlan, Caitleen, Caitlen, Caitlene, Caitlenn, Caitline, Caitlinn, Caitlon, Caitlyn, Catlee, Catleen, Catleene, Catlin

CAITLYN, Caitlynn (Irish) alternate forms of Caitlin. See also Kaitlyn.
Caitlyne, Caitlynne, Catelyn, Catlyn, Catlynn, Catlynne

CALA (Arabic) castle, fortress. See also Callie, Kala.
Calah, Calan, Calla, Callah

CALANDRA (Greek) lark.
Calan, Calandrea, Calandria, Caleida, Calendra, Calendre, Kalandra, Kalandria

CALEIGH, Caley (American) alternate forms of Caeley.
Caileigh, Caleah

CALI, Calli (Greek) alternate forms of Callie. See also Kali.
Calee

CALIDA (Spanish) warm; ardent.
Calina, Calinda, Callida, Callinda, Kalida

CALLIE (Greek, Arabic) a familiar form of Cala, Callista. See also Kalli.
Cal, Cali, Calie, Callee, Calley, Calli, Cally, Caly *Califsinra*

CALLISTA (Greek) most beautiful. See also Kallista.
Calesta, Calista, Callie, Calysta

CALVINA (Latin) bald. A feminine form of Calvin.
Calvine, Calvinetta, Calvinette

CALYPSO (Greek) concealer. Botany: a white orchid with purple or yellow markings. Mythology: the sea nymph who held Odysseus captive for seven years.
Caly, Lypsie, Lypsy

CAM (Vietnamese) sweet citrus.
Kam

CAMARA (American) a form of Cameron.
Camera, Cameri, Cameria, Camira, Camry

CAMBERLY (American) a form of Kimberly.
Camber, Camberlee, Camberleigh

CAMBRIA (Latin) from Wales. See also Kambria.
Camberry, Cambreia, Cambie, Cambrea, Cambree, Cambrie, Cambrina, Cambry, Cambrya, Cami

CAMDEN (Scottish) winding valley.
Camdyn

CAMELLIA (Italian) evergreen tree or shrub.
Camala, Camalia, Camallia, Camela, Camelia, Camelita, Camella, Camellita, Cami, Kamelia, Kamellia

CAMEO (Latin) gem or shell on which a portrait is carved.
Cami, Kameo

CAMERON (Scottish) crooked nose. See also Kameron, Kamryn.
Camara, Cameran, Cameren, Camira, Camiran, Camiron, Camryn

CAMI (French) a short form of Camille. See also Kami.
Camey, Camie, Cammi, Cammie, Cammy, Cammye, Camy

CAMILA, Camilla (Italian) forms of Camille. See also Kamila, Mila.
Camia, Camilia, Camillia, Camilya, Cammilla, Chamelea, Chamelia, Chamika, Chamila, Chamilia

CAMILLE (French) young ceremonial attendant. See also Millie.
Cam, Cami, Camiel, Camielle, Camil, Camila, Camile, Camill, Cammille, Cammillie, Cammilyn, Cammyl, Cammyll, Camylle, Chamelle, Chamille, Kamille

CAMISHA (American) a combination of Cami + Aisha.
Cameasha, Cameesha, Cameisha, Camesa, Camesha, Cameshaa, Cameshia, Camiesha, Camyeshia

CAMRI, Camrie (American) short forms of Camryn. See also Kamri.
Camrea, Camree, Camrey, Camry

CAMRYN (American) a form of Cameron. See also Kamryn.
Camri, Camrin, Camron, Camrynn

CAMYLLE (French) an alternate form of Camille.
Camyle, Camyll

CANDACE (Greek) glittering white; glowing. History: the name and title of the queens of ancient Ethiopia. See also Dacey, Kandace.
Cace, Canace, Canda, Candas, Candece, Candelle, Candi, Candiace, Candice, Candyce

CANDI, Candy (American) familiar forms of Candace, Candice, Candida. See also Kandi.
Candee, Candie

CANDICE, Candis (Greek) alternate forms of Candace.
Candes, Candi, Candias, Candies, Candise, Candiss, Candus

CANDIDA (Latin) bright white.
Candeea, Candi, Candia, Candide, Candita

CANDRA (Latin) glowing. See also Kandra.
Candrea, Candria

CANDYCE (Greek) an alternate form of Candace.
Candys, Candyse, Cyndyss

CANTARA (Arabic) small crossing.
Cantarah

CANTRELLE (French) song.
Cantrella

CAPRI (Italian) a short form of Caprice. Geography: an island off the west coast of Italy. See also Kapri.
Capria, Caprie, Capry

CAPRICE (Italian) fanciful.
Cappi, Caprece, Caprecia, Capresha, Capricia, Capriese, Caprina, Capris, Caprise, Caprisha, Capritta

CARA (Latin) dear. (Irish) friend. See also Karah.
Caira, Caragh, Carah, Caralee, Caranda, Carey, Carra

CARALEE (Irish) an alternate form of Cara.
Caralea, Caraleigh, Caralia, Caralie, Carely

CARALYN (English) a form of Caroline.
Caralin, Caraline, Caralynn, Caralynna, Caralynne

CARESSA (French) a form of Carissa.
Caresa, Carese, Caresse, Carissa, Charessa, Charesse, Karessa

CAREY (Welsh) a familiar form of Cara, Caroline, Karen, Katherine. See also Carrie, Kari.
Caree, Cari, Carrey, Cary

CARI, Carie (Welsh) alternate forms of Carey, Kari.

CARINA (Greek) a familiar form of Cora. (Italian) dear little one. (Swedish) a form of Karen.
Carena, Carinah, Carine, Carinna

CARINE (Italian) an alternate form of Carina.
Carin, Carinn, Carinne

CARISA, Carrisa (Greek) alternate forms of Carissa.
Carise, Carisha, Carisia, Charisa

CARISSA (Greek) beloved. See also Karissa.
Caressa, Carisa, Carrissa, Charissa

CARITA (Latin) charitable.
Caritta, Karita, Karitta

CARLA (Latin) an alternate form of Carol, Caroline. (German) farmer. (English) strong and womanly. See also Karla.
Carila, Carilla, Carleta, Carlia, Carliqua, Carliyle, Carlonda, Carlyjo, Carlyle, Carlysle

CARLEE, Carleigh, Carley (English) alternate forms of Carly. See also Karlee.
Carle, Carlea, Carleah, Carleh

CARLEEN, Carlene (English) forms of Caroline. See also Karlene.
Carlaen, Carlaena, Carleena, Carlen, Carlena, Carlenna, Carline, Carlyn, Carlyne

CARLI, Carlie (English) alternate forms of Carly. See also Karli.

CARLIN (Latin) a short form of Caroline. (Irish) little champion.
Carlan, Carlana, Carlandra, Carlina, Carlinda, Carline, Carling, Carllan, Carlyn, Carllen, Carrlin

CARLISA (American) an alternate form of Carlissa.
Carilis, Carilise, Carilyse, Carleesia, Carlesia, Carletha, Carlethe, Carlicia, Carlis, Carlise, Carlisha, Carlisia, Carlyse

CARLISSA (American) a combination of Carla + Lissa.
Carleeza, Carlisa, Carliss, Carlissah, Carlisse, Carlissia, Carlista

CARLOTTA (Italian) a form of Charlotte.
Carletta, Carlita, Carlota

CARLY (English) a familiar form of Caroline, Charlotte. See also Karli.
Carlee, Carli, Carlie, Carlye

CARLYN, Carlynn (Irish) alternate forms of Carlin.
Carlyna, Carlynne

CARMELA, Carmella (Hebrew) garden; vineyard. Bible: Mount Carmel in Israel is often thought of as paradise. See also Karmel.
Carma, Carmalla, Carmarit, Carmel, Carmeli, Carmelia, Carmelina, Carmelit, Carmelle, Carmellia, Carmellina, Carmesa, Carmesha, Carmi, Carmie, Carmiel, Carmil, Carmila, Carmile, Carmilla, Carmille, Carmisha, Leeta, Lita

CARMELIT (Hebrew) an alternate form of Carmela.
Carmaletta, Carmalit, Carmalita, Carmelita, Carmelitha, Carmelitia, Carmellit, Carmellita, Carmellitha, Carmellitia

CARMEN (Latin) song. Religion: Santa Maria del Carmen—Saint Mary of Mount Carmel—is one of the titles of the Virgin Mary. See also Karmen.
Carma, Carmaine, Carman, Carmelina, Carmencita, Carmene, Carmi, Carmia, Carmin, Carmina, Carmine, Carmita, Carmon, Carmynn, Charmaine

CAROL (German) farmer. (French) song of joy. (English) strong and womanly. A feminine form of Carl, Charles. See also Charlene, Kalle, Karoll.
Carel, Cariel, Caro, Carola, Carole, Carolenia, Carolinda, Caroline, Caroll, Carrie, Carrol, Carroll, Caryl

CAROLANE, Carolann, Carolanne (American) forms of Caroline.
Carolan, Carol Ann, Carole-Anne

CAROLE (English) an alternate form of Carol.
Carolee, Karole, Karrole

CAROLINA (Italian) a form of Caroline. See also Karolina.
Carilena, Carlena, Carlina, Caroleena, Caroleina, Carolena, Carrolena

CAROLINE (French) little and womanly. See also Carla, Carleen, Carlin, Karolina.
Caralin, Caraline, Carileen, Carilene, Carilin, Cariline, Carling, Carly, Caro, Carolann, Caroleen, Carolin, Carolina, Carolyn, Carrie, Carroleen, Carrolene, Carrolin, Carroline, Cary, Charlene

CAROLYN (English) a form of Caroline. See also Karolyn.
Carilyn, Carilynn, Carilynne, Carlyn, Carlynn, Carlynne, Carolyne, Carolynn, Carolynne, Carrolyn, Carrolynn, Carrolynne

CARON (Welsh) loving, kindhearted, charitable.
Caronne, Carron, Carrone

CARRA (Irish) an alternate form of Cara.
Carrah

CARRIE (English) a familiar form of Carol, Caroline. See also Carey, Kari, Karri.
Carree, Carrey, Carri, Carria, Carry, Cary

CARSON (English) daughter of Carr.
Carsen, Carsyn

CARTER (English) cart driver.

CARYL (Latin) a form of Carol.
Caryle, Caryll, Carylle

CARYN (Danish) a form of Karen.
Caren, Carren, Carrin, Carryn, Caryna, Caryne, Carynn

CARYS (Welsh) love.
Caris, Caryse, Ceris, Cerys

CASANDRA (Greek) an alternate form of Cassandra.
Casandera, Casandre, Casandrea, Casandrey, Casandri, Casandria, Casanndra, Casaundra, Casaundre, Casaundri, Casaundria, Casondra, Casondre, Casondri, Casondria

CASEY (Greek) a familiar form of Acacia. (Irish) brave. See also Kasey.
Cacy, Cascy, Casie, Casse, Cassee, Cassey, Cassye, Casy, Cayce, Cayse, Caysee, Caysy

CASIDY (Irish) an alternate form of Cassidy.
Casidee, Casidi

CASIE (Irish) an alternate form of Casey.
Caci, Caesi, Caisie, Casci, Cascie, Casi, Cayci, Caysi, Caysie, Cazzi

CASS (Greek) a short form of Cassandra.

CASSADY (Irish) an alternate form of Cassidy.
Casadee, Casadi, Casadie, Cassaday, Cassadee, Cassadey, Cassadi, Cassadie, Cassadina

CASSANDRA (Greek) helper of men. Mythology: a prophetess of ancient Greece whose prophesies were not believed. See also Kassandra, Sandra, Sandy, Zandra.
Casandra, Cass, Cassandre, Cassandri, Cassandry, Cassaundra, Cassie, Cassondra

CASSAUNDRA (Greek) an alternate form of Cassandra.
Cassaundre, Cassaundri, Cassundra, Cassundre, Cassundri, Cassundria

CASSIA (Greek) spicy cinnamon. See also Kasia.
Casia, Cass, Casya

CASSIDY (Irish) clever. See also Kassidy.
Casidy, Cassady, Casseday, Cassiddy, Cassidee, Cassidi, Cassidie, Cassity

CASSIE, Cassey, Cassi (Greek) familiar forms of Cassandra, Catherine. See also Kassie.
Cassee, Cassii, Cassy, Casy

CASSIOPEIA (Greek) clever. Mythology: the wife of the Ethiopian king Cepheus; the mother of Andromeda.
Cassio

CASSONDRA (Greek) an alternate form of Cassandra.
Cassondre, Cassondri, Cassondria

CATALINA (Spanish) a form of Catherine. See also Katalina.
Cataleen, Catalena, Catalene, Catalin, Catalyn, Catalyna, Cateline

CATARINA (German) a form of Catherine.
Catarena, Catarin, Catarine, Caterin, Caterina, Caterine

CATELYN (Irish) an alternate form of Caitlin.
Catelin, Cateline, Catelyne, Catelynn

CATHARINE (Greek) an alternate form of Catherine.
Catharen, Catharin, Catharina, Catharyn

CATHERINE (Greek) pure. (English) a form of Katherine.
Cat, Catalina, Catarina, Cate, Cathann, Cathanne, Catharine, Cathenne, Catheren, Catherene, Catheria, Catherin, Catherina, Catheryn, Catheryne, Cathi, Cathleen, Cathrine, Cathryn, Cathy, Catlaina, Catreeka, Catrelle, Catrice, Catricia, Catrika, Catrina

CATHI, Cathy (Greek) familiar forms of Catherine, Cathleen. See also Kathy.
Catha, Cathe, Cathee, Cathey, Cathie

CATHLEEN (Irish) a form of Catherine. See also Caitlin, Kathleen.
Caithlyn, Cathaleen, Cathelin, Cathelina, Cathelyn, Cathi, Cathleana, Cathleene, Cathlene, Cathleyn, Cathlin, Cathline, Cathlyn, Cathlyne, Cathlynn, Cathy

CATHRINE (Greek) an alternate form of Catherine.

CATHRYN (Greek) an alternate form of Catherine.
Cathryne, Cathrynn, Catryn

CATRINA (Slavic) a form of Catherine, Katrina.
Caitriana, Caitriona, Catina, Catreen, Catreena, Catrene, Catrenia, Catrin, Catrine, Catrinia, Catriona, Catroina

CAYLA (Hebrew) an alternate form of Kayla.
Caylea, Caylia

CAYLEE, Caylie (American) alternate forms of Caeley, Cailey, Cayley.
Cayle, Cayleigh, Cayli, Cayly

CEARA (Irish) an alternate form of Ciara.
Ceaira, Ceairah, Ceairra, Cearaa, Cearie, Cearah, Cearra, Cera

CECELIA (Latin) an alternate form of Cecilia. See also Sheila.
Caceli, Cacelia, Cece, Ceceilia, Ceceli, Cecelia, Cecelie, Cecely, Cecelyn, Cecette, Cescelia, Cescelie

CECILIA (Latin) blind. A feminine form of Cecil. See also Cicely, Cissy, Secilia, Selia, Sissy.
Cacilia, Caecilia, Cecelia, Cecil, Cecila, Cecile, Cecilea, Cecilija, Cecilla, Cecille, Cecillia, Cecily, Cecilya, Ceclia, Cecylia, Cee, Ceil, Ceila, Ceilagh, Ceileh, Ceileigh, Ceilena, Celia, Cesilia, Cicelia

CECILY (Latin) an alternate form of Cecilia.
Cacilie, Cecilee, Ceciley, Cecilie, Cescily, Cicely, Cilley

CEIL (Latin) a short form of Cecilia.
Ceel, Ciel

CEIRA, Ceirra (Irish) alternate forms of Ciara.
Ceire

CELENA (Greek) an alternate form of Selena.
Celeena, Celene, Celenia, Celine, Cena

CELENE (Greek) an alternate form of Celena.
Celeen

CELESTE (Latin) celestial, heavenly.
Cele, Celeeste, Celense, Celes, Celesia, Celesley, Celest, Celesta, Celestia, Celestial, Celestin, Celestina, Celestine, Celestinia, Celestyn, Celestyna, Cellest, Celleste, Selestina

CELIA (Latin) a short form of Cecilia.
Ceilia, Celie

CELINA (Greek) an alternate form of Celena. See also Selina.
Caleena, Calena, Calina, Celena, Celinda, Celinka, Celinna, Celka, Cellina

CELINE (Greek) an alternate form of Celena.
Caline, Celeen, Celene, Céline, Cellinn

CERA (French) a short form of Cerise.
Cerea, Ceri, Ceria, Cerra

CERELLA (Latin) springtime.
Cerelisa, Ceres

CERISE (French) cherry; cherry red.
Cera, Cerese, Cerice, Cericia, Cerissa, Cerria, Cerrice, Cerrina, Cerrita, Cerryce, Ceryce, Cherise

CESILIA (Latin) an alternate form of Cecilia.
Cesia, Cesya

CHABLIS (French) a dry, white wine. Geography: a region in France where wine grapes are grown.
Chabeli, Chabelly, Chabely, Chablee, Chabley, Chabli

CHADEE (French) from Chad, a country in north central Africa. See also Sade.
Chaday, Chadday, Chade, Chadea, Chadi

CHAI (Hebrew) life.
Chae, Chaela, Chaeli, Chaella, Chaena, Chaia

CHAKA (Sanskrit) an alternate form of Chakra. See also Shaka.
Chakai, Chakia, Chakka, Chakkah

CHAKRA (Sanskrit) circle of energy.
Chaka, Chakara, Chakaria, Chakena, Chakina, Chakira, Chakrah, Chakria, Chakriya, Chakyra

CHALICE (French) goblet.
Chalace, Chalcie, Chalece, Chalicea, Chalie, Chaliese, Chalis, Chalisa, Chalise, Chalisk, Chalissa, Chalisse, Challa, Challaine, Challis, Challisse, Challysse, Chalsey, Chalyce, Chalyn, Chalyse, Chalyssa, Chalysse

CHALINA (Spanish) a form of Rose.
Chaline, Chalini

CHALONNA (American) a combination of the prefix Cha + Lona.
Chalon, Chalona, Chalonda, Chalonn, Chalonne, Chalonte, Shalon

CHAMBRAY (French) a lightweight fabric.
Chambrae, Chambre, Chambree, Chambrée, Chambrey, Chambria, Chambrie

CHAN (Cambodian) sweet-smelling tree.

CHANA (Hebrew) an alternate form of Hannah.

Chana (cont.)
Chanae, Chanai, Chanay, Chanea, Chanie

CHANCEY (English) chancellor; church official. A feminine form of Chauncey.
Chance, Chancee, Chancie, Chancy

CHANDA (Sanskrit) great goddess. Religion: the name assumed by the Hindu goddess Devi. See also Shanda.
Chandee, Chandey, Chandi, Chandie, Chandin

CHANDELLE (French) candle.
Chandal, Chandel, Shandal, Shandel

CHANDLER (Hindi) moon.
Chandlar, Chandlier, Chandlor, Chandlyr

CHANDRA (Sanskrit) moon. Religion: one of the names of the Hindu goddess Shakti. See also Shandra.
Chandrae, Chandray, Chandre, Chandrea, Chandrelle, Chandria

CHANEL (English) channel. See also Shanel.
Chanal, Chaneel, Chaneil, Chanele, Chanell, Channal, Channel, Chenelle

CHANELL, Chanelle (English) alternate forms of Chanel.
Channell, Shanell

CHANISE (American) an alternate form of Shanice.
Chanisse, Chenice, Chenise

CHANNA (Hindi) chickpea.
Channah

CHANTAL (French) song.
Chandal, Chantaal, Chantael, Chantala, Chantale, Chantall,

Chantalle, Chantara, Chantaral, Chantasia, Chante, Chanteau, Chantel, Chantle, Chantoya, Chantrill, Chauntel

CHANTE (French) a short form of Chantal.
Chanta, Chantae, Chantai, Chantay, Chantaye, Chanté, Chantéa, Chantee, Chanti, Chantia, Chaunte, Chauntea, Chauntéa, Chauntee

CHANTEL, Chantell, Chantelle (French) alternate forms of Chantal. See also Shantel.
Chanteese, Chantela, Chantele, Chantella, Chanter, Chantey, Chantez, Chantrel, Chantrell, Chantrelle, Chatell

CHANTILLY (French) fine lace. See also Shantille.
Chantiel, Chantielle, Chantil, Chantila, Chantilée, Chantill, Chantille

CHANTREA (Cambodian) moon; moonbeam.
Chantra, Chantrey, Chantri, Chantria

CHANTRICE (French) singer. See also Shantrice.
Chantreese, Chantress

CHARDAE, Charde (Punjabi) charitable. (French) short forms of Chardonnay. See also Shardae.
Charda, Chardai, Charday, Chardea, Chardee, Chardée, Chardese, Chardey, Chardie

CHARDONNAY (French) a dry white wine. Geography: a wine-making region in France.
Char, Chardae, Chardnay, Chardney, Chardon, Chardonae, Chardonai, Chardonay, Chardonaye, Chardonee, Chardonna, Chardonnae,

Chardonnai, Chardonnee, Chardonnée, Chardonney, Shardonay, Shardonnay

CHARIS (Greek) grace; kindness.
Charece, Chareece, Chareeze, Charese, Chari, Charice, Charie, Charish, Charisse

CHARISSA, Charisse (Greek) forms of Charity.
Charesa, Charese, Charessa, Charesse, Charis, Charisa, Charise, Charisha, Charissee, Charista, Charyssa

CHARITY (Latin) charity, kindness.
Chariety, Charis, Charissa, Charisse, Charista, Charita, Chariti, Charitie, Sharity

CHARLA (French, English) a short form of Charlene, Charlotte.
Char, Charlea

CHARLAINE (English) an alternate form of Charlene.
Charlaina, Charlane, Charlanna, Charlayna, Charlayne

CHARLEE, Charley (German, English) alternate forms of Charlie.
Charle, Charleigh

CHARLENE (English) little and womanly. A form of Caroline. See also Carol, Karla, Sharlene.
Charla, Charlaine, Charlean, Charleen, Charleene, Charleesa, Charlena, Charlenae, Charlesena, Charline, Charlyn, Charlyne, Charlynn, Charlynne, Charlzina, Charoline

CHARLIE (German, English) strong and womanly. A feminine form of Charles.

Charlee, Charley, Charli, Charyl, Chatty, Sharli, Sharlie

CHARLOTTE (French) little and womanly. A form of Caroline. Literature: Charlotte Brontë was a British novelist and poet best known for her novel *Jane Eyre*. See also Karlotte, Lotte, Sharlotte, Tottie.
Carlotta, Carly, Chara, Charil, Charl, Charla, Charlet, Charlett, Charletta, Charlette, Charlisa, Charlita, Charlott, Charlotta, Charlottie, Charlotty, Charolet, Charolette, Charolot, Charolotte

CHARMAINE (French) a form of Carmen. See also Sharmaine.
Charamy, Charma, Charmae, Charmagne, Charmaigne, Charmain, Chamaine, Charmalique, Charman, Charmane, Charmar, Charmara, Charmayane, Charmayne, Charmeen, Charmeine, Charmene, Charmese, Charmian, Charmin, Charmine, Charmion, Charmisa, Charmon, Charmyn, Charmyne, Charmynne

CHARNETTE (American) a combination of Charo + Annette.
Charnetta, Charnita

CHARNIKA (American) a combination of Charo + Nika.
Charneka, Charniqua, Charnique

CHARO (Spanish) a familiar form of Rosa.

CHARYANNA (American) a combination of Charo + Anna.
Charian, Charyian, Cheryn

CHASIDY, Chassidy (Latin) alternate forms of Chastity.

Chasa Dee, Chasadie, Chasady, Chasidee, Chasidey, Chasidie, Chassedi, Chassidi, Chasydi

CHASITY (Latin) an alternate form of Chastity.
Chasiti, Chasitie, Chasitty, Chassey, Chassie, Chassiti, Chassity, Chassy

CHASTITY (Latin) pure.
Chasidy, Chasity, Chasta, Chastady, Chastidy, Chastin, Chastitie, Chastney, Chasty

CHAUNTEL (French) an alternate form of Chantal.
Chaunta, Chauntae, Chauntay, Chaunte, Chauntell, Chauntelle, Chawntel, Chawntell, Chawntelle, Chontelle

CHAVA (Hebrew) life. (Yiddish) bird. Bible: the original name of Eve.
Chabah, Chavae, Chavah, Chavalah, Chavarra, Chavarria, Chave, Chavé, Chavette, Chaviva, Chavvis, Hava, Kaÿa

CHAVELLA (Spanish) an alternate form of Isabel.
Chavel, Chaveli, Chavell, Chavelle, Chevelle, Chavely, Chevie

CHAVI (Gypsy) girl.
Chavali

CHAVON (Hebrew) an alternate form of Jane.
Chavona, Chavonda, Chavonn, Chavonne, Shavon

CHAVONNE (Hebrew) an alternate form of Chavon. (American) a combination of the prefix Cha + Yvonne.
Chavondria, Chavonna, Chevon, Chevonn, Chevonna

CHAYA (Hebrew) life; living.
Chaike, Chaye, Chayka, Chayla, Chaylah, Chaylea, Chaylee, Chaylene, Chayra

CHELCI, Chelcie (English) alternate forms of Chelsea.
Chelce, Chelcee, Chelcey, Chelcy

CHELSEA (English) seaport. See also Kelsi, Shelsea.
Chelci, Chelese, Chelesia, Chelsa, Chelsae, Chelsah, Chelse, Chelseah, Chelsee, Chelsey, Chelsia, Chelsie, Chesea, Cheslee, Chessea

CHELSEE (English) an alternate form of Chelsea.
Chelsei, Chelseigh

CHELSEY, Chelsy (English) alternate forms of Chelsea. See also Kelsey.
Chelcy, Chelsay, Chelssy, Chelssey, Chelsye, Chesley

CHELSIE (English) an alternate form of Chelsea.
Chelli, Chellie, Chellise, Chellsie, Chelsi, Chelssie, Cheslie, Chessie

CHENELLE (English) an alternate form of Chanel.
Chenel, Chenell

CHENOA (Native American) white dove.
Chenee, Chenika, Chenita, Chenna, Chenoah

CHER (French) beloved, dearest. (English) a short form of Cherilyn.
Chere, Cheri, Cherie, Sher

CHERELLE, Cherrelle (French) alternate forms of Cheryl. See also Sherelle.
Charell, Charelle, Cherell, Cherrel, Cherrell

CHERESE (Greek) an alternate form of Cherish.
Chereese, Cheresa, Cheresse, Cherice

CHERI, Cherie (French) familiar forms of Cher.
Cheree, Chérie, Cheriee, Cherri, Cherrie

CHERILYN (English) a combination of Cheryl + Lynn.
Cher, Cheralyn, Chereen, Chereena, Cherilynn, Cherlyn, Cherlynn, Cherralyn, Cherrilyn, Cherrylyn, Cherylene, Cherylin, Cheryline, Cheryl-Lyn, Cheryl-Lynn, Cheryl-Lynne, Cherylyn, Cherylynn, Cherylynne, Sherilyn

CHERISE (French) a form of Cherish. See also Sharice, Sherice.
Charisa, Charise, Cherece, Chereese, Cheresa, Cherice, Cheriss, Cherissa, Cherisse, Cherrise

CHERISH (English) dearly held, precious.
Charish, Charisha, Cheerish, Cherise, Cherishe, Cherrish, Sherish

CHEROKEE (Native American) a tribal name.
Cherika, Cherkita, Cherrokee, Sherokee

CHERRY (Latin) a familiar form of Charity. (French) cherry; cherry red.
Chere, Cheree, Cherey, Cherida, Cherita, Cherrey, Cherrita, Cherry-Ann, Cherry-Anne, Cherrye, Chery, Cherye

CHERYL (French) beloved. See also Sheryl.
Charel, Charil, Charyl, Cherelle, Cherrelle, Cheryl-Ann, Cheryl-

Anne, Cheryle, Cherylee, Cheryll, Cherylle, Cheryl-Lee

CHESAREY (American) a form of Desiree.
Chesarae, Chessa

CHESNA (Slavic) peaceful.
Chesnee, Chesney, Chesnie, Chesny

CHESSA (American) a short form of Chesarey.
Chessi, Chessie, Chessy

CHEYANNE (Cheyenne) an alternate form of Cheyenne.
Cheyan, Cheyana, Cheyane, Cheyann, Cheyanna, Cheyeana, Cheyeannna, Cheyeannne

CHEYENNE (Cheyenne) a tribal name. See also Shaianne, Sheyenne, Shianne, Shyann.
Cheyanne, Cheyeene, Cheyena, Cheyene, Cheyenna, Cheyna, Chi, Chi-Anna, Chie, Chyanne

CHEYLA (American) a form of Sheila.
Cheylan, Cheyleigh, Cheylo

CHEYNA (American) a short form of Cheyenne.
Chey, Cheye, Cheyne, Cheynee, Cheyney, Cheynna

CHIARA (Italian) a form of Clara.
Cheara, Chiarra

CHIKA (Japanese) near and dear.
Chikaka, Chikako, Chikara, Chikona

CHIKU (Swahili) chatterer.

CHINA (Chinese) fine porcelain. Geography: a country in eastern Asia. See also Ciana, Shina.

Chinaetta, Chinah, Chinasa, Chinda, Chinea, Chinesia, Chinita, Chinna, Chinwa, Chyna, Chynna

CHINIRA (Swahili) God receives.
Chinara, Chinarah, Chinirah

CHINUE (Ibo) God's own blessing.

CHIQUITA (Spanish) little one. See also Shiquita.
Chaqueta, Chaquita, Chica, Chickie, Chicky, Chikata, Chikita, Chiqueta, Chiquila, Chiquite, Chiquitha, Chiquithe, Chiquitia, Chiquitta

CHIYO (Japanese) eternal.
Chiya

CHLOE (Greek) blooming, verdant. Mythology: the goddess of agriculture.
Chloé, Chlöe, Chloee, Chloie, Cloe, Kloe

CHLORIS (Greek) pale. Mythology: the only daughter of Niobe to escape the vengeful arrows of Apollo and Artemis. See also Loris.
Cloris, Clorissa

CHO (Korean) beautiful.
Choe

CHOLENA (Native American) bird.

CHRIKI (Swahili) blessing.

CHRIS (Greek) a short form of Christina. See also Kris.
Chrys, Cris

CHRISSA (Greek) a short form of Christina. See also Khrissa.
Chrysa, Chryssa, Crissa, Cryssa

CHRISSY (English) a familiar form of Christina.
Chrisie, Chrissee, Chrissie, Crissie, Khrissy

CHRISTA (German) a short form of Christina. History: Christa McAuliffe, an American school teacher, was the first civilian on a U.S. space flight. See also Krista.
Chrysta, Crista, Crysta

CHRISTABEL (Latin, French) beautiful Christian.
Christabell, Christabella, Christabelle, Christable, Cristabel, Kristabel

CHRISTAIN (Greek) an alternate form of Christina.
Christana, Christann, Christanna

CHRISTAL (Latin) an alternate form of Crystal. (Scottish) a form of Christina.
Christalene, Christalin, Christaline, Christall, Christalle, Christalyn, Christelle, Christle, Chrystal

CHRISTELLE (French) a form of Christal.
Christel, Christele, Christell, Chrystel, Chrystelle

CHRISTEN, Christin (Greek) alternate forms of Christina. See also Kristen.
Christan, Christyn, Chrystan, Chrysten, Chrystyn, Crestienne

CHRISTENA, Christen (Greek) alternate forms of Christina.

CHRISTI, Christie (Greek) short forms of Christina, Christine. See also Kristi.
Christy, Chrysti, Chrystie, Chrysty, Kristi

CHRISTIAN, Christiana, Christianna (Greek) alternate forms of Christina. See also Kristian, Krystian.
Christiane, Christiann, Christi-Ann, Christianne, Christi-Anne, Christianni, Christiaun, Christiean, Christien, Christiena, Christienne, Christinan, Christy-Ann, Christy-Anne, Crystian, Chrystyann, Chrystyanne, Crystiann, Crystianne

CHRISTIN (Greek) a short form of Christina.
Christen, Chrystin

CHRISTINA (Greek) Christian; anointed. See also Khristina, Kristina, Stina, Tina.
Chris, Chrissa, Chrissy, Christa, Christain, Christal, Christeena, Christella, Christen, Christena, Christi, Christian, Christie, Christin, Christinaa, Christine, Christinea, Christinia, Christinna, Christinnah, Christna, Christy, Christyn, Christyna, Christynna, Chrystina, Chrystyna, Cristeena, Cristena, Cristina, Crystina, Chrystena, Cristena

CHRISTINE (French, English) a form of Christina. See also Kirsten, Kristen, Kristine.
Chrisa, Christeen, Christen, Christene, Christi, Christie, Christy, Chrystine, Cristeen, Cristene, Cristine, Crystine

CHRISTOPHE (Greek) Christ-bearer. A feminine form of Christopher.

CHRISTY (English) a short form of Christina, Christine.
Cristy

CHRISTYN (Greek) an alternate form of Christina.
Christyne

CHRYS (English) a form of Chris.
Krys

CHRYSTAL (Latin) an alternate form of Christal.
Chrystale, Chrystalla, Chrystallina, Chrystallynn,

CHU HUA (Chinese) chrysanthemum.

CHUMANI (Lakota) dewdrops.
Chumany

CHUN (Burmese) nature's renewal.

CHYANNE, Chyenne (Cheyenne) alternate forms of Cheyenne.
Chyan, Chyana, Chyane, Chyann, Chyanna, Chyeana, Chyenn, Chyenna, Chyennee

CHYNA, Chynna (Chinese) alternate forms of China.

CIANA (Chinese) an alternate form of China. (Italian) a form of Jane.
Cian, Ciandra, Ciann, Cianna

CIARA, Ciarra (Irish) black. See also Sierra.
Ceara, Chiairah, Ciaara, Ciaera, Ciaira, Ciarah, Ciaria, Ciarrah, Cieara, Ciearra, Ciearria, Ciera, Cierra, Cioria, Cyarra

CICELY (English) a form of Cecilia. See also Sissy.
Cicelia, Cicelie, Ciciley, Cicilia, Cicilie, Cicily, Cile, Cilka, Cilla, Cilli, Cillie, Cilly

CIDNEY (French) an alternate form of Sydney.
Cidnee, Cidni, Cidnie

CIERA, Cierra (Irish) alternate forms of Ciara, Ciarra.

Ciera, Cierra (cont.)
Ceira, Cierah, Ciere, Cieria, Cierrah, Cierre, Cierria, Cierro

CINDERELLA (French, English) little cinder girl. Literature: a fairy tale heroine.
Cindella

CINDY (Greek) moon. (Latin) a familiar form of Cynthia. See also Sindy.
Cindee, Cindi, Cindie, Cyndi

CINTHIA, Cinthya (Greek) alternate forms of Cynthia.
Cinthiya, Cintia

CIRA (Spanish) a form of Cyrilla.

CISSY (American) a familiar form of Cecelia, Cicely.
Cissey, Cissi, Cissie

CLAIRE (French) a form of Clara.
Clair, Klaire, Klarye

CLAIRISSA (Greek) an alternate form of Clarissa.
Clairisa, Clairisse, Claraissa

CLARA (Latin) clear; bright. Music: Clara Shumann was a famous nineteenth-century German composer. See also Chiara, Klara.
Claira, Claire, Clarabelle, Clare, Claresta, Clarice, Clarie, Clarina, Clarinda, Clarine, Clarissa, Clarita

CLARABELLE (Latin) bright and beautiful.
Clarabella, Claribel, Claribell

CLARE (English) a form of Clara.

CLARIE (Latin) a familiar form of Clara.
Clarey, Clari, Clary

CLARICE (Italian) a form of Clara.
Claris, Clarise, Clarisse, Claryce, Cleriese, Klarice, Klarise

CLARISA (Greek) an alternate form of Clarissa.
Claresa, Clarise, Clarisia

CLARISSA (Greek) brilliant. (Italian) a form of Clara. See also Klarissa.
Clairissa, Clarecia, Claressa, Claresta, Clarisa, Clarissia, Claritza, Clarizza, Clarrisa, Clarrissa, Clerissa

CLARITA (Spanish) a form of Clara.
Clairette, Clareta, Claretta, Clarette, Claritza

CLAUDETTE (French) a form of Claudia.
Clauddetta

CLAUDIA (Latin) lame. A feminine form of Claude. See also Gladys, Klaudia.
Claudeen, Claudel, Claudelle, Claudette, Claudex, Claudiana, Claudiane, Claudie, Claudie-Anne, Claudina, Claudine

CLAUDIE (Latin) an alternate form of Claudia.
Claudee

CLEA (Greek) an alternate form of Cleo, Clio.

CLEMENTINE (Latin) merciful. A feminine form of Clement.
Clemence, Clemencia, Clemencie, Clemency, Clementia, Clementina, Clemenza, Clemette

CLEO (Greek) a short form of Cleopatra.
Chleo, Clea

CLEONE (Greek) glorious.
Cleonie, Cleonna, Cliona

CLEOPATRA (Greek) her father's fame. History: a great Egyptian queen.
Cleo

CLETA (Greek) illustrious.

CLIO (Greek) proclaimer; glorifier. Mythology: the muse of history.
Clea

CLOE (Greek) an alternate form of Chloe.
Clo, Cloei, Cloey, Cloie

CLOTILDA (German) heroine.

COCO (Spanish) coconut. See also Koko.

CODI, CODY (English) cushion. See also Kodi.
Coady, Codee, Codey, Codia, Codie

COLBY (English) coal town. Geography: a region in England known for cheese-making. See also Kolby.
Cobi, Cobie, Colbi, Colbie

COLETTE (Greek, French) a familiar form of Nicole.
Coe, Coetta, Coletta, Collet, Collete, Collett, Colletta, Collette, Kolette, Kollette

COLLEEN (Irish) girl. See also Kolina.
Coe, Coel, Cole, Coleen, Colene, Coley, Coline, Colleene, Collen, Collene, Collie, Collina, Colline, Colly

COLLINA (Irish) an alternate form of Colleen.
Colena, Colina, Colinda

CONCETTA (Italian) pure. Religion: refers to the Immaculate Conception.
Concettina, Conchetta

CONCHITA (Spanish) conception.
Chita, Conceptia, Concha, Conciana

CONCORDIA (Latin) harmonious. Mythology: the goddess governing the peace after war.
Con, Cordae, Cordaye

CONNIE (Latin) a familiar form of Constance.
Con, Connee, Conni, Conny, Konnie, Konny

CONNOR (Scottish) wise. (Irish) praised; exhalted.
Connar, Conner, Connery, Conor

CONSTANCE (Latin) constant; firm. History: Constance Motley was the first African-American woman to be appointed as a U.S. federal judge. See also Konstance, Kosta.
Connie, Constancia, Constancy, Constanta, Constantia, Constantina, Constantine, Constanza, Constynse

CONSTANZA (Spanish) a form of Constance.
Constanz, Constanze

CONSUELO (Spanish) consolation. Religion: Santa Maria del Consuelo—Saint Mary of Consolation—is a name for the Virgin Mary.
Consolata, Consuela, Consuella, Consula, Conzuelo, Konsuela, Konsuelo

CORA (Greek) maiden. Mythology: the daughter of Demeter, the goddess of agriculture. See also Kora.
Corah, Coralee, Coretta, Corissa, Corey, Corra

CORABELLE (American) a combination of Cora + Belle.
Corabel, Corabella

CORAL (Latin) coral. See also Koral.
Coraal, Corral

CORALEE (American) a combination of Cora + Lee.
Coralea, Cora-Lee, Coralena, Coralene, Coraley, Coralie, Coraline, Coraly, Coralyn, Corella, Corilee, Koralie

CORALIE (American) an alternate form of Coralee.
Corali, Coralia, Coralina, Coralynn, Coralynne

CORAZON (Spanish) heart.

CORBIN (Latin) raven.
Corbe, Corbi, Corby, Corbyn, Corbynn

CORDASHA (American) a combination of Cora + Dasha.

CORDELIA (Latin) warm hearted. (Welsh) sea jewel. See also Delia, Della.
Cordae, Cordelie, Cordett, Cordette, Cordi, Cordilia, Cordilla, Cordula, Kordelia, Kordula

CORDI (Welsh) a short form of Cordelia.
Cordey, Cordia, Cordie, Cordy

CORETTA (Greek) a familiar form of Cora.
Coreta, Corette, Correta, Corretta, Corrette, Koretta, Korretta

COREY, Cory (Greek) familiar forms of Cora. (Irish) from the hollow. See also Kori.
Coree, Cori, Correy, Correye, Corry

CORI, Corie, Corrie (Irish) alternate forms of Corey.

CORIANN, Corianne (American) combinations of Cori + Ann, Cori + Anne.
Corian, Coriane, Cori-Ann, Corri, Corrie-Ann, Corrianne, Corrie-Anne

CORINA, Corinna (Greek) familiar forms of Corinne. See also Korina.
Coreena, Coriana, Corianna, Corinda, Correna, Corrinna, Coryna

CORINNE (Greek) maiden.
Coreen, Coren, Corin, Corina, Corine, Corinee, Corinn, Corinna, Corrina, Coryn, Corynn, Corynne

CORISSA (Greek) a familiar form of Cora.
Coresa, Coressa, Corisa, Coryssa, Korissa

CORLISS (English) cheerful; good hearted.
Corlisa, Corlise, Corlissa, Corly, Korliss

CORNELIA (Latin) horn colored. A feminine form of Cornelius. See also Kornelia, Nelia, Nellie.
Carna, Carniella, Corneilla, Cornela, Cornelie, Cornella, Cornelle, Cornie, Cornilear, Cornisha, Corny

CORRINA, Corrine (Greek) alternate forms of Corinne.
Correen, Corren, Corrin, Corrinn, Corrinna, Corrinne, Corrinne, Corryn

CORTNEY (English) an alternate form of Courtney.
Cortne, Cortnea, Cortnee, Cortneia, Cortni, Cortnie, Cortny, Cortnye, Corttney

COSETTE (French) a familiar form of Nicole.
Cosetta, Cossetta, Cossette, Cozette

COURTENAY (English) an alternate form of Courtney.
Courtaney, Courtany, Courteney, Courteny

COURTNEE, Courtnie (English) alternate forms of Courtney.
Courtne, Courtnée, Courtnei, Courtneigh, Courtni, Courtnii

COURTNEY (English) from the court. See also Kortney, Kourtney.
Cortney, Courtena, Courtenay, Courtene, Courtnae, Courtnay, Courtnee, Courtny, Courtonie

CRISBELL (American) a combination of Crista + Belle.
Crisbel, Cristabel

CRISTA, Crysta (Italian) forms of Christa.
Cristah

CRISTAL (Latin) an alternate form of Crystal.
Cristalie, Cristalina, Cristalle, Cristel, Cristela, Cristelia, Cristella, Cristelle, Cristhie, Cristle

CRISTEN, Cristin (Irish) forms of Christen, Christin. See also Kristin.
Cristan, Cristyn, Crystan, Crysten, Crystin, Crystyn

CRISTINA, Cristine (Greek) alternate forms of Christina. See also Kristina.
Cristiona, Cristy

CRISTY (English) a familiar form of Cristina. An alternate form of Christy. See also Kristy.
Cristey, Cristi, Cristie, Crysti, Crystie, Crysty

CRYSTAL (Latin) clear, brilliant glass. See also Kristal, Krystal.
Christal, Chrystal, Chrystal-Lynn, Chrystel, Cristal, Crystala, Crystale, Crystalee, Crystalin, Crystall, Crystalle, Crystaly, Crystel, Crystela, Crystelia, Crystelle, Crysthelle, Crystl, Crystle, Crystol, Crystole, Crystyl

CRYSTALIN (American) a form of Crystal.
Crystal-Ann, Cristalanna, Crystal-Anne, Cristalina, Cristallina, Cristalyn, Crystallynn, Crystallynne, Cristilyn, Crystalina, Crystal-Lee, Crystal-Lynn, Crystalyn, Crystalynn

CRYSTINA (Greek) an alternate form of Christina.
Crystin, Crystine, Crystyn, Crystyna, Crystyne

CURRAN (Irish) heroine.
Cura, Curin, Curina, Curinna

CYBELE (Greek) an alternate form of Sybil.
Cybel, Cybil, Cybill, Cybille

CYDNEY (French) an alternate form of Sydney.
Cydne, Cydnee, Cydnei, Cydni, Cydnie

CYERRA (Irish) a form of Ciara.
Cyera, Cyerria

CYNDI (Greek) an alternate form of Cindy.

Cynda, Cyndal, Cyndale, Cyndall, Cyndee, Cyndel, Cyndia, Cyndie, Cyndle, Cyndy

CYNTHIA (Greek) moon. Mythology: another name for Artemis, the moon goddess. See also Hyacinth, Kynthia.
Cindy, Cinthia, Cyneria, Cynethia, Cynithia, Cynthea, Cynthiana, Cynthiann, Cynthie, Cynthria, Cynthy, Cynthya, Cyntia, Cyntreia, Cythia, Synthia

CYRILLA (Greek) ladylike. A feminine form of Cyril.
Cerelia, Cerella, Cira, Cirilla, Cyrella, Cyrille

DACEY (Greek) a familiar form of Candace. (Irish) southerner.
Dacee, Dacei, Daci, Dacia, Dacie, Dacy, Daicee, Daici, Daicie, Daicy, Daycee, Daycie, Daycy

DACIA (Irish) an alternate form of Dacey.
Daciah

DAE (English) day. See also Dai.

DAEJA (French) an alternate form of Déja.
Daejah, Daejia

DAELYNN (American) a combination of Dae + Lynn.
Daeleen, Daelena, Daelin, Daelyn, Daelynne

DAESHANDRA (American) a combination of Dae + Shandra.
Daeshandria, Daeshaundra, Daeshaundria, Daeshawndra, Daeshawndria, Daeshondra, Daeshondria

DAESHAWNA (American) a combination of Dae + Shawna.
Daeshan, Daeshaun, Daeshauna, Daeshavon, Daeshawn, Daeshawntia, Daeshon, Daeshona

DAESHONDA (American) a combination of Dae + Shonda.
Daeshanda, Daeshawnda

DAFNY (American) a form of Daphne.
Dafany, Daffany, Daffie, Daffy, Dafna, Dafne, Dafney, Dafnie

DAGMAR (German) glorious.
Dagmara

DAGNY (Scandinavian) day.
Dagna, Dagnanna, Dagne, Dagney, Dagnie

DAHLIA (Scandinavian) valley. Botany: a perennial flower. See also Daliah.
Dahliah, Dahlya, Dahlye

DAI (Japanese) great. See also Dae.
Day, Daye

DAIJA, Daijah (French) alternate forms of Déja.
Daijaah, Daijea, Daijha, Daijhah, Dayja

DAISHA (American) a form of Dasha.
Daesha, Daishae, Daishia, Daishya, Daisia

DAISY (English) day's eye. Botany: a white and yellow flower.
Daisee, Daisey, Daisi, Daisia, Daisie, Dasey, Dasi, Dasie, Dasy, Daysi, Deisy

DAJA, Dajah (French) alternate forms of Déja.
Dajae, Dajai, Daje, Dajha, Dajia

DAKAYLA (American) a combination of the prefix Da + Kayla.
Dakala, Dakila

DAKIRA (American) a combination of the prefix Da + Kira.
Dakara, Dakaria, Dakarra, Dakirah, Dakyra

DAKOTA (Native American) a tribal name.
Dakkota, Dakoda, Dakotah, Dakotha, Dakotta, Dekoda, Dekota, Dekotah, Dekotha

DALE (English) valley.
Dael, Dahl, Daile, Daleleana, Dalena, Dalina, Dayle

DALIA, Daliah (Hebrew) branch. See also Dahlia.
Daelia, Dailia, Daleah, Daleia, Dalialah, Daliyah

DALILA (Swahili) gentle.
Dalela, Dalida, Dalilah, Dalilia

DALISHA (American) a form of Dallas.
Dalisa, Dalishea, Dalishia, Dalishya, Dalisia, Dalissia

DALLAS (Irish) wise.
Dalis, Dalise, Dalisha, Dalisse, Dallace, Dallis, Dallise, Dallus, Dallys, Dalyce, Dalys

DAMARIS (Greek) gentle girl. See also Maris.

Dama, Damar, Damara, Damarius, Damary, Damarylis, Damarys, Dameress, Dameris, Damiris, Dammaris, Dammeris, Damris, Demaras, Demaris

DAMIANA (Greek) tamer, soother. A feminine form of Damian.
Daimenia, Daimiona, Damia, Damiann, Damianna, Damianne, Damien, Damienne, Damiona, Damon, Demion

DAMICA (French) friendly.
Damee, Dameeka, Dameka, Damekah, Damicah, Damicia, Damicka, Damie, Damieka, Damika, Damikah, Damyka, Demeeka, Demeka, Demekah, Demica, Demicah

DAMITA (Spanish) small noblewoman.
Damee, Damesha, Dameshia, Damesia, Dametia, Dametra, Dametrah

DAMONICA (American) a combination of the prefix Da + Monica.
Damonec, Damoneke, Damonik, Damonika, Damonique, Diamoniqua, Diamonique

DANA (English) from Denmark; bright as day.
Daina, Dainna, Danah, Danaia, Danan, Danarra, Dane, Danean, Danna, Dayna

DANAE (Greek) Mythology: the mother of Perseus.
Danaë, Danay, Danayla, Danays, Danai, Danea, Danee, Dannae, Denae, Denee

DANALYN (American) a combination of Dana + Lynn.
Danalee, Donaleen

DANEIL (Hebrew) an alternate form of Danielle.
Daneal, Daneala, Daneale, Daneel, Daneela, Daneila

DANELLA (American) a form of Danielle.
Danayla, Danela, Danelia, Danelle, Danna, Donella, Donnella

DANELLE (Hebrew) an alternate form of Danielle.
Danael, Danalle, Danel, Danele, Danell, Danella, Donelle, Donnelle

DANESHA, Danisha (American) alternate forms of Danessa.
Daneisha, Daneshia, Daniesha, Danishia

DANESSA (American) a combination of Danielle + Vanessa. See also Doneshia.
Danasia, Danesa, Danesha, Danessia, Daniesa, Danisa, Danissa

DANESSIA (American) an alternate form of Danessa.
Danesia, Danieshia, Danisia, Danissia

DANETTE (American) a form of Danielle.
Danetra, Danett, Danetta, Donnita

DANI (Hebrew) a familiar form of Danielle.
Danee, Danie, Danne, Dannee, Danni, Dannie, Danny, Dannye, Dany

DANIA, Danya (Hebrew) short forms of Danielle.
Daniah, Danja, Dannia, Danyae

DANICA, Danika (Hebrew) alternate forms of Danielle. (Slavic) morning star.

Daneca, Daneeka, Daneekah, Danicah, Danicka, Danieka, Danikah, Danikla, Danneeka, Dannica, Dannika, Dannikah, Danyka, Denica, Donica, Donika, Donnaica, Donnica, Donnika

DANICE (American) a combination of Danielle + Janice.
Donice

DANIELA (Italian) a form of Danielle.
Daniellah, Dannilla, Danijela

DANIELAN (Spanish) a form of Danielle.

DANIELLE (Hebrew, French) God is my judge. A feminine form of Daniel.
Daneen, Daneil, Daneille, Danelle, Dani, Danial, Danialle, Danica, Daniel, Daniela, Danielan, Daniele, Danielka, Daniell, Daniella, Danilka, Danille, Danit, Dannielle, Danyel, Donniella

DANILLE (American) a form of Danielle.
Danila, Danile, Danilla, Dannille

DANIT (Hebrew) an alternate form of Danielle.
Danett, Danis, Danisha, Daniss, Danita, Danitra, Danitrea, Danitria, Danitza, Daniz

DANNA (Hebrew) a short form of Danella.
Dannah

DANIELLA (English) an alternate form of Dana.
Danka, Danniella, Danyella

DANNIELLE (Hebrew, French) an alternate form of Danielle.
Danniel, Danniele, Danniell

DANYEL, Danyell, Danyelle (American) forms of Danielle.
Daniyel, Danyae, Danyail, Danyaile, Danyal, Danyale, Danyea, Danyele, Danyiel, Danyielle, Danyle, Donnyale, Donnyell, Donyale, Donyell

DAPHNE (Greek) laurel tree.
Dafny, Daphane, Daphany, Dapheney, Daphna, Daphnee, Daphnique, Daphnit, Daphny

DAPHNEE (Greek) an alternate form of Daphne.
Daphaney, Daphanie, Daphney, Daphni, Daphnie

DARA (Hebrew) compassionate.
Dahra, Daira, Dairah, Darah, Daraka, Daralea, Daralee, Daraleigh, Daralie, Daravie, Darda, Darice, Darisa, Darissa, Darja, Darra, Darrah

DARBY (Irish) free. (Scandinavian) deer estate.
Darb, Darbe, Darbee, Darbi, Darbie, Darbra, Darbye

DARCELLE (French) a form of Darci.
Darcel, Darcell, Darcella, Darselle

DARCI, Darcy (Irish) dark. (French) fortress.
Darcee, Darcelle, Darcey, Darcie, Darsey, Darsi, Darsie

DARIA (Greek) wealthy. A feminine form of Darius.
Dari, Dariya, Darria, Darya, Daryia

DARIAN, Darrian (Greek) alternate forms of Daron.
Dariana, Dariane, Dariann, Darianna, Darianne, Dariyan, Dariyanne, Darriana, Darriane, Darriann, Darrianna, Darrianne, Derrian, Driana

DARIELLE (French) an alternate form of Daryl.
Dariel, Dariela, Dariell, Darriel, Darrielle

DARIEN, Darrien (Greek) alternate forms of Daron.
Dariene, Darienne, Darriene

DARILYNN (American) a form of Darlene.
Daralin, Daralyn, Daralynn, Daralynne, Darilin, Darilyn, Darilynne, Darlin, Darlyn, Darlynn, Darlynne, Darylin, Darylyn, Darylynn, Darylynne

DARION, Darrion (Irish) alternative forms of Daron.
Dariona, Darione, Darionna, Darionne, Darriona, Darrionna

DARLA (English) a short form of Darlene.
Darlecia, Darli, Darlice, Darlie, Darlis, Darly, Darlys

DARLENE (French) little darling. See also Daryl.
Darilynn, Darla, Darlean, Darlee, Darleen, Darleene, Darlena, Darlenia, Darlenne, Darletha, Darlin, Darline, Darling, Darlyn, Darlynn, Darlynne

DARNEE (Irish) a familiar form of Darnelle.

DARNELLE (English) hidden place.
Darnee, Darnel, Darnell, Darnella, Darnesha, Darnetta, Darnette, Darnice, Darniece, Darnita, Darnyell

DARNESHA, Darnisha
(American) forms of Darnelle.
Darneisha, Darneishia, Darneshea, Darneshia, Darnesia, Darniesha, Darnishia, Darnisia, Darrenisha

DARON (Irish) great. A feminine form of Darren.
Darian, Darien, Darion, Daronica, Daronice, Darron, Daryn

DARSELLE (French) an alternate form of Darcelle.
Darsel, Darsell, Darsella

DARU (Hindi) pine tree.

DARYL (French) a short form of Darlene. (English) beloved.
Darelle, Darielle, Daril, Darilynn, Darrel, Darrell, Darrelle, Darreshia, Darryl, Darryll, Daryll, Darylle

DARYN (Greek) gifts. (Irish) great. A feminine form of Darren.
Daron, Daryan, Daryne, Darynn, Darynne

DASHA, Dasia (Russian) forms of Dorothy.
Daisha, Dashae, Dashenka, Dashia, Dashiah, Dasiah, Daysha

DASHAWNA (American) a combination of the prefix Da + Shawna.
Dashawn, Dashawnna, Dashay, Dashell, Dayshana, Dayshawnna, Dayshona, Deshawna

DASHIKI (Swahili) loose-fitting shirt worn in Africa.
Dashi, Dashika, Dashka, Desheka, Deshiki

DASHONDA (American) a combination of the prefix Da + Shonda.
Dashawnda, Dishante

DAVALINDA (American) a combination of Davida + Linda.
Davalynda, Davelinda, Davilinda, Davylinda

DAVALYNDA (American) an alternate form of Davalinda.
Davelynda, Davilynda, Davylynda

DAVALYNN (American) a combination of Davida + Lynn.
Davalin, Davalyn, Davalynne, Davelin, Davelyn, Davelynn, Davelynne, Davilin, Davilyn, Davilynn, Davilynne, Dayleen, Devlyn

DAVIDA (Hebrew) beloved. A feminine form of David. See also Vida.
Daveta, Davetta, Davette, Davika, Davita

DAVINA (Scottish) a form of Davida. See also Vina.
Dava, Davannah, Davean, Davee, Daveen, Daveena, Davene, Daveon, Davey, Davi, Daviana, Davie, Davin, Davinder, Davine, Davineen, Davinia, Davinna, Davonna, Davria, Devean, Deveen, Devene, Devina

DAVISHA (American) a combination of the prefix Da + Aisha.
Daveisha, Davesia, Davis, Davisa

DAVONNA (Scottish, English) an alternate form of Davina, Devonna.
Davion, Daviona, Davionna, Davon, Davona, Davonda, Davone, Davonia, Davonne, Davonnia

DAWN (English) sunrise, dawn.
Dawana, Dawandrea, Dawanna, Dawin, Dawna, Dawne, Dawnee, Dawnetta, Dawnisha, Dawnlynn, Dawnn, Dawnrae

DAWNA (English) an alternate form of Dawn.
Dawnna, Dawnya

DAWNYELLE (American) a combination of Dawn + Danielle.
Dawnele, Dawnell, Dawnelle, Dawnyel, Dawnyella

DAWNISHA (American) a form of Dawn.
Dawnesha, Dawni, Dawniell, Dawnielle, Dawnisia, Dawniss, Dawnita, Dawnnisha, Dawnysha, Dawnysia

DAYANA (Latin) an alternate form of Diana.
Dayanara, Dayani, Dayanna, Dayanne, Dayanni, Deyanaira, Dyani, Dyanna, Dyia

DAYLE (English) an alternate form of Dale.
Dayla, Daylan, Daylea, Daylee

DAYNA (Scandinavian) a form of Dana.
Daynah, Dayne, Daynna, Deyna

DAYSHA (American) a form of Dasha.
Daysa, Dayshalie, Daysia, Deisha

DAYSI, Deysi (English) alternate forms of Daisy.
Daysee, Daysia, Daysie, Daysy, Deysia, Deysy

DAYTON, Daytona (English) day town; bright, sunny town.
Daytonia

DEANA (Latin) divine. (English) valley. A feminine form of Dean.
Deanah, Deane, Deanielle, Deanisha, Deanna, Deeana, Deeann, Deeanna, Deena

DEANDRA (American) a combination of Dee + Andrea.
Dandrea, Deandre, Deandré, Deandrea, Deandree, Deandreia, Deandria, Deanndra,

Deaundra, Deaundria, Deeandra, Deyaneira, Deondra, Diandra, Diandre, Diandrea, Diondria, Dyandra

DEANGELA (Italian) a combination of the prefix De + Angela.
Deangala, Deangalique, Deangle

DEANNA (Latin) an alternate form of Deana, Diana.
Deaana, Deahana, Deandra, Deandre, Déanna, Deannia, Deeanna, Deena

DEANNE (Latin) an alternate form of Diane.
Deahanne, Deane, Deann, Déanne, Deeann, Dee-Ann, Deeanne

DEBBIE (Hebrew) a short form of Deborah.
Debbee, Debbey, Debbi, Debby, Debee, Debi, Debie

DEBORAH (Hebrew) bee. Bible: a great Hebrew prophetess.
Deb, Debbie, Debbora, Debborah, Deberah, Debor, Debora, Deboran, Deborha, Deborrah, Debra, Debrena, Debrina, Debroah, Devora, Dobra

DEBRA (American) a short form of Deborah.
Debbra, Debbrah, Debrah, Debrea, Debria

DEDRA (American) a form of Deirdre.
Deeddra, Deedra, Deedrea, Deedrie

DEDRIANA (American) a combination of Dedra + Adriana.
Dedranae

DEE (Welsh) black, dark.
De, Dea, Deah, Dede, Dedie, Deea, Deedee, Dee Dee, Didi

DEENA (American) a form of Deana, Dena, Dinah.

DEIDRA, Deidre (Irish) alternate forms of Deirdre.
Deidrah, Deidrea, Deidrie, Diedra, Diedre, Dierdra

DEIRDRE (Irish) sorrowful; wanderer.
Dedra, Deerdra, Deerdre, Deidra, Deidre, Deirdree, Didi, Diedra, Dierdre, Diérdre, Dierdrie

DEISY (English) an alternate form of Daisy.
Deisi, Deissy

DEITRA (Greek) a short form of Demetria.
Deetra, Detria

DÉJA (French) before.
Daeja, Daija, Deejay, Dejae, Déjah, Dejai, Dejanae, Dejanelle, Dejon

DEJANAE (French) an alternate form of Déja.
Dajahnae, Dajona, Dejana, Dejanah, Dejanae, Dejanai, Dejanay, Dejane, Dejanea, Dejanee, Dejanna, Dejannaye, Dejena, Dejonae

DEJON (French) an alternate form of Déja.
Daijon, Dajan, Dejone, Dejonee, Dejonelle, Dejonna

DEKA (Somali) pleasing.
Dekah

DELACY (American) a combination of the prefix De + Lacy.
Delaceya

DELAINEY (Irish) an alternate form of Delaney.
Delaine, Delainee, Delaini, Delainie, Delainy

DELANA (German) noble protector.
Dalanna, Dalayna, Daleena, Dalena, Dalenna, Dalina, Dalinda, Dalinna, Delaina, Delania, Delanya, Delayna, Deleena, Delena, Delenya, Delina, Dellaina

DELANEY (Irish) descendant of the challenger. (English) an alternate form of Adeline.
Dalaney, Dalania, Dalene, Daleney, Daline, Del, Delainey, Delane, Delanee, Delanie, Delany, Delayne, Delayney, Delaynie, Deleani, Déline, Della, Dellaney

DELANIE (Irish) an alternate form of Delaney.
Delani

DELFINA (Greek) an alternate form of Delphine. (Spanish) dolphin.
Delfeena, Delfine

DELIA (Greek) visible; from Delos. (German, Welsh) a short form of Adelaide, Cordelia. Mythology: a festival of Apollo held every five years in ancient Greece.
Dehlia, Delea, Deli, Deliah, Deliana, Delianne, Delinda, Dellia, Dellya, Delya

DELICIA (English) delightful.
Delecia, Delesha, Delice, Delisa, Delise, Delisha, Delishia, Delisiah, Delya, Delys, Delyse, Delysia, Doleesha

DELILAH (Hebrew) brooder. Bible: the companion of Samson. See also Lila.
Dalialah, Dalila, Daliliah, Delila, Delilia

DELLA (English) a short form of Adelaide, Cordelia, Delaney.

Del, Dela, Dell, Delle, Delli, Dellie, Dells

DELORES (Spanish) an alternate form of Dolores.
Delora, Delore, Deloria, Delories, Deloris, Delorise, Delorita, Delsie

DELPHINE (Greek) from Delphi. See also Delfina.
Delpha, Delphe, Delphi, Delphia, Delphina, Delphinia, Delvina

DELSIE (English) a familiar form of Delores.
Delsa, Delsey, Delza

DELTA (Greek) door. Linguistics: the fourth letter in the Greek alphabet. Geography: a triangular land mass at the mouth of a river.
Delte, Deltora, Deltoria, Deltra

DEMETRIA (Greek) cover of the earth. Mythology: Demeter was the Greek goddess of the harvest.
Deitra, Demeta, Demeteria, Demetra, Demetriana, Demetrianna, Demetrias, Demetrice, Demetriona, Demetris, Demetrish, Demetrius, Demi, Demita, Demitra, Demitria, Dymitra

DEMI (Greek) a short form of Demetria. (French) half.
Demia, Demiah, Demii, Demmi, Demmie, Demy

DENA (Hebrew) an alternate form of Dinah. (English, Native American) valley. See also Deana.
Deane, Deena, Deeyn, Denae, Denah, Dene, Denea, Deney, Denna, Deonna

DENAE (Hebrew) an alternate form of Dena.
Denaé, Denay, Denee, Deneé

DENI (French) a short form of Denise.
Deney, Denie, Denni, Dennie, Denny, Dinnie, Dinny

DENICA, Denika (Slavic) alternate forms of Danica, Danika.
Denikah, Denikia

DENISE (French) Mythology: follower of Dionysus, the god of wine. A feminine form of Dennis.
Danice, Danise, Denese, Deni, Denice, Denicy, Deniece, Denisha, Denisse, Denize, Dennise, Dennys, Denyce, Denys, Denyse

DENISHA (American) a form of Denise.
Deneesha, Deneichia, Deneisha, Deneishea, Denesha, Deneshia, Deniesha, Denishia

DENISSE (French) an alternate form of Denise.
Denesse, Denissa

DEONNA (English) an alternate form of Dena.
Deon, Deona, Deonah, Deondra, Deonne

DERIKA (German) ruler of the people. A feminine form of Derek.
Dereka, Derekia, Derica, Dericka, Derrica, Derricka, Derrika

DERRY (Irish) redhead.
Deri, Derie

DERYN (Welsh) bird.
Derien, Derienne, Derion, Derin, Deron, Derren, Derrin, Derrine, Derrion, Derriona, Deryne

DESARAE (French) an alternate form of Desiree.
Desara, Desarai, Desaraie, Desaray, Desare, Desaré, Desarea, Desaree, Desarie, Dezarae

DESERAE, Desirae (French) alternate forms of Desiree.
Desera, Deserai, Deseray, Desere, Deseree, Deseret, Deseri, Deserie, Deserrae, Deserray, Deserré, Dessirae, Dezeray, Dezere, Dezerea, Dezrae, Dezyrae

DESHAWNA (American) a combination of the prefix De + Shawna.
Dashawna, Deshan, Deshane, Deshaun, Deshawn, Desheania, Deshona, Deshonna

DESHAWNDA (American) a combination of the prefix De + Shawnda.
Deshanda, Deshandra, Deshaundra, Deshawndra, Deshonda

DESI (French) a short form of Desiree.
Désir, Desira, Dezi, Dezia, Dezzia, Dezzie

DESIREE (French) desired, longed for. See also Dessa.
Chesarey, Desarae, Deserae, Desi, Desirae, Desirah, Desirai, Desiray, Desire, Desirea, Desireah, Desirée, Désirée, Desirey, Desiri, Desray, Desree, Dessie, Dessire, Dezarae, Dezirae, Deziree

DESSA (Greek) wanderer. (French) an alternate form of Desiree.

DESTA (Ethiopian) happy. (French) a short form of Destiny.
Desti, Destie, Desty

DESTANY (French) an alternate form of Destiny.
Destanee, Destaney, Destani, Destanie, Destannee. Destannie

DESTINEE, Destini, Destinie (French) alternate forms of Destiny.
Desteni, Destiana, Destine, Destinée, Destnie

DESTINEY (French) an alternate form of Destiny.

DESTINY (French) fate.
Desnine, Desta, Destany, Destenee, Destenie, Desteny, Destin, Destinee, Destiney, Destini, Destinie, Destonie, Destynee, Dezstany

DESTYNEE, Destyni (French) alternate forms of Destiny.
Desty, Destyn, Destyne, Destyne, Destynie

DEVA (Hindi) divine. Religion: the Hindu moon goddess.
Deeva

DEVAN (Irish) an alternate form of Devin.
Devana, Devane, Devanee, Devaney, Devani, Devanie, Devann, Devanna, Devannae, Devanne, Devany

DEVI (Hindi) goddess. Religion: the Hindu goddess of power and destruction.

DEVIN (Irish) poet.
Devan, Deven, Devena, Devenje, Deveny, Devine, Devinn, Devinne, Devyn

DEVON (English) a short form of Devonna.
Deaven, Devion, Devione, Devionne, Devone, Devoni, Devonne

DEVONNA (English) from Devonshire.
Davonna, Devon, Devona, Devonda, Devondra, Devonia

DEVORA (Hebrew) an alternate form of Deborah.
Deva, Devorah, Devra, Devrah

DEVYN (Irish) an alternate form of Devin.
Deveyn, Devyne, Devynn, Devynne

DEXTRA (Latin) adroit, skillful.
Dekstra, Dextria

DEZARAE, Dezirae, Deziree (French) alternate forms of Desiree.
Dezaraee, Dezarai, Dezaray, Dezare, Dezaree, Dezarey, Dezerie, Deziray, Dezirea, Dezirée, Dezorae, Dezra

DI (Latin) a short form of Diana, Diane.
Dy

DIA (Latin) a short form of Diana, Diane.

DIAMOND (Latin) precious gem.
Diamantina, Diamon, Diamonda, Diamonde, Diamonia, Diamonique, Diamonte, Diamontina, Dyamond

DIANA (Latin) divine. Mythology: the goddess of the hunt, the moon, and fertility. See also Deanna, Deanne, Dyan.
Daiana, Daianna, Dayana, Dayanna, Di, Dia, Dianah, Dianalyn, Dianarose, Dianatris, Dianca, Diandra, Diane, Dianelis, Diania, Dianielle, Dianita, Dianna, Dianys, Didi

DIANE, Dianne (Latin) alternate forms of Diana.
Deane, Deanne, Deeane, Deeanne, Di, Dia, Diahann, Dian, Diani, Dianie, Diann

DIANNA (Latin) an alternate form of Diana.
Diahanna, Diannah

DIANTHA (Greek) divine flower.
Diandre, Dianthe

DIEDRA (Irish) an alternate form of Deirdre.
Didra, Diedre

DILLAN (Irish) loyal, faithful.
Dillon, Dillyn

DILYS (Welsh) perfect; true.

DINA (Hebrew) a short form of Dinah.
Dinna, Dyna

DINAH (Hebrew) vindicated. Bible: a daughter of Jacob and Leah.
Dina, Dinnah, Dynah

DINKA (Swahili) people.

DIONNA (Greek) an alternative form of Dionne.
Deona, Deondra, Deonia, Deonna, Deonyia, Diona, Diondra, Diondrea

DIONNE (Greek) divine queen. Mythology: the mother of Aphrodite, the goddess of love.
Deonne, Dion, Dione, Dionee, Dionis, Dionna, Dionte

DIOR (French) golden.
Diora, Diore, Diorra, Diorre

DITA (Spanish) a form of Edith.
Ditka, Ditta

DIVINIA (Latin) divine.
Devina, Devinae, Devinia, Devinie, Devinna, Diveena, Divina, Divine, Diviniea, Divya

DIXIE (French) tenth. (English) wall; dike. Geography: a nickname for the American South.
Dix, Dixee, Dixi, Dixy

DIZA (Hebrew) joyful.
Ditza, Ditzah, Dizah

DODIE (Greek) a familiar form of Dorothy. (Hebrew) beloved.
Doda, Dode, Dodee, Dodi, Dody

DOLLY (American) a short form of Dolores, Dorothy.
Dol, Doll, Dollee, Dolley, Dolli, Dollie, Dollina

DOLORES (Spanish) sorrowful. Religion: Santa Maria de los Dolores—Saint Mary of the Sorrows—is a name for the Virgin Mary. See also Lola.
Delores, Deloria, Dolly, Dolorcitas, Dolorita, Doloritas

DOMINICA, Dominika (Latin) belonging to the Lord. A feminine form of Dominic. See also Mika.
Domenica, Domenika, Domineca, Domineka, Dominga, Domini, Dominick, Dominicka, Dominique, Dominixe, Domino, Dominyika, Domka, Domnicka, Domonica, Domonice, Domonika

DOMINIQUE, Domonique (French) forms of Dominica, Dominika.
Domanique, Domeneque, Domenique, Domineque, Dominiqua, Domino, Dominoque, Dominque, Dominuque, Domique, Domminique, Domoniqua

DOMINO (English) a short form of Dominica, Dominique.

DONA (Italian) an alternate form of Donna. (English)

world leader; proud ruler. A feminine form of Donald.
Donae, Donah, Donalda, Donaldina, Donelda, Donellia, Doni

DOÑA (Italian) an alternate form of Donna.
Donail, Donalea, Donalisa, Donay, Doni, Donia, Donie, Donise, Donitrae

DONATA (Latin) gift.
Donatha, Donato, Donatta, Donetta, Donette, Donita, Donnette, Donnita, Donte

DONDI (American) a familiar form of Donna.
Dondra, Dondrea, Dondria

DONESHIA, Donisha (American) alternate forms of Danessa.
Donasha, Donashay, Doneisha, Doneishia, Donesha, Donisa, Donisha, Donishia, Donneshia, Donnisha

DONNA (Italian) lady.
Doña, Dondi, Donnae, Donnalee, Donnalen, Donnay, Donne, Donnell, Donni, Donnie, Donnise, Donny, Dontia, Donya

DONNIELLA (American) a form of Danielle.
Donella, Doniele, Doniell, Doniella, Donielle, Donnella, Donnielle, Donnyella, Donyelle

DORA (Greek) gift. A short form of Adora, Eudora, Pandora, Theodora.
Dorah, Doralia, Doralie, Doralisa, Doraly, Doralynn, Doran, Dorchen, Dore, Dorece, Doree, Doreece, Doreen, Dorelia, Dorella, Dorelle, Doresha, Doressa, Doretta, Dori, Dorielle, Dorika, Doriley, Dorilis, Dorinda, Dorion, Dorita, Doro, Dory

DORALYNN (English) a combination of Dora + Lynn.
Doralin, Doralyn, Doralynne, Dorlin

DOREEN (Greek) an alternate form of Dora. (Irish) moody, sullen. (French) golden.
Doreena, Dorena, Dorene, Dorina, Dorine

DORETTA (American) a form of Dora, Dorothy.
Doretha, Dorette, Dorettie

DORI, Dory (American) familiar forms of Dora, Doria, Doris, Dorothy.
Dore, Dorey, Dorie, Dorree, Dorri, Dorrie, Dorry

DORIA (Greek) an alternate form of Dorian.
Dori

DORIAN (Greek) from Doris, Greece.
Dorean, Doriana, Doriane, Doriann, Dorianna, Dorianne, Dorin, Dorina, Dorriane

DORINDA (Spanish) a form of Dora.

DORIS (Greek) sea. Mythology: wife of Nereus and mother of the Nereids, or sea nymphs.
Dori, Dorice, Dorisa, Dorise, Dorris, Dorrise, Dorrys, Dory, Dorys

DOROTHEA (Greek) an alternate form of Dorothy. See also Thea.
Dorethea, Dorotea, Doroteya, Dorotha, Dorothia, Dorotthea, Dorthea, Dorthia

DOROTHY (Greek) gift of God. See also Dasha, Dodie, Lolotea, Theodora.
Dasya, Do, Doa, Doe, Dolly, Doortje, Dorathy, Dordei, Dordi, Doretta, Dori, Dorika, Doritha, Dorka, Dorle, Dorlisa, Doro, Dorolice, Dorosia, Dorota, Dorothea, Dorothee, Dorothi, Dorothie, Dorottya, Dorte, Dortha, Dorthy, Dory, Dosi, Dossie, Dosya, Dottie

DORRIT (Greek) dwelling. (Hebrew) generation.
Dorit, Dorita, Doritt

DOTTIE, Dotty (Greek) familiar forms of Dorothy.
Dot, Dottee

DREW (Greek) courageous; strong. (Latin) a short form of Drusilla.
Dru, Drue

DRINKA (Spanish) a form of Alexandria.
Dreena, Drena, Drina

DRUSI (Latin) a short form of Drusilla.
Drucey, Druci, Drucie, Drucy, Drusey, Drusie, Drusy

DRUSILLA (Latin) descendant of Drusus, the strong one. See also Drew.
Drewsila, Drucella, Drucill, Drucilla, Druscilla, Druscille, Drusi

DULCE (Latin) sweet.
Delcina, Delcine, Douce, Doucie, Dulcea, Dulcey, Dulci, Dulcia, Dulciana, Dulcibel, Dulcibella, Dulcie, Dulcine, Dulcinea, Dulcy, Dulse, Dulsea

DULCINEA (Spanish) sweet. Literature: Don Quixote's love interest.

DUSCHA (Russian) soul; sweetheart; term of endearment.
Duschah, Dusha, Dushenka

DUSTI, Dusty (English) short forms of Dustine.
Dustee, Dustie

DUSTINE (German) valiant fighter. (English) brown rock, quarry. A feminine form of Dustin.
Dusteena, Dusti, Dustin, Dustina, Dustyn

DYAMOND, Dymond (Latin) alternate forms of Diamond.
Dyamin, Dyamon, Dyamone, Dymin, Dymon, Dymonde, Dymone, Dymonn

DYANA (Latin) an alternate form of Diana. (Native American) deer.
Dyan, Dyane, Dyani, Dyann, Dyanna, Dyanne

DYLAN (Welsh) sea.
Dylaan, Dylaina, Dylana, Dylane, Dylanee, Dylanie, Dylann, Dylanna, Dylen, Dylin, Dyllan, Dylynn

DYLLIS (Welsh) sincere.
Dilys, Dylis, Dylys

DYNASTY (Latin) powerful ruler.
Dynastee, Dynasti, Dynastie

DYSHAWNA (American) a combination of the prefix Dy + Shawna.
Dyshanta, Dyshawn, Dyshonda, Dyshonna

EARLENE (Irish) pledge. (English) noblewoman. A feminine form of Earl.
Earla, Earlean, Earlecia, Earleen, Earlena, Earlina, Earlinda, Earline, Erla, Erlana, Erlene, Erlenne, Erlina, Erlinda, Erline, Erlisha

EARTHA (English) earthy.
Ertha

EASTER (English) Easter time. History: a name for a child born on Easter.
Eastan, Eastlyn, Easton

EBONE, Ebonee (Greek) alternate forms of Ebony.
Abonee, Ebanee, Eboné, Ebonea, Ebonne, Ebonnee

EBONI, Ebonie (Greek) alternate forms of Ebony.
Ebanie, Ebeni, Ebonni, Ebonnie

EBONY (Greek) a hard, dark wood.
Abony, Eban, Ebanie, Ebany, Ebbony, Ebone, Eboney, Eboni, Ebonie, Ebonique, Ebonisha, Ebonye, Ebonyi

ECHO (Greek) repeated sound. Mythology: the nymph who pined for the love of Narcissus until only her voice remained.
Echoe, Ecko, Ekko, Ekkoe

EDA (Irish, English) a short form of Edana, Edith.

EDANA (Irish) ardent; flame.
Eda, Edan, Edanna

EDDA (German) an alternate form of Hedda.
Etta

EDDY (American) a familiar form of Edwina.
Eady, Eddi, Eddie, Edy

EDELINE (English) noble; kind.
Adeline, Edelyne, Ediline, Edilyne

EDEN (Babylonian) a plain. (Hebrew) delightful. Bible: the earthly paradise.
Eaden, Ede, Edena, Edene, Edenia, Edin, Edyn

EDIE (English) a familiar form of Edith.
Eadie, Edi, Edy, Edye, Eyde, Eydie

EDITH (English) rich gift. See also Dita.
Eadith, Eda, Ede, Edetta, Edette, Edie, Edit, Edita, Edite, Editha, Edithe, Editta, Ediva, Edyta, Edyth, Edytha, Edythe

EDNA (Hebrew) rejuvenation. Mythology: the wife of Enoch, according to ancient eastern legends.
Adna, Adnisha, Ednah, Edneisha, Edneshia, Ednisha, Ednita, Edona

EDRIANNA (Greek) an alternate form of Adrienne.
Edria, Edriana, Edrina

EDWINA (English) prosperous friend. A feminine form of Edwin. See also Winnie.
Eddy, Edina, Edweena, Edwena, Edwine, Edwyna, Edwynn

EFFIA (Ghanian) born on Friday.

EFFIE (Greek) spoken well of. (English) a short form of Alfreda, Euphemia.
Effi, Effia, Effy, Ephie

EILEEN (Irish) a form of Helen. See also Aileen, Ilene.
Eilean, Eileena, Eileene, Eilena, Eilene, Eiley, Eilie, Eilieh, Eilina, Eiline, Eilleen, Eillen, Eilyn, Eleen, Elene

EKATERINA (Russian) a form of Katherine.
Ekaterine, Ekaterini

ELA (Polish) a form of Adelaide.

ELAINA (French) a form of Helen.
Elainea, Elainia, Elainna

ELAINE (French) a form of Helen. See also Lainey, Laine.
Eilane, Elain, Elaina, Elaini, Elan, Elana, Elane, Elania, Elanie, Elanit, Elauna, Elayna, Ellaine

ELANA (Greek) a short form of Eleanor. See also Ilana, Lana.
Elan, Elanee, Elaney, Elani, Elania, Elanie, Elanna, Elanni

ELAYNA (French) an alternate form of Elaina.
Elayn, Elaynah, Elayne, Elayni

ELBERTA (English) a form of Alberta.
Elbertha, Elberthina, Elberthine, Elbertina, Elbertine

ELDORA (Spanish) golden, gilded.
Eldoree, Eldorey, Eldori, Eldoria, Eldorie, Eldory

ELEANOR (Greek) light. An alternate form of Helen. History: Anna Eleanor Roosevelt was a U.S. delegate to the United Nations, a writer, and the thirty-second First Lady of the U.S. See also Elana, Ella, Ellen, Leanore, Lena, Lenore, Leonore, Leora, Nellie, Nora, Noreen.
Elana, Elanor, Elanore, Eleanora, Eleanore, Elena, Eleni, Elenor, Elenorah, Elenore, Eleonor, Eleonore, Elianore, Elinor, Elinore, Elladine, Ellenor, Ellie, Elliner, Ellinor, Ellinore, Elna, Elnore, Elynor, Elynore

ELEANORA (Greek) an alternate form of Eleanor. See also Lena.
Elenora, Eleonora, Elianora, Ellenora, Ellenorah, Elnora, Elynora

ELECTRA (Greek) shining; brilliant. Mythology: the daughter of Agamemnon, leader of the Greeks in the Trojan War.
Elektra

ELENA (Greek) an alternate form of Eleanor. (Italian) a form of Helen.
Eleana, Eleen, Eleena, Elen, Elene, Elenitsa, Elenka, Elenna, Elenoa, Elenola, Elina, Ellena, Lena

ELENI (Greek) a familiar form of Eleanor.
Elenie, Eleny

ELEORA (Hebrew) the Lord is my light.
Eliora, Elira, Elora

ELEXIS (Greek) an alternate form of Alexis.
Elexas, Elexes, Elexess, Elexeya, Elexia, Elexiah

ELEXUS (Greek) an alternate form of Alexius, Alexus.
Elexius, Elexsus, Elexxus, Elexys

ELFRIDA (German) peaceful. See also Freda.
Elfrea, Elfreda, Elfredda, Elfreeda, Elfreyda, Elfrieda, Elfryda

ELGA (German) an alternate form of Helga. (Norwegian) pious.
Elgiva

ELIA (Hebrew) a short from of Eliana.
Eliah

ELIANA (Hebrew) my God has answered me. A feminine form of Eli, Elijah. See also Iliana.
Elia, Eliane, Elianna, Ellianna, Liana, Liane

ELIANE (Hebrew) an alternate form of Eliana.
Elianne, Elliane, Ellianne

ELICIA (Hebrew) an alternate form of Elisha. See also Alicia.
Elecia, Elica, Elicea, Elicet, Elichia, Eliscia, Elisia, Elissia, Ellecia, Ellicia

ELIDA, Elide (Latin) alternate forms of Alida.
Elidee, Elidia, Elidy

ELISA (Spanish, Italian, English) a short form of Elizabeth. See also Alisa, Ilisa.
Elecea, Eleesa, Elesa, Elesia, Elisia, Elisya, Ellisa, Ellisia, Ellissa, Ellissia, Ellissya, Ellisya, Elysa, Elysia, Elyssia, Elyssya, Elysya, Lisa

ELISABETH (Hebrew) an alternate form of Elizabeth.

Elisabet, Elisabeta, Elisabethe, Elisabetta, Elisabette, Elisabith, Elisebet, Elisheba, Elisheva

ELISE (French, English) a short form of Elizabeth, Elysia. See also Ilise, Liese, Lisette, Lissie.
Eilis, Eilise, Elese, Élise, Elisee, Elisie, Elisse, Elizé, Ellice, Ellise, Ellyce, Ellyse, Ellyze, Elsey, Elsie, Elsy, Elyce, Elyci, Elyse, Elyze, Lisel, Lisl, Lison

ELISHA (Greek) an alternate form of Alisha. (Hebrew) consecrated to God. See also Ilisha, Lisha.
Eleacia, Eleasha, Eleesha, Eleisha, Elesha, Eleshia, Eleticia, Elicia, Elishah, Elisheva, Elishia, Elishua, Eliska, Ellesha, Ellexia, Ellisha, Elsha, Elysha, Elyshia

ELISSA, Elyssa (Greek, English) forms of Elizabeth. Short forms of Melissa. See also Alissa, Alyssa, Lissa.
Elissah, Ellissa, Ellyssa, Ilissa, Ilyssa

ELITA (Latin, French) chosen. See also Lida, Lita.
Elitia, Elitia, Elitie, Ellita, Ellitia, Ellitie, Ilida, Ilita, Litia

ELIZA (Hebrew) a short form of Elizabeth. See also Aliza.
Eliz, Elizaida, Elizalina, Elize, Elizea

ELIZABET (Hebrew) an alternate form of Elizabeth.
Elizabete, Elizabette

ELIZABETH (Hebrew) consecrated to God. Bible: the mother of John the Baptist. See also Bess, Beth, Betsy, Betty, Elsa, Ilse, Libby, Liese, Liesel,

Lisa, Lisbeth, Lisette, Lissa, Lissie, Liz, Liza, Lizabeta, Lizabeth, Lizbeth, Lizina, Lizzy, Veta, Yelisabeta, Zizi. *Alizabeth, Eliabeth, Elisa, Elisabeth, Elise, Elissa, Eliza, Elizabee, Elizabet, Elizaveta, Elizebeth, Elka, Elsabeth, Elsbeth, Elschen, Elspeth, Elysabeth, Elzbieta, Elzsébet, Helsa, Ilizzabet, Lusa*

ELIZAVETA (Polish, English) a form of Elizabeth. *Elisavet, Elisaveta, Elisavetta, Elisveta, Elizavet, Elizavetta, Elizveta, Elsveta, Elzveta*

ELKA (Polish) a form of Elizabeth. *Ilka*

ELKE (German) a form of Adelaide, Alice. *Elki, Ilki*

ELLA, Elle (Greek) short forms of Eleanor. (English) elfin; beautiful fairy-woman. *Ellah, Ellamae, Ellia, Ellie*

ELLEN (English) a form of Eleanor, Helen. *Elen, Elenee, Eleny, Elin, Elina, Elinda, Ellan, Ellena, Ellene, Ellie, Ellin, Ellon, Ellyn, Ellynn, Ellynne, Elyn*

ELLICE (English) an alternate form of Elise. *Ellecia, Ellyce, Elyce*

ELLIE, Elly (English) short forms of Eleanor, Ella, Ellen. *Ele, Elie, Ellee, Elleigh, Elli*

ELMA (Turkish) sweet fruit.

ELMIRA (Arabic, Spanish) an alternate form of Almira. *Elmeera, Elmera, Elmeria, Elmyra*

ELNORA (American) a combination of Ella + Nora.

ELODIE (American) a form of Melody. *Elodee, Elodia, Elody*

ELOISE (French) a form of Louise. *Elois, Eloisa, Eloisia*

ELORA (American) a short form of Elnora. *Ellora, Elloree, Elorie*

ELSA (Hebrew) a short form of Elizabeth. (German) noble. See also Ilse. *Ellsa, Ellse, Else, Elsia, Elsie, Elsje*

ELSBETH (German) a form of Elizabeth. *Elsbet, Elzbet, Elzbieta*

ELSIE (German) a familiar form of Elsa, Helsa. *Ellsie, Elsie, Ellsy, Elsi, Elsy*

ELSPETH (Scottish) a form of Elizabeth. *Elspet, Elspie*

ELVA (English) elfin. See also Alva, Alvina. *Elvia, Elvie*

ELVINA (English) an alternate form of Alvina. *Elvenea, Elvinea, Elvinia, Elvinna*

ELVIRA (Latin) white; blond. (German) closed up. (Spanish) elfin. Geography: the town in Spain that hosted the first Ecumenical Council in 300 A.D. *Elva, Elvera, Elvire, Elwira, Vira*

ELYSE (Latin) an alternate form of Elysia. *Ellysa, Ellyse, Elyce, Elys, Elysee, Elysse*

ELYSIA (Latin) sweet; blissful. Mythology: Elysium was the dwelling place of happy souls. *Elise, Elishia, Ellicia, Elycia, Elyssa, Ilysha, Ilysia*

ELYSSA (Latin) an alternate form of Elysia. *Ellyssa*

EMALEE (Latin) an alternate form of Emily. *Emaili, Emalea, Emaleigh, Emali, Emalia, Emalie*

EMANI (Arabic) an alternate form of Iman. *Eman, Emane, Emaneé, Emanie, Emann*

EMANUELLE (Hebrew) an alternate form of Emmanuelle. *Emanual, Emanuel, Emanuela, Emanuella*

EMBER (French) an alternate form of Amber. *Emberlee, Emberly*

EMELIA, Emelie (Latin) alternate forms of Emily. *Emellie*

EMELY (Latin) an alternate form of Emily. *Emelly*

EMERALD (French) bright green gemstone. *Emelda, Esmeralda*

EMERY (German) industrious leader. *Emeri, Emerie*

EMILEE, Emilie (English) forms of Emily. *Emile, Emilea, Emileigh, Émilie, Emiliee, Emillee, Emillie, Emméie, Emmilee, Emylee*

EMILIA (Italian) a form of Amelia, Emily.
Emalia, Emelia, Emila

EMILY (Latin) flatterer. (German) industrious. A feminine form of Emil. See also Amelia, Emma, Millie.
Eimile, Em, Emaily, Emalee, Emeli, Emelia, Emelie, Emelita, Emely, Emilee, Emiley, Emili, Emilia, Emilie, Émilie, Emilis, Emilka, Emillie, Emilly, Emmaline, Emmaly, Emmélie, Emmey, Emmi, Emmie, Emmilly, Emmily, Emmy, Emmye, Emyle

EMILYANN (American) a combination of Emily + Ann.
Emileane, Emileann, Emileanna, Emileanne, Emiliana, Emiliann, Emilianna, Emilianne, Emillyane, Emillyann, Emillyanna, Emillyanne, Emliana, Emliann, Emlianna, Emlianne

EMMA (German) a short form of Emily. See also Amy.
Em, Ema, Emmah, Emmy

EMMALEE (American) a combination of Emma + Lee. A form of Emily.
Emalea, Emalee, Emilee, Emmalea, Emmalei, Emmaleigh, Emmaley, Emmali, Emmalia, Emmalie, Emmaliese, Emmalyse, Emylee

EMMALINE (French) a form of Emily.
Emalina, Emaline, Emelina, Emeline, Emilienne, Emilina, Emiline, Emmalina, Emmalene, Emmeline, Emmiline

EMMALYNN (American) a combination of Emma + Lynn.
Emelyn, Emelyne, Emelynne, Emilyn, Emilynn, Emilynne, Emlyn, Emlynn, Emlynne, Emmalyn, Emmalynne

EMMANUELLE (Hebrew) God is with us. A feminine form of Emmanuel.
Emanuelle, Emmanuela, Emmanuella

EMMY (German) a familiar form of Emma.
Emi, Emie, Emiy, Emmi, Emmie, Emmye, Emy

EMMYLOU (American) a combination of Emmy + Lou.
Emlou, Emmalou, Emmelou, Emmilou, Emylou

ENA (Irish) a form of Helen.
Enna

ENID (Welsh) life; spirit.

ENRICA (Spanish) a form of Henrietta. See also Rica.
Enrieta, Enrietta, Enrika, Enriqua, Enriqueta, Enriquetta, Enriquette

EPPIE (English) a familiar form of Euphemia.
Effie, Effy, Eppy

ERICA (Scandinavian) ruler of all. (English) brave ruler. A feminine form of Eric. See also Arica, Rica, Ricki.
Ericca, Ericha, Ericka, Errica

ERICKA, Erika (Scandanavian) alternate forms of Erica.
Erickah, Erikaa, Erikah, Erikka, Erricka, Errika, Eyka, Erykka, Eyrika

ERIN (Irish) peace. History: another name for Ireland. See also Arin.
Earin, Earrin, Eran, Eren, Erena, Erene, Ereni, Eri, Erian, Erina, Erine, Erinetta, Erinn, Errin, Eryn

ERINN (Irish) an alternate form of Erin.
Erinna, Erinne

ERMA (Latin) a short form of Ermine, Hermina. See also Irma.
Ermelinda

ERMINE (Latin) an alternate form of Hermina.
Erma, Ermin, Ermina, Erminda, Erminia, Erminie

ERNA (English) a short form of Ernestine.

ERNESTINE (English) earnest, sincere. A feminine form of Ernest.
Erna, Ernaline, Ernesia, Ernesta, Ernestina, Ernesztina

ERYN (Irish) an alternate form of Erin.
Eiryn, Eryne, Erynn, Erynne

ESHE (Swahili) life.
Eisha, Esha

ESMÉ (French) a familiar form of Esmeralda. A form of Amy.
Esma, Esme, Esmëe

ESMERALDA (Greek, Spanish) a form of Emerald.
Emelda, Esmé, Esmerelda, Esmerilda, Esmiralda, Ezmerelda, Ezmirilda

ESPERANZA (Spanish) hope. See also Speranza.
Esparanza, Espe, Esperance, Esperans, Esperansa, Esperanta, Esperanz, Esperenza

ESSENCE (Latin) life; existence.
Essa, Essenc, Essencee, Essences, Essenes, Essense, Essynce

ESSIE (English) a short form of Estelle, Esther.
Essa, Essey, Essie, Essy

ESTEE (English) a short form of Estelle, Esther.
Esta, Estée, Esti

ESTEFANI, Estefania, Estefany (Spanish) forms of Stephanie.
Estafania, Estefana, Estefane, Estefanie

ESTELLE (French) a form of Esther. See also Stella, Trella.
Essie, Estee, Estel, Estela, Estele, Esteley, Estelina, Estelita, Estell, Estella, Estellina, Estellita, Esthella

ESTEPHANIE (Spanish) a form of Stephanie.
Estephania, Estephani, Estephany

ESTHER (Persian) star. Bible: the Jewish captive whom Ahasuerus made his queen. See also Hester.
Essie, Estee, Ester, Esthur, Eszter, Eszti

ESTRELLA (French) star.
Estrela, Estrelinha, Estrell, Estrelle, Estrellita

ETHANA (Hebrew) strong; firm. A feminine form of Ethan.

ETHEL (English) noble.
Ethelda, Ethelin, Etheline, Ethelle, Ethelyn, Ethelynn, Ethelynne, Ethyl

ÉTOILE (French) star.

ETTA (German) little. (English) a short form of Henrietta.
Etka, Etke, Etti, Ettie, Etty, Itke, Itta

EUDORA (Greek) honored gift. See also Dora.

EUGENIA (Greek) born to nobility. A feminine form of Eugene. See also Gina.

Eugenie, Eugenina, Eugina, Evgenia

EUGENIE (Greek) an alternate form of Eugenia.
Eugenee, Eugénie

EULALIA (Greek) well spoken. See also Ula.
Eula, Eulalee, Eulalie, Eulalya, Eulia

EUN (Korean) silver.

EUNICE (Greek) happy; victorious. Bible: the mother of Saint Timothy. See also Unice.
Euna, Eunique, Eunise, Euniss

EUPHEMIA (Greek) spoken well of, in good repute. History: a fourth-century Christian martyr.
Effam, Effie, Eppie, Eufemia, Euphan, Euphemie, Euphie

EURYDICE (Greek) wide, broad. Mythology: the wife of Orpheus.
Euridice, Euridyce, Eurydyce

EUSTACIA (Greek) productive. (Latin) stable; calm. A feminine form of Eustace. See also Stacey.
Eustasia

EVA (Greek) a short form of Evangelina. (Hebrew) an alternate form of Eve. See also Ava, Chava.
Éva, Evah, Evalea, Evalee, Evike

EVALINE (French) a form of Evelyn.
Evalin, Evalina, Evalyn, Evalynn, Eveleen, Evelene, Evelina, Eveline

EVANGELINA (Greek) bearer of good news.

Eva, Evangelene, Evangelia, Evangelica, Evangeline, Evangelique, Evangelyn, Evangelynn

EVANIA (Greek) a feminine form of Evan. (Irish) young warrior.
Evan, Evana, Evanka, Evann, Evanna, Evanne, Evany, Eveania, Evvanne, Evvunea, Evyan

EVE (Hebrew) life. An alternate form of Chava. Bible: the first woman created by God. (French) a short form of Evonne. See also Hava, Naeva, Vica, Yeva.
Eva, Evie, Evita, Evuska, Evyn, Ewa, Yeva

EVELIN (English) an alternate form of Evelyn.
Evelina, Eveline

EVELYN (English) hazelnut.
Avalyn, Aveline, Evaleen, Evalene, Evaline, Evalyn, Evalynn, Evalynne, Eveleen, Evelin, Evelyna, Evelyne, Evelynn, Evelynne, Evline, Ewalina

EVERETT (German) couragrous as a boar.

EVETTE (French) an alternate form of Yvette. A familiar form of Evonne. See also Ivette.
Evett

EVIE (Hungarian) a form of Eve.
Evey, Evi, Evicka, Evike, Evka, Evuska, Evvie, Evvy, Evy, Ewa

EVITA (Spanish) a form of Eve.

EVLINE (English) an alternate form of Evelyn.
Evleen, Evlene, Evlin, Evlina, Evlyn, Evlynn, Evlynne

EVONNE (French) an alternate form of Yvonne. See also Ivonne.
Evanne, Eve, Evenie, Evenne, Eveny, Evette, Evin, Evon, Evona, Evone, Evoni, Evonna, Evonnie, Evony, Evyn, Evynn, Eyona, Eyvone

EZRI (Hebrew) helper; strong.
Ezra, Ezria

FABIA (Latin) bean grower. A feminine form of Fabian.
Fabiana, Fabienne, Fabiola, Fabra, Fabria

FABIANA (Latin) an alternate form of Fabia.
Fabyana

FABIENNE (Latin) an alternate form of Fabia.
Fabian, Fabiann, Fabianne, Fabiene, Fabreanne

FABIOLA, Faviola (Latin) alternate forms of Fabia.
Fabiole, Fabyola, Faviana, Faviolha

FAITH (English) faithful; fidelity. See also Faye, Fidelity.
Fayth, Faythe

FAIZAH (Arabic) victorious.

FALDA (Icelandic) folded wings.
Faida, Fayda

FALINE (Latin) catlike.
Faleen, Falena, Falene, Falin, Falina, Fallyn, Fallyne, Faylina, Fayline, Faylyn, Faylynn, Faylynne, Felenia, Felina

FALLON (Irish) grandchild of the ruler.
Falan, Falen, Fallan, Fallen, Fallonne, Falon, Falyn, Falynn, Falynne, Phalon

FANCY (French) betrothed. (English) whimsical; decorative.
Fanchette, Fanchon, Fanci, Fancia, Fancie

FANNIE, Fanny (American) familiar forms of Frances.
Fan, Fanette, Fani, Fania, Fannee, Fanney, Fanni, Fannia, Fany, Fanya

FANTASIA (Greek) imagination.
Fantasy, Fantasya, Fantaysia, Fantazia, Fiantasi

FARAH, Farrah (English) beautiful; pleasant.
Fara, Farra, Fayre

FAREN, Farren (English) wanderer.
Faran, Fare, Farin, Faron, Farrahn, Farran, Farrand, Farrin, Farron, Farryn, Farye, Faryn, Feran, Ferin, Feron, Ferran, Ferren, Ferrin, Ferron, Ferryn

FATIMA (Arabic) daughter of the Prophet. History: the daughter of Muhammad.
Fatema, Fathma, Fatimah, Fatime, Fatma, Fatmah, Fatme, Fattim

FAWN (French) young deer.
Faun, Fawna, Fawne

FAWNA (French) an alternate form of Fawn.
Fauna, Fawnia, Fawnna

FAYE (French) fairy; elf. (English) an alternate form of Faith.
Fae, Fay, Fayann, Fayanna, Fayette, Fayina, Fey

FAYOLA (Nigerian) lucky.
Fayla, Feyla

FELECIA (Latin) an alternate form of Felicia.
Flecia

FELICA (Spanish) a short form of Felicia.
Falisa, Felisa, Felisca, Felissa, Feliza

FELICE (Latin) a short form of Felicia.
Felece, Felicie, Felise, Felize, Felyce, Felysse

FELICIA (Latin) fortunate; happy. A feminine form of Felix. See also Lecia, Phylicia.
Falecia, Faleshia, Falicia, Fela, Felecia, Felica, Felice, Felicidad, Feliciona, Felicity, Felicya, Felisea, Felisha, Felisia, Felisiana, Felissya, Felita, Felixia, Felizia, Felka, Fellcia, Felycia, Felysia, Felyssia, Fleasia, Fleichia, Fleishia, Flichia

FELICITY (English) a form of Felicia.
Falicity, Felicita, Felicitas, Félicité, Feliciti, Felisita, Felisity

FELISHA (Latin) an alternate form of Felicia.
Faleisha, Falesha, Falisha, Falleshia, Feleasha, Feleisha, Felesha, Felishia, Fellishia, Felysha, Flisha

FEMI (French) woman. (Nigerian) love me.
Femie, Femmi, Femmie, Femy

FEODORA (Greek) gift of God. A feminine form of Theodore.
Fedora, Fedoria

FERN (German) a short form of Fernanda. (English) fern.
Ferne, Ferni, Fernlee, Fernleigh, Fernley, Fernly

FERNANDA (German) daring, adventurous. A feminine form of Ferdinand. See also Andee, Nan.
Ferdie, Ferdinanda, Ferdinande, Fern, Fernande, Fernandette, Fernandina, Nanda

FIALA (Czech) violet flower.

FIDELIA (Latin) an alternate form of Fidelity.
Fidela, Fidele, Fidelina

FIDELITY (Latin) faithful, true. See also Faith.
Fidelia, Fidelita

FIFI (French) a familiar form of Josephine.
Feef, Feefee, Fifine

FILIPPA (Italian) a form of Philippa.
Felipa, Filipa, Filippina, Filpina

FILOMENA (Italian) a form of Philomena.
Fila, Filah, Filemon

FIONA (Irish) fair, white.
Fionna

FIONNULA (Irish) white shouldered. See also Nola, Nuala.
Fenella, Fenula, Finella, Finola, Finula

FLAIR (English) style; verve.
Flaire, Flare

FLANNERY (Irish) redhead. Literature: Flannery O'Connor was a renowned American writer.
Flan, Flann, Flanna

FLAVIA (Latin) blond, golden haired.
Flavere, Flaviar, Flavie, Flavien, Flavienne, Flaviere, Flavio, Flavyere, Fulvia

FLAVIE (Latin) an alternate form of Flavia.
Flavi

FLEUR (French) flower.
Fleure, Fleuree, Fleurette

FLO (American) a short form of Florence.

FLORA (Latin) flower. A short form of Florence. See also Lore.
Fiora, Fiore, Fiorenza, Flor, Florann, Florella, Florelle, Floren, Floria, Floriana, Florianna, Florica, Florimel

FLORENCE (Latin) blooming; flowery; prosperous. History: Florence Nightingale, a British nurse, is considered the founder of modern nursing. See also Florida.
Fiorenza, Flo, Flora, Florance, Florencia, Florency, Florendra, Florentia, Florentina, Florentyna, Florenza, Floretta, Florette, Florie, Florina, Florine, Floris, Flossie

FLORIA (Basque) a form of Flora.
Flori, Florria

FLORIDA (Spanish) a form of Florence.
Floridia, Florinda, Florita

FLORIE (English) a familiar form of Florence.
Flore, Flori, Florri, Florrie, Florry, Flory

FLORIS (English) a form of Florence.
Florisa, Florise

FLOSSIE (English) a familiar form of Florence.
Floss, Flossi, Flossy

FOLA (Yoruba) honorable.

FONDA (Latin) foundation. (Spanish) inn.
Fondea, Fonta

FONTANNA (French) fountain.
Fontaine, Fontana, Fontane, Fontanne, Fontayne

FORTUNA (Latin) fortune; fortunate.
Fortoona, Fortune

FRAN (Latin) a short form of Frances.
Frain, Frann

FRANCES (Latin) free; from France. See also Paquita.
Fanny, Fran, Franca, France, Francee, Francena, Francesca, Francess, Francesta, Franceta, Francetta, Francette, Francine, Francis, Francisca, Françoise, Frankie, Frannie, Franny

FRANCESCA (Italian) a form of Frances.
Franceska, Francessca, Francesta, Franchesca, Franzetta

FRANCHESCA (Italian) an alternate form of Francesca.
Cheka, Chekka, Chesca, Cheska, Francheca, Francheka, Franchelle, Franchesa, Francheska, Franchessca, Franchesska

FRANCI (Hungarian) a familiar form of Francine.
Francey, Francie, Francy

FRANCINE (French) a form of Frances.
Franceen, Franceine, Franceline, Francene, Francenia, Franci, Francin, Francina, Francyne

FRANCIS (Latin) an alternate form of Frances.
Francise, Franncia, Francys

FRANCISCA (Italian) a form of Frances.
Franciska, Franciszka, Frantiska, Franziska

FRANÇOISE (French) a form of Frances.

FRANKIE (American) a familiar form of Frances.
Francka, Francki, Franka, Frankey, Franki, Frankia, Franky, Frankye

FRANNIE, Franny (English) familiar forms of Frances.
Frani, Frania, Franney, Franni, Frany

FREDA, Freida, Frida (German) short forms of Alfreda, Elfrida, Frederica, Sigfreda.
Frayda, Fredda, Fredella, Fredia, Fredra, Freeda, Freeha, Freia, Frida, Frideborg, Frieda

FREDDI, Freddie (English) familiar forms of Frederica, Winifred.
Fredda, Freddy, Fredi, Fredia, Fredy, Frici

FREDERICA (German) peaceful ruler. A feminine form of Frederick. See also Alfreda, Rica, Ricki.
Farica, Federica, Freda, Fredalena, Fredaline, Freddi, Freddie, Frederickina, Frederika, Frederike, Frederina, Frederine, Frederique, Fredith, Fredora, Fredreca, Fredrica, Fredricah, Fredricia, Freida, Fritzi, Fryderica

FREDERIKA (German) an alternate form of Frederica.
Fredericka, Fredreka, Fredricka, Fredrika, Fryderyka

FREDERIKE (German) an alternate form of Frederica.
Fredericke, Friederike

FREDERIQUE (French) a form of Frederica.
Frédérique, Rike

FREJA (Scandinavian) noblewoman. Mythology: the Norse goddess of love.
Fraya, Freya

FRITZI (German) a familiar form of Frederica.
Friezi, Fritze, Fritzie, Fritzinn, Fritzline, Fritzy

GABRIEL, Gabriele (French) alternate forms of Gabrielle.
Gabbriel, Gabbryel, Gabreal, Gabreale, Gabreil, Gabrial, Gabryel

GABRIELA, Gabriella (Italian) alternate forms of Gabrielle.
Gabriala, Gabrialla, Gabrielia, Gabriellia, Gabrila, Gabrilla, Gabryella

GABRIELLE (French) devoted to God. A feminine form of Gabriel.
Gabbrielle, Gabielle, Gabrealle, Gabriana, Gabriel, Gabriela, Gabriele, Gabriell, Gabriella, Gabrille, Gabrina, Gabriylle, Gabryell, Gabryelle, Gaby, Gavriella

GABY (French) a familiar form of Gabrielle.
Gabbey, Gabbi, Gabbie, Gabby, Gabey, Gabi, Gabie, Gavi, Gavy

GADA (Hebrew) lucky.
Gadah

GAEA (Greek) planet Earth. Mythology: the Greek goddess of Earth.
Gaia, Gaiea, Gaya

GAETANA (Italian) from Gaeta. Geography: a region in southern Italy.
Gaetan, Gaétane, Gaetanne

GAGANDEEP (Sikh) sky's light.
Gagandip, Gagnadeep, Gagndeep

GAIL (Hebrew) a short form of Abigail. (English) merry, lively.
Gael, Gaela, Gaelle, Gaila, Gaile, Gale, Gayla, Gayle

GALA (Norwegian) singer.
Galla

GALEN (Greek) healer; calm. (Irish) little and lively.
Gaelen, Gaellen, Galyn, Gaylaine, Gayleen, Gaylen, Gaylene, Gaylyn

GALENA (Greek) healer; calm.

GALI (Hebrew) hill; fountain; spring.
Galice, Galie

GALINA (Russian) a form of Helen.
Gailya, Galayna, Galenka, Galia, Galiana, Galiena, Galinka, Galochka, Galya, Galyna

GANESA (Hindi) fortunate. Religion: the Hindu god of wisdom and luck.

GANYA (Hebrew) garden of the lord.
Gana, Gani, Gania, Ganice, Ganit

GARDENIA (English) Botany: a sweet-smelling flower.
Deeni, Denia, Gardena, Gardinia

GARLAND (French) wreath of flowers.

GARNET (English) dark red gem.
Garnetta, Garnette

GARYN (English) spear carrier. A feminine form of Gary.
Garan, Garen, Garra, Garryn

GASHA (Russian) a familiar form of Agatha.
Gashka

GAVRIELLA (Hebrew) a form of Gabrielle.
Gavila, Gavilla, Gavrid, Gavrieela, Gavriela, Gavrielle, Gavrila, Gavrilla

GAY (French) merry.
Gae, Gai, Gaye

GAYLE (English) an alternate form of Gail.
Gayla

GAYNA (English) a familiar form of Guinevere.
Gaynah, Gayner, Gaynor

GEELA (Hebrew) joyful.
Gela, Gila

GEENA (American) a form of Gena.
Geania, Geeana, Geeanna

GELYA (Russian) angelic.

GEMA, Gemma (Latin, Italian) jewel, precious stone. See also Jemma.
Gem, Gemmey, Gemmie, Gemmy

GEMINI (Greek) twin.
Gemelle, Gemima, Gemina, Geminine, Gemmina

GEN (Japanese) spring. A short form of names beginning with "Gen."

GENA (French) a form of Gina. A short form of Geneva, Genevieve, Iphigenia.
Geanna, Geena, Geenah, Gen, Genae, Genah, Genai, Genea, Geneja, Geni, Genia, Genie

GENEEN (Scottish) an alternate form of Jeanine.
Geanine, Geannine, Gen, Genene, Genine, Gineen, Ginene

GENELL (American) an alternate form of Jenelle.

GENESIS (Latin) origin; birth.
Genes, Genese, Genesha, Genesia, Genesiss, Genessa, Genesse, Genessie, Genessis, Genicis, Genises, Genysis, Yenesis

GENEVA (French) juniper tree. A short form of Genevieve. Geography: a city in Switzerland.
Geena, Gen, Gena, Geneieve, Geneiva, Geneive, Geneve, Ginneva, Janeva, Jeaneva, Jeneva

GENEVIEVE (German, French) an alternate form of Guinevere. See also Gwendolyn.
Gen, Gena, Genaveeve, Genaveve, Genavie, Genavieve, Genavive, Geneva, Geneveve, Genevie, Geneviéve, Genevievre, Genevive, Genovieve, Genvieve, Ginette, Gineveve, Ginevieve, Ginevive, Guinevieve, Guinivive, Gwenevieve, Gwenivive, Jennavieve

GENEVRA (French, Welsh) an alternate form of Guinevere.
Gen, Genever, Genevera, Ginevra

GENICE (American) a form of Janice.
Gen, Genece, Geneice, Genesa, Genesee, Genessia, Genis, Genise

GENITA (American) an alternate form of Janita.
Gen, Genet, Geneta

GENNA (English) a form of Jenna.
Gen, Gennae, Gennay, Genni, Gennie, Genny

GENNIFER (American) a form of Jennifer.
Gen, Genifer, Ginnifer

GENOVIEVE (French) an alternate form of Genevieve.
Genoveva, Genoveve, Genovive

GEORGEANNA (English) a combination of Georgia + Anna.
Georgana, Georganna, Georgeana, Georgiana, Georgianna, Georgyanna, Giorgianna

GEORGEANNE (English) a combination of Georgia + Anne.
Georgann, Georganne, Georgean, Georgeann, Georgie, Georgyann, Georgyanne

GEORGENE (English) a familiar form of Georgia.
Georgeena, Georgeina, Georgena, Georgenia, Georgiena, Georgienne, Georgina, Georgine

GEORGETTE (French) a form of Georgia.
Georgeta, Georgett, Georgetta, Georjetta

GEORGIA (Greek) farmer. A feminine form of George. Art: Georgia O'Keeffe was an American painter known especially for her paintings of flowers. Geography: a southern American state; a country in Eastern Europe. See also Jirina, Jorja.
Georgene, Georgette, Georgie, Giorgia

GEORGIANNA (English) an alternate form of Georgeanna.
Georgiana, Georgiann, Georgianne, Georgie, Georgieann, Georgionna

GEORGIE (English) a familiar form of Georgeanne, Georgia, Georgianna.
Georgi, Georgy, Giorgi

GEORGINA (English) a form of Georgia.
Georgena, Georgene, Georgine, Giorgina, Jorgina

GERALDINE (German) mighty with a spear. A feminine form of Gerald. See also Dena, Jeraldine.
Geralda, Geraldina, Geraldyna, Geraldyne, Gerhardine, Geri, Gerianna, Gerianne, Gerrilee, Giralda

GERALYN (American) a combination of Geraldine + Lynn.
Geralisha, Geralynn, Gerilyn, Gerrilyn

GERARDO (English) brave spearwoman.
Gerardine

GERDA (German) a familiar form of Gertrude. (Norwegian) protector.
Gerta

GERI (American) a familiar form of Geraldine. See also Jeri.
Gerri, Gerrie, Gerry

GERMAINE (French) from Germany. See also Jermaine.
Germain, Germana, Germanee, Germani, Germanie, Germaya, Germine

GERTIE (German) a familiar form of Gertrude.
Gert, Gertey, Gerti, Gerty

GERTRUDE (German) beloved warrior. See also Trudy.
Gerda, Gerta, Gertie, Gertina, Gertraud, Gertrud, Gertruda

GERVAISE (French) skilled with a spear. A feminine form of Jarvis.

GESSICA (Italian) a form of Jessica.
Gesica, Gesika, Gess, Gesse, Gessy

GEVA (Hebrew) hill.
Gevah

GHADA (Arabic) young; tender.
Gada

GHITA (Italian) pearly.
Gita

GIANNA (Italian) a short form of Giovanna. See also Jianna, Johana.
Geona, Geonna, Giana, Gianella, Gianetta, Gianina, Gianinna, Gianne, Giannee, Giannella, Giannetta, Gianni, Giannie, Giannina, Gianny, Gianoula

GIGI (French) a familiar form of Gilberte.
Geegee, G.G., Giggi

GILANA (Hebrew) joyful.
Gila, Gilah

GILBERTE (German) brilliant; pledge; trustworthy. A feminine form of Gilbert. See also Berti.
Gigi, Gilberta, Gilbertina, Gilbertine, Gill

GILDA (English) covered with gold.
Gilde, Gildi, Gildie, Gildy

GILL (Latin, German) a short form of Gilberte, Gillian.
Gili, Gilli, Gillie, Gilly

GILLIAN (Latin) an alternate form of Jillian.
Gila, Gilana, Gilenia, Gili, Gilian, Gill, Gilliana, Gilliane, Gilliann, Gillianna, Gillianne, Gillie, Gilly, Gillyan, Gillyane, Gillyann, Gillyanne, Gyllian, Lian

GIN (Japanese) silver. A short form of names beginning with "Gin."

GINA (Italian) a short form of Angelina, Eugenia, Regina, Virginia. See also Jina.
Gena, Gin, Ginah, Ginai, Ginna

GINETTE (English) a form of Genevieve.
Gin, Ginata, Ginett, Ginetta, Ginnetta, Ginnette

GINGER (Latin) flower; spice. A familiar form of Virginia.
Gin, Ginja, Ginjer, Ginny

GINIA (Latin) a familiar form of Virginia.
Gin

GINNIFER (Welsh) an alternate form of Jennifer. (English) white; smooth; soft.
Gin, Ginifer

GINNY (English) a familiar form of Ginger, Virginia. See also Jin, Jinny.
Gin, Gini, Ginney, Ginni, Ginnie, Giny, Gionni, Gionny

GIORDANA (Italian) a form of Jordana.

GIORGIANNA (English) an alternate form of Georgeanna.
Giorgina

GIOVANNA (Italian) a form of Jane.
Geovana, Geovanna, Geovonna, Giavanna, Giavonna, Giovana, Giovanne, Giovanni, Giovannica, Giovonna, Givonnie, Jeveny

GISA (Hebrew) carved stone.
Gazit, Gissa

GISELA (German) an alternate form of Giselle.
Gisella, Gissela, Gissella

GISELLE (German) pledge; hostage. See also Jizelle.
Ghisele, Gisel, Gisela, Gisele, Geséle, Giseli, Gisell, Gissell, Gisselle, Gizela, Gysell

GISSEL, Gisselle (German) alternate forms of Giselle.
Gissell

GITA (Polish) a short form of Margaret. (Yiddish) good.
Gitka, Gitta, Gituska

GITANA (Spanish) gypsy; wanderer.

GITTA (Irish) a short form of Bridget.
Getta

GIULIA (Italian) a form of Julia.
Giulana, Giuliana, Giulianna, Giulliana, Guila, Guiliana, Guilietta

GIZELA (Czech) a form of Giselle.
Gizel, Gizele, Gizella, Gizelle, Gizi, Giziki, Gizus

GLADIS (Irish) an alternate form of Gladys.
Gladi, Gladiz

GLADYS (Latin) small sword. (Irish) princess. (Welsh) a form of Claudia. Botany: a gladiolus flower.
Glad, Gladis, Gladness, Gladwys, Glady, Gwladys

GLENDA (Welsh) a form of Glenna.
Glanda, Glennda, Glynda

GLENNA (Irish) valley, glen. A feminine form of Glenn. See also Glynnis.
Glenda, Glenetta, Glenina, Glenine, Glenn, Glenne, Glennesha, Glennia, Glennie, Glenora, Gleny, Glyn

GLENNESHA (American) a form of Glenna.
Glenesha, Glenisha, Glennisha, Glennishia

GLORIA (Latin) glory. History: Gloria Steinem, a leading American feminist, founded *Ms.* magazine.
Gloresha, Gloriah, Gloribel, Gloriela, Gloriella, Glorielle, Gloris, Glorisha, Glorvina, Glory

GLORIANNE (American) a combination of Gloria + Anne.
Gloriana, Gloriane, Gloriann, Glorianna

GLORY (Latin) an alternate form of Gloria.
Glorey, Glori, Glorie

GLYNNIS (Welsh) a form of Glenna.
Glenice, Glenis, Glenise, Glenyse, Glennis, Glennys, Glenwys, Glenys, Glenyss, Glinnis, Glinys, Glynesha, Glynice, Glynis, Glynisha, Glyniss, Glynitra, Glynys, Glynyss

GOLDA (English) gold. History: Golda Meir was a Russian-born politician who served as Prime Minister of Israel.
Goldarina, Golden, Goldie, Goldina

GOLDIE (English) a familiar form of Golda.
Goldi, Goldy

GOMA (Swahili) joyful dance.

GRACE (Latin) graceful.
Engracia, Graca, Gracia, Gracie, Graciela, Graciella, Gracinha, Graice, Grata, Gratia, Gray, Grayce, Grecia

GRACEANNE (English) a combination of Grace + Anne.
Graceann, Graceanna, Gracen, Graciana, Gracianna, Gracin, Gratiana

GRACIA (Spanish) a form of Grace.
Gracea, Grecia

GRACIE (English) a familiar form of Grace.
Gracee, Gracey, Graci, Gracy, Graecie, Graysie

GRANT (English) great; giving.

GRAYSON (English) bailiff's daughter.
Graison, Graisyn, Grasien, Grasyn, Graysen

GRAZIA (Latin) an alternate form of Grace.
Graziella, Grazielle, Graziosa, Grazyna

GRECIA (Latin) an alternate form of Grace.

GREER (Scottish) vigilant. A feminine form of Gregory.
Grear, Grier

GRETA (German) a short form of Gretchen, Margaret.
Greatal, Greatel, Greeta, Gretal, Grete, Gretel, Gretha, Grethal, Grethe, Grethel, Gretta, Grette, Grieta, Gryta, Grytta

GRETCHEN (German) a form of Margaret.
Greta, Gretchin, Gretchyn

GRICELDA (German) an alternate form of Griselda.
Gricelle

GRISEL (German) a short form of Griselda.
Grisell, Griselle, Grissel, Grissele, Grissell, Grizel

GRISELDA (German) gray woman warrior. See also Selda, Zelda.
Gricelda, Grisel, Griseldis, Griseldys, Griselys, Grishilda, Grishilde, Grisselda, Grissely, Grizelda

GUADALUPE (Arabic) river of black stones. See also Lupe.
Guadalup, Guadelupe, Guadlupe, Guadulupe, Gudalupe

GUDRUN (Scandinavian) battler. See also Runa.
Gudren, Gudrin, Gudrinn, Gudruna

GUILLERMA (Spanish) a form of Wilhelmina.
Guilla, Guillermina

GUINEVERE (French, Welsh) white wave; white phantom. Literature: the wife of King Arthur. See also Gayna, Genevieve, Genevra, Jennifer, Winifred, Wynne.
Generva, Genn, Ginette, Guenevere, Guenna, Guinivere, Guinna, Gwen, Gwenevere, Gwenivere, Gwynnevere

GUNDA (Norwegian) female warrior.
Gundala, Gunta

GURIT (Hebrew) innocent baby.

GURLEEN (Sikh) follower of the guru.

GURPREET (Punjabi) religion.
Gurprit

GUSTA (Latin) a short form of Augusta.
Gus, Gussi, Gussie, Gussy, Gusti, Gustie, Gusty

GWEN (Welsh) a short form of Guinevere, Gwendolyn.
Gwenesha, Gweness, Gweneta, Gwenetta, Gwenette, Gweni, Gwenisha, Gwenita, Gwenn, Gwenna, Gwennie, Gwenny

GWENDA (Welsh) a familiar form of Gwendolyn.
Gwinda, Gwynda, Gwynedd

GWENDOLYN (Welsh) white wave; white browed; new moon. Literature: the wife of Merlin, the magician. See also Genevieve, Gwyneth, Wendy.
Guendolen, Gwen, Gwendalin, Gwenda, Gwendalee, Gwendaline, Gwendalyn, Gwendalynn, Gwendela, Gwendelyn, Gwendelynn, Gwendilyn, Gwendolen, Gwendolene, Gwendolin, Gwendoline, Gwendolyne, Gwendolynn, Gwendolynne, Gwendylan, Gwyndolyn, Gwynndolen

GWYN (Welsh) a short form of Gwyneth.
Gwinn, Gwinne, Gwynn, Gwynne

GWYNETH (Welsh) an alternate form of Gwendolyn. See also Winnie, Wynne.
Gweneth, Gwenith, Gwenneth, Gwennyth, Gwenyth, Gwyn, Gwynneth

GYPSY (English) wanderer.
Gipsy, Gypsie, Jipsi

HABIBA (Arabic) beloved.
Habibah, Habibeh

HACHI (Japanese) eight; good luck.
Hachiko, Hachiyo

HADARA (Hebrew) adorned with beauty.
Hadarah

HADASSAH (Hebrew) myrtle tree.
Hadas, Hadasah, Hadassa, Haddasa, Haddasah

HADIYA (Swahili) gift.
Hadaya, Hadia, Hadiyah, Hadiyyah

HADLEY (English) field of heather.
Hadlea, Hadlee, Hadleigh, Hadli, Hadlie, Hadly

HADRIANE (Greek, Latin) an alternate form of Adrienne.

*Hadriana, Hadrianna,
Hadrianne, Hadriene, Hadrienne*

HAELEY (English) an alternate
form of Hailey.
*Haelee, Haeleigh, Haeli, Haelie,
Haelleigh, Haelli, Haellie, Haely*

HAGAR (Hebrew) forsaken;
stranger. Bible: Sarah's
handmaiden, the mother of
Ishmael.
Haggar

HAIDEE (Greek) modest.
*Hady, Haide, Haidi, Haidy,
Haydee, Haydy*

HAIDEN (English) heather-
covered hill. A feminine form
of Hadden.
*Haden, Hadyn, Haeden, Haidn,
Haidyn*

HAILEE (English) an alternate
form of Hayley.
Haile, Hailei, Haileigh, Haillee

HAILEY (English) an alternate
form of Hayley.
*Haeley, Haiely, Hailea, Hailley,
Hailly, Haily*

HAILI, Hailie (English) alternate
forms of Hayley.
Haille, Hailli, Haillie

HALDANA (Norwegian) half-
Danish.

HALEE (English) an alternate
form of Haley.
*Hale, Halea, Haleah, Haleh,
Halei*

HALEIGH (English) an alternate
form of Haley.

HALEY (Scandinavian) heroine.
See also Hailey, Hayley.
*Halee, Haleigh, Hali, Halley,
Hallie, Haly, Halye*

HALI, Halie (English) alternate
forms of Haley.
Haliegh

HALIA (Hawaiian) in loving
memory.

HALIMAH (Arabic) gentle;
patient.
Halima, Halime

HALINA (Russian) a form of
Helen.
*Haleen, Haleena, Halena,
Halinka*

HALLA (African) unexpected
gift.
Hala, Hallah, Halle

HALLEY (English) an alternate
form of Haley.
Hally, Hallye

HALLIE (Scandinavian) an
alternate form of Haley.
Hallee, Hallei, Halleigh, Halli

HALONA (Native American)
fortunate.
Halonah, Haloona, Haona

HALSEY (English) Hall's island.
Halsea, Halsie

HAMA (Japanese) shore.

HANA, Hanah (Japanese)
flower. (Arabic) happiness.
(Slavic) forms of Hannah.
*Hanae, Hanan, Haneen,
Hanicka, Hanin, Hanita, Hanka*

HANAKO (Japanese) flower
child.

HANIA (Hebrew) resting place.
*Haniya, Hanja, Hannia, Hanniah,
Hanya*

HANNA (Hebrew) an alternate
form of Hannah.

HANNAH (Hebrew) gracious.
Bible: the mother of Samuel.
See also Anci, Anezka, Ania,
Anka, Ann, Anna, Annalie,
Anneka, Chana, Nina, Nusi.
*Hana, Hanna, Hanneke,
Hannele, Hanni, Hannon, Honna*

HANNI (Hebrew) a familiar
form of Hannah.
Hani, Hanne, Hannie, Hanny

HAPPY (English) happy.
Happi

HARA (Hindi) tawny. Religion:
another name for the Hindu
goddess Shiva, the destroyer.

HARLEE, Harleigh, Harlie
(English) alternate forms of
Harley.
Harlei, Harli

HARLEY (English) meadow of
the hare. See also Arleigh.
Harlee, Harleey, Harly

HARLEYANN (English) a combi-
nation of Harley + Ann.
*Harlann, Harlanna, Harlanne,
Harleen, Harlene, Harleyanna,
Harleyanne, Harliann, Harlianna,
Harlianne, Harlina, Harline*

HARMONY (Latin) harmonious.
*Harmene, Harmeni, Harmon,
Harmonee, Harmonei, Harmoni,
Harmonia, Harmonie*

HARPREET (Punjabi) devoted
to God.
Harprit

HARRIET (French) ruler of the
household. (English) an alternate form of Henrietta.
Literature: Harriet Beecher
Stowe was an American
writer noted for her novel
Uncle Tom's Cabin.

Harriet *(cont.)*
Harri, Harrie, Harriett, Harrietta, Harriette, Harriot, Harriott, Hattie

HARU (Japanese) spring.

HASANA (Swahili) she arrived first. A name used for the first-born female twin. See also Huseina.
Hasanna, Hasna, Hassana, Hassna, Hassona

HASINA (Swahili) good.
Haseena, Hasena, Hassina

HATEYA (Moquelumnan) foot-prints.

HATTIE (English) familiar forms of Harriet, Henrietta.
Hatti, Hatty, Hetti, Hettie, Hetty

HAUSU (Moquelumnan) like a bear yawning upon awakening.

HAVA (Hebrew) an alternate form of Chava. See also Eve.
Havah, Havvah

HAVEN (English) an alternate form of Heaven.
Havan, Havana, Havanna, Havannah, Havyn

HAVIVA (Hebrew) beloved.
Havalee, Havelah, Havi, Hayah

HAYDEN (English) an alternate form of Haiden.
Hayde, Haydin, Haydn, Haydon,

HAYFA (Arabic) shapely.

HAYLEE, Hayleigh, Haylie (English) alternate forms of Hayley.
Hayle, Haylea, Haylei, Hayli, Haylle, Hayllie

HAYLEY (English) hay meadow. See also Hailey, Haley.
Hailee, Haili, Haylee, Hayly

HAZEL (English) hazelnut tree; commanding authority.
Hazal, Hazaline, Haze, Hazeline, Hazell, Hazelle, Hazen, Hazyl

HEATHER (English) flowering heather.
Heath, Heatherlee, Heatherly

HEAVEN (English) place of beauty and happiness. Bible: where God and angels are said to dwell.
Haven, Heavan, Heavenly, Heavin, Heavon, Heavyn, Hevean, Heven, Hevin

HEDDA (German) battler. See also Edda, Hedy.
Heda, Hedaya, Hedia, Hedvick, Hedvig, Hedvika, Hedwig, Hedwiga, Heida, Hetta

HEDY (Greek) delightful; sweet. (German) a familiar form of Hedda.
Heddey, Heddi, Heddie, Heddy, Hede, Hedi

HEIDI, Heidy (German) short forms of Adelaide.
Heida, Heide, Heidee, Heidie, Heydy, Hidee, Hidi, Hidie, Hidy, Hiede, Hiedi, Hydi

HELEN (Greek) light. See also Aileen, Aili, Alena, Eileen, Elaina, Elaine, Eleanor, Ellen, Galina, Ila, Ilene, Ilona, Jelena, Leanore, Leena, Lelya, Lenci, Lene, Liolya, Nellie, Nitsa, Olena, Onella, Yalena, Yelena.
Elana, Ena, Halina, Hela, Hele, Helena, Helene, Helle, Hellen, Helli, Hellin, Hellon, Hellyn, Helon

HELENA (Greek) an alternate form of Helen. See also Ilena.
Halena, Halina, Helaina, Helana, Helania, Helayna, Heleana, Heleena, Helenia, Helenka, Helenna, Helina, Hellanna, Hellena, Hellenna, Helona, Helonna

HELENE (French) a form of Helen.
Helaine, Helanie, Helayne, Heleen, Heleine, Hèléne, Helenor, Heline, Hellenor

HELGA (German) pious. (Scandinavian) an alternate form of Olga. See also Elga.

HELKI (Native American) touched.
Helkey, Helkie, Helky

HELMA (German) a short form of Wilhelmina.
Halma, Helme, Helmi, Helmine, Hilma

HELOISE (French) a form of Louise.
Héloïse, Hlois

HELSA (Danish) a form of Elizabeth.
Helse, Helsey, Helsi, Helsie, Helsy

HELTU (Moquelumnan) like a bear reaching out.

HENNA (English) a familiar form of Henrietta.
Hena, Henaa, Henah, Heni, Henia, Henny, Henya

HENRIETTA (English) ruler of the household. A feminine form of Henry. See also Enrica, Etta, Yetta.
Harriet, Hattie, Hatty, Hendrika, Heneretta, Henka, Henna, Hennrietta, Hennriette, Henretta, Henrica, Henrie, Henrieta, Henriete, Henriette,

Henrika, Henrique, Henriquetta, Henryetta, Hetta, Hettie

HERA (Greek) queen; jealous. Mythology: the queen of heaven and the wife of Zeus.

HERMIA (Greek) messenger. A feminine form of Hermes.

HERMINA (Latin) noble. (German) soldier. A feminine form of Herman. See also Erma, Ermine, Irma.
Herma, Hermenia, Hermia, Herminna

HERMIONE (Greek) earthy.
Hermalina, Hermia, Hermina, Hermine, Herminia

HERMOSA (Spanish) beautiful.

HERTHA (English) child of the earth.
Heartha, Hirtha

HESTER (Dutch) a form of Esther.
Hessi, Hessie, Hessye, Hesther, Hettie

HESTIA (Persian) star. Mythology: the Greek goddess of the hearth and home.
Hestea, Hesti, Hestie, Hesty

HETA (Native American) racer.

HETTA (German) an alternate form of Hedda. (English) a familiar form of Henrietta.

HETTIE (German) a familiar form of Hester, Henrietta.
Hetti, Hetty

HILARY, Hillary (Greek) cheerful, merry. See also Alair.
Hilaree, Hilari, Hilaria, Hilarie, Hilery, Hiliary, Hillaree, Hillari, Hillarie, Hilleary, Hilleree, Hilleri,

Hillerie, Hillery, Hillianne, Hilliary, Hillory

HILDA (German) a short form of Brunhilda, Hildegarde.
Helle, Hilde, Hildey, Hildie, Hildur, Hildy, Hulda, Hylda

HILDEGARDE (German) fortress.
Hilda, Hildagard, Hildagarde, Hildegard, Hildred

HINDA (Hebrew) hind; doe.
Hindey, Hindie, Hindy, Hynda

HISA (Japanese) long-lasting.
Hisae, Hisako, Hisay

HITI (Eskimo) hyena.
Hitty

HOA (Vietnamese) flower; peace.
Ho, Hoai

HOLA (Hopi) seed-filled club.

HOLLEY (English) an alternate form of Holly.
Holleah, Hollee

HOLLI, Hollie (English) alternate forms of Holly.
Holeigh, Holleigh

HOLLIS (English) near the holly bushes.
Hollise, Hollyce, Holyce

HOLLY (English) holly tree.
Holley, Holli, Hollie, Hollye

HOLLYANN (English) a combination of Holly + Ann.
Holliann, Hollianna, Hollianne, Hollyanne, Hollyn

HOLLYN (English) a short form of Hollyann.
Holin, Holeena, Hollina, Hollynn

HONEY (Latin) a familiar form of Honora. (English) sweet.
Honalee, Hunney, Hunny

HONG (Vietnamese) pink.

HONORA (Latin) honorable. See also Nora, Onora.
Honey, Honner, Honnor, Honnour, Honor, Honorah, Honorata, Honore, Honoree, Honoria, Honorina, Honorine, Honour, Honoure

HOPE (English) hope.
Hopey, Hopi, Hopie

HORTENSE (Latin) gardener. See also Ortensia.
Hortencia, Hortensia

HOSHI (Japanese) star.
Hoshie, Hoshiko, Hoshiyo

HUA (Chinese) flower.

HUATA (Moquelumnan) basket carrier.

HUNTER (English) hunter.
Hunta, Huntar, Huntter

HUONG (Vietnamese) flower.

HUSEINA (Swahili) an alternate form of Hasana.

HYACINTH (Greek) Botany: a plant with colorful, fragrant flowers. See also Cynthia, Jacinda.
Giacinta, Hyacintha, Hyacinthe, Hyacinthia, Hyacinthie, Hycinth, Hycynth

HYDI, Hydeia (German) alternate forms of Heidi.
Hyde, Hydea, Hydee, Hydia, Hydie, Hydiea

HYE (Korean) graceful.

IAN (Hebrew) God is gracious.
Iaian, Iain, Iana, Iann, Ianna, Iannel, Iyana

IANTHE (Greek) violet flower.
Iantha, Ianthia, Ianthina

ICESS (Egyptian) an alternate form of Isis.
Ices, Icesis, Icesse, Icey, Icia, Icis, Icy

IDA (German) hardworking. (English) prosperous.
Idah, Idaia, Idalia, Idalis, Idaly, Idamae, Idania, Idarina, Idarine, Idaya, Ide, Idelle, Idette, Idys

IDALINA (English) a combination of Ida + Lina.
Idaleena, Idaleene, Idalena, Idalene, Idaline

IDALIS (English) an alternate form of Ida.
Idalesse, Idalise, Idaliz, Idallas, Idallis, Idelis, Idelys, Idialis

IDEASHIA (American) a combination of Ida + Iesha.
Idasha, Idaysha, Ideesha, Idesha

IDELLE (Welsh) a form of Ida.
Idell, Idella, Idil

IESHA (American) a form of Aisha.
Ieachia, Ieaisha, Ieasha, Ieashe, Ieesha, Ieeshia, Ieisha, Ieishia, Iescha, Ieshah, Ieshea, Iesheia, Ieshia, Iiesha, Iisha

IGNACIA (Latin) fiery, ardent. A feminine form of Ignatius.
Ignacie, Ignasha, Ignashia, Ignatia, Ignatzia

IKIA (Hebrew) God is my salvation. (Hawaiian) a feminine form of Isaiah.
Ikaisha, Ikea, Ikeea, Ikeia, Ikeisha, Ikeishi, Ikeishia, Ikesha, Ikeshia, Ikeya, Ikeyia, Ikiea, Ikiia

ILA (Hungarian) a form of Helen.

ILANA (Hebrew) tree.
Ilaina, Ilane, Ilani, Ilania, Ilainie, Illana, Illane, Illani, Ilania, Illanie, Ilanit

ILEANA (Hebrew) an alternate form of Iliana.
Ilea, Ileah, Ileane, Ileanna, Ileanne, Illeana

ILENA (Greek) an alternate form of Helena.
Ileana, Ileena, Ileina, Ilina, Ilyna

ILENE (Irish) a form of Helen. See also Aileen, Eileen.
Ileen, Ileene, Iline, Ilyne

ILIANA (Greek) from Troy.
Ileana, Ili, Ilia, Iliani, Illiana, Illiani, Illianna, Illyana, Illyanna

ILIMA (Hawaiian) flower of Oahu.

ILISA (Scottish, English) an alternate form of Alisa, Elisa.
Ilicia, Ilissa, Iliza, Illisa, Illissa, Illysa, Illyssa, Ilycia, Ilysa, Ilysia, Ilyssa, Ilyza

ILISE (German) a form of Elise.
Ilese, Illytse, Ilyce, Ilyse

ILISHA (Hebrew) an alternate form of Alisha, Elisha. See also Lisha.
Ileshia, Ilishia, Ilysha, Ilyshia

ILKA (Hungarian) a familiar form of Ilona.
Ilke, Milka, Milke

ILONA (Hungarian) a form of Helen.
Ilka, Illona, Illonia, Illonya, Ilonka, Ilyona

ILSE (German) a form of Elizabeth. See also Elsa.
Ilsa, Ilsey, Ilsie, Ilsy

IMA (German) a familiar form of Amelia. (Japanese) presently.

IMALA (Native American) strong minded.

IMAN (Arabic) believer.
Aman, Imana, Imane, Imani

IMANI (Arabic) an alternate form of Iman.
Amani, Emani, Imahni, Imanie, Imanii, Imonee, Imoni

IMELDA (German) warrior.
Imalda, Irmhilde, Melda

IMENA (African) dream.
Imee, Imene

IMOGENE (Latin) image, likeness.
Emogen, Emogene, Imogen, Imogenia, Imojean, Imojeen, Innogen, Innogene

INA (Irish) a form of Agnes.
Ena, Inanna, Inanne

INDIA (Hindi) from India.
Indea, Indeah, Indee, Indeia, Indeya, Indi, Indiah, Indian, Indiana, Indianna, Indie, Indieya, Indiya, Indy, Indya

INDIGO (Latin) dark blue color.
Indiga, Indygo

INDIRA (Hindi) splendid. Religion: the god of heaven.

History: Indira Nehru Gandi was an Indian politician and prime minister.
Indiara, Indra, Indre, Indria

INES, Inez (Spanish) forms of Agnes. See also Ynez.
Inés, Inesa, Inesita, Inésita, Inessa

INGA (Scandinavian) a short form of Ingrid.
Ingaberg, Ingaborg, Inge, Ingeberg, Ingeborg, Ingela

INGRID (Scandinavian) hero's daughter; beautiful daughter.
Inga, Inger

INOA (Hawaiian) name.

IOANA (Romanian) a form of Joan.
Ioani, Ioanna

IOLA (Greek) dawn; violet colored. (Welsh) worthy of the Lord.
Iole, Iolee, Iolia

IOLANA (Hawaiian) soaring like a hawk.

IOLANTHE (English) a form of Yolanda. See also Jolanda.
Iolanda, Iolande

IONA (Greek) violet flower.
Ione, Ioney, Ioni, Ionia, Iyona, Iyonna

IPHIGENIA (Greek) sacrifice. Mythology: the daughter of the Greek leader Agamemnon. See also Gena.

IRENE (Greek) peaceful. Mythology: the goddess of peace. See also Orina, Rena, Rene, Yarina.
Irén, Irien, Irina, Jereni

IRINA (Russian) a form of Irene.
Eirena, Erena, Ira, Irana, Iranda, Iranna, Irena, Irenea, Irenka, Iriana, Irin, Irinia, Irinka, Irona, Ironka, Irusya, Iryna, Irynka, Rina

IRIS (Greek) rainbow. Mythology: the goddess of the rainbow and messenger of the gods.
Irisa, Irisha, Irissa, Irita, Irys, Iryssa

IRMA (Latin) an alternate form of Erma.
Irmina, Irminia

ISABEAU (French) a form of Isabel.

ISABEL (Spanish) consecrated to God. A form of Elizabeth. See also Bel, Belle, Chavella, Ysabel.
Isabal, Isabeau, Isabeli, Isabelita, Isabella, Isabelle, Ishbel, Isobel, Issie, Izabel, Izabele, Izabella

ISABELLA (Italian) a form of Isabel.
Isabela, Isabelia, Isabello

ISABELLE (French) a form of Isabel.
Isabele, Isabell

ISADORA (Latin) gift of Isis.
Isidora

ISELA (Scottish) an alternate form of Isla.
Isel

ISHA (American) a form of Aisha.
Ishae, Ishana, Ishanaa, Ishanda, Ishanee, Ishaney, Ishani, Ishanna, Ishaun, Ishawna, Ishaya, Ishenda, Ishia, Iysha

ISHI (Japanese) rock.
Ishiko, Ishiyo, Shiko, Shiyo

ISIS (Egyptian) supreme goddess. Mythology: the goddess of the moon, maternity, and fertility.
Icess, Issis, Isys

ISLA (Scottish) Geography: the Isla River in Scotland.
Isela

ISOBEL (Spanish) an alternate form of Isabel.
Isobell, Isobella, Isobelle

ISOKA (Benin) gift from god.
Soka

ISOLDE (Welsh) fair lady. Literature: a princess in the Arthurian legends; a heroine in the medieval romance *Tristan and Isolde*. See also Yseult.
Isolda, Isolt, Izolde

ISSIE (Spanish) a familiar form of Isabel.
Isa, Issi, Issy, Iza

ITA (Irish) thirsty.

ITALIA (Italian) from Italy.
Itali, Italie, Italy, Italya

ITAMAR (Hebrew) palm island.
Isamar, Isamari, Isamaria, Ithamar, Ittamar

ITZEL (Spanish) protected.
Itcel, Itchel, Itesel, Itsel, Itssel, Itza, Itzallana, Itzayana, Itzell, Ixchel

IVA (Slavic) a short form of Ivana.
Ivah

IVANA (Slavic) God is gracious. A feminine form of Ivan. See also Yvanna.

Ivana *(cont.)*
Iva, Ivanah, Ivania, Ivanka, Ivanna, Ivannia, Ivany

IVEREM (Tiv) good fortune; blessing.

IVETTE (French) an alternate form of Yvette. See also Evette.
Ivet, Ivete, Iveth, Ivetha, Ivett, Ivetta

IVONNE (French) an alternate form of Yvonne. See also Evonne.
Ivon, Ivona, Ivone, Ivonna, Iwona, Iwonka, Iwonna, Iwonne

IVORY (Latin) made of ivory.
Ivoory, Ivori, Ivorie, Ivorine, Ivree

IVRIA (Hebrew) from the land of Abraham.
Ivriah, Ivrit

IVY (English) ivy tree.
Ivey, Ivie

IYABO (Yoruba) mother has returned.

IYANA, Iyanna (Hebrew) alternate forms of Ian.
Iyanah, Iyannah, Iyannia

IZABELLA (Spanish) an alternate form of Isabel.
Izabela, Izabell, Izabellah, Izabelle, Izobella

IZUSA (Native American) white stone.

JABREA, Jabria (American) a combination of the prefix Ja + Brea.
Jabreal, Jabree, Jabreea, Jabreena, Jabrelle, Jabreona, Jabri, Jabriah, Jabriana, Jabrie, Jabriel, Jabrielle, Jabrienna, Jabrina

JACALYN (American) a form of Jacqueline.
Jacalynn, Jacolyn, Jacolyne, Jacolynn

JACELYN (American) a form of Jocelyn.
Jaceline, Jacelyne, Jacelynn, Jacilyn, Jacilyne, Jacilynn, Jacylyn, Jacylyne, Jacylynn

JACEY, Jacy (Greek) familiar forms of Jacinda. (American) combinations of the initials J. + C.
Jace, Jac-E, Jacee, Jaci, Jacie, Jacylin, Jaice, Jaicee

JACI, Jacie (Greek) alternate forms of Jacey.
Jacci, Jacia, Jacie, Jaciel, Jaici, Jaicie

JACINDA, Jacinta (Greek) beautiful, attractive. (Spanish) a form of Hyacinth.
Jacenda, Jacenta, Jacey, Jacinthe, Jacintia, Jacynthe, Jakinda, Jaxine

JACINTHE (Spanish) an alternate form of Jacinda.
Jacinte, Jacinth, Jacintha

JACKALYN (American) a form of Jacqueline.
Jackalene, Jackalin, Jackaline, Jackalynn, Jackalynne, Jackelin, Jackeline, Jackelyn, Jackelynn, Jackelynne, Jackilin, Jackilyn, Jackilynn, Jackilynne, Jackolin, Jackoline, Jackolyn, Jackolynn, Jackolynne

JACKELINE, Jackelyn (American) forms of Jacqueline.
Jackelin, Jackelline, Jackellyn, Jockeline

JACKI, Jackie (American) familiar forms of Jacqueline.
Jackee, Jackey, Jackia, Jackielee, Jacky, Jackye

JACKLYN (American) a short form of Jacqueline.
Jacklin, Jackline, Jacklyne, Jacklynn, Jacklynne

JACKQUEL (French) an alternate form of Jacqueline.
Jackqueline, Jackquetta, Jackquiline, Jackquilyn, Jackquilynn, Jackquilynne

JACLYN (American) a short form of Jacqueline.
Jacleen, Jaclin, Jacline, Jaclyne, Jaclynn

JACOBI (Hebrew) supplanter, substitute. A feminine form of Jacob.
Coby, Jacoba, Jacobee, Jacobette, Jacobia, Jacobina, Jacoby, Jacolbi, Jacolbia, Jacolby

JACQUALINE (French) an alternate form of Jacqueline.
Jacqualin, Jacqualine, Jacqualyn, Jacqualyne, Jacqualynn

JACQUELIN (French) an alternate form of Jacqueline.
Jacquelina

JACQUELINE (French) supplanter, substitute; little Jacqui. A feminine form of Jacques.
Jacalyn, Jackalyn, Jackeline, Jacki, Jacklyn, Jackquel, Jaclyn, Jacqueena, Jacqueine, Jacquel, Jacqueleen, Jacquelene, Jacquelin, Jacquelyn, Jacquelynn, Jacquena, Jacquene, Jacquenetta, Jacquenette, Jacqui, Jacquiline, Jacquine, Jakelin, Jaquelin, Jaqueline, Jaquelyn, Jocqueline

JACQUELYN, Jacquelynn (French) alternate forms of Jacqueline.
Jackquelyn, Jackquelynn, Jacquelyne, Jacquelynne,

JACQUI (French) a short form of Jacqueline.
Jacquay, Jacqué, Jacquee, Jacqueta, Jacquete, Jacquetta, Jacquette, Jacquie, Jacquise, Jacquita, Jaquay, Jaqui, Jaquie, Jaquiese, Jaquina, Jaquita

JACQULIN, Jacqulyn (American) forms of Jacqueline.
Jackquilin, Jacqul, Jacqulin, Jacqulyne, Jacqulynn, Jacqulynne, Jacquoline

JACQUILINE (French) an alternate form of Jacqueline.
Jacquil, Jacquilin, Jacquilyn, Jacquilyne, Jacquilynn

JACYNTHE (Spanish) an alternate form of Jacinda.
Jacynda, Jacynta, Jacynth, Jacyntha

JADA (Spanish) an alternate form of Jade.
Jadah, Jadda, Jadae, Jadzia, Jadziah, Jaeda, Jaedra, Jayda

JADE (Spanish) jade.
Jada, Jadea, Jadeann, Jadee, Jaden, Jadera, Jadi, Jadie, Jadienne, Jady, Jadyn, Jaedra, Jaida, Jaide, Jaiden, Jayde, Jayden

JADELYN (American) a combination of Jade + Lynn.
Jadalyn, Jadelaine, Jadeline, Jadelyne, Jadelynn, Jadielyn

JADEN (Spanish) an alternate form of Jade.
Jadeen, Jadena, Jadene, Jadeyn, Jadin, Jadine, Jaeden, Jaedine

JADYN (Spanish) an alternate form of Jade.
Jadynn, Jaedyn, Jaedynn

JAE (Latin) jaybird. (French) a familiar form of Jacqueline.
Jaea, Jaey, Jaya

JAEL (Hebrew) mountain goat; climber. See also Yael.
Jaela, Jaelee, Jaeli, Jaelie, Jaelle, Jahla, Jahlea

JAELYN, Jaelynn (American) a combination of Jae + Lynn.
Jaeleen, Jaelin, Jaelinn, Jaelyn, Jailyn, Jalyn, Jalynn, Jayleen, Jaylyn, Jaylynn, Jaylynne

JAFFA (Hebrew) an alternate form of Yaffa.
Jaffice, Jaffit, Jafit, Jafra

JAHA (Swahili) dignified.
Jahaida, Jahaira, Jaharra, Jahayra, Jahida, Jahira, Jahitza

JAI (Tai) heart.

JAIDA, Jaide (Spanish) alternate forms of Jade.
Jaidah, Jaidan

JAIDEN, Jaidyn (Spanish) alternate forms of Jade.
Jaidey, Jaidi, Jaidin, Jaidon

JAILYN (American) an alternate form of Jaelyn.
Jaileen, Jailen, Jailene, Jailin, Jailine

JAIME (French) I love.
Jaima, Jaimee, Jaimey, Jaimie, Jaimini, Jaimme, Jaimy, Jamee

JAIMEE (French) an alternate form of Jaime.

JAIMIE (French) an alternate form of Jaime.
Jaimi, Jaimmie

JAIRA (Spanish) Jehovah teaches.
Jairah, Jairy

JAKEISHA (American) a combination of Jakki + Aisha.
Jakeisia, Jakesha, Jakisha

JAKELIN (American) a form of Jacqueline.
Jakeline, Jakelyn, Jakelynn, Jakelynne

JAKKI (American) an alternate form of Jacki, Jackie.
Jakala, Jakea, Jakeela, Jakeida, Jakeita, Jakela, Jakelia, Jakell, Jakena, Jaketta, Jakevia, Jaki, Jakia, Jakiah, Jakira, Jakita, Jakiya, Jakiyah, Jakke, Jakkia

JALEESA (American) an alternate form of Jalisa.
Jaleasa, Jalece, Jalecea, Jaleesah, Jaleese, Jaleesia, Jaleisa, Jaleisha, Jaleisya

JALENA (American) a combination of Jane + Lena.
Jalaina, Jalana, Jalani, Jalanie, Jalayna, Jalean, Jaleen, Jaleena, Jaleene, Jalen, Jalene, Jalina, Jaline, Jallena, Jalyna, Jelayna, Jelena, Jelina, Jelyna

JALESA, Jalessa (American) alternate forms of Jalisa.
Jalese, Jalesha, Jaleshia, Jalesia

JALIA, Jalea (American) combination of Jae + Leah.
Jaleah, Jalee, Jaleea, Jaleeya, Jaleia, Jalitza

JALILA (Arabic) great.
Jalile

JALISA, Jalissa (American) combinations of Jae + Lisa.
Jaleesa, Jalesa, Jalise, Jalisha, Jalisia, Jalysa

JALYN, Jalynn (American) combinations of Jae + Lynn. See also Jaylyn.
Jaelin, Jaeline, Jaelyn, Jaelyne, Jaelynn, Jaelynne, Jalin, Jaline, Jalyne, Jalynne

JALYSA (American) an alternate form of Jalisa.
Jalyse, Jalyssa, Jalyssia

JAMAICA (Spanish) Geography: an island in the Caribbean.
Jameca, Jamecia, Jameica, Jameika, Jameka, Jamica, Jamika, Jamoka, Jemaica, Jemika, Jemyka

JAMANI (American) a form of Jami.
Jamana

JAMARIA (American) combinations of Jae + Maria.
Jamar, Jamara, Jamarea, Jamaree, Jamari, Jamarie, Jameira, Jamerial, Jamira

JAMECIA (Spanish) an alternate form of Jamaica.

JAMEE (French) an alternate form of Jaime.

JAMEIKA, Jameka (Spanish) alternate forms of Jamaica.
Jamaika, Jamaka, Jamecka, Jamekia, Jamekka

JAMESHA (American) a form of Jami.
Jameisha, Jamese, Jameshia, Jameshyia, Jamesia, Jamesica, Jamesika, Jamesina, Jamessa, Jameta, Jametta, Jamiesha, Jamisha, Jammesha, Jammisha

JAMEY (English) an alternate form of Jami, Jamie.

JAMI, Jamie (Hebrew) supplanter, substitute. (English) feminine forms of James.
Jama, Jamani, Jamay, Jamesha, Jamey, Jamia, Jamii, Jamis, Jamise, Jammie, Jamy, Jamye, Jayme, Jaymee, Jaymie

JAMIA (English) an alternate form of Jami, Jamie.
Jamea, Jamiah, Jamiea, Jamiya, Jamiyah, Jamya, Jamyah

JAMICA (Spanish) an alternate form of Jamaica.
Jamika

JAMILA (Arabic) beautiful. See also Yamila.
Jahmela, Jahmelia, Jahmil, Jahmilla, Jameela, Jameelah, Jameeliah, Jameila, Jamela, Jamelia, Jameliah, Jamell, Jamella, Jamelle, Jamely, Jamelya, Jamiela, Jamielee, Jamilah, Jamilee, Jamilia, Jamiliah, Jamilla, Jarnillah, Jamille, Jamillia, Jamilya, Jamyla, Jemeela, Jemelia, Jemila, Jemilla

JAMILYNN (English) a combination of Jami + Lynn.
Jamielin, Jamieline, Jamielyn, Jamielyne, Jamielynn, Jamielynne, Jamilin, Jamiline, Jamilyn, Jamilyne, Jamilynne

JAMMIE (American) a form of Jami.
Jammi, Jammice, Jammise

JAMONICA (American) a combination of Jamie + Monica.
Jamoni

JAMYLIN (American) a form of Jamilynn.
Jamylin, Jamyline, Jamylyn, Jamylyne, Jamylynn, Jamylynne, Jaymylin, Jaymyline, Jaymylyn, Jaymylyne, Jaymylynn, Jaymylynne

JAN (English) a short form of Jane, Janet, Janice.
Jania, Jandy

JANA (Slavic) a form of Jane. See also Yana.
Janalee, Janalisa, Janna, Janne

JANAE, Janay (American) forms of Jane.
Janaé, Janaea, Janaeh, Janah, Janai, Janaya, Janaye, Janea, Janee, Janée, Jannae, Jannay, Jenae, Jenay, Jenaya, Jennae, Jennay, Jennaya, Jennaye

JANAI (American) an alternate form of Janae.
Janaiah, Janaira, Janaiya

JANALYNN (American) a combination of Jana + Lynn.
Janalin, Janaline, Janalyn, Janalyne, Janalynne

JANAN (Arabic) heart; soul.
Jananee, Janani, Jananie, Janann, Jananni

JANE (Hebrew) God is gracious. A feminine form of John. See also Chavon, Jean, Joan, Juanita, Seana, Shana, Shawna, Sheena, Shona, Shunta, Sinead, Zaneta, Zanna, Zhana.

Jaine, Jan, Jana, Janae, Janay, Janelle, Janessa, Janet, Jania, Janice, Janie, Janika, Janine, Janis, Janka, Jannie, Jasia, Jayna, Jayne, Jenica

JANEL, Janell (French) alternate forms of Janelle.
Janiel, Jannel, Jannell, Janyll, Jaynel, Jaynell

JANELLE (French) a form of Jane.
Janel, Janela, Janele, Janelis, Janell, Janella, Janelli, Janellie, Janelly, Janely, Janelys, Janielle, Janille, Jannelle, Jannellies, Jaynelle

JANESHA (American) an alternate form of Janessa.
Janeisha, Janeshia, Janiesha, Janisha, Janishia, Jannesha, Jannisha, Janysha, Jenesha, Jenisha, Jennisha

JANESSA (American) a form of Jane.
Janeesa, Janesa, Janesea, Janesha, Janesia, Janeska, Janessi, Janessia, Janiesa, Janissa, Jannesa, Jannessa, Jannisa, Jannissa, Janyssa, Jenesa, Jenessa, Jenissa, Jennisa, Jennissa

JANET (English) a form of Jane. See also Jessie, Yanet.
Jan, Janeta, Janete, Janeth, Janett, Janette, Jannet, Janot, Jante, Janyte

JANETH (English) an alternate form of Janet.
Janetha, Janith, Janneth

JANETTE, Jannette (French) forms of Janet.
Janett, Janetta, Jannett, Jannetta

JANICE (Hebrew) God is gracious. (English) a familiar

form of Jane. See also Genice.
Jan, Janece, Janecia, Janeice, Janiece, Janizzette, Jannice, Janniece, Janyce, Jenice, Jhanice, Jynice

JANIE (English) a familiar form of Jane.
Janey, Jani, Janiyh, Jannie, Janny, Jany

JANIKA (Slavic) a form of Jane.
Janaca, Janeca, Janecka, Janeika, Janeka, Janica, Janick, Janicka, Janieka, Janikka, Janikke, Janique, Janka, Jankia, Jannica, Jannick, Jannika, Janyca, Jenica, Jenicka, Jenika, Jeniqua, Jenique, Jennica, Jennika, Jonika

JANINE (French) a form of Jane.
Janean, Janeann, Janeanne, Janeen, Janenan, Janene, Janina, Jannen, Jannina, Jannine, Jannyne, Janyne, Jeannine, Jeneen, Jenine

JANIS (English) a form of Jane.
Janees, Janese, Janesey, Janess, Janesse, Janise, Jannis, Jannise, Janys, Jenesse, Jenis, Jennise, Jennisse

JANITA (American) a form of Juanita. See also Genita.
Janitra, Janitza, Janneta, Jaynita, Jenita, Jennita

JANNA (Hebrew) a short form of Johana. (Arabic) harvest of fruit.
Janaya, Janaye, Jannae, Jannah, Jannai

JANNIE (English) a familiar form of Jan, Jane.
Janney, Janny

JAQUANA (American) a combination of Jacqueline + Anna.

Jaqua, Jaquai, Jaquanda, Jaquania, Jaquanna

JAQUELEN (American) a form of Jacqueline.
Jaquala, Jaquera, Jaqulene, Jaquonna

JAQUELIN, Jaqueline (French) alternate forms of Jacqueline.
Jaqualin, Jaqualine, Jaquelina, Jaquline, Jaquella

JAQUELYN (French) an alternate form of Jacqueline.
Jaquelyne, Jaquelynn, Jaquelynne

JARDENA (Hebrew) an alternate form of Jordan. (French, Spanish) garden.
Jardan, Jardana, Jardane, Jarden, Jardenia, Jardin, Jardine, Jardyn, Jardyne

JARIAN (American) a combination of Jane + Marian.

JARITA (Arabic) earthen water jug.
Jara, Jaretta, Jari, Jaria, Jarica, Jarida, Jarietta, Jarika, Jarina, Jaritta, Jaritza, Jarixa, Jarnita, Jarrika, Jarrine

JAS (American) a short form of Jasmine.
Jase, Jass, Jaz, Jazz, Jazze, Jazzi

JASIA (Polish) a form of Jane.
Jaisha, Jasa, Jasea, Jasha, Jashae, Jashala, Jashona, Jashonte, Jasie, Jassie, Jaysa

JASLEEN, Jaslyn (Latin) alternate forms of Jocelyn.
Jaslene, Jaslien, Jaslin, Jasline, Jaslynn, Jaslynne

JASMAIN (Persian) an alternate form of Jasmine.
Jasmaine, Jasmane, Jassmain, Jassmaine

JASMARIE (American) a combination of Jasmine + Marie.
Jasmari

JASMIN (Persian) an alternate form of Jasmine.
Jasimin, Jasman, Jasmeen, Jasmen, Jasmon, Jassmin, Jassminn

JASMINE (Persian) jasmine flower. See also Jessamine, Yasmin.
Jas, Jasma, Jasmain, Jasme, Jasmeet, Jasmene, Jasmin, Jasmina, Jasminne, Jasmira, Jasmit, Jasmyn, Jassma, Jassmin, Jassmine, Jassmit, Jassmon, Jassmyn, Jazmin, Jazmyn, Jazzmin

JASMYN, Jasmyne (Persian) alternate forms of Jasmine.
Jasmynn, Jasmynne, Jassmyn

JASPREET (Punjabi) virtuous.
Jaspar, Jasparit, Jasparita, Jasper, Jasprit, Jasprita, Jasprite

JATARA (American) a combination of Jane + Tara.
Jataria, Jatarra, Jatori, Jatoria

JAVANA (Malayan) from Java.
Javanna, Javanne, Javona, Javonna, Jawana, Jawanna, Jawn

JAVIERA (Spanish) owner of a new house. A feminine form of Javier. See also Xaviera.
Javeera, Viera

JAVONA, Javonna (Malayan) alternate forms of Javana.
Javon, Javonda, Javone, Javoni, Javonne, Javonni, Javonya

JAYA (Hindi) victory.
Jaea, Jaia

JAYCEE (American) a combination of the initials J. + C.
Jacee, Jacey, Jaci, Jacie, Jacy, Jayce, Jaycey, Jayci, Jaycie, Jaycy

JAYDA (Spanish) an alternate form of Jada.
Jaydah, Jeyda

JAYDE (Spanish) an alternate form of Jade.
Jayd

JAYDEE (American) a combination of the initials J. + D.
Jadee, Jadey, Jadi, Jadie, Jady, Jaydey, Jaydi, Jaydie, Jaydy

JAYDEN (Spanish) an alternate form of Jade.
Jaydeen, Jaydene, Jaydin, Jaydn, Jaydon

JAYE (Latin) jaybird.
Jae, Jay

JAYLA (American) a short form of Jaylene.
Jaylaa, Jaylah, Jayli, Jaylia, Jayliah, Jaylie

JAYLENE (American) an alternate form of Jaylyn.
Jayelene, Jayla, Jaylan, Jayleana, Jaylee, Jayleen, Jayleene, Jaylen, Jaylenne

JAYLIN (American) an alternate form of Jaylyn.
Jayline, Jaylinn

JAYLYN, Jaylynn (American) combinations of Jaye + Lynn. See also Jalyn.
Jaylene, Jaylin, Jaylyne, Jaylynne

JAYME, Jaymie (English) alternate forms of Jami.
Jaymi, Jaymia, Jaymine, Jaymini

JAYMEE, Jaymi (English) alternate forms of Jami.

JAYNA (Hebrew) an alternate form of Jane.
Jaynae, Jaynah, Jaynna

JAYNE (Hindi) victorious. (English) a form of Jane.
Jayn, Jaynie, Jaynne

JAYNIE (English) a familiar form of Jayne.
Jaynee, Jayni

JAZLYN (American) a combination of Jazmin + Lynn.
Jasleen, Jazaline, Jazalyn, Jazleen, Jazlene, Jazlin, Jazline, Jazlon, Jazlynn, Jazlynne, Jazzalyn, Jazzleen, Jazzlene, Jazzlin, Jazzline, Jazzlyn, Jazzlynn, Jazzlynne

JAZMIN, Jazmine (Persian) alternate forms of Jasmine.
Jazmaine, Jazman, Jazmen, Jazminn, Jazmon, Jazzmit

JAZMYN, Jazmyne (Persian) alternate forms of Jasmine.
Jazmynn, Jazmynne, Jazzmyn, Jazzmyne

JAZZMIN, Jazzmine (Persian) alternate forms of Jasmine.
Jazzman, Jazzmeen, Jazzmen, Jazzmene, Jazzmenn, Jazzmon

JEAN, Jeanne (Scottish) God is gracious. Forms of Jane, Joan. See also Kini.
Jeana, Jeanann, Jeancie, Jeane, Jeaneia, Jeanette, Jeaneva, Jeanice, Jeanie, Jeanine, Jeanmaria, Jeanmarie, Jeanna, Jeanné, Jeannie, Jeannita, Jeannot, Jeantelle

JEANA, Jeanna (Scottish) alternate forms of Jean.
Jeanae, Jeannae, Jeannia

JEANETTE, Jeannett (French) forms of Jean.

Jeanet, Jeanete, Jeanett, Jeanetta, Jeanita, Jeannete, Jeannetta, Jeannette, Jeannita, Jenet, Jenett, Jenette, Jennet, Jennett, Jennetta, Jennette, Jennita, Jinetta, Jinette

JEANIE, Jeannie (Scottish) a familiar form of Jean.
Jeannee, Jeanney, Jeani, Jeanny, Jeany

JEANINE, Jenine (Scottish) alternate forms of Jean. See also Geneen.
Jeaneane, Jeaneen, Jeanene, Jeanina, Jeannina, Jeannine, Jennine

JELENA (Russian) a form of Helen. See also Yelena.
Jalaine, Jalane, Jalani, Jalanna, Jalayna, Jalayne, Jaleen, Jaleena, Jaleene, Jalena, Jalene, Jelaina, Jelaine, Jelana, Jelane, Jelani, Jelanni, Jelayna, Jelayne, Jelean, Jeleana, Jeleen, Jeleena, Jelene

JELISA (American) a combination of Jean + Lisa.
Jalissa, Jelesha, Jelessa, Jelise, Jelissa, Jellese, Jellice, Jelysa, Jelyssa, Jillisa, Jillissa, Julissa

JEM (Hebrew) a short form of Jemima.
Gem, Jemi, Jemia, Jemiah, Jemie, Jemm, Jemmi, Jemmy

JEMIMA (Hebrew) dove.
Jamim, Jamima, Jem, Jemimah, Jemma

JEMMA (Hebrew) a short form of Jemima. (English) a form of Gemma.
Jemmia, Jemmiah, Jemmie, Jemmy

JENA, Jenae (Arabic) alternate forms of Jenna.

Jenah, Jenai, Jenal, Jenay, Jenaya, Jenea

JENDAYA (Zimbabwean) thankful.
Daya, Jenda, Jendayah

JENELLE (American) a combination of Jenny + Nell.
Genell, Jeanell, Jeanelle, Jenall, Jenalle, Jenel, Jenela, Jenele, Jenell, Jenella, Jenille, Jennel, Jennell, Jennella, Jennelle, Jennielle, Jennille, Jinelle, Jinnell

JENESSA (American) an alternate form of Jenisa.
Jenesa, Jenese, Jenesia, Jenessia, Jennesa, Jennese, Jennessa, Jinessa

JENICA (Romanian) a form of Jane.
Jeneca, Jenika, Jenikka, Jennica, Jennika

JENIFER, Jeniffer (Welsh) alternate forms of Jennifer.
Jenefer

JENILEE (American) a combination of Jennifer + Lee.
Jenalea, Jenalee, Jenaleigh, Jenaly, Jenelea, Jenelee, Jeneleigh, Jenely, Jenelly, Jenileigh, Jenily, Jennalee, Jennely, Jennielee, Jennilea, Jennilee, Jennilie

JENISA (American) a combination of Jennifer + Nisa.
Jenessa, Jenisha, Jenissa, Jenisse, Jennisa, Jennise, Jennisha, Jennissa, Jennisse, Jennysa, Jennyssa, Jenysa, Jenyse, Jenyssa, Jenysse

JENKA (Czech) a form of Jane.

JENNA (Arabic) small bird. (Welsh) a short form of Jennifer. See also Gen.

Jena, Jennae, Jennah, Jennal, Jennat, Jennay, Jennaya, Jennaye, Jhenna

JENNI, Jennie (Welsh) familiar forms of Jennifer.
Jeni, Jenne, Jenné, Jennee, Jenney, Jennia, Jennier, Jennita, Jennora, Jensine

JENNIFER (Welsh) white wave; white phantom. An alternate form of Guinevere. See also Gennifer, Ginnifer, Yenifer.
Jen, Jenifer, Jeniffer, Jenipher, Jenna, Jennafer, Jenni, Jenniferanne, Jenniferlee, Jenniffe, Jenniffer, Jenniffier, Jennifier, Jennilee, Jenniphe, Jennipher, Jenny, Jennyfer

JENNILEE (American) a combination of Jenny + Lee.
Jennalea, Jennalee, Jennielee, Jennilea, Jennilie, Jinnalee

JENNILYN, Jennilynn (American) a combination of Jenni + Lynn.
Jennalin, Jennaline, Jennalyn, Jenalynann, Jenelyn, Jenilyn, Jennalyne, Jennalynn, Jennalynne, Jennilin, Jenniline, Jennilyne, Jennilynne

JENNY (Welsh) a familiar form of Jennifer.
Jenney, Jenni, Jennie, Jeny, Jinny

JENNYFER (Welsh) an alternate form of Jennifer.
Jenyfer

JERALDINE (English) a form of Geraldine.
Jeraldeen, Jeraldene, Jeraldina, Jeraldyne, Jeralee, Jeri

JERENI (Russian) a form of Irene.
Jerena, Jerenae, Jerina

123

JERI, Jerri, Jerrie (American) short forms of Jeraldine. See also Geri.
Jera, Jerae, JeRae, Jeree, Jeriel, Jerilee, Jerinda, Jerra, Jerrah, Jerrece, Jerree, Jerriann, Jerrilee, Jerrine, Jerry, Jerrylee, Jerryne, Jerzy

JERICA (American) a combination of Jeri + Erica.
Jereca, Jerecka, Jerice, Jericka, Jerika, Jerrica, Jerrice, Jeryka

JERILYN (American) a combination of Jeri + Lynn.
Jeralin, Jeraline, Jeralyn, Jeralyne, Jeralynn, Jeralynne, Jerelin, Jereline, Jerelyn, Jerelyne, Jerelynn, Jerelynne, Jerilin, Jeriline, Jerilyne, Jerilynn, Jerilynne, Jerrilin, Jerriline, Jerrilyn, Jerrilyne, Jerrilynn, Jerrilynne, Jerrylea

JERMAINE (French) an alternate form of Germaine.
Jermain, Jerman, Jermanay, Jermanaye, Jermane, Jermanee, Jermani, Jermanique, Jermany, Jermayne, Jermecia, Jermia, Jermice, Jermicia, Jermika, Jermila

JERRICA (American) an alternate form of Jerica.
Jerreka, Jerricah, Jerricca, Jerricha, Jerricka, Jerrieka, Jerrika

JERUSHA (Hebrew) inheritance.
Jerushah, Yerusha

JESENIA, Jessenia (Arabic) flower.
Jescenia, Jessennia, Jessenya

JESICA, Jesika (Hebrew) alternate forms of Jessica.
Jesicca, Jesikah, Jesikkah

JESSA (American) a short form of Jessalyn, Jessamine, Jessica.
Jesa, Jesha, Jessah

JESSALYN (American) a combination of Jessica + Lynn.
Jesalin, Jesaline, Jesalyn, Jesalyne, Jesalynn, Jesalynne, Jesilin, Jesiline, Jesilyn, Jesilyne, Jesilynn, Jesilynne, Jessa, Jessalin, Jessaline, Jessalyne, Jessalynn, Jessalynne, Jesselin, Jesseline, Jesselyn, Jesselyne, Jesselynn, Jesselynne, Jesslyn

JESSAMINE (French) a form of Jasmine.
Jessa, Jessamin, Jessamon, Jessamy, Jessamyn, Jessemin, Jessemine, Jessimin, Jessimine, Jessmin, Jessmine, Jessmon, Jessmy, Jessmyn

JESSE, Jessi (Hebrew) alternate forms of Jessie.
Jese, Jesi, Jesie

JESSECA (Hebrew) an alternate form of Jessica.
Jesseeca, Jesseeka

JESSICA (Hebrew) wealthy. A feminine form of Jesse. Literature: a name perhaps invented by Shakespeare for a character in his play *The Merchant of Venice*. See also Gessica, Yessica.
Jesica, Jesika, Jessa, Jessaca, Jessca, Jesscia, Jesseca, Jessia, Jessicah, Jessicca, Jessicia, Jessicka, Jessie, Jessika, Jessiqua, Jessy, Jessyca, Jessyka, Jezeca, Jezica, Jezika, Jezyca

JESSIE, Jessy (Hebrew) short forms of Jessica. (Scottish) forms of Janet.
Jescie, Jesey, Jess, Jesse, Jessé, Jessee, Jessey, Jessi, Jessia, Jessiya, Jessye

JESSIKA (Hebrew) an alternate form of Jessica.
Jessieka

JESSLYN (American) an alternate form of Jessalyn.
Jessilyn, Jessilynn, Jesslin, Jesslynn, Jesslynne

JESSYCA, Jessyka (Hebrew) alternate forms of Jessica.

JÉSUSA (Hebrew) God is my salvation. (Spanish) a feminine form of Jésus.

JETTA (English) jet black gem. (American) a familiar form of Jevette.
Jeta, Jetia, Jetje, Jette, Jettie

JEVETTE (American) a combination of Jean + Yvette.
Jetta, Jeva, Jeveta, Jevetta

JEWEL (French) precious gem.
Jewelann, Jewelia, Jeweliana, Jeweliann, Jewelie, Jewell, Jewelle, Jewellee, Jewellene, Jewellie, Juel, Jule

JEZEBEL (Hebrew) unexalted; impure. Bible: the wife of King Ahab.
Jesibel, Jessabel, Jessebel, Jez, Jezabel, Jezabella, Jezabelle, Jezebell, Jezebella, Jezebelle

JIANNA (Italian) an alternate form of Gianna.
Jiana, Jianina, Jianine, Jianni, Jiannini

JIBON (Hindi) life.

JILL (English) a short form of Jillian.
Jil, Jilli, Jillie, Jilly

JILLAINE (Latin) an alternate form of Jillian.
Jilaine, Jilane, Jilayne, Jillana, Jillane, Jillann, Jillanne, Jillayne

JILLEEN (Irish) a form of Jillian.
Jileen, Jilene, Jiline, Jillene, Jillenne, Jilline, Jillyn

JILLIAN (Latin) youthful. An alternate form of Julia. See also Gillian.
Jilian, Jiliana, Jiliann, Jilianna, Jilianne, Jilienna, Jilienne, Jill, Jillaine, Jilliana, Jilliane, Jilliann, Jillianne, Jileen, Jillien, Jillienne, Jillion, Jilliyn

JIMI (Hebrew) supplanter, substitute. (American) a feminine form of Jimmy.
Jimae, Jimaria, Jimee, Jimella, Jimena, Jimia, Jimiah, Jimie, Jimiyah, Jimmeka, Jimmet, Jimmi, Jimmia, Jimmie

JIMISHA (American) a combination of Jimi + Aisha.
Jimica, Jimicia, Jimmicia, Jimysha

JIN (Japanese) tender. (American) a short form of Ginny, Jinny.

JINA (Italian) an alternate form of Gina. (Swahili) baby with a name.
Jena, Jinae, Jinan, Jinda, Jinna, Jinnae

JINNY (Scottish) a familiar form of Jenny. (American) a familiar form of Virginia. See also Ginny.
Jin, Jinnee, Jinney, Jinni, Jinnie

JIRINA (Czech) a form of Georgia.
Jirah, Jireh

JIZELLE (American) a form of Giselle.
Jessel, Jezel, Jezell, Jezella, Jezelle, Jisel, Jisela, Jisell, Jisella, Jiselle, Jissel, Jissell, Jissella, Jisselle, Jizel, Jizella, Joselle

JO (American) a short form of Joanna, Jolene, Josephine.
Joangie, Joetta, Joette, Joey

JOAN (Hebrew) God is gracious. An alternate form of Jane. History: Joan of Arc was a fifteenth-century heroine and resistance fighter. See also Ioana, Jean, Juanita, Siobahn.
Joane, Joaneil, Joanel, Joanelle, Joanie, Joanmarie, Joann, Joannanette, Joanne, Joannel, Joanny, Jonni

JOANA, Joanna (English) a form of Joan. See also Yoanna.
Janka, Jhoana, Jo, Jo-Ana, Joandra, Joanka, Joananna, Jo-Anie, Joanka, Jo-Anna, Joannah, Jo-Annie, Joeana, Joeanna, Johana, Johanna, Johannah

JOANIE, Joannie (Hebrew) familiar forms of Joan.
Joanee, Joani, Joanni, Joenie, Johanie, Johnnie, Joni

JOANNE (English) a form of Joan.
Joanann, Joananne, Joann, Jo-Ann, Jo-Anne, Joayn, Joeann, Joeanne

JOANNY (Hebrew) a familiar form of Joan.
Joany

JOAQUINA (Hebrew) God will establish.
Joaquine

JOBETH (English) a combination of Jo + Beth.
Joby

JOBY (Hebrew) afflicted. A feminine form of Job. (English) a familiar form of Jobeth.
Jobey, Jobi, Jobie, Jobina, Jobita, Jobrina, Jobye, Jobyna

JOCACIA (American) a combination of Joy + Acacia.

JOCELIN, Joceline (Latin) alternate forms of Jocelyn.
Jocelina, Jocelinn

JOCELYN (Latin) joyous. See also Yocelin, Yoselin.
Jacelyn, Jasleen, Jocelin, Jocelle, Jocelyne, Jocelynn, Joci, Jocia, Jocilyn, Jocilynn, Jocinta, Joclyn, Joclynn, Josalyn, Joscelin, Joselin, Joselyn, Joshlyn, Josilin, Jossalin, Josselyn, Joycelyn

JOCELYNE (Latin) an alternate form of Jocelyn.
Joceline, Jocelynne, Joclynne

JODI, Jodie, Jody (American) familiar forms of Judith.
Jodee, Jodele, Jodell, Jodelle, Jodevea, Jodey, Jodia, Jodiee, Jodilee, Jodi-Lee, Jodilynn, Jodi-Lynn, Joedi, Joedy

JODIANN (American) a combination of Jodi + Ann.
Jodene, Jodi-Ann, Jodianna, Jodi-Anna, Jodianne, Jodi-Anne, Jodine, Jodyann, Jody-Ann, Jodyanna, Jody-Anna, Jodyanne, Jody-Anne, Jodyne

JOELLE (Hebrew) God is willing. A feminine form of Joel.
Joela, Joele, Joelee, Joeli, Joelia, Joelie, Joell, Joella, Joëlle, Joelli, Joelly, Joely, Joyelle

JOELYNN (American) a combination of Joelle + Lynn.
Joeleen, Joelene, Joeline, Joellen, Joellyn, Joelyn, Joelyne

JOHANA, Johanna, Johannah (German) forms of Joanna. See also Gianna.
Janna, Joahna, Johanah, Johanka, Johanne, Johnna, Johonna, Jonna, Joyhanna, Joyhannah

JOHANIE, Johannie (Hebrew) alternate forms of Joanie.
Johani, Johanni, Johanny, Johany

JOHNNA, Jonna (American) forms of Johana, Joanna.
Jahna, Jahnaya, Jhona, Jhonna, Johna, Johnda, Johnnielynn, Johnnie-Lynn, Johnnquia, Joncie, Jonda, Jondrea, Jontel, Jutta

JOHNNIE (Hebrew) an alternate form of Joanie.
Johni, Johnie, Johnni, Johnny

JOHNNESSA (American) a combination of Johnna + Nessa.
Jahnessa, Johneatha, Johnecia, Johnesha, Johnetra, Johnisha, Johnishi, Johnnise, Jonyssa

JOI (Latin) an alternate form of Joy.
Joia, Joie

JOKLA (Swahili) beautiful robe.

JOLANDA (Greek) an alternate form of Yolanda. See also Iolanthe.
Jola, Jolan, Jolán, Jolande, Jolander, Jolanka, Jolánta, Jolantha, Jolanthe

JOLEEN, Joline (English) alternate forms of Jolene.
Joleena, Joleene, Jolleen, Jollene

JOLENE (Hebrew) God will add, God will increase. (English) a form of Josephine.
Jo, Jolaine, Jolana, Jolane, Jolanna, Jolanne, Jolanta, Jolayne, Jole, Jolean, Joleane, Joleen, Jolena, Joléne, Jolenna, Jolin, Jolina, Jolinda, Joline, Jolinn, Jolinna, Jolleane, Jolleen, Jolline

JOLIE (French) pretty.
Jole, Jolea, Jolee, Joleigh, Joley, Joli, Jolibeth, Jollee, Jollie, Jolly, Joly, Jolye

JOLISA (American) a combination of Jo + Lisa.
Joleesa, Joleisha, Joleishia, Jolieasa, Jolise, Jolisha, Jolisia, Jolissa, Jolysa, Jolyssa, Julissa

JOLYNN (American) a combination of Jo + Lynn.
Jolyn, Jolyne, Jolynne

JONATHA (Hebrew) gift of God. A feminine form of Jonathan.
Johnasha, Johnasia, Jonesha, Jonisha

JONELLE (American) a combination of Joan + Elle.
Jahnel, Jahnell, Jahnelle, Johnel, Johnell, Johnella, Johnelle, Jonel, Jonell, Jonella, Jonyelle, Jynell, Jynelle

JONESHA, Jonisha (American) forms of Jonatha.
Joneisha, Jonesa, Joneshia, Jonessa, Jonisa, Jonishia, Jonneisha, Jonnesha, Jonnessia

JONI (American) a familiar form of Joan.
Jona, Jonae, Jonai, Jonann, Jonati, Joncey, Jonci, Joncie, Jonice, Jonie, Jonilee, Joni-lee, Jonis, Jony

JONIKA (American) a form of Janika.
Johnica, Johnique, Johnquia, Johnnica, Johnnika, Joneeka, Joneika, Jonica, Joniqua, Jonique

JONINA (Hebrew) dove. A feminine form of Jonah. See also Yonina.
Jona, Jonita, Jonnina

JONITA (Hebrew) an alternate form of Jonina. See also Yonita.
Johnetta, Johnette, Johnita, Johnittia, Jonati, Jonetia, Jonetta, Jonette, Jonit, Jonnita, Jonta, Jontae, Jontaé, Jontaya

JONNI, Jonnie (American) familiar forms of Joan.
Jonny

JONQUIL (Latin, English) Botany: an ornamental plant with fragrant yellow flowers.
Jonquelle, Jonquie, Jonquill, Jonquille

JONTEL (American) an alternate form of Johnna.
Jontaya, Jontell, Jontelle, Jontia, Jontila, Jontrice

JORA (Hebrew) autumn rain.
Jorah

JORDAN (Hebrew) descending. See also Jardena.
Jordain, Jordaine, Jordana, Jordane, Jordann, Jordanna, Jordanne, Jordany, Jordea, Jordee, Jorden, Jordi, Jordian, Jordie, Jordin, Jordon, Jordyn, Jori, Jorie, Jourdan

JORDANA, Jordanna (Hebrew) alternate forms of Jordan. See also Giordana, Yordana.
Jordannah, Jordina, Jordonna, Jourdana, Jourdanna

JORDEN, Jordin, Jordon (Hebrew) alternate forms of Jordan.
Jordenne, Jordine

JORDYN (Hebrew) an alternate form of Jordan.
Jordyne, Jordynn, Jordynne

JORI, Jorie (Hebrew) familiar forms of Jordan.
Jorai, Jorea, Joree, Jorée, Jorey, Jorian, Jorin, Jorina, Jorine, Jorita, Jorre, Jorrey, Jorri, Jorrian, Jorrie, Jorry, Jory

JORIANN (American) a combination of Jori + Ann.
Jori-Ann, Jorianna, Jori-Anna, Jorianne, Jori-Anne, Jorriann, Jorrianna, Jorrianne, Jorryann, Jorryanne, Joryann, Joryanna, Joryanne

JORJA (American) a form of Georgia.
Jeorgi, Jeorgia, Jorgana, Jorgi, Jorgia, Jorgina, Jorjana, Jorji

JOSALYN (Latin) an alternate form of Jocelyn.
Josalene, Josalin, Josalind, Josaline, Josalynn, Joshalyne

JOSCELIN, Joscelyn (Latin) alternate forms of Jocelyn.
Josceline, Joscelyne, Joscelynn, Joscelynne, Joselin, Joseline, Joselyn, Joselyne, Joselynn, Joselynne, Joshlyn

JOSEE, Josée (American) familiar forms of Josephine.
Joesee, Josey, Josi, Josina, Josy, Jozee

JOSEFINA (Spanish) a form of Josephine.
Josefa, Josefena, Joseffa, Josefine

JOSELIN, Joseline (Latin) alternate forms of Jocelyn.
Joselina, Joselinne, Josielina

JOSELLE (American) an alternate form of Jizelle.
Joesell, Jozelle

JOSELYN, Joslyn (Latin) alternate forms of Jocelyn.
Joselene, Joselyne, Joselynn, Joshely, Josiline, Josilyn

JOSEPHINE (French) God will add, God will increase. A feminine form of Joseph. See also Fifi, Pepita, Yosepha.
Fina, Jo, Joey, Josee, Josée, Josefina, Josepha, Josephe, Josephene, Josephin, Josephina, Josephyna, Josephyne, Josette, Josey, Josie, Jozephine, Jozie, Sefa

JOSETTE (French) a familiar form of Josephine.
Joesette, Josetta, Joshetta, Jozette

JOSEY, Josie (Hebrew) familiar forms of Josephine.
Josi, Josse, Jossee, Jossie, Josy, Josye

JOSHANN (American) a combination of Joshlyn + Ann.
Joshana, Joshanna, Joshanne

JOSHLYN (Latin) an alternate form of Jocelyn. (Hebrew) God is my salvation. A feminine form of Joshua.
Joshalin, Joshalyn, Joshalynn, Joshalynne, Joshelle, Joshleen, Joshlene, Joshlin, Joshline, Joshlyne, Joshlynn, Joshlynne

JOSIANE, Josianne (American) combinations of Josie + Anne.
Josian, Josie-Ann, Josieann

JOSILIN, Joslin (Latin) alternate forms of Jocelyn.
Josielina, Josiline, Josilyn, Josilyne, Josilynn, Josilynne, Joslin, Josline, Joslyn, Joslyne, Joslynn, Joslynne

JOSSALIN (Latin) an alternate form of Jocelyn.
Jossaline, Jossalyn, Jossalynn, Jossalynne, Josselyn, Josslin, Jossline

JOSSELYN (Latin) an alternate form of Jocelyn.
Josselen, Josselin, Josseline, Jossellen, Jossellin, Jossellyn, Josselyne, Josselynn, Josselynne, Josslyn, Josslyne, Josslynn, Josslynne

JOURDAN (Hebrew) an alternate form of Jordan.
Jourdain, Jourdann, Jourdanne, Jourden, Jourdian, Jourdon, Jourdyn

JOVANA (Latin) an alternate form of Jovanna.
Jeovana, Jouvan, Jovan, Jovanah, Jovena, Jovian, Jowan, Jowana

JOVANNA (Latin) majestic. A feminine form of Jovan. (Italian) an alternate form of Giovanna. Mythology: Jove, also known as Jupiter, was the supreme Roman god.
Jeovanna, Jovado, Joval, Jovana, Jovann, Jovannie, Jovena, Jovina, Jovon, Jovonda, Jovonia, Jovonna, Jovonnah, Jovonne, Jowanna

JOVANNIE (Italian) a familiar form of Jovanna.
Jovanee, Jovani, Jovanie, Jovanne, Jovanni, Jovanny, Jovonnie

JOVITA (Latin) jovial.
Joveda, Joveta, Jovetta, Jovida, Jovitta

JOY (Latin) joyous.
Joe, Joi, Joya, Joye, Joyeeta, Joyella, Joyia, Joyous, Joyvina

JOYANNE (American) a combination of Joy + Anne.
Joyan, Joyann, Joyanna,

JOYCE (Latin) joyous. A short form of Joycelyn.
Joice, Joycey, Joycie, Joyous, Joysel

JOYCELYN (American) a form of Jocelyn.
Joycelin, Joyceline, Joycelyne, Joycelynn, Joycelynne

JOYLYN (American) a combination of Joy + Lynn.
Joyleen, Joylene, Joylin, Joyline, Joylyne, Joylynn, Joy-Lynn, Joylynne

JOZIE (Hebrew) a familiar form of Josephine.
Jozee, Jozée, Jozi, Jozy

JUANA (Spanish) a short form of Juanita.
Juanell, Juaney, Juanika, Juanit, Juanna, Juannia

JUANDALYN (Spanish) an alternate form of Juanita.
Jualinn, Juandalin, Juandaline, Juandalyne, Juandalynn, Juandalynne

JUANITA (Spanish) a form of Jane, Joan. See also Kwanita, Nita, Waneta, Wanika.
Juana, Juandalyn, Juaneice, Juanequa, Juanesha, Juanice, Juanicia, Juaniqua, Juanisha, Juanishia

JUCI (Hungarian) a form of Judy.
Jucika

JUDITH (Hebrew) praised. Mythology: the slayer of Holofernes, according to ancient eastern legend. A feminine form of Judah. See also Yehudit, Yudita.
Giuditta, Ioudith, Jodi, Jodie, Jody, Jude, Judine, Judit, Judita, Judite, Juditha, Judithe, Judy, Judyta, Jutka

JUDY (Hebrew) a familiar form of Judith.
Juci, Judi, Judie, Judye

JUDYANN (American) a combination of Judy + Ann.
Judana, Judiann, Judianna, Judianne, Judyanna, Judyanne

JULA (Polish) a form of Julia.
Julca, Julcia, Juliska, Julka

JULENE (Basque) a form of Julia. See also Yulene.
Julena, Julina, Juline, Julinka, Juliska, Julleen, Jullena, Jullene, Julyne

JULIA (Latin) youthful. A feminine form of Julius. See also Giulia, Jill, Jillian, Sulia, Yulia.
Iulia, Jula, Julea, Juleah, Julene, Juliah, Juliana, Juliann, Julica, Julie, Juliea, Juliet, Julija, Julina, Juline, Julisa, Julissa, Julita, Juliya, Julka, Julyssa

JULIANA (Czech, Spanish), Julianna (Hungarian) forms of Julia.
Julieana, Julieanna, Juliena, Julliana, Jullianna, Julyana, Julyanna, Yuliana

JULIANN, Julianne (English) forms of Julia.
Julean, Juleann, Julian, Juliane, Julieann, Julie-Ann, Julieanne, Julie-Anne, Julien, Juliene, Julienn, Julienne, Jullian

JULIE (English) a form of Julia.
Juel, Jule, Julee, Juli, Julie-Lynn, Julie-Mae, Julle, Jullee, Jullie, Jully, July

JULIET, Juliette (French) forms of Julia.
Julet, Julieta, Juliett, Julietta, Jullet, Julliet, Jullietta

JULISA, Julissa (Latin) alternate forms of Julia.
Julis, Julisha, Julysa, Julyssa

JULITA (Spanish) a form of Julia.
Julitta, Julyta

JUMARIS (American) a combination of Julie + Maris.

JUN (Chinese) truthful.

JUNE (Latin) born in the sixth month.
Juna, Junea, Junel, Junell, Junella, Junelle, Junette, Juney, Junia, Junie, Juniet, Junieta, Junietta, Juniette, Junina, Junita

JUNO (Latin) queen. Mythology: the goddess of heaven.

JUSTICE (Latin) an alternate form of Justine.
Justis, Justise, Justiss, Justisse, Justus, Justyce, Justys

JUSTINA (Italian) a form of Justine.
Jestena, Jestina, Justinna, Justyna

JUSTINE (Latin) just, righteous. A feminine form of Justin.
Giustina, Jestine, Juste, Justi, Justice, Justie, Justina, Justinn, Justy, Justyn, Justyne, Justynn, Justynne

KACEY, Kacy (Irish) brave. (American) alternate forms of Casey. A combination of the initials K. + C.
K. C., Kace, Kacee, Kaci, Kacie, Kaicee, Kaicey, Kasey, Kasie, Kaycee, Kayci, Kaycie

KACHINA (Native American) sacred dancer.
Kachine

KACI, Kacie (American) alternate forms of Kacey, Kacy.
Kasci, Kaycie, Kaysie

KACIA (Greek) a short form of Acacia.
Kaycia, Kaysia

KADEDRA (American) a combination of Kady + Dedra.
Kadeadra, Kadedrah, Kadedria, Kadeedra, Kadeidra, Kadeidre, Kadeidria

KADEJAH (Arabic) an alternate form of Kadijah.
Kadeija, Kadeijah, Kadejá, Kadejia

KADELYN (American) a combination of Kady + Lynn.

KADESHA (American) a combination of Kady + Aisha.
Kadeesha, Kadeeshia, Kadeesia, Kadeesiah, Kadeezia, Kadesa, Kadesheia, Kadeshia, Kadesia, Kadessa, Kadezia

KADIE (English) an alternate form of Kady.
Kadi, Kadia, Kadiah

KADIJAH (Arabic) trustworthy.
Kadajah, Kadeeja, Kadeejah, Kadija

KADISHA (American) an alternate form of Kadesha.
Kadiesha, Kadieshia, Kadishia, Kadisia, Kadysha, Kadyshia

KADY (English) an alternate form of Katy. A combination of the initials K. + D. See also Cady.
K. D., Kade, Kadee, Kadey, Kadie, Kadya, Kadyn, Kaidi, Kaidy, Kayde, Kaydee, Kaydey, Kaydi, Kaydie, Kaydy

KAEDÉ (Japanese) maple leaf.

KAELA (Hebrew, Arabic) beloved, sweetheart. A short form of Kalila, Kelila.
Kaelah, Kaelea, Kaeleah, Kaelee, Kaeli, Kayla

KAELEE, Kaeli (American) forms of Kaela.
Kaelei, Kaeleigh, Kaeley, Kaelia, Kaelie, Kaelii, Kaelly, Kaely, Kaelye

KAELIN (American) an alternate form of Kaelyn.
Kaeleen, Kaelene, Kaelina, Kaelinn, Kalan

KAELYN (American) a combination of Kae + Lynn. See also Caelin, Kaylyn.
Kaelan, Kaelen, Kaelin, Kaelynn, Kaelynne

KAETLYN (Irish) an alternate form of Kaitlin.
Kaetlin, Kaetlynn

KAGAMI (Japanese) mirror.

KAHSHA (Native American) fur robe.
Kasha, Kashae, Kashia

KAI (Hawaiian) sea. (Hopi, Navaho) willow tree.
Kae, Kaie

KAIA (Greek) earth. Mythology: Gaia was the earth goddess.
Kaiah, Kaija

KAILA (Hebrew) laurel; crown.
Kailah, Kailea, Kaileah, Kailee, Kailey, Kayla

KAILEE, Kailey (American) familiar forms of Kaila. Alternate forms of Kaylee.
Kaile, Kaileh, Kaileigh, Kaili, Kailia, Kailie, Kailli, Kaillie, Kaily, Kailya

KAILYN, Kailynn (American) forms of Kaitlin.
Kailan, Kaileen, Kaileena, Kailen, Kailena, Kailene, Kaileyne, Kailin, Kailina, Kailon, Kailynne

KAIROS (Greek) last, final, complete. Mythology: the last goddess born to Jupiter.
Kaira, Kairra

KAISHAWN (American) a combination of Kai + Shawna.
Kaeshun, Kaisha, Kaishala, Kaishon

KAITLIN (Irish) pure. An alternate form of Caitlin. See also Katelin.
Kaetlyn, Kailyn, Kailynn, Kaitlan, Kaitland, Kaitleen, Kaitlen, Kaitlind, Kaitlinn, Kaitlinne, Kaitlon, Kaytlin

KAITLYN, Kaitlynn (Irish) an alternate form of Caitlyn.
Kaitelynne, Kaitlynne

KAIYA (Japanese) forgiveness.
Kaiyah, Kaiyia

KALA (Arabic) a short form of Kalila. An alternate form of Cala.
Kalah, Kalla, Kallah

KALAMA (Hawaiian) torch.

KALANI (Hawaiian) chieftain; sky.
Kailani, Kalanie, Kaloni

KALARE (Latin, Basque) bright; clear.

KALEA (Hawaiian) bright; clear.
Kahlea, Kahleah, Kailea, Kaileah, Kaleah, Kaleeia, Kaleia, Kalia, Kallea, Kalleah, Kaylea, Kayleah, Khalea, Khaleah

KALEE, Kaleigh, Kaley, Kalie (American) alternate forms of Caley, Kaylee.
Kalei, Kalleigh, Kalley, Kally, Kaly

KALEI (Hawaiian) flower wreath.
Kahlei, Kailei, Kallei, Kaylei, Khalei

KALENA (Hawaiian) pure. See also Kalina.
Kaleen, Kaleena, Kalene, Kalenea, Kalenna

KALERE (Swahili) short woman.
Kaleer

KALI (Sanskrit) energy; black goddess; time the destroyer. (Hawaiian) hesitating. Religion: a name for the Hindu goddess Shakti. See also Cali.
Kalee, Kaleigh, Kaley, Kalie, Kallee, Kalley, Kalli, Kallie, Kally, Kallye, Kaly

KALIA (Hawaiian) an alternate form of Kalea.
Kaliah, Kaliea, Kalieya

KALIFA (Somali) chaste; holy.

KALILA (Arabic) beloved, sweetheart. See also Kaela.
Kahlila, Kala, Kaleela, Kalilla, Kaylil, Kaylila, Kelila, Khalila, Khalilah, Khalillah, Kylila, Kylilah, Kylillah

KALINA (Slavic) flower. (Hawaiian) a form of Karen. See also Kalena.
Kalin, Kalinna, Kalyna, Kalynah, Kalynna

KALINDA (Hindi) sun.
Kaleenda, Kalindi, Kalynda, Kalyndi

KALISA (American) a combination of Kate + Lisa.
Kalise, Kalissa, Kalysa, Kalyssa

KALISHA (American) a combination of Kate + Aisha.
Kaleesha, Kaleisha, Kalishia

KALISKA (Moquelumnan) coyote chasing deer.

KALLAN (Slavic) stream, river.
Kalahn, Kalan, Kalen, Kallen, Kallon, Kalon

KALLE (Finnish) a form of Carol.
Kaille, Kaylle

KALLI, Kallie (Greek) alternate forms of Callie. Familiar forms of Kalliope, Kallista, Kalliyan.
Kalle, Kallee, Kalley, Kallita, Kally

KALLIOPE (Greek) beautiful voice. Mythology: Calliope was the muse of epic poetry.
Kalli, Kallie, Kallyope

KALLISTA (Greek) an alternate form of Callista.
Kalesta, Kalista, Kallesta, Kalli, Kallie, Kallysta, Kaysta

KALLIYAN (Cambodian) best.
Kalli, Kallie

KALTHA (English) marigold, yellow flower.

KALUWA (Swahili) forgotten one.
Kalua

KALYCA (Greek) rosebud.
Kalica, Kalika, Kaly

KALYN, Kalynn (American) alternate forms of Kaylyn, Kaylynn.
Kalin, Kallen, Kallin, Kallon, Kallyn, Kalyne, Kalynne

KAMA (Sanskrit) loved one. Religion: the Hindu god of love.

KAMALA (Hindi) lotus.
Kamalah, Kammala

KAMALI (Mahona) spirit guide; protector.
Kamalie

KAMARIA (Swahili) moonlight.
Kamar, Kamara, Kamarae, Kamaree, Kamari, Kamariah, Kamarie, Kamariya, Kamariyah, Kamarya

KAMATA (Moquelumnan) gambler.

KAMBRIA (Latin) an alternate form of Cambria.
Kambra, Kambrie, Kambriea, Kambry

KAMEA (Hawaiian) one and only; precious.
Kameah, Kameo, Kamiya

KAMEKE (Swahili) blind.

KAMEKO (Japanese) turtle child. Mythology: the turtle symbolizes longevity.

KAMERON (American) a form of Cameron.
Kameran, Kamri

KAMI (Italian, North African) a short form of Kamila, Kamilah. (Japanese) divine aura. See also Cami.
Kamie, Kammi, Kammie, Kammy, Kammye, Kamy

KAMILA (Slavic) a form of Camila. See also Millie.
Kameela, Kamela, Kamelia, Kamella, Kami, Kamilah, Kamilia, Kamilka, Kamilla, Kamille, Kamma, Kammilla, Kamyla

KAMILAH (North African) perfect.
Kameela, Kameelah, Kami, Kamillah, Kammilah

KAMIYA (Hawaiian) an alternate form of Kamea.
Kamia, Kamiah, Kamiyah

KAMRI (American) a short form of Kameron. See also Camri.
Kamree, Kamrey, Kamrie, Kamry, Kamrye

KAMRYN (American) a form of Cameron. See also Camryn.
Kameryn, Kamren, Kamrin, Kamron, Kamrynn

KANANI (Hawaiian) beautiful.
Kana, Kanae, Kanan

KANDA (Native American) magical power.

KANDACE, Kandice (Greek) glittering white; glowing. (American) alternate forms of Candace, Candice.
Kandas, Kandess, Kandi, Kandis, Kandise, Kandiss, Kandus, Kandyce, Kandys, Kandyse

KANDI (American) a familiar form of Kandace, Kandice. See also Candi.
Kandhi, Kandia, Kandie, Kandy, Kendi, Kendie, Kendy, Kenndi, Kenndie, Kenndy

KANDRA (American) a form of Kendra. See also Candra.
Kandrea, Kandree, Kandria

KANE (Japanese) two right hands.

KANEISHA, Kanisha (American) alternate forms of Keneisha.
Kaneasha, Kanecia, Kaneesha, Kanesah, Kanesha, Kaneshea, Kaneshia, Kanessa, Kaneysha, Kaniece, Kanishia

KANENE (Swahili) a little important thing.

KANI (Hawaiian) sound.

KANIKA (Mwera) black cloth.
Kanica, Kanicka

KANNITHA (Cambodian) angel.

KANOA (Hawaiian) free.

KANYA (Hindi) virgin. (Tai) young lady. Religion: a name for the Hindu goddess Shakti.
Kanea, Kania, Kaniya, Kanyia

KAPRI (American) an alternate form of Capri.
Kapre, Kapree, Kapria, Kaprice, Kapricia, Kaprisha, Kaprisia

KAPUA (Hawaiian) blossom.

KAPUKI (Swahili) first-born daughter.

KARA (Greek, Danish) pure. An alternate form of Katherine.
Kaira, Kairah, Karah, Karalea, Karaleah, Karalee, Karalie, Kari, Karra

KARAH (Greek, Danish) an alternate form of Kara. (Irish, Italian) an alternate form of Cara.
Karrah

KARALYNN (English) a combination of Kara + Lynn.
Karalin, Karaline, Karalyn, Karalyne, Karalynne

KARELLE (American) a form of Carol.
Karel, Kareli, Karell, Karely

KAREN (Greek) pure. An alternate form of Katherine. See also Carey, Carina, Caryn.
Kaaren, Kalina, Karaina, Karan, Karena, Karin, Karina, Karine, Karna, Karon, Karren, Karron, Karyn, Kerron, Koren

KARENA (Scandinavian) a form of Karen.
Kareen, Kareena, Kareina, Karenah, Karene, Karreen, Karreena, Karrena, Karrene

KARESSA (French) an alternate form of Caressa.

KARI (Greek) pure. (Danish) a form of Caroline, Katherine. See also Carey, Cari, Carrie.
Karee, Karey, Karia, Kariah, Karie, Karrey, Karri, Karrie, Karry, Kary

KARIANE, Karianne (American) combinations of Kari + Anne.
Karian, Kariana, Kariann, Karianna

KARIDA (Arabic) untouched, pure.
Kareeda, Karita

KARILYNN (American) a combination of Kari + Lynn.
Kareelin, Kareeline, Kareelinn, Kareelyn, Kareelyne, Kareelynn, Kareelynne, Karilin, Kariline,

Karilynn *(cont.)*
Karilinn, Karilyn, Karilyne, Karilynne, Karylin, Karyline, Karylinn, Karylyn, Karylyne, Karylynn, Karylynne

KARIMAH (Arabic) generous.
Kareema, Kareemah, Karima, Karime

KARIN (Scandinavian) a form of Karen.
Kaarin, Kareen, Karina, Karine, Karinne, Karrin, Kerrin

KARINA (Russian) a form of Karen.
Kaarina, Karinna, Karrina, Karryna, Karyna, Karynna

KARINE (Russian) a form of Karen.
Karrine, Karryne, Karyne

KARIS (Greek) graceful.
Karess, Karice, Karise, Karisse, Karris, Karys, Karyss

KARISSA (Greek) an alternate form of Carissa.
Karese, Karesse, Karisa, Karisha, Karishma, Karisma, Karissimia, Kariza, Karrisa, Karrissa, Karysa, Karyssa, Kerisa

KARLA (German) an alternate form of Carla. (Slavic) a short form of Karoline.
Karila, Karilla, Karle, Karlene, Karlicka, Karlinka, Karlisha, Karlisia, Karlitha, Karlla, Karlon, Karlyn

KARLEE, Karleigh (American) alternate forms of Karley, Karly. See also Carlee.
Karlea, Karleah, Karlei

KARLENE, Karlyn (American) forms of Karla. See also Carleen.
Karleen, Karlen, Karlena, Karlign, Karlin, Karlina, Karlinna, Karlyan, Karlynn, Karlynne

KARLEY, Karly (Latin) little and womanly. (American) forms of Carly.
Karlee, Karley, Karlie, Karlyan, Karlye

KARLI, Karlie (American) alternate forms of Karley, Karly. See also Carli.

KARLOTTE (American) a form of Charlotte.
Karlita, Karletta, Karlette, Karlotta

KARMA (Hindi) fate, destiny; action.

KARMEL (Hebrew) an alternate form of Carmela.
Karmeita, Karmela, Karmelina, Karmella, Karmelle, Karmiella, Karmielle, Karmyla

KARMEN (Latin) song. A form of Carmen.
Karman, Karmencita, Karmin, Karmina, Karmine, Karmita, Karmon, Karmyn, Karmyne

KAROLANE (American) a combination of Karoll + Anne.
Karolan, Karolann, Karolanne, Karol-Anne

KAROLINA, Karoline (Slavic) forms of Caroline. See also Carolina.
Karaleen, Karalena, Karalene, Karalin, Karaline, Karileen, Karilena, Karilene, Karilin, Karilina, Kariline, Karleen, Karlen, Karlena, Karlene, Karling, Karoleena, Karolena, Karolinka, Karroleen, Karrolena, Karrolene, Karrolin, Karroline

KAROLL (Slavic) a form of Carol.
Karel, Karilla, Karily, Karol, Karola, Karole, Karoly, Karrol, Karyl, Kerril

KAROLYN (American) a form of Carolyn.
Karalyn, Karalyna, Karalynn, Karalynne, Karilyn, Karilyna, Karilynn, Karilynne, Karlyn, Karlynn, Karlynne, Karolyna, Karolynn, Karolynne, Karrolyn, Karrolyna, Karrolynn, Karrolynne

KARRI, Karrie (American) forms of Carrie.
Kari, Karie, Karry, Kary

KARSEN, Karsyn (English) daughter of Kar. Feminine forms of Carson.
Karson

KARUNA (Hindi) merciful.

KARYN (American) a form of Karen.
Karyne, Karynn, Karynna, Kerrynn, Kerrynne

KASA (Hopi) fur robe.

KASANDRA (Greek) an alternate form of Kassandra.
Kasander, Kasandria, Kasandra, Kasaundra, Kasondra, Kasoundra

KASEY, Kasie (Irish) brave. (American) forms of Casey, Kacey.
Kaisee, Kaisie, Kasci, Kascy, Kasee, Kasi, Kassee, Kassey, Kasy, Kasya, Kaysci, Kaysea, Kaysee, Kaysey, Kaysi, Kaysie, Kaysy

KASHAWNA (American) a combination of Kate + Shawna.
Kasha, Kashae, Kashana, Kashanna, Kashauna, Kashawn, Kasheana, Kasheanna, Kasheena, Kashena, Kashonda, Kashonna

KASHMIR (Sanskrit)
Geography: a state in India.
*Cashmere, Kashmear, Kashmere,
Kashmia, Kashmira, Kasmir,
Kasmira, Kazmir, Kazmira*

KASI (Hindi) from the holy city.

KASIA (Polish) a form of
Katherine. See also Cassia.
*Kashia, Kasiah, Kasian,
Kasienka, Kasja, Kaska, Kassa,
Kassia, Kassya, Kasya*

KASINDA (Umbundu) our last
baby.

KASSANDRA (Greek) an alter-
nate form of Cassandra.
*Kassandr, Kassandre,
Kassandré, Kassaundra, Kassi,
Kassondra, Kassondria,
Kassundra, Kazandra,
Khrisandra, Krisandra,
Krissandra*

KASSI, Kassie (American)
familiar forms of Kassandra,
Kassidy. See also Cassie.
Kassey, Kassia, Kassy

KASSIDY (Irish) clever.
(American) an alternate form
of Cassidy.
*Kassadee, Kassadi, Kassadie,
Kassadina, Kassady, Kasseday,
Kassedee, Kassi, Kassiddy,
Kassidee, Kassidi, Kassidie,
Kassity, Kassydi*

KATALINA (Irish) an alternate
form of Caitlin. See also
Catalina.
*Kataleen, Kataleena, Katalena,
Katalin, Katalyn, Katalynn*

KATARINA (Czech) a form of
Katherine.
*Kata, Katareena, Katarena,
Katarin, Katarine, Katarinna,
Katarinne, Katarrina, Kataryna,
Katarzyna, Katinka, Katrika,
Katrinka*

KATE (Greek) pure. (English) a
short form of Katherine.
*Kait, Kata, Katee, Kati, Katica,
Katie, Katka, Katy, Katya*

KATEE, Katey (English) familiar
forms of Kate, Katherine.

KATELIN (Irish) an alternate
form of Caitlin. See also
Kaitlin.
*Kaetlin, Katalin, Katelan,
Kateland, Kateleen, Katelen,
Katelene, Katelind, Kateline,
Katelinn, Katelun, Kaytlin*

KATELYN, Katelynn (Irish) alter-
nate forms of Caitlin.
*Kaetlyn, Kaetlynn, Kaetlynne,
Katelyne, Katelynne, Kaytlyn,
Kaytlynn, Kaytlynne*

KATERINA (Slavic) a form of
Katherine.
*Katenka, Katerine, Katerini,
Katerinka*

KATHARINE (Greek) an alter-
nate form of Katherine.
*Katharaine, Katharin, Katharina,
Katharyn*

KATHERINE (Greek) pure. See
also Carey, Catherine,
Ekaterina, Kara, Karen, Kari,
Kasia, Katerina, Yekaterina.
*Ekaterina, Ekatrinna, Kasienka,
Kasin, Kat, Katarina, Katchen,
Kate, Katee, Kathann,
Kathanne, Katharine,
Kathereen, Katheren,
Katherene, Katherenne,
Katherin, Katherina, Katheryn,
Katheryne, Kathi, Kathleen,
Kathrine, Kathryn, Kathy,
Kathyrine, Katia, Katina,
Katlaina, Katoka, Katreeka,
Katrina, Kay, Kitty*

KATHI, Kathy (English) familiar
forms of Katherine, Kathleen.
See also Cathi.

*Kaethe, Katha, Kathe, Kathee,
Kathey, Kathi, Kathie, Katka,
Katla, Kató*

KATHLEEN (Irish) a form of
Katherine. See also Cathleen.
*Katheleen, Kathelene, Kathi,
Kathileen, Kathlean, Kathleena,
Kathleene, Kathlene, Kathlin,
Kathlina, Kathlyn, Kathlyne,
Kathlynn, Kathy, Katleen*

KATHRINE (Greek) an alternate
form of Katherine.
*Kathreen, Kathreena, Kathrene,
Kathrin, Kathrina*

KATHRYN (English) a form of
Katherine.
*Kathren, Kathryne, Kathrynn,
Kathrynne*

KATI (Estonian) a form of Kate.
Katja, Katya, Katye

KATIA, Katya (Russian) forms
of Katherine.
*Cattiah, Katiya, Kattia, Kattiah,
Katyah*

KATIE (English) a familiar form
of Kate.
*Katee, Kati, Kātia, Katti, Kattie,
Katy, Kayte, Kaytee, Kaytie*

KATILYN (Irish) an alternate
form of Katlyn.
Katilin, Katilynn

KATLIN (Irish) an alternate
form of Katlyn.
Katlina, Katline

KATLYN (Greek) pure. (Irish) an
alternate form of Katelin.
*Kaatlain, Katilyn, Katland,
Katlin, Katlynd, Katlyne, Katlynn,
Katlynne*

KATRIEL (Hebrew) God is my
crown.
*Katrelle, Katri, Katrie, Katry,
Katryel*

KATRINA (German) a form of Katherine. See also Catrina, Trina.
Katreen, Katreena, Katrene, Katri, Katrice, Katricia, Katrien, Katrin, Katrine, Katrinia, Katriona, Katryn, Katryna, Kattrina, Kattryna, Katus, Katuska

KATY (English) a familiar form of Kate. See also Cady.
Kady, Katey, Katty, Kayte

KAULANA (Hawaiian) famous.
Kaula, Kauna, Kahuna

KAVERI (Hindi) Geographical: a sacred river in India.

KAVINDRA (Hindi) poet.

KAWENA (Hawaiian) glow.
Kawana, Kawona

KAY (Greek) rejoicer. (Teutonic) a fortified place. (Latin) merry. A short form of Katherine.
Caye, Kae, Kai, Kaye, Kayla

KAYA (Hopi) wise child. (Japanese) resting place.
Kaja, Kayah, Kayia

KAYCEE (American) a combination of the initials K. + C.
Kayce, Kaysee, Kaysey, Kaysi, Kaysie, Kaysii

KAYDEE (American) a combination of the initials K. + D.
Kayda, Kayde, Kayden, Kaydi, Kaydie

KAYLA (Arabic, Hebrew) laurel; crown. An alternate form of Kaela, Kaila. See also Cayla.
Kaylah, Kaylea, Kaylee, Kayleen, Kaylene, Kaylia, Keila, Keyla

KAYLAH (Arabic, Hebrew) an alternate form of Kayla.
Kayleah, Kaylia, Keylah

KAYLAN, Kaylen (Hebrew) alternate forms of Kayleen.
Kaylana, Kayland, Kaylani, Kaylann, Kaylean, Kayleana, Kayleanna, Kaylenn

KAYLEE (American) a form of Kayla. See also Caeley, Kalee.
Kailee, Kayle, Kayleigh, Kayley, Kayli, Kaylie

KAYLEEN, Kaylene (Hebrew) beloved, sweetheart. Alternate forms of Kayla.
Kaylan, Kayleena, Kayleene, Kaylen, Kaylena

KAYLEIGH (American) an alternate form of Kaylee.
Kaylei

KAYLEY, Kayli, Kaylie (American) alternate forms of Kaylee.

KAYLIN (American) an alternate form of Kaylyn.
Kaylon

KAYLYN, Kaylynn (American) combinations of Kay + Lynn. See also Kaelyn.
Kalyn, Kalynn, Kayleen, Kaylene, Kaylin, Kaylyna, Kaylyne, Kaylynne

KAYTLIN, Kaytlyn (Irish) alternate forms of Kaitlin.
Kaytlan, Kaytlann, Kaytlen, Kaytlyne, Kaytlynn, Kaytlynne

KEAIRA (Irish) an alternate form of Keara.
Keair, Keairah, Keairra, Keairre, Keairrea

KEALA (Hawaiian) path.

KEANA, Keanna (German) bold; sharp. (Irish) beautiful. Feminine forms of Keane.
Keanah, Keanne, Keanu, Keenan, Keeyana, Keeyanah, Keeyanna, Keeyona. Keeyonna, Keiana, Keianna, Keona, Keonna

KEANDRA, Keondra (American) forms of Kenda.
Keandrah, Keandre, Keandrea, Keandria, Kedeana, Kedia, Keonda, Keondre, Keondria

KEARA (Irish) dark; black. Religion: an Irish saint.
Keaira, Kearah, Kearia, Kearra, Keera, Keerra, Keiara, Keiarah, Keiarra, Keira, Kera

KEARSTEN, Keirsten (Greek) alternate forms of Kirstin.
Kearstin, Kearston, Kearstyn, Keirstan, Keirstein, Keirstin, Keirston, Keirstyn, Keirstynne

KEELEY, Keely (Irish) alternate forms of Kelly.
Kealee, Kealey, Keali, Kealie, Keallie, Kealy, Keela, Keelan, Keele, Keelee, Keeleigh, Keeli, Keelia, Keelie, Keellie, Keelye, Keighla, Keilee, Keileigh, Keiley, Keilly, Kiela, Kiele, Kieley, Kielly, Kiely

KEELYN (Irish) an alternate form of Kellyn.
Kealyn, Keelin, Keilan, Kielyn

KEENA (Irish) brave.
Keenya, Kina

KEESHA (American) an alternate form of Keisha.
Keesa, Keeshae, Keeshana, Keeshanne, Keeshawna, Keeshonna, Keeshya, Keiosha

KEI (Japanese) reverent.

KEIANA, Keianna (Irish) alternate forms of Keana, Keanna.
Keiann, Keiannah, Keionna

KEIKI (Hawaiian) child.
Keikana, Keikann, Keikanna, Keikanne

KEIKO (Japanese) happy child.

KEILA (Arabic, Hebrew) an alternate form of Kayla.
Keilah, Kela, Kelah

KEILANI (Hawaiian) glorious chief.
Kaylani, Keilan, Keilana, Keilany, Kelana, Kelanah, Kelane, Kelani, Kelanie

KEIRA (Irish) an alternate form of Keara.
Keiara, Keiarra, Keirra, Keirrah, Kera, Keyeira

KEISHA (American) a short form of Keneisha.
Keasha, Keashia, Keesha, Keishaun, Keishauna, Keishawn, Kesha, Keysha, Kiesha, Kisha, Kishanda

KEITA (Scottish) woods; enclosed place.
Keiti

KEKONA (Hawaiian) second-born child.

KELCEY, Kelci, Kelcie
(Scottish) alternate forms of Kelsey.
Kelse, Kelcee, Kelcy

KELILA (Hebrew) crown, laurel. See also Kaela, Kayla, Kalila.
Kelilah, Kelula

KELLEY (Irish) an alternate form of Kelly.

KELLI, Kellie (Irish) familiar forms of Kelly.
Keleigh, Keli, Kelia, Keliah, Kelie, Kellee, Kelleigh, Kellia, Kellisa

KELLY (Irish) brave warrior. See also Caeley.
Keeley, Keely, Kelley, Kelley, Kelli, Kellie, Kellye

KELLYANNE (Irish) a combination of Kelly + Anne.
Kelliann, Kellianne, Kellyann

KELLYN (Irish) a combination of Kelly + Lyn.
Keelyn, Kelleen, Kellen, Kellene, Kellina, Kelline, Kellynn, Kellynne

KELSEA (Scottish) an alternate form of Kelsey.
Kelcea, Kelcia, Kelsa, Kelsae, Kelsay, Kelse

KELSEY (Scandinavian, Scottish) ship island. (English) an alternate form of Chelsey.
Kelcey, Kelda, Kellsee, Kellsei, Kellsey, Kellsie, Kellsy, Kelsea, Kelsei, Kelsey, Kelsi, Kelsie, Kelsy, Kelsye

KELSI, Kelsie, Kelsy (Scottish) forms of Chelsea.
Kalsie, Kelci, Kelcie, Kellsi

KENDA (English) water baby. (Dakota) magical power. Astrology: a child born under Cancer, Scorpio, or Pisces.
Keandra, Kendra, Kennda

KENDAL (English) an alternate form of Kendall.
Kendahl, Kendale, Kendalie, Kendalin, Kendalyn, Kendalynn, Kendel, Kendele, Kendil, Kindal

KENDALL (English) ruler of the valley.
Kendal, Kendalla, Kendalle, Kendell, Kendelle, Kendera,
Kendia, Kendyl, Kinda, Kindall, Kindi, Kindle, Kynda, Kyndal, Kyndall, Kyndel

KENDRA (English) an alternate form of Kenda.
Kandra, Kendrah, Kendre, Kendrea, Kendreah, Kendria, Kenndra, Kentra, Kentrae, Kindra, Kyndra

KENDYL (English) an alternate form of Kendall.
Kendyle, Kendyll

KENEISHA (American) a combination of the prefix Ken + Aisha.
Kaneisha, Keisha, Keneesha, Kenesha, Keneshia, Kenisha, Kenneisha, Kennesha, Kenneshia, Keosha, Kineisha

KENENZA (English) an alternate form of Kennice.
Kenza

KENIA (Hebrew) an alternate form of Kenya.
Keniya, Kennia

KENISHA (American) an alternate form of Keneisha.
Kenisa, Kenise, Kenishia, Kenissa, Kennisa, Kennisha, Kennysha

KENNA (Irish) a short form of Kennice.

KENNEDY (Irish) helmeted chief. History: John F. Kennedy was the thirty-fifth U.S. president.
Kenedee, Kenedey, Kenedi, Kenedie, Kenedy, Kenidee, Kenidi, Kenidie, Kenidy, Kennadee, Kennadi, Kennadie, Kennady, Kennedee, Kennedey, Kennedi, Kennedie, Kennidee, Kennidi, Kennidy, Kynnedi

KENNICE (English) beautiful. A feminine form of Kenneth.
Kanice, Keneese, Kenenza, Kenese, Kennise

KENYA (Hebrew) animal horn. Geography: a country in Africa.
Keenya, Kenia, Kenja, Kenyah, Kenyana, Kenyatta, Kenyia

KENYATTA (American) a form of Kenya.
Kenyata, Kenyatah, Kenyatte, Kenyattia, Kenyatta, Kenyette

KENZIE (Scottish) light skinned. (Irish) a short form of Mackenzie.
Kenzea, Kenzee, Kenzey, Kenzi, Kenzia, Kenzy, Kinzie

KEONA, Keonna (Irish) alternate forms of Keana.
Keiona, Keionna, Keoana, Keoni, Keonia, Keonnah, Keonni, Keonnia

KEOSHA (American) a short form of Keneisha.
Keoshae, Keoshi, Keoshia, Keosia

KERANI (Hindi) sacred bells. See also Rani.
Kera, Kerah, Keran, Kerana

KEREN (Hebrew) animal's horn.
Kerrin, Keryn

KERENSA (Cornish) loving, affectionate.
Karensa, Karenza, Kerenza

KERI, Kerri, Kerrie (Irish) alternate forms of Kerry.
Keriann, Kerianne, Kerriann, Kerrianne

KERRY (Irish) dark haired. Geography: a county in Ireland.

Keary, Keiry, Keree, Kerey, Keri, Kerri, Kerrie, Kerryann, Kerryanne, Kery, Kiera, Kierra

KERSTIN (Scandinavian) an alternate form of Kirsten.
Kerstan, Kerste, Kerstein, Kersten, Kerstie, Kerstien, Kerston, Kerstyn, Kerstynn

KESARE (Latin) long haired. (Basque) a feminine form of Caesar.

KESHA (American) an alternate form of Keisha.
Keshah, Keshal, Keshala, Keshan, Keshana, Keshara, Keshawn, Keshawna, Keshawnna

KESHIA (American) an alternate form of Keisha. A short form of Keneisha.
Kecia, Keishia, Keschia, Keshea, Kesia, Kesiah, Kessia, Kessiah

KESI (Swahili) born during difficult times.

KESSIE (Ashanti) chubby baby.
Kess, Kessa, Kesse, Kessey, Kessi

KEVYN (Irish) beautiful. A feminine form of Kevin.
Keva, Kevan, Keven, Kevia, Keviana, Kevinna, Kevina, Kevion, Kevionna, Kevon, Kevona, Kevone, Kevonia, Kevonna, Kevonne, Kevonya, Kevynn

KEYANA, Keyanna (American) alternate forms of Kiana.
Keya, Keyanah, Keyanda, Keyandra, Keyannah

KEYARA (Irish) an alternate form of Kiara.
Keyarah, Keyari, Keyarra, Keyera, Keyerah, Keyerra

KEYONA, Keyonna (American) alternate forms of Kiana.
Keyonda, Keyondra, Keyonnia, Keyonnie

KEYSHA (American) an alternate form of Keisha.
Keyosha, Keyoshia, Keyshana, Keyshanna, Keyshawn, Keyshawna, Keyshia, Keyshla, Keyshona, Keyshonna

KEZIAH (Hebrew) cinnamonlike spice. Bible: one of the daughters of Job.
Kazia, Kaziah, Ketzi, Ketzia, Ketziah, Kezi, Kezia, Kizzy

KHADIJAH (Arabic) trustworthy. History: Muhammed's first wife.
Khadaja, Khadajah, Khadeeja, Khadeejah, Khadeja, Khadejah, Khadejha, Khadija, Khadije, Khadijia, Khadijiah

KHALIDA (Arabic) immortal, everlasting.
Khali, Khalia, Khaliah, Khalidda, Khalita

KHRISSA (American) a form of Chrissa.
Khrishia, Khryssa, Krisha, Krisia, Krissa, Krysha, Kryssa

KHRISTINA (Russian, Scandinavian) a form of Kristina, Christina.
Khristeen, Khristen, Khristin, Khristine, Khyristya, Khristyana, Khristyna, Khrystyne

KI (Korean) arisen.

KIA (African) season's beginning. (American) a short form of Kiana.
Kiah

KIANA (American) a combination of the prefix Ki + Ana.

Keanna, Keiana, Keyana, Keyona, Khiana, Khianah, Khianna, Ki, Kiahna, Kiane, Kiani, Kiania, Kianna, Kiauna, Kiandra, Kiandria, Kiauna, Kiaundra, Kiyana, Kyana

KIANNA (American) an alternate form of Kiana.
Kiannah, Kianne, Kianni

KIARA (Irish) little and dark. A feminine form of Kieran.
Keyara, Kiarra, Kieara, Kiearah, Kiearra, Kyara

KIARIA, Kiarra, Kichi (Japanese) fortunate.

KIELE (Hawaiian) gardenia; fragrant blossom.
Kiela, Kieley, Kieli, Kielli, Kielly

KIERA, Kierra (Irish) alternate forms of Kerry.
Kierana, Kieranna, Kierea

KIERSTEN, Kierstin (Scandanavian) alternate forms of Kirsten.
Keirstan, Kerstin, Kierstan, Kierston, Kierstyn, Kierstynn

KIKI (Spanish) a familiar form of names ending in "queta."

KIKU (Japanese) chrysanthemum.
Kiko

KILEY (Irish) attractive; from the straits.
Kilea, Kilee, Kileigh, Kili, Kilie, Kylee, Kyli, Kylie

KIM (Vietnamese) needle. (English) a short form of Kimberly.
Kima, Kimette, Kym

KIMANA (Shoshone) butterfly.
Kiman, Kimani

KIMBER (English) a short form of Kimberly.
Kimbra

KIMBERLEE, Kimberley (English) alternate forms of Kimberly.
Kimbalee, Kimberlea, Kimberlei, Kimberleigh, Kimbley

KIMBERLY (English) chief, ruler.
Cymberly, Cymbre, Kim, Kimba, Kimbely, Kimber, Kimbereley, Kimberely, Kimberlee, Kimberli, Kimberlie, Kimberlyn, Kimbery, Kimbria, Kimbrie, Kimbry, Kimmie, Kymberly

KIMBERLYN (English) an alternate form of Kimberly.
Kimberlin, Kimberlynn

KIMI (Japanese) righteous.
Kimia, Kimika, Kimiko, Kimiyo, Kimmi, Kimmie, Kimmy

KIMMIE (English) a familiar form of Kimberly.
Kimee, Kimme, Kimmee, Kimmi, Kimmy, Kimy

KINA (Hawaiian) from China.

KINEISHA (American) an alternate form of Keneisha.
Kineesha, Kinesha, Kineshia, Kinisha, Kinishia

KINETA (Greek) energetic.
Kinetta

KINI (Hawaiian) a form of Jean.
Kina

KINSEY (English) offspring; relative.
Kinsee, Kinsley, Kinza, Kinze, Kinzee, Kinzey, Kinzi, Kinzie, Kinzy

KINSLEY (American) a form of Kinsey.
Kinslee, Kinslie, Kinslyn

KIOKO (Japanese) happy child.
Kiyo, Kiyoko

KIONA (Native American) brown hills.
Kionah, Kioni, Kionna

KIRA (Persian) sun. (Latin) light. A feminine form of Cyrus.
Kirah, Kiri, Kiria, Kiro, Kirra, Kirrah, Kirri

KIRAN (Hindi) ray.

KIRBY (Scandinavian) church village. (English) cottage by the water.
Kirbee, Kirbi

KIRIMA (Eskimo) hill.

KIRSI (Hindi) amaranth blossoms.
Kirsie

KIRSTA (Scandinavian) an alternate form of Kirsten.

KIRSTEN (Greek) Christian; annointed. (Scandinavian) a form of Christine.
Karsten, Kearsten, Keirstan, Kerstin, Kiersten, Kirsteni, Kirsta, Kirstan, Kirstene, Kirstie, Kirstin, Kirston, Kirsty, Kirstyn, Kjersten, Kursten, Kyersten, Kyrsten, Kyrstin

KIRSTIN (Scandinavian) an alternate form of Kirsten.
Karstin, Kirsteen, Kirstien, Kirstine

KIRSTIE, Kirsty (Scandinavian) familiar forms of Kirsten.
Kerstie, Kirsta, Kirste, Kirstee, Kirstey, Kirsti, Kjersti, Kyrsty

KIRSTYN (Greek) an alternate form of Kirsten.
Kirstynn

KISA (Russian) kitten.
Kisha, Kiska, Kissa, Kiza

KISHI (Japanese) long and happy life.

KISSA (Ugandan) born after twins.

KITA (Japanese) north.

KITRA (Hebrew) crowned.

KITTY (Greek) a familiar form of Katherine.
Ketter, Ketti, Ketty, Kit, Kittee, Kitteen, Kittey, Kitti, Kittie

KIWA (Japanese) borderline.

KIYANA (American) an alternate form of Kiana.
Kiya, Kiyah, Kiyan, Kiyani, Kiyanna, Kiyenna

KIZZY (American) a familiar form of Keziah.
Kezi, Kissie, Kizzi, Kizzie

KLARA (Hungarian) a form of Clara.
Klára, Klari, Klarika

KLARISE (German) an alternate form of Klarissa.
Klarice, Kláris, Klaryce

KLARISSA (German) clear, bright. (Italian) an alternate form of Clarissa.
Klarisa, Klarise, Klarrisa, Klarrissa, Klarrissia, Klarisza, Klarysa, Klaryssa, Kleresa

KLAUDIA (American) a form of Claudia.
Klaudija

KLOE (American) a form of Chloe.
Khloe, Kloee, Kloey, Klohe, Kloie

KODI (American) a form of Codi.
Kodee, Kodey, Kodie, Kody, Kodye, Koedi

KOFFI (Swahili) born on Friday.
Kaffe, Kaffi, Koffe, Koffie

KOKO (Japanese) stork. See also Coco.

KOLBY (American) a form of Colby.
Kobie, Koby, Kolbee, Kolbey, Kolbi, Kolbie

KOLINA (Swedish) a form of Katherine. See also Colleen.
Koleen, Koleena, Kolena, Kolene, Koli, Kolleen, Kollena, Kollene, Kolyn, Kolyna

KONA (Hawaiian) lady. (Hindi) angular. Astrology: born under the sign of Capricorn.
Koni, Konia

KONSTANCE (Latin) an alternate form of Constance.
Konstantina, Konstantine, Konstanza, Konstanze

KORA (Greek) an alternate form of Cora.
Korah, Kore, Koren, Koressa, Koretta, Korra

KORAL (American) a form of Coral.
Korel, Korele, Korella, Korilla, Korral, Korrel, Korrell, Korrelle

KORI (American) a short form of Korina. See also Corey, Cori.
Koree, Korey, Koria, Korie, Korri, Korrie, Korry, Kory

KORINA (Greek) an alternate form of Corina.
Koreena, Korena, Koriana, Korianna, Korine, Korinna, Korreena, Korrina, Korrinna, Koryna, Korynna

KORINE (Greek) an alternate form of Korina.
Koreen, Korene, Koriane, Korianne, Korin, Korinn, Korinne, Korrin, Korrine, Korrinne, Korryn, Korrynne, Koryn, Koryne, Korynn

KORNELIA (Latin) an alternate form of Cornelia.
Karniela, Karniella, Karnis, Kornelija, Kornelis, Kornelya, Korny

KORTNEY (English) an alternate form of Courtney.
Kortnay, Kortnee, Kortni, Kortnie, Kortny

KOSMA (Greek) order; universe.
Cosma

KOSTA (Latin) a short form of Constance.
Kostia, Kostusha, Kostya

KOTO (Japanese) harp.

KOURTNEY (American) a form of Courtney.
Kourtnay, Kourtne, Kourtnee, Kourtnei, Kourtneigh, Kourtni, Kourtny, Kourtynie

KRIS (American) a short form of Kristine. An alternate form of Chris.
Khris, Krissy

KRISSY (American) a familiar form of Kris.
Krissey, Krissi, Krissie

KRISTA (Czech) a form of Christina. See also Christa.
Khrissa, Khrista, Khryssa, Khrysta, Krissa, Kryssa, Krysta

KRISTAL (Latin) an alternate form of Crystal.
Kristale, Kristall, Kristill, Kristl, Kristle, Kristy

KRISTAN (Greek) an alternate form of Kristen.
Kristana, Kristanna, Kristanne, Kriston, Krystan, Krystane

KRISTEN (Greek) Christian; annointed. (Scandinavian) a form of Christine.
Christen, Kristan, Kristene, Kristien, Kristin, Kristyn, Krysten

KRISTI, Kristie (Scandinavian) short forms of Kristine.
Christi

KRISTIAN, Kristiana (Greek) Christian; anointed. Alternate forms of Christian.
Khristian, Kristian, Kristiane, Kristiann, Kristi-Ann, Kristianna, Kristianne, Kristi-Anne, Kristienne, Kristyan, Kristyana, Kristy-Ann, Kristy-Anne

KRISTIN (Scandinavian) an alternate form of Kristen. See also Cristen.
Kristiin, Krystin

KRISTINA (Greek) Christian; annointed. (Scandinavian) a form of Christina. See also Cristina.
Khristina, Kristena, Kristina, Kristeena, Kristena, Kristinka, Krystina

KRISTINE (Scandinavian) a form of Christine.
Kris, Kristeen, Kristene, Kristi, Kristie, Kristy, Krystine, Krystyne

KRISTY (American) a familiar form of Kristine, Krystal. See also Cristy.
Kristi, Kristia, Kristie, Krysia, Krysti

KRISTYN (Greek) an alternate form of Kristen.
Kristyne, Kristynn

KRYSTA (Polish) a form of Krista.
Krystah, Krystka

KRYSTAL (American) clear, brilliant glass. A form of Crystal.
Kristabel, Kristal, Krystalann, Krystalanne, Krystale, Krystall, Krystalle, Krystel, Krystil, Krystle, Krystol

KRYSTALEE (American) a combination of Krystal + Lee.
Kristalea, Kristaleah, Kristalee, Krystalea, Krystaleah, Krystlea, Krystleah, Krystlee, Krystlelea, Krystleleah, Krystlelee

KRYSTALYNN (American) a combination of Krystal + Lynn.
Kristaline, Kristalyn, Kristalynn, Kristilyn, Kristilynn, Kristlyn, Krystaleen, Krystalene, Krystalin, Krystalina, Krystallyn, Krystalyn, Krystalynne

KRYSTEL (Latin) an alternate form of Krystal.
Kristel, Kristell, Kristelle, Krystelle

KRYSTEN (Greek) an alternate form of Kristen.
Krystene, Krystyn, Krystyne

KRYSTIAN, Krystiana (Greek) alternate forms of Christian.
Krystiana, Krystianna, Krystianne, Krysty-Ann, Krystyan, Kristyana, Krystyanna, Krystyanne, Krysty-Anne, Krystyen

KRYSTIN (Czech) a form of Kristin.

KRYSTINA (Greek) an alternate form of Kristina.
Krysteena, Krystena, Krystyna, Krystynka

KRYSTLE (American) an alternate form of Krystal.
Krystl, Krystyl

KUDIO (Swahili) born on Monday.

KUMA (Japanese) bear.

KUMIKO (Japanese) girl with braids.
Kumi

KUMUDA (Sanskrit) lotus flower.

KUNIKO (Japanese) child from the country.

KUNTO (Twi) third-born.

KURI (Japanese) chestnut.

KUSA (Hindi) God's grass.

KWANITA (Zuni) a form of Juanita.

KWASHI (Swahili) born on Sunday.

KWAU (Swahili) born on Thursday.

KYANA (American) an alternate form of Kiana.
Kyanah, Kyani, Kyann, Kyanna, Kyanne, Kyanni, Kyeana, Kyeanna

KYARA (Irish) an alternate form of Kiara.
Kiyara, Kiyera, Kiyerra, Kyarah, Kyaria, Kyarie, Kyarra, Kyera, Kyerra

KYLA (Irish) attractive. (Yiddish) crown; laurel.
Khyla, Kylah, Kylea, Kyleah, Kylia

KYLE (Irish) attractive.
Kial, Kiele, Kylee, Kyleigh, Kylene, Kylie

KYLEE (Irish) a familiar form of Kyle.
Kylea, Kyleah, Kylie, Kyliee

KYLEIGH (Irish) an alternate form of Kyle.
Kyliegh

KYLENE (Irish) an alternate form of Kyle.
Kyleen, Kylen, Kylyn, Kylynn

KYLIE (West Australian Aboriginal) curled stick; boomerang. (Irish) a familiar form of Kyle.
Keiley, Keilley, Keilly, Keily, Kiley, Kye, Kylee, Kyley, Kyli, Kyllie

KYMBERLY (English) an alternate form of Kimberly.
Kymber, Kymberlee, Kymberleigh, Kymberley, Kymberli, Kymberlie, Kymberlyn, Kymberlynn, Kymberlynne

KYNDAL, Kyndall (English) alternate forms of Kendall.
Kyndahl, Kyndalle, Kyndel, Kyndell, Kyndelle, Kyndle, Kyndol

KYNTHIA (Greek) an alternate form of Cynthia.
Kyndi

KYOKO (Japanese) mirror.

KYRA (Greek) ladylike. An alternate form of Cyrilla.
Keera, Keira, Kira, Kyrah, Kyrene, Kyria, Kyriah, Kyriann, Kyrie

LACEY, Lacy (Greek) familiar forms of Larissa. (Latin) cheerful.
Lacee, Laci, Lacie, Lacye

LACHANDRA (American) a combination of the prefix La + Chandra.
Lachanda, Lachandice

LACI, Lacie (Latin) alternate forms of Lacey.
Lacia, Laciann, Lacianne

LACRECIA (Latin) an alternate form of Lucretia.
Lacrasha, Lacreash, Lacreasha, Lacreashia, Lacreisha, Lacresha, Lacreshia, Lacresia, Lacretia, Lacricia, Lacriesha, Lacrisah, Lacrisha, Lacrishia, Lacrissa

LADA (Russian) Mythology: the goddess of beauty.

LADASHA (American) a combination of the prefix La + Dasha.
Ladaesha, Ladaisa, Ladaisha, Ladaishea, Ladaishia, Ladashiah, Ladaseha, Ladashia, Ladasia, Ladassa, Ladaysha, Ladesha, Ladisha, Ladosha

LADEIDRA (American) a combinatione of the prefix La + Deidra.
Ladedra, Ladiedra

LADONNA (American) a combination of the prefix La + Donna.
Ladan, Ladana, Ladon, Ladona, Ladonne, Ladonya

LAELA (Arabic, Hebrew) an alternate form of Leila.
Lael, Laelle

LAHELA (Hawaiian) a form of Rachel.

LAILA (Arabic) an alternate form of Leila.
Lailah, Laili, Lailie

LAINE, Layne (French) short forms of Elaine.
Lain, Laina, Lainah, Lainee, Lainna, Layna

LAINEY, Layney (French) familiar forms of Elaine.
Laini, Lainie, Laynee, Layni, Laynie

LAJILA (Hindi) shy, coy.

LAJUANA (American) a combination of the prefix La + Juana.
Lajuanna, Lawana, Lawanna, Lawanza, Lawanze, Laweania

LAKA (Hawaiian) attractive; seductive; tame. Mythology: the goddess of the hula dance.

LAKAYLA (American) a combination of the prefix La + Kayla.
Lakala, Lakaya, Lakeila, Lakela, Lakella

LAKEISHA (American) a combination of the prefix La + Keisha. See also Lekasha.
Lakaiesha, Lakaisha, Lakasha, Lakashia, Lakaysha, Lakaysia,

Lakeasha, Lakecia, Lakeesh, Lakeesha, Lakeeshia, Lakesha, Lakeshia, Lakeysha, Lakezia, Lakicia, Lakieshia, Lakisha

LAKEN, Lakin, Lakyn (American) short forms of Lakendra.
Lakena, Lakyna, Lakynn

LAKENDRA (American) a combination of the prefix La + Kendra.
Lakanda, Lakedra, Laken, Lakenda

LAKENYA (American) a combination of the prefix La + Kenya.
Lakeena, Lakeenna, Lakeenya, Lakena, Lakenia, Lakinja, Lakinya, Lakwanya, Lekenia, Lekenya

LAKESHA, Lakeshia, Lakisha (American) alternate forms of Lakeisha.
Lakecia, Lakeesha, Lakesa, Lakese, Lakeseia, Lakeshya, Lakesi, Lakesia, Lakeyshia, Lakiesha

LAKETA (American) a combination of the prefix La + Keita.
Lakeeta, Lakeetah, Lakeita, Lakeitha, Lakeithia, Laketha, Laketia, Laketta, Lakieta, Lakietha, Lakita, Lakitia, Lakitra, Lakitri, Lakitta

LAKIA (Arabic) found treasure.
Lakiea, Lakkia

LAKOTA (Dakota) a tribal name.
Lakoda, Lakohta, Lakotah

LAKRESHA (American) a form of Lucretia.
Lacresha, Lacreshia, Lacresia, Lacretia, Lacrisha, Lakreshia, Lakrisha, Lekresha, Lekresia

LAKYA (Hindi) born on Thursday.
Lakeya, Lakeyah, Lakieya, Lakiya, Lakyia

LALA (Slavic) tulip.
Lalah, Lalla

LALASA (Hindi) love.

LALEH (Persian) tulip.
Lalah

LALI (Spanish) a form of Lulani.
Lalia, Lalli, Lally

LALITA (Greek) talkative. (Sanskrit) charming; candid. Religion: a name for the Hindu goddess Shakti.

LALLIE (English) babbler.
Lalli, Lally

LAMESHA (American) a combination of the prefix La + Mesha.
Lamees, Lameesha, Lameise, Lameisha, Lameshia, Lamisha, Lamishia, Lemisha

LAMIA (German) bright land. A feminine form of Lambert.
Lama, Lamiah

LAMIS (Arabic) soft to the touch.
Lamese, Lamise

LAMONICA (American) a combination of the prefix La + Monica.
Lamoni, Lamonika

LAMYA (Arabic) dark lipped.
Lama

LAN (Vietnamese) flower.

LANA (Latin) woolly. (Irish) attractive, peaceful. A short form of Alana, Elana. (Hawaiian) floating; bouyant.
Lanae, Lanai, Lanata, Lanay, Laneah, Laneetra, Lanette, Lanna, Lannah

LANDA (Basque) another name for the Virgin Mary.

LANDON (English) open, grassy meadow.
Landan, Landen, Landin, Landyn, Landynne

LANDRA (German, Spanish) counselor.
Landrea

LANE (English) narrow road.
Laina, Laney, Layne

LANEISHA (American) a combination of the prefix La + Keneisha.
Laneasha, Lanecia, Laneesha, Laneise, Laneishia, Lanesha, Laneshe, Laneshea, Laneshia, Lanesia, Lanessa, Lanesse, Lanisha, Lanishia

LANEY (English) a familiar form of Lane.
Lanie, Lanni, Lanny, Lany

LANI (Hawaiian) sky; heaven. A short form of Atalanta, 'Aulani, Leilani.
Lanee, Lanei, Lania, Lanie, Lanita, Lanney, Lanni, Lannie

LAPORSHA (American) a combination of the prefix La + Porsha.
Laporcha, Laporche, Laporscha, Laporsche, Laporschia, Laporshe, Laporshia, Laportia

LAQUEENA (American) a combination of the prefix La + Queenie.
Laqueen, Laquena, Laquenetta, Laquinna

LAQUINTA (American) a combination of the prefix La + Quintana.
Laquanta, Laqueinta, Laquenda, Laquenta, Laquinda

LAQUISHA (American) a combination of the prefix La + Queisha.
Laquasha, Laquaysha, Laqueisha, Laquesha, Laquiesha

LAQUITA (American) a combination of the prefix La + Queta.
Laqeita, Laqueta, Laquetta, Laquia, Laquiata, Laquieta, Laquitta, Lequita

LARA (Greek) cheerful. (Latin) shining; famous. Mythology: the daughter of the river god Almo. A short form of Laraine, Larissa, Laura.
Larae, Larah, Laretta, Larette

LARAINE (Latin) an alternate form of Lorraine.
Lara, Laraene, Larain, Larane, Larayn, Larayne, Laraynna, Larein, Lareina, Lareine, Laren, Larenn, Larenya, Lauraine, Laurraine

LARINA (Greek) seagull.
Larena, Larine

LARISA (Greek) an alternate form of Larissa.
Lareesa, Lareese, Laresa, Laris, Larise, Larisha, Larrisa, Larysa, Laurisa

LARISSA (Greek) cheerful. See also Lacey.
Lara, Laressa, Larisa, Larissah, Larrissa, Larryssa, Laryssa, Laurissa, Laurissah

LARK (English) skylark.

LASHAE, Lashay (American) combinations of the prefix La + Shay.
Lasha, Lashai, Lashaia, Lashaya, Lashaye, Lashea

LASHANA (American) a combination of the prefix La + Shana.
Lashanay, Lashane, Lashanna, Lashannon, Lashona, Lashonna

LASHANDA (American) a combination of the prefix La + Shanda.
Lashandra, Lashanta, Lashante

LASHAWNA (American) a combination of the prefix La + Shawna.
Lashaun, Lashauna, Lashaune, Lashaunna, Lashaunta, Lashawn, Lashawnd, Lashawnda, Lashawndra, Lashawne, Lashawnia, Leshawn, Leshawna

LASHONDA (American) a combination of the prefix La + Shonda.
Lachonda, Lashaunda, Lashaundra, Lashon, Lashond, Lashonde, Lashondia, Lashondra, Lashonta, Lashunda, Lashundra, Lashunta, Lashunte, Leshande, Leshandra, Leshondra, Leshundra

LATANYA (American) a combination of the prefix La + Tanya.
Latana, Latandra, Latania, Latanja, Latanna, Latanua, Latonshia

LATARA (American) a combination of the prefix La + Tara.

LATASHA (American) a combination of the prefix La + Tasha.
Latacha, Latacia, Latai, Lataisha, Latashia, Latasia, Lataysha, Letasha, Letashia, Letasiah

LATAVIA (American) a combination of the prefix La + Tavia.

LATEEFAH (Arabic) pleasant. (Hebrew) pat, caress.
Lateefa, Latifa, Latifah, Latipha

LATESHA (American) a form of Letitia.
Lataeasha, Lateasha, Lateashia, Latecia, Lateicia, Lateisha, Latesa, Lateshia, Latessa, Lateysha, Latisa, Latissa, Leteisha, Leteshia

LATIA (American) a combination of the prefix La + Tia.
Latea, Lateia, Lateka

LATIKA (Hindi) elegant.
Lateeka, Lateka

LATISHA (Latin) joy. An alternate form of Leticia. (American) a combination of the prefix La + Tisha.
Laetitia, Laetizia, Latashia, Lateasha, Lateashia, Latecia, Lateesha, Lateicia, Lateisha, Latice, Laticia, Latiesha, Latishia, Latishya, Latissha, Latitia, Latysha

LATONA (Latin) Mythology: the powerful goddess who bore Apollo and Diana.
Latonna, Latonnah

LATONYA (Latin) an alternate form of Latona. (American) a combination of the prefix La + Tonya.
Latoni, Latonia

LATORIA (American) a combination of the prefix La + Tori.

Latoira, Latorio, Latorja, Latorray, Latorreia, Latory, Latorya, Latoyra, Latoyria

LATOSHA (American) a combination of the prefix La + Tosha.
Latoshia, Latoshya, Latosia

LATOYA (American) a combination of the prefix La + Toya.
Latoia, Latoiya, LaToya, Latoyia, Latoye, Latoyia, Latoyita, Latoyo

LATRICE (American) a combination of the prefix La + Trice.
Latrece, Latreece, Latreese, Latresa, Latrese, Latressa, Letreece, Letrice

LATRICIA (American) a combination of the prefix La + Tricia.
Latrecia, Latresh, Latresha, Latreshia, Latrica, Latrisha, Latrishia

LAURA (Latin) crowned with laurel. A feminine form of Laurence.
Lara, Laurah, Lauralee, Laurelen, Laurella, Lauren, Lauricia, Laurie, Laurka, Laury, Lauryn, Lavra, Lolly, Lora, Loretta, Lori, Lorinda, Lorna, Loura

LAUREL (Latin) laurel tree.
Laural, Laurell, Laurelle, Lorel, Lorelle

LAUREN (English) a form of Laura.
Lauran, Laureen, Laurena, Laurene, Laurien, Laurin, Laurine, Lawren, Loren, Lorena

LAURENCE (Latin) crowned with laurel.
Laurencia, Laurens, Laurent, Laurentana, Laurentina, Lawrencia

LAURIANNA (English) a combination of Laurie + Anne.
Laurana, Laurann, Laureana, Laureanne, Laureen, Laureena, Laurian, Lauriana, Lauriane, Laurianna, Laurie Ann, Laurie Anne, Laurina

LAURIE (English) a familiar form of Laura.
Lari, Larilia, Laure, Lauré, Lauri, Lawrie

LAURY (English) a familiar form of Laura.

LAURYN (English) a familiar form of Laura.
Laurynn

LAVEDA (Latin) cleansed, purified.
Lavare, Lavetta, Lavette

LAVELLE (Latin) cleansing.
Lavella

LAVENA (Latin) an alternate form of Lavina. (Irish, French) joy.

LAVERNE (Latin) springtime. (French) grove of alder trees. See also Verna.
Laverine, Lavern, Laverna, La Verne

LAVINA (Latin) purified; woman of Rome. See also Vina.
Lavena, Lavenia, Lavinia, Lavinie, Levenia, Levinia, Livinia, Louvinia, Lovina, Lovinia

LAVONNA (American) a combination of the prefix La + Yvonne.
Lavon, Lavonda, Lavonder, Lavondria, Lavone, Lavonia, Lavonica, Lavonn, Lavonne, Lavonnie, Lavonya

LAWAN (Tai) pretty.
Lawanne

LAWANDA (American) a combination of the prefix La + Wanda.
Lawonda, Lawynda

LAYCE (American) a form of Lacey.
Laycee, Layci, Laycia, Laycie, Laysa, Laysea, Laysie

LAYLA (Hebrew, Arabic) an alternate form of Leila.
Laylah, Layli, Laylie

LE (Vietnamese) pearl.

LEA (Hawaiian) Mythology: the goddess of canoe makers.

LEAH (Hebrew) weary. Bible: the wife of Jacob. See also Lia.
Lea, Léa, Lee, Leea, Leeah, Leia

LEALA (French) faithful, loyal.
Lealia, Lealie, Leial

LEAN, Leann, Leanne (English) forms of Leeann, Lian.
Leana, Leane, Leanna

LEANDRA (Latin) like a lioness.
Leanda, Leandre, Leandrea, Leandria, Leeanda, Leeandra

LEANNA, Leeanna (English) alternate forms of Liana.
Leana, Leeana, Leianna

LEANORE (Greek) an alternate form of Eleanor. (English) a form of Helen.
Leanora, Lanore

LECIA (Latin) a short form of Felecia.
Leasia, Leecia, Leesha, Leesia, Lesha, Leshia, Lesia

LEDA (Greek) lady. Mythology: the Queen of Sparta and the mother of Helen of Troy.
Ledah, Lyda, Lydah

LEE (Chinese) plum. (Irish) poetic. (English) meadow. A short form of Ashley, Leah.
Lea, Leigh

LEEANN, Leeanne (English) a combination of Lee + Ann. A form of Lian.
Leane, Leean, Leian, Leiann, Leianne

LEENA (Estonian) a form of Helen.

LEEZA (Hebrew) a short form of Aleeza. (English) an alternate form of Lisa, Liza.
Leesa

LEI (Hawaiian) a familiar form of Leilani.

LEIGH, Leigha (English) alternate forms of Lee.
Leighann, Leighanna, Leighanne

LEIKO (Japanese) arrogant.

LEILA (Hebrew) dark beauty; night. (Arabic) born at night. Literature: the heroine of the epic Persian poem *Leila and Majnum*. See also Laela, Layla, Lila.
Laila, Leela, Leelah, Leilah, Leilia, Lela, Lelah, Leland, Lelia, Leyla

LEILANI (Hawaiian) heavenly flower; heavenly child.
Lailanee, Lailani, Lailanie, Lailany, Lailoni, Lani, Lei, Leilany, Leiloni, Leilony, Lelani, Lelania

LEIRE (Basque) Religion: another name for the Virgin Mary.

LEKASHA (American) an alternate form of Lakeishia.
Lekeesha, Lekeisha, Lekesha, Lekeshia, Lekesia, Lekicia, Lekisha

LELI (Swiss) a form of Magdalen.
Lelie

LELIA (Greek) fair speech.
Leliah, Lelika, Lelita, Lellia

LELYA (Russian) a form of Helen.

LENA (Greek) a short form of Eleanor. (Hebrew) dwelling or lodging. (Latin) temptress. (Norwegian) illustrious. Music: Lena Horne, a well-known African-American singer.
Lenah, Lene, Lenee, Leni, Lenka, Lenna, Lennah, Lina, Linah

LENCI (Hungarian) a form of Helen.
Lency

LENE (German) a form of Helen.
Leni, Line

LENEISHA (American) a combination of the prefix Le + Keneisha.
Lenece, Lenesha, Leniesha, Lenieshia, Leniesia, Leniessia, Lenisa, Lenise, Lenisha, Lennise, Lennisha, Lynesha

LENIA (German) an alternate form of Leona.
Lenayah, Lenda, Lenea, Leneen, Lenna, Lennah, Lennea, Leny

LENITA (Latin) gentle.
Leneta, Lenette, Lennette

LENORE (Greek, Russian) a form of Eleanor.
Lenni, Lenor, Lenora, Lenorah

LEONA (German) brave as a lioness. A feminine form of Leon. See also Lona.
Lenia, Leoine, Leola, Leolah, Leonae, Leonah, Leondra, Leone, Leonelle, Leonia, Leonice, Leonicia, Leonie, Leonissa, Leonna, Leonne, Liona

LEONIE (German) a familiar form of Leona.
Leoni, Léonie, Leony

LEONORE (Greek) an alternate form of Eleanor. See also Nora.
Leonor, Leonora, Leonorah, Léonore

LEONTINE (Latin) like a lioness.
Leona, Leonine, Leontyne, Léontyne

LEORA (Greek) a familiar form of Eleanor. (Hebrew) light. See also Liora.
Leorah, Leorit

LEOTIE (Native American) prairie flower.

LERA (Russian) a short form of Valera.
Lerka

LESLEY (Scottish) gray fortress.
Leslea, Leslee, Leslie, Lesly, Lezlee, Lezley

LESLIE (Scottish) an alternate form of Lesley.
Leslei, Lesleigh, Lesli, Lesslie, Lezli

LESLY (Scottish) an alternate form of Lesley.
Leslye, Lessly, Lezly

LETA (Greek) a short form of Aleta. (Latin) glad. (Swahili) bringer.
Lita, Lyta

LETICIA (Latin) joy. See also Latisha, Tisha.
Laticia, Leisha, Leshia, Let, Leta, Letesa, Letesha, Leteshia, Letha, Lethia, Letice, Letichia, Letisha, Letishia, Letisia, Letissa, Letita, Letitia, Letiticia, Letiza, Letizia, Letty, Letycia, Loutitia

LETTY (English) a familiar form of Leticia.
Letta, Letti, Lettie

LEVANA (Hebrew) moon; white. (Latin) risen. Mythology: the goddess of newborn babies.
Lévana, Levania, Levanna, Levenia, Lewana, Livana

LEVANI (Fijian) anointed with oil.

LEVIA (Hebrew) joined, attached.
Leevya, Levi, Levie

LEVINA (Latin) flash of lightning.
Levene

LEVONA (Hebrew) spice, incense.
Leavonia, Levonat, Levonna, Levonne, Livona

LEWANA (Hebrew) an alternate form of Levana.
Lebhanah, Lewanna

LEXANDRA (Greek) a short form of Alexandra.
Lisandra

LEXI, Lexie (Greek) familiar forms of Alexandra.
Leksi, Lexey, Lexy

LEXIA (Greek) a familiar form of Alexandra.
Leska, Lesya, Lexa, Lexane, Lexina, Lexine

LEXIS (Greek) a short form of Alexius, Alexus.
Laexis, Lexius, Lexsis, Lexxis

LEXUS (Greek) a short form of Alexis.
Lexuss, Lexxus, Lexyss

LEYA (Spanish) loyal. (Tamil) the constellation Leo.
Leyah, Leyla

LIA (Greek) bringer of good news. (Hebrew, Dutch, Italian) dependent. See also Leah.
Liah

LIAN (Chinese) graceful willow. (Latin) a short form of Gillian, Lillian.
Lean, Leeann, Liane, Liann, Lianne

LIANA, Lianna (Hebrew) short forms of Eliana. (Latin) youth. (French) bound, wrapped up; tree covered with vines. (English) meadow.
Leanna

LIANE, Lianne (Hebrew) short forms of Eliane. (English) forms of Lian.
Leeanne

LIBBY (Hebrew) a familiar form of Elizabeth.
Ibby, Lib, Libbee, Libbey, Libbie

LIBERTY (Latin) free.
Liberti, Libertie

LICIA (Greek) a short form of Alicia.
Licha, Lishia, Lisia, Lycia

LIDA (Greek) happy. (Latin) a short form of Alida, Elita. (Slavic) loved by people.
Leeda, Lidah, Lidochka, Lyda

LIDE (Latin, Basque) life.

LIDIA (Greek) an alternate form of Lydia.

Lidea, Lidi, Lidija, Lidiya, Lidka, Lidya

LIEN (Chinese) lotus.
Lienne

LIESABET (German) a short form of Elizabeth.
Liesbeth, Lisbete

LIESE (German) a familiar form of Elise, Elizabeth.
Liesa, Lieschen, Lise

LIESEL (German) a familiar form of Elizabeth.
Leesel, Leesl, Leezel, Leezl, Liesl, Liezel, Liezl, Lisel

LILA (Arabic) night. (Hindi) free will of god. (Persian) lilac. A short form of Dalila, Delilah, Lillian.
Lilah, Lilia, Lyla, Lylah

LILAC (Sanskrit) lilac; blue-purple.

LILIA (Persian) an alternate form of Lila.
Lili

LILIAN (Latin) an alternate form of Lillian.
Liliane, Liliann, Lilianne

LILIANA (Latin) an alternate form of Lillian.
Lileana, Lilliana, Lilianna, Lilliana, Lillianna

LILIBETH (English) a combination of Lilly + Beth.
Lilibet, Lillibeth, Lillybeth, Lilybet, Lilybeth

LILITH (Arabic) of the night; night demon. Mythology: the first wife of Adam, according to ancient eastern legends.
Lillis, Lily

LILLIAN (Latin) lily flower.
Lian, Lil, Lila, Lilas, Lileane, Lilia, Lilian, Liliana, Lilias, Liliha, Lilja, Lilla, Lilli, Lillia, Lilliane, Lilliann, Lillianne, Lillyann, Lis, Liuka

LILLYANN (Latin) an alternate form of Lilian. (English) a combination of Lilly + Ann.
Lillyan, Lillyanne, Lily, Lilyan, Lilyana, Lilyann, Lilyanna, Lilyanne

LILY (Latin, Arabic) a familiar form of Lilith, Lillian, Lillyann.
Lil, Lîle, Lili, Lilie, Lilijana, Lilika, Lilike, Liliosa, Lilium, Lilka, Lille, Lilli, Lillie, Lilly

LIMBER (Tiv) joyful.

LIN (Chinese) beautiful jade. (English) a short form of Lynn.
Linh, Linn

LINA (Greek) light. (Latin) an alternate form of Lena. (Arabic) tender.

LINDA (Spanish) pretty.
Lind, Lindy, Linita, Lynda

LINDSAY (English) an alternate form of Lindsey.
Lindsi, Linsay, Lyndsay

LINDSEY (English) linden tree island; camp near the stream.
Lind, Lindsea, Lindsee, Lindsi, Linsey, Lyndsey, Lynsey

LINDSI (American) a familiar form of Lindsay, Lindsey.
Lindsie, Lindsy, Lindze, Lindzee, Lindzey, Lindzy

LINDY (Spanish) a familiar form of Linda.
Linde, Lindee, Lindey, Lindi, Lindie

LINETTE (Welsh) idol. (French) bird.
Lanette, Linet, Linnet, Linnetta, Linnette, Lyannette, Lynette

LING (Chinese) delicate, dainty.

LINNEA (Scandinavian) lime tree. History: the national flower of Sweden.
Lin, Linae, Linea, Linnae, Linnaea, Linneah, Lynea, Lynnea

LINSEY (English) an alternate form of Lindsey.
Linsea, Linsee, Linsi, Linsie, Linsy, Linzee, Linzey, Linzi, Linzie, Linzy, Linzzi, Lynsey

LIOLYA (Russian) a form of Helen.

LIORA (Hebrew) light. See also Leora.

LIRIT (Hebrew) poetic; lyrical, musical.

LIRON (Hebrew) my song.
Leron, Lerone, Lirone

LISA (Hebrew) consecrated to God. (English) a short form of Elizabeth.
Leeza, Liesa, Liisa, Lise, Lisenka, Lisette, Liszka, Litsa, Lysa

LISBETH (English) a short form of Elizabeth.
Lisbet

LISE (German) a form of Lisa.

LISETTE, Lissette (French) forms of Lisa. (English) familiar forms of Elise, Elizabeth.
Liset, Liseta, Lisete, Liseth, Lisett, Lisetta, Lisettina, Lisset, Lissete, Lissett, Lizet, Lizette, Lysette

LISHA (Hebrew) a short form of Alisha, Elisha, Ilisha. (Arabic) darkness before midnight.
Lishe

LISSA (Greek) honey bee. A short form of Elissa, Elizabeth, Melissa, Millicent.
Lyssa

LISSIE (American) a familiar form of Allison, Elise, Elizabeth.
Lissee, Lissey, Lissi, Lissy, Lissye

LITA (Latin) a familiar form of names ending in "lita."
Leta, Litah, Litta

LITONYA (Moquelumnan) darting hummingbird.

LIV (Latin) a short form of Livia, Olivia.

LIVANA (Hebrew) an alternate form of Levana. Astrological: born under the sign of Cancer.
Livna, Livnat

LIVIA (Hebrew) crown. A familiar form of Olivia. (Latin) olive.
Levia, Liv, Livie, Livy, Livya, Livye

LIVIYA (Hebrew) brave lioness; royal crown.
Leviya, Levya, Livya

LIVONA (Hebrew) an alternate form of Levona.

LIZ (English) a short form of Elizabeth.

LIZA (American) a short form of Elizabeth.
Leeza, Lizela, Lizka, Lyza

LIZABETA (Russian) a form of Elizabeth.
Lizabetah, Lizaveta, Lizonka

LIZABETH (English) a short form of Elizabeth.
Lisabet, Lisabeth, Lisabette, Lizabette

LIZBETH (English) a short form of Elizabeth.
Lizbet, Lizbett

LIZET, Lizette (French) alternate forms of Lisette.
Lizet, Lizete, Lizeth, Lizett, Lizzet, Lizzeth, Lizzette

LIZINA (Latvian) a familiar form of Elizabeth.

LIZZY (American) a familiar form of Elizabeth.
Lizzie, Lizy

LOGAN (Irish) meadow.
Logann, Loganne, Logen, Loghan, Logun, Logyn, Logynn

LOIS (German) famous warrior. An alternate form of Louise.

LOLA (Spanish) a familiar form of Carlota, Dolores, Louise.
Lolah, Lolita

LOLITA (Spanish) sorrowful. A familiar form of Lola.
Lita, Lulita

LOLLY (English) a familiar form of Laura.

LOLOTEA (Zuni) a form of Dorothy.

LOMASI (Native American) pretty flower.

LONA (Latin) lioness. (German) a short form of Leona. (English) solitary.
Loni, Lonna

LONDON (English) fortress of the moon. Geography: the capital of Great Britain.
Landyn, Londen, Londun, Londyn

LONI (American) a form of Lona.
Lonee, Lonie, Lonni, Lonnie

LORA (Latin) crowned with laurel. (American) a form of Laura.
Lorah, Lorane, Lorann, Lorra, Lorrah, Lorrane

LORE (Latin) a short form of Flora. (Basque) flower.
Lor

LORELEI (German) alluring. Mythology: the siren of the Rhine River who lured sailors to their deaths. See also Lurleen.
Loralee, Loralei, Lorali, Loralie, Loralyn, Loreal, Lorelea, Loreli, Lorilee, Lorilyn

LORELLE (American) a form of Laurel.

LOREN (American) an alternate form of Lauren.
Loreen, Lorena, Lorin, Lorne, Lorren, Lorrin, Lorryn, Loryn, Lorynn, Lorynne

LORENA (English) an alternate form of Lauren, Loren.
Lorene, Lorenea, Lorenia, Lorenna, Lorina, Lorrina, Lorrine, Lurana

LORENZA (Latin) an alternate form of Laura.
Laurencia, Laurentia, Laurentina

LORETTA (English) a familiar form of Laura.
Larretta, Lauretta, Laurette, Loretah, Lorette, Lorita, Lorretta, Lorrette

LORI (Latin) crowned with laurel. (French) a short form of Lorraine. (American) a familiar form of Laura.
Loree, Lorey, Loria, Lorianna, Lorianne, Lorie, Lorree, Lorri, Lorrie, Lory

LORIN (American) an alternate form of Loren.
Lorine

LORINDA (Spanish) a form of Laura.

LORIS (Greek) a short form of Chloris. (Latin) thong. (Dutch) clown.
Laurice, Laurys, Lorice

LORNA (Latin) crowned with laurel. An alternate form of Laura. Literature: probably coined by Richard Blackmore in his novel *Lorna Doone*.
Lorrna

LORRAINE (Latin) sorrowful. (French) from Lorraine. See also Rayna.
Laraine, Lorain, Loraine, Lorayne, Lorein, Loreine, Lori, Lorine, Lorrain, Lorraina, Lorrayne, Lorreine

LOTTE (German) a short form of Charlotte.
Lotie, Lotta, Lottchen, Lottey, Lottie, Lotty, Loty

LOTUS (Greek) lotus.

LOU (American) a short form of Louise, Luella.
Lu

LOUAM (Ethiopian) sleep well.

LOUISA (English) a familiar form of Louise. Literature: Louisa May Alcott was an American writer and reformer best known for her novel *Little Women*.

Louisa *(cont.)*
Aloisa, Eloisa, Heloisa, Lou, Louisian, Louisane, Louisina, Louiza, Lovisa, Luisa, Luiza, Lujza, Lujzika

LOUISE (German) famous warrior. A feminine form of Louis. See also Alison, Eloise, Heloise, Lois, Lola, Ludovica, Luella, Lulu.
Loise, Lou, Louisa, Louisette, Louisiane, Louisine, Lowise, Loyce, Loyise, Luise

LOURDES (French) from Lourdes, France. Geography: a town in France. Religion: a place where the Virgin Mary was said to have appeared.

LOVE (English) love; kindness; charity.
Lovely, Lovewell, Lovey, Lovie, Lovy, Luv, Luvvy

LOVISA (German) an alternate form of Louisa.

LUANN (Hebrew, German) graceful woman warrior. (Hawaiian) happy; relaxed. (American) a combination of Louise + Anne.
Louann, Louanne, Lu, Lua, Luan, Luane, Luanna, Luanne, Luanni, Luannie

LUANNA (German) an alternate form of Luann.
Lewanna, Louanna, Luana, Luwana

LUBOV (Russian) love.
Luba, Lubna, Lubochka, Lyuba, Lyubov

LUCERNE (Latin) lamp; circle of light. Geography: a lake in Switzerland.
Lucerna, Lucero

LUCERO (Latin) an alternate form of Lucerne.

LUCETTA (English) a familiar form of Lucy.
Lucette

LUCIA (Italian, Spanish) a form of Lucy.
Luciana, Lucianna

LUCIE (French) a familiar form of Lucy.

LUCILLE (English) a familiar form of Lucy.
Lucila, Lucile, Lucilla

LUCINDA (Latin) a familiar form of Lucy. See also Cindy.

LUCINE (Basque) a form of Lucy. (Arabic) moon.
Lucienne, Lucina, Lucyna, Lukene, Lusine, Luzine

LUCITA (Spanish) a form of Lucy.
Lusita

LUCRETIA (Latin) rich; rewarded.
Lacrecia, Lucrece, Lucréce, Lucrecia, Lucreecia, Lucresha, Lucreshia, Lucrezia, Lucrisha, Lucrishia

LUCREZIA (Italian) a form of Lucretia. History: Lucrezia Borgia was the Duchess of Ferrara and a patron of learning and the arts.

LUCY (Latin) light; bringer of light. A feminine form of Lucius.
Luca, Luce, Lucetta, Luci, Lucia, Lucida, Lucie, Lucija, Lucika, Lucille, Lucinda, Lucine, Lucita, Luciya, Lucya, Luzca, Luzi

LUDMILLA (Slavic) loved by the people. See also Mila.
Ludie, Ludka, Ludmila, Lyuba, Lyudmila

LUDOVICA (German) an alternate form of Louise.
Ludovika, Ludwiga

LUELLA (German) a familiar form of Louise. (English) elf.
Loella, Lou, Louella, Ludella, Luelle, Lula, Lulu

LUISA (Spanish) a form of Louisa.

LULANI (Polynesian) highest point of heaven.

LULU (Arabic) pearl. (German) a familiar form of Louise, Luella. (English) soothing, comforting. (Native American) hare.
Loulou, Lula, Lulie

LUNA (Latin) moon.
Lunetta, Lunette, Lunneta, Lunnete

LUPE (Latin) wolf. (Spanish) a short form of Guadalupe.
Lupi, Lupita, Luppi

LUPITA (Latin) an alternate form of Lupe.

LURLEEN, Lurlene (German) alternate forms of Lorelei. (Scandinavian) war horn.
Lura, Lurette, Lurline

LUSA (Finnish) a form of Elizabeth.

LUSELA (Moquelumnan) like a bear swinging its foot when licking it.

LUVENA (Latin, English) little; beloved.
Lovena, Lovina, Luvenia, Luvina

LUYU (Moquelumnan) like a pecking bird.

LUZ (Spanish) light. Religion: Santa Maria de Luz is another name for the Virgin Mary.
Luzi, Luzija

LYCORIS (Greek) twilight.

LYDA (Greek) a short form of Lidia, Lydia.

LYDIA (Greek) from Lydia, an ancient land once ruled by Midas. (Arabic) strife.
Lidia, Lidija, Lidiya, Lyda, Lydie, Lydië

LYLA (French) island. (English) a feminine form of Lyle.
Lila, Lilah

LYNDA (Spanish) pretty. (American) a form of Linda.
Lyndah, Lynde, Lyndi, Lynnda

LYNDELL (English) an alternate form of Lynelle.
Lyndall, Lyndel, Lyndella

LYNDI (Spanish) a familiar form of Lynda.
Lyndee, Lindie, Lyndy, Lynndie, Lynndy

LYNDSAY (American) a form of Lindsay.
Lyndsaye

LYNDSEY (English) linden tree island; camp near the stream. (American) a form of Lindsey.
Lyndsea, Lyndsee, Lyndsi, Lyndsie, Lyndsy, Lyndzee, Lyndzey, Lyndzi, Lyndzie, Lynndsie

LYNELLE (English) pretty.
Linel, Linell, Linnell, Lyndell, Lynel, Lynell, Lynella, Lynnell

LYNETTE (Welsh) idol. (English) a form of Linette.
Lynett, Lynetta, Lynnet, Lynnette

LYNN, Lynne (English) waterfall; pool below a waterfall.
Lin, Lina, Linley, Linn, Lyn, Lynlee, Lynley, Lynna, Lynnae, Lynnea

LYNNELL (English) an alternate form of Lynelle.
Linnell, Lynnelle

LYNSEY (American) an alternate form of Lyndsey.
Lynnsey, Lynnzey, Lynsie, Lynsy, Lynzee, Lynzey, Lynzi, Lynzie, Lynzy

LYRA (Greek) lyre player.
Lyre, Lyric, Lyrica, Lyrie, Lyris

LYSANDRA (Greek) liberator. A feminine form of Lysander.
Lisandra, Lysandre, Lytle

LYSANNE (American) a combination of Lysandra + Anne.
Lisanne, Lizanne

MAB (Irish) joyous. (Welsh) baby. Literature: the name of the Fairy Queen in Edmund Spenser's epic romance *The Faerie Queene.*
Mabry

MABEL (Latin) lovable. A short form of Amabel.
Mabelle, Mable, Mabyn, Maible, Maybel, Maybeline, Maybelle, Maybull

MACAWI (Dakota) generous; motherly.

MACAYLA (American) an alternate form of Makayla.
Macaela, Macaila, Macala, Macalah, Macaylah, Macayle, Macayli, Mackayla

MACEY, Macie, Macy (Polish) familiar forms of Macia.
Macee, Maci, Macye

MACHAELA (Hebrew) an alternate form of Mickaela.
Machael, Machaelah, Machaelie, Machaila, Machala, Macheala

MACHIKO (Japanese) fortunate child.
Machi

MACIA (Polish) a form of Miriam.
Macelia, Macey, Machia, Macie, Macy, Masha, Mashia

MACKENNA (American) a form of Mackenzie.
Mackena, Makenna, Mckenna

MACKENZIE (Irish) daughter of the wise leader. See also Kenzie.
Macenzie, Mackenna, Mackensi, Mackensie, Mackenze, Mackenzee, Mackenzey, Mackenzi, Mackenzia, Mackenzy, Mackenzye, Mackinsey, Mackynze, Makenzie, McKenzie, Mckinzie, Mekenzie, Mykenzie

MACKINSEY (Irish) an alternate form of Mackenzie.

Mackinsey *(cont.)*
Mackinsie, Mackinze, Mackinzee, Mackinzey, Mackinzi, Mackinzie

MADA (English) a short form of Madaline, Magdalen.
Madda, Mahda

MADALINE (English) an alternate form of Madeline.
Mada, Madailéin, Madaleen, Madaleine, Madalene, Madalin, Madaline

MADALYN (Greek) an alternate form of Madeline.
Madalyne, Madalynn, Madalynne

MADDIE (English) a familiar form of Madeline.
Maddi, Maddy, Mady, Maidie, Maydey

MADDISON (English) an alternate form of Madison.
Maddisan, Maddisen, Maddisson, Maddisyn, Maddyson

MADELAINE (French) a form of Madeline.
Madelane, Madelayne

MADELEINE (French) a form of Madeline.
Madalaine, Madalayne, Madelaine, Madelein, Madeliene

MADELENA (English) an alternate form of Madeline.
Madalaina, Madalena, Madalina, Maddalena, Madelaina, Madeleina, Madelina, Madelyna

MADELINE (Greek) high tower. (English) from Magdala, England. An alternate form of Magdalen. See also Lena, Lina, Maud.

Madaline, Madalyn, Maddie, Madel, Madelaine, Madeleine, Madelena, Madelene, Madelia, Madella, Madelle, Madelon, Madelyn, Madge, Madilyn, Madlen, Madlin, Madline, Madlyn, Madolyn, Maida

MADELYN (Greek) an alternate form of Madeline.
Madelyne, Madelynn, Madelynne, Madilyn, Madlyn, Madolyn

MADGE (Greek) a familiar form of Madeline, Margaret.
Madgi, Madgie, Mady

MADILYN (Greek) an alternate form of Madeline.
Madilen, Madiline, Madilyne, Madilynn

MADISEN (English) an alternate form of Madison.
Madisan, Madisin, Madissen, Madisun

MADISON (English) good; daughter of Maud.
Maddison, Madisen, Madisson, Madisyn, Madyson, Mattison

MADISYN (English) an alternate form of Madison.
Madissyn, Madisynn, Madisynne

MADOLYN (Greek) an alternate form of Madeline.
Madoline, Madolyne, Madolynn, Madolynne

MADONNA (Latin) my lady.
Madona

MADRONA (Spanish) mother.
Madre, Madrena

MADYSON (English) an alternate form of Madison.
Madysen, Madysun

MAE (English) an alternate form of May. History: Mae

Jemison was the first African-American woman in space.
Maelea, Maeleah, Maelen, Maelle, Maeona

MAEGAN (Irish) an alternate form of Megan.
Maegen, Maeghan, Maegin

MAEKO (Japanese) honest child.
Mae, Maemi

MAEVE (Irish) joyous. History: a first-century queen of Ireland. See also Mavis.
Maevi, Maevy, Maive, Mayve

MAGALI, Magaly (Hebrew) from the high tower.
Magalie, Magally

MAGAN, Magen (Greek) alternate forms of Megan.
Maggen, Maggin

MAGDA (Czech, Polish, Russian) a form of Magdalen.
Mahda, Makda

MAGDALEN (Greek) high tower. Bible: Magdala was the home of Saint Mary Magdalen. See also Madeline, Malena, Marlene.
Mada, Magda, Magdala, Magdaleen, Magdalena, Magdalene, Magdaline, Magdalyn, Magdalynn, Magdelane, Magdelene, Magdeline, Magdelyn, Magdlen, Magdolna, Maggie, Magola, Maighdlin, Mala, Malaine

MAGDALENA (Greek) an alternate form of Magdalen.
Magdalina, Magdelana, Magdelena, Magdelina

MAGENA (Native American) coming moon.

MAGGIE (Greek) pearl.
(English) a familiar form of
Magdalen, Margaret.
Mag, Magge, Maggee, Maggi,
Maggia, Maggie, Maggiemae,
Maggy, Magi, Magie, Mags

MAGGY, Meggy (English) alternate forms of Maggie.
Maggey, Magy

MAGNOLIA (Latin) flowering
tree. See also Nollie.
Nola

MAHAL (Filipino) love.

MAHALA (Arabic) fat, marrow;
tender. (Native American)
powerful woman.
Mahalah, Mahalar, Mahalla,
Mahela, Mahila, Mahlah,
Mahlaha, Mehala, Mehalah

MAHALIA (American) a form of
Mahala.
Mahaley, Mahaliah, Mahalie,
Mahayla, Mahaylah, Mahaylia,
Mahelea, Maheleah, Mahelia,
Mahilia, Mehalia

MAHARENE (Ethiopian) forgive
us.

MAHESA (Hindi) great lord.
Religion: a name for the
Hindu goddess Shiva.
Maheesa, Mahisa

MAHILA (Sanskrit) woman.

MAHINA (Hawaiian) moon glow.

MAHIRA (Hebrew) energetic.
Mahri

MAHOGONY (Spanish) rich;
strong.
Mahagony, Mahoganey,
Mahogani, Mahoganie,
Mahogany, Mahogney, Mahogny,
Mohogany, Mohogony

MAI (Japanese) brightness.
(Vietnamese) flower. (Navajo)
coyote.

MAIA (Greek) mother; nurse.
(English) kinswoman; maid-
en. Mythology: the loveliest
of the Pleiades, the seven
daughters of Atlas, and the
mother of Hermes. See also
Maya.
Maiah, Maie, Maiya

MAIDA (Greek) a short form of
Madeline. (English) maiden.
Maidel, Mayda, Maydena

MAIJA (Finnish) a form of Mary.
Maiji, Maikki

MAIKA (Hebrew) a familiar
form of Michaela.
Maikala, Maikka, Maiko

MAIRA, Maire (Irish) forms of
Mary.
Maairah, Mair, Mairi, Mairim,
Mairin, Mairona, Mairwen

MAISIE (Scottish) a familiar
form of Margaret.
Maisa, Maise, Maisey, Maisi,
Maisy, Maizie, Maycee, Maysie,
Mayzie, Mazey, Mazie, Mazy,
Mazzy, Mysie, Myzie

MAITA (Spanish) a form of
Martha.
Maite, Maitia

MAITLYN (American) a combi-
nation of Maita + Lynn.
Maitlan, Maitland, Maitlynn,
Mattilyn

MAIYA (Greek) an alternate
form of Maia.
Maiyah

MAJA (Arabic) a short form of
Majidah.

Majal, Majalisa, Majalyn,
Majalynn

MAJIDAH (Arabic) splendid.
Maja, Majida

MAKAELA, Makaila (American)
forms of Michaela.
Makaelah, Makaelee, Makaella,
Makaely, Makail, Makailah,
Makailee, Makailla, Makaillah,
Makealah, Makell

MAKALA (Hawaiian) myrtle.
Makalae, Makalah, Makalai,
Makalea, Makalee, Makaleh,
Makaleigh, Makaley, Makalia,
Makalie, Makalya, Makela,
Makelah, Makell, Makella

MAKANA (Hawaiian) gift,
present.

MAKANI (Hawaiian) wind.

MAKARA (Hindi) born during
the lunar month of Capricorn.

MAKAYLA (American) a form of
Michaela.
Macayla, Makaylah, Makaylee,
Makayleigh, Makayli, Makaylia,
Makaylla, Makell, Makyla,
Makylah, Mckayla, Mekayla,
Mikayla

MAKELL (American) a short
form of Makaela, Makala,
Makayla.
Makele, Makelle, Mckell, Mekel

MAKENNA (American) an alternate form of Mackenna.
Makena, Makennah, Mikenna

MAKENZIE (Irish) an alternate
form of Mackenzie.
Makense, Makensey, Makensie,
Makenze, Makenzee, Makenzey,
Makenzi, Makenzy, Makenzye,
Makinzey, Makynzey, Mekenzie,
Mykenzie

MALA (Greek) a short form of Magdalen.
Malana, Malee, Mali

MALANA (Hawaiian) bouyant, light.

MALAYA (Filipino) free.
Malayaa, Malayah, Malayna, Malea, Maleah

MALENA (Swedish) a familiar form of Magdalen.
Malen, Malenna, Malin, Malina, Maline, Malini, Malinna

MALHA (Hebrew) queen.
Maliah, Malkah, Malkia, Malkiah, Malkie, Malkiya, Malkiyah, Miliah

MALI (Tai) jasmine flower. (Hungarian) a short form of Malika.
Malea, Malee, Maley

MALIA (Hawaiian, Zuni) a form of Mary. (Spanish) a form of Maria.
Malea, Maleah, Maleeya, Maleeyah, Maleia, Maliah, Maliasha, Malie, Maliea, Maliya, Maliyah, Malli, Mally

MALIKA (Hungarian) industrious.
Malak, Maleeka, Maleka, Mali, Maliaka, Malik, Malikah, Malikee, Maliki, Malikia, Malky

MALINA (Hebrew) tower. (English) from Magdala, England. (Native American) soothing.
Malin, Maline, Malina, Malinna, Mallie

MALINDA (Greek) an alternate form of Melinda.
Malinde, Malinna, Malynda

MALINI (Hindi) gardener. Religion: the Hindu god of the earth.
Maliny

MALISSA (Greek) an alternate form of Melissa.
Malisa, Malisah, Malyssa

MALLALAI (Pashto) beautiful.

MALLEY (American) a familiar form of Mallory.
Mallee, Malli, Mallie, Mally, Maly

MALLORIE (French) an alternate form of Mallory.
Malerie, Mallari, Mallerie, Malloreigh, Mallori

MALLORY (German) army counselor. (French) unlucky.
Maliri, Mallary, Mallauri, Mallery, Malley, Malloree, Mallorey, Mallorie, Malorie, Malory, Malorym, Malree, Malrie, Mellory

MALORIE, Malory (German) alternate forms of Mallory.
Malarie, Maloree, Malori, Melorie, Melory

MALVA (English) a form of Melba.
Malvi, Malvy

MALVINA (Scottish) a form of Melvina. Literature: a name created by the eighteenth-century romantic poet James MacPherson.
Malvane, Malvi

MAMIE (American) a familiar form of Margaret.
Mame, Mamee, Mami, Mammie, Mamy, Mamye

MAMO (Hawaiian) saffron flower; yellow bird.

MANA (Hawaiian) psychic; sensitive.
Manal, Manali, Manna, Mannah

MANAR (Arabic) guiding light.
Manayra

MANDA (Latin) a short form of Amanda. (Spanish) woman warrior.
Mandy

MANDARA (Hindi) calm. Religion: a Hindu mythical tree that makes worries disappear.

MANDEEP (Punjabi) enlightened.

MANDISA (Xhosa) sweet.

MANDY (Latin) lovable. A familiar form of Amanda, Manda, Melinda.
Mandee, Mandi, Mandie

MANETTE (French) a form of Mary.

MANGENA (Hebrew) song, melody.
Mangina

MANI (Chinese) a mantra repeated in Tibetan Buddhist prayer to impart understanding.
Manee

MANKA (Polish, Russian) a form of Mary.

MANON (French) a familiar form of Marie.
Mannon

MANPREET (Punjabi) mind full of love.
Manprit

MANSI (Hopi) plucked flower.
Mancey, Manci, Mancie, Mansey, Mansie, Mansy

MANUELA (Spanish) a form of Emmanuelle.
Manuala, Manuelita, Manuella, Manuelle

MANYA (Russian) a form of Mary.

MARA (Greek) a short form of Amara. (Slavic) a form of Mary.
Mahra, Marae, Marah, Maralina, Maraline, Marra

MARABEL (English) a form of Mirabel.
Marabella, Marabelle

MARANDA (Latin) an alternate form of Miranda.

MARAYA (Hebrew) an alternate form of Mariah.
Mareya

MARCELA (Latin) an alternate form of Marcella.
Marcele, Marcelen, Marcelia, Marcelina, Marceline, Maricela

MARCELEN (English) a form of Marcella.
Marcelen, Marcelin, Marcelina, Marceline, Marcellin, Marcellina, Marcelline, Marcelyn, Marcilen

MARCELLA (Latin) martial, warlike. Mythology: Mars was the god of war. A feminine form of Marcellus.
Mairsil, Marca, Marce, Marceil, Marcela, Marcelen, Marcell, Marcelle, Marcello, Marcena, Marchella, Marchelle, Marci, Marcia, Marcie, Marciella, Marcile, Marcilla, Marcille, Marella, Marsella, Marselle, Marsiella

MARCENA (Latin) an alternate form of Marcella, Marcia.
Maracena, Marceen, Marcene, Marcenia, Marceyne, Marcina

MARCI, Marcie (English) familiar forms of Marcella, Marcia.
Marca, Marcee, Marcita, Marcy, Marsi, Marsie

MARCIA (Latin) martial, warlike. An alternate form of Marcella. See also Marquita.
Marcena, Marchia, Marci, Marciale, Marcie, Marcsa, Marsha, Martia

MARCIANN (American) a combination of Marci + Ann.
Marciane, Marcianna, Marcianne, Marcyane, Marcyanna, Marcyanne

MARCILYNN (American) a combination of Marci + Lynn.
Marcilen, Marcilin, Marciline, Marcilyn, Marcilyne, Marcilynne, Marcylen, Marcylin, Marcyline, Marcylyn, Marcylyne, Marcylynn, Marcylynne

MARCY (English) an alternate form of Marci.
Marsey, Marsy

MARDI (French) born on Tuesday. (Aramaic) a familiar form of Martha.

MARE (Irish) a form of Mary.
Mair, Maire

MARELDA (German) renowned warrior.
Marella, Marilda

MAREN (Latin) sea. (Aramaic) a form of Mary. See also Marina.
Marin, Marine, Marinn, Miren

MARESA, Maressa (Latin) alternate forms of Marisa.
Maresha, Meresa

MARETTA (English) a familiar form of Margaret.
Maret, Marette

MARGARET (Greek) pearl. History: Margaret Hilda Thatcher served as British prime minister. See also Gita, Greta, Gretchen, Marjorie, Markita, Meg, Megan, Peggy, Reet, Rita.
Madge, Maergrethe, Maggie, Maisie, Mamie, Maretta, Marga, Margalo, Marganit, Margara, Maretha, Margarett, Margarette, Margarida, Margarit, Margarita, Margaro, Margaux, Marge, Margeret, Margeretta, Margerette, Margery, Margetta, Margiad, Margie, Margisia, Margit, Margo, Margot, Margret, Marguerite, Meta

MARGARIT (Greek) an alternate form of Margaret.
Margalide, Margalit, Margalith, Margarid, Margaritt, Margerit

MARGARITA (Italian, Spanish) a form of Margaret.
Margareta, Margaretta, Margarida, Margaritis, Margaritta, Margeretta, Margharita, Margherita, Margrieta, Margrita, Marguarita, Marguerita, Margurita

MARGAUX (French) a form of Margaret.
Margeaux

MARGE (English) a short form of Margaret, Marjorie.
Margie

MARGERY (English) a form of Margaret.
Margerie, Margorie

MARGIE (English) a familiar form of Marge, Margaret.
Margey, Margi, Margy

MARGIT (Hungarian) a form of Margaret.
Marget, Margette, Margita

MARGO, Margot (French) forms of Margaret.
Mago, Margaro

MARGRET (German) a form of Margaret.
Margreta, Margrete, Margreth, Margrett, Margretta, Margrette, Margrieta, Margrita

MARGUERITE (French) a form of Margaret.
Margarete, Margaretha, Margarethe, Margarite, Margerite, Marguaretta, Marguarette, Marguarite, Marguerette, Margurite

MARI (Japanese) ball. (Spanish) a form of Mary.

MARIA (Hebrew) bitter; sea of bitterness. (Italian, Spanish) a form of Mary.
Maie, Malia, Marea, Mareah, Mariabella, Mariae, Mariesa, Mariessa, Mariha, Marija, Mariya, Mariyah, Marja, Marya

MARIAH (Hebrew) an alternate form of Mary. See also Moriah.
Maraia, Maraya, Mariyah, Marriah, Meriah

MARIAM (Hebrew) an alternate form of Miriam.
Mariama, Mariame, Mariem, Meryam

MARIAN (English) an alternate form of Maryann.
Mariana, Mariane, Mariann, Marianne, Mariene, Marion, Marrian, Marriann

MARIANA, Marianna (Spanish) forms of Marian.
Marriana, Marrianna, Maryana, Maryanna

MARIANE, Marianne (English) alternate forms of Marian.
Marrianne, Maryanne

MARIBEL (French) beautiful. (English) a combination of Maria + Bell.
Marabel, Marbelle, Mariabella, Maribella, Maribelle, Maridel, Marybel, Marybella, Marybelle

MARICE (Italian) a form of Mary. See also Maris.
Marica, Marise, Marisse

MARICELA (Latin) an alternate form of Marcella.
Maricel, Mariceli, Maricelia, Maricella, Maricely

MARIDEL (English) a form of Maribel.

MARIE (French) a form of Mary.
Maree, Marietta, Marrie

MARIEL, Marielle (German, Dutch) forms of Mary.
Marial, Marieke, Marielana, Mariele, Marieli, Marielie, Marieline, Mariell, Mariellen, Marielsie, Mariely, Marielys

MARIELA, Mariella (German, Dutch) forms of Mary.

MARIETTA (Italian) a familiar form of Marie.
Maretta, Marette, Mariet, Mariette, Marrietta

MARIEVE (American) a combination of Mary + Eve.

MARIGOLD (English) Botany: a plant with yellow or orange flowers.
Marygold

MARIKA (Dutch, Slavic) a form of Mary.
Marica, Marieke, Marija, Marijke, Marikah, Marike, Marikia, Marikka, Mariska, Mariske, Marrika, Maryk, Maryka, Merica, Merika

MARIKO (Japanese) circle.

MARILEE (American) a combination of Mary + Lee.
Marili, Marilie, Marily, Marrilee, Marylea, Marylee, Merrilee, Merrili, Merrily

MARILLA (Hebrew, German) a form of Mary.
Marella, Marelle

MARILOU (American) an alternate form of Marylou.
Marilu, Mariluz

MARILYN (Hebrew) Mary's line or descendants. See also Merilyn.
Maralin, Maralyn, Maralyne, Maralynn, Maralynne, Marelyn, Marilin, Marillyn, Marilyne, Marilynn, Marilynne, Marlyn, Marolyn, Marralynn, Marrilin, Marrilyn, Marrilynn, Marrilynne, Marylin, Marylinn, Marylyn, Marylyne, Marylynn, Marylynne

MARINA (Latin) sea. See also Maren.
Mareena, Marena, Marenka, Marinae, Marinah, Marinda, Marindi, Marinka, Marinna, Marrina, Maryna, Merina, Mirena

MARINI (Swahili) healthy; pretty.

MARION (French) a form of Mary.
Marrian, Marrion, Maryon, Maryonn

MARIS (Greek) a short form of Amaris, Damaris. (Latin) sea. See also Marice.

Maries, Marise, Marris, Marys, Maryse, Meris

MARISA (Latin) sea.
Maresa, Mariesa, Mariessa, Marisela, Marissa, Marita, Mariza, Marrisa, Marrissa, Marysa, Maryse, Maryssa, Merisa

MARISELA (Latin) an alternate form of Marisa.
Mariseli, Marisella, Marishelle, Marissela

MARISHA (Russian) a familiar form of Mary.
Mareshah, Marishenka, Marishka, Mariska

MARISOL (Spanish) sunny sea.
Marise, Marizol, Marysol

MARISSA (Latin) an alternate form of Maris, Marisa.
Maressa, Marisa, Marisha, Marissah, Marisse, Marizza, Marrissa, Marrissia, Maryssa, Merissa, Morissa

MARIT (Aramaic) lady.
Marita, Marite

MARITA (Spanish) a form of Marissa.
Marité, Maritha

MARITZA (Arabic) blessed.
Maritsa, Maritssa

MARIYAN (Arabic) purity.
Mariya, Mariyah, Mariyana, Mariyanna

MARJA (Finnish) a form of Mary.
Marjae, Marjatta, Marjie

MARJAN (Persian) coral. (Polish) a form of Mary.
Marjaneh, Marjanna

MARJIE (Scottish) a familiar form of Marjorie.
Marje, Marjey, Marji, Marjy

MARJOLAINE (French) marjoram.

MARJORIE (Greek) a familiar form of Margaret. (Scottish) a form of Mary.
Majorie, Marge, Margeree, Margerey, Margerie, Margery, Margorie, Margory, Marjarie, Marjary, Marjerie, Marjery, Marjie, Marjorey, Marjori, Marjory

MARKAYLA (American) a combination or Mary + Kayla.
Marka, Markaiah, Markaya, Markayel, Markeela, Markel

MARKEISHA (English) a combination of Mary + Keisha.
Markasha, Markeisa, Markeisia, Markesha, Markeshia, Markesia, Markiesha, Markisha, Markishia, Marquesha

MARKITA (Czech) a form of Margaret.
Marka, Markeah, Markeda, Markee, Markeeta, Marketa, Marketta, Marki, Markia, Markie, Markieta, Markita, Markitha, Markketta, Merkate

MARLA (English) a short form of Marlena, Marlene.
Marlah, Marlea, Marleah

MARLANA (English) a form of Marlena.
Marlaena, Marlaina, Marlainna, Marlania, Marlanna, Marlayna, Marleana

MARLEE (English) a form of Marlene.
Marlea, Marleah, Marleigh

MARLENA (German) a form of Marlene.
Marla, Marlaina, Marlana, Marlanna, Marleena, Marlina, Marlinda, Marlyna, Marna

MARLENE (Greek) high tower. (Slavic) a form of Magdalen.
Marla, Marlaine, Marlane, Marlayne, Marlee, Marleen, Marleene, Marlen, Marlena, Marlenne, Marley, Marlin, Marline, Marlyne

MARLEY (English) a familiar form of Marlene.
Marlee, Marli, Marlie, Marly

MARLIS (English) a combination of Maria + Lisa.
Marles, Marlisa, Marlise, Marlys, Marlyse, Marlyssa

MARLO (English) a form of Mary.
Marlon, Marlow, Marlowe

MARLYN (Hebrew) a short form of Marilyn.
Marlynn, Marlynne

MARMARA (Greek) sparkling, shining.
Marmee

MARNI (Hebrew) an alternate form of Marnie.
Marnia, Marnique

MARNIE (Hebrew) a short form of Marnina.
Marna, Marnay, Marne, Marnee, Marney, Marni, Marnisha, Marnja, Marny, Marnya, Marnye

MARNINA (Hebrew) rejoice.

MAROULA (Greek) a form of Mary.

MARQUISE (French) noblewoman.

Marquise (cont.)
Markese, Marquees, Marquese, Marquice, Marquies, Marquiese, Marquis, Marquisa, Marquisee, Marquisha, Marquisse, Marquiste

MARQUISHA (American) a form of Marquise.
Marquiesha, Marquisia

MARQUITA (Spanish) a form of Marcia.
Marquatte, Marqueda, Marquedia, Marquee, Marqueita, Marquet, Marqueta, Marquetta, Marquette, Marquia, Marquida, Marquietta, Marquitra, Marquitia, Marquitta

MARRIM (Chinese) tribal name in Manpur state.

MARSALA (Italian) from Marseille, France.
Marsali, Marseilles

MARSHA (English) a form of Marcia.
Marcha, Marshae, Marshay, Marshel, Marshele, Marshell, Marshia, Marshiela

MARTA (English) a short form of Martha, Martina.
Martá, Martä, Marte, Martia, Marttaha, Merta

MARTHA (Aramaic) lady; sorrowful. Bible: a sister of the Virgin Mary. See also Mardi.
Maita, Marta, Martaha, Marth, Marthan, Marthe, Marthy, Marti, Marticka, Martita, Mattie, Matty, Martus, Martuska, Masia

MARTI (English) a familiar form of Martha, Martina.
Martie, Marty

MARTINA (Latin) martial, war-like. A feminine form of Martin. See also Tina.

Marta, Martel, Martella, Martelle, Martene, Marthena, Marthina, Marthine, Marti, Martine, Martinia, Martino, Martisha, Martosia, Martoya, Martricia, Martrina, Martyna, Martyne, Martynne

MARTIZA (Arabic) blessed.

MARU (Japanese) round.

MARUCA (Spanish) a form of Mary.
Maruja, Maruska

MARVELLA (French) marvelous.
Marva, Marvel, Marvela, Marvele, Marvelle, Marvely, Marvetta, Marvette, Marvia, Marvina

MARY (Hebrew) bitter; sea of bitterness. An alternate form of Miriam. Bible: the mother of Jesus. See also Maija, Malia, Maren, Mariah, Marjorie, Maura, Maureen, Miriam, Mitzi, Moira, Mollie, Muriel.
Maira, Maire, Manette, Manka, Manon, Manya, Mara, Mare, Maree, Maren, Marella, Marelle, Mari, Maria, Maricara, Marice, Marie, Mariel, Mariela, Marika, Marilla, Marilyn, Marion, Mariquilla, Mariquita, Marisha, Marja, Marjan, Marlo, Maroula, Maruca, Marye, Maryla, Marynia, Masha, Mavra, Mendi, Mérane, Meridel, Mhairie, Mirja, Molara, Morag, Moya

MARYA (Arabic) purity; bright whiteness.
Maryah

MARYAM (Hebrew) an alternate form of Miriam.
Maryama

MARYANN, Maryanne (English) combinations of Mary + Ann.

Marian, Marryann, Maryan, Meryem

MARYBETH (American) a combination of Mary + Beth.
Maribeth, Maribette

MARYELLEN (American) a combination of Mary + Ellen.
Mariellen

MARYJANE (American) a combination of Mary + Jane.

MARYJO (American) a combination of Mary + Jo.
Marijo, Maryjoe

MARYKATE (American) a combination of Mary + Kate.
Mary-Kate

MARYLOU (American) a combination of Mary + Lou.
Marilou, Marylu

MARYSSA (Latin) an alternate form of Marissa.
Maryse, Marysia

MASAGO (Japanese) sands of time.

MASANI (Luganda) gap toothed.

MASHA (Russian) a form of Mary.
Mashka, Mashenka

MASHIKA (Swahili) born during the rainy season.
Masika

MATANA (Hebrew) gift.
Matat

MATHENA (Hebrew) gift of God. (English) a feminine form of Matthau.

MATHILDE (German) an alternate form of Matilda.
Mathilda

MATILDA (German) powerful battler. See also Maud, Tilda, Tillie.
Máda, Mahaut, Maitilde, Malkin, Mat, Matelda, Mathilde, Matilde, Mattie, Matty, Matusha, Matylda

MATRIKA (Hindi) mother. Religion: a name for the Hindu goddess Shakti.
Matrica

MATSUKO (Japanese) pine tree.

MATTEA (Hebrew) gift of God.
Matea, Mathea, Mathia, Matia, Matte, Matthea, Matthia, Mattia, Matya

MATTIE, Matty (English) familiar forms of Martha, Matilda.
Matte, Mattey, Matti, Mattye

MATUSHA (Spanish) a form of Matilda.
Matuja, Matuxa

MAUD, Maude (English) short forms of Madeline, Matilda. See also Madison.
Maudie, Maudine, Maudlin

MAURA (Irish) dark. An alternate form of Mary, Maureen. See also Moira.
Maurah, Maure, Maurette, Mauricette, Maurita

MAUREEN (French) dark. (Irish) a form of Mary.
Maura, Maurene, Maurine, Mo, Moreen, Morena, Morene, Morine, Morreen, Moureen

MAURELLE (French) dark; elfin.
Mauriel, Mauriell, Maurielle

MAURISE (French) dark skinned; moor; marshland. A feminine form of Maurice.
Maurisa, Maurissa, Maurita, Maurizia

MAUSI (Native American) plucked flower.

MAUVE (French) violet colored.

MAVIS (French) song thrush bird. See also Maeve.
Mavies, Mavin, Mavine, Mavon, Mavra

MAXIE (English) a familiar form of Maxine.
Maxi, Maxy

MAXINE (Latin) greatest. A feminine form of Maximillian.
Max, Maxa, Maxeen, Maxena, Maxene, Maxie, Maxima, Maxime, Maximiliane, Maxina, Maxna, Maxyne

MAY (Latin) great. (Arabic) discerning. (English) flower; month of May. See also Mae, Maia.
Maj, Mayberry, Maybeth, Mayday, Maydee, Maydena, Maye, Mayela, Mayella, Mayetta, Mayrene

MAYA (Hindi) God's creative power. (Greek) mother; grandmother. (Latin) great. An alternate form of Maia.
Mayam, Mya

MAYBELINE (Latin) a familiar form of Mabel.

MAYGAN, Maygen (Irish) an alternate form of Megan.
Mayghan, Maygon

MAYLYN (American) a combination of May + Lynn.
Mayelene, Mayleen, Maylen, Maylene, Maylin, Maylon, Maylynn, Maylynne

MAYOREE (Tai) beautiful.
Mayra, Mayree, Mayariya

MAYRA (Tai) an alternate form of Mayoree.

MAYSA (Arabic) walks with a proud stride.

MAYSUN (Arabic) beautiful.

MAZEL (Hebrew) lucky.
Mazal, Mazala, Mazella

MCKAYLA (American) an alternate form of Makayla.
Mckaela, Mckaila, Mckala, Mckaylah, Mckayle, Mckaylee, Mckayleh, Mckayleigh, Mckayli, Mckaylia, Mckaylie

MCKELL (American) an alternate form of Makell.
Mckelle

MCKENNA (American) an alternate form of Mackenna.
Mckena, Mckennah, Mckinna, Mckinnah

MCKENZIE (Scottish) an alternate form of Mackenzie.
Mckennzie, Mckensee, Mckensey, McKensi, Mckensi, Mckensie, Mckensy, Mckenze, Mckenzee, Mckenzey, Mckenzi, Mckenzy, Mckenzye, Mekensie, Mekenzi, Mekenzie

MCKINLEY (Irish) daughter of the learned ruler.
Mckinlee, Mckinleigh, Mckinlie, Mckinnley

MCKINZIE (Irish) an alternate form of Mackenzie.
Mckinsey, Mckinze, Mckinzea, Mckinzee, Mckinzi, Mckinzy, Mckynze, Mckynzie

MEAD, Meade (Greek) honey wine.

MEAGAN (Irish) an alternate form of Megan.

Meagan (cont.)
Maegan, Meagain, Meagann, Meagen, Meagin, Meagnah, Meagon

MEAGHAN (Welsh) a form of Megan.
Maeghan, Meaghann, Meaghen, Meahgan

MEARA (Irish) mirthful.

MEDA (Native American) prophet; priestess.

MEDEA (Greek) ruling. (Latin) middle. Mythology: a sorceress who helped Jason get the Golden Fleece.
Medeia

MEDINA (Arabic) History: the site of Muhammed's tomb.
Medinah

MEDORA (Greek) mother's gift. Literature: a character in Lord Byron's poem "Corsair."

MEENA (Hindi) blue semi-precious stone; bird.

MEG (English) a short form of Margaret, Megan.

MEGAN (Greek) pearl; great. (Irish) a form of Margaret.
Maegan, Magan, Magen, Meagan, Meaghan, Magen, Maygan, Maygen, Meg, Megane, Megann, Megean, Megen, Meggan, Meggen, Meggie, Meghan, Megyn, Meygan

MEGANE (Irish) an alternate form of Megan.
Magana, Meganna, Meganne

MEGARA (Greek) first. Mythology: Hercules's first wife.

MEGGIE (English) a familiar form of Margaret, Megan.
Meggi, Meggy

MEGHAN (Welsh) a form of Megan.
Meeghan, Meehan, Megha, Meghana, Meghane, Meghann, Meghanne, Meghean, Meghen, Mehgan, Mehgen

MEHADI (Hindi) flower.

MEHIRA (Hebrew) speedy; energetic.
Mahira

MEHITABEL (Hebrew) benefited by trusting God.
Mehetabel, Mehitabelle, Hetty, Hitty

MEHRI (Persian) kind; lovable; sunny.

MEI (Chinese) a short form of Meiying. (Hawaiian) great.
Meiko

MEIRA (Hebrew) light.
Meera

MEIT (Burmese) affectionate.

MEIYING (Chinese) beautiful flower.
Mei

MEKA (Hebrew) a familiar form of Michaela.

MEKAYLA (American) an alternate form of Makayla.
Mekaela, Mekaila, Mekayela, Mekaylia

MEL (Portuguese, Spanish) sweet as honey.

MELA (Hindi) religious service. (Polish) a form of Melanie.

MELANA (Russian) a form of Melanie.
Melanna, Melashka, Melenka, Milana

MELANIE (Greek) dark skinned.
Malania, Malanie, Meila, Meilani, Meilin, Melaine, Melainie, Melana, Melane, Melanee, Melaney, Melani, Melania, Mélanie, Melanka, Melanney, Melannie, Melany, Melanya, Melasya, Melayne, Melenia, Mella, Mellanie, Melonie, Melya, Milena, Milya

MELANTHA (Greek) dark flower.

MELBA (Greek) soft; slender. (Latin) mallow flower.
Malva, Melva

MELE (Hawaiian) song; poem.

MELESSE (Ethiopian) eternal.
Mellesse

MELIA (German) a short form of Amelia.
Melcia, Melea, Meleah, Meleia, Meleisha, Meli, Meliah, Melida, Melika, Mema

MELINA (Latin) canary yellow. (Greek) a short form of Melinda.
Melaina, Meleana, Meleena, Melena, Meline, Melinia, Melinna, Melynna

MELINDA (Greek) honey. See also Linda, Melina, Mindy.
Maillie, Malinda, Melinde, Melinder, Mellinda, Melynda, Melyne, Milinda, Milynda, Mylenda, Mylinda, Mylynda

MELIORA (Latin) better.
Melior, Meliori, Mellear, Melyor, Melyora

MELISA (Greek) an alternate form of Melissa.
Melesa, Mélisa, Melise, Melisha, Melishia, Melisia, Meliza, Melizah, Mellisa, Melosa, Milisa, Mylisa, Mylisia

MELISANDE (French) a form of Melissa, Millicent.
Lisandra, Malisande, Malissande, Malyssandre, Melesande, Melisandra, Melisandre, Mélisandré, Melisenda, Melissande, Melissandre, Mellisande, Melond, Melysande, Melyssandre

MELISSA (Greek) honey bee. See also Elissa, Lissa, Melisande, Millicent.
Malissa, Mallissa, Melessa, Meleta, Melisa, Mélissa, Melisse, Melissia, Mellie, Mellissa, Melly, Melyssa, Milissa, Millie, Milly, Missy, Molissia, Mollissa, Mylissa, Mylissia

MELITA (Greek) a form of Melissa. (Spanish) a short form of Carmelita.
Malita, Meleeta, Melitta, Melitza, Melletta, Molita

MELLY (American) a familiar form of names beginning with "Mel." See also Millie.
Meli, Melie, Melli, Mellie

MELODY (Greek) melody. See also Elodie.
Meladia, Melodee, Melodey, Melodi, Melodia, Melodie, Melodyann, Melodye

MELONIE (American) an alternate form of Melanie.
Melloney, Mellonie, Mellony, Melonee, Meloney, Meloni, Melonie, Melonnie, Melony

MELOSA (Spanish) sweet; tender.

MELVINA (Irish) armored chief. A feminine form of Melvin. See also Malvina.
Melevine, Melva, Melveen, Melvena, Melvene, Melvonna

MELYNE (Greek) a short form of Melinda.
Melyn, Melynn, Melynne

MELYSSA (Greek) an alternate form of Melissa.

MENA (Greek) a short form of Philomena. (German, Dutch) strong. History: Mena was the first king of Egypt.
Menah

MENDI (Basque) a form of Mary.
Menda, Mendy

MERANDA (Latin) an alternate form of Miranda.
Merana, Merandah, Merandia, Merannda

MÉRANE (French) a form of Mary.
Meraine, Merrane

MERCEDES (Latin) reward, payment. (Spanish) merciful.
Mercades, Mercadez, Mercadie, Meceades, Merced, Mercede, Mercedees, Mercedeez, Mercedez, Mercedies, Mercedis, Mersade, Mersades

MERCIA (English) a form of Marcia. History: the name of an ancient British kingdom.

MERCY (English) compassionate, merciful. See also Merry.
Mercey, Merci, Mercie, Mercille, Mersey

MEREDITH (Welsh) protector of the sea.
Meredeth, Meredithe, Meredy, Meredyth, Meredythe, Meridath, Merideth, Meridie, Meridith, Merridie, Merridith, Merry

MERI (Finnish) sea. (Irish) a short form of Meriel.

MERIEL (Irish) shining sea.
Meri, Merial, Meriol, Meryl

MERILYN (English) a combination of Merry + Lynn. See also Marilyn.
Merelyn, Merlyn, Merralyn, Merrelyn, Merrilyn

MERISSA (Latin) an alternate form of Marissa.
Merisa, Merisha

MERLE (Latin, French) blackbird.
Merl, Merla, Merlina, Merline, Merola, Murle, Myrle, Myrleen, Myrlene, Myrline

MERRY (English) cheerful, happy. A familiar form of Mercy, Meredith.
Merie, Merree, Merri, Merrie, Merrielle, Merrilee, Merrili, Merrilyn, Merris, Merrita

MERYL (German) famous. (Irish) shining sea. An alternate form of Meriel, Muriel.
Meral, Merel, Merrall, Merrell, Merril, Merrile, Merrill, Merryl, Meryle, Meryll

MESHA (Hindi) born in the lunar month of Aries.
Meshal

META (German) a short form of Margaret.
Metta, Mette, Metti

MHAIRIE (Scottish) a form of Mary.
Mhaire, Mhairi, Mhari, Mhary

MIA (Italian) mine. A familiar form of Michaela, Michelle.
Mea, Meah, Miah

MICAELA (Hebrew) an alternate form of Michaela.
Macaela, Micaella, Micaila, Micala, Miceala

MICAH (Hebrew) a short form of Michaela. Bible: one of the Old Testament prophets.
Meecah, Mica, Micha, Mika, Myca, Mycah

MICAYLA, Michayla (Hebrew) alternate forms of Michaela.
Micayle, Micaylee, Michaylah

MICHAELA (Hebrew) who is like God? A feminine form of Michael.
Machaela, Maika, Makaela, Makaila, Makala, Makayla, Mia, Micaela, Micayla, Michael, Michaelann, Michala, Michayla, Michealia, Michaelina, Michaeline, Michaell, Michaella, Michaelyn, Michaila, Michal, Michala, Micheal, Micheala, Michelia, Michelina, Michelle, Michely, Michelyn, Micheyla, Micheline, Micki, Miguela, Mikaela, Mikala, Misha, Mycala, Mychael, Mychal

MICHALA (Hebrew) an alternate form of Michaela.
Michalann, Michale, Michalene, Michalin, Mchalina, Michalisha, Michalla, Michalle, Michayla, Michayle, Michela

MICHELE (Italian) a form of Michaela.
Michaelle, Michal, Michela

MICHELLE (French) who is like God? A form of Michaela. See also Shelley.
Machealle, Machele, Machell, Machella, Machelle, Mechelle, Meichelle, Meschell, Meshell, Meshelle, Mia, Michel, Michéle, Michell, Michella, Michellene, Michellyn, Mischel, Mischelle, Mishael, Mishaela, Mishayla, Mishell, Mishelle, Mitchele, Mitchelle

MICHI (Japanese) righteous way.
Miche, Michee, Michiko

MICKI (American) a familiar form of Michaela.
Mickee, Mickeeya, Mickia, Mickie, Micky, Mickya, Miquia

MIDORI (Japanese) green.

MIEKO (Japanese) prosperous.
Mieke

MIELIKKI (Finnish) pleasing.

MIETTE (French) small; sweet.

MIGINA (Omaha) new moon.

MIGNON (French) cute; graceful.
Mignonette, Minnionette, Minnonette, Minyonette, Minyonne

MIGUELA (Spanish) a form of Michaela.
Micquel, Miguelina, Miguelita, Miquel, Miquela, Miquella

MIKA (Hebrew) an alternate form of Micah. (Japanese) new moon. (Russian) God's child. (Native American) wise racoon.
Mikah, Mikka

MIKAELA (Hebrew) an alternate form of Michaela.
Mekaela, Mekala, Mickael, Mickaela, Mickala, Mickalla, Mickeel, Mickell, Mickelle, Mikael, Mikail, Mikaila, Mikal, Mikalene, Mikalovna, Mikalyn, Mikayla, Mikea, Mikeisha, Mikeita, Mikel, Mikela, Mikele, Mikell, Mikella, Mikesha, Mikeya, Mikhaela, Mikie, Mikiela, Mikkel, Mikyla, Mykaela

MIKALA (Hebrew) an alternate form of Michaela.
Mickala, Mikalah, Mikale, Mikalea, Mikalee, Mikaleh

MIKAYLA (American) a form of Mikaela.
Mekayla, Mickayla, Mikala, Mikayle, Mikyla

MIKHAELA (American) a form of Mikaela.
Mikhail, Mikhaila, Mikhala, Mikhalea, Mikhayla, Mikhelle

MIKI (Japanese) flower stem.
Mikia, Mikiala, Mikie, Mikita, Mikiyo, Mikki, Mikkie, Mikkiya, Mikko, Miko

MILA (Italian, Slavic) a short form of Camilla, Ludmilla. (Russian) dear one.
Milah, Milla

MILADA (Czech) my love.
Mila, Milady

MILAGROS (Spanish) miracle.
Mila, Milagritos, Milagro, Milagrosa, Mirari

MILANA (Italian) from Milan, Italy.
Milan, Milane, Milani, Milanka, Milanna, Milanne

MILDRED (English) gentle counselor.
Mil, Mila, Mildrene, Mildrid, Millie, Milly

MILENA (Greek, Hebrew, Russian) a form of Ludmilla, Magdalen, Melanie.
Mila, Milène, Milenia, Milenny, Milini, Millini

MILETA (German) generous, merciful. A feminine form of Milo.

MILIA (German) industrious. A short form of Amelia, Emily.
Mila, Milka, Milla, Milya

MILIANI (Hawaiian) caress.
Milanni, Miliany

MILILANI (Hawaiian) heavenly caress.
Milliani

MILISSA (Greek) an alternate form of Melissa.
Milessa, Milisa, Millisa, Millissa

MILKA (Czech) a form of Amelia.
Milica, Milika

MILLICENT (Greek) an alternate form of Melissa. (English) industrious. See also Lissa, Melisande.
Melicent, Meliscent, Mellicent, Mellisent, Melly, Milicent, Milisent, Millie, Milliestone, Millisent, Milly, Milzie, Missy

MILLIE, Milly (English) familiar forms of Amelia, Camille, Emily, Kamila, Melissa, Mildred, Millicent.
Mili, Milla, Millee, Milley, Millie, Mylie

MIMA (Burmese) woman.
Mimma

MIMI (French) a familiar form of Miriam.

MINA (German) love. (Persian) blue sky. (Hindi) born in the lunar month of Pisces. (Arabic) harbor. (Japanese) south. A short form of names ending in "mina."
Meena, Mena, Min

MINAL (Native American) fruit.

MINDA (Hindi) knowledge.

MINDY (Greek) a familiar form of Melinda.
Mindee, Mindi, Mindie, Mindyanne, Mindylee, Myndy

MINE (Japanese) peak; mountain range.
Mineko

MINERVA (Latin) wise. Mythology: the goddess of wisdom.
Merva, Minivera, Minnie, Myna

MINETTE (French) faithful defender
Minnette, Minnita

MINKA (Polish) a short form of Wilhelmina.

MINNA (German) a short form of Wilhelmina.
Mina, Minka, Minnie, Minta

MINNIE (American) a familiar form of Mina, Minerva, Minna, Wilhelmina.
Mini, Minie, Minne, Minni, Minny

MINOWA (Native American) singer.
Minowah

MINTA (English) Literature: originally coined by playwright Sir John Vanbrugh in his comedy *The Confederacy.*
Minty

MINYA (Osage) older sister.

MIO (Japanese) three times as strong.

MIRA (Latin) wonderful. (Spanish) look, gaze. A short form of Almira, Amira, Marabel, Mirabel, Miranda.
Mirae, Mirra, Mirah

MIRABEL (Latin) beautiful.
Mira, Mirabell, Mirabella, Mirabelle, Mirable

MIRACLE (Latin) wonder, marvel.

MIRANDA (Latin) strange; wonderful; admirable. Literature: the heroine of Shakespeare's *The Tempest.* See also Randi.
Maranda, Marenda, Meranda, Mira, Miran, Miranada, Mirandia, Mirinda, Mirindé, Mironda, Mirranda, Muranda, Myranda

MIREILLE (Hebrew) God spoke. (Latin) wonderful.
Mireil, Mirel, Mirella, Mirelle, Mirelys, Mireya, Mireyda, Mirielle, Mirilla, Myrella, Myrilla

MIREYA (Hebrew) an alternate form of Mireille.
Mireea, Miriah, Miryah

MIRI (Gypsy) a short form of Miriam.
Miria, Miriah

MIRIAM (Hebrew) bitter, sea of bitterness. Bible: the original form of Mary. See also Macia, Mimi, Mitzi.
Mairwen, Mariam, Maryam, Miram, Mirham, Miri, Miriain, Miriama, Miriame, Mirian, Mirit, Mirjam, Mirjana, Mirriam, Mirrian, Miryam, Miryan, Myriam

MISHA (Russian) a form of Michaela.
Mischa, Mishae

MISSY (English) a familiar form of Melissa, Millicent.
Missi, Missie

MISTY (English) shrouded by mist.
Missty, Mistee, Mistey, Misti, Mistie, Mistin, Mistina, Mistral, Mistylynn, Mystee, Mysti, Mystie

MITRA (Hindi) god of daylight. (Persian) angel.
Mita

MITUNA (Moquelumnan) like a fish wrapped up in leaves.

MITZI (German) a form of Mary, Miriam.
Mieze, Mitzee, Mitzie, Mitzy

MIWA (Japanese) wise eyes.
Miwako

MIYA (Japanese) temple.
Miyah, Miyana, Miyanna

MIYO (Japanese) beautiful generation.
Miyoko, Miyuko

MIYUKI (Japanese) snow.

MOANA (Hawaiian) ocean; fragrance.

MOCHA (Arabic) chocolate-flavored coffee.
Moka

MODESTY (Latin) modest.
Modesta, Modeste, Modestia, Modestie, Modestina, Modestine, Modestus

MOESHA (American) a short form of Monisha.
Myesha

MOHALA (Hawaiian) flowers in bloom.
Moala

MOIRA (Irish) great. A form of Mary. See also Maura.
Moirae, Moirah, Moire, Moya, Moyra, Moyrah

MOLARA (Basque) a form of Mary.

MOLLIE, Molly (Irish) familiar forms of Mary.
Moli, Molie, Moll, Mollee, Molley, Molli, Mollissa

MONA (Greek) a short form of Monica, Ramona, Rimona. (Irish) noble.
Moina, Monah, Mone, Monea, Monna, Moyna

MONET (French) Art: Claude Monet was a leading French impressionist remembered for his paintings of water lilies.
Monae, Monay, Monee

MONICA (Greek) solitary. (Latin) advisor.
Mona, Monca, Monee, Monia, Monic, Monice, Monicia, Monicka, Monika, Monique, Monise, Monn, Monnica, Monnie, Monya

MONIFA (Yoruba) I have my luck.

MONIKA (German) a form of Monica.
Moneka, Monieka, Monike, Monnika

MONIQUE (French) a form of Monica.
Moneeke, Moneik, Moniqua, Moniquea, Moniquie, Munique

MONISHA (American) a combination of Monica + Aisha.
Moesha, Moneisha, Monishia

MONTANA (Spanish) mountain.
Montanna

MORA (Spanish) blueberry.
Morae, Morea, Moria, Morita

MORELA (Polish) apricot.
Morelia, Morelle

MORENA (Irish) a form of Maureen.

MORGAN (Welsh) seashore. Literature: Morgan Le Fay was the half-sister of King Arthur.
Morgana, Morgance, Morgane, Morganetta, Morganette, Morganica, Morgann, Morganna, Morganne, Morgen, Morghan, Morgyn, Morrigan

MORGHAN (Welsh) an alternate form of Morgan.
Morghen, Morghin, Morghyn

MORIAH (Hebrew) God is my teacher. (French) dark skinned. Bible: the name of the mountain on which the temple of Solomon was built. See also Mariah.
Moria, Moriel, Morit, Morria, Morriah

MORIE (Japanese) bay.

MOROWA (Akan) queen.

MORRISA (Latin) dark skinned; moor; marshland. A feminine form of Morris.
Morisa, Morissa, Morrissa

MOSELLE (Hebrew) drawn from the water. A feminine form of Moses. (French) a white wine.
Mozelle

MOSI (Swahili) first-born.

MOSWEN (Tswana) white.

MOUNA (Arabic) wish, desire.
Moona, Moonia, Mounia, Muna, Munia

MRENA (Slavic) white eyes.
Mren

MUMTAZ (Arabic) distinguished.

MURA (Japanese) village.

MURIEL (Arabic) myrrh. (Irish) shining sea. A form of Mary. See also Meryl.
Merial, Meriel, Meriol, Merrial, Merriel, Muire, Murial, Muriell, Murielle

MUSETTA (French) little bagpipe.
Musette

MUSLIMAH (Arabic) devout believer.

MYA (Burmese) emerald.
My, Myah, Myia, Myiah

MYESHA (American) an alternate form of Moesha.
Myeisha, Myeshia, Myiesha, Myisha

MYKAELA, Mykayla (American) forms of Mikaela.
Mykael, Mykaila, Mykal, Mykala, Mykaleen, Mykel, Mykela, Mykyla

MYLA (English) merciful.

MYLENE (Greek) dark.
Mylaine, Mylana, Mylee, Myleen

MYRA (Latin) fragrant ointment. A feminine form of Myron.
Mayra, Myrena, Myria

MYRANDA (Latin) an alternate form of Miranda.
Myrandah, Myrandia, Myrannda

MYRIAM (American) a form of Miriam.
Myriame, Myryam

MYRNA (Irish) beloved.
Merna, Mirna, Morna, Muirna

MYRTLE (Greek) dark green shrub.
Mertis, Mertle, Mirtle, Myrta, Myrtia, Myrtias, Myrtice, Myrtie, Myrtilla, Myrtis

NABILA (Arabic) born to nobility.
Nabeela, Nabiha, Nabilah

NADDA (Arabic) generous; dewy.
Nada

NADETTE (French) a short form of Bernadette.

NADIA (French, Slavic) hopeful.
Nadea, Nadenka, Nadezhda, Nadiah, Nadie, Nadija, Nadijah, Nadine, Nadiya, Nadiyah, Nadja, Nadjae, Nadjah, Nadka, Nadusha, Nady, Nadya

NADINE (French, Slavic) a form of Nadia.
Nadean, Nadeana, Nadeen, Nadena, Nadene, Nadien, Nadin, Nadina, Nadyne, Naidene, Naidine

NADIRA (Arabic) rare, precious.
Naadirah, Nadirah

NAEVA (French) a form of Eve.
Nahvon

NAFUNA (Luganda) born feet first.

NAGIDA (Hebrew) noble; prosperous.
Nagda, Nageeda

NAHID (Persian) Mythology: another name for Venus, the goddess of love and beauty.

NAHIMANA (Dakota) mystic.

NAIDA (Greek) water nymph.
Naiad, Naiya, Nayad, Nyad

NAILA (Arabic) successful.
Nailah

NAIRI (Armenian) land of canyons. History: a name for ancient Armenia.
Naira, Naire, Nayra

NAIYA (Greek) an alternate form of Naida.
Naia, Naiyana, Naja, Najah, Naya

NAJAM (Arabic) star.
Naja, Najma

NAJILA (Arabic) brilliant eyes.
Naja, Najah, Najia, Najja, Najla

NAKEISHA (American) a combination of the prefix Na + Keisha.
Nakeesha, Nakesha, Nakeshea, Nakeshia, Nakeysha, Nakiesha, Nakisha, Nekeisha

NAKEITA (American) a form of Nikita.
Nakeeta, Nakeitha, Nakeithra, Nakeitra, Nakeitress, Nakeitta, Nakeittia, Naketta, Nakieta, Nakitha, Nakitia, Nakitta, Nakyta

NAKIA (Arabic) pure.
Nakea, Nakeia, Nakeya, Nakeyah, Nakeyia, Nakiah, Nakiaya, Nakiea, Nakiya, Nakiyah, Nekia

NAKITA (American) a form of Nikita.
Nakkita, Naquita

NALANI (Hawaiian) calm as the heavens.
Nalanie, Nalany

NAMI (Japanese) wave.
Namika, Namiko

NAN (German) a short form of Fernanda. (English) an alternate form of Ann.
Nana, Nanice, Nanine, Nanna, Nanon

NANA (Hawaiian) spring.

NANCI (English) an alternate form of Nancy.
Nancie, Nancsi, Nansi

NANCY (English) gracious. A familiar form of Nan.
Nainsi, Nance, Nancee, Nancey, Nanci, Nancine, Nancye, Nanette, Nanice, Nanncey, Nanncy, Nanouk, Nansee, Nansey, Nanuk

NANETTE (French) a form of Nancy.
Nan, Nanete, Nannette, Nettie, Nineta, Ninete, Ninetta, Ninette, Nini, Ninita, Ninnetta, Ninnette, Nynette

NANI (Greek) charming. (Hawaiian) beautiful.
Nanni, Nannie, Nanny

NAOMI (Hebrew) pleasant, beautiful. Bible: a friend of Ruth.
Naoma, Naomia, Naomie, Naomy, Navit, Neoma, Neomi, Noami, Noemi, Noma, Nomi, Nyomi

NAOMIE (Hebrew) an alternate form of Naomi.
Naome, Naomee, Noemie

NARA (Greek) happy. (English) north. (Japanese) oak.
Narah

NARCISSA (Greek) daffodil. A feminine form of Narcissus. Mythology: the youth who fell in love with his own reflection.
Narcessa, Narcisa, Narcisse, Narcyssa, Narissa, Narkissa

NARELLE (Australian) woman from the sea.
Narel

NARI (Japanese) thunder.
Narie, Nariko

NARMADA (Hindi) pleasure giver.

NASHAWNA (American) a combination of the prefix Na + Shawna.
Nashan, Nashana, Nashanda, Nashaun, Nashauna, Nashaunda, Nashauwna, Nashawn, Nasheena, Nashounda, Nashuana

NASHOTA (Native American) double; second-born twin.

NASTASIA (Greek) an alternate form of Anastasia.
Nastasha, Nastashia, Nastasja, Nastassa, Nastassia, Nastassiya, Nastassja, Nastassya, Nastasya, Nastazia, Nastisija, Nastka, Nastusya, Nastya

NASYA (Hebrew) miracle.
Nasia, Nasyah

NATA (Sanskrit) dancer. (Latin) swimmer. (Polish, Russian) a form of Natalie. (Native American) speaker; creator. See also Nadia.
Natia, Natka, Natya

NATACHA (Russian) an alternate form of Natasha.
Natachia, Natacia, Naticha

NATALEE, Natali (Latin) alternate forms of Natalie.
Natale, Nataleh, Nataleigh, Nattlee

NATALIA (Russian) a form of Natalie. See also Talia.
Nacia, Natala, Natalea, Nataliia, Natalija, Natalina, Nataliya, Nataliyah, Natalja, Natalka, Natallea, Natallia, Natalya, Nathalia, Natka

NATALIE (Latin) born on Christmas day. See also Nata, Natasha, Noel, Talia.
Nat, Natalee, Natali, Natalia, Nataliee, Nataline, Natalle, Natallie, Nataly, Natelie, Nathalie, Nathaly, Natie, Natilie, Natlie, Nattalie, Nattilie

NATALINE (Latin) an alternate form of Natalie.
Natalene, Nataléne, Natalyn

NATALLE (French) a form of Natalie.
Natale

NATALY (Latin) an alternate form of Natalie.
Nathaly, Natally, Natallye

NATANE (Arapaho) daughter.
Natanne

NATANIA (Hebrew) gift of God. A feminine form of Nathan.
Natanya, Natée, Nathania, Nathenia, Netania, Nethania

NATARA (Arabic) sacrifice.
Natori, Natoria

NATASHA (Russian) a form of Natalie. See also Stacey, Tasha.
Nahtasha, Natacha, Natasa, Natascha, Natashah, Natashea, Natashenka, Natashia, Natashiea, Natashja, Natashka,

Natasia, Natassia, Natassija, Natassja, Natasza, Natausha, Natawsha, Natesha, Nateshia, Nathasha, Nathassha, Natisha, Natishia, Natosha, Netasha, Notosha

NATESA (Hindi) godlike; goddess. Religion: another name for the Hindu goddess Shakti.
Natisa, Natissa

NATHALIE, Nathaly (Latin) alternate forms of Natalie.
Nathalee, Nathali, Nathalia, Nathalya

NATIE (English) a familiar form of Natalie.
Nati, Natti, Nattie, Natty

NATOSHA (Russian) an alternate form of Natasha.
Natoshia, Natoshya, Netosha, Notosha

NAVA (Hebrew) beautiful; pleasant.
Navah, Naveh, Navit

NAYELY (Irish) an alternate form of Neila.
Naeyli, Nayelia, Nayelli, Nayelly, Nayla

NEALA (Irish) an alternate form of Neila.
Nayela, Naylea, Naylia, Nealia, Neela, Neelia, Neila

NECHA (Spanish) a form of Agnes.
Necho

NECI (Hungarian) fiery, intense.
Necia, Necie

NEDA (Slavic) born on Sunday.
Nedah, Nedi, Nedia, Neida

NEDDA (English) prosperous guardian. A feminine form of Edward.
Neddi, Neddie, Neddy

NEELY (Irish) a familiar form of Neila, Nelia.
Nealee, Nealie, Nealy, Neelee, Neeley, Neeli, Neelie, Neili, Neilie

NEEMA (Swahili) born during prosperous times.

NEENA (Spanish) an alternate form of Nina.
Neenah, Nena

NEILA (Irish) champion. A feminine form of Neil. See also Neala, Neely.
Nayely, Neilah, Neile, Neilia, Neilla, Neille

NEKEISHA (American) an alternate form of Nakeisha.
Nechesa, Neikeishia, Nekesha, Nekeshia, Nekiesha, Nekisha, Nekysha

NEKIA (Arabic) an alternate form of Nakia.
Nekeya, Nekiya, Nekiyah, Nekya, Nekiya

NELIA (Spanish) yellow. (Latin) a familiar form of Cornelia.
Neelia, Neely, Neelya, Nela, Neli, Nelka, Nila

NELLE (Greek) stone.

NELLIE, Nelly (English) familiar forms of Cornelia, Eleanor, Helen, Prunella.
Nel, Neli, Nell, Nella, Nelley, Nelli, Nellianne, Nellice, Nellis, Nelma

NENET (Egyptian) born near the sea. Mythology: the goddess of the sea.

NEOLA (Greek) youthful.
Neolla

NEONA (Greek) new moon.

NEREIDA (Greek) an alternate form of Nerine.
Nereyda, Nereyida, Nerida

NERINE (Greek) sea nymph.
Nereida, Nerina, Nerita, Nerline

NERISSA (Greek) sea nymph. See also Rissa.
Narice, Narissa, Nerice, Nerisa, Nerisse, Nerrisa, Nerys, Neryssa

NESSA (Greek) a short form of Agnes. (Scandinavian) promontory. See also Nessie.
Nesa, Nesha, Neshia, Nesiah, Nessia, Nesta, Nevsa, Neysa, Neysha, Neyshia

NESSIE (Greek) a familiar form of Agnes, Nessa, Vanessa.
Nese, Neshie, Nesho, Nesi, Ness, Nessi, Nessy, Nest, Neys

NETA (Hebrew) plant, shrub. See also Nettie.
Netia, Netta, Nettia

NETIS (Native American) trustworthy.

NETTIE (French) a familiar form of Annette, Nanette, Antoinette.
Neti, Netie, Netta, Netti, Netty, Nety

NEVA (Spanish) snow. (English) new. Geography: a river in Russia.
Neiva, Neve, Nevia, Neyva, Nieve, Niva, Nivea, Nivia

NEVADA (Spanish) snow. Geography: a western American state.
Neiva, Neva

NEVINA (Irish) worshipper of the saint. A feminine form of Nevin. History: a well-known Irish saint.
Neveen, Nevein, Nevena, Neveyan, Nevin, Nivena

NEYLAN (Turkish) fulfilled wish.
Neya, Neyla

NEZA (Slavic) a form of Agnes.

NIA (Irish) a familiar form of Neila. Mythology: a legendary Welsh woman.
Neya, Niah, Niajia, Niya, Nya

NIABI (Osage) fawn.

NICHELLE (American) a combination of Nicole + Michelle. Culture: Nichelle Nichols was the first African-American woman featured in a television drama *Star Trek*.
Nichele, Nichell, Nishelle

NICHOLE (French) an alternate form of Nicole.
Nichol, Nichola, Nicholas, Nicholle

NICKI (French) a familiar form of Nicole.
Nicci, Nickey, Nickeya, Nickia, Nickie, Nickiya, Nicky, Niki

NICKOLE (French) an alternate form of Nicole.
Nickol

NICOLA (Italian) a form of Nicole.
Nacola, Necola, Nichola, Nickola, Nicolea, Nicolla, Nikkola, Nikola, Nikolia, Nykola

NICOLE (French) victorious people. A feminine form of Nicholas. See also Colette, Cosette, Nikita.
Nacole, Necole, Nica, Nichole, Nicia, Nicki, Nickole, Nicol, Nicola, Nicolette, Nicoli, Nicolie, Nicoline, Nicolle, Nikayla, Nikelle, Nikki, Niquole, Nocole, Nycole

NICOLETTE (French) an alternate form of Nicole.
Nicholette, Nicoletta, Nicollete, Nicollette, Nikkolette, Nikoleta, Nikoletta, Nikolette

NICOLINE (French) a familiar form of Nicole.
Nicholine, Nicholyn, Nicoleen, Nicolene, Nicolina, Nicolyn, Nicolyne, Nicolynn, Nicolynne, Nikolene, Nikolina, Nikoline

NICOLLE (French) an alternate form of Nicole.
Nicholle

NIDA (Omaha) Mythology: an elflike creature.
Nidda

NIDIA (Latin) nest.
Nidi, Nidya

NIESHA (Scandinavian) an alternate form of Nissa. (American) pure.
Neisha, Neishia, Neissia, Nesha, Neshia, Nesia, Nessia, Niessia, Nisha, Nyesha

NIGE (Latin) dark night. A feminine form of Nigel.
Nigea, Nigela, Nija, Nijae, Nijah

NIKA (Russian) belonging to God.
Nikka

NIKAYLA, Nikelle (American) forms of Nicole.
Nikeille, Nikel, Nikela, Nikelie

NIKE (Greek) victorious. Mythology: the goddess of victory.

NIKI (Russian) a short form of Nikita.
Nikia, Nikiah

NIKITA (Russian) victorious people. A form of Nicole.
Nakeita, Nakita, Niki, Nikitah, Nikitia, Nikitta, Nikki, Nikkita, Niquita, Niquitta

NIKKI (American) a familiar form of Nicole, Nikita.
Nicki, Nikia, Nikkea, Nikkey, Nikkia, Nikkiah, Nikkie, Nikko, Nikky

NIKOLE (French) an alternate form of Nicole.
Nikkole, Nikkolie, Nikola, Nikole, Nikolena, Nicolia, Nikolina, Nikolle

NILA (Latin) Geography: the Nile River in Egypt. (Irish) an alternate form of Neila.
Nilah, Nilesia, Nyla

NILI (Hebrew) Botany: a pea plant that yields indigo.

NIMA (Hebrew) thread. (Arabic) blessing.
Nema, Niama, Nimali

NINA (Hebrew) a familiar form of Hannah. (Spanish) girl. (Native American) mighty.
Neena, Ninah, Ninacska, Ninja, Ninna, Ninon, Ninosca, Ninoshka

NINON (French) a form of Nina.

NIREL (Hebrew) light of God.
Nirali, Nirelle

NIRVELI (Hindi) water child.

NISA (Arabic) woman.

NISHA (American) an alternate form of Niesha, Nissa.
Niasha, Nishay

NISHI (Japanese) west.

NISSA (Hebrew) sign, emblem. (Scandinavian) friendly elf; brownie. See also Nyssa.
Nisha, Nisse, Nissie, Nissy

NITA (Hebrew) planter. (Spanish) a short form of Anita, Juanita. (Choctaw) bear.
Nitai, Nitha, Nithai, Nitika

NITARA (Hindi) deeply rooted.

NITASHA (American) a form of Natasha.
Nitasia, Niteisha, Nitisha, Nitishia

NITSA (Greek) a form of Helen.

NITUNA (Native American) daughter.

NITZA (Hebrew) flower bud.
Nitzah, Nitzana, Nitzanit, Niza, Nizah

NIXIE (German) water sprite.

NIYA (Irish) an alternate form of Nia.
Niyah, Niyana, Niyia, Nyia

NIZANA (Hebrew) an alternate form of Nitza.
Nitzana, Nitzania, Zana

NOEL (Latin) Christmas. See also Natalie.
Noël, Noela, Noelani, Noele, Noeleen, Noelene, Noelia, Noeline, Noelle, Noelyn, Noelynn, Nohely, Noleen, Novelenn, Novelia, Nowel, Noweleen, Nowell

NOELANI (Hawaiian) beautiful one from heaven.
Noela

NOELLE (French) Christmas. A form of Noel.

Noell, Noella, Noelleen, Noelly, Noellyn

NOEMI (Hebrew) an alternate form of Naomi.
Noam, Noemie, Noemy, Nohemi, Nomi

NOEMIE (Hebrew) an alternate form of Noemi.

NOEMY (Hebrew) an alternate form of Noemi.
Noamy

NOGA (Hebrew) morning light.

NOHELY (Latin) an alternate form of Noel.
Noeli, Noelie, Noely, Nohal, Noheli

NOKOMIS (Dakota) moon daughter.

NOLA (Latin) small bell. (Irish) famous; noble. A short form of Fionnula. A feminine form of Nolan.
Nuala

NOLETA (Latin) unwilling.
Nolita

NOLLIE (English) a familiar form of Magnolia.
Nolia, Nolle, Nolley, Nolli, Nolly

NOMA (Hawaiian) a form of Norma.

NONA (Latin) ninth.
Nonah, Noni, Nonia, Nonie, Nonna, Nonnah, Nonya

NOOR (Aramaic) an alternate form of Nura.
Noorie, Nour, Nur

NORA (Greek) light. A familiar form of Eleanor, Honora, Leonore.
Norah, Noreen

NOREEN (Irish) a form of Eleanor, Nora. (Latin) a familiar form of Norma.
Noorin, Noreena, Noreene, Noren, Norena, Norene, Norina, Norine, Nureen

NORELL (Scandinavian) from the north.
Narell, Narelle, Norela, Norelle, Norely

NORI (Japanese) law, tradition.
Noria, Norico, Noriko, Norita

NORMA (Latin) rule, precept.
Noma, Noreen, Normi, Normie

NOVA (Latin) new. A short form of Novella, Novia. (Hopi) butterfly chaser. Astronomy: a star that releases bright bursts of energy.

NOVELLA (Latin) newcomer.
Nova, Novela

NOVIA (Spanish) sweetheart.
Nova, Novka, Nuvia

NU (Burmese) tender. (Vietnamese) girl.
Nue

NUALA (Irish) a short form of Fionnula.
Nola, Nula

NUELA (Spanish) a form of Amelia.

NUNA (Native American) land.

NUNCIATA (Latin) messenger.
Nunzia

NURA (Aramaic) light.
Noor, Noora, Noorah, Noura, Nurah

NURIA (Aramaic) the Lord's light.
Nuri, Nuriel, Nurin

NURITA (Hebrew) Botany: a flower with red and yellow blossoms.
Nurit

NURU (Swahili) daylight.

NUSI (Hungarian) a form of Hannah.

NUWA (Chinese) mother goddess. Mythology: the creator of mankind and order.

NYA (Irish) an alternate form of Nia.
Nyaa, Nyah, Nyia

NYCOLE (French) an alternate form of Nicole.
Nychelle, Nycolette, Nycolle

NYDIA (Latin) nest.
Nyda

NYESHA (American) an alternate form of Niesha.
Nyeisha, Nyeshia

NYLA (Irish) an alternate form of Nila.
Nylah

NYOKO (Japanese) gem, treasure.

NYOMI (Hebrew) an alternate form of Naomi.
Nyome, Nyomee, Nyomie

NYREE (Maori) sea.
Nyra, Nyrie

NYSSA (Greek) beginning. See also Nissa.
Nisha, Nissi, Nissy, Nyasia, Nysa

NYUSHA (Russian) a form of Agnes.
Nyushenka, Nyushka

OBA (Yoruba) Mythology: the goddess who rules the rivers.

OBELIA (Greek) needle.

OCEANA (Greek) ocean. Mythology: Oceanus was the god of water.
Ocean, Oceananna, Oceane, Oceania, Oceanna, Oceanne, Oceaonna, Oceon

OCTAVIA (Latin) eighth. A feminine form of Octavio. See also Tavia.
Octabia, Octaviah, Octaviais, Octavice, Octavie, Octavienne, Octavio, Octavious, Octavise, Octavya, Octivia, Otavia, Ottavia

ODEDA (Hebrew) strong; courageous.

ODELE (Greek) melody, song.
Odelet, Odelette, Odell, Odelle

ODELIA (Greek) ode; melodic. (Hebrew) I will praise God. (French) wealthy. A feminine form of Odell. See also Odetta.
Oda, Odeelia, Odeleya, Odelina, Odelinda, Odelyn, Odila, Odile, Odilia

ODELLA (English) wood hill.
Odela, Odelle, Odelyn

ODERA (Hebrew) plough.

ODESSA (Greek) odyssey, long voyage.
Adesha, Adeshia, Adessa, Adessia, Odessia

ODETTA (German, French) a form of Odelia.
Oddetta, Odette

ODINA (Algonquin) mountain.

OFELIA (Greek) an alternate form of Ophelia.
Ofeelia, Ofilia

OFIRA (Hebrew) gold.
Ofarrah, Ophira

OFRA (Hebrew) an alternate form of Aphra.
Ofrat

OGIN (Native American) wild rose.

OHANNA (Hebrew) God's gracious gift.

OKALANI (Hawaiian) heaven.
Okilani

OKI (Japanese) middle of the ocean.
Okie

OKSANA (Latin) an alternate form of Osanna.
Oksanna

OLA (Greek) a short form of Olesia. (Scandinavian) ancestor. A feminine form of Olaf.

OLATHE (Native American) beautiful.
Olathia

OLEDA (Spanish) an alternate form of Alida. See also Leda.
Oleta, Olida, Olita

OLENA (Russian) a form of Helen.

Oleena, Olenka, Olenna, Olenya, Olya

OLESIA (Greek) an alternate form of Alexandra.
Cesya, Ola, Olecia, Oleesha, Oleishia, Olesha, Olesya, Olexa, Olice, Olicia, Olisha, Olishia, Ollicia

OLETHA (Scandinavian) nimble.
Oleta, Yaletha

OLETHEA (Latin) truthful. See also Alethea.
Oleta

OLGA (Scandinavian) holy. See also Helga, Olivia.
Olenka, Olia, Olja, Ollya, Olva, Olya

OLIANA (Polynesian) oleander.

OLINA (Hawaiian) filled with happiness.

OLINDA (Greek) an alternate form of Yolanda. (Latin) scented. (Spanish) protector of property.

OLISA (Ibo) God.

OLIVE (Latin) olive tree.
Oliff, Oliffe, Olivet, Olivette

OLIVIA (Latin) olive tree. (English) a form of Olga. See also Liv, Livia.
Alivia, Alyvia, Olevia, Oliva, Olivea, Oliveia, Olivetta, Olivi, Olivianne, Olivya, Oliwia, Ollie, Olva, Olyvia

OLLIE (English) a familiar form of Olivia.
Olla, Olly, Ollye

OLWEN (Welsh) white footprint.
Olwenn, Olwin, Olwyn, Olwyne, Olwynne

OLYMPIA (Greek) heavenly.
Olimpia, Olympe, Olympie

OLYVIA (Latin) an alternate form of Olivia.

OMA (Hebrew) reverent. (German) grandmother. (Arabic) highest. A feminine form of Omar.

OMAIRA (Arabic) red.
Omar, Omara, Omarah, Omari, Omaria, Omarra

OMEGA (Greek) last, final, end. Linguistics: the last letter in the Greek alphabet.

ONA (Latin, Irish) an alternate form of Oona, Una. (English) river.

ONATAH (Iroquois) daughter of the earth and the corn spirit.

ONAWA (Native American) wide awake.
Onaja, Onajah

ONDINE (Latin) an alternate form of Undine.
Ondene, Ondina, Ondyne

ONDREA (Czech) a form of Andrea.
Ohndrea, Ohndreea, Ohndreya, Ohndria, Ondraya, Ondreana, Ondreea, Ondreya, Ondria, Ondrianna, Ondriea

ONEIDA (Native American) eagerly awaited.
Onida, Onyda

ONELLA (Hungarian) a form of Helen.

ONESHA (American) a combination of Ondrea + Aisha.
Oneshia, Onesia, Onessa, Onessia, Onethia, Oniesha, Onisha

ONI (Yoruba) born on holy ground.
Onnie

ONORA (Latin) an alternate form of Honora.
Onoria, Onorine, Ornora

OONA (Latin, Irish) an alternate form of Una.
Ona, Onna, Onnie, Oonagh, Oonie

OPA (Choctaw) owl.

OPAL (Hindi) precious stone.
Opale, Opalina, Opaline

OPHELIA (Greek) helper. Literature: Hamlet's love interest in the Shakespearean play *Hamlet*.
Filia, Ofelia, Ophélie, Ophilia, Phelia

OPRAH (Hebrew) an alternate form of Orpah.
Ophra, Ophrah, Opra

ORA (Greek) an alternate form of Aura. (Latin) prayer. (Spanish) gold. (English) seacoast.
Orah, Orlice, Orra

ORABELLA (Latin) an alternate form of Arabella.
Orabel, Orabela, Orabelle

ORALEE (Hebrew) the Lord is my light. See also Yareli.
Areli, Orali, Oralit, Orelie, Orlee, Orli, Orly

ORALIA (French) a form of Aurelia. See also Oriana.
Oralis, Oriel, Orielda, Orielle, Oriena, Orlena, Orlene

OREA (Greek) mountains.
Oreal, Oria, Oriah

ORELA (Latin) announcement from the gods; oracle.
Oreal, Orella, Orelle, Oriel, Orielle

ORENDA (Iroquois) magical power.

ORETHA (Greek) an alternate form of Aretha.
Oreta, Oretta, Orette

ORIANA (Latin) dawn, sunrise. (Irish) golden.
Orane, Orania, Orelda, Orelle, Ori, Oria, Orian, Oriane, Orianna, Orieana, Oryan

ORINA (Russian) a form of Irene.
Orya, Oryna

ORINDA (Hebrew) pine tree. (Irish) light skinned, white. A feminine form of Oren.
Orenda

ORINO (Japanese) worker's field.
Ori

ORIOLE (Latin) golden; black and orange bird.
Auriel, Oriel, Oriell, Oriella, Oriola

ORLA (Irish) golden woman.
Orlagh, Orlie, Orly

ORLANDA (German) famous throughout the land. A feminine form of Orlando.
Orlandia, Orlantha, Orlenda, Orlinda

ORLENDA (Russian) eagle.

ORLI (Hebrew) light.
Orlice, Orlie, Orly

ORMANDA (Latin) noble. (German) mariner, seaman. A feminine form of Orman.
Orma

ORNICE (Hebrew) cedar tree. (Irish) pale; olive colored.
Orna, Ornah, Ornat, Ornette, Ornit

ORPAH (Hebrew) runaway. See also Oprah.
Orpa, Orpha, Orphie

ORQUIDEA (Spanish) orchid.
Orquidia

ORSA (Greek) an alternate form of Ursula. (Latin) bear-like. A feminine form of Orson. See also Ursa.
Orsaline, Orse, Orsel, Orselina, Orseline, Orsola

ORTENSIA (Italian) a form of Hortense.

ORVA (French) golden; worthy. (English) brave friend.

OSANNA (Latin) praise the Lord.
Oksana, Osana

OSEN (Japanese) one thousand.

OSEYE (Benin) merry.

OSMA (English) devine protector. A feminine form of Osmond.
Ozma

OTILIE (Czech) lucky heroine.
Otila, Otilia, Otka, Ottili, Otylia

OVIA (Latin, Danish) egg.

OWENA (Welsh) born to nobility; young warrior. A feminine form of Owen.

OYA (Moquelumnan) called forth.

OZ (Hebrew) strength.

OZARA (Hebrew) treasure, wealth.

PACA (Spanish) a short form of Pancha. See also Paka.

PADGET (French) an alternate form of Page.
Padgett, Paget, Pagett

PADMA (Hindi) lotus.

PAGE (French) young assistant.
Padget, Pagen, Pagi, Payge

PAIGE (English) young child.
Payge

PAISLEY (Scottish) patterned fabric made in Paisley, Scotland.
Paislay, Paislee, Paisleyann, Paisleyanne, Paizlei, Paizleigh, Paizley, Pasley, Pazley

PAITON (English) warrior's town.
Paiten, Paityn, Paityne, Paiyton, Paten, Patton

PAKA (Swahili) kitten. See also Paca.

PAKUNA (Moquelumnan) deer bounding while running downhill.

PALILA (Polynesian) bird.

PALLAS (Greek) wise. Mythology: another name for Athena, the goddess of wisdom.

PALMA (Latin) palm tree.
Pallma, Palmira

PALMIRA (Spanish) a form of Palma.
Pallmirah, Pallmyra, Palmer, Palmyra

PALOMA (Spanish) dove. See also Aloma.
Palloma, Palometa, Palomita, Paluma, Peloma

PAMELA (Greek) honey.
Pam, Pama, Pamala, Pamalla, Pamelia, Pamelina, Pamella, Pamila, Pamilla, Pammela, Pammi, Pammie, Pammy, Pamula

PANCHA (Spanish) free; from France. A feminine form of Pancho.
Paca, Panchita

PANDITA (Hindi) scholar.

PANDORA (Greek) highly gifted. Mythology: a young woman who received many gifts from the gods, such as beauty, wisdom, and creativity. See also Dora.
Pandi, Pandorah, Pandorra, Pandorrah, Pandy, Panndora, Panndorah, Panndorra, Panndorrah

PANSY (Greek) flower; fragrant. (French) thoughtful.
Pansey, Pansie

PANTHEA (Greek) all the gods.
Pantheia, Pantheya

PANYA (Swahili) mouse; tiny baby. (Russian) a familiar form of Stephanie.
Panyia

PANYIN (Fanti) older twin.

PAOLA (Italian) a form of Paula.
Paoli, Paolina

PAPINA (Moquelumnan) vine growing on an oak tree.

PAQUITA (Spanish) a form of Frances.
Paqua

PARI (Persian) fairy eagle

PARIS (French) Geography: the capital of France. Mythology: the Trojan prince who started the Trojan war by abducting Helen.
Parice, Paries, Parisa, Parise, Parish, Parisha, Pariss, Parissa, Parisse, Parris, Parys, Parysse

PARKER (English) park keeper.
Park, Parke

PARRIS (French) an alternate form of Paris.
Parrise, Parrish, Parrisha, Parrys, Parrysh

PARTHENIA (Greek) virginal.
Partheenia, Parthenie, Parthinia, Pathina

PARVENEH (Persian) butterfly.

PASCALE (French) born on Easter or Passover. A feminine form of Pascal.
Pascalette, Pascaline, Pascalle, Paschale, Paskel

PASHA (Greek) sea.
Palasha, Pascha, Pasche, Pashae, Pashe, Pashel, Pashka, Pasia, Passia

PASSION (Latin) passion.
Pashion, Pashonne, Pasion, Passionaé, Passionate, Passionette

PASUA (Swahili) born by Caesarean section.

PAT (Latin) a short form of Patricia, Patsy

PATI (Moquelumnan) fish baskets made of willow branches.

PATIA (Latin, English) a familiar form of Patience, Patricia. (Gypsy, Spanish) leaf.

PATIENCE (English) patient.
Paciencia, Patia, Patiance, Patient, Patince, Patishia

PATRA (Greak, Latin) an alternate form of Petra.

PATRICE (French) a form of Patricia.
Patrease, Patrece, Patreece, Patreese, Patreice, Patriece, Patryce, Pattrice

PATRICIA (Latin) noblewoman. A feminine form of Patrick. See also Payton, Peyton, Tricia, Trisha, Trissa.
Pat, Patia, Patresa, Patrica, Patrice, Patricea, Patriceia, Patrichea, Patriciana, Patricianna, Patricja, Patricka, Patrickia, Patrisha, Patrishia, Patrisia, Patrissa, Patrizia, Patrizzia, Patrycia, Patrycja, Patsy, Patty

PATSY (Latin) a familiar form of Patricia.
Pat, Patsey, Patsi

PATTY (English) a familiar form of Patricia.
Patte, Pattee, Patti, Pattie

PAULA (Latin) small. A feminine form of Paul. See also Pavla, Polly.
Paliki, Paola, Paulane, Paulann, Paule, Paulette, Paulina, Pauline, Paulla, Pavia

PAULETTE (Latin) a familiar form of Paula.
Paulet, Paulett, Pauletta, Paulita, Paullett, Paulletta, Paullette

PAULINA (Slavic) a form of Paula.
Paulena, Paulene, Paulenia, Pauliana, Paulianne, Paullena, Paulyna, Pawlina, Polena, Polina, Polinia

PAULINE (Latin) a familiar form of Paula.
Pauleen, Paulene, Paulien, Paulin, Paulyne, Paulynn, Pouline

PAUSHA (Hindi) lunar month of Capricorn.

PAVLA (Czech, Russian) a form of Paula.
Pavlina, Pavlinka

PAXTON (Latin) peaceful town.
Paxtin, Paxtynn

PAYGE (English) an alternate form of Paige.

PAYTON (Irish) a form of Patricia.
Paydon, Paytan, Payten, Paytin, Paytn, Paytton

PAZ (Spanish) peace.

PAZI (Ponca) yellow bird.

PAZIA (Hebrew) golden.
Paz, Paza, Pazice, Pazit

PEACE (English) peaceful.

PEARL (Latin) jewel.
Pearle, Pearleen, Pearlena, Pearlene, Pearlette, Pearlina, Pearline, Pearlisha, Pearlyn, Perl, Perla, Perle, Perlette, Perlie, Perline, Perlline

PEGGY (Greek) a familiar form of Margaret.
Peg, Pegeen, Pegg, Peggey, Peggi, Peggie, Pegi

PEKE (Hawaiian) a form of Bertha.

PELA (Polish) a short form of Penelope.
Pele

PELAGIA (Greek) sea.
Pelage, Pelageia, Pelagie, Pelga, Pelgia, Pellagia

PELIPA (Zuni) a form of Philippa.

PEMBA (Bambara) the power that controls all life.

PENDA (Swahili) loved.

PENELOPE (Greek) weaver. Mythology: the clever and loyal wife of Odysseus, a Greek hero.
Pela, Pen, Penelopa, Penna, Pennelope, Penny, Pinelopi

PENI (Carrier) mind.

PENINAH (Hebrew) pearl.
Penina, Peninit, Peninnah, Penny

PENNY (Greek) a familiar form of Penelope, Peninah.
Penee, Peni, Penney, Penni, Pennie

PEONY (Greek) flower.
Peonie

PEPITA (Spanish) a familiar form of Josephine.
Pepa, Pepi, Peppy, Peta

PEPPER (Latin) condiment from the pepper plant.

PERAH (Hebrew) flower.

PERDITA (Latin) lost. Literature: a character in Shakespeare's play *The Winter's Tale*.
Perdida, Perdy

PERFECTA (Spanish) flawless.

PERI (Greek) mountain dweller. (Persian) fairy or elf.
Perita

PERLA (Latin) an alternate form of **Pearl**.
Pearla

PERLIE (Latin) a familiar form of Pearl.
Pearley, Pearlie, Pearly, Perley, Perli, Perly, Purley, Purly

PERNELLA (Greek, French) rock. (Latin) a short form of Petronella.
Parnella, Pernel, Pernell, Pernelle

PERRI (Greek, Latin) small rock; traveler. (French) pear tree. (Welsh) daughter of Harry. A feminine form of Perry.
Perre, Perrey, Perriann, Perrie, Perrin, Perrine, Perry

PERSEPHONE (Greek) springtime. Mythology: the goddess of spring.
Persephanie, Persephany, Persephonie

PERSIS (Latin) from Persia.
Perssis, Persy

PETA (Blackfoot) golden eagle.

PETRA (Greek, Latin) small rock. A short form of Petronella. A feminine form of Peter.
Patra, Pet, Peta, Petena, Peterina, Petraann, Petrice, Petrina, Petrine, Petrova, Petrovna, Pier, Pierce, Pietra

PETRONELLA (Greek) small rock. (Latin) of the Roman clan Petronius.
Pernella, Peternella, Petra, Petrona, Petronela, Petronella, Petronelle, Petronia, Petronija, Petronilla, Petronille

PETULA (Latin) seeker.
Petulah

PETUNIA (Native American) flower.

PEYTON (Irish) an alternate form of Patricia.
Peyden, Peydon, Peyten, Peytyn

PHAEDRA (Greek) bright.
Faydra, Phae, Phaidra, Phe, Phedre

PHALLON (Irish) an alternate form of Fallon.
Phalaine, Phalen, Phallan, Phallie, Phalon, Phalyn

PHEBE (Greek) an alternate form of Phoebe.
Pheba, Pheby

PHEODORA (Greek, Russian) an alternate form of Feodora.
Phedora, Phedorah, Pheodorah, Pheydora, Pheydorah

PHILANA (Greek) lover of mankind. A feminine form of Philander.
Phila, Philanna, Philene, Philiane, Philina, Philine

PHILANTHA (Greek) lover of flowers.

PHILICIA (Latin) an alternate form of Phylicia.
Philecia, Philesha, Philica, Philicha, Philycia

PHILIPPA (Greek) lover of horses. A feminine form of Philip. See also Filippa.
Phil, Philipa, Philippe, Phillipina, Phillippine, Phillie, Philly, Pippa, Pippy

PHILOMENA (Greek) love song; loved one. Bible: a first-century saint. See also Filomena, Mena.
Philoméne, Philomina

PHOEBE (Greek) shining.
Phaebe, Phebe, Pheobe, Phoebey

PHYLICIA (Greek) a form of Felicia. (Latin) fortunate; happy.
Philicia, Phylecia, Phylesha, Phylesia, Phylica, Phylisha, Phylisia, Phylissa, Phyllecia, Phyllicia, Phyllisha, Phyllisia, Phyllissa, Phyllyza

PHYLLIDA (Greek) an alternate form of Phyllis.
Fillida, Philida, Phillida, Phillyda

PHYLLIS (Greek) green bough.
Filise, Fillys, Fyllis, Philis, Phillis, Philliss, Philys, Philyss, Phylis, Phyllida, Phyllis, Phylliss, Phyllys

PIA (Italian) devout.

PIEDAD (Spanish) devoted; pious.

PIER (French) a form of Petra.
Pierette, Pierrette, Pierra, Pierre

PIERCE (English) a form of Petra.

PILAR (Spanish) pillar, column. Religion: honoring the Virgin Mary, the pillar of the Catholic Church.
Peelar, Pilár, Pillar

PING (Chinese) duckweed. (Vietnamese) peaceful.

PINGA (Hindi) bronze; dark. Religion: another name for the Hindu goddess Shakti.

PIPER (English) pipe player.

PIPPA (English) a short form of Phillipa.

PIPPI (French) rosy cheeked.
Pippen, Pippie, Pippin, Pippy

PITA (African) fourth daughter.

PLACIDIA (Latin) serene.
Placida

PLEASANCE (French) pleasant.
Pleasence

POLLA (Arabic) poppy.
Pola

POLLY (Latin) a familiar form of Paula.
Paili, Pali, Pauli, Paulie, Pauly, Poll, Pollee, Polley, Polli, Pollie

POLLYAM (Hindi) goddess of the plague. Religion: the Hindu name invoked to ward off bad spirits.

POLLYANNA (English) a combination of Polly + Anna. Literature: an overly optimistic heroine created by Eleanor Poiter.

POLOMA (Choctaw) bow.

POMONA (Latin) apple. Mythology: the goddess of fruit and fruit trees.

PONI (African) second daughter.

POPPY (Latin) poppy flower.
Popi, Poppey, Poppi, Poppie

PORA, Poria (Hebrew) fruitful.

PORCHA (Latin) an alternate form of Portia.
Porchae, Porchai, Porche, Porchia, Porcia

PORSCHA, Porsche (German) forms of Portia.
Porcsha, Porcshe, Porschah, Porsché, Porschea, Porschia, Pourche

PORSHA (Latin) an alternate form of Portia.
Porshai, Porshay, Porshe, Porshea, Porshia

PORTIA (Latin) offering. Literature: the heroine of Shakespeare's play *The Merchant of Venice*.
Porcha, Porscha, Porsche, Porsha, Portiea

PRECIOUS (French) precious; dear.
Pracious, Preciouse, Precisha, Prescious, Preshious, Presious

PRESLEY (English) priest's meadow.
Preslea, Preslee, Preslei, Presli, Preslie, Presly, Preslye, Pressley, Presslie, Pressly

PRIMA (Latin) first, beginning; first child.
Prema, Primalia, Primetta, Primina, Priminia

PRIMAVERA (Italian, Spanish) spring.

PRIMROSE (English) primrose flower.
Primula

PRINCESS (English) daughter of royalty.
Princcess, Princes, Princesa, Princessa, Princetta, Princie, Princilla

PRISCILLA (Latin) ancient.
Cilla, Piri, Precila, Precilla, Prescilla, Presilla, Pressilia, Pricila, Pricilla, Pris, Prisca, Priscela, Priscella, Priscila, Priscilia, Priscill, Priscille, Priscillia, Prisella, Prisila, Prisilla, Prissila, Prissilla, Prissy, Pryscylla, Prysilla

PRISSY (Latin) a familiar form of Priscilla.
Prisi, Priss, Prissi, Prissie

PRIYA (Hindi) beloved; sweet natured.
Pria

PROCOPIA (Latin) declared leader. A feminine form of Prokopius.

PROMISE (Latin) promise, pledge.
Promis, Promiss, Promys, Promyse

PRU (Latin) a short form of Prudence.
Prue

PRUDENCE (Latin) cautious; discreet.
Pru, Prudencia, Prudens, Prudy

PRUDY (Latin) a familiar form of Prudence.
Prudee, Prudi, Prudie

PRUNELLA (Latin) brown; little plum. See also Nellie.
Prunela

PSYCHE (Greek) soul. Mythology: a beautiful mortal loved by Eros, the Greek god of love.

PUA (Hawaiian) flower.

PUALANI (Hawaiian) heavenly flower.
Puni

PURITY (English) purity.
Pura, Pureza, Purisima

PYRALIS (Greek) fire.
Pyrene

QADIRA (Arabic) powerful.
Kadira

QAMRA (Arabic) moon.
Kamra

QITARAH (Arabic) fragrant.

QUAASHIE (Ewe) born on Sunday.

QUADEISHA (American) a combination of Qadira + Aisha.
Qudaisha, Quadaishia, Quadajah, Quadasha, Quadasia, Quadayshia, Quadaza, Quadejah, Quadesha, Quadeshia, Quadiasha, Quaesha

QUANEISHA (American) a combination of the prefix Qu + Niesha.
Quaneasa, Quanece, Quanecia, Quaneice, Quanesha, Quanisha, Quansha, Quarnisha, Queisha, Qwanisha, Qynisha

QUANESHA (American) an alternate form of Quaneisha.

Quamesha, Quaneesha, Quaneshia, Quanesia, Quanessa, Quanessia, Quannesha, Quanneshia, Quannezia, Quayneshia, Quinesha

QUANIKA (American) a combination of the prefix Qu + Nika.
Quanikka, Quanikki, Quaniqua, Quanique, Quantenique, Quawanica, Queenika, Queenique

QUANISHA (American) an alternate form of Quaneisha.
Quaniesha, Quanishia, Quaynisha, Queenisha, Quenisha, Quenishia

QUARTILLA (Latin) fourth.
Quantilla

QUBILAH (Arabic) agreeable.

QUEEN (English) queen. See also Quinn.
Queena, Queenie, Quenna

QUEENIE (English) an alternate form of Queen.
Queenation, Queeneste, Queeny

QUEISHA (American) a short form of Quaneisha.
Qeysha, Queshia, Queysha

QUENBY (Scandinavian) feminine.

QUENISHA (American) a combination of Queen + Aisha.
Queneesha, Quenesha, Quennisha, Quensha, Quinesha, Quinisha

QUENNA (English) an alternate form of Queen.
Quenell, Quenessa

QUERIDA (Spanish) dear; beloved.

QUESTA (French) searcher.

QUETA (Spanish) a short form of names ending in "queta" or "quetta."
Quenetta, Quetta

QUIANA (American) a combination of the prefix Qu + Anna.
Quian, Quianah, Quianda, Quiane, Quiani, Quianita, Quianna, Quianne, Quionna

QUINBY (Scandinavian) queen's estate.

QUINCY (Irish) fifth.
Quincee, Quincey, Quinci, Quincia, Quincie

QUINELLA (Latin) an alternate form of Quintana.

QUINESHA, Quinisha (American) alternate forms of Quenisha.
Quineshia, Quinessa, Quinessia, Quinisa, Quinishia, Quinnesha, Quinneshia, Quinnisha, Quneasha, Quonesha, Quonisha, Quonnisha

QUINETTA (Latin) an alternate form of Quintana.
Queenetta, Queenette, Quinette, Quinita, Quinnette

QUINN (German, English) queen. See also Queen.
Quin, Quinna, Quinne, Quynn

QUINSHAWNA (American) a combination of Quinn + Shauna.
Quinshea

QUINTANA (Latin) fifth. (English) queen's lawn. A feminine form of Quentin, Quintin. See also Quinella, Quinetta.

Quinntina, Quinta, Quintanna, Quintara, Quintarah, Quintia, Quintila, Quintilla, Quintina, Quintona, Quintonice

QUINTESSA (Latin) essence. See also Tess.
Quintaysha, Quintesa, Quintesha, Quintessia, Quintice, Quinticia, Quintisha, Quintosha

QUINTRELL (American) a combination of Quinn + Trella.
Quintela, Quintella, Quintrelle

QUITERIE (Latin, French) tranquil.
Quita

QWANISHA (American) an alternate form of Quaneisha.
Qwanechia, Qwanesha, Qwanessia, Qwantasha

RABECCA (Hebrew) an alternate form of Rebecca.
Rabecka, Rabeca, Rabekah

RABI (Arabic) breeze.
Rabia, Rabiah

RACHAEL (Hebrew) an alternate form of Rachel.
Rachaele, Rachaell, Rachail, Rachalle

RACHEAL (Hebrew) an alternate form of Rachel.

RACHEL (Hebrew) female sheep. Bible: the wife of Jacob. See also Lahela, Rae, Rochelle.
Racha, Rachael, Rachal, Racheal, Rachela, Rachelann, Rachele, Rachelle, Racquel, Raechel, Rahel, Rahela, Rahil, Raiche, Raquel, Rashel, Rashelle, Ray, Raycene, Raychel, Raychelle, Rey, Ruchel

RACHELLE (French) a form of Rachel. See also Shelley.
Rachalle, Rachell, Rachella, Raechell, Raechelle, Raeshelle, Rashel, Rashele, Rashell, Rashelle, Raychell, Rayshell, Ruchelle

RACQUEL (French) a form of Rachel.
Rackel, Racquell, Racquella, Racquelle

RADELLA (German) counselor.

RADEYAH (Arabic) content, satisfied.
Radeeyah, Radhiya, Radiah, Radiyah

RADINKA (Slavic) full of life; happy, glad.

RADMILLA (Slavic) worker for the people.

RADWA (Arabic) Geography: a mountain in Medina, Saudi Arabia.

RAE (English) doe. (Hebrew) a short form of Rachel.
Raeh, Raeneice, Raeneisha, Raesha, Ray, Raye, Rayetta, Rayette, Rayma, Rey

RAEANN (American) a combination of Rae + Ann. See also Rayanne.
Raea, Raean, Raeanna, Raeannah, Raeona, Reanna, Raeanne

RAECHEL (Hebrew) an alternate form of Rachel.
Raechael, Raechal, Raechele, Raechell, Raechyl

RAEDEN (Japanese) Mythology: the thunder god. A feminine form of Raiden.
Raeda, Raedeen

RAEGAN (Irish) an alternate form of Reganne.
Raegen, Raegene, Raegine, Raegyn

RAELENE (American) a combination of Rae + Lee.
Rael, Raela, Raelani, Raele, Raeleah, Raelee, Raeleen, Raeleia, Raeleigh, Raeleigha, Raelein, Raelene, Raelennia, Raelesha, Raelin, Raelina, Raelle, Raelyn, Raelynn

RAELYN, Raelynn (American) alternate forms of Raelene.
Raelynda, Raelyne, Raelynne

RAENA (German) an alternate form of Raina.
Raenah, Raenia, Raenie, Raenna, Raeonna, Raeyauna, Raeyn, Raeyonna

RAEVEN (English) an alternate form of Raven.
Raevin, Raevion, Raevon, Raevonna, Raevyn, Raevynne, Raewyn, Raewynne, Raivan, Raiven, Raivin, Raivyn

RAFA (Arabic) happy; prosperous.

RAFAELA (Hebrew) an alternate form of Raphaela.
Rafaelia, Rafaella

RAGAN (Irish) an alternate form of Reganne.
Ragean, Rageane, Rageen, Ragen, Ragene, Rageni, Ragenna, Raggan, Raygan, Raygen, Raygene, Rayghan, Raygin

RAGINE (English) an alternate form of Regina.
Raegina, Ragin, Ragina, Raginee

RAGNILD (Scandinavian) Mythology: a warrior goddess.
Ragna, Ragnell, Ragnhild, Rainell, Renilda, Renilde

RAHEEM (Punjabi) compassionate God.
Raheema, Rahima

RÁIDAH (Arabic) leader.

RAINA (German) mighty. (English) a short form of Regina. See also Rayna.
Raeinna, Raena, Raheena, Rain, Rainah, Rainai, Raine, Rainea, Rainna, Reanna

RAINBOW (English) rainbow.
Rainbeau, Rainbeaux, Rainbo, Raynbow

RAINE (Latin) a short form of Regina. An alternate form of Raina, Rane.
Rainee, Rainey, Raini, Rainie, Rainy, Reyne

RAISA (Russian) a form of Rose.
Raisah, Raissa, Raiza, Raysa, Rayza, Razia

RAIZEL (Yiddish) a form of Rose.
Rayzil, Razil, Reizel, Resel

RAJA (Arabic) hopeful.
Raia, Rajaah, Rajae, Rajah, Rajai

RAKU (Japanese) pleasure.

RALEIGH (Irish) an alternate form of Riley.
Ralea, Raleiah, Raley

RAMA (Hebrew) lofty, exalted. (Hindi) godlike. Religion: another name for the Hindu goddess Shiva.
Ramah

RAMAN (Spanish) an alternate form of Ramona.

RAMANDEEP (Sikh) covered by the light of the Lord's love.

RAMLA (Swahili) fortuneteller.
Ramlah

RAMONA (Spanish) mighty; wise protector. See also Mona.
Raman, Ramonda, Raymona, Romona, Romonda

RAMSEY (English) ram's island.
Ramsha, Ramsi, Ramsie, Ramza

RAN (Japanese) water lily. (Scandinavian) destroyer. Mythology: the sea goddess who destroys.

RANA (Sanskrit) royal. (Arabic) gaze, look.
Rahna, Rahni, Rani

RANAIT (Irish) graceful; prosperous.
Rane, Renny

RANDALL (English) protected.
Randa, Randah, Randal, Randalee, Randel, Randell, Randelle, Randi, Randilee, Randilynn, Randlyn, Randy, Randyl

RANDI, Randy (English) familiar forms of Miranda, Randall.
Rande, Randee, Randeen, Randene, Randey, Randie, Randii

RANE (Scandinavian) queen.
Raine

RANI (Sanskrit) queen. (Hebrew) joyful. A short form of Kerani.
Rahni, Ranee, Raney, Rania, Ranie, Ranice, Ranique, Ranni, Rannie

RANITA (Hebrew) song; joyful.
Ranata, Ranice, Ranit, Ranite, Ranitta, Ronita

RANIYAH (Arabic) gazing.
Ranya, Ranyah

RAPA (Hawaiian) moonbeam.

RAPHAELA (Hebrew) healed by God. Bible: one of the four archangels.
Rafaella, Raphaella, Raphaelle

RAPHAELLE (French) a form of Raphaela.
Rafaelle, Raphael, Raphaele

RAQUEL (French) a form of Rachel.
Rakel, Rakhil, Rakhila, Raqueal, Raquela, Raquella, Raquelle, Rickelle, Rickquel, Ricquel, Ricquelle, Rikell, Rikelle, Rockell

RASHA (Arabic) young gazelle.
Rahshea, Rahshia, Rashae, Rashai, Rashea, Rashi, Rashia

RASHAWNA (American) a combination of the prefix Ra + Shawna.
Rashana, Rashanae, Rashanah, Rashanda, Rashane, Rashani, Rashanna, Rashanta, Rashaun, Rashauna, Rashaunda, Rashaundra, Rashaune, Rashawn, Rashawnda, Rashawnna, Rashon, Rashona, Rashonda, Rashunda

RASHEL, Rashelle (American) forms of Rachel.
Rashele, Rashell, Rashella

RASHIDA (Swahili, Turkish) righteous.
Rahshea, Rahsheda, Rahsheita, Rashdah, Rasheda, Rashedah, Rasheeda, Rasheedah, Rasheeta, Rasheida, Rashidah, Rashidi

RASHIEKA (Arabic) descended from royalty.
Rasheeka, Rasheika, Rasheka, Rashika, Rasika

RASIA (Greek) rose.

RATANA (Tai) crystal.
Ratania, Ratanya, Ratna, Rattan, Rattana

RATRI (Hindi) night. Religion: another name for the Hindu goddess Shakti.

RAULA (French) wolf counselor. A feminine form of Raoul.
Raoula, Raulla, Raulle

RAVEN (English) blackbird.
Raeven, Raveen, Raveena, Raveenn, Ravena, Ravene, Ravenn, Ravenna, Ravennah, Ravenne, Raveon, Ravin, Ravon, Ravyn, Rayven, Revena

RAVIN (English) an alternate form of Raven.
Ravi, Ravina, Ravine, Ravinne, Ravion,

RAVYN (English) an alternate form of Raven.
Ravynn

RAWNIE (Gypsy) fine lady.
Rawan, Rawna, Rhawnie

RAYA (Hebrew) friend.
Raia, Raiah, Raiya, Ray, Rayah

RAYANNE (American) an alternate form of Raeann.
Rayane, Ray-Ann, Rayan, Rayana, Rayann, Rayanna,

Rayanne (cont.)
Rayeanna, Rayona, Rayonna, Reyan, Reyana, Reyann, Reyanna, Reyanne

RAYCHEL, Raychelle (Hebrew) alternate forms of Rachel.
Raychael, Raychele, Raychell, Raychil

RAYLENE (American) a combination of Rae + Lyn.
Ralina, Rayel, Rayele, Rayelle, Rayleana, Raylee, Rayleen, Rayleigh, Raylena, Raylin, Raylinn, Raylona, Raylyn, Raylynn, Raylynne

RAYMONDE (German) wise protector. A feminine form of Raymond.
Rayma, Raymae, Raymie

RAYNA (Scandinavian) mighty. (Yiddish) pure, clean. (French) a familiar form of Lorraine. (English) king's advisor. A feminine form of Reynold. See also Raina.
Raynah, Rayne, Raynell, Raynelle, Raynette, Rayona, Rayonna, Reyna

RAYVEN (English) an alternate form of Raven.
Rayvan, Rayvana, Rayvein, Rayvenne, Rayveona, Rayvin, Rayvon, Rayvonia

RAYYA (Arabic) thirsty no longer.

RAZI (Aramaic) secretive.
Rayzil, Rayzilee, Raz, Razia, Raziah, Raziela, Razilee, Razili

RAZIYA (Swahili) agreeable.

REA (Greek) poppy flower.
Reah

REAGAN (Irish) an alternate form of Reganne.
Reagen, Reaghan, Reagine

REANNA (German, English) an alternate form of Raina. (American) an alternate form of Raeann.
Reannah

REANNE (American) an alternate form of Raeann, Reanna.
Reana, Reane, Reann, Reannan, Reanne, Reannen, Reannon, Reeana

REBA (Hebrew) fourth-born child. A short form of Rebecca. See also Reva, Riva.
Rabah, Reeba, Rheba

REBECA (Hebrew) an alernate form of Rebecca.
Rebbeca, Rebecah

REBECCA (Hebrew) tied, bound. Bible: the wife of Isaac. See also Becca, Becky.
Rabecca, Reba, Rebbecca, Rebeca, Rebeccah, Rebeccea, Rebeccka, Rebecha, Rebecka, Rebeckah, Rebeckia, Rebecky, Rebekah, Rebeque, Rebi, Reveca, Riva, Rivka

REBEKAH (Hebrew) an alternate form of Rebecca.
Rebeka, Rebekha, Rebekka, Rebekkah, Rebekke, Revecca, Reveka, Revekka, Rifka

REBI (Hebrew) a familiar form of Rebecca.
Rebbie, Rebe, Rebie, Reby, Ree, Reebie

REENA (Greek) peaceful.
Reen, Reenie, Rena, Reyna

REET (Estonian) a form of Margaret.
Reatha, Reta, Retha

REGAN (Irish) an alternate form of Reganne.
Regane, Reghan

REGANNE (Irish) little ruler. A feminine form of Reagan.
Raegan, Ragan, Reagan, Regin

REGGIE (English) a familiar form of Regina.
Reggi, Reggy, Regi, Regia, Regie

REGINA (Latin) queen. (English) king's advisor. A feminine form of Reginald. Geography: the capital of Saskatchewan. See also Gina.
Ragine, Raina, Raine, Rega, Regena, Regennia, Reggie, Regiena, Regine, Reginia, Regis, Reina, Rena

REGINE (Latin) an alternate form of Regina.
Regin

REI (Japanese) polite, well behaved.
Reiko

REILLY (Irish) an alternate form of Riley.
Reilee, Reileigh, Reiley, Reili, Reilley, Reily

REINA (Spanish) a short form of Regina. See also Reyna.
Reinah, Reine, Reinette, Reinie, Reinna, Reiny, Reiona, Renia, Rina

REKHA (Hindi) thin line.
Reka, Rekia, Rekiah, Rekiya

REMEDIOS (Spanish) remedy.

REMI (French) from Rheims.
Raymi, Remee, Remie, Remy

REMINGTON (English) raven estate.
Remmington

REN (Japanese) arranger; water lily; lotus.

RENA (Hebrew) song; joy. A familiar form of Irene, Regina, Renata, Sabrina, Serena.
Reena, Rina, Rinna, Rinnah

RENAE (French) an alternate form of Renée.
Renay

RENATA (French) an alternate form of Renée.
Ranata, Rena, Renada, Renatta, Renita, Rennie, Renyatta, Rinada, Rinata

RENE (Greek) a short form of Irene, Renée.
Reen, Reenie, Reney, Rennie

RENÉE (French) born again.
Renae, Renata, Renay, Rene, Renea, Reneigh, Renell, Renelle, Renne

RENITA (French) an alternate form of Renata.
Reneeta, Renetta, Renitza

RENNIE (English) a familiar form of Renata.
Reni, Renie, Renni

RESEDA (Spanish) fragrant mignonette blossom.

RESHAWNA (American) a combination of the prefix Re + Shawna.
Resaunna, Reshana, Reshaunda, Reshawnda, Reshawnna, Reshonda, Reshonn, Reshonta

RESI (German) a familiar form of Theresa.
Resia, Ressa, Resse, Ressie, Reza, Rezka, Rezi

RETA (African) shaken.
Reeta, Retta, Rheta, Rhetta

REUBENA (Hebrew) behold a daughter. A feminine form of Reuben.
Reubina, Reuvena, Rubena, Rubenia, Rubina, Rubine, Rubyna

REVA (Latin) revived. (Hebrew) rain; one-fourth. An alternate form of Reba, Riva.
Ree, Reeva, Revia, Revida

REVECA, Reveka (Slavic) forms of Rebecca, Rebekah.
Reve, Revecca, Revekka, Rivka

REXANNE (American) queen. A feminine form of Rex.
Rexan, Rexana, Rexann, Rexanna

REYHAN (Turkish) sweet-smelling flower.

REYNA (Greek) peaceful. (English) an alternate form of Reina.
Reyana, Reyanna, Reyni, Reynna

REYNALDA (German) king's advisor. A feminine form of Reynold.

RÉZ (Latin, Hungarian) copper-colored hair.

REZA (Czech) a form of Theresa.
Rezi, Rezka

RHEA (Greek) brook, stream. Mythology: the mother of Zeus.
Rheá, Rhéa, Rhealyn, Rheanna, Rhia, Rhianna

RHEANNA, Rhianna (Greek) alternate forms of Rhea.
Rheana, Rheann, Rheanne, Rhiana, Rhiauna

RHIAN (Welsh) a short form of Rhiannon.
Rhianne, Rhyan, Rhyann, Rhyanne, Rian, Riane, Riann, Rianne, Riayn

RHIANNON (Welsh) witch; nymph; goddess.
Rheannan, Rheannin, Rheannon, Rheanon, Rhian, Rhianen, Rhianna, Rhiannan, Rhiannen, Rhianon, Rhianwen, Rhinnon, Rhyanna, Riana, Riannon, Rianon

RHODA (Greek) from Rhodes.
Rhode, Rhodeia, Rhodie, Rhody, Roda, Rodi, Rodie, Rodina

RHONA (Scottish) powerful, mighty. (English) king's advisor. A feminine form of Ronald.
Rhonae, Rhonnie

RHONDA (Welsh) grand.
Rhondene, Rhondiesha, Ronda, Ronelle, Ronnette

RIA (Spanish) river.
Riah

RIANA, Rianna (Irish) short forms of Briana.
Reana, Reanna, Rhianna, Rhyanna, Riana, Rianah

RICA (Spanish) a short form of Erica, Frederica, Ricarda. See also Enrica, Sandrica, Terrica, Ulrica.
Ricca, Rieca, Riecka, Rieka, Rikka, Riqua, Rycca

RICARDA (Spanish) rich and powerful ruler. A feminine form of Richard.
Rica, Richanda, Richarda, Richi, Ricki

RICHAEL (Irish) saint.

RICHELLE (German, French) a form of Ricarda.
Richel, Richela, Richele, Richell, Richella, Richia

RICKELLE (American) a form of Raquel.
Rickel, Rickela, Rickell

RICKI, Rikki (American) familiar forms of Erica, Frederica, Ricarda.
Rica, Ricci, Riccy, Rici, Rickee, Rickia, Rickie, Rickilee, Rickina, Rickita, Ricky, Ricquie, Riki, Rikia, Rikita, Rikka, Rikke, Rikkia, Rikkie, Rikky, Riko

RICQUEL (American) a form of Raquel.
Rickquell, Ricquelle, Rikell, Rikelle

RIDA (Arabic) favored by God.

RIHANA (Arabic) sweet basil.
Rhiana, Rhianna, Riana, Rianna

RIKA (Swedish) ruler.
Ricka

RILEE (Irish) an alternate form of Riley.
Rielee, Rielle

RILEY (Irish) valiant.
Raleigh, Reilly, Rieley, Rielly, Riely, Rilee, Rileigh, Rilie

RILLA (German) small brook.

RIMA (Arabic) white antelope.
Reem, Reema, Reemah, Rema, Remah, Rhymia, Rim, Ryma

RIMONA (Hebrew) pomegranate. See also Mona.

RIN (Japanese) park. Geography: a Japanese village.
Rini, Rynn

RINA (English) a short form of names ending in "rina."
Reena, Rena

RINAH (Hebrew) joyful.
Rina

RIONA (Irish) saint.

RISA (Latin) laughter.
Reesa, Resa

RISHA (Hindi) born during the lunar month of Taurus.
Rishah, Rishay

RISHONA (Hebrew) first.
Rishina, Rishon

RISSA (Greek) a short form of Nerissa.
Risa, Rissah, Ryssa, Ryssah

RITA (Sanskrit) brave; honest. (Greek) a short form of Margarita.
Reatha, Reda, Reeta, Reida, Reitha, Rheta, Riet, Ritah, Ritamae, Ritamarie

RITSA (Greek) a familiar form of Alexandra.
Ritsah, Ritsi, Ritsie, Ritsy

RIVA (Hebrew) a short form of Rebecca. (French) river bank. See also Reba, Reva.
Rivalee, Rivi, Rivvy

RIVER (Latin, French) stream, water.
Rivana, Rivanna, Rivers, Riviane

RIVKA (Hebrew) a short form of Rebecca.
Rivca, Rivcah, Rivkah

RIZA (Greek) a form of Theresa.
Riesa, Rizus, Rizza

ROANNA (American) a combination of Rose + Anna.
Ranna, Roana, Roanda, Roanne

ROBBI, Robbie (English) familiar forms of Roberta.
Robby, Robbye, Robey, Robi, Robia, Roby

ROBERTA (English) famous brilliance. A feminine form of Robert. See also Bobbette, Bobbi, Robin.
Roba, Robbi, Robbie, Robena, Robertena, Robertina

ROBIN (English) robin. An alternate form of Roberta.
Robann, Robbin, Robeen, Roben, Robena, Robian, Robina, Robine, Robinette, Robinia, Robinn, Robinta, Robyn

ROBINETTE (English) a familiar form of Robin.
Robernetta, Robinet, Robinett, Robinita

ROBYN (English) an alternate form of Robin.
Robbyn, Robbynn, Robyne, Robynn, Robynne

ROCHELLE (Hebrew) an alternate form of Rachel. (French) large stone. See also Shelley.
Reshelle, Roch, Rocheal, Rochealle, Rochel, Rochele, Rochell, Rochella, Rochette, Rockelle, Roshele, Roshell, Roshelle

ROCIO (Spanish) dewdrops.
Rocío

RODERICA (German) famous ruler. A feminine form of Roderick.
Rica, Rika, Rodericka, Roderika, Rodreicka, Rodricka, Rodrika

RODNAE (English) island clearing.
Rodna, Rodnetta, Rodnicka

RODNEISHA (American) a combination of Rodnae + Aisha.
Rodesha, Rodisha, Rodishah, Rodnecia, Rodnesha, Rodneshia, Rodneycia, Rodneysha, Rodnisha

ROHANA (Hindi) sandalwood. (American) a combination of Rose + Hannah.
Rochana, Rohena

ROHINI (Hindi) woman.

ROLANDA (German) famous throughout the land. A feminine form of Roland.
Ralna, Rolande, Rolando, Rolaunda, Roleesha, Rolene, Rolinda, Rollande, Rolonda

ROLENE (German) an alternate form of Rolanda.
Rolaine, Rolena, Rolleen, Rollene

ROMA (Latin) from Rome.
Romai, Rome, Romeise, Romeka, Romelle, Romesha, Rometta, Romia, Romilda, Romilla, Romina, Romini, Romma, Romonia

ROMAINE (French) from Rome.
Romana, Romanda, Romanelle, Romania, Romanique, Romany, Romayne, Romona, Romy

ROMY (French) a familiar form of Romaine. (English) a familiar form of Rosemary.
Romi, Romie

RONA (Scandinavian) a short form of Rhona.
Rhona, Roana, Ronalda, Ronna, Ronnae, Ronnay, Ronne, Ronni, Ronsy

RONAELE (Greek) Eleanor spelled backwards.
Ronalee, Ronni, Ronnie, Ronny

RONDA (Welsh) an alternate form of Rhonda.
Rondai, Rondesia, Rondi, Rondie, Ronelle, Ronnette, Ronni, Ronnie, Ronny

RONDELLE (French) short poem.
Rhondelle, Rondel, Ronndelle

RONEISHA (American) a combination of Rhonda + Aisha.
Roneasha, Ronecia, Ronee, Roneeka, Roneesha, Roneice, Ronese, Ronesha, Roneshia, Ronesia, Ronessa, Ronessia, Ronichia, Ronicia, Roniesha, Ronisha, Ronneisha, Ronnesa, Ronnesha, Ronneshia, Ronni, Ronnie, Ronniesha, Ronny

RONELLE (Welsh) an alternate form of Rhonda, Ronda.
Ranell, Ranelle, Ronel, Ronella, Ronielle, Ronnella, Ronnelle

RONISHA (American) an alternate form of Roneisha.
Ronise, Ronnise, Ronnisha, Ronnishia

RONLI (Hebrew) joyful.
Ronia, Ronice, Ronit, Ronlee, Ronlie, Ronni, Ronnie, Ronny

RONNETTE (Welsh) a familiar form of Rhonda, Ronda.
Ronetta, Ronette, Ronit, Ronita, Ronnetta, Ronni, Ronnie, Ronny

RONNI, Ronnie, Ronny (American) familiar forms of Veronica and names beginning with "Ron."
Rone, Ronee, Roni, Ronnee, Ronney

RORI, Rory (Irish) famous brilliance; famous ruler. Feminine forms of Robert, Roderick.
Rorie

ROS, Roz (English) short forms of Rosalind, Rosalyn.
Rozz, Rozzey, Rozzi, Rozzie, Rozzy

ROSA (Italian, Spanish) a form of Rose. History: Rosa Parks inspired the American civil rights movement by refusing to give up her bus seat to a white man in Montgomery, Alabama. See also Charo, Roza.

ROSABEL (French) beautiful rose.
Rosabelia, Rosabella, Rosabelle, Rosebelle

ROSALBA (Latin) white rose.
Rosalva, Roselba

ROSALIE (English) a form of Rosalind.
Rosalea, Rosalee, Rosaleen, Rosaleigh, Rosalene, Rosalia, Rosealee, Rosealie, Roselee, Roseli, Roselia, Roselie, Roseley, Rosely, Rosilee, Rosli, Rozali, Rozália, Rozalie, Rozele

ROSALIND (Spanish) fair rose.
Ros, Rosalie, Rosalinda, Rosalinde, Rosalyn, Rosalynd, Rosalynde, Roselind, Roselyn, Rosie, Roz, Rozalind, Rozland

ROSALINDA (Spanish) an alternate form of Rosalind.
Rosalina

ROSALYN (Spanish) an alternate form of Rosalind.
Ros, Rosaleen, Rosalin, Rosaline, Rosalyne, Rosalynn, Rosalynne, Rosilyn, Roslin,

Rosalyn *(cont.)*
Roslyn, Roslyne, Roslynn, Roz, Rozalyn, Rozlyn

ROSAMOND (German) famous guardian.
Rosamund, Rosamunda, Rosemonde, Rozamond

ROSANNA, Roseanna (English) combinations of Rose + Anna.
Ranna, Roanna, Rosana, Rosannah, Roseana, Roseannah, Rosehanah, Rosehannah, Rosie, Rossana, Rossanna, Rozana, Rozanna

ROSANNE, Roseanne (English) combinations of Rose + Ann.
Roanne, Rosan, Rosann, Roseann, Rose Ann, Rose Anne, Rossann, Rossanne, Rozann, Rozanne

ROSARIO (Filipino, Spanish) rosary.
Rosarah, Rosaria, Rosarie, Rosary, Rosaura

ROSE (Latin) rose. See also Chalina, Raisa, Raizel, Roza.
Rada, Rasia, Rasine, Rois, Róise, Rosa, Rosea, Rosella, Roselle, Roses, Rosetta, Rosie, Rosina, Rosita, Rosse

ROSELANI (Hawaiian) heavenly rose.

ROSELYN (Spanish) an alternate form of Rosalind.
Roseleen, Roselene, Roselin, Roseline, Roselyne, Roselynn, Roselynne

ROSEMARIE (English) a combination of Rose + Marie.
Rosamaria, Rosamarie, Rosemari, Rosemaria, Rose Marie

ROSEMARY (English) a combination of Rose + Mary.
Romi, Romy

ROSETTA (Italian) a form of Rose.
Roseta, Rosette

ROSHAN (Sanskrit) shining light.

ROSHAWNA (American) a combination of Rose + Shawna.
Roshan, Roshana, Roshanda, Roshani, Roshann, Roshanna, Roshanta, Roshaun, Roshauna, Roshaunda, Roshawn, Roshawnda, Roshawnna, Roshona, Roshonda, Roshowna, Roshunda

ROSIE (English) a familiar form of Rosalind, Rosanna, Rose.
Rosey, Rosi, Rosio, Rosse, Rosy, Rozsi, Rozy

ROSINA (English) a familiar form of Rose.
Rosena, Rosenah, Rosene, Rosheen, Rozena, Rozina

ROSITA (Spanish) a familiar form of Rose.
Roseeta, Roseta, Rozeta, Rozita, Rozyte

ROSLYN (Scottish) an alternate form of Rossalyn.
Roslin, Roslynn, Rosslyn, Rosslynn

ROSSALYN (Scottish) cape; promontory.
Roslyn, Rosselyn, Rosylin, Roszaliyn

ROWAN (English) tree with red berries. (Welsh) an alternate form of Rowena.
Rowana

ROWENA (Welsh) fair haired. (English) famous friend. Literature: Ivanhoe's love interest in Sir Walter Scott's novel *Ivanhoe*.
Ranna, Ronni, Row, Rowan, Rowe, Roweena, Rowen, Rowina

ROXANA, Roxanna (Persian) alternate forms of Roxann, Roxanne.
Rocsana, Roxannah

ROXANN, Roxanne (Persian) sunrise. Literature: the heroine of Edmond Rostand's play *Cyrano de Bergerac*.
Rocxann, Roxan, Roxana, Roxane, Roxanna, Roxianne, Roxy

ROXY (Persian) a familiar form of Roxann.
Roxi, Roxie

ROYALE (English) royal.
Royal, Royalene, Royalle, Roylee, Roylene, Ryal, Ryale

ROYANNA (English) queenly, royal. A feminine form of Roy.
Roya

ROZA (Slavic) a form of Rosa.
Roz, Rozalia, Roze, Rozel, Rozele, Rozell, Rozella, Rozelli, Rozia, Rozsa, Rozsi, Rozyte, Rozza, Rozzie

ROZENE (Native American) rose blossom.
Rozena, Rozina, Rozine, Ruzena

RUANA (Hindi) stringed musical instrument.
Ruan, Ruon

RUBENA (Hebrew) an alternate form of Reubena.
Rubenia, Rubina, Rubine, Rubinia, Rubyn, Rubyna

RUBI (French) an alternate form of Ruby.
Ruba, Rubbie, Rubee, Rubia, Rubie

RUBY (French) precious stone.
Rubby, Rubetta, Rubette, Rubey, Rubi, Rubiann, Rubyann, Rubye

RUCHI (Hindi) one who wishes to please.

RUDEE (German) famous wolf. A feminine form of Rudolph.
Rudeline, Rudell, Rudella, Rudi, Rudie, Rudina, Rudy

RUDRA (Hindi) seeds of the rudraksha plant.

RUE (German) famous. (French) street. (English) regretful; strong-scented herbs.
Ru, Ruey

RUFFINA (Italian) redhead.
Rufeena, Rufeine, Rufina, Ruphyna

RUI (Japanese) affectionate.

RUKAN (Arabic) steady; confident.

RULA (Latin, English) ruler.

RUNA (Norwegian) secret; flowing.
Runna

RUPERTA (Spanish) a form of Roberta.

RUPINDER (Sanskrit) beautiful.

RURI (Japanese) emerald.
Ruriko

RUSALKA (Czech) wood nymph. (Russian) mermaid.

RUSSHELL (French) redhead; fox colored. A feminine form of Russell.
Rushell, Rushelle, Russellynn, Russhelle

RUSTI (English) redhead.
Russet, Rustie, Rusty

RUTH (Hebrew) friendship. Bible: friend of Naomi.
Rutha, Ruthalma, Ruthe, Ruthella, Ruthetta, Ruthie, Ruthven

RUTHANN (American) a combination of Ruth + Ann.
Ruthan, Ruthanna, Ruthannah, Ruthanne, Ruthina, Ruthine

RUTHIE (Hebrew) a familiar form of Ruth.
Ruthey, Ruthi, Ruthy

RUZA (Czech) rose.
Ruzena, Ruzenka, Ruzha, Ruzsa

RYAN, Ryann (Irish) little ruler.
Raiann, Raianne, Rhyann, Riana, Riane, Ryana, Ryane, Ryanna, Ryanne, Rye, Ryen, Ryenne

RYBA (Czech) fish.

RYLEE (Irish) valiant.
Rye, Ryelee, Rylea, Ryleigh, Ryley, Rylie, Rylina, Rylyn

RYLEIGH, Rylie (Irish) alternate forms of Rylee.
Ryelie, Ryli, Rylleigh, Ryllie

RYLEY (Irish) an alternate form of Rylee.
Ryeley, Rylly, Ryly

RYO (Japanese) dragon.
Ryoko

SAARAH (Arabic) princess.

SABA (Greek) a form of Sheba. (Arabic) morning.
Sabaah, Sabah, Sabba, Sabbah

SABI (Arabic) young girl.

SABINA (Latin) History: the Sabine were a tribe in ancient Italy. See also Bina.
Sabeen, Sabena, Sabienne, Sabin, Sabine, Sabinka, Sabinna, Sabiny, Saby, Sabyne, Savina, Sebina, Sebinah

SABIYA (Arabic) morning; eastern wind.
Saba, Sabaya, Sabiyah

SABLE (English) sable; sleek.
Sabel, Sabela, Sabella

SABRA (Hebrew) thorny cactus fruit. History: a name for native-born Israelis, who were said to be hard on the outside and soft and sweet on the inside. (Arabic) resting.
Sabera, Sabira, Sabrah, Sabre, Sabrea, Sabreah, Sabree, Sabreea, Sabri, Sabria, Sabriah, Sabriya, Sebra

SABREENA (English) an alternate form of Sabrina.
Sabreen, Sabrena, Sabrene

SABRINA (Latin) boundary line. (Hebrew) a familiar form of Sabra. (English) princess. See also Bree, Brina, Rena, Zabrina.
Sabre, Sabreena, Sabrinas, Sabrinah, Sabrine, Sabrinia, Sabrinna, Sabryna, Sebree, Sebrina, Subrina

SABRYNA (English) an alternate form of Sabrina.
Sabrynna

SACHA (Russian) an alternate form of Sasha.
Sache, Sachia

SACHI (Japanese) blessed; lucky.
Saatchi, Sachie, Sachiko

SADA (Japanese) chaste. (English) a form of Sadie.
Sadá, Sadah, Sadako

SADE (Hebrew) an alternate form of Chadee, Sarah, Shardae, Sharday.
Sâde, Sadé, Sadea, Sadee, Shaday

SADELLA (American) a combination of Sade + Ella.
Sadelle, Sydel, Sydell, Sydella, Sydelle

SADHANA (Hindi) devoted.

SADIE (Hebrew) a familiar form of Sarah. See also Sada.
Saddie, Sadee, Sadey, Sadi, Sadiey, Sady, Sadye, Saide, Saidee, Saidey, Saidi, Saidia, Saidie, Saidy, Sayde, Saydee, Seidy

SADIRA (Persian) lotus tree. (Arabic) star.
Sadra

SADIYA (Arabic) lucky, fortunate.
Sadi, Sadia, Sadiah, Sadiyah, Sadiyyah, Sadya

SADZI (Carrier) sunny disposition.

SAFFRON (English) Botany: a plant with purple or white flowers whose orange stigmas are used as a spice.
Safron

SAFIYA (Arabic) pure; serene; best friend.
Safa, Safeya, Saffa, Safia, Safiyah

SAGARA (Hindi) ocean.

SAGE (English) wise. Botany: an herb with healing powers.
Sagia, Saige, Salvia

SAHARA (Arabic) desert; wilderness.
Sahar, Saharah, Sahari, Saheer, Saher, Sahira, Sahra, Sahrah

SAI (Japanese) talented.
Saiko

SAIDA (Hebrew) an alternate form of Sarah. (Arabic) happy; fortunate.
Saidah

SAIGE (English) an alternate form of Sage.

SAIRA (Hebrew) an alternate form of Sara.
Sairah, Sairi

SAKAË (Japanese) prosperous.

SAKARI (Hindi) sweet.
Sakkara

SAKI (Japanese) cloak; rice wine.

SAKTI (Hindi) energetic. An alternate form of Shakti.

SAKUNA (Native American) bird.

SAKURA (Japanese) cherry blossom; wealthy; prosperous.

SALA (Hindi) sala tree. Religion: the sacred tree under which Buddha died.

SALALI (Cherokee) squirrel.

SALAMA (Arabic) peaceful. See also Zulima.

SALENA (French) an alternate form of Salina.
Saleana, Saleen, Saleena, Salene, Salenna, Sallene

SALIMA (Arabic) safe and sound; healthy.
Saleema, Salema, Salim, Salimah, Salma

SALINA (French) solemn, dignified.
Salena, Salin, Salinah, Salinda, Saline

SALLIANN (English) a combination of Sally + Ann.
Sallian, Sallianne, Sallyann, Sally-Ann, Sallyanne, Sally-Anne

SALLY (English) princess. A familiar form of Sarah. History: Sally Ride, an American astronaut, became the first U.S. woman in space.
Sal, Salaid, Sallee, Salletta, Sallette, Salley, Salli, Sallie

SALOME (Hebrew) peaceful. History: Salome Alexandra was a ruler of ancient Judea. Bible: the sister of King Herod.
Saloma, Salomé, Salomey, Salomi

SALVADORA (Spanish) savior.

SALVIA (Latin) a form of Sage. (Spanish) healthy; saved.
Sallvia, Salviana, Salviane, Salvina, Salvine

SAMALA (Hebrew) asked of God.
Samale, Sammala

SAMANTA (Hebrew) an alternate form of Samantha.
Samantah, Smanta

SAMANTHA (Aramaic) listener. (Hebrew) told by God.
Sam, Samana, Samanath, Samanatha, Samanitha, Samanithia, Samanta, Samanth, Samanthe, Samanthi, Samanthia, Samatha, Sami, Sammanth, Sammantha, Semantha, Simantha, Smantha, Symantha

SAMARA (Latin) elm-tree seed.
Saimara, Samaira, Samar, Samarah, Samari, Samaria, Samariah, Samarie, Samarra, Samarrea, Samary, Samera, Sameria, Samira, Sammar, Sammara, Samora

SAMATHA (Hebrew) an alternate form of Samantha.
Sammatha

SAMEH (Hebrew) listener. (Arabic) forgiving.
Samaiya, Samaya

SAMI (Hebrew) a short form of Samantha, Samuela. (Arabic) praised.
Samia, Samiah, Samiha, Samina, Sammey, Sammi, Sammie, Sammijo, Sammy, Sammyjo, Samya, Samye

SAMIRA (Arabic) entertaining.
Samirah, Samire, Samiria, Samirra, Samyra

SAMONE (Hebrew) an alternate form of Simone.
Samoan, Samoane, Samon, Samona, Samoné, Samonia

SAMUELA (Hebrew) heard God, asked of God. A feminine form of Samuel.
Samala, Samelia, Samella, Sami, Samielle, Samille, Sammile, Samuelle

SAMUELLE (Hebrew) an alternate form of Samuela.
Samuella

SANA (Arabic) mountaintop; splendid; brilliant.
Sanaa, Sanáa, Sanaah, Sane, Sanah

SANCIA (Spanish) holy, sacred.
Sanceska, Sancha, Sancharia, Sanchia, Sancie, Santsia, Sanzia

SANDEEP (Punjabi) enlightened.
Sandip

SANDI (Greek) a familiar form of Sandra.
Sandee, Sandia, Sandie, Sandiey, Sandine, Sanndie

SANDRA (Greek) defender of mankind. A short form of Alexandra, Cassandra. History: Sandra Day O'Connor was the first woman appointed to the U.S. Supreme Court. See also Zandra.
Sahndra, Sandi, Sandira, Sandrea, Sandria, Sandrica, Sandy, Sanndra, Saundra

SANDREA (Greek) an alternate form of Sandra.
Sandreea, Sandreia, Sandrell, Sandria, Sanndria

SANDRICA (Greek) an alternate form of Sandra. See also Rica.
Sandricka, Sandrika

SANDRINE (Greek) an alternate form of Alexandra.
Sandreana, Sandrene, Sandrenna, Sandrianna, Sandrina

SANDY (Greek) a familiar form of Cassandra, Sandra.
Sandya, Sandye

SANNE (Hebrew, Dutch) lily.
Sanea, Saneh, Sanna, Sanneen

SANTANA (Spanish) saint.
Santa, Santaniata, Santanna, Santanne, Santena, Santenna, Shantana

SANTINA (Spanish) little saint.
Santinia

SANURA (Swahili) kitten.
Sanora

SANUYE (Moquelumnan) red clouds at sunset.

SANYA (Sanskrit) born on Saturday.
Saneiya, Sania, Sanyia

SANYU (Luganda) happiness.

SAPATA (Native American) dancing bear.

SAPPHIRA (Hebrew) a form of Sapphire.
Safira, Sapheria, Saphira, Saphyra, Sephira

SAPPHIRE (Greek) blue gemstone.
Saffire, Saphire, Saphyre, Sapphira

SARA (Hebrew) an alternate form of Sarah.

Sara (cont.)
Saira, Sarae, Saralee, Sarra,
Sera

SARAH (Hebrew) princess.
Bible: the wife of Abraham
and mother of Isaac. See
also Sadie, Saida, Sally,
Saree, Sharai, Shari, Zara,
Zarita.
Sahra, Sara, Saraha, Sarahann,
Sarahi, Sarai, Sarann, Saray,
Sarha, Sariah, Sarina, Sarita,
Sarolta, Sarotte, Sarrah, Sasa,
Sayra, Sorcha

SARAI, Saray (Hebrew) alternate forms of Sarah.
Saraya

SARALYN (American) a combination of Sarah + Lynn.
Saralena, Saraly, Saralynn

SAREE (Hebrew) a familiar
form of Sarah. (Arabic) noble.
Sareeka, Sareka, Sari, Sarika,
Sarka, Sarri, Sarrie, Sary

SARIAH (Hebrew) an alternate
form of Sarah.
Saria, Sarie

SARILA (Turkish) waterfall.

SARINA (Hebrew) a familiar
form of Sarah.
Sareen, Sareena, Saren,
Sarena, Sarene, Sarenna, Sarin,
Sarine, Sarinna, Sarinne

SARITA (Hebrew) a familiar
form of Sarah.
Saretta, Sarette, Sarit, Saritia,
Saritta

SAROLTA (Hungarian) a form of
Sarah.

SAROTTE (French) a form of
Sarah.

SARRAH (Hebrew) an alternate
form of Sarah.
Sarra

SASA (Hungarian) a form of
Sarah, Sasha. (Japanese)
assistant.

SASHA (Russian) defender of
mankind. A short form of
Alexandra. See also Zasha.
Sacha, Sahsha, Sasa, Sascha,
Saschae, Sashae, Sashah,
Sashai, Sashana, Sashay,
Sashea, Sashel, Sashenka,
Sashey, Sashi, Sashia, Sashira,
Sashsha, Sashya, Sasjara,
Sauscha, Sausha, Shasha,
Shashi, Shashia

SASS (Irish) Saxon.
Sassie, Sassoon, Sassy

SATARA (American) a combina-
tion of Sarah + Tara.
Sataria, Satarra, Sateriaa,
Saterra, Saterria

SATIN (French) smooth, shiny.
Satinder

SATINKA (Native American)
sacred dancer.

SATO (Japanese) sugar.
Satu

SAUNDRA (English) a form of
Sandra, Sondra.
Saundee, Saundi, Saundie,
Saundy

SAURA (Hindi) sun worshiper.
Astrology: born under the
sign of Leo.

SAVANA, Savanna (Spanish)
alternate forms of Savannah.
Saveena, Savhana, Savhanna,
Savina, Savine, Savona,
Savonna

SAVANAH (Spanish) an alternate form of Savannah.
Savhannah

SAVANNAH (Spanish) treeless
plain.
Sahvannah, Savana, Savanah,
Savanha, Savanna, Savannha,
Savauna, Savonnah, Savonne,
Sevan, Sevanah, Sevanh,
Sevann, Sevanna, Svannah

SAWA (Japanese) swamp.
(Moquelumnan) stone.

SAWYER (English) wood worker.
Sawyar, Sawyor

SAYDE, Saydee (Hebrew) alternate forms of Sadie.
Saydi, Saydia, Saydie, Saydy

SAYO (Japanese) born at night.

SAYRA (Hebrew) an alternate
form of Sarah.
Sayrah, Sayre, Sayri

SCARLETT (English) bright red.
Literature: Scarlett O'Hara is
the heroine of Margaret
Mitchell's novel *Gone with
the Wind.*
Scarlet, Scarlette, Scarlotte,
Skarlette

SCHYLER (Dutch) sheltering.
Schuyla, Schuyler, Schuylia,
Schylar

SCOTTI (Scottish) from
Scotland. A feminine form of
Scott.
Scota, Scotia, Scottie, Scotty

SEANA, Seanna (Irish) forms of
Jane. See also Shauna,
Shawna.
Seaana, Sean, Seane, Seann,
Seannae, Seannah, Seannalisa,
Seanté, Sianna, Sina

SEBASTIANE (Greek) venerable. (Latin) revered. (French) a feminine form of Sebastian.
Sebastene, Sebastia, Sebastian, Sebastiana, Sebastien, Sebastienne

SEBLE (Ethiopian) autumn.

SEBRINA (English) an alternate form of Sabrina.
Sebrena, Sebrenna, Sebria, Sebriana

SECILIA (Latin) an alternate form of Cecilia.
Saselia, Sasilia, Sesilia, Sileas

SECUNDA (Latin) second.

SEDA (Armenian) forest voices.

SEDNA (Eskimo) well-fed. Mythology: the goddess of sea animals.

SEELIA (English) a form of Sheila.

SEEMA (Greek) sprout. (Afghani) sky; profile.
Seemah, Sima, Simah

SEFA (Swiss) a familiar form of Josefina.

SEIRRA (Irish) an alternate form of Sierra.
Seiara, Seiarra, Seira, Seirria

SEKI (Japanese) wonderful.
Seka

SELA (English) a short form of Selena.
Seeley, Selah

SELAM (Ethiopian) peaceful.

SELDA (German) a short form of Griselda. (Yiddish) an alternate form of Zelda.
Seldah, Selde, Sellda, Selldah

SELENA (Greek) moon. Mythology: Selene was the goddess of the moon. See also Celena.
Saleena, Sela, Selana, Seleana, Seleena, Selen, Selenah, Selene, Séléné, Selenia, Selenna, Selina, Sena, Syleena, Sylena

SELENE (Greek) an alternate form of Selena.
Seleni, Selenie, Seleny

SELIA (Latin) a short form of Cecilia.
Seel, Seil, Sela, Silia

SELIMA (Hebrew) peaceful. A feminine form of Solomon.
Selema, Selemah, Selimah

SELINA (Greek) an alternate form of Celina, Selena.
Selie, Selin, Selinda, Seline, Selinia, Selinka, Sellina, Selyna, Selyne, Selynne, Sylina

SELMA (German) devine protector. (Irish) fair, just. (Scandinavian) divinely protected. (Arabic) secure. A feminine form of Anselm. See also Zelma.
Sellma, Sellmah, Selmah

SEMA (Turkish) heaven; divine omen.
Semaj

SEN (Japanese) Mythology: a magical forest elf that lives for thousands of years.

SENALDA (Spanish) sign.
Sena, Senda, Senna

SENECA (Iroquoian) a tribal name.
Senaka, Seneka, Senequa, Senequae, Senequai, Seneque

SEPTIMA (Latin) seventh.

SEQUOIA (Cherokee) giant redwood tree.
Seqoiyia, Seqouyia Seqoya, Sequoi, Sequoiah, Sequora, Sequoya, Sequoyah, Sikoya

SERAFINA (Hebrew) burning; ardent. Bible: Seraphim are the highest order of angels.
Sarafina, Serafine, Seraphe, Seraphin, Seraphina, Seraphine, Seraphita, Serapia Serofina

SERENA (Latin) peaceful. See also Rena.
Sarina, Saryna, Seraina, Serana, Sereen, Sereina, Seren, Serenah, Serene, Serenea, Serenia, Serenna, Serina, Serreana, Serrena Serrenna

SERENITY (Latin) peaceful.
Serenidy, Serenitee, Serenitey, Sereniti, Serenitiy Serinity, Serrennity

SERILDA (Greek) armed warrior woman.

SERINA (Latin) an alternate form of Serena.
Sereena, Serin Serine, Serreena, Serrin, Serrina, Seryna

SEVILLA (Spanish) from Seville.
Sevilie

SHABA (Spanish) rose.
Shabana, Shabina

SHADA (Native American) pelican.
Shadae, Shadea, Shadeana, Shadee, Shadi, Shadia, Shadian, Shadie, Shadiya, Shaida

SHADAY (American) a form of Sade.

Shaday (cont.)
Shadai, Shadaia, Shadaya, Shadayna, Shadei, Shadeziah, Shaiday

SHADRIKA (American) a combination of the prefix Sha + Rika.
Shadreeka, Shadreka, Shadrica, Shadricka, Shadrieka

SHAE (Irish) an alternate form of Shea.
Shaenel, Shaeya, Shai, Shaia

SHAELEE (Irish) an alternate form of Shea.
Shaeleigh, Shaeley, Shaelie, Shaely

SHAELYN (Irish) an alternate form of Shea.
Shael, Shaelaine, Shaelan, Shaelanie, Shaelanna, Shaeleen, Shaelene, Shaelin, Shaeline, Shaelyne, Shaelynn, Shae-Lynn, Shaelynne

SHAFIRA (Swahili) distinguished.
Shaffira

SHAHAR (Arabic) moonlit.
Shahara

SHAHINA (Arabic) falcon.
Shaheen, Shaheena, Shahi, Shahin

SHAHLA (Afghani) beautiful eyes.
Shaila, Shailah, Shalah

SHAIANNE (Cheyenne) an alternate form of Cheyenne.
Shaeen, Shaeine, Shaian, Shaiana, Shaiandra, Shaiane, Shaiann, Shaianna

SHAILA (Latin) an alternate form of Sheila.
Shaela, Shaelea, Shaeyla, Shailah, Shailee, Shailey, Shaili, Shailie, Shailla, Shaily, Shailyn, Shailynn

SHAINA (Yiddish) beautiful.
Shaena, Shainah, Shaine, Shainna, Shajna, Shanie, Shayna, Shayndel, Sheina, Sheindel

SHAJUANA (American) a combination of the prefix Sha + Juanita. See also Shawanna.
Shajuan, Shajuanda, Shajuanita, Shajuanna, Shajuanza

SHAKA (Hindi) an alternate form of Shakti. A short form of names beginning with "Shak." See also Chaka.
Shakah, Shakha

SHAKARAH (American) a combination of the prefix Sha + Kara.
Shacara, Shacari, Shaccara, Shaka, Shakari, Shakkara, Shikara

SHAKAYLA (Arabic) an alternate form of Shakila.
Shakaela, Shakail, Shakaila, Shakala

SHAKEENA (American) a combination of the prefix Sha + Keena.
Shaka, Shakeina, Shakeyna, Shakina, Shakyna

SHAKEITA (American) a combination of the prefix Sha + Keita. See also Shaqueita.
Shaka, Shakeeta, Shakeitha, Shakeithia, Shaketa, Shaketha, Shakethia, Shaketia, Shakita, Shakitra, Sheketa, Shekita, Shikita, Shikitha

SHAKERA (Arabic) an alternate form of Shakira.
Chakeria, Shakeira, Shakeirra, Shakerah, Shakeria, Shakeriah, Shakeriay, Shakerra, Shakerri, Shakerria, Shakerya, Shakeryia, Shakeyra

SHAKIA (American) a combination of the prefix Sha + Kia.
Shakeeia, Shakeeyah, Shakeia, Shakeya, Shakiya, Shekeia, Shekia, Shekiah, Shikia

SHAKILA (Arabic) pretty.
Chakila, Shaka, Shakayla, Shakeela, Shakeena, Shakela, Shakelah, Shakilah, Shakyla, Shekila, Shekilla, Shikeela

SHAKIRA (Arabic) thankful. A feminine form of Shakir.
Shaakira, Shacora, Shaka, Shakeera, Shakeerah, Shakeeria, Shakera, Shakiera, Shakierra, Shakir, Shakirah, Shakirat, Shakirea, Shakirra, Shakora, Shakuria, Shakyra, Shaquira, Shekiera, Shekira, Shikira

SHAKTI (Hindi) divine woman. Religion: the Hindu goddess who controls time and destruction.
Sakti, Shaka, Sita

SHAKYRA (Arabic) an alternate form of Shakira.
Shakyria

SHALANA (American) a combination of the prefix Sha + Lana.
Shalaana, Shalain, Shalaina, Shalaine, Shaland, Shalanda, Shalane, Shalann, Shalaun, Shalauna, Shalayna, Shalayne, Shalaynna, Shallan, Shelan, Shelanda

SHALEAH (American) a combination of the prefix Sha + Leah.
Shalea, Shalee, Shaleea, Shalia, Shaliah

SHALEISHA (American) a combination of the prefix Sha + Aisha.
Shalesha, Shalesia, Shalicia, Shalisha

SHALENA (American) a combination of the prefix Sha + Lena.
Shaleana, Shaleen, Shaleena, Shalen, Shálena, Shalene, Shalené, Shalenna, Shalina, Shalinda, Shaline, Shalini, Shalinna, Shelayna, Shelayne, Shelena

SHALISA (American) a combination of the prefix Sha + Lisa.
Shalesa, Shalese, Shalessa, Shalice, Shalicia, Shaliece, Shalise, Shalisha, Shalishea, Shalisia, Shalissa, Shalisse, Shalyce, Shalys, Shalyse

SHALITA (American) a combination of the prefix Sha + Lita.
Shaleta, Shaletta, Shalida, Shalitta

SHALONA (American) a combination of the prefix Sha + Lona.
Shalon, Shalone, Shálonna, Shalonne

SHALONDA (American) a combination of the prefix Sha + Ondine.
Shalonde, Shalondine, Shalondra, Shalondria

SHALYN (American) a combination of the prefix Sha + Lynn.
Shalin, Shalina, Shalinda, Shaline, Shalyna, Shalynda, Shalyne, Shalynn, Shalynne

SHAMARA (Arabic) ready for battle.
Shamar, Shamarah, Shamare, Shamarea, Shamaree, Shamari,

Shamaria, Shamariah, Shamarra, Shamarri, Shammara, Shamora, Shamori, Shamorra, Shamorria, Shamorriah

SHAMEKA (American) a combination of the prefix Sha + Meka.
Shameaka, Shameakah, Shameca, Shamecca, Shamecha, Shamecia, Shameika, Shameke, Shamekia

SHAMIKA (American) a combination of the prefix Sha + Mika.
Shameeca, Shameeka, Shamica, Shamicia, Shamicka, Shamieka, Shamikia

SHAMIRA (Hebrew) precious stone. A feminine form of Shamir.
Shamir, Shamiran, Shamiria, Shamyra

SHAMIYA (American) a combination of the prefix Sha + Mia.
Shamea, Shamia, Shamiah, Shamiyah, Shamyia, Shamyiah, Shamyne

SHANA (Hebrew) God is gracious (Irish) a form of Jane.
Shaana, Shan, Shanae, Shanda, Shandi, Shane, Shania, Shanna, Shannah, Shauna, Shawna

SHANAE (Irish) an alternate form of Shana.
Shanay, Shanea

SHANDA (American) a form of Chanda, Shana.
Shandae, Shandah, Shandra, Shannda

SHANDI (English) a familiar form of Shana.
Shandee, Shandeigh, Shandey, Shandice, Shandie

SHANDRA (American) an alternate form of Shanda. See also Chandra.
Shandrea, Shandreka, Shandri, Shandria, Shandriah, Shandrice, Shandrie, Shandry

SHANE (Irish) an alternate form of Shana.
Shanea, Shaneah, Shanee, Shanée, Shanie

SHANEISHA (American) a combination of the prefix Sha + Aisha.
Shanesha, Shaneshia, Shanessa, Shanisha, Shanissha

SHANEKA (American) an alternate form of Shanika.
Shanecka, Shaneeka, Shaneekah, Shaneequa, Shaneeque, Shaneika, Shaneikah, Shanekia, Shanequa, Shaneyka, Shonneka

SHANEL, Shanell, Shanelle (American) forms of Chanel.
Schanel, Schanell, Shanella, Shanelly, Shannel, Shannell, Shannelle, Shenel, Shenela, Shenell, Shenelle, Shenelly, Shinelle, Shonelle, Shynelle

SHANETA (American) a combination of the prefix Sha + Neta.
Seanette, Shaneeta, Shanetha, Shanethis, Shanetta, Shanette, Shineta, Shonetta

SHANI (Swahili) marvelous.

SHANIA (American) a form of Shana.
Shanasia, Shanaya, Shaniah, Shaniya, Shanya, Shenia

SHANICE (American) a form of Janice. See also Chanise.
Chenise, Shanece, Shaneese, Shaneice, Shanese, Shanicea,

Shanice (cont.)
Shaniece, Shanise, Shanneice, Shannice, Shanyce, Sheneice

SHANIDA (American) a combination of the prefix Sha + Ida.
Shaneeda, Shannida

SHANIKA (American) a combination of the prefix Sha + Nika.
Shaneka, Shanica, Shanicca, Shanicka, Shanieka, Shanike, Shanikia, Shanikka, Shanikqua, Shanikwa, Shaniqua, Shenika, Shineeca, Shonnika

SHANIQUA (American) an alternate form of Shanika.
Shaniqa, Shaniquah, Shanique, Shaniquia, Shaniquwa, Shaniqwa, Shenequa, Sheniqua, Shinequa, Shiniqua

SHANISE (American) an alternate form of Shanice.
Shanisa, Shanisha, Shanisia, Shanissa, Shanisse, Shineese

SHANITA (American) a combination of the prefix Sha + Nita.
Shanitha, Shanitra, Shanitta, Shinita

SHANLEY (Irish) hero's child.
Shanlee, Shanleigh, Shanlie, Shanly

SHANNA (Irish) an alternate form of Shana, Shannon.
Shanea, Shannah, Shannea

SHANNEN (Irish) an alternate form of Shannon.
Shanen, Shanena, Shanene

SHANNON (Irish) small and wise.
Shanan, Shanadoah, Shann, Shanna, Shannan, Shanneen, Shannen, Shannie, Shannin, Shannyn, Shanon

SHANTA, Shantae, Shante (French) alternate forms of Chantal.
Shantai, Shantay, Shantaya, Shantaye, Shanté, Shantea, Shantee, Shantée, Shanteia

SHANTAL (American) an alternate form of Shantel.
Shantall, Shontal

SHANTANA (American) a form of Santana.
Shantan, Shantanae, Shantanell, Shantanickia, Shantanika, Shantanna

SHANTARA (American) a combination of the prefix Sha + Tara.
Shantaria, Shantarra, Shantera, Shanteria, Shanterra, Shantira, Shontara, Shuntara

SHANTECA (American) a combination of the prefix Sha + Teca.
Shantecca, Shanteka, Shantika, Shantikia

SHANTEL, Shantell (American) song. Forms of Chantel.
Seantelle, Shanntell, Shanta, Shantal, Shantae, Shantale, Shante, Shanteal, Shanteil, Shantele, Shantella, Shantelle, Shantrell, Shantyl, Shantyle, Shauntel, Shauntell, Shauntelle, Shauntrel, Shauntrell, Shauntrella, Shentel, Shentelle, Shontal, Shontalla, Shontalle, Shontel, Shontelle

SHANTERIA (American) an alternate form of Shantara.
Shanterica, Shanterria, Shanterrie, Shantieria, Shantirea, Shonteria

SHANTESA (American) a combination of the prefix Sha + Tess.

Shantese, Shantice, Shantise, Shantisha, Shontecia, Shontessia

SHANTIA (American) a combination of the prefix Sha + Tia.
Shanteya, Shanti, Shantida, Shantie, Shaunteya, Shauntia, Shontia

SHANTILLE (American) a form of Chantilly.
Shanteil, Shantil, Shantilli, Shantillie, Shantilly, Shantyl, Shantyle

SHANTINA (American) a combination of the prefix Sha + Tina.
Shanteena, Shontina

SHANTORA (American) a combination of the prefix Sha + Tory.
Shantoia, Shantori, Shantoria, Shantory, Shantorya, Shantoya, Shanttoria

SHANTRICE (American) a combination of the prefix Sha + Trice. See also Chantrice.
Shantrece, Shantrecia, Shantreece, Shantreese, Shantrese, Shantress, Shantrezia, Shantricia, Shantriece, Shantris, Shantrisse, Shontrice

SHANY (Swahili) marvellous, wonderful.
Shaney, Shannai, Shannea, Shanni, Shannia, Shannie, Shanny, Shanya

SHAPPA (Native American) red thunder.

SHAQUANDA (American) a combination of the prefix Sha + Wanda.
Shaquan, Shaquana, Shaquand, Shaquandey, Shaquandra, Shaquandria, Shaquanera,

Shaquani, Shaquania, Shaquanna, Shaquanta, Shaquantae, Shaquantay, Shaquante, Shaquantia, Shaquona, Shaquonda, Shaquondra, Shaquondria

SHAQUEITA, Shaquita (American) alternate forms of Shakeita.
Shaqueta, Shaquetta, Shaquette, Shaquitta, Shequida, Shequita, Shequittia

SHAQUILA, Shaquilla (American) forms of Shakila.
Shaquail, Shaquia, Shaquil, Shaquilah, Shaquile, Shaquill, Shaquillah, Shaquille, Shaquillia, Shequela, Shequele, Shequila, Shquiyla

SHAQUIRA (American) a form of Shakira.
Shaquirah, Shaquire, Shaquirra, Shaqura, Shaqurah, Shaquri

SHARA (Hebrew) a short form of Sharon.
Shaara, Sharah, Sharal, Sharala, Sharalee, Sharlyn, Sharlynn, Sharra, Sharrah

SHARAI (Hebrew) princess. An alternate form of Sarah. See also Sharon.
Sharae, Sharaé, Sharah, Sharaiah, Sharay, Sharaya, Sharayah

SHARAN (Hindi) protector.
Sharaine, Sharanda, Shararjeet

SHARDAE, Sharday (Punjabi) charity. (Yoruba) honored by royalty. (Arabic) runaway. An alternate form of Chardae.
Sade, Shadae, Sharda, Shar-Dae, Shardai, Shar-Day, Sharde, Shardea, Shardee, Shardée, Shardei, Shardeia, Shardey

SHAREE (English) a form of Shari.
Shareen, Shareena, Sharine

SHARI (French) beloved, dearest. An alternate form of Cheri. (Hungarian) a form of Sarah. See also Sharita, Sheree, Sherry.
Shara, Share, Sharee, Sharia, Shariah, Sharian, Shariann, Sharianne, Sharie, Sharra, Sharree, Sharri, Sharrie, Sharry, Shary

SHARICE (French) an alternate form of Cherise.
Shareese, Sharesse, Sharese, Sharica, Sharicka, Shariece, Sharis, Sharise, Sharish, Shariss, Sharissa, Sharisse, Sharyse

SHARIK (African) child of God.

SHARISSA (American) a form of Sharice.
Sharesa, Sharessia, Sharisa, Sharisha, Shereeza, Shericia, Sherisa, Sherissa

SHARITA (French) a familiar form of Shari. (American) a form of Charity. See also Sherita.
Shareeta, Sharrita

SHARLA (French) a short form of Sharlene, Sharlotte.

SHARLENE (French) little and womanly. A form of Charlene.
Scharlane, Scharlene, Shar, Sharla, Sharlaina, Sharlaine, Sharlane, Sharlanna, Sharlee, Sharleen, Sharleine, Sharlena, Sharleyne, Sharline, Sharlyn, Sharlyne, Sharlynn, Sharlynne, Sherlean, Sherleen, Sherlene, Sherline

SHARLOTTE (American) a form of Charlotte.

Sharlet, Sharlett, Sharlott, Sharlotta

SHARMA (American) a short form of Sharmaine.
Sharmae, Sharme

SHARMAINE (American) a form of Charmaine.
Sharma, Sharmain, Sharman, Sharmane, Sharmanta, Sharmayne, Sharmeen, Sharmene, Sharmese, Sharmin, Sharmine, Sharmon, Sharmyn

SHARNA (Hebrew) an alternate form of Sharon.
Sharnae, Sharnay, Sharne, Sharnea, Sharnease, Sharnee, Sharneese, Sharnell, Sharnelle, Sharnese, Sharnett, Sharnetta, Sharnise

SHARON (Hebrew) desert plain. An alternate form of Sharai.
Shaaron, Shara, Sharai, Sharan, Shareen, Sharen, Shari, Sharin, Sharna, Sharonda, Sharone, Sharran, Sharren, Sharrin, Sharron, Sharrona, Sharyn, Sharyon, Sheren, Sheron, Sherryn

SHARONDA (Hebrew) an alternate form of Sharon.
Sharronda, Sheronda, Sherrhonda

SHARRONA (Hebrew) an alternate form of Sharon.
Sharona, Sharone, Sharonia, Sharonna, Sharony, Sharronne, Sheron, Sherona, Sheronna, Sherron, Sherronna, Sherronne, Shirona

SHATARA (Hindi) umbrella. (Arabic) good; industrious. (American) a combination of Sharon + Tara.

Shatara *(cont.)*
Shatarea, Shatari, Shataria, Shatarra, Shataura, Shateira, Shatera, Shaterah, Shateria, Shaterra, Shaterri, Shaterria, Shatherian, Shatierra, Shatiria

SHATORIA (American) a combination of the prefix Sha + Tory.
Shatora, Shatorea, Shatori, Shatorri, Shatorria, Shatory, Shatorya, Shatoya

SHAUNA (Hebrew) God is gracious. (Irish) an alternate form of Shana. See also Seana, Shona.
Shaun, Shaunah, Shaunda, Shaune, Shaunee, Shauneen, Shaunelle, Shaunette, Shauni, Shaunice, Shaunicy, Shaunie, Shaunika, Shaunisha, Shaunna, Shaunnea, Shaunta, Shaunua, Shaunya

SHAUNDA (Irish) an alternate form of Shauna. See also Shanda, Shawnda, Shonda.
Shaundal, Shaundala, Shaundel, Shaundela, Shaundell, Shaundelle, Shaundra, Shaundrea, Shaundree, Shaundria, Shaundrice

SHAUNTA (Irish) an alternate form of Shauna. See also Shawnta, Shonta.
Schunta, Shauntae, Shauntay, Shaunte, Shauntea, Shauntee, Shauntée, Shaunteena, Shauntei, Shauntia, Shauntier, Shauntrel, Shauntrell, Shauntrella

SHAVON (American) an alternate form of Shavonne.
Schavon, Schevon, Shavan, Shavana, Shavaun, Shavona, Shavonda, Shavone, Shavonia, Shivon

SHAVONNE (American) a combination of the prefix Sha + Yvonne. See also Siobhan.
Shavanna, Shavon, Shavondra, Shavonn, Shavonna, Shavonni, Shavonnia, Shavonnie, Shavontae, Shavonte, Shavonté, Shavoun, Shivaun, Shivawn, Shivonne, Shyvon, Shyvonne

SHAWANNA (American) a combination of the prefix Sha + Wanda. See also Shajuana, Shawna.
Shawan, Shawana, Shawanda, Shawante, Shiwani

SHAWNA (Hebrew) God is gracious. (Irish) a form of Jane. An alternate form of Shana, Shauna. See also Seana, Shona.
Sawna, Shaw, Shawn, Shawnae, Shawnai, Shawnea, Shawnee, Shawneen, Shawneena, Shawnell, Shawnette, Shawnna, Shawnra, Shawnta, Sheona, Siân, Siana, Sianna

SHAWNDA (Irish) an alternate form of Shawna. See also Shanda, Shaunda, Shonda.
Shawndal, Shawndala, Shawndan, Shawndel, Shawndra, Shawndrea, Shawndree, Shawndreel, Shawndrell, Shawndria

SHAWNEE (Irish) an alternate form of Shawna.
Shawne, Shawneea, Shawney, Shawni, Shawnic

SHAWNIKA (American) a combination of Shawna + Nika.
Shawnaka, Shawnequa, Shawneika, Shawnicka

SHAWNTA (Irish) an alternate form of Shawna. See also Shaunta, Shonta.

Shawntae, Shawntay, Shawnte, Shawnté, Shawntee, Shawntell, Shawntelle, Shawnteria, Shawntia, Shawntil, Shawntile, Shawntill, Shawntille, Shawntina, Shawntish, Shawntrese, Shawntriece

SHAY, Shaye (Irish) alternate forms of Shea.
Shaya, Shayah, Shayda, Shayha, Shayia, Shayla, Shey, Sheye

SHAYLA (Irish) an alternate form of Shay.
Shaylagh, Shaylah, Shaylain, Shaylan, Shaylea, Shayleah, Shaylla, Shaylyn, Sheyla

SHAYLEE (Irish) an alternate form of Shea.
Shaylei, Shayleigh, Shayley, Shayli, Shaylie, Shayly, Shealy

SHAYLYN (Irish) an alternate form of Shea.
Shaylin, Shaylina, Shaylinn, Shaylynn, Shaylynne, Shealyn, Sheylyn

SHAYNA (Hebrew) beautiful. A form of Shaina.
Shaynae, Shaynah, Shayne, Shaynee, Shayney, Shayni, Shaynie, Shaynna, Shaynne, Shayny, Sheana, Sheanna

SHEA (Irish) fairy palace.
Shae, Shay, Shaylee, Shaylyn, Shealy, Shaelee, Shaelyn, Shealyn, Sheann, Sheannon, Sheanta, Sheaon, Shearra, Sheatara, Shcaunna, Sheavon

SHEBA (Hebrew) a short form of Bathsheba. Geography: an ancient country of South Arabia.
Saba, Sabah, Shebah, Sheeba

SHEENA (Hebrew) God is gracious. (Irish) a form of Jane.

Sheenagh, Sheenah, Sheenan, Sheeneal, Sheenika, Sheenna, Sheina, Shena, Shiona

SHEILA (Latin) blind. (Irish) a form of Cecelia. See also Cheyla, Zelizi.
Seelia, Seila, Selia, Shaila, Sheela, Sheelagh, Sheelah, Sheilagh, Sheilah, Sheileen, Sheiletta, Sheilia, Sheillynn, Sheilya, Shela, Shelagh, Shelah, Shelia, Shiela, Shila, Shilah, Shilea, Shyla

SHELBI, Shelbie (English) alternate forms of Shelby.
Shelbbie, Shellbi, Shellbie

SHELBY (English) ledge estate.
Chelby, Schelby, Shel, Shelbe, Shelbee, Shelbey, Shelbi, Shelbie, Shelbye, Shellby

SHELDON (English) farm on the ledge.
Sheldina, Sheldine, Sheldrina, Sheldyn, Shelton

SHELEE (English) an alternate form of Shelley.
Shelee, Sheleen, Shelena, Sheley, Sheli, Shelia, Shelina, Shelinda, Shelita

SHELISA (American) a combination of Shelley + Lisa.
Sheleza, Shelica, Shelicia, Shelise, Shelisse, Sheliza

SHELLEY, Shelly (English) meadow on the ledge. (French) familiar forms of Michelle. See also Rochelle.
Shelee, Shell, Shella, Shellaine, Shellana, Shellany, Shellee, Shellene, Shelli, Shellian, Shelliann, Shellie, Shellina

SHELSEA (American) a form of Chelsea.

Shellsea, Shellsey, Shelsey, Shelsie, Shelsy

SHENA (Irish) an alternate form of Sheena.
Shenada, Shenae, Shenah, Shenay, Shenda, Shene, Shenea, Sheneda, Shenee, Sheneena, Shenica, Shenika, Shenina, Sheniqua, Shenita, Shenna, Shennae, Shennah, Shenoa

SHERA (Aramaic) light.
Sheera, Sheerah, Sherae, Sherah, Sheralee, Sheralle, Sheralyn, Sheralynn, Sheralynne, Sheray, Sheraya

SHEREE (French) beloved, dearest. An alternate form of Shari.
Scherie, Sheeree, Shere, Shereé, Sherrelle, Shereen, Shereena

SHERELLE (French) an alternate form of Cherelle, Sheryl.
Sherel, Sherell, Sheriel, Sherrel, Sherrell, Sherrelle, Shirelle

SHERI, Sherri (French) alternate forms of Sherry.
Sheria, Sheriah, Sherie, Sherrie

SHERIAN (American) a combination of Sheri + Ann.
Sherianne, Sherrina

SHERICE (French) an alternate form of Cherise.
Scherise, Sherece, Shereece, Sherees, Shereese, Sherese, Shericia, Sherise, Sherisse, Sherrish, Sherryse, Sheryce

SHERIDAN (Irish) wild.
Sherida, Sheridane, Sherideen, Sheriden, Sheridian, Sheridon, Sherridan, Sherridon

SHERIKA (Punjabi) relative. (Arabic) easterner.

Shereka, Sherica, Shericka, Sherrica, Sherricka, Sherrika

SHERISSA (French) a form of Sherry, Sheryl.
Shereeza, Sheresa, Shericia, Sherrish

SHERITA (French) a form of Sherry, Sheryl. See also Sharita.
Shereta, Sheretta, Sherette, Sherrita

SHERLEEN (French, English) an alternate form of Sheryl, Shirley.
Sherileen, Sherlene, Sherlin, Sherlina, Sherline, Sherlyn, Sherlyne, Sherlynne, Shirlena, Shirlene, Shirlina, Shirlyn

SHERRY (French) beloved, dearest. An alternate form of Shari. A familiar form of Sheryl. See also Sheree.
Sherey, Sheri, Sherissa, Sherrey, Sherri, Sherria, Sherriah, Sherrie, Sherye, Sheryy

SHERYL (French) beloved. An alternate form of Cheryl. A familiar form of Shirley. See also Sherry.
Sharel, Sharil, Sharilyn, Sharyl, Sharyll, Sheral, Sherell, Sheriel, Sheril, Sherill, Sherily, Sherilyn, Sherissa, Sherita, Sherleen, Sherral, Sherrelle, Sherril, Sherrill, Sherryl, Sherylly

SHERYLYN (American) a combination of Sheryl + Lynn. See also Cherilyn.
Sharolin, Sharolyn, Sharyl-Lynn, Sheralyn, Sherilyn, Sherilynn, Sherilynne, Sherralyn, Sherralynn, Sherrilyn, Sherrilynn, Sherrilynne, Sherrylyn, Sherryn, Sherylanne

SHEVONNE (American) a combination of the prefix She + Yvonne.
Shevaun, Shevon, Shevonda, Shevone

SHEYENNE (Cheyenne) an alternate form of Cheyenne. See also Shyann, Shyanne.
Shayhan, Sheyan, Sheyane, Sheyann, Sheyanna, Sheyannah, Sheyanne, Sheyen, Sheyene, Shiante, Shyanne

SHIANNE (Cheyenne) an alternate form of Cheyenne.
She, Shian, Shiana, Shianah, Shianda, Shiane, Shiann, Shianna, Shiannah, Shiany, Shieana, Shieann, Shieanne, Shiena, Shiene, Shienna

SHIFRA (Hebrew) beautiful.
Schifra, Shifrah

SHIKA (Japanese) gentle deer.
Shi, Shikah, Shikha

SHILO (Hebrew) God's gift. Geography: a site near Jerusalem. Bible: a sanctuary for the Israelites where the Ark of the Covenant was kept.
Shiloh

SHINA (Japanese) virtuous; wealthy. (Chinese) an alternate form of China.
Shinae, Shinay, Shine, Shinna

SHINO (Japanese) bamboo stalk.

SHIQUITA (American) a form of Chiquita.
Shiquata, Shiquitta

SHIRA (Hebrew) song.
Shirah, Shiray, Shire, Shiree, Shiri, Shirit, Shyra

SHIRLENE (English) an alternate form of Shirley.
Shirleen, Shirline, Shirlynn

SHIRLEY (English) bright meadow. See also Sheryl.
Sherlee, Sherleen, Sherley, Sherli, Sherlie, Shir, Shirl, Shirlee, Shirlie, Shirly, Shirlly, Shurlee, Shurley

SHIVANI (Hindi) life and death.
Shiva, Shivana, Shivanie, Shivanna

SHIZU (Japanese) silent.
Shizue, Shizuka, Shizuko, Shizuyo

SHONA (Irish) a form of Jane. An alternate form of Shana, Shauna, Shawna.
Shiona, Shonagh, Shonah, Shonalee, Shonda, Shone, Shonee, Shonette, Shoni, Shonie, Shonna, Shonnah, Shonta

SHONDA (Irish) an alternate form of Shona. See also Shanda, Shaunda, Shawnda.
Shondalette, Shondalyn, Shondel, Shondelle, Shondi, Shondia, Shondie, Shondra, Shondreka, Shounda

SHONTA (Irish) an alternate form of Shona. See also Shaunta, Shawnta.
Shontá, Shontae, Shontai, Shontalea, Shontasia, Shontavia, Shontaviea, Shontay, Shontaya, Shonte, Shonté, Shontedra, Shontee, Shonteral, Shonti, Shontol, Shontoy, Shontrail, Shountáe

SHOSHANA (Hebrew) lily. An alternate form of Susan.
Shosha, Shoshan, Shoshanah, Shoshane, Shoshanha, Shoshann, Shoshanna, Shoshannah, Shoshauna, Shoshaunah, Shoshawna, Shoshona, Shoshone, Shoshonee, Shoshoney, Shoshoni, Shoushan, Shushana, Sosha, Soshana

SHU (Chinese) kind, gentle.

SHUG (American) a short form of Sugar.

SHULA (Arabic) flaming, bright.
Shulah

SHULAMITH (Hebrew) peaceful. See also Sula.
Shulamit, Sulamith

SHUNTA (Irish) an alternate form of Shonta.
Shuntae, Shunté, Shuntel, Shuntell, Shuntelle, Shuntia

SHURA (Russian) a form of Alexandra.
Schura, Shurah, Shuree, Shureen, Shurelle, Shuritta, Shurka, Shurlana

SHYANN, Shyanne (Cheyenne) alternate forms of Cheyenne. See also Sheyenne.
Shyan, Shyana, Shyandra, Shyane, Shynee, Shyanna, Shyannah, Shye, Shyene, Shyenna, Shyenne

SHYLA (English) an alternate form of Sheila.
Shya, Shyah, Shylah, Shylan, Shylayah, Shylana, Shylane, Shyle, Shyleah, Shylee, Shyley, Shyli, Shylia, Shylie, Shylo, Shyloe, Shyloh, Shylon, Shylyn

SHYRA (Hebrew) an alternate form of Shira.
Shyrae, Shyrah, Shyrai, Shyrie, Shyro

SIARA (Irish) an alternate form of Sierra.
Siarah, Siarra, Siarrah, Sieara

SIANNA (Irish) an alternate form of Seana.
Sian, Siana, Sianae, Sianai, Sianey, Siannah, Sianne, Sianni, Sianny, Siany

SIBETA (Moquelumnan) finding a fish under a rock.

SIBLEY (Greek) an alternate form of Sybil. (English) sibling; friendly.
Sybley

SIDNEY (French) an alternate form of Sydney.
Sidne, Sidnee, Sidnei, Sidneya, Sidni, Sidnie, Sidny, Sidnye

SIDONIA (Hebrew) enticing.
Sydania, Syndonia

SIDONIE (French) from Saint Denis, France. Geography: an ancient Phoenician city. See also Sydney.
Sedona, Sidaine, Sidanni, Sidelle, Sidoine, Sidona, Sidonae, Sidonia, Sidony

SIDRA (Latin) star child.
Sidrah, Sidras

SIENNA (American) a form of Ciana.
Seini, Siena

SIERA (Irish) an alternte form of Sierra.
Sierah, Sieria

SIERRA (Irish) black. (Spanish) saw toothed. Geography: a rugged range of mountains that, when viewed from a distance, has a jagged profile. See also Ciara.
Seara, Searria, Seera, Seirra, Siara, Siearra, Siera, Sierrah, Sierre, Sierrea, Sierriah, Syerra

SIGFREDA (German) victorious peace. See also Freda.
Sigfreida, Sigfrida, Sigfrieda, Sigfryda

SIGMUNDA (German) victorious protector.
Sigmonda

SIGNE (Latin) sign, signal. (Scandinavian) a short form of Sigourney.
Sig, Signa, Signy, Singna, Singne

SIGOURNEY (English) victorious conquerer.
Signe, Sigournee, Sigourny

SIGRID (Scandinavian) victorious counselor.
Siegrid, Siegrida, Sigritt

SIHU (Native American) flower; bush.

SIKO (African) crying baby.

SILVIA (Latin) an alternate form of Sylvia.
Silivia, Silva, Silvya

SIMCHA (Hebrew) joyful.

SIMONE (Hebrew) she heard. (French) a feminine form of Simon.
Samone, Siminie, Simmi, Simmie, Simmona, Simmone, Simoane, Simona, Simonetta, Simonette, Simonia, Simonina, Simonne, Somone, Symone

SIMRAN (Sikh) absorbed in God.
Simren, Simrin, Simrun

SINA (Irish) an alternate form of Seana.
Seena, Sinai, Sinaia, Sinan, Sinay

SINCLAIRE (French) prayer. Religion: name honoring Saint Clair.
Sinclair

SINDY (American) a form of Cindy.
Sinda, Sindal, Sindee, Sindi, Sindia, Sindie, Sinnedy, Synda, Syndal, Syndee, Syndey, Syndi, Syndia, Syndie, Syndy

SINEAD (Irisn) a form of Jane.
Seonaid, Sine, Sinéad

SIOBHAN (Irish) a form of Joan. See also Shavonne.
Shibahn, Shibani, Shibhan, Shioban, Shobana, Shobha, Shobhana, Siobahn, Siobhana, Siobhann, Siobhon, Siovaun, Siovhan

SIRENA (Greek) enchanter. Mythology: sirens were half-woman, half-bird creatures whose singing so enchanted sailors, they crashed their ships into nearby rocks.
Sireena, Sirene, Sirine, Syrena, Syrenia, Syrenna, Syrina

SISIKA (Native American) songbird.

SISSY (American) a familiar form of Cecelia.
Sisi, Sisie, Sissey, Sissie

SITA (Hindi) an alternate form of Shakti.
Sitah, Sitarah, Sitha, Sithara

SITI (Swahili) respected woman.

SKYE (Arabic) water giver. (Dutch) a short form of Skyler. Geography. an island in the Hebrides, Scotland.
Ski, Skie, Skii, Skky, Sky, Skya, Skyy

SKYLAR (Dutch) an alternate form of Skyler.
Skyela, Skyelar, Skyla, Skylair, Skyylar

SKYLER (Dutch) sheltering.
Skila, Skilah, Skye, Skyeler, Skyelur, Skyla, Skylar, Skylee, Skylena, Skyli, Skylia, Skylie, Skylin, Skyllar, Skylor, Skylyn, Skylynn, Skylyr, Skyra

SLOANE (Irish) warrior.
Sloan, Sloanne

SOCORRO (Spanish) helper.

SOFIA (Greek) an alternate form of Sophia. See also Zofia, Zsofia.
Sofeea, Sofeeia, Soffi, Sofi, Soficita, Sofie, Sofija, Sofiya, Sofka, Sofya

SOLADA (Tai) listener.

SOLANA (Spanish) sunshine.
Solande, Solanna, Soleil, Solena, Soley, Solina, Solinda

SOLANGE (French) dignified.

SOLEDAD (Spanish) solitary.
Sole, Soleda

SOLENNE (French) solemn, dignified.
Solaine, Solene, Soléne, Solenna, Solina, Soline, Solonez, Souline, Soulle

SOMA (Hindi) lunar. Astrological: born under the sign of Cancer.

SOMMER (English) summer; summoner. (Arabic) black. See also Summer.
Somara, Somer, Sommar, Sommara, Sommers

SONDRA (Greek) defender of mankind. A short form of Alexandra.
Saundra, Sondre, Sonndra, Sonndre

SONIA (Russian, Slavic) an alternate form of Sonya.
Sonica, Sonida, Sonita, Sonna, Sonni, Sonnia, Sonnie, Sonny

SONJA (Scandinavian) a form of Sonya.
Sonjae, Sonjia

SONYA (Greek) wise. (Russian, Slavic) a form of Sophia.
Sonia, Sonja, Sonnya, Sonyae, Sunya

SOOK (Korean) pure.

SOPHEARY (Cambodian) beautiful girl.

SOPHIA (Greek) wise. See also Sonya, Zofia.
Sofia, Sophie

SOPHIE (Greek) a familiar form of Sophia. See also Zocha.
Sophey, Sophi, Sophy

SOPHRONIA (Greek) wise; sensible.
Soffrona, Sofronia

SORA (Native American) chirping songbird.

SORAYA (Persian) princess.
Suraya

SORREL (French) reddish brown. Botany: a wild herb.

SOSO (Native American) tree squirrel dining on pine nuts; chubby-cheeked baby.

SOUZAN (Persian) burning fire.
Sousan, Souzanne

SPENCER (English) dispenser of provisions.
Spenser

SPERANZA (Italian) a form of Esperanza.
Speranca

SPRING (English) springtime.
Spryng

STACEY, Stacy (Greek) resurrection. (Irish) a short form of Anastasia, Eustacia, Natasha.
Stace, Stacee, Staceyan, Staceyann, Staicy, Stasey, Stasya, Stayce, Staycee, Staci, Steacy

STACI, Stacie (Greek) alternate forms of Stacey.
Stacci, Stacia, Stayci

STACIA (English) a short form of Anastasia.
Stasia, Staysha

STARLA (English) an alternate form of Starr.
Starrla

STARLEEN (English) an alternate form of Starr.
Starleena, Starlena, Starlene, Starlin, Starlyn, Starlynn, Starrlen

STARLEY (English) a familiar form of Starr.
Starle, Starlee, Staly

STARLING (English) bird.

STARR (English) star.
Star, Staria, Starisha, Starla, Starleen, Starlet, Starlette, Starley, Starlight, Starre, Starri, Starria, Starrika, Starrsha, Starsha, Starshanna, Startish

STASYA (Greek) a familiar form of Anastasia. (Russian) a form of Stacey.
Stasa, Stasha, Stashia, Stasia, Stasja, Staska

STEFANI, Steffani (Greek) alternate forms of Stephanie.
Stafani, Stefanni, Steffane, Steffanee, Stefini, Stefoni

STEFANIE (Greek) an alternate form of Stephanie.
Stafanie, Staffany, Stefane, Stefanee, Stefaney, Stefania, Stefanié, Stefanija, Stefannie, Stefcia, Stefenie, Steffanie, Steffi, Stefinie, Stefka

STEFANY, Steffany (Greek) alternate forms of Stephanie.
Stefanny, Stefanya, Steffaney

STEFFI (Greek) a familiar form of Stefanie, Stephanie.
Stefa, Stefcia, Steffee, Steffie, Steffy, Stefi, Stefka, Stefy, Stepha, Stephi, Stephie, Stephy

STELLA (Latin) star. (French) a familiar form of Estelle.
Steile, Stellina

STEPANIA (Russian) a form of Stephanie.
Stepa, Stepahny, Stepanida, Stepanie, Stepanyda, Stepfanie, Stephana

STEPHANI (Greek) an alternate form of Stephanie.
Stephania, Stephanni

STEPHANIE (Greek) crowned. A feminine form of Stephan. See also Estefani, Estephanie, Panya, Stevie, Zephania.
Stamatios, Stefani, Stefanie, Stefany, Steffie, Stepania, Stephaija, Stephaine, Stephanas, Stephane, Stephanee, Stephani, Stephanida, Stéphanie, Stephanine, Stephann, Stephannie, Stephany, Stephene, Stephenie, Stephianie, Stephney, Stesha, Steshka, Stevanee

STEPHANY (Greek) an alternate form of Stephanie.
Stephaney, Stephanye

STEPHENE (Greek) an alternate form of Stephanie.
Stephina, Stephine, Stephyne

STEPHENIE (Greek) an alternate form of Stephanie.
Stephena, Stephenee, Stepheney, Stepheni, Stephenny, Stepheny, Stephine, Stephinie

STEPHNEY (Greek) an alternate form of Stephanie.
Stephne, Stephni, Stephnie, Stephny

STERLING (English) valuable; silver penny.

STEVIE (Greek) a familiar form of Stephanie.
Steva, Stevana, Stevanee, Stevee, Stevena, Stevey, Stevi, Stevy, Stevye

STINA (German) a form of Christina.
Steena, Stena, Stine, Stinna

STOCKARD (English) stockyard.

STORMIE (English) an alternate form of Stormy.
Stormee, Stormi, Stormii

STORMY (English) impetuous by nature.
Storm, Storme, Stormey, Stormie, Stormm

SUCHIN (Tai) beautiful thought.

SUE (Hebrew) a short form of Susan, Susanna.

SUEANN, Sueanna (American) combinations of Sue + Ann, Sue + Anna.
Suann, Suanna, Suannah, Suanne, Sueanne

SUELA (Spanish) consolation.
Suelita

SUGAR (American) sweet as sugar.
Shug

SUGI (Japanese) cedar tree.

SUKE (Hawaiian) a form of Susan.

SUKEY (Hawaiian) a familiar form of Susan.
Suka, Sukee, Suki, Sukie, Suky

SUKHDEEP (Sikh) light of peace and bliss.
Sukhdip

SUKI (Japanese) loved one. (Moquelumnan) eagle eyed.
Sukie

SULA (Greek, Hebrew) a short form of Shulamith, Ursula. (Icelandic) large seabird.

SULETU (Moquelumnan) soaring bird.

SULIA (Latin) an alternate form of Julia.
Suliana

SULWEN (Welsh) bright as the sun.

SUMALEE (Tai) beautiful flower.

SUMATI (Hindi) unity.

SUMAYA (American) a combination of Sue + Maya.
Sumayah, Sumayya, Sumayyah

SUMI (Japanese) elegant, refined.
Sumiko

SUMMER (English) summertime. See also Sommer.
Sumer, Summar, Summerann, Summerbreeze, Summerhaze, Summerine, Summerlee, Summerlin, Summerlyn, Summerlynn, Summers, Sumrah, Summyr, Sumyr

SUN (Korean) obedient.
Suncance, Sundee, Sundeep, Sundi, Sundip, Sundrenea, Sunta, Sunya

SUNEE (Tai) good.
Suni

SUN-HI (Korean) good; joyful.

SUNI (Zuni) native; member of our tribe.
Sunita, Sunitha, Suniti, Sunne, Sunni, Sunnie, Sunnilei

SUNKI (Hopi) swift.
Sunkia

SUNNY (English) bright, cheerful.
Sunni, Sunnie

SUNSHINE (English) sunshine.
Sunshyn, Sunshyne

SURATA (Pakistani) blessed joy.

SURI (Todas) pointy nose.
Suree, Surena, Surenia

SURYA (Pakistani) Mythology: a sun god.
Suria, Suriya, Surra

SUSAMMI (French) a combination of Susan + Aimee.
Suzami, Suzamie, Suzamy

SUSAN (Hebrew) lily. See also Shoshana, Sukey, Zsa Zsa, Zusa.
Sawsan, Siusan, Sosan, Sosana, Sue, Suesan, Sueva, Suisan, Suke, Susana, Susann, Susanna, Suse, Susen, Susette, Susie, Suson, Suzan, Suzanna, Suzannah, Suzanne, Suzette

SUSANA (Hebrew) an alternate form of Susan.
Susanah, Susane

SUSANNA, Susannah (Hebrew) alternate forms of Susan. See also Xuxa, Zanna, Zsuzsanna.
Sonel, Sosana, Sue, Suesanna, Susana, Susanah, Susanka, Susette, Susie, Suzanna

SUSE (Hawaiian) a form of Susan.

SUSETTE (French) a familiar form of Susan, Susanna.
Susetta

SUSIE, Suzie (American) familiar forms of Susan, Susanna.
Suse, Susey, Susi, Sussi, Sussy, Susy, Suze, Suzi, Suzy, Suzzie

SUZANNA, Suzannah (Hebrew) alternate forms of Susan.
Suzana, Suzenna, Suzzanna

SUZANNE (English) a form of Susan.
Susanne, Suszanne, Suzane, Suzann, Suzzane, Suzzann, Suzzanne

SUZETTE (French) a form of Susan.
Suzetta, Suzzette

SUZU (Japanese) little bell.
Suzue, Suzuko

SUZUKI (Japanese) bell tree.

SVETLANA (Russian) bright light.
Sveta, Svetochka

SYÀ (Chinese) summer.

SYBELLA (English) a form of Sybil.
Sebila, Sibbella, Sibeal, Sibel, Sibell, Sibella, Sibelle, Sibilla, Sibylla, Sybel, Sybelle, Sybila, Sybilla

SYBIL (Greek) prophet. Mythology: sibyls were oracles who relayed the messages of the gods. See also Cybele, Sibley.
Sib, Sibbel, Sibbie, Sibbill, Sibby, Sibeal, Sibel, Sibyl, Sibylle, Sibylline, Sybella, Sybille, Syble

SYDNEE (French) an alternate form of Sydney.
Sydne, Sydnea, Sydnei

SYDNEY (French) from Saint Denis, France. A feminine form of Sidney. See also Sidonie.
Cidney, Cydney, Sidney, Sy, Syd, Sydel, Sydelle, Sydna, Sydnee, Sydni, Sydnie, Sydny, Sydnye, Syndona, Syndonah

SYDNI, Sydnie (French) alternate forms of Sydney.

SYING (Chinese) star.

SYLVANA (Latin) forest.
Silvaine, Silvana, Silvanna, Silviane, Sylva, Sylvaine, Sylvanah, Sylvania, Sylvanna, Sylvie, Sylvina, Sylvinnia, Sylvonah, Sylvonia, Sylvonna

SYLVIA (Latin) forest. Literature: Sylvia Plath was a well-known American writer and poet. See also Silvia, Xylia.
Sylvette, Sylvie, Sylwia

SYLVIANNE (American) a combination of Sylvia + Anne.
Sylvian

SYLVIE (Latin) a familiar form of Sylvia.
Silvi, Silvie, Silvy, Sylvi

SYMONE (Hebrew) an alternate form of Simone.
Symmeon, Symmone, Symona, Symoné, Symonne

SYMPHONY (Greek) symphony, harmonious sound.
Symfoni, Symphanie, Symphany, Symphanée, Symphoni, Symphoni

SYREETA (Hindi) good traditions. (Arabic) companion.
Syretta, Syrrita

TABATHA (Greek, Aramaic) an alternate form of Tabitha.
Tabathe, Tabathia, Tabbatha

TABBY (English) a familiar form of Tabitha.
Tabbi

TABIA (Swahili) talented.
Tabea

TABETHA (Greek, Aramaic) an alternate form of Tabitha.

TABINA (Arabic) follower of Muhammed.

TABITHA (Greek, Aramaic) gazelle.
Tabatha, Tabbee, Tabbetha, Tabbey, Tabbi, Tabbie, Tabbitha, Tabby, Tabetha, Tabiatha, Tabita, Tabithia, Tabotha, Tabtha, Tabytha

TABYTHA (Greek, Aramaic) an alternate form of Tabitha.
Tabbytha

TACEY (English) a familiar form of Tacita.
Tace, Tacee, Taci, Tacy, Tacye

TACI (Zuni) washtub. (English) an alternate form of Tacey.
Tacia, Taciana, Tacie

TACITA (Latin) silent.
Tacey

TADITA (Omaha) runner.
Tadeta, Tadra

TAELOR (English) an alternate form of Taylor.
Taelar, Taeler, Taellor, Taelore, Taelyr

TAESHA (Latin) an alternate form of Tisha. (American) a combination of the prefix Ta + Aisha.
Tadasha, Taeshayla, Taeshia, Taheisha, Tahisha, Taiesha, Taisha, Taishae, Teasha, Teashia, Teisha, Tesha

TAFFY (Welsh) beloved.
Taffia, Taffine, Taffye, Tafia, Tafisa, Tafoya

TAHIRA (Arabic) virginal, pure.
Taheera, Taheerah, Tahera, Tahere, Taheria, Taherri, Tahiara, Tahirah, Tahireh

TAHLIA (Greek, Hebrew) an alternate form of Talia.
Tahleah, Tahleia

TAILOR (English) an alternate form of Taylor.
Tailar, Tailer, Taillor, Tailyr

TAIMA (Native American) loud thunder.
Taimi, Taimia, Taimy

TAIPA (Moquelumnan) flying quail.

TAITE (English) cheerful.
Tate, Tayte, Tayten

TAJA (Hindi) crown.
Taiajára, Taija, Tajae, Tajah, Tahai, Tehya, Teja, Tejah, Tejal

TAKA (Japanese) honored.

TAKALA (Hopi) corn tassel.

TAKARA (Japanese) treasure.
Takarah, Takaria, Takarra, Takra

TAKAYLA (American) a combination of the prefix Ta + Kayla.
Takayler, Takeyli

TAKEISHA (American) a combination of the prefix Ta + Keisha.
Takecia, Takesha, Takeshia, Takesia, Takisha, Takishea, Takishia, Tekeesha, Tekeisha, Tekeshi, Tekeysia, Tekisha, Tikesha, Tikisha, Tokesia, Tykeisha

TAKENYA (Hebrew) animal horn. (Moquelumnan) falcon. (American) a combination of the prefix Ta + Kenya.
Takenia, Takenja

TAKERIA (American) an alternate form of Takira.
Takera, Takeri, Takerian, Takerra, Takerria, Takierria, Takoria

TAKI (Japanese) waterfall.
Tiki

199

TAKIA (Arabic) worshiper.
Takeia, Takeiyah, Takeya, Takeyah, Takhiya, Takiah, Takija, Takiya, Takiyah, Takkia, Takya, Takyah, Takyia, Taqiyya, Taquaia, Taquaya, Taquiia, Tekeiya, Tekeiyah, Tekeyia, Tekiya, Tekiyah, Tikia, Tykeia, Tykia

TAKILA (American) a form Tequila.
Takayla, Takeila, Takela, Takelia, Takella, Takeyla, Takiela, Takilah, Takilla, Takilya, Takyla, Takylia, Tatakyla, Tehilla, Tekeila, Tekela, Tekelia, Tekilaa, Tekilia, Tekilla, Tekilyah, Tekla

TAKIRA (American) a combination of the prefix Ta + Kira.
Takara, Takarra, Takeara, Takeera, Takeira, Takeirah, Takera, Takiara, Takiera, Takierah, Takierra, Takirah, Takiria, Takirra, Takora, Takyra, Takyrra, Taquera, Taquira, Tekeria, Tikara, Tikira, Tykera

TALA (Native American) stalking wolf.

TALASI (Hopi) corn tassel.
Talasea, Talasia

TALEAH (American) a form of Talia.
Talaya, Talayah, Talayia, Talea, Taleana, Taleea, Taleéi, Talei, Taleia, Taleiya, Tylea, Tyleah, Tylee

TALEISHA (American) a combination of Talia + Aisha.
Taileisha, Taleise, Talesha, Talicia, Taliesha, Talisa, Talisha, Talysha, Telisha, Tilisha, Tyleasha, Tyleisha, Tylicia, Tylisha, Tylishia

TALENA (American) a combination of the prefix Ta + Lena.
Talayna, Talihna, Taline, Tallenia, Talná, Tilena, Tilene, Tylena

TALESHA (American) an alternate form of Taleisha.
Taleesha, Talesa, Talese, Taleshia, Talesia, Tallese, Tallesia, Tylesha, Tyleshia, Tylesia

TALIA (Greek) blooming. (Hebrew) dew from heaven. (Latin, French) birthday. A short form of Natalie. See also Thalia.
Tahlia, Taleah, Taliah, Taliatha, Taliea, Taliyah, Talley, Tallia, Tallya, Talya, Tylia

TALINA (American) a combination of Talia + Lina.
Talin, Talinda, Taline, Tallyn, Talyn, Talynn, Tylina, Tyline

TALISA (English) an alternate form of Tallis.
Talisha, Talishia, Talisia, Talissa, Talysa, Talysha, Talysia, Talyssa

TALITHA (Arabic) young girl.
Taleetha, Taletha, Talethia, Taliatha, Talita, Talithia, Taliya, Telita, Tiletha

TALIYAH (Greek) an alternate form of Talia.
Taleya, Taleyah, Talieya, Talliyah, Talya, Talyah, Talyia

TALLEY (French) a familiar form of Talia.
Tali, Talle, Tallie, Tally, Taly, Talye

TALLIS (French, English) forest.
Talice, Talisa, Talise, Tallys

TALLULAH (Choctaw) leaping water.
Tallou, Talula

TAM (Vietnamese) heart.

TAMA (Japanese) jewel.
Tamaa, Tamah, Tamaiah, Tamala, Tema

TAMAKA (Japanese) bracelet.
Tamaki, Tamako, Timaka

TAMAR (Hebrew) a short form of Tamara. (Russian) History: a twelfth-century Georgian queen.
Tamer, Tamor, Tamour

TAMARA (Hebrew) palm tree. See also Tammy.
Tamar, Tamará, Tamarae, Tamarah, Tamaria, Tamarin, Tamarla, Tamarra, Tamarria, Tamarrian, Tamarsha, Tamary, Tamera, Tamira, Tamma, Tammara, Tamora, Tamoya, Tamra, Tamura, Tamyra, Temara, Temarian, Thama, Thamar, Thamara, Thamarra, Timara, Tomara, Tymara

TAMASSA (Hebrew) an alternate form of Thomasina.
Tamasin, Tamasine, Tamsen, Tamsin, Tamzen, Tamzin

TAMEKA (Aramaic) twin.
Tameca, Tamecia, Tamecka, Tameeka, Tamekia, Tamiecka, Tamieka, Temeka, Timeeka, Timeka, Tomeka, Tomekia, Trameika, Tymeka, Tymmeeka, Tymmeka

TAMERA (Hebrew) an alternate form of Tamara.
Tamer, Tamerai, Tameran, Tameria, Tamerra, Tammera, Thamer, Timera

TAMESHA (American) a combination of the prefix Ta + Mesha.
Tameesha, Tameisha, Tameshia, Tameshkia, Tameshya, Tamisha, Tamishia, Tamnesha, Temisha, Timesha, Timisha, Tomesha, Tomiese, Tomise, Tomisha, Tramesha, Tramisha, Tymesha

TAMIKA (Japanese) an alternate form of Tamiko.

Tamica, Tamieka, Tamikah, Tamikia, Tamikka, Tammika, Tamyka, Timika, Timikia, Tomika, Tymika, Tymmicka

TAMIKO (Japanese) child of the people.
Tami, Tamika, Tamike, Tamiqua, Tamiyo, Tammiko

TAMILA (American) a combination of the prefix Ta + Mila.
Tamala, Tamela, Tamelia, Tamilla, Tamille, Tamillia, Tamilya

TAMIRA (Hebrew) an alternate form of Tamara.
Tamir, Tamirae, Tamirah, Tamiria, Tamirra, Tamyra, Tamyria, Tamyrra

TAMMI, Tammie (English) alternate forms of Tammy.
Tameia, Tami, Tamia, Tamiah, Tamie, Tamijo, Tamiya

TAMMY (Hebrew) a familiar form of Tamara. (English) twin.
Tamilyn, Tamlyn, Tammee, Tammey, Tammi, Tammie, Tamy, Tamya

TAMRA (Hebrew) a short form of Tamara.
Tammra, Tamrah

TAMSIN (English) a short form of Thomasina.

TANA (Slavic) a short form of Tanya.
Taina, Tanae, Tanaeah, Tanah, Tanairi, Tanairy, Tanalia, Tanara, Tanavia, Tanaya, Tanaz, Tanna, Tannah

TANDY (English) team.
Tanda, Tandalaya, Tandi, Tandie, Tandis, Tandra, Tandrea, Tandria

TANEISHA, Tanesha (American) combinations of the prefix Ta + Nesha.

Tahniesha, Taineshia, Tanasha, Tanashia, Tanaysia, Taneasha, Taneesha, Taneshea, Taneshia, Taneshya, Tanesia, Tanesian, Tanessa, Tanessia, Taniesha, Tannesha, Tanneshia, Tanniecia, Tanniesha, Tantashea

TANEYA (Russian, Slavic) an alternate form of Tanya.
Tanea, Taneah, Tanee, Taneé, Taneia

TANGIA (American) a combination of the prefix Ta + Angela.
Tangela, Tangi, Tangie, Tanja, Tanji, Tanjia, Tanjie

TANI (Japanese) valley. (Slavic) stand of glory. A familiar form of Tania.
Tahnee, Tahni, Tahnie, Tanee, Taney, Tanie, Tany

TANIA (Russian, Slavic) fairy queen. A form of Tanya, Titania.
Taneea, Tani, Taniah, Tanija, Tanika, Tanis, Taniya, Tannia, Tannis, Tanniya, Tannya, Tarnia

TANIEL (American) a combination of Tania + Danielle.
Taniele, Tanielle, Teniel, Teniele, Tenielle

TANIKA (American) a form of Tania.
Tanikka, Tanikqua, Taniqua, Tanique, Tannica, Tianeka, Tianika

TANIS, Tannis (Slavic) forms of Tania, Tanya.
Tanas, Tanese, Taniese, Tanise, Tanisia, Tanka, Tannese, Tanniece, Tanniese, Tannis, Tannise, Tannus, Tannyce, Tenice, Tenise, Tenyse, Tiannis, Tonise, Tranice, Tranise, Tynice, Tyniece, Tyniese, Tynise

TANISHA (American) a combination of the prefix Ta + Nisha.
Tahniscia, Tahnisha, Tanasha, Tanashea, Tanicha, Taniesha, Tanish, Tanishah, Tanishia, Tanitia, Tannicia, Tannisha, Tenisha, Tenishka, Tinisha, Tonisha, Tonnisha, Tynisha

TANISSA (American) a combination of the prefix Tania + Nissa.
Tanesa, Tanisa, Tannesa, Tannisa, Tennessa, Tranissa

TANITA (American) a combination of the prefix Ta + Nita.
Taneta, Tanetta, Tanitra, Tanitta, Teneta, Tenetta, Tenita, Tenitta, Tyneta, Tynetta, Tynette, Tynita, Tynitra, Tynitta

TANITH (Phoenician) Mythology: the goddess of love.
Tanitha

TANNER (English) leather worker, tanner.
Tannor

TANSY (Greek) immortal. (Latin) tenacious, persistent.
Tancy, Tansee, Tansey, Tanshay, Tanzey

TANYA (Russian, Slavic) fairy queen. A short form of Tatiana.
Tahnee, Tahnya, Tana, Tanaya, Taneya, Tania, Tanis, Taniya, Tanka, Tannis, Tannya, Tanoya, Tany, Tanyia, Taunya, Tawnya, Thanya

TAO (Chinese, Vietnamese) peach.

TARA (Aramaic) throw; carry. (Irish) rocky hill. (Arabic) a measurement.

Tara *(cont.)*
Taira, Tairra, Taraea, Tarah, Taráh, Tarai, Taralee, Tarali, Tarasa, Tarasha, Taraya, Tarha, Tari, Tarra, Taryn, Tayra, Tehra

TARANEH (Persian) melody.

TAREE (Japanese) arching branch.
Tarea, Tareya, Tari, Taria

TARI (Irish) a familiar form of Tara.
Taria, Tarika, Tarila, Tarilyn, Tarin, Tarina, Tarita

TARISSA (American) a combination of Tara + Rissa.
Taris, Tarisa, Tarise, Tarisha

TARRA (Irish) an alternate form of Tara.
Tarrah

TARYN (Irish) an alternate form of Tara.
Taran, Tareen, Tareena, Taren, Tarene, Tarin, Tarina, Tarren, Tarrena, Tarrin, Tarrina, Tarron, Tarryn, Taryna

TASARLA (Gypsy) dawn.

TASHA (Greek) born on Christmas day. (Russian) a short form of Natasha. See also Tashi, Tosha.
Tacha, Tachiana, Tahsha, Tasenka, Tashae, Tashana, Tashay, Tashe, Tashee, Tasheka, Tashka, Tasia, Taska, Taysha, Thasha, Tiaisha, Tysha

TASHANA (American) a combination of the prefix Ta + Shana.
Tashan, Tashanda, Tashani, Tashanika, Tashanna, Tashiana, Tashianna, Tashina, Tishana, Tishani, Tishanna, Tishanne, Toshanna, Toshanti, Tyshana

TASHARA (American) a combination of the prefix Ta + Shara.
Tashar, Tasharah, Tasharia, Tasharna, Tasharra, Tashera, Tasherey, Tasheri, Tasherra, Tashira, Tashirah

TASHAWNA (American) a combination of the prefix Ta + Shawna.
Tashauna, Tashauni, Tashaunie, Tashaunna, Tashawanna, Tashawn, Tashawnda, Tashawnna, Tashawnnia, Tashonda, Tashondra, Tiashauna, Tishawn, Tishunda, Tishunta, Toshauna, Toshawna, Tyshauna, Tyshawna

TASHEENA (American) a combination of the prefix Ta + Sheena.
Tasheana, Tasheeana, Tasheeni, Tashena, Tashenna, Tashennia, Tasheona, Tashina, Tisheena, Tosheena, Tysheana, Tysheena, Tyshyna

TASHELLE (American) a combination of the prefix Ta + Shelley.
Tachell, Tashell, Techell, Techelle, Teshell, Teshelle, Tochell, Tochelle, Toshelle, Tychell, Tychelle, Tyshell, Tyshelle

TASHI (Slavic) a form of Tasha. (Hausa) a bird in flight.
Tashia, Tashie, Tashika, Tashima, Tashiya

TASIA (Slavic) a familiar form of Tasha.
Tachia, Tashea, Tasiya, Tassi, Tassia, Tassiana, Tassie, Tasya

TASSOS (Greek) an alternate form of Theresa.

TATA (Russian) a familiar form of Tatiana.
Tate, Tatia

TATE (English) a short form of Tatum. An alternate form of Taite, Tata.

TATIANA (Slavic) fairy queen. A feminine form of Tatius. See also Tanya, Tiana.
Tata, Tatania, Tatanya, Tateana, Tati, Tatia, Tatianna, Tatie, Tatihana, Tatiyana, Tatjana, Tatyana, Tiatiana

TATIANNA (Slavic) an alternate form of Tatiana.
Taitiann, Taitianna, Tateanna, Tateonna, Tationna

TATIYANA (Slavic) an alternate form of Tatiana.
Tateyana, Tatiayana, Tatiyanna, Tatiyona, Tatiyonna

TATUM (English) cheerful.
Tate, Tatumn

TATYANA (Slavic) an alternate form of Tatiana.
Tatyanah, Tatyani, Tatyanna, Tatyannah, Tatyona, Tatyonna

TAURA (Latin) bull. Astrology: Taurus is a sign of the zodiac.
Taurae, Tauria, Taurina

TAURI (English) an alternate form of Tory.
Taure, Taurie, Taury

TAVIA (Latin) a short form of Octavia. See also Tawia.
Taiva, Tauvia, Tava, Tavah, Tavita

TAVIE (Scottish) twin. A feminine form of Tavish.
Tavey, Tavi

TAWANNA (American) a combination of the prefix Ta + Wanda.
Taiwana, Taiwanna, Taquana, Taquanna, Tawan, Tawana, Tawanda, Tawanne, Tequana, Tequanna, Tequawna, Tewanna, Tewauna, Tiquana, Tiwanna, Tiwena, Towanda, Towanna, Tywania, Tywanna

TAWIA (African) born after twins. (Polish) a form of Tavia.

TAWNI (English) an alternate form of Tawny.
Tauni, Taunia, Tawnia, Tawnie, Tawnnie, Tiawni

TAWNY (Gypsy) little one. (English) brownish yellow, tan.
Tahnee, Tany, Tauna, Tauné, Taunisha, Tawnee, Tawnesha, Tawney, Tawni, Tawnyell, Tiawna

TAWNYA (American) a combination of Tawny + Tonya.
Tawna

TAYA, Taye (English) short forms of Taylor.
Tay, Tayah, Tayana, Tayiah, Tayna, Tayra, Taysha, Taysia, Tayva, Tayvonne, Teya, Teyanna, Teyona, Teyuna, Tiaya, Tiya, Tiyah, Tiyana, Tye

TAYLA (English) a short form of Taylor.
Taylah, Tayleah, Taylee, Tayleigh, Taylie, Teila

TAYLAR (English) an alternate form of Taylor.
Talar, Tayla, Taylah, Taylare, Tayllar

TAYLER (English) an alternate form of Taylor.
Tayller

TAYLOR (English) tailor.
Taelor, Tailor, Taiylor, Talor, Talora, Taya, Taye, Tayla, Taylar, Tayler, Tayllor, Tayllore, Tayloir, Taylorann, Taylore, Taylorr, Taylour, Taylur, Teylor

TAZU (Japanese) stork; longevity.
Taz, Tazi, Tazia

TEAGAN (Welsh) beautiful, attractive.
Taegen, Teage, Teagen, Teaghan, Teaghanne, Teaghen, Teagin, Teague, Teegan, Teeghan, Tegan, Tegwen, Teigan, Tejan, Tiegan, Tigan, Tijan, Tijana

TEAIRA (Latin) an alternate form of Tiara.
Teairra, Teairre, Teairria, Teara, Tearah, Teareya, Teari, Tearia, Teariea, Tearra, Tearria

TEAL (English) river duck; blue green.
Teala, Teale, Tealia, Tealisha

TEANNA (American) a combination of the prefix Te + Anna. An alternate form of Tina.
Tean, Teana, Teanah, Teann, Teannah, Teanne, Teaunna, Teena, Teuana

TECA (Hungarian) a form of Theresa.
Techa, Teka, Tica, Tika

TECLA (Greek) God's fame.
Tekla, Theckla

TEDDI (Greek) a familiar form of Theodora.
Tedde, Teddey, Teddie, Teddy, Tedi, Tediah, Tedy

TEDRA (Greek) a short form of Theodora.
Teddra, Teddreya, Tedera, Teedra, Teidra

TEGAN (Welsh) an alternate form of Teagan.
Tega, Tegen, Teggan, Teghan, Tegin, Tegyn, Teigen

TELISHA (American) an alternate form of Taleisha.
Teleesha, Teleisia, Telesa, Telesha, Teleshia, Telesia, Telicia, Telisa, Telishia, Telisia, Telissa, Telisse, Tellisa, Tellisha, Telsa, Telysa

TEMIRA (Hebrew) tall.
Temora, Timora

TEMPEST (French) stormy.
Tempesta, Tempeste, Tempestt, Tempist, Tempistt, Tempress, Tempteste

TENESHA, Tenisha (American) combinations of the prefix Te + Niesha.
Tenecia, Teneesha, Teneisha, Teneshia, Tenesia, Tenessa, Teneusa, Teniesha, Tenishia

TENNILLE (American) a combination of the prefix Te + Nellie.
Taniel, Tanille, Teneal, Teneil, Teneille, Teniel, Tenille, Tenneal, Tenneill, Tenneille, Tennia, Tennie, Tennielle, Tennile, Tineal, Tiniel, Tonielle, Tonille

TEODORA (Czech) a form of Theodora.
Teadora

TEONA, Teonna (Greek) alternate forms of Tiana, Tianna.
Teon, Teoni, Teonia, Teonie, Teonney, Teonnia, Teonnie

TEQUILA (Spanish) an alcoholic cocktail. See also Takila.
Taquela, Taquella, Taquila, Taquilla, Tequilia, Tequilla, Tiquila, Tiquilia

TERA, Terra (Latin) earth. (Japanese) swift arrow.
Terah, Terai, Teria, Terrae, Terrah, Terria, Tierra

TERALYN (American) a combination of Terri + Lynn.
Taralyn, Teralyn, Teralynn, Terralin, Terralyn

TERESA (Greek) reaper. An alternate form of Theresa. See also Tressa.
Taresa, Taressa, Tarissa, Terasa, Tercza, Tereasa, Tereatha, Terese, Teresea, Teresha, Teresia, Teresina, Teresita, Tereska, Tereson, Teressa, Teretha, Tereza, Terezia, Terezie, Terezilya, Terezinha, Terezka, Terezsa, Terisa, Terisha, Teriza, Terrasa, Terresa, Terresha, Terresia, Terressa, Terrosina, Tersa, Tersea, Teruska, Terza, Teté, Tyresa, Tyresia

TERESE (Greek) an alternate form of Teresa.
Tarese, Taress, Taris, Tarise, Tereece, Tereese, Teress, Terez, Teris, Terrise

TERI (Greek) reaper. A familiar form of Theresa.
Terie

TERRELLE (Greek) an alternate form of Theresa.
Tarrell, Teral, Terall, Terel, Terell, Teriel, Terral, Terrall, Terrell, Terrella, Terriel, Terriell, Terrielle, Terrill, Terryelle, Terryl, Terryll, Terrylle, Teryl, Tyrell, Tyrelle

TERRENE (Latin) smooth. A feminine form of Terrence.
Tareena, Tarena, Teran, Teranee, Tereena, Terena, Terencia, Terene, Terenia, Terentia, Terina, Terran, Terren, Terrena, Terrin,

Terrina, Terron, Terrosina, Terryn, Terun, Teryn, Teryna, Terynn, Tyreen, Tyrene

TERRI (Greek) reaper. A familiar form of Theresa.
Terree, Terria, Terrie

TERRIANN (American) a combination of Terri + Ann.
Teran, Terian, Teriann, Terianne, Teriyan, Terria, Terrian, Terrianne, Terryann

TERRIANNA (American) a combination of Terri + Anna.
Teriana, Terianna, Terriana, Terriauna, Terrina, Terriona, Terrionna, Terriyana, Terriyanna, Terryana, Terryauna, Tyrina

TERRICA (American) a combination of Terri + Erica. See also Rica.
Tereka, Terica, Tericka, Terika, Terreka, Terricka, Terrika, Tyrica, Tyricka, Tyrika, Tyrikka, Tyronica

TERRY (Greek) a short form of Theresa.
Tere, Teree, Terelle, Terene, Teri, Terie, Terrey, Terri, Terrie, Terrye, Tery

TERRY-LYNN (American) a combination of Terry + Lynn.
Terelyn, Terelynn, Terri-Lynn, Terrilynn, Terrylynn

TERTIA (Latin) third.
Tercia, Tercina, Tercine, Terecena, Tersia, Terza

TESS (Greek) a short form of Quintessa, Theresa.
Tes, Tese

TESSA (Greek) reaper. A short form of Theresa.
Tesa, Tesah, Tesha, Tesia, Tessah, Tessia, Tezia

TESSIE (Greek) a familiar form of Theresa.
Tesi, Tessey, Tessi, Tessy, Tezi

TETSU (Japanese) strong as iron.

TETTY (English) a familiar form of Elizabeth.

TEVY (Cambodian) angel.
Teva

TEYLOR (English) an alternate form of Taylor.
Teighlor, Teylar

THADDEA (Greek) courageous. (Latin) praiser. A feminine form of Thaddeus.
Thada, Thadda

THALASSA (Greek) sea, ocean.

THALIA (Greek) an alternate form of Talia. Mythology: the Muse of comedy.
Thaleia, Thalie, Thalya

THANA (Arabic) happy occasion.
Thaina, Thania, Thanie

THANH (Vietnamese) bright blue. (Punjabi) good place.
Thantra, Thanya

THAO (Vietnamese) respectful of parents.

THEA (Greek) goddess. A short form of Althea.
Theo

THELMA (Greek) willful.
Thelmalina

THEMA (African) queen.

THEODORA (Greek) gift of God. See also Dora, Dorothy, Feodora.

Taedra, Teddi, Tedra, Teodora, Teodory, Teodosia, Theda, Thedorsha, Thedrica, Theo, Theodore, Theodoria, Theodorian, Theodosia, Theodra

THEONE (Greek) gift of God.
Theondra, Theoni, Theonie

THEOPHANIA (Greek) God's appearance. See also Tiffany.
Theo, Theophanie

THEOPHILA (Greek) loved by God.
Theo

THERESA (Greek) reaper. See also Resi, Reza, Riza, Tassos, Teca, Terrelle, Tracey, Tracy, Zilya.
Teresa, Teri, Terri, Terry, Tersea, Tess, Tessa, Tessie, Theresia, Theresina, Theresita, Theressa, Thereza, Therisa, Therissie, Thersa, Thersea, Tresha, Tressa, Trice

THERESE (Greek) an alternate form of Theresa.
Terese, Thérése, Theresia, Theressa, Therra, Therressa, Thersa

THETA (Greek) Linguistics: a letter in the Greek alphabet.

THETIS (Greek) disposed. Mythology: the mother of Achilles.

THI (Vietnamese) poem.
Thia, Thy, Thya

THIRZA (Hebrew) pleasant.
Therza, Thirsa, Thirzah, Thursa, Thurza, Thyrza, Tirshka, Tirza

THOMASINA (Hebrew) twin. A feminine form of Thomas. See also Tamassa.

Tamsin, Thomasa, Thomasia, Thomasin, Thomasine, Thomazine, Thomencia, Thomethia, Thomisha, Thomsina, Toma, Tomasa, Tomasina, Tomasine, Tomina, Tommie, Tommina

THORA (Scandinavian) thunder. A feminine form of Thor.
Thordia, Thordis, Thorri, Thyra, Tyra

THUY (Vietnamese) gentle.

TIA (Greek) princess. (Spanish) aunt.
Téa, Teah, Teeya, Teia, Ti, Tiakeisha, Tialeigh, Tiamarie, Tianda, Tiandria, Tiante, Tiia, Tiye, Tyja

TIANA, Tianna (Greek) princess. (Latin) short forms of Tatiana.
Teana, Teanna, Tiahna, Tianah, Tiane, Tianea, Tianee, Tiani, Tiann, Tiannah, Tianne, Tianni, Tiaon, Tiauna, Tiena, Tiona, Tionna, Tiyana

TIARA (Latin) crowned.
Teair, Teaira, Teara, Téare, Tearia, Tearria, Teearia, Teira, Teirra, Tiaira, Tiare, Tiarea, Tiareah, Tiari, Tiaria, Tiarra, Tiera, Tierra, Tyara

TIARRA (Latin) an alternate form of Tiara.
Tiairra, Tiarrah, Tyarra

TIAUNA (Greek) an alternate form of Tiana.
Tiaunah, Tiaunia, Tiaunna

TIBERIA (Latin) Geography: the Tiber River in Italy.
Tib, Tibbie, Tibby

TICHINA (American) a combination of the prefix Ti + China.
Tichian, Tichin, Tichinia

TIDA (Tai) daughter.

TIERA, Tierra (Latin) alternate forms of Tiara.
Tieara, Tiéra, Tierah, Tierre, Tierrea, Tierria

TIERNEY (Irish) noble.
Tieranae, Tierani, Tieranie, Tieranni, Tierany, Tiernan, Tiernee, Tierny

TIFF (Latin) a short form of Tiffani, Tiffanie, Tiffany.

TIFFANI, Tiffanie (Latin) alternate forms of Tiffany.
Tephanie, Tifanee, Tifani, Tifanie, Tiff, Tiffanee, Tiffayne, Tiffeni, Tiffenie, Tiffennie, Tiffiani, Tiffianie, Tiffine, Tiffini, Tiffinie, Tiffni, Tiffy, Tiffynie, Tifni

TIFFANY (Greek) a short form of Theophania. (Latin) trinity. See also Tyfany.
Taffanay, Taffany, Tifaney, Tifany, Tiff, Tiffaney, Tiffani, Tiffanie, Tiffanny, Tiffeney, Tiffiany, Tiffiney, Tiffiny, Tiffnay, Tiffney, Tiffny, Tiffy, Tiphanie, Triffany

TIFFY (Latin) a familiar form of Tiffani, Tiffany.
Tiffey, Tiffi, Tiffie

TIJUANA (Spanish) Geography: a border town in Mexico.
Tajuana, Tajuanna, Thejuana, Tiajuana, Tiajuanna, Tiawanna

TILDA (German) a short form of Matilda.
Tilde, Tildie, Tildy, Tylda, Tyldy

TILLIE (German) a familiar form of Matilda.
Tilia, Tilley, Tilli, Tillia, Tilly, Tillye

TIMI (English) a familiar form of Timothea.
Timia, Timie, Timmi, Timmie

TIMOTHEA (English) honoring God. A feminine form of Timothy.
Thea, Timi

TINA (Spanish, American) a short form of Augustine, Martina, Christina, Valentina.
Teanna, Teena, Teina, Tena, Tenae, Tinai, Tine, Tinea, Tinia, Tiniah, Tinna, Tinnia, Tyna, Tynka

TINBLE (English) sound bells make.
Tynble

TINESHA (American) a combination of the prefix Ti + Niesha.
Timnesha, Tinecia, Tineisha, Tinesa, Tineshia, Tinessa, Tinisha, Tinsia

TINISHA (American) an alternate form of Tenesha.
Tiniesha, Tinieshia, Tinishia, Tinishya

TIONA, Tionna (American) forms of Tiana.
Teona, Teonna, Tionda, Tiondra, Tiondre, Tioné, Tionette, Tioni, Tionia, Tionie, Tionja, Tionnah, Tionne, Tionya, Tyonna

TIPHANIE (Latin) an alternate form of Tiffany.
Tiphanee, Tiphani, Tiphany

TIPONYA (Native American) great horned owl.
Tipper

TIPPER (Irish) water pourer. (Native American) a short form of Tiponya.

TIRA (Hindi) arrow.
Tirah, Tirea, Tirena

TIRTHA (Hindi) ford.

TIRZA (Hebrew) pleasant.
Thersa, Thirza, Tierza, Tirsa, Tirzah, Tirzha, Tyrzah

TISA (Swahili) ninth-born.
Tisah, Tysa, Tyssa

TISH (Latin) a short form of Tisha.

TISHA (Latin) joy. A short form of Leticia.
Taesha, Tesha, Teisha, Tiesha, Tieshia, Tish, Tishal, Tishia, Tysha, Tyshia

TITA (Greek) giant. (Spanish) a short form of names ending in "tita." A feminine form of Titus.

TITANIA (Greek) giant. Mythology: the Titans were a race of giants.
Tania, Teata, Titanna, Titanya, Titiana, Tiziana, Tytan, Tytania, Tytiana

TITIANA (Greek) an alternate form of Titania.
Titianay, Titiania, Titianna, Titiayana, Titionia, Titiyana, Titiyanna, Tityana

TIVONA (Hebrew) nature lover.

TIWA (Zuni) onion.

TIYANA (Greek) an alternate form of Tiana.
Tiyan, Tiyani, Tiyania, Tiyanna, Tiyonna

TOBI (Hebrew) God is good. A feminine form of Tobias.
Tobe, Tobee, Tobey, Tobie, Tobit, Toby, Tobye, Tova, Tovah, Tove, Tovi, Tybi, Tybie

TOCARRA (American) a combination of the prefix To + Cara.
Tocara, Toccara

TOINETTE (French) a short form of Antoinette.
Toinetta, Tola, Tonetta, Tonette, Toni, Toniette, Twanette

TOKI (Japanese) hopeful.
Toko, Tokoya, Tokyo

TOLA (Polish) a form of Toinette.
Tolsia

TOMI (Japanese) rich.
Tomie, Tomiju

TOMMIE (Hebrew) a short form of Thomasina.
Tomme, Tommi, Tommia, Tommy

TOMO (Japanese) intelligent.
Tomoko

TONESHA (American) a combination of the prefix To + Niesha.
Toneisha, Toneisheia, Tonesha, Tonesia, Toniece, Tonisha, Tonneshia

TONI (Greek) flourishing. (Latin) praiseworthy. A short form of Antoinette, Antonia, Toinette.
Tonee, Toney, Tonia, Tonie, Toniee, Tonni, Tonnie, Tony, Tonye

TONIA (Latin, Slavic) an alternate form of Toni, Tonya.
Tonea, Toniah, Toniea, Tonja, Tonje, Tonna, Tonni, Tonnia, Tonnie, Tonnja

TONISHA (American) an alternate form of Tonesha.
Toniesha, Tonisa, Tonise, Tonisia, Tonnisha

TONYA (Slavic) fairy queen.
Tonia, Tonnya, Tonyea, Tonyetta, Tonyia

TOPAZ (Latin) golden yellow gem.

TOPSY (English) on top.
Literature: a slave in Harriet
Beecher Stowe's novel *Uncle
Tom's Cabin*.
Toppsy, Topsey, Topsie

TORA (Japanese) tiger.

TORI (Japanese) bird. (English)
an alternate form of Tory.
*Toria, Toriana, Torie, Torri, Torrie,
Torrita*

TORIA (English) an alternate
form of Tori.
Toriah, Torria

TORIANA (English) an alternate
form of Tori.
*Torian, Toriane, Toriann,
Torianna, Torianne, Toriauna,
Torin, Torina, Torine, Torinne,
Torion, Torionna, Torionne,
Toriyanna, Torrina*

TORIE, Torrie (English) alternate forms of Tori.
Tore, Toree, Torei, Torre, Torree

TORILYN (English) a combination of Tori + Lynn.
Torilynn, Torrilyn, Torrilynn

TORRI (English) an alternate
form of Tori.

TORY (Latin) a short form of
Victoria. (English) victorious.
*Tauri, Torey, Tori, Torrey, Torreya,
Torry, Torrye, Torya, Torye, Toya*

TOSHA (Punjabi) armaments.
(Polish) a familiar form of
Antonia. (Russian) an alter-
nate form of Tasha.
*Toshea, Toshia, Toshiea,
Toshke, Tosia, Toska*

TOSHI (Japanese) mirror
image.
Toshie, Toshiko, Toshikyo

TOSKI (Hopi) squash bug.

TOTSI (Hopi) moccasins.

TOTTIE (English) a familiar
form of Charlotte.
Tota, Totti, Totty

TOVAH (Hebrew) good.
Tova, Tovia

TOYA (Spanish) a form of Tory.
*Toia, Toyanika, Toyanna, Toyea,
Toylea, Toyleah, Toylenn, Toylin,
Toylyn*

TRACEY (Greek) a familiar
form of Theresa. (Latin)
warrior.
*Trace, Tracee, Tracell, Traci,
Tracie, Tracy, Traice, Trasey,
Treesy*

TRACI, Tracie (Latin) alternate
forms of Tracey.
*Tracia, Tracilee, Tracilyn,
Tracilynn, Tracina, Traeci*

TRACY (Greek) a familiar form
of Theresa. (Latin) warrior.
Treacy

TRALENA (Latin) a combination
of Tracy + Lena.
*Traleen, Tralene, Tralin, Tralinda,
Tralyn, Tralynn, Tralynne*

TRANESHA (American) a com-
bination of the prefix Tra +
Niesha.
*Traneice, Traneis, Traneise,
Traneisha, Tranese, Traneshia,
Tranice, Traniece, Traniesha,
Tranisha, Tranishia*

TRASHAWN (American) a com-
bination of the prefix Tra +
Shawn.
*Trashan, Trashana, Trashauna,
Trashon, Trayshauna*

TRAVA (Czech) spring grasses.

TREASURE (Latin) treasure,
wealth; valuable.
*Treasa, Treasur, Treasuré,
Treasury*

TRELLA (Spanish) a familiar
form of Estelle.

TRESHA (Greek) an alternate
form of Theresa.
*Trescha, Trescia, Treshana,
Treshia*

TRESSA (Greek) a short form
of Theresa. See also Teresa.
*Treaser, Tresa, Tresca, Trese,
Treska, Tressia, Tressie, Trez,
Treza, Trisa*

TREVINA (Irish) prudent.
(Welsh) homestead. A femi-
nine form of Trevor.
*Treva, Trevanna, Trevena,
Trevenia, Treveon, Trevia,
Treviana, Trevien, Trevin, Trevona*

TREVONA (Irish) an alternate
form of Trevina.
*Trevion, Trevon, Trevonia,
Trevonna, Trevonne, Trevonye*

TRIANA (Greek) an alternate
form of Trina. (Latin) third.
Tria, Triann, Trianna, Trianne

TRICE (Greek) a short form of
Theresa.
Treece

TRICIA (Latin) an alternate
form of Trisha.
*Trica, Tricha, Trichelle, Tricina,
Trickia*

TRILBY (English) soft hat.
Tribi, Trilbie, Trillby

TRINA (Greek) pure. A short
form of Katrina. (Hindi)
points of sacred kusa grass.
*Treena, Treina, Trenna, Triana,
Trinia, Trinchen, Trind, Trinda,*

Trina *(cont.)*
Trine, Trinette, Trini, Trinica, Trinice, Triniece, Trinika, Trinique, Trinisa, Tryna

TRINI (Greek) an alternate form of Trina.
Trinia, Trinie

TRINITY (Latin) triad. Religion: the Father, the Son, and the Holy Spirit.
Trinita, Trinite, Trinitee, Triniti, Trinnette, Trinty

TRISH (Latin) a short form of Beatrice, Trisha.
Trishell, Trishelle

TRISHA (Latin) noblewoman. A familiar form of Patricia. (Hindi) thirsty. See also Tricia.
Treasha, Trish, Trishann, Trishanna, Trishanne, Trishara, Trishia, Trishna, Trissha, Trycia

TRISSA (Latin) a familiar form of Patricia.
Trisa, Trisanne, Trisia, Trisina, Trissi, Trissie, Trissy, Tryssa

TRISTA (Latin) a short form of Tristen.
Trisatal, Tristess, Tristia, Trysta, Trystia

TRISTAN (Latin) bold.
Trista, Tristane, Tristanni, Tristany, Tristen, Tristian, Tristiana, Tristin, Triston, Trystan, Trystyn

TRISTEN (Latin) an alternate form of Tristan.
Tristene, Trysten

TRISTIN (Latin) an alternate form of Tristan.
Tristina, Tristine, Tristinye, Tristn, Trystin

TRISTON, Trystyn (Latin) alternate forms of Tristan.
Tristony, Trystyn

TRIXIE (American) a familiar form of Beatrice.
Tris, Trissie, Trissina, Trix, Trixi, Trixy

TROYA (Irish) foot soldier.
Troi, Troia, Troiana, Troiya, Troy

TRUDEL (Dutch) a form of Trudy.

TRUDY (German) a familiar form of Gertrude.
Truda, Trude, Trudel, Trudessa, Trudey, Trudi, Trudie

TRYCIA (latin) an alternate form of Trisha.

TRYNA (Greek) an alternate form of Trina.
Tryane, Tryanna, Trynee

TRYNE (Dutch) pure.
Trine

TSIGANA (Hungarian) an alternate form of Zigana.
Tsigane, Tzigana, Tzigane

TU (Chinese) jade.

TUESDAY (English) second day of the week.
Tuesdae, Tuesdea, Tuesdee, Tuesdey, Tusdai

TULA (Hindi) born in the lunar month of Capricorn.
Tulah, Tulla, Tullah, Tuula

TULLIA (Irish) peaceful, quiet.
Tulia, Tulliah

TULSI (Hindi) basil, a sacred Hindi herb.
Tulsia

TURQUOISE (French) blue green, semi-precious stone originally brought to Europe through Turkey.
Turkois, Turkoise, Turkoys, Turkoyse

TUSA (Zuni) prairie dog.

TUYEN (Vietnamese) angel.

TUYET (Vietnamese) snow.

TWYLA (English) woven of double thread.
Twila, Twilla

TYANNA (American) a combination of the prefix Ty + Anna.
Tya, Tyana, Tyann, Tyannah, Tyanne, Tyannia

TYEISHA (American) an alternate form of Tyesha.
Tyeesha, Tyeishia, Tyieshia, Tyisha, Tyishea, Tyishia

TYESHA (American) a combination of the prefix Ty + Aisha.
Tyasha, Tyashia, Tyasia, Tyasiah, Tyeisha, Tyeshia, Tyeyshia, Tyisha

TYFANY (American) a short form of Tiffany.
Tyfani, Tyfanny, Tyffani, Tyffanni, Tyffany, Tyffini, Typhanie, Typhany

TYKEISHA (American) an alternate form of Takeisha.
Tkeesha, Tykeisa, Tykeishia, Tykesha, Tykeshia, Tykeysha, Tykeza, Tykisha

TYKERA (American) an alternate form of Takira.
Tykeira, Tykeirah, Tykereiah, Tykeria, Tykeriah, Tykerria, Tykiera, Tykierra, Tykira, Tykiria, Tykirra

TYLER (English) tailor.
Tyller, Tylor

TYNA (Czech) a short form of Kristina.
Tynae, Tynea, Tynia

TYNE (English) river.
Tine, Tyna, Tynelle, Tynessa, Tynetta

TYNESHA (American) a combination of the prefix Ty + Niesha.
Tynaise, Tynece, Tyneicia, Tynesa, Tynesha, Tyneshia, Tynessia, Tyniesha, Tynisha, Tyseisha

TYNISHA (American) an alternate form of Tynesha.
Tyneisha, Tyneisia, Tynisa, Tynise, Tynishi

TYRA (Scandinavian) battler. Mythology: Tyr was the god of battle.
Tyraa, Tyrah, Tyran, Tyree, Tyria

TYSHANNA (American) a combination of the prefis Ty + Shawna.
Tyshana, Tyshanae, Tyshane, Tyshaun, Tyshaunda, Tyshawn, Tyshawna, Tyshawnah, Tyshawnda, Tyshawnna, Tysheann, Tysheanna, Tyshonia, Tyshonna, Tyshonya

TYTIANA (Greek) an alternate form of Titania.
Tytana, Tytanna, Tyteana, Tyteanna, Tytianna, Tytianni, Tytionna, Tytiyana, Tytiyanna, Tytyana, Tytyauna

U (Korean) gentle.

UDELE (English) prosperous.
Uda, Udella, Udelle, Yudelle

ULA (Basque) the Virgin Mary. (Irish) sea jewel. (Spanish) a short form of Eulalia. (Scandinavian) wealthy.
Uli, Ulla

ULANI (Polynesian) cheerful.
Ulana, Ulane

ULIMA (Arabic) astute; wise.
Ullima

ULLA (Latin) a short form of Ursula. (German, Swedish) willful.
Ulli

ULRICA (German) wolf ruler; ruler of all. A feminine form of Ulric. See also Rica.
Ulka, Ullrica, Ullricka, Ullrika, Ulrika, Ulrike

ULTIMA (Latin) last, endmost, farthest.

ULULANI (Hawaiian) heavenly inspiration.

ULVA (German) wolf.

UMA (Hindi) mother. Religion: another name for the Hindu goddess Shakti.

UMAY (Turkish) hopeful.
Umai

UMEKO (Japanese) plum blossom child; patient.
Ume, Umeyo

UNA (Latin) one; united. (Irish) a form of Agnes. (Hopi) good memory. See also Oona.
Unna, Uny

UNDINE (Latin) little wave. Mythology: the Undines were water sprites. See also Ondine.
Undeen, Undene

UNICE (English) a form of Eunice.

UNIKA (American) a form of Unique.
Unica, Unicka, Unik, Unikqua, Unikue

UNIQUE (Latin) only one.
Unika, Uniqia, Uniqua, Uniquia

UNITY (English) unity.
Uinita, Unita, Unitee

UNN (Norwegian) she who is loved.

UNNA (German) woman.

URANIA (Greek) heavenly. Mythology: the Muse of astronomy.
Urainia, Uranie, Uraniya, Uranya

URBANA (Latin) city dweller.
Urbanah, Urbanna

URIKA (Omaha) useful to everyone.
Ureka

URIT (Hebrew) bright.
Urice

URSA (Greek) a short form of Ursula. (Latin) an alternate form of Orsa.
Ursey, Ursi, Ursie, Ursy

URSULA (Greek) little bear. See also Sula, Ulla, Vorsila.
Irsaline, Ursa, Ursala, Ursel, Ursela, Ursella, Ursely, Ursilla, Ursillane, Ursola, Ursule, Ursulina, Ursuline, Urszula, Urszuli, Urzula

USHA (Hindi) sunrise.

USHI (Chinese) ox. Astrology: a sign of the zodiac.

UTA (German) rich. (Japanese) poem.
Utako

UTINA (Native American) woman of my country.
Utahna, Utona, Utonna

VAIL (English) valley.
Vale, Vayle

VAL (Latin) a short form of Valentina, Valerie.

VALA (German) singled out.
Valla

VALARIE (Latin) an alternate form of Valerie.
Valarae, Valaree, Valarey, Valari, Valaria, Vallarie

VALDA (German) famous ruler. A feminine form of Valdemar.
Valida, Velda

VALENCIA (Spanish) strong. Geography: a region in eastern Spain.
Valecia, Valence, Valenica, Valentia, Valenzia

VALENE (Latin) a short form of Valentina.
Valaine, Valean, Valeda, Valeen, Valen, Valena, Valeney, Valien, Valina, Valine, Vallan, Vallen

VALENTINA (Latin) strong. History: Valentina Tereshkova, a Soviet cosmonaut, was the first woman in space. See also Tina, Valene, Valli.
Val, Valantina, Vale, Valenteen, Valentena, Valentijn, Valentin, Valentine, Valiaka, Valtina, Valyn, Valynn

VALERA (Russian) a form of Valerie. See also Lera.

VALERIA (Latin) an alternate form of Valerie.
Valaria, Valeriana, Valeriane, Veleria

VALERIE (Latin) strong.
Vairy, Val, Valarie, Vale, Valera, Valeree, Valeri, Valeria, Valérie, Valery, Valka, Valleree, Valleri, Vallerie, Valli, Vallirie, Valora, Valorie, Valry, Valya, Velerie, Waleria

VALERY (Latin) an alternate form of Valerie.
Valerye, Vallary, Vallery

VALESKA (Slavic) glorious ruler. A feminine form of Vladislav.
Valesca, Valese, Valeshia, Valeshka, Valezka, Valisha

VALLI (Latin) a familiar form of Valentina, Valerie. Botany: a plant native to India.
Vallie, Vally

VALMA (Finnish) loyal defender.

VALONIA (Latin) shadow valley.
Vallon, Valona

VALORA (Latin) an alternate form of Valerie.
Valoria, Valorya, Velora

VALORIE (Latin) an alternate form of Valerie.
Vallori, Vallory, Valori, Valory

VANDA (German) an alternate form of Wanda.
Vandana, Vandella, Vandetta, Vandi, Vannda

VANESA (Greek) an alternate form of Vanessa.
Vanesha, Vaneshah, Vanesia, Vanisa

VANESSA (Greek) butterfly. Literature: a name invented by Jonathan Swift as a nickname for Esther Vanhomrigh. See also Nessie.
Van, Vanassa, Vanesa, Vaneshia, Vanesse, Vanessia, Vanessica, Vanetta, Vaneza, Vaniece, Vaniessa, Vanija, Vanika, Vanissa, Vanita, Vanna, Vannesa, Vannessa, Vanni, Vannie, Vanny, Varnessa, Venessa

VANETTA (English) a form of Vanessa.
Vaneta, Vanita, Vanneta, Vannetta, Vannita, Venetta

VANIA, Vanya (Russian) familiar forms of Anna.
Vanija, Vanina, Vaniya, Vanja, Vanka, Vannia

VANITY (English) vain.
Vaniti, Vanitty

VANNA (Greek) a short form of Vanessa. (Cambodian) golden.
Vana, Vanae, Vanelly, Vannah, Vannalee, Vannaleigh, Vannie, Vanny

VANNESA, Vannessa (Greek) alternate forms of Vanessa.
Vannesha, Vanneza

VANORA (Welsh) white wave.
Vannora

VANTRICE (American) a combination of the prefix Van + Trice.
Vantrece, Vantricia, Vantrisa, Vantrissa

VARDA (Hebrew) rose.
Vadit, Vardia, Vardice, Vardina, Vardis, Vardit

VARVARA (Latin) a form of Barbara.
Vara, Varenka, Varina, Varinka, Varya, Varyusha, Vava, Vavka

VASHTI (Persian) lovely. Bible: the wife of Ahasuerus, king of Persia.
Vashtee, Vashtie, Vashty

VEANNA (American) a combination of the prefix Ve + Anna.
Veeana, Veena, Veenaya, Veeona

VEDA (Sanskrit) wise. Religion: the Vedas are the sacred writings of Hinduism.
Vedad, Vedis, Veeda, Veida, Veleda, Vida

VEDETTE (Italian) sentry; scout. (French) movie star.
Vedetta

VEGA (Arabic) falling star.

VELDA (German) an alternate form of Valda.

VELIKA (Slavic) great, wondrous.

VELMA (German) a familiar form of Vilhelmina.
Valma, Vellma, Vilma, Vilna

VELVET (English) velvety.

VENECIA (Italian) from Venice.
Vanecia, Vanetia, Veneise, Venesa, Venesha, Venesher, Venesse, Venessia, Venetia, Venette, Venezia, Venice, Venicia, Veniece, Veniesa, Venise, Venisha, Venishia, Venita, Venitia, Venize, Vennesa, Vennice, Vennisa, Vennise, Vonitia, Vonizia

VENESSA (Latin) a form of Vanessa.
Veneese, Venesa, Venese, Veneshia, Venesia, Venisa, Venissa, Vennessa

VENUS (Latin) love. Mythology: the goddess of love and beauty.
Venis, Venusa, Venusina, Vinny

VERA (Latin) true. (Slavic) faith. A short form of Elvera, Veronica. See also Verena, Wera.
Vara, Veera, Veira, Veradis, Verasha, Vere, Verka, Verla, Viera, Vira

VERBENA (Latin) sacred plants including olive, laurel, and myrtle.
Verbeena, Verbina

VERDA (Latin) young, fresh.
Verdi, Verdie, Viridiana, Viridis

VERDAD (Spanish) truthful.

VERENA (Latin) truthful. A familiar form of Vera, Verna.
Verene, Verenis, Vereniz, Verina, Verine, Verinka, Veroshka, Verunka, Verusya, Virna

VERENICE (Latin) an alternate form of Varonica.
Verenis, Verenise, Vereniz

VERITY (Latin) truthful.
Verita, Veritie

VERLENE (Latin) a combination of Veronica + Lena.
Verleen, Verlena, Verlin, Verlina, Verlinda, Verline, Verlyn

VERNA (Latin) springtime. (French) a familiar form of Laverne. See also Verena, Wera.
Verasha, Verla, Verne, Vernetia, Vernetta, Vernette, Vernia, Vernice, Vernita, Verusya, Viera, Virida, Virna, Virnell

VERNICE (Latin) a form of Bernice, Verna.
Vernese, Vernesha, Verneshia, Vernessa, Vernica, Vernicca, Verniece, Vernika, Vernique, Vernis, Vernise, Vernisha, Vernisheia, Vernissia

VERONICA (Latin) true image. See also Ronni, Weronika.
Varonica, Vera, Veranique, Verenice, Verhonica, Verinica, Verohnica, Veron, Verona Verone, Veronic, Véronic, Veronice, Veronika, Veronique, Véronique, Veronne, Veronnica, Veruszhka, Vironica, Vron Vronica

VERONIKA (Latin) an alternate form of Veronica.
Varonika, Veronick, Véronick, Veronik, Veronike, Veronka, Veronkia, Veruka

VERONIQUE, Véronique
(French) forms of Veronica.

VESPERA (Latin) evening star.

VESTA (Latin) keeper of the house. Mythology: the goddess of the home.
Vessy, Vest, Vesteria

VETA (Slavic) a familiar form of Elizabeth.
Veeta, Vita

VI (Latin, French) a short form of Viola, Violet.
Vye

VIANCA (Spanish) a form of Bianca.
Vianeca, Vianica

VIANEY (American) a familiar form of Vianna.
Vianney, Viany

VIANNA (American) a combination of Vi + Anna.
Viana, Vianey, Viann, Vianne

VICA (Hungarian) a form of Eve.

VICKI, Vickie (Latin) familiar forms of Victoria.
Vic, Vicci, Vicke, Vickee, Vickiana, Vickilyn, Vickki, Vicky, Vika, Viki, Vikie, Vikki, Vikky

VICKY (Latin) a familiar form of Victoria.
Viccy, Vickey, Viky, Vikkey, Vikky

VICTORIA (Latin) victorious. See also Tory, Wicktoria, Wisia.
Vicki, Vicky, Victoire, Victoriana, Victorianna, Victorie, Victorina, Victorine, Victoriya, Victorria, Victorriah, Victory, Victorya, Viktoria, Vitoria, Vyctoria

VIDA (Sanskrit) an alternate form of Veda. (Hebrew) a short form of Davida.
Vidamarie

VIDONIA (Portuguese) branch of a vine.
Vedonia, Vidonya

VIENNA (Latin) Geography: the capital of Austria.
Veena, Vena, Venna, Vienette, Vienne, Vina

VIKTORIA (Latin) an alternate form of Victoria.
Viktorie, Viktorija, Viktorina, Viktorine, Viktorka

VILHELMINA (German) an alternate form of Wilhelmina.
Velma, Vilhelmine, Vilma

VILLETTE (French) small town.
Vietta

VILMA (German) a short form of Vilhemina.

VINA (Hebrew) a short form of Davina. (Hindi) Mythology: a musical instrument played by the Hindu goddess of wisdom. (Spanish) vineyard. See also Lavina. (English) a short form of Alvina.
Veena, Vena, Viña, Vinesha, Vinessa, Vinia, Viniece, Vinique, Vinisha, Viñita, Vinna, Vinni, Vinnie, Vinny, Vinora, Vyna

VINCENTIA (Latin) victor, conqueror. A feminine form of Vincent.
Vicenta, Vincenta, Vincentena, Vincentina, Vincentine, Vincenza, Vincy, Vinnie

VIÑITA (Spanish) an alternate form of Vina.

Viñeet, Viñeeta, Viñetta, Viñette, Viñitha, Viñta, Viñti, Viñtia, Vyñetta, Vyñette

VIOLA (Latin) violet; stringed instrument in the violin family. Literature: the heroine of Shakespeare's play *Twelfth Night*.
Vi, Violaine, Violanta, Violante, Viole, Violeine

VIOLET (French) Botany: a plant with purplish blue flowers.
Vi, Violeta, Violette, Vyolet, Vyoletta, Vyolette

VIOLETA (French) an alternate form of Violet.
Violetta

VIRGILIA (Latin) rod bearer, staff bearer. A feminine form of Virgil.
Virgillia

VIRGINIA (Latin) pure, virginal. Literature: Virginia Woolf was a well-known British writer. See also Gina, Ginger, Ginny, Jinny.
Verginia, Verginya, Virge, Virgen, Virgenia, Virgenya, Virgie, Virgine, Virginie, Virginië, Virginio, Virginnia, Virgy, Virjeana

VIRGINIE (French) a form of Virginia.

VIRIDIANA (Latin) an alternate form of Viridis.

VIRIDIS (Latin) green.
Virdis, Virida, Viridia, Viridiana

VIRTUE (Latin) virtuous.

VITA (Latin) life.
Veeta, Veta, Vitaliana, Vitalina, Vitel, Vitella, Vitia, Vitka, Vitke

VITORIA (Spanish) a form of Victoria.
Vittoria

VIV (Latin) a short form of Vivian.

VIVA (Latin) a short form of Aviva, Vivian.
Vica, Vivan, Vivva

VIVECA (Latin) an alternate form of Vivian.
Viv, Vivecca, Vivecka, Viveka, Vivica, Vivieca, Vyveca

VIVIAN (Latin) full of life.
Vevay, Vevey, Viv, Viva, Viveca, Vivee, Vivi, Vivia, Viviana, Viviane, Viviann, Vivianne, Vivie, Vivien, Vivienne, Vivina, Vivion, Vivyan, Vivyann, Vivyanne, Vyvyan, Vyvyann, Vyvyanne

VIVIANA (Latin) an alternate form of Vivian.
Viv, Vivianna, Vivyana, Vyvyana

VONDRA (Czech) loving woman.
Vonda, Vondrea

VONEISHA (American) a combination of Yvonne + Aisha.
Voneishia, Vonesha, Voneshia

VONNA (French) an alternate form of Yvonne.
Vona

VONNY (French) a familiar form of Yvonne.
Vonney, Vonni, Vonnie

VONTRICIA (American) a combination of Yvonne + Tricia.
Vontrece, Vontrese, Vontrice, Vontriece

VORSILA (Greek) an alternate form of Ursula.
Vorsilla, Vorsula, Vorsulla, Vorsyla

WADD (Arabic) beloved.

WAHEEDA (Arabic) one and only.

WAINANI (Hawaiian) beautiful water.

WAKANA (Japanese) plant.

WAKANDA (Dakota) magical power.
Wakenda

WAKEISHA (American) a combination of the prefix Wa + Keisha.
Wakeishia, Wakesha, Wakeshia, Wakesia

WALAD (Arabic) newborn.
Waladah, Walidah

WALDA (German) powerful; famous. A feminine form of Waldo.
Waldina, Waldine, Walida, Wallda, Welda

WALERIA (Polish) a form of Valerie.
Wala

WALKER (English) cloth; walker.
Wallker

WALLIS (English) from Wales. A feminine form of Wallace.
Wallie, Walliss, Wally, Wallys

WANDA (German) wanderer. See also Wendy.
Vanda, Wahnda, Wandah, Wandely, Wandie, Wandis, Wandja, Wandzia, Wannda, Wonda, Wonnda

WANDIE (German) a familiar form of Wanda.
Wandi, Wandy

WANETA (Native American) charger. See also Juanita.
Waneeta, Wanita, Wanite, Wanneta, Waunita, Wonita, Wonnita, Wynita

WANETTA (English) pale face.
Wanette, Wannetta, Wannette

WANIKA (Hawaiian) a form of Juanita.
Wanicka

WARDA (German) guardian. A feminine form of Ward.
Wardah, Wardeh, Wardena, Wardenia, Wardia, Wardine

WASHI (Japanese) eagle.

WATTAN (Japanese) homeland.

WAUNA (Moquelumnan) snow geese honking.
Waunakee

WAVA (Slavic) a form of Barbara.

WAVERLY (English) quaking aspen-tree meadow.
Waverley, Waverli, Wavierlee

WAYNESHA (American) a combination of Waynette + Niesha.
Wayneesha, Wayneisha, Waynie, Waynisha

WAYNETTE (English) wagon maker. A feminine form of Wayne.

Waynette *(cont.)*
Waynel, Waynelle, Waynetta, Waynlyn

WEEKO (Dakota) pretty girl.

WEHILANI (Hawaiian) heavenly adornment.

WENDA (Welsh) an alternate form of Wendy.
Wendaine, Wendayne

WENDELLE (English) wanderer.
Wendaline, Wendall, Wendalyn, Wendeline, Wendella, Wendelline, Wendelly

WENDI (Welsh) an alternate form of Wendy.
Wendie

WENDY (Welsh) white; light skinned. A familiar form of Gwendolyn, Wanda.
Wenda, Wende, Wendee, Wendey, Wendi, Wendye, Wuendy

WERA (Polish) a form of Vera. See also Verna.
Wiera, Wiercia, Wierka

WERONIKA (Polish) a form of Veronica.
Weronikra

WESISA (Musoga) foolish.

WESLEE (English) western meadow. A feminine form of Wesley.
Weslea, Wesleigh, Weslene, Wesley, Wesli, Weslia, Weslie, Weslyn

WHITLEY (English) white field.
Whitely, Whitlee, Whitleigh, Whitlie, Whittley

WHITNEY (English) white island.
Whiteney, Whitne, Whitné, Whitnee, Whitneigh, Whitnie, Whitny, Whitnye, Whytne, Whytney, Witney

WHITNIE (English) an alternate form of Whitney.
Whitani, Whitnei, Whitni, Whytni, Whytnie

WHITTNEY (English) an alternate form of Whitney.
Whittaney, Whittanie, Whittany, Whitteny, Whittnay, Whittnee, Whittney, Whittni, Whittnie

WHOOPI (English) happy; excited.
Whoopie, Whoopy

WICKTORIA (Polish) a form of Victoria.
Wicktorja, Wiktoria, Wiktorja

WILDA (German) untamed. (English) willow.
Willda, Wylda

WILEEN (English) a short form of Wilhelmina.
Wilene, Willeen, Willene

WILHELMINA (German) determined guardian. A feminine form of Wilhelm, William. See also Billie, Guillerma, Helma, Minka, Minna, Minnie.
Vilhelmina, Wileen, Wilhelmine, Willa, Willamina, Willamine, Willemina, Willette, Williamina, Willie, Willmina, Willmine, Wilma, Wimina

WILIKINIA (Hawaiian) a form of Virginia.

WILLA (German) a short form of Wilhelmina.
Willabella, Willette, Williabelle

WILLETTE (English) a familiar form of Wilhelmina, Willa.
Wiletta, Wilette, Willetta, Williette

WILLIE (English) a familiar form of Wilhelmina.
Willi, Willina, Willisha, Willishia, Willy

WILLOW (English) willow tree.
Willough

WILMA (German) a short form of Wilhelmina.
Williemae, Wilmanie, Wilmayra, Wilmetta, Wilmette, Wilmina, Wilmyne, Wylma

WILONA (English) desired.
Willona, Willone, Wilone

WIN (German) a short form of Winifred. See also Edwina.
Wyn

WINDA (Swahili) hunter.

WINDY (English) windy.
Windee, Windey, Windi, Windie, Wyndee, Wyndy

WINEMA (Moquelumnan) woman chief.

WINIFRED (German) peaceful friend. (Welsh) an alternate form of Guinevere. See also Freddi, Una, Winnie.
Win, Winafred, Winefred, Winefride, Winfreda, Winfrieda, Winiefrida, Winifrid, Winifryd, Winnafred, Winnefred, Winniefred, Winnifred, Winnifrid, Wynafred, Wynifred, Wynnifred

WINNA (African) friend.
Winnah

WINNIE (English) a familiar form of Edwina, Gwyneth, Winnifred, Winona, Wynne. History: Winnie Mandela kept the anti-aparteid movement alive in South Africa while her husband, Nelson Mandela, was imprisoned. Literature:

the lovable bear in A. A.
Milne's children's story
Winnie the Pooh.
Wina, Winne, Winney, Winni,
Winny, Wynnie

WINOLA (German) charming
friend.
Wynola

WINONA (Lakota) oldest
daughter.
Wanona, Wenona, Wenonah,
Winnie, Winonah, Wynonna

WINTER (English) winter.
Wintr, Wynter

WIRA (Polish) a form of Elvira.
Wiria, Wirke

WISIA (Polish) a form of
Victoria.
Wicia, Wikta

WREN (English) wren, songbird.

WYANET (Native American)
legendary beauty.
Wyaneta, Wyanita, Wynette

WYNNE (Welsh) white, light
skinned. A short form of
Blodwyn, Guinivere, Gwyneth.
Winnie, Wyn, Wynn

WYNONNA (Lakota) an alternate form of Winona.
Wynnona, Wynona

WYNTER (English) an alternate
form of Winter.
Wynteria

WYOMING (Native American)
Geography: a western
American state.
Wy, Wye, Wyoh, Wyomia

XANDRA (Greek) an alternate
form of Zandra. (Spanish) a
short form of Alexandra.
Xander, Xandrea, Xandria

XANTHE (Greek) yellow, blond.
See also Zanthe.
Xanne, Xantha, Xanthia,
Xanthippe

XANTHIPPE (Greek) an alter-
nate form of Xanthe. History:
Socrates's wife.
Xantippie

XAVIERA (Basque) owner of
the new house. (Arabic)
bright. A feminine form of
Xavier. See also Javiera,
Zaviera.
Xavia, Xaviére, Xavyera, Xiveria

XELA (Quiché) my mountain
home.

XENA (Greek) an alternate
form of Xenia.

XENIA (Greek) hospitable. See
also Zena, Zina.
Xeenia, Xena, Xenea, Xenya,
Xinia

XIANG (Chinese) fragrant.

XIOMARA (Teutonic) glorious
forest.
Xiomaris, Xiomayra

XIU MEI (Chinese) beautiful
plum.

XOCHITL (Aztec) place of many
flowers.
Xochil, Xochilt, Xochilth, Xochiti

XUAN (Vietnamese) spring.

XUXA (Portuguese) a familiar
form of Susanna.

XYLIA (Greek) a form of Sylvia.
Xylina, Xylona

YACHNE (Hebrew) hospitable.

YADIRA (Hebrew) friend.
Yadirah, Yadirha, Yadyra

YAEL (Hebrew) strength of
God. See also Jael.
Yaeli, Yaella, Yeala

YAFFA (Hebrew) beautiful. See
also Jaffa.
Yafeal, Yaffit, Yafit

YAHAIRA (Hebrew) an alternate form of Yakira.
Yahara, Yahayra, Yahira

YAJAIRA (Hebrew) an alternate
form of Yakira.
Yahaira, Yajara, Yajayra, Yajhaira

YAKIRA (Hebrew) precious;
dear.
Yahaira, Yajaira

YALANDA (Greek) an alternate form of Yolanda.
Yalando, Yalonda, Ylana, Ylanda

YALENA (Greek, Russian) an alternate form of Helen. See also Lena, Yelena.

YALETHA (American) a form of Oletha.
Yelitsa

YAMARY (American) a combination of the prefix Ya + Mary.
Yamairy, Yamarie, Yamaris, Yamayra

YAMELIA (American) an alternate form of Amelia.
Yameily, Yamelya, Yamelys

YAMILA (Arabic) an alternate form of Jamila.
Yamela, Yamely, Yamil, Yamile, Yamilet, Yamiley, Yamilla, Yamille

YAMINAH (Arabic) right, proper.
Yamina, Yamini, Yemina, Yeminah, Yemini

YAMKA (Hopi) blossom.

YAMUNA (Hindi) sacred river.

YANA (Slavic) an alternate form of Jana.
Yanae, Yanah, Yanay, Yanaye, Yanesi, Yanet, Yaneth, Yaney, Yani, Yanik, Yanina, Yanis, Yanisha, Yanitza, Yanixia, Yanna, Yannah, Yanni, Yannica, Yannick, Yannina

YANABA (Navajo) brave.

YANELI (American) a combination of the prefix Ya + Nellie.
Yanela, Yanelis, Yaneliz, Yanelle, Yanelli, Yanely, Yanelys

YANET (American) a form of Janet.

Yanete, Yaneth, Yanethe, Yanette, Yannet, Yanneth, Yannette

YÁNG (Chinese) sun.

YARELI (American) a form of Oralee.
Yarely, Yaresly

YARINA (Slavic) a form of Irene.
Yaryna

YARITZA (American) a combination of Yana + Ritsa.
Yaritsa, Yaritza

YARKONA (Hebrew) green.

YARMILLA (Slavic) market trader.

YASHIRA (Afghani) hamble; takes it easy. (Arabic) wealthy. A feminine form of Yasir.

YASMEEN (Persian) an alternate form of Yasmin.
Yasemeen, Yasemin, Yasmeena, Yasmen, Yasmene, Yasmeni, Yasmenne, Yassmeen, Yassmen

YASMIN, Yasmine (Persian) jasmine flower. Alternate forms of Jasmine.
Yashmine, Yasiman, Yasimine, Yasma, Yasmain, Yasmaine, Yasmina, Yasminda, Yasmon, Yasmyn, Yazmin, Yesmean, Yesmeen, Yesmin, Yesmina, Yesmine, Yesmyn

YASU (Japanese) resting, calm.
Yasuko, Yasuyo

YAZMIN (Persian) an alternate form of Yasmin.
Yazmeen, Yazmen, Yazmene, Yazmina, Yazmine, Yazmyn, Yazmyne, Yazzmien, Yazzmine, Yazzmine, Yazzmyn

YECENIA (Arabic) an alternate form of Yesenia.

YEHUDIT (Hebrew) an alternate form of Judith.
Yudit, Yudita, Yuta

YEI (Japanese) flourishing.

YEIRA (Hebrew) light.

YEKATERINA (Russian) a form of Katherine.

YELENA (Russian) a form of Helen, Jelena. See also Lena, Yalena.
Yeleana, Yelen, Yelenna, Yelenne, Yelina, Ylena, Ylenia, Ylenna

YELISABETA (Russian) a form of Elizabeth.
Yelizaveta

YEMENA (Arabic) from Yemen.
Yemina

YEN (Chinese) yearning; desirous.
Yeni, Yenih, Yenny

YENENE (Native American) shaman.

YENIFER (Welsh) an alternate form of Jennifer.
Yenefer, Yennifer

YEO (Korean) mild.
Yee

YEPA (Native American) snow girl.

YERA (Basque) Religion: a name for the Virgin Mary.

YESENIA (Arabic) flower.
Yasenya, Yecenia, Yesinia, Yesnia, Yessenia

YESICA (Hebrew) an alternate form of Jessica.
Yesika, Yesiko

YESSENIA (Arabic) an alternate form of Yesenia.
Yessena, Yessenya, Yissenia

YESSICA (Hebrew) an alternate form of Jessica.
Yessika, Yesyka

YETTA (English) a short form of Henrietta.
Yette, Yitta, Yitty

YEVA (Ukrainian) a form of Eve.

YIESHA (Arabic, Swahili) an alternate form of Aisha.
Yiasha

YÍN (Chinese) silver.

YNEZ (Spanish) a form of Agnes. See also Inez.
Ynes, Ynesita

YOANNA (Hebrew) an alternate form of Joanna.
Yoana, Yohana, Yohanka, Yohanna, Yohannah

YOCELIN, Yocelyn (Latin) alternate forms of Jocelyn.
Yoceline, Yocelyne, Yuceli

YOI (Japanese) born in the evening.

YOKI (Hopi) bluebird.
Yokie

YOKO (Japanese) good girl
Yo

YOLIE (Greek) a familiar form of Yolanda.
Yola, Yoley, Yoli, Yoly

YOLANDA (Greek) violet flower. See also Iolanthe, Jolanda, Olinda.
Yalanda, Yolie, Yolaine, Yolana, Yoland, Yolande, Yolane, Yolanna, Yolantha, Yolanthe,

Yolette, Yolonda, Yorlanda, Youlanda, Yulanda, Yulonda

YOLUTA (Native American) summer flower.

YOMARA (American) a combination of Yolanda + Tamara.
Yomaira, Yomarie, Yomira

YON (Burmese) rabbit. (Korean) lotus blossom.
Yona, Yonna

YONÉ (Japanese) wealth; rice.

YONINA (Hebrew) an alternate form of Jonina.
Yona, Yonah

YONITA (Hebrew) an alternate form of Jonita.
Yonat, Yonati, Yonit

YOOMEE (Coos) star.
Yoome

YORDANA (Basque) descendant. See also Jordana.

YORI (Japanese) reliable.
Yoriko, Yoriyo

YOSELIN (Latin) an alternate form of Jocelyn.
Yoseline, Yoselyn, Yosselin, Yosseline, Yosselyn

YOSEPHA (Hebrew) a form of Josephine.
Yosefa, Yosifa, Yuseffa

YOSHI (Japanese) good; respectful.
Yoshie, Yoshiko, Yoshiyo

YOVELA (Hebrew) joyful heart; rejoicer.

YSABEL (Spanish) an alternate form of Isabel.
Ysabell, Ysabella, Ysabelle, Ysbel, Ysbella, Ysobel

YSANNE (American) a combination of Ysabel + Ann.
Ysande, Ysann, Ysanna

YSEULT (German) ice rule. (Irish) fair; light skinned. (Welsh) an alternate form of Isolde.
Yseulte, Ysolt

YUANA (Spanish) an alternate form of Juana.
Yuan, Yuanna

YUDELLE (English) an alternate form of Udele
Yudela, Yudell, Yudella

YUDITA (Russian) a form of Judith.
Yudit, Yudith, Yuditt

YUKI (Japanese) snow.
Yukie, Yukiko, Yukiyo

YULENE (Basque) a form of Julia.
Yuleen

YULIA (Russian) a form of Julia.
Yula, Yulenka, Yulinka, Yulka, Yulya

YULIANA (Spanish) an alternate form of Juliana.
Yulenia, Yuliani

YURI (Japanese) lily.
Yuree, Yuriko, Yuriyo

YVANNA (Slavic) an alternate form of Ivana.
Yvan, Yvana, Yvannia

YVETTE (French) a familiar form of Yvonne. See also Evette, Ivette.
Yavette, Yevett, Yevette, Yevetta, Yvet, Yveta, Yvett, Yvetta

YVONNE (French) young archer. (Scandanavian) yew wood; bow wood. A feminine form of Ivar. See also Evonne, Ivonne, Vonna, Vonny, Yvette.
Yavanda, Yavanna, Yavanne, Yavonda, Yavonna, Yavonne, Yveline, Yvon, Yvone, Yvonna, Yvonnah, Yvonnia, Yvonnie, Yvonny

ZABRINA (American) an alternate form of Sabrina.
Zabreena, Zabrinia, Zabrinna, Zabryna

ZACHARIE (Hebrew) God remembered. A feminine form of Zachariah.
Zacari, Zacceaus, Zacchaea, Zachary, Zachoia, Zackaria, Zackeisha, Zackeria, Zakaria, Zakaya, Zakeshia, Zakiah, Zakiria, Zakiya, Zakiyah, Zechari

ZACHARY (Hebrew) an alternate form of Zacharie.
Zackery, Zakary

ZADA (Arabic) fortunate, prosperous.
Zaida, Zayda, Zayeda

ZAFINA (Arabic) victorious.

ZAFIRAH (Arabic) successful; victorious.

ZAHAR (Hebrew) daybreak; dawn.

Zahara, Zaharra, Zahera, Zahira, Zahirah, Zeeherah

ZAHAVAH (Hebrew) golden.
Zachava, Zachavah, Zechava, Zechavah, Zehava, Zehavi, Zehavit, Zeheva, Zehuva

ZAHRA (Swahili) flower. (Arabic) white.
Zahara, Zahraa, Zahrah, Zahreh, Zahria

ZAIRA (Hebrew) an alternate form of Zara.
Zaire, Zairea, Zirrea

ZAKIA (Swahili) smart. (Arabic) chaste.
Zakea, Zakeia, Zakiah, Zakiya

ZAKIRA (Hebrew) an alternate form of Zacharie.
Zaakira, Zakiera, Zakierra, Zakir, Zakirah, Zakiria, Zakiriya, Zykarah, Zykera, Zykeria, Zykerria, Zykira, Zykuria

ZAKIYA (Arabic) an alternate form of Zakia.
Zakeya, Zakeyia, Zakiyaa, Zakiyah, Zakiyya, Zakiyyah, Zakkiyya, Zakkiyyah, Zakkyyah

ZALIKA (Swahili) born to royalty.
Zuleika

ZALTANA (Native American) high mountain.

ZANDRA (Greek) an alternate form of Sandra.
Zahndra, Zandrea, Zandria, Zandy, Zanndra, Zondra

ZANETA (Spanish) a form of Jane. A feminine form of Zane.
Zanita, Zanitra

ZANNA (Spanish) a form of Jane. (English) a short form of Susanna.

Zaina, Zainah, Zainna, Zana, Zanae, Zanah, Zanella, Zanette, Zannah, Zannette, Zannia, Zannie

ZANTHE (Greek) an alternate form of Xanthe.
Zanth, Zantha

ZARA (Hebrew) an alternate form of Sarah, Zora.
Zaira, Zarah, Zarea, Zaree, Zareea, Zareen, Zareena, Zareh, Zareya, Zari, Zaria, Zariya, Zarria

ZARIFA (Arabic) successful.

ZARITA (Spanish) a form of Sarah.

ZASHA (Russian) an alternate form of Sasha.
Zascha, Zashenka, Zashka, Zasho

ZAVIERA (Spanish) a form of Xaviera.
Zavera, Zavirah

ZAWATI (Swahili) gift.

ZAYIT (Hebrew) olive.

ZAYNAH (Arabic) beautiful.
Zayn, Zayna

ZEA (Latin) grain.

ZELDA (German) a short form of Griselda. (Yiddish) gray haired. See also Selda.
Zelde, Zella, Zellda

ZELENE (English) sunshine.
Zeleen, Zelena, Zeline

ZELIA (Spanish) sunshine.
Zele, Zelene, Zelie, Zélie, Zelina

ZELIZI (Basque) a form of Sheila.

ZELMA (German) an alternate form of Selma.

ZEMIRAH (Hebrew) song of joy.

ZENA (Greek) an alternate form of Xenia. (Ethiopian) news. (Persian) woman. See also Zina.
Zanae, Zanah, Zeena, Zeenat, Zeenet, Zeenia, Zeenya, Zein, Zeina, Zenah, Zenana, Zenea, Zenia, Zenna, Zennah, Zennia, Zenya

ZENAIDE (Greek) Mythology: a daughter of Zeus.
Zenaida, Zenaïde, Zenayda, Zenochka

ZENDA (Persian) sacred; feminine.

ZENOBIA (Greek) sign, symbol. History: a queen who ruled the city of Palmyra in the Arabian desert.
Zeba, Zeeba, Zenobie, Zenovia

ZEPHANIA, Zephanie (Greek) alternate forms of Stephanie.
Zepania, Zephanas, Zephany

ZEPHYR (Greek) west wind.
Zefiryn, Zephra, Zephria, Zephyer, Zephyrine

ZERA (Hebrew) seeds.
Zerah, Zeriah

ZERDALI (Turkish) wild apricot.

ZERLINA (Latin, Spanish) beautiful dawn. Music: a character in Mozart's opera *Don Giovanni*.
Zerla, Zerlinda

ZERRIN (Turkish) golden.
Zerren

ZETA (English) rose. Linguistics: the last letter in the Greek alphabet.
Zayit, Zetana, Zetta

ZETTA (Portuguese) rose.

ZHANA, Zhane (Slavic) forms of Jane.
Zhanae, Zhanay, Zhanaya, Zhané, Zhanea, Zhanee, Zhaney, Zhani, Zhaniah, Zhanna

ZHEN (Chinese) chaste.

ZIA (Latin) grain. (Arabic) light.
Zea

ZIGANA (Hungarian) gypsy girl. See also Tsigana.
Zigane

ZIHNA (Hopi) one who spins tops.

ZILLA (Hebrew) shadow.
Zila, Zillah, Zylla

ZILPAH (Hebrew) dignified. Bible: Jacob's wife.
Zilpha, Zylpha

ZILYA (Russian) a form of Theresa.

ZIMRA (Hebrew) song of praise.
Zamora, Zemira, Zemora, Zimria

ZINA (Greek) an alternate form of Xenia, Zena. (African) secret spirit. (English) hospitable.
Zinah, Zine

ZINNIA (Latin) Botany: a plant with beautiful, rayed, colorful flowers.
Zinia, Zinny, Zinnya, Zinya

ZIPPORAH (Hebrew) bird. Bible: Moses' wife.
Zipora, Ziporah, Zipporia, Ziproh

ZITA (Spanish) rose. (Arabic) mistress. A short form of names ending in "sita" or "zita."
Zeeta, Zyta, Zytka

ZIVA (Hebrew) bright; radiant.
Zeeva, Ziv, Zivanka, Zivi, Zivit

ZIZI (Hungarian) a familiar form of Elizabeth.
Zsi Zsi

ZOCHA (Polish) an alternate form of Sophie.

ZOE (Greek) life.
Zoé, Zoë, Zoee, Zoelie, Zoeline, Zoelle, Zoey, Zoi, Zoie, Zowe, Zowey, Zowie, Zoya

ZOEY (Greek) an alternate form of Zoe.
Zooey

ZOFIA (Slavic) an alternate form of Sophia. See also Sofia.
Zofka, Zsofia

ZOHAR (Hebrew) shining, brilliant.
Zoheret

ZOHRA (Hebrew) blossom.

ZOHREH (Persian) happy.
Zahreh, Zohrah

ZOLA (Italian) piece of earth.
Zoela, Zoila

ZONA (Latin) belt, sash.
Zonia

ZONDRA (Greek) an alternate form of Zandra.
Zohndra

ZORA (Slavic) aurora; dawn. See also Zara.
Zorah, Zorana, Zoreen, Zoreena, Zorna, Zorra, Zorrah, Zorya

ZORINA (Slavic) golden.
Zorana, Zori, Zorie, Zorine, Zorna, Zory

ZOYA (Slavic) a form of Zoe.
Zoia, Zoyara, Zoyechka, Zoyenka, Zoyya

ZSA ZSA (Hungarian) a familiar form of Susan.
Zhazha

ZSOFIA (Hungarian) a form of Sofia.
Zofia, Zsofi, Zsofika

ZSUZSANNA (Hungarian) a form of Susanna.
Zsuska, Zsuzsa, Zsuzsi, Zsuzsika, Zsuzska

ZUDORA (Sanskrit) laborer.

ZULEIKA (Arabic) brilliant.
Zeleeka, Zul, Zulay, Zulekha, Zuleyka

ZULIMA (Arabic) an alternate form of Salama.
Zuleima, Zulema, Zulemah, Zulimah

ZURAFA (Arabic) lovely.
Ziraf, Zuruf

ZURI (Basque) white; light skinned. (Swahili) beautiful.
Zuria, Zurie, Zurisha, Zury

ZUSA (Czech, Polish) a form of Susan.
Zuzana, Zuzanka, Zuzia, Zuzka, Zuzu

ZUWENA (Swahili) good.
Zwena

ZYTKA (Polish) rose.

BOYS' NAMES

AAKASH (Hindi) an alternate form of Akash.

AARON (Hebrew) enlightened. (Arabic) messenger. Bible: the brother of Moses and the first high priest of the Jews. See also Ron.
Aahron, Aaran, Aaren, Aareon, Aarin, Aaronn, Aarron, Aaryn, Aeron, Aharon, Ahran, Ahren, Aranne, Arek, Aren, Ari, Arin, Aron, Aronek, Aronne, Aronos, Arran, Arron

ABAN (Persian) Mythology: a figure associated with water and the arts.

ABASI (Swahili) stern.

ABBEY (Hebrew) a familiar form of Abe.
Abey, Abbie, Abby

ABBOTT (Hebrew) father; abbot.
Ab, Abba, Abbah, Abbán, Abbé, Abbot, Abott

ABBUD (Arabic) devoted.

ABDIRAHMAN (Arabic) an alternate form of Abdulrahman.
Abdirehman

ABDUL (Arabic) servant.
Abdal, Abdeel, Abdel, Abdoul, Abdual, Abdull, Abul

ABDULAZIZ (Arabic) servant of the Mighty.
Abdelazim, Abdelaziz, Abdulazaz, Abdulazeez

ABDULLAH (Arabic) servant of Allah.
Abdalah, Abdalla, Abdallah, Abduala, Abdualla, Abduallah, Abdulah, Abdulahi, Abdulha, Abdulla, Abdullahi

ABDULRAHMAN (Arabic) servant of the Merciful.
Abdelrahim, Abdelrahman, Abdirahman, Abdolrahem, Abdularahman, Abdurrahman, Abdurram

ABE (Hebrew) a short form of Abel, Abraham.

ABEL (Hebrew) breath. (Assyrian) meadow. (German) a short form of Abelard. Bible: Adam and Eve's second son.
Abe, Abele, Abell, Able, Adal, Avel

ABELARD (German) noble; resolute.
Ab, Abalard, Abel, Abelardo, Abelhard, Abilard, Adalard, Adelard

ABI (Turkish) older brother.

ABIAH (Hebrew) God is my father.
Abia, Abiel, Abija, Abijah, Abisha, Abishai, Aviya, Aviyah

ABIE (Hebrew) a familiar form of Abraham.

ABIEL (Hebrew) an alternate form of Abiah.

ABIR (Hebrew) strong.

ABISHA (Hebrew) gift of God.
Abijah, Abishai

ABNER (Hebrew) father of light. Bible: the commander of King Saul's army.
Ab, Avner, Ebner

ABRAHAM (Hebrew) father of many nations. Bible: the first Hebrew patriarch. See also Avram, Bram, Ibrahim.
Abarran, Abe, Aberham, Abey, Abhiram, Abie, Abrahaim, Abrahame, Abrahamo, Abrahan, Abrahán, Abraheem, Abrahem, Abrahim, Abrahm, Abram, Abramo, Abrán, Abrao, Arram, Avram

ABRAHAN (Hebrew) an alternate form of Abraham.
Abrahon

ABRAM (Hebrew) a short form of Abraham. See also Bram.
Abramo, Abrams, Avram

ABSALOM (Hebrew) father of peace. Bible: the son of King David. See also Avshalom, Axel.
Absalaam, Absalon, Abselon, Absolum

ACAR (Turkish) bright.

ACE (Latin) unity.
Acer, Acey, Acie

ACHILLES (Greek) Mythology: a hero of the Trojan war. Literature: the hero of Homer's epic *The Iliad*.
Achill, Achille, Achillea, Achillios, Akil, Akili, Akilles

ACKERLEY (English) meadow of oak trees.
Accerley, Ackerlea, Ackerleigh, Ackersley, Acklea, Ackleigh, Ackley, Acklie

ACTON (English) oak-tree settlement.

ADAHY (Cherokee) in the woods.

ADAIR (Scottish) oak-tree ford.
Adaire, Adare

ADAM (Phoenician) man; mankind. (Hebrew) earth; man of the red earth. Bible: the first man created by God. See also Adamson, Addison, Damek, Keddy, Macadam.
Ad, Adama, Adamec, Adamo, Adão, Adas, Addam, Addams, Addis, Addy, Adem, Adham, Adhamh, Adné, Adok, Adomas

ADAMEC (Czech) a form of Adam.
Adamek, Adamik, Adamka, Adamko, Adamok

ADAMSON (Hebrew) son of Adam.
Adams, Adamsson, Addamson

ADAN (Irish) an alternate form of Aidan.
Aden, Adian, Adin

ADAR (Syrian) ruler, prince. (Hebrew) noble; exalted.
Addar

ADARIUS (American) a combination of Adam + Darius.
Adareus, Adarias, Adarrius, Adarro, Adarruis, Adaruis, Adauris

ADDISON (English) son of Adam.
Addis, Addisen, Addisun, Addyson, Adison, Adisson, Adyson

ADDY (Hebrew) a familiar form of Adam, Adlai. (German) a familiar form of Adelard.
Addey, Addi, Addie, Ade, Adi

ADE (Yoruba) royal.

ADELARD (German) noble; courageous.
Adal, Adalar, Adalard, Addy, Adel, Adél, Adelar

ADEN (Arabic) Geography: a region in southern Yemen. (Irish) an alternate form of Aidan, Aiden.

ADHAM (Arabic) black.

ADIL (Arabic) just; wise.
Adeel, Adeele

ADIN (Hebrew) pleasant.

ADIR (Hebrew) majestic; noble.
Adeer

ADIV (Hebrew) pleasant; gentle.
Adeev

ADLAI (Hebrew) my ornament.
Ad, Addy, Adley

ADLER (German) eagle.
Ad, Addler, Adlar

ADLI (Turkish) just; wise.

ADMON (Hebrew) peony.

ADNAN (Arabic) pleasant.
Adnaan

ADNEY (English) noble's island.
Adny

ADOLF (German) noble wolf. History: Adolf Hitler led Germany to defeat in World War II. See also Dolf.
Ad, Adolfo, Adolfus, Adolph

ADOLFO (Spanish) a form of Adolf.
Adolpho

ADOLPH (German) an alternate form of Adolf.
Adolphe, Adolpho, Adolphus, Adulphus

ADOM (Akan) help from God.

ADON (Greek) a short form of Adonis. (Hebrew) Lord.

ADONIS (Greek) highly attractive. Mythology: the attractive youth loved by Aphrodite.
Adon, Adonnis, Adonys

ADRI (Indo-Pakistani) rock. (Hindi) Religion: a minor Hindu god.
Adrey

ADRIAN (Greek) rich. (Latin) dark. (Swedish) a short form of Hadrian.
Adarian, Ade, Adorjan, Adrain, Adreian, Adreyan, Adri, Adriaan, Adriane, Adriann, Adrianne, Adriano, Adriean, Adrien, Adrik, Adrion, Adrionn, Adrionne, Adron, Adryan, Adryn, Adryon

ADRIANO (Italian) a form of Adrian.
Adrianno

ADRIEL (Hebrew) member of God's flock.
Adrial

ADRIEN (French) a form of Adrian.
Adriene, Adrienne

ADRIK (Russian) a form of Adrian.
Adric

AENEAS (Greek) praised. Literature: the Trojan hero of Virgil's epic *Aeneid*. See also Eneas.

AFRAM (African) Geography: a river in Ghana, Africa.

AFTON (English) from Afton, England.
Affton

AGAMEMNON (Greek) resolute. Mythology: the King of Mycenae who led the Greeks in the Trojan War.

AGNI (Hindi) Religion: the Hindu fire god.

AGU (Ibo) leopard.

AGUSTIN (Latin) an alternate form of Augustine.
Agostino, Agoston, Aguistin, Agustine, Agustis, Agusto, Agustus

AHAB (Hebrew) father's brother. Literature: the captain of the Pequod in Herman Melville's novel *Moby Dick*.

AHANU (Native American) laughter.

AHDIK (Native American) caribou; reindeer.

AHEARN (Scottish) lord of the horses. (English) heron.
Ahearne, Aherin, Ahern, Aherne, Hearn

AHIR (Turkish) last.

AHMAD (Arabic) most highly praised. See also Muhammad.
Achmad, Achmed, Ahamad, Ahamada, Ahamed, Ahmaad, Ahmaud, Amad, Amahd, Amed

AHMED (Swahili) praiseworthy.

AHSAN (Arabic) charitable.

AIDAN (Irish) fiery.
Adan, Aden, Aiden, Aydan, Ayden, Aydin

AIDEN, Ayden (Irish) an alternate form of Aidan.
Aden, Aidon, Aidyn, Aydean

AIKEN (English) made of oak.
Aicken, Aikin, Ayken, Aykin

AIMERY (German) an alternate form of Emery.
Aime, Aimerey, Aimeric, Amerey, Aymeric, Aymery

AIMON (French) house. (Irish) an alternate form of Eamon.

AINDREA (Irish) a form of Andrew.
Aindreas

AINSLEY (Scottish) my own meadow.
Ainsleigh, Ainslie, Ansley, Aynslee, Aynsley, Aynslie

AIZIK (Russian) a form of Isaac.

AJALA (Yoruba) potter.

AJAY (Punjabi) victorious; undefeatable. (American) a combination of the initials A. + J.
Aj, Aja, Ajae, Ajai, Ajaye, Ajaz, Ajé, Ajee, Ajit

AJIT (Sanskrit) unconquerable.
Ajeet, Ajith

AKAR (Turkish) flowing stream.
Akara

AKASH (Hindi) sky.
Aakash, Akasha, Akshay

AKBAR (Arabic) great.

AKECHETA (Sioux) warrior.

AKEEM, Akim (Hebrew) short forms of Joachim.
Achim, Ackeem, Ackim, Ahkieme, Akeam, Akee, Akiem, Akima, Arkeem

AKEMI (Japanese) dawn.

AKIL (Arabic) intelligent. Geography: a river in the Basque region.
Ahkeel, Akeel, Akeil, Akeyla, Akhil, Akiel, Akila, Akilah, Akile, Akili

AKINS (Yoruba) brave.

AKIRA (Japanese) intelligent.
Akihito, Akio, Akiyo

AKIVA (Hebrew) an alternate form of Jacob.
Akiba, Kiva

AKMAL (Arabic) perfect.

AKSEL (Norwegian) father of peace.
Aksell

AKSHAY (American) a form of Akash.
Akshaj, Akshaya

AKSHAT (Sanskrit) uninjurable.

AKULE (Native American) he looks up.

AL (Irish) a short form of Alan, Albert, Alexander.

ALADDIN (Arabic) height of faith. Literature: the hero of a story in the *Arabian Nights*.
Ala, Alaa, Alaaddin, Aladean, Aladin, Aladino

ALAIN (French) a form of Alan.
Alaen, Alainn, Alayn, Allain

ALAIRE (French) joyful.

ALAM (Arabic) universe.

ALAN (Irish) handsome; peaceful.
Ailan, Ailin, Al, Alaan, Alain, Alair, Aland, Alande, Alando, Alani, Alann, Alano, Alanson, Alante, Alao, Allan, Allen, Alon, Alun

ALARIC (German) ruler of all. See also Ulrich.
Alarick, Alarico, Alarik, Aleric, Allaric, Allarick, Alric, Alrick, Alrik

ALASTAIR (Scottish) a form of Alexander.
Alaisdair, Alaistair, Alaister, Alasdair, Alasteir, Alaster, Alastor, Aleister, Alester, Alistair, Allaistar, Allastair, Allaster, Allastir, Allysdair, Alystair

ALBAN (Latin) from Alba, Italy, a city on a white hill.
Albain, Albany, Albean, Albein, Alby, Auban, Auben

ALBERN (German) noble; courageous.

ALBERT (German, French) noble and bright. See also Elbert, Ulbrecht.
Adelbert, Ailbert, Al, Albertik, Alberto, Alberts, Albie, Albrecht, Alby, Alvertos, Aubert

ALBERTO (Italian) a form of Albert.
Berto

ALBIE, Alby (German, French) familiar forms of Albert.
Albee, Albi

ALBIN (Latin) an alternate form of Alvin.
Alben, Albeno, Albinek, Albino, Albins, Albinson, Alby, Auben

ALBION (Latin) white cliffs. Geography: a reference to the white cliffs in Dover, England.

ALCOTT (English) old cottage.
Alcot, Alkot, Alkott, Allcot, Allcott, Allkot, Allkott

ALCANDOR (Greek) manly; strong.

ALDAIR (German, English) an alternate form of Alder.
Aldahir, Aldayr

ALDEN (English) old; wise protector.
Aldan, Aldean, Aldin, Aldous, Elden

ALDER (German, English) alder tree.
Aldair

ALDO (Italian) old; elder.

ALDOUS (German) a form of Alden.
Aldis, Aldo, Aldon, Aldus, Elden

ALDRED (English) old; wise counselor.
Alldred, Eldred

ALDRICH (English) wise counselor.
Aldric, Aldrick, Aldridge, Aldrige, Aldritch, Alldric, Alldrich, Alldrick, Alldridge, Eldridge

ALDWIN (English) old friend.
Aldwyn, Eldwin

ALEC, Alek (Greek) short forms of Alexander.
Aleck, Alekko, Elek

ALEJÁNDRO (Spanish) a form of Alexander.
Alejándra, Aléjo, Alexjándro

ALEKSANDAR, Aleksander (Greek) alternate forms of Alexander.
Aleksandor, Aleksandr, Aleksandras, Aleksandur

ALEKSEI (Russian) a form of Alexander.
Aleks, Aleksey, Aleksi, Aleksis, Aleksy, Alexei, Alexey

ALEKZANDER, Alexzander (Greek) alternate forms of Alexander.
Alekxander, Alekxzander, Alexkzandr, Alexzandr, Alexzandyr

ALEM (Arabic) wise.

ALERIC (German) an alternate form of Alaric.
Alerick, Alleric, Allerick

ALERON (Latin) winged.

ALESSANDRO (Italian) a form of Alexander.
Alessand, Allessandro

ALEX (Greek) a short form of Alexander.
Alax, Alix, Allax, Allex, Elek

ALEXANDER (Greek) defender of mankind. History: Alexander the Great was the conquerer of the Greek Empire. See also Alastair, Alistair, Iskander, Jando, Leks, Lex, Lexus, Macallister, Oleksandr, Olés, Sander, Sándor, Sandro, Sandy, Sasha, Xan, Xander, Zander, Zindel.
Al, Alec, Alecsandar, Alejándro, Alek, Alekos, Aleksandar, Aleksander, Aleksei, Alekzander, Alessandro, Alex, Alexandar, Alexandor, Alexandr, Alexandre, Alexandro, Alexandros, Alexi, Alexis, Alexxander, Alexzander, Alic, Alick, Alisander, Alixander,

ALEXANDRE (French) a form of Alexander.

ALEXANDRO (Greek) an alternate form of Alexander.
Alexandras, Alexandros, Alexandru

ALEXI (Greek) a short form of Alexander.
Alexe, Alexee, Alexey, Alexie, Alexio, Alexy

ALEXIS (Greek) a short form of Alexander.
Alexei, Alexes, Alexey, Alexios, Alexius, Alexiz, Alexsis, Alexsus, Alexus

ALFIE (English) a familiar form of Alfred.
Alfy

ALFONSO (Italian, Spanish) a form of Alphonse.
Affonso, Alfons, Alfonse, Alfonsus, Alfonza, Alfonzo, Alfonzus

ALFORD (English) old river ford.

ALFRED (English) elf counselor; wise counselor. See also Fred.
Ailfrid, Ailfryd, Alf, Alfeo, Alfie, Alfredo, Alured

ALFREDO (Italian, Spanish) a form of Alfred.
Alfrido

ALGER (German) noble spearman. (English) a short form of Algernon. See also Elger.
Algar, Allgar

ALGERNON (English) bearded, wearing a moustache.
Algenon, Alger, Algie, Algin, Algon

ALGIE (English) a familiar form of Algernon.
Algee, Algia, Algy

ALGIS (German) spear.

ALI (Arabic) greatest. (Swahili) exalted.
Aly

ALIC (Greek) a short form of Alexander.
Alick, Aliek, Alik, Aliko

ALIM (Arabic) scholar.

ALISANDER (Greek) an alternate form of Alexander.
Alissander, Alissandre, Alsandair, Alsandare, Alsander

ALISTAIR (English) a form of Alexander.
Alisdair, Alistaire, Alistar, Alister, Allistair, Allistar, Allister, Allistir, Alstair

ALIXANDER (Greek) an alternate form of Alexander.
Alixandre, Alixandru, Alixzander

ALLAN (Irish) an alternate form of Alan.
Allayne

ALLARD (English) noble, brave.
Alard, Ellard

ALLEN (Irish) an alternate form of Alan.
Alen, Alley, Alleyn, Alleyne, Allie, Allin, Allon, Allyn

ALMON (Hebrew) widower.

ALOIS (German) a short form of Aloysius.
Aloys

ALOISIO (Spanish) a form of Louis.

ALOK (Sanskrit) victorious cry.

ALON (Hebrew) oak.

ALONSO, Alonzo (Spanish) forms of Alphonse.
Alano, Alanzo, Alon, Alonza, Elonzo, Lon, Lonnie, Lonso, Lonzo

ALOYSIUS (German) famous warrior. An alternate form of Louis.
Alaois, Alois, Aloisius, Aloisio

ALPHONSE (German) noble and eager.
Alf, Alfie, Alfonso, Alonzo, Alphons, Alphonsa, Alphonso, Alphonsus, Alphonza, Alphonzus, Fonzie

ALPHONSO (Italian) a form of Alphonse.
Alphanso, Alphonzo, Fonso

ALPIN (Irish) attractive.
Alpine

ALROY (Spanish) king.

ALSTON (English) noble's settlement.
Allston, Alstun

ALTAIR (Greek) star. (Arabic) flying eagle.

ALTMAN (German) old man.
Altmann, Atman

ALTON (English) old town.
Alten

ALVA (Hebrew) sublime.
Alvah

ALVAN (German) an alternate form of Alvin.
Alvand

ALVAR (Swedish) Botany: a small shrub native to Sweden. (English) army of elves.
Alvara

ALVARO (Spanish) just; wise.

ALVERN (Latin) spring.
Elvern

ALVIN (Latin) white; light skinned. (German) friend to all; noble friend; friend of elves. See also Albin, Elvin.
Aloin, Aluin, Aluino, Alvan, Alven, Alvie, Alvino, Alvy, Alvyn, Alwin, Elwin

ALVIS (Scandinavian) all-knowing.

ALWIN (German) an alternate form of Alvin.
Ailwyn, Alwyn, Alwynn, Aylwin

AMADEO (Italian) a form of Amadeus.

AMADEUS (Latin) loves God. Music: Wolfgang Amadeus Mozart was a famous eighteenth-century Austrian composer.
Amad, Amadeaus, Amadée, Amadeo, Amadei, Amadio, Amadis, Amado, Amador, Amadou, Amando, Amedeo, Amodaos

AMAL (Hebrew) worker. (Arabic) hopeful.

AMANDEEP (Punjabi) light of peace.
Amandip, Amanjit, Amanjot, Amanpreet

AMANDO (French) a form of Amadeus.
Amand, Amandio, Amaniel, Amato

AMANI (Arabic) believer.
Amanee

AMAR (Punjabi) immortal. (Arabic) builder.
Amare, Amaree, Amari, Amario, Amaris, Amarjit, Amaro,

Amarpreet, Amarri, Ammar, Ammer

AMATO (French) loved.
Amatto

AMBAR (Sanskrit) sky.
Amber

AMBROSE (Greek) immortal.
Ambie, Ambroise, Ambros, Ambrosi, Ambrosio, Ambrosius, Ambrus, Amby

AMEER (Hebrew) an alternate form of Amir.
Ameir, Amer, Amere

AMERIGO (Teutonic) industrious. History: Amerigo Vespucci was the explorer for whom America is named.
Americo, Americus

AMES (French) friend.

AMICUS (English, Latin) beloved friend.
Amico

AMIEL (Hebrew) God of my people.
Ammiel

AMIN (Hebrew, Arabic) trustworthy; honest. (Hindi) faithful.
Amine

AMIR (Hebrew) proclaimed. (Punjabi) wealthy; king's minister. (Arabic) prince.
Aamer, Aamir, Ameer, Amire, Amiri

AMISH (Sanskrit) honest.

AMIT (Punjabi) unfriendly. (Arabic) highly praised.
Amitan, Amreet

AMMON (Egyptian) hidden. Mythology: the ancient god

associated with reproduction and life.
Amman

AMOL (Hindi) priceless, valuable.
Amul

AMON (Hebrew) trustworthy; faithful.

AMORY (German) an alternate form of Emory.
Amery, Amor

AMOS (Hebrew) burdened, troubled. Bible: an Old Testament prophet.
Amose

AMRAM (Hebrew) mighty nation.
Amarien, Amran, Amren

AMRIT (Sanskrit) nectar.

AN (Chinese, Vietnamese) peaceful.
Ana

ANAND (Hindi) blissful.
Ananda, Anant, Ananth

ANASTASIUS (Greek) resurrection.
Anas, Anastacio, Anastacios, Anastagio, Anastas, Anastase, Anastasi, Anastasio, Anastasios, Anastice, Anastisis, Anaztáz, Athanasius

ANATOLE (Greek) east.
Anatol, Anatoley, Anatoli, Anatolijus, Anatolio, Anatoliy, Anatoly, Anitoly

ANCHALI (Taos) painter.

ANDERS (Swedish) a form of Andrew.
Ander

ANDERSON (Swedish) son of Andrew.
Andersen

ANDONIOS (Greek) an alternate form of Anthony.
Andoni, Andonis, Andonny

ANDOR (Hungarian) a form of Andrew.

ANDRÁS (Hungarian) a form of Andrew.
Andraes, Andri, Andris, Andrius, Andriy, Aundras, Aundreas

ANDRE, André (French) forms of Andrew.
Andra, Andrae, Andrecito, Andree, Andrei, Aundre, Aundré

ANDREA (Greek) an alternate form of Andrew.
Andrean, Andreani, Andrian

ANDREAS (Greek) an alternate form of Andrew.
Andres, Andries

ANDREI (Bulgarian, Romanian, Russian) a form of Andrew.
Andreian, Andrej, Andrey, Andreyan, Andrie, Aundrei

ANDRES (Spanish) a form of Andrew.
Andras, Andrés, Andrez

ANDREW (Greek) strong; manly; courageous. Bible: one of the Twelve Apostles. See also Bandi, Drew, Endre, Evangelos, Kendrew, Ondro.
Aindrea, Anders, Andery, Andonis, Andor, András, Andre, André, Andrea, Andreas, Andrei, Andres, Andrews, Andru, Andrue, Andrus, Andy, Anker, Anndra, Antal, Audrew

ANDROS (Polish) sea. Mythology: the god of the sea.
Andris, Andrius, Andrus

ANDY (Greek) a short form of Andrew.
Andino, Andis, Andje

ANEURIN (Welsh) honorable; gold. See also Nye.
Aneirin

ANFERNEE (Greek) an alternate form of Anthony.
Anferney, Anfernie, Anferny, Anfranee, Anfrene, Anfrenee, Anpherne

ANGEL (Greek) angel. (Latin) messenger. See also Gotzon.
Ange, Angell, Angelo, Angie, Angy

ANGELO (Italian) a form of Angel.
Angeleo, Angelito, Angello, Angelos, Anglo

ANGUS (Scottish) exceptional; outstanding. Mythology: Angus Og was the Celtic god of laughter, love, and wisdom. See also Ennis, Gus.
Aeneas, Aonghas

ANH (Vietnamese) peace; safety.

ANIBAL (Phoenician) an alternate form of Hannibal.

ANIL (Hindi) wind god.
Aneel, Anel, Aniel, Aniello

ANKA (Turkish) phoenix.

ANKER (Danish) a form of Andrew.
Ankur

ANNAN (Scottish) brook. (Swahili) fourth-born son.

ANNAS (Greek) gift from God.
Anis, Anish, Anna, Annais

ANNO (German) a familiar form of Johann.

ANOKI (Native American) actor.

ANSEL (French) follower of a nobleman.
Ancell, Ansa, Ansell

ANSELM (German) divine protector. See also Elmo.
Anse, Anselme, Anselmi, Anselmo

ANSIS (Latvian) an alternate form of Janis.

ANSLEY (Scottish) an alternate form of Ainsley.
Anslea, Anslee, Ansleigh, Anslie, Ansly, Ansy

ANSON (German) divine. (English) Anne's son.
Ansun

ANTAL (Hungarian) a form of Anthony.
Antek, Anti, Antos

ANTARES (Greek) giant, red star. Astronomy: the brightest star in the constellation Scorpio.
Antar, Antario, Antarious, Antarius, Antarr, Antarus

ANTAVAS (Lithuanian) a form of Anthony.
Antae, Antaeus, Antavious, Antavius, Ante, Anteo

ANTHANY (Latin, Greek) an alternate form of Anthony.
Antanee, Antanie, Antenee, Anthan, Antheny, Anthine, Anthney

ANTHONIE (Latin, Greek) an alternate form of Anthony.
Anthone, Anthonee, Anthoni, Anthonia

ANTHONY (Latin) praiseworthy. (Greek) flourishing. See also Tony.
Anathony, Andonios, Andor, András, Anothony, Antal, Antavas, Anfernee, Anthany, Anthawn, Anthey, Anthian, Anthino, Anthone, Anthoney, Anthonie, Anthonio, Anthonu, Anthonysha, Anthoy, Anthyoine, Anthyonny, Antione, Antjuan, Antoine, Anton, Antonio, Antony, Antwan, Antwon

ANTIONE (French) a form of Anthony.
Antion, Antionio, Antionne, Antiono

ANTJUAN (Spanish) a form of Anthony.
Antajuan, Anthjuan, Antuan, Antuane

ANTOAN (Vietnamese) safe, secure.

ANTOINE (French) a form of Anthony.
Anntoin, Anthoine, Antoiné, Antoinne, Atoine

ANTON (Slavic) a form of Anthony.
Anthon, Antone, Antonn, Antonne, Antons, Antos

ANTONIO (Italian) a form of Anthony. See also Tino, Tonio.
Anthonio, Antinio, Antoinio, Antoino, Antonello, Antoneo, Antonin, Antonín, Antonino, Antonnio, Antonios, Antonius, Antonyia, Antonyio, Antonyo

ANTONY (Latin) an alternate form of Anthony.

Antin, Antini, Antius, Antoney, Antoni, Antonie, Antonin, Antonios, Antonius, Antonyia, Antonyio, Antonyo, Anty

ANTTI (Finnish) manly.
Anthey, Anthi, Anti

ANTWAN (Arabic) a form of Anthony.
Antaw, Antawan, Antawn, Anthawn, Antowan, Antowaun, Antowine, Antowne, Antowyn, Antuwan, Antwain, Antwaina, Antwaine, Antwainn, Antwaion, Antwane, Antwann, Antwanne, Antwarn, Antwaun, Antwen, Antwian, Antwine, Antwuan, Antwun, Antwyné

ANTWON (Arabic) a form of Anthony.
Antown, Antuwon, Antwion, Antwione, Antwoan, Antwoin, Antwoine, Antwone, Antwonn, Antwonne, Antwoun, Antwyon, Antwyone, Antyon, Antyonne, Antywon

ANWAR (Arabic) luminous.
Anour, Anouar, Anwi

APIATAN (Kiowa) wooden lance.

APOLLO (Greek) manly. Mythology: the god of prophecy, healing, music, poetry, truth, and the sun. See also Polo.
Apolinar, Apolinario, Apollos, Apolo, Apolonio, Appollo

AQUILA (Latin, Spanish) eagle.
Acquilla, Aquil, Aquilas, Aquileo, Aquiles, Aquilino, Aquilla, Aquille, Aquillino

ARALDO (Spanish) a form of Harold.
Aralodo, Aralt, Aroldo, Arry

ARAM (Syrian) high, exalted.
Ara, Aramia, Arra, Arram

ARAMIS (French) Literature: one of the title characters in Alexandre Dumas's novel *The Three Musketeers*.
Airamis, Aramith, Aramys

ARAN (Tai) forest.

ARCHER (English) bowman.
Archie

ARCHIBALD (German) bold. See also Arkady.
Arch, Archaimbaud, Archambault, Archibaldo, Archibold, Archie

ARCHIE (German, English) a familiar form of Archer, Archibald.
Archy

ARDAL (Irish) a form of Arnold.
Ardale

ARDELL (Latin) eager; industrious.
Ardel

ARDEN (Latin) ardent; fiery.
Ard, Ardan, Ardene, Ardian, Ardie, Ardin, Ardn, Arduino

ARDON (Hebrew) bronzed.

AREN (Danish) eagle; ruler.

ARETINO (Greek, Italian) victorious.

ARGUS (Danish) watchful, vigilant.
Agos

ARI (Greek) a short form of Aristotle. (Hebrew) a short form of Ariel.
Aria, Arias, Arie, Arieh, Arih, Arij, Ario, Arri, Ary, Arye

ARIAN (Greek) an alternate form of Arion.

Ariana, Ariane, Ariann, Arianne, Arrian, Aryan

ARIC (German) an alternate form of Richard. (Scandinavian) an alternate form of Eric.
Aaric, Arec, Areck, Arich, Arick, Ariek, Arik, Arrek, Arric, Arrick, Arrik, Aryk

ARIEL (Hebrew) lion of God. Bible: another name for Jerusalem. Literature: the name of a spirit in the Shakespearean play *The Tempest.*
Airel, Arel, Areli, Ari, Ariell, Ariya, Ariyel, Arrial, Arriel

ARIES (Greek) Mythology: Ares was the Greek god of war. (Latin) ram.
Ares, Arie, Ariez

ARIF (Arabic) knowledgeable.
Areef

ARION (Greek) enchanted. Mythology: a magic horse. (Hebrew) melodious.
Arian, Arien, Ario, Arione, Aryon

ARISTIDES (Greek) son of the best.
Aris, Aristedes, Aristeed, Aristide, Aristides, Aristidis

ARISTOTLE (Greek) best; wise. History: a third-century B.C. philosopher who tutored Alexander the Great.
Ari, Aris, Aristito, Aristo, Aristokles, Aristotelis

ARJUN (Hindi) white, milk-colored.
Arjen, Arjin, Arju, Arjuna, Arjune

ARKADY (Russian) a form of Archibald.
Arcadio, Arkadi, Arkadij, Arkadiy

ARKIN (Norwegian) son of the eternal king.
Aricin, Arkeen, Arkyn

ARLEDGE (English) lake with the hares.
Arlidge, Arlledge

ARLEN (Irish) pledge.
Arlan, Arland, Arlend, Arlin, Arlinn, Arlyn, Arlynn

ARLEY (English) a short form of Harley.
Arleigh, Arlie, Arly

ARLO (German) an alternate form of Charles. (Spanish) barberry. (English) fortified hill. An alternate form of Harlow.

ARMAN (Persian) desire, goal.
Armaan, Armahn, Armaine

ARMAND (Latin) noble. (German) soldier. An alternate form of Herman. See also Mandek.
Armad, Arman, Armanda, Armando, Armands, Armanno, Armaude, Armenta, Armond

ARMANDO (Spanish) a form of Armand.
Armondo

ARMANI (Hebrew) an alternate form of Armon.
Arman, Armann, Armoni, Armonie, Armonio, Armonni, Armony

ARMON (Hebrew) high fortress, stronghold.
Armani, Armen, Armin, Armino, Armonn, Armons

ARMSTRONG (English) strong arm.

ARNAUD (French) a form of Arnold.
Arnauld, Arnault, Arnoll

ARNE (German) an alternate form of Arnold.
Arna, Arnay, Arnel, Arnele, Arnell, Arnelle

ARNETTE (English) little eagle.
Arnat, Arnet, Arnett, Arnetta, Arnot, Arnott

ARNIE (German) a familiar form of Arnold.
Arney, Arni, Arnny, Arny

ARNO (German) eagle wolf. (Czech) a short form of Ernest.
Arnou, Arnoux

ARNOLD (German) eagle ruler.
Ardal, Arnald, Arnaldo, Arnaud, Arne, Arnie, Arno, Arnol, Arnoldas, Arnoldo, Arnoll, Arndt, Arnulfo

ARNON (Hebrew) rushing river.
Arnan

ARNULFO (German) an alternate form of Arnold.

ARON, Arron (Hebrew) alternate forms of Aaron.
Arrion

AROON (Tai) dawn.

ARRAN (Hebrew) an alternate form of Aaron. (Scottish) island dweller. Geography: an island off the coast of Scotland.
Arren, Arrin, Arryn, Aryn

ARRIGO (Italian) a form of Harry.
Alrigo, Arrighetto

ARRIO (Spanish) warlike.
Ario, Arrow, Arryo, Aryo

ARSENIO (Greek) masculine; virile. History: Saint Arsenius was a teacher in the Roman Empire.
Arsen, Arsène, Arsenius, Arseny, Arsinio

ARSHA (Persian) venerable.

ART (English) a short form of Arthur.

ARTEMUS (Greek) gift of Artemis. Mythology: Artemis was the goddess of the hunt and the moon.
Artemas, Artemio, Artemis, Artimas, Artimis, Artimus

ARTHUR (Irish) noble; lofty hill. (Scottish) bear. (English) rock. (Icelandic) follower of Thor. See also Turi.
Art, Artair, Artek, Arth, Arther, Arthor, Artie, Artor, Arturo, Artus, Aurthar, Aurther, Aurthur

ARTIE (English) a familiar form of Arthur.
Arte, Artian, Artis, Arty, Atty

ARTURO (Italian) a form of Arthur.
Arthuro, Artur

ARUN (Cambodian, Hindi) sun.
Aruns

ARUNDEL (English) eagle valley.

ARVE (Norwegian) heir, inheritor.

ARVEL (Welsh) wept over.
Arval, Arvell, Arvelle

ARVID (Hebrew) wanderer. (Norwegian) eagle tree. See also Ravid.
Arv, Arvad, Arve, Arvie, Arvind, Arvinder, Arvydas

ARVIN (German) friend of the people; friend of the army.
Arv, Arvie, Arvind, Arvinder, Arvon, Arvy

ARYEH (Hebrew) lion.

ASA (Hebrew) physician, healer. (Yoruba) falcon.
Asaa, Ase

ASÁD (Arabic) lion.
Asaad, Asad, Asid, Assad, Azad

ASADEL (Arabic) prosperous.
Asadour, Asadul, Asael

ASCOT (English) eastern cottage; style of necktie. Geography: a famous race-track near Windsor castle.

ASGARD (Scandinavian) court of the gods.

ASH (Hebrew) ash tree.
Ashby

ASHANTI (Swahili) from a tribe in West Africa.
Ashan, Ashani, Ashante, Ashantee, Ashaunte

ASHBY (Scandinavian) ash-tree farm. (Hebrew) an alternate form of Ash.
Ashbey

ASHER (Hebrew) happy; blessed.
Ashar, Ashor, Ashur

ASHFORD (English) ash-tree ford.
Ash, Ashtin

ASHLEY (English) ash-tree meadow.
Ash, Asheley, Ashelie, Ashely, Ashlan, Ashlee, Ashleigh, Ashlen, Ashlie, Ashlin, Ashling, Ashlinn, Ashlone, Ashly, Ashlyn, Ashlynn, Aslan

ASHON (Swahili) seventh-born son.

ASHTON (English) ash-tree settlement.
Ashtan, Ashten, Ashtian, Ashtin, Ashtion, Ashtonn, Ashtun, Ashtyn

ASHUR (Swahili) Mythology: the principle Assyrian deity.

ASHWANI (Hindi) first. Religion: the first of the twenty-seven galaxies revolving around the moon.
Ashwan

ASHWIN (Hindi) star.

ASIEL (Hebrew) created by God.

ASKER (Turkish) soldier.

ASPEN (English) aspen tree.

ASTON (English) eastern town.
Asten, Astin

ASWAD (Arabic) dark skinned, black.

ATA (Fante) twin.

ATEK (Polish) a form of Tanek.

ATHAN (Greek) immortal.

ATHERTON (English) town by a spring.

ATID (Tai) sun.

ATIF (Arabic) caring.
Ateef, Atef

ATLAS (Greek) lifted; carried. Mythology: Atlas was forced to carry the world on his shoulders as a punishment for feuding with Zeus.

ATLEY (English) meadow.
Atlea, Atlee, Atleigh, Atli, Attley

ATTILA (Gothic) little father. History: the Hun leader who conquered the Goths.
Atalik, Atila, Atilio, Atilla, Atiya, Attal, Attilio

ATWATER (English) at the water's edge.

ATWELL (English) at the well.

ATWOOD (English) at the forest.

ATWORTH (English) at the farmstead.

AUBERON (German) an alternate form of Oberon.
Auberron, Aubrey

AUBREY (German) noble; bear-like. (French) a familiar form of Auberon. See also Avery.
Aubary, Aube, Aubery, Aubie, Aubré, Aubree, Aubreii, Aubrie, Aubry, Aubury

AUBURN (Latin) reddish brown.

AUDEN (English) old friend.

AUDIE (German) noble; strong. (English) a familiar form of Edward.
Audi, Audiel, Audley, Audy

AUDON (French) old; rich.
Audelon

AUDREY (English) noble strength.
Audra, Audre, Audrea, Audrius, Audry

AUDRIC (English) wise ruler.
Audrick, Audrik

AUDUN (Scandinavian) deserted, desolate.

AUGIE (Latin) a familiar form of August.
Auggie, Augy

AUGUST (Latin) a short form of Augustine, Augustus.
Agosto, Augie, Auguste, Augusto

AUGUSTINE (Latin) majestic. Religion: Saint Augustine was the first Archbishop of Canterbury. See also Austin, Gus, Tino.
August, Agustin, Augustin, Augustinas, Augustino, Austen, Austin, Auston, Austyn

AUGUSTUS (Latin) majestic; venerable. History: a name used by Roman emperors such as Augustus Caesar.
August

AUKAI (Hawaiian) seafarer.

AUNDRE (Greek) an alternate form of Andre.
Aundrae, Aundray, Aundrea, Aundrey, Aundry

AUREK (Polish) golden haired.

AURELIO (Latin) a short form of Aurelius.
Aurel, Aurele, Aureli, Aurellio

AURELIUS (Latin) golden. History: Marcus Aurelius Antoninus was a second-century A.D. philosopher and emperor of Rome.
Arelian, Areliano, Aurèle, Aureliano, Aurelien, Aurêlien, Aurelio, Aurey, Auriel, Aury

AURICK (German) protecting ruler.
Auric

AUSTEN, Auston, Austyn (Latin) short forms of Augustine.
Austan, Austun, Austyne

AUSTIN (Latin) a short form of Augustine.
Astin, Austine, Oistin, Ostin

AVEL (Greek) breath.

AVENT (French) born during Advent.
Aventin, Aventino

AVERILL (French) born in April. (English) boar-warrior.
Ave, Averel, Averell, Averiel, Averil, Averyl, Averyll, Avrel, Avrell, Avrill, Avryll

AVERY (English) a form of Aubrey.
Avary, Aveary, Avere, Averee, Averey, Averi, Averie, Avrey, Avry

AVI (Hebrew) God is my father.
Avian, Avidan, Avidor, Aviel, Avion

AVIV (Hebrew) youth; springtime.

AVNER (Hebrew) an alternate form of Abner.
Avneet, Avniel

AVRAM (Hebrew) an alternate form of Abraham, Abram.
Arram, Avraam, Avraham, Avrahom, Avrohom, Avrom, Avrum

AVSHALOM (Hebrew) father of peace. See also Absalom.
Avsalom

AWAN (Native American) somebody.

AXEL (Latin) axe. (German) small oak tree; source of life. (Scandinavian) a form of Absalom.

Axel *(cont.)*
Aksel, Ax, Axe, Axell, Axil, Axill, Axl, Axle, Axyle

AYDIN (Turkish) intelligent.

AYERS (English) heir to a fortune.

AYINDE (Yoruba) we gave praise and he came.

AYLMER (English) an alternate form of Elmer.
Aillmer, Ailmer, Allmer, Ayllmer

AYMIL (Greek) an alternate form of Emil.

AYMON (French) a form of Raymond.

AYO (Yoruba) happiness.

AZAD (Turkish) free.

AZEEM (Arabic) an alternate form of Azim.
Aseem, Asim

AZI (Nigerian) youth.

AZIM (Arabic) defender.
Azeem

'AZIZ (Arabic) strong.

AZIZI (Swahili) precious.

AZRIEL (Hebrew) God is my aid.

AZURIAH (Hebrew) aided by God.
Azaria, Azariah, Azuria

BADEN (German) bather.
Baeden, Bayden, Baydon

BAHIR (Arabic) brilliant, dazzling.

BAHRAM (Persian) ancient king.

BAILEY (French) bailiff, steward.
Bail, Bailee, Bailie, Bailio, Baillie, Baily, Bailye, Baley, Bayley

BAIN (Irish) a short form of Bainbridge.
Baine, Bayne, Baynn

BAINBRIDGE (Irish) fair bridge.
Bain, Baynbridge, Bayne, Baynebridge

BAIRD (Irish) bard, traveling minstrel; poet.
Bairde, Bard

BAKARI (Swahili) noble promise.
Bacari, Baccari, Bakarie

BAKER (English) baker. See also Baxter.
Bakir, Bakory, Bakr

BAL (Sanskrit) child born with lots of hair.

BALASI (Basque) flat footed.

BALBO (Latin) stammerer.
Bailby, Balbi, Ballbo

BALDEMAR (German) bold; famous.
Baldemer, Baldomero, Baumar, Baumer

BALDER (Scandinavian) bald. Mythology: the Norse god of light, summer, and innocence.
Baldier, Baldur, Baudier

BALDRIC (German) brave ruler.
Baldrick, Baudric

BALDWIN (German) bold friend.
Bald, Baldovino, Balduin, Baldwinn, Baldwyn, Baldwynn, Balldwin, Baudoin

BALFOUR (Scottish) pasture land.
Balfor, Balfore

BALIN (Hindi) mighty soldier.
Bali, Baylen, Baylin, Baylon, Valin

BALLARD (German) brave; strong.
Balard

BALRAJ (Hindi) strongest.

BALTAZAR (Greek) an alternate form of Balthasar.
Baltasar

BALTHASAR (Greek) God save the king. Bible: one of the Three Wise Men.
Badassare, Baldassare, Baltazar, Balthasaar, Balthazar, Balthazzar, Baltsaros, Belshazar, Belshazzar, Boldizsár

BANCROFT (English) bean field.
Ban, Bancrofft, Bank, Bankroft, Banky, Binky

BANDI (Hungarian) a form of Andrew.
Bandit

BANE (Hawaiian) a form of Bartholomew.

BANNER (Scottish, English) flag bearer.
Bannor, Banny

BANNING (Irish) small and fair.
Bannie, Banny

BARAK (Hebrew) lightning bolt. Bible: the valiant warrior who helped Deborah.
Barrak

BARAN (Russian) ram.
Baren

BARASA (Kikuyu) meeting place.

BARCLAY (Scottish, English) birch tree meadow.
Bar, Barcley, Barklay, Barkley, Barklie, Barrclay, Berkeley

BARD (Irish) an alternate form of Baird.
Bar, Barde, Bardia, Bardiya, Barr

BARDOLF (German) bright wolf. Literature: the name of a drunken fool who appeared in four Shakespearean plays.
Bardo, Bardolph, Bardou, Bardoul, Bardulf, Bardulph

BARDRICK (Teutonic) axe ruler.
Bardric, Bardrik

BARIS (Turkish) peaceful.

BARKER (English) lumberjack; advertiser at a carnival.

BARLOW (English) bare hillside.
Barlowe, Barrlow, Barrlowe

BARNABAS (Greek, Hebrew, Aramaic, Latin) son of the missionary. Bible: disciple of Paul.
Bane, Barna, Barnaba, Barnabus, Barnaby, Barnebas, Barnebus, Barney

BARNABY (English) a form of Barnabas.
Barnabe, Barnabé, Barnabee, Barnabey, Barnabi, Barnabie, Bernabé, Burnaby

BARNARD (English) a form of Bernard.
Barn, Barnard, Barnhard, Barnhardo

BARNES (English) bear; son of Barnett.

BARNETT (English) nobleman; leader.
Barn, Barnet, Barney, Baronet, Baronett, Barrie, Barron, Barry

BARNEY (English) a familiar form of Barnabas, Barnett.
Barnie, Barny

BARNUM (German) barn; storage place. (English) baron's home.
Barnham

BARON (German, English) nobleman, baron.
Baaron, Barion, Baronie, Barrin, Barrion, Barron, Baryn, Bayron, Berron

BARRETT (German) strong as a bear.
Bar, Baret, Barrat, Barret, Barretta, Barrette, Barry, Berrett, Berrit

BARRIC (English) grain farm.
Barrick, Beric, Berric, Berrick, Berrik

BARRINGTON (English) Geography: a town in England.

BARRY (Welsh) son of Harry. (Irish) spear, marksman. (French) gate, fence.
Baris, Barri, Barrie, Barris, Bary

BART (Hebrew) a short form of Bartholomew, Barton.
Barrt, Bartel, Bartie, Barty

BARTHOLOMEW (Hebrew) son of Talmaí. Bible: one of the Twelve Apostles. See also Jerney, Parlan, Parthalán.
Balta, Bane, Bart, Bartek, Barth, Barthel, Barthelemy, Barthélemy, Barthélmy, Bartho, Bartholo, Bartholomaus, Bartholome, Bartholomeo, Bartholomeus, Bartholomieu, Bartimous, Bartlet, Barto, Bartolome, Bartolomé, Bartolomeo, Bartolomeô, Bartolommeo, Bartome, Bartz, Bat

BARTLET (English) a form of Bartholomew.
Bartlett, Bartley

BARTO (Spanish) a form of Bartholomew.
Bardo, Bardol, Bartol, Bartoli, Bartolo, Bartos

BARTON (English) barley farm; Bart's town.
Barrton, Bart

BARTRAM (English) an alternate form of Bertram.
Barthram

BARUCH (Hebrew) blessed.
Boruch

BASAM (Arabic) smiling.
Basem, Basim, Bassam

BASIL (Greek, Latin) royal, kingly. Religion: a saint and leading scholar of the early Christian Church. Botany: an

Basil (cont.)
herb used in cooking. See also Vasilis, Wasili.
Bas, Basal, Base, Baseal, Basel, Basle, Basile, Basilio, Basilios, Basilius, Bassel, Bazek, Bazel, Bazil, Bazyli

BASIR (Turkish) intelligent, discerning.
Bashar, Basheer, Bashir, Bashiyr, Bechir, Bhasheer

BASSETT (English) little person.
Basett, Basit, Basset, Bassit

BASTIEN (German) a short form of Sebastian.
Baste, Bastiaan, Bastian, Bastion

BAT (English) a short form of Bartholomew.

BAUL (Gypsy) snail.

BAVOL (Gypsy) wind; air.

BAXTER (English) an alternate form of Baker.
Bax, Baxie, Baxty, Baxy

BAY (Vietnamese) seventh son. (French) chestnut brown color; evergreen tree. (English) howler.

BAYARD (English) reddish brown hair.
Baiardo, Bay, Bayardo, Bayerd, Bayrd

BAYLEY (French) an alternate form of Bailey.
Baylee, Bayleigh, Baylie, Bayly

BEACAN (Irish) small.
Beacán, Becan

BEACHER (English) beech trees.
Beach, Beachy, Beech, Beecher, Beechy

BEAGAN (Irish) small.
Beagen, Beagin

BEALE (French) an alternate form of Beau.
Beal, Beall, Bealle, Beals

BEAMAN (English) beekeeper.
Beamann, Beamen, Beeman, Beman

BEAMER (English) trumpet player.

BEASLEY (English) field of peas.

BEATTIE (Latin) blessed; happy; bringer of joy. A masculine form of Beatrice.
Beatie, Beatty, Beaty

BEAU (French) handsome.
Beale, Beaux, Bo

BEAUFORT (French) beautiful fort.

BEAUMONT (French) beautiful mountain.

BEAUREGARD (French) handsome; beautiful; well regarded.

BEAVER (English) beaver.
Beav, Beavo, Beve, Bevo

BEBE (Spanish) baby.

BECK (English, Scandinavian) brook.
Beckett

BEDE (English) prayer. Religion: the patron saint of scholars.

BELA (Czech) white. (Hungarian) bright.
Béla, Belaal, Belal, Belall, Belay, Bellal

BELDEN (French, English) pretty valley.
Beldin, Beldon, Bellden, Belldon

BELEN (Greek) arrow.

BELL (French) handsome. (English) bell ringer.

BELLAMY (French) beautiful friend.
Belamy, Bell, Bellamey, Bellamie

BELLO (African) helper or promoter of Islam

BELMIRO (Portuguese) good looking; attractive.

BEM (Tiv) peace.
Behm

BEN (Hebrew) a short form of Benjamin.
Behn, Benio, Benn, Benne, Benno

BEN-AMI (Hebrew) son of my people.
Baram, Barami

BENEDICT (Latin) blessed. See also Venedictos, Venya.
Benci, Bendick, Bendict, Bendino, Bendix, Bendrick, Benedetto, Benedick, Benedicto, Benedictus, Benedikt, Bengt, Benito, Benoit

BENEDIKT (German, Slavic) a form of Benedict.
Bendek, Bendik, Benedek, Benedik

BENGT (Scandinavian) a form of Benedict.
Beng, Benke, Bent

BENIAM (Ethiopian) a form of Benjamin.
Beneyam, Beniamin, Beniamino

BENITO (Italian) a form of Benedict. History: Benito Mussolini led Italy during World War II.

Benedo, Benino, Benno, Beno, Betto, Beto

BENJAMEN (Hebrew) an alternate form of Benjamin.
Benejamen, Benjermen, Benjjmen

BENJAMIN (Hebrew) son of my right hand. See also Peniamina, Veniamin.
Behnjamin, Bejamin, Bemjiman, Ben, Benejaminas, Bengamin, Beniam, Benja, Benjahmin, Benjaim, Benjam, Benjamaim, Benjaman, Benjamen, Benjamine, Benjaminn, Benjamino, Benjamon, Benjamyn, Benjamynn, Benjemin, Benjermain, Benjermin, Benji, Benjie, Benjiman, Benjy, Benkamin, Bennjamin, Benny, Benyamin, Benyamino, Binyamin, Mincho

BENJIMAN (Hebrew) an alternate form of Benjamin.
Benjimen, Benjimin, Benjimon, Benjmain

BENJIRO (Japanese) enjoys peace.

BENNETT (Latin) little blessed one.
Benet, Benett, Bennet, Benette, Bennete, Bennette

BENNY (Hebrew) a familiar form of Benjamin.
Bennie

BENO (Hebrew) son. (Mwera) band member.

BENOIT (French) a form of Benedict. (English) Botany: a yellow, flowering rose plant.
Benott

BENONI (Hebrew) son of my sorrow. Bible: Ben-Oni was the son of Jacob and Rachel.
Ben-Oni

BENSON (Hebrew) son of Ben. A short form of Ben Zion.
Bensan, Bensen, Benssen, Bensson

BENTLEY (English) moor; coarse grass meadow.
Bent, Bentlea, Bentlee, Bentlie, Lee

BENTON (English) Ben's town; town on the moors.
Bent

BENZI (Hebrew) a familiar form of Ben Zion.

BEN ZION (Hebrew) son of Zion.
Benson, Benzi

BEPPE (Italian) a form of Joseph.
Beppy

BER (English) boundary. (Yiddish) bear.

BEREDEI (Russian) a form of Hubert.
Berdry, Berdy, Beredej, Beredy

BERG (German) mountain.
Berdj, Berge, Bergh, Berje

BERGEN (German, Scandinavian) hill dweller.
Bergin, Birgin

BERGER (French) shepherd.

BERGREN (Scandinavian) mountain stream.
Berg

BERK (Turkish) solid, rugged.

BERKELEY (English) an alternate form of Barclay.
Berk, Berkely, Berkie, Berkley, Berklie, Berkly, Berky

BERL (German) an alternate form of Burl.
Berle, Berlie, Berlin, Berlyn

BERLYN (German) boundary line. See also Burl.
Berlin, Burlin

BERN (German) a short form of Bernard.
Berne

BERNAL (German) strong as a bear.
Bernald, Bernaldo, Bernel, Bernhald, Bernhold, Bernold

BERNARD (German) brave as a bear. See also Bjorn.
Barnard, Bear, Bearnard, Benek, Ber, Berend, Bern, Bernabé, Bernadas, Bernardel, Bernardin, Bernardo, Bernardus, Bernardyn, Bernarr, Bernat, Bernek, Bernal, Bernel, Bernerd, Berngards, Bernhard, Bernhards, Bernhardt, Bernie, Bjorn, Burnard

BERNARDO (Spanish) a form of Bernard.
Barnardino, Barnardo, Barnhardo, Benardo, Bernardino, Bernhardo, Berno, Burnardo, Nardo

BERNIE (German) a familiar form of Bernard.
Berney, Berni, Berny, Birney, Birnie, Birny, Burney

BERRY (English) berry; grape.
Berrie

BERSH (Gypsy) one year.

BERT (German, English) bright, shining. A short form of Berthold, Berton, Bertram, Bertrand, Egbert, Filbert.
Bertie, Bertus, Birt, Burt

BERTHOLD (German) bright; illustrious; brilliant ruler.
Bert, Berthoud, Bertold, Bertolde

BERTIE (English) a familiar form of Bert, Egbert.
Bertie, Berty, Birt, Birtie, Birty

BERTÍN (Spanish) distinguished friend.
Berti

BERTO (Spanish) a short form of Alberto.

BERTON (English) bright settlement; fortified town.
Bert

BERTRAM (German) bright; illustrious. (English) bright raven. See also Bartram.
Beltran, Beltrán, Beltrano, Bert, Berton, Bertrae, Bertraim, Bertraum, Bertron

BERTRAND (German) bright shield.
Bert, Bertran, Bertrando, Bertranno

BERWYN (English) harvest son; powerful friend. Astrology: a name for babies born under the signs of Virgo, Capricorn, and Taurus.
Berwin, Berwynn, Berwynne

BEVAN (Welsh) son of Evan.
Beavan, Beaven, Beavin, Bev, Beve, Beven, Bevin, Bevo, Bevon

BEVERLY (English) beaver meadow.
Beverlea, Beverleigh, Beverley, Beverlie

BEVIS (French) from Beauvais, France; bull.
Beauvais, Bevys

BHAGWANDAS (Hindi) servant of God.

BICKFORD (English) axe-man's ford.

BIENVENIDO (Filipino) welcome.

BIJAN (Persian) ancient hero.
Bihjan, Bijann, Bijhan, Bijhon, Bijon

BILAL (Arabic) chosen.
Bila, Bilaal, Bilale, Bile, Bilel, Billaal, Billal

BILL (German) a short form of William.
Bil, Billee, Billijo, Billye, Byll, Will

BILLY (German) a familiar form of Bill, William.
Bille, Billey, Billie, Billy, Bily, Willie

BINAH (Hebrew) understanding; wise.
Bina

BING (German) kettle-shaped hollow.

BINH (Vietnamese) peaceful.

BINKENTIOS (Greek) a form of Vincent.

BINKY (English) a familiar form of Bancroft, Vincent.
Bink, Binkentios, Binkie

BIRCH (English) white; shining; birch tree.
Birk, Burch

BIRGER (Norwegian) rescued.

BIRKEY (English) island with birch trees.
Birk, Birkie, Birky

BIRKITT (English) birch-tree coast.
Birk, Birket, Birkit, Burket, Burkett, Burkitt

BIRLEY (English) meadow with the cow barn.
Birlee, Birlie, Birly

BIRNEY (English) island with a brook.
Birne, Birnie, Birny, Burney, Burnie, Burny

BIRTLE (English) hill with birds.

BISHOP (Greek) overseer. (English) bishop.
Bish, Bishup

BJORN (Scandinavian) a form of Bernard.
Bjarne

BLACKBURN (Scottish) black brook.

BLADE (English) knife, sword.
Bladen, Bladon, Bladyn, Blae, Blaed, Blayde

BLADIMIR (Russian) an alternate form of Vladimir.
Bladimer

BLAINE (Irish) thin, lean. (English) river source.
Blain, Blane, Blayne

BLAIR (Irish) plain, field. (Welsh) place.
Blaire, Blare, Blayr, Blayre

BLAISE, Blaize (French) forms of Blaze.
Ballas, Balyse, Blais, Blaisot, Blas, Blase, Blasi, Blasien, Blasius, Blass, Blaz, Blaze, Blayz, Blayze, Blayzz

BLAKE (English) attractive; dark.
Blaik, Blaike, Blakely, Blakeman, Blakey, Blayke

BLAKELY (English) dark meadow.
Blakelee, Blakeleigh, Blakeley, Blakelie, Blakelin, Blakelyn, Blakeny, Blakley, Blakney

BLANCO (Spanish) light skinned, white, blond.

BLANE (Irish) an alternate form of Blaine.
Blaney, Blanne

BLAYNE (Irish) an alternate form of Blaine.
Blayn, Blayney

BLAZE (Latin) stammerer. (English) flame; trail mark made on a tree.
Balázs, Biaggio, Biagio, Blaise, Blaize, Blazen, Blazer

BLISS (English) blissful; joyful.

BLY (Native American) high.

BLYTHE (English) carefree; merry, joyful.
Blithe, Blyth

BO (English) a form of Beau, Beauregard. (German) a form of Bogart.
Boe

BOAZ (Hebrew) swift; strong.
Bo, Boas, Booz, Bos, Boz

BOB (English) a short form of Robert.
Bobb, Bobby, Bobek, Rob

BOBBY (English) a familiar form of Bob, Robert.
Bobbey, Bobbi, Bobbie, Bobbye, Boby

BOBEK (Czech) a form of Bob, Robert.

BODEN (Scandinavian) sheltered. (French) messenger, herald.
Bodie, Bodin, Bodine, Bodyne, Boe

BODIE (Scandinavian) a familiar form of Boden.
Boddie, Bode, Bodee, Bodey, Bodhi, Bodi, Boedee, Boedi, Boedy

BODIL (Norwegian) mighty ruler.

BODUA (Akan) animal's tail.

BOGART (German) strong as a bow. (Irish, Welsh) bog, marshland.
Bo, Bogey, Bogie, Bogy

BOHDAN (Ukranian) a form of Donald.
Bogdan, Bogdashka, Bogdon, Bohden, Bohdon

BONARO (Italian, Spanish) friend.
Bona, Bonar

BONAVENTURE (Italian) good luck.

BOND (English) tiller of the soil.
Bondie, Bondon, Bonds, Bondy

BONIFACE (Latin) do-gooder.
Bonifacio, Bonifacius, Bonifacy

BOOKER (English) book-maker; book lover; Bible lover.
Bookie, Books, Booky

BOONE (Latin, French) good. History: Daniel Boone was an American frontiersman.
Bon, Bone, Bonne, Boonie, Boony

BOOTH (English) hut. (Scandinavian) temporary dwelling.
Boot, Boote, Boothe

BORAK (Arabic) lightning. Mythology: the horse that carried Muhammed to seventh heaven.

BORDEN (French) cottage. (English) valley of the boar; boar's den.
Bord, Bordie, Bordy

BORG (Scandinavian) castle.

BORIS (Slavic) battler, warrior. Religion: the patron saint of Moscow.
Boriss, Borja, Borris, Borya, Boryenka, Borys

BORKA (Russian) fighter.
Borkinka

BOSEDA (Tiv) born on Saturday.

BOSLEY (English) grove of trees.

BOTAN (Japanese) blossom, bud.

BOUREY (Cambodian) country.

BOURNE (Latin, French) boundary. (English) brook, stream.

BOUTROS (Arabic) a form of Peter.

BOWEN (Welsh) son of Owen.
Bow, Bowe, Bowie

BOWIE (Irish) yellow haired. History: Colonel James Bowie was an American scout.
Bow, Bowen

BOYCE (French) woods, forest.
Boice, Boise, Boy, Boycey, Boycie

BOYD (Scottish) yellow haired.
Boid, Boyde

BRAD (English) a short form of Bradford, Bradley.
Bradd, Brade

BRADBURN (English) broad stream.

BRADEN (English) broad valley.
Bradan, Bradden, Bradeon, Bradin, Bradine, Bradyn, Braeden, Braiden, Brayden, Bredan, Bredon

BRADFORD (English) broad river crossing.
Brad, Braddford, Ford

BRADLEE (English) an alternate form of Bradley.
Bradlea, Bradleigh, Bradlie

BRADLEY (English) broad meadow.
Brad, Braddly, Bradlay, Bradlee, Bradly, Bradlyn, Bradney

BRADLY (English) an alternate form of Bradley.

BRADON (English) broad hill.
Braedon, Braidon, Braydon

BRADSHAW (English) broad forest.

BRADY (Irish) spirited. (English) broad island.
Bradey, Bradi, Bradie, Bradye, Braidy

BRADYN (English) an alternate form of Braden.
Bradynne, Breidyn

BRAEDEN, Braiden (English) alternate forms of Braden.

BRAEDON (English) an alternate form of Bradon.
Breadon

BRAGI (Scandinavian) poet. Mythology: the god of poetry and music.
Brage

BRAHAM (Hindi) creator.
Braheem, Braheim, Brahiem, Brahima, Brahm

BRAINARD (English) bold raven; prince.
Brainerd

BRAM (Hebrew) a short form of Abraham, Abram. (Scottish) bramble, brushwood.
Brame, Bramm, Bramdon

BRAMWELL (English) bramble-bush spring.
Brammel, Brammell, Bramwel, Bramwyll

BRANCH (Latin) paw; claw; tree branch.

BRAND (English) firebrand; sword. A short form of Brandon.
Brandall, Brande, Brandel, Brandell, Brander, Brandley, Brandol, Brandt, Brandy, Brann

BRANDEIS (Czech) dweller on a burned clearing.
Brandis

BRANDEN (English) beacon valley.
Brandden, Brandene, Brandin, Brandine, Brandyn, Breandan

BRANDON (English) beacon hill.
Bran, Brand, Brandan, Branddon, Brandone, Brandonn, Brandyn, Branndan, Branndon, Brannon, Breandon, Brendon

BRANDT (English) an alternate form of Brant.

BRANDY (Dutch) brandy.
Branddy, Brandey, Brandi, Brandie

BRANDYN (English) an alternate form of Branden.
Brandynn

BRANNON (Irish) a form of Brandon.
Branen, Brannan, Brannen, Branon

BRANSON (English) son of Brandon, Brant.
Bransen, Bransin, Brantson

BRANT (English) proud.
Brandt, Brannt, Brante, Brantley, Branton

BRANTLEY (English) an alternate form of Brant.
Brantlie, Brantly, Brentlee, Brentley, Brently

BRAULIO (Italian) a form of Brawley.
Brauli, Brauliuo

BRAWLEY (English) meadow on the hillside.
Braulio , Brawlee, Brawly

BRAXTON (English) Brock's town.
Brax, Braxdon, Braxston, Braxten, Braxtin, Braxxton

BRAYAN (Irish, Scottish) an alternate form of Brian.
Brayn, Brayon

BRAYDEN (English) an alternate form of Braden.
Braydan, Braydn, Bradyn, Breydan, Breyden, Brydan, Bryden

BRAYDON (English) an alternate form of Bradon.
Braydoon, Brydon, Breydon

BRECK (Irish) freckled.
Brec, Breckan, Brecken, Breckie, Breckin, Breckke, Breckyn, Brek, Brexton

BREDE (Scandinavian) iceberg, glacier.

BRENCIS (Latvian) a form of Lawrence.
Brence

BRENDAN (Irish) little raven. (English) sword.
Breandan, Bren, Brenden, Brendis, Brendon, Brendyn, Brenn, Brennan, Brennen, Brenndan, Brenyan, Bryn

BRENDEN (Irish) an alternate form of Brendan.
Bren, Brendene, Brendin, Brendine, Brennden

BRENDON (English) an alternate form of Brandon.
Brenndon

BRENNAN, Brennen (English, Irish) alternate forms of Brendan.
Bren, Brenan, Brenen, Brenin, Brenn, Brenna, Brennann, Brenner, Brennin, Brennon, Brennor, Brennyn, Brenon

BRENT (English) a short form of Brenton.
Brendt, Brente, Brentson, Brentt

BRENTON (English) steep hill.
Brent, Brentan, Brenten, Brentin, Brentten, Brentton, Brentyn

BRET, Brett (Scottish) from Great Britain. See also Britton.

Bhrett, Braten, Braton, Brayton, Bretin, Bretley, Bretlin, Breton, Brettan, Brette, Bretten, Bretton, Brit, Britt

BREWSTER (English) brewer.
Brew, Brewer, Bruwster

BREYON (Irish, Scottish) an alternate form of Brian.
Breon, Breyan

BRIAN (Irish, Scottish) strong; virtuous; honorable. History: Brian Boru was the most famous Irish king. See also Palaina.
Brayan, Breyon, Briana, Briann, Brianna, Brianne, Briano, Briant, Briante, Briaun, Briayan, Brien, Brience, Brient, Brin, Briny, Brion, Bryan, Bryen

BRIAR (French) heather.
Brier, Brierly, Bryar, Bryer, Bryor

BRICE (Welsh) alert; ambitious. (English) son of Rice.
Bricen, Briceton, Bryce

BRICK (English) bridge.
Bricker, Bricklen, Brickman, Brik

BRIDGER (English) bridge builder.
Bridd, Bridge, Bridgeley, Bridgely

BRIGHAM (English) covered bridge. (French) troops, brigade.
Brig, Brigg, Briggs, Brighton

BRIGHTON (English) bright town.
Breighton, Bright, Brightin, Bryton

BRION (Irish, Scottish) an alternate form of Brian.
Brieon, Brione, Brionn, Brionne

BRIT, Britt (Scottish) alternate forms of Bret, Brett. See also Britton.
Brit, Brityce

BRITTON (Scottish) from Great Britain. See also Bret, Brett, Brit, Britt.
Britain, Briten, Britian, Britin, Briton, Brittain, Brittan, Britten, Brittian, Brittin, Britton

BROCK (English) badger.
Broc, Brocke, Brockett, Brockie, Brockley, Brockton, Brocky, Brok, Broque

BROD (English) a short form of Broderick.
Brode, Broden

BRODERICK (Welsh) son of the famous ruler. (English) broad ridge. See also Roderick.
Brod, Broddie, Brodderick, Brodderrick, Broddy, Broderic, Broderrick, Brodrick,

BRODIE (Irish) an alternate form of Brody.
Brodi, Broedi

BRODRICK (Welsh, English) an alternate form of Broderick.
Broddrick, Brodric, Brodryck

BRODY (Irish) ditch; canal builder.
Brodee, Broden, Brodey, Brodie, Broedy

BROGAN (Irish) a heavy work shoe.
Brogen, Broghan, Broghen

BROMLEY (English) brushwood meadow.

BRON (Afrikaans) source.

BRONISLAW (Polish) weapon of glory.

BRONSON (English) son of Brown.
Bransen, Bransin, Branson, Bron, Bronnie, Bronnson, Bronny, Bronsan, Bronsen, Bronsin, Bronsonn, Bronsson, Bronsun, Bronsyn, Brunson

BROOK (English) brook, stream.
Brooke, Brooker, Brookin, Brooklyn

BROOKS (English) son of Brook.
Brookes, Broox

BROWN (English) brown; bear.

BRUCE (French) brushwood thicket; woods.
Brucey, Brucy, Brue, Bruis

BRUNO (German, Italian) brown haired; brown skinned.
Brunon, Bruns

BRYAN (Irish) strong; virtuous; honorable. An alternate form of Brian.
Brayan, Bryann, Bryant, Bryen

BRYANT (Irish) an alternate form of Bryan.
Bryent

BRYCE (Welsh) an alternate form of Brice.
Brycen, Bryceton, Bryson, Bryston

BRYON (German) cottage. (English) bear.
Bryeon, Bryn, Bryne, Brynn, Brynne, Bryone

BRYSON (Welsh) son of Brice.
Brysan, Brysen, Brysun, Brysyn

BRYTON (English) an alternate form of Brighton.
Brayten, Brayton, Breyton, Bryeton, Brytan, Bryten, Brytin, Brytten, Brytton

BUBBA (German) a boy.
Babba, Babe, Bebba

BUCK (German, English) male deer.
Buckie, Buckley, Buckner, Bucko, Bucky

BUCKLEY (English) deer meadow.
Bucklea, Bucklee

BUCKMINSTER (English) preacher.

BUD (English) herald, messenger.
Budd, Buddy

BUDDY (American) a familiar form of Bud.
Budde, Buddey, Buddie

BUELL (German) hill dweller. (English) bull.

BUFORD (English) ford near the castle.
Burford

BURGESS (English) town dweller; shopkeeper.
Burg, Burges, Burgh, Burgiss, Burr

BURIAN (Ukrainian) lives near weeds.

BURKE (German, French) fortress, castle.
Berk, Berke, Birk, Bourke, Burk, Burkley

BURL (German) a short form of Berlyn. (English) cup bearer; wine servant; knot in a tree.
Berl, Burley, Burlie, Byrle

BURLEIGH (English) meadow with knotted tree trunks.
Burlee, Burley, Burlie, Byrleigh, Byrlee

BURNE (English) brook.
Beirne, Burn, Burnell, Burnett, Burney, Byrn, Byrne

BURNEY (English) island with a brook. A familiar form of Rayburn.

BURR (Swedish) youth. (English) prickly plant.

BURRIS (English) town dweller.

BURT (English) an alternate form of Bert. A short form of Burton.
Burrt, Burtt, Burty

BURTON (English) fortified town.
Berton, Burt

BUSBY (Scottish) village in the thicket; tall military hat made of fur.
Busbee, Buzby, Buzz

BUSTER (American) hitter, puncher.

BUTCH (American) a short form of Butcher.

BUTCHER (English) butcher.
Butch

BUZZ (Scottish) a short form of Busby.
Buzzy

BYFORD (English) by the ford.

BYRAM (English) cattleyard.

BYRD (English) birdlike.
Bird, Birdie, Byrdie

BYRNE (English) an alternate form of Burne.
Byrn, Byrnes

BYRON (French) cottage. (English) barn.
Beyren, Beyron, Biren, Biron, Buiron, Byram, Byran, Byrann, Byren, Byrom, Byrone

CABLE (French, English) rope maker.
Cabell

CADAO (Vietnamese) folk song.

CADBY (English) warrior's settlement.

CADDOCK (Welsh) eager for war.

CADE (Welsh) a short form of Cadell.
Cady

CADELL (Welsh) battler.
Cade, Cadel, Cedell

CADEN (American) a form of Kadin.
Cadan, Caddon, Cadian, Cadien, Cadin, Cadon, Cadyn, Caeden, Caedon, Caid, Caiden, Cayden

CADMUS (Greek) from the east. Mythology: the founder of the city of Thebes.

CAELAN (Scottish) a form of Nicholas.
Cael, Caelon, Caelyn, Cailan, Cailean, Caillan, Cailun, Cailyn, Calan, Calen, Caleon, Caley, Calin, Callan, Callon, Callyn, Calon, Calyn, Caylan, Cayley

CAESAR (Latin) long haired. History: a title for Roman emperors. See also Kaiser, Kesar, Sarito.
Caesarae, Caesear, Caeser, Caezar, Caseare, Ceasar, Cesar, Ceseare, Cezar, Cézar, Czar, Seasar

CAHIL (Turkish) young, naive.

CAI (Welsh) a form of Gaius
Caio, Caius, Caw

CAIN (Hebrew) spear; gatherer. Bible: Adam and Eve's oldest son. See also Kabil, Kane, Kayne.
Cainaen, Cainan, Caine, Cainen, Caineth, Cayn, Cayne

CAIRN (Welsh) landmark made of piled-up stones.
Cairne, Carn, Carne

CAIRO (Arabic) Geography: the capital of Egypt.
Kairo

CAL (Latin) a short form of Calvert, Calvin.

CALDER (Welsh, English) brook, stream.

CALDWELL (English) cold well.

CALE (Hebrew) a short form of Caleb.

CALEB (Hebrew) dog; faithful. (Arabic) bold, brave. Bible: a companion of Moses and Joshua. See also Kaleb, Kayleb.
Caeleb, Calab, Calabe, Cale, Caley, Calib, Calieb, Callob, Calob, Calyb, Cayleb, Caylebb, Caylib, Caylob

CALEN, Calin (Scottish) alternate forms of Caelan.

Caelen, Caelin Caellin, Cailen, Cailin, Caillin, Calean, Callen, Caylin

CALEY (Irish) a familiar form of Caleb.
Calee, Caleigh

CALHOUN (Irish) narrow woods. (Scottish) warrior.
Colhoun, Colhoune, Colquhoun

CALLAHAN (Irish) Religion: a Catholic saint.
Calahan, Callaghan

CALLUM (Irish) dove.
Callam, Calum, Calym

CALVERT (English) calf herder.
Cal, Calbert, Calvirt

CALVIN (Latin) bald. See also Kalvin, Vinny.
Cal, Calv, Calvien, Calvon, Calvyn

CAM (Gypsy) beloved. (Scottish) a short form of Cameron.
Camm, Cammie, Cammy, Camy

CAMARON (Scottish) an alternate form of Cameron.
Camar, Camari, Camaran, Camaren

CAMDEN (Scottish) winding valley.
Kamden

CAMERON (Scottish) crooked nose. See also Kameron.
Cam, Camaron, Cameran, Cameren, Camerin, Cameroun, Camerron, Camerson, Camerun, Cameryn, Camiren, Camiron, Cammeron, Camron

CAMILLE (French) young ceremonial attendant.
Camile

243

CAMILO (Latin) child born to freedom; noble.
Camiel, Camillo, Camillus

CAMPBELL (Latin, French) beautiful field. (Scottish) crooked mouth.
Cam, Camp, Campy

CAMRON (Scottish) a short form of Cameron.
Camren, Cammrin, Cammron, Camran, Camreon, Camrin, Camryn, Camrynn

CANAAN (French) an alternate form of Cannon. History: an ancient region between the Jordan River and the Mediterranean Sea.
Canan, Canen, Caynan

CANDIDE (Latin) pure; sincere.
Candid, Candido, Candonino

CANNON (French) church official; large gun. See also Kannon.
Canaan, Cannan, Cannen, Cannin, Canning, Canon

CANUTE (Latin) white haired. (Scandinavian) knot. History: an ancient Danish king who won a battle at Knutsford. See also Knute.
Cnut, Cnute

CAPPI (Gypsy) good fortune.

CAR (Irish) a short form of Carney.

CAREY (Greek) pure. (Welsh) castle; rocky island. See also Karey.
Care, Caree, Cari, Carre, Carree, Carrie, Cary

CARL (German) farmer. (English) strong and manly.

An alternate form of Charles. A short form of Carlton. See also Carroll, Kale, Kalle, Karl, Karlen, Karol.
Carle, Carles, Carless, Carlis, Carll, Carlo, Carlos, Carlson, Carlston, Carlus, Carolos

CARLIN (Irish) little champion.
Carlan, Carlen, Carley, Carlie, Carling, Carlino, Carly

CARLISLE (English) Carl's island.
Carlyle, Carlysle

CARLITO (Spanish) a familiar form of Carlos.
Carlitos

CARLO (Italian) a form of Carl, Charles.
Carolo

CARLOS (Spanish) a form of Carl, Charles.
Carlito

CARLTON (English) Carl's town.
Carl, Carleton, Carllton, Carlston, Carltonn, Carltton, Charlton

CARMEL (Hebrew) vineyard, garden. See also Carmine.
Carmello, Carmelo, Karmel

CARMICHAEL (Scottish) follower of Michael.

CARMINE (Latin) song; crimson. (Italian) a form of Carmel.
Carmain, Carmaine, Carman, Carmen, Carmon

CARNELIUS (Greek, Latin) an alternate form of Cornelius.
Carnealius, Carneilius, Carnellius, Carnilious

CARNELL (English) defender of the castle.

CARNEY (Irish) victorious. (Scottish) fighter. See also Kearney.
Car, Carny, Karney

CARR (Scandinavian) marsh. See also Kerr.
Karr

CARRICK (Irish) rock.
Carooq, Carricko

CARRINGTON (Welsh) rocky town.

CARROLL (German) an alternate form of Carl. (Irish) champion.
Carel, Carell, Cariel, Cariell, Carol, Carole, Carolo, Carols, Carollan, Carolus, Carrol, Cary, Caryl

CARSON (English) son of Carr.
Carsen, Carsino, Carrson, Karson

CARSTEN (Greek) an alternate form of Karsten.
Carston

CARTER (English) cart driver.
Cart

CARTWRIGHT (English) cart builder.

CARVELL (French, English) village on the marsh.
Carvel, Carvelle, Carvellius

CARVER (English) wood-carver; sculptor.

CARY (Welsh) an alternate form of Carey.
Carray, Carry

CASE (Irish) a short form of Casey. (English) a short form of Casimir.

CASEY (Irish) brave.
Case, Casie, Casy, Cayse, Caysey, Kacey, Kasey

CASH (Latin) vain. (Slavic) a short form of Casimir.
Cashe

CASIMIR (Slavic) peacemaker.
Cachi, Cas, Case, Cash, Cashemere, Cashi, Cashmeire, Cashmere, Casimere, Casimire, Casimiro, Castimer, Kasimir, Kazio

CASPER (Persian) treasurer. (German) imperial. See also Gaspar, Jasper, Kasper.
Caspar, Cass

CASS (Irish, Persian) a short form of Casper, Cassidy.

CASSIDY (Irish) clever; curly haired. See also Kazio.
Casidy, Cass, Cassady, Cassie, Kassidy

CASSIE (Irish) a familiar form of Cassidy.
Casi, Casie, Casio, Cassey, Cassy, Casy

CASSIUS (Latin, French) box; protective cover.
Cassia, Cassio, Cazzie

CASTLE (Latin) castle.
Cassle, Castel

CASTOR (Greek) beaver. Astrology: one of the twins in the constellation Gemini. Mythology: one of the patron saints of sailors.
Caster, Caston

CATER (English) caterer.

CATO (Latin) knowledgeable, wise.
Caton, Catón

CAVAN (Irish) handsome. See also Kevin.
Caven, Cavin, Cavan, Cawoun

CAYDEN (American) an alternate form of Caden.
Cayde, Caydin

CAYLAN (Scottish) an alternate form of Caelan.
Caylans, Caylen, Caylon

CAZZIE (American) a familiar form of Cassius.
Caz, Cazz, Cazzy

CEASAR (Latin) an alternate form of Caesar.
Ceaser

CECIL (Latin) blind.
Cece, Cecile, Cecilio, Cecilius, Cecill, Celio, Siseal

CEDRIC (English) battle chieftain. See also Kedrick, Rick.
Cad, Caddaric, Ced, Cederic, Cedrec, Cédric, Cedrick, Cedryche, Sedric

CEDRICK (English) an alternate form of Cedric.
Ceddrick, Cederick, Cederrick, Cedirick, Cedrik

CEEJAY (American) a combination of the initials C. + J.
Cejay, C.J.

CEMAL (Arabic) attractive.

CEPHAS (Latin) small rock. Bible: the term used by Jesus to describe Peter.
Cepheus, Cephus

CERDIC (Welsh) beloved.
Caradoc, Caradog, Ceredig, Ceretic

CEREK (Greek) an alternate form of Cyril. (Polish) lordly.

CESAR (Spanish) a form of Caesar.
Casar, César, Cesare, Cesareo, Cesario, Cesaro, Cessar

CESTMIR (Czech) fortress.

CEZAR (Slavic) a form of Caesar.
Cézar, Cezary, Cezek, Chezrae, Sezar

CHACE (French) an alternate form of Chase.
Chayce

CHAD (English) warrior. A short form of Chadwick. Geography: a country in north-central Africa.
Ceadd, Chaad, Chadd, Chaddie, Chaddy, Chade, Chadleigh, Chadler, Chadley, Chadlin, Chadlyn, Chadmen, Chado, Chadron, Chady

CHADRICK (German) mighty warrior.
Chaddrick, Chaderic, Chaderick, Chadrack, Chadric

CHADWICK (English) warrior's town.
Chad, Chaddwick, Chadvic, Chadwyck

CHAGO (Spanish) a form of Jacob.
Chango, Chanti

CHAIM (Hebrew) life. See also Hyman.
Chai, Chaimek, Haim, Khaim

CHAISE (French) an alternate form of Chase.
Chais, Chaisen, Chaison

CHAL (Gypsy) boy; son.
Chalie, Chalin

CHALMERS (Scottish) son of the lord.
Chalmer, Chalmr, Chamar, Chamarr

CHAM (Vietnamese) hard worker.
Chams

CHAN (Sanskrit) shining. (Spanish) an alternate form of Juan.
Chann, Chano, Chayo

CHANAN (Hebrew) cloud.

CHANCE (English) a short form of Chancellor, Chauncey.
Chanc, Chancee, Chancey, Chancie, Chancy, Chanse, Chansy, Chants, Chantz, Chanze, Chanz, Chaynce

CHANCELLOR (English) record-keeper.
Chance, Chancelar, Chancelen, Chanceleor, Chanceler, Chanceller, Chancelor, Chanselor, Chanslor

CHANDER (Hindi) moon.
Chand, Chandan, Chandany, Chandara, Chandon

CHANDLER (English) candle maker.
Chandelar, Chandlan, Chandlar, Chandlier, Chandlor, Chandlyr

CHANE (Swahili) dependable.

CHANEY (French) oak.
Chayne, Cheaney, Cheney, Cheyn, Cheyne, Cheyney

CHANKRISNA (Cambodian) sweet-smelling tree.

CHANNING (English) wise. (French) canon; church official.
Chane, Chann

CHANSE (English) an alternate form of Chance.
Chans, Chansey

CHANTE (French) singer.
Chant, Chantha, Chanthar, Chantra, Chantry, Shantae

CHAPMAN (English) merchant.
Chap, Chappie, Chappy

CHARLES (German) farmer. (English) strong and manly. See also Carl, Searlas, Tearlach, Xarles.
Arlo, Chareles, Charels, Charlese, Carlo, Carlos, Charl, Charle, Charlen, Charlie, Charlot, Charlz, Charlzell, Chaz, Chick, Chip, Chuck

CHARLIE (German, English) a familiar form of Charles.
Charle, Charlee, Charley, Charli, Charly

CHARLTON (English) a form of Carlton.
Charlesten, Charleston, Charleton, Charlotin

CHARRO (Spanish) cowboy.

CHASE (French) hunter.
Chace, Chaise, Chasen, Chason, Chass, Chasse, Chastan, Chasten, Chastin, Chastinn, Chaston, Chasyn, Chayse

CHASKA (Sioux) first-born son.

CHAUNCEY (English) chancellor; church official.
Chan, Chance, Chancey, Chaunce, Chauncei, Chauncy, Chaunecy, Chaunesy, Chaunszi

CHAVEZ (Hispanic) a surname used as a first name.

Chavaz, Chaves, Chaveze, Chavies, Chavis, Chavius, Chevez, Cheveze, Cheviez, Chevious, Chevis, Chivass, Chivez

CHAYSE (French) an alternate form of Chase.
Chaysea, Chaysen, Chayson, Chaysten

CHAYTON (Lakota) falcon.

CHAZ (English) a familiar form of Charles.
Chas, Chasz, Chaze, Chazwick, Chazy, Chazz, Chez

CHÉ (Spanish) a familiar form of José. History: Ché Guevarra was a revolutionary who fought at Fidel Castro's side in Cuba.
Chay

CHECHA (Spanish) a familiar form of Jacob.

CHECHE (Spanish) a familiar form of Joseph.

CHEN (Chinese) great, tremendous.

CHENCHO (Spanish) a familiar form of Lawrence.

CHEPE (Spanish) a familiar form of Joseph.
Cepito

CHEROKEE (Cherokee) people of a different speech.
Cherrakee

CHESMU (Native American) gritty.

CHESTER (English) a short form of Rochester.
Ches, Cheslav, Cheston, Chet

CHET (English) a short form of Chester.
Chett, Chette

CHEUNG (Chinese) good luck.

CHEVALIER (French) horseman, knight.
Chev, Chevy

CHEVY (French) a familiar form of Chevalier. Geography: Chevy Chase is a town in Maryland. Culture: a short form of Chevrolet, an American automobile.
Chev, Chevey, Chevi, Chevie, Chevvy, Chewy

CHEYENNE (Cheyenne) a tribal name.
Chayann, Chayanne, Cheyeenne, Cheyene, Chyenne, Shayan

CHI (Chinese) younger generation. (Nigerian) personal guardian angel.

CHICK (English) a familiar form of Charles.
Chic, Chickie, Chicky

CHICO (Spanish) boy.

CHIK (Gypsy) earth.

CHIKE (Ibo) God's power.

CHIKO (Japanese) arrow; pledge.

CHILO (Spanish) a familiar form of Francisco.

CHILTON (English) farm by the spring.
Chil, Chill, Chillton, Chilt

CHIM (Vietnamese) bird.

CHINUA (Ibo) God's blessing.
Chino, Chinou

CHIOKE (Ibo) gift of God.

CHIP (English) a familiar form of Charles.
Chipman, Chipper

CHIRAM (Hebrew) exalted; noble.

CHRIS (Greek) a short form of Christian, Christopher. See also Kris.
Chriss, Christ, Chrys, Cris, Crist

CHRISTAIN (Greek) an alternate form of Christian.
Christai, Christan, Christane, Christaun, Christein

CHRISTIAN (Greek) follower of Christ; anointed. See also Jaan, Kerstan, Khristian, Kit, Krister, Kristian, Krystian.
Chretien, Chris, Christa, Christain, Christé, Christen, Christensen, Christiaan, Christiana, Christiane, Christiann, Christianna, Christianno, Christiano, Christianos, Christien, Christin, Christino, Christion, Christon, Christos, Christyan, Christyon, Chritian, Chrystian, Cristian, Crystek

CHRISTIEN (Greek) an alternate form of Christian.
Christienne, Christinne, Chrystien

CHRISTOFER (Greek) an alternate form of Christopher.
Christafer, Christafur, Christefor, Christerfer, Christifer, Christoffer, Christofher, Christofper, Chrystofer

CHRISTOFF (Russian) a form of Christopher.
Chrisof, Christif, Christof, Cristofe

CHRISTOPHE (French) a form of Christopher.
Christoph

CHRISTOPHER (Greek) Christ-bearer. Religion: the patron saint of travelers and drivers. See also Kester, Kit, Kristopher, Risto, Stoffel, Tobal, Topher.
Chris, Chrisopherson, Christapher, Christepher, Christerpher, Christhoper, Christipher, Christobal, Christofer, Christoff, Christoforo, Christoher, Christopehr, Christoper, Christophe, Christopherr, Christophor, Christophoros, Christophr, Christophre, Christophyer, Christophyr, Christorpher, Christos, Christovao, Christpher, Christphere, Christphor, Christpor, Christrpher, Chrystopher, Cristobal

CHRISTOPHOROS (Greek) an alternate form of Christopher.
Christoforo, Christoforos, Christophor, Christophorus, Christphor, Cristoforo, Cristopher

CHRISTOS (Greek) an alternate form of Christopher. See also Khristos.

CHUCHO (Hebrew) a familiar form of Jesus.

CHUCK (American) a familiar form of Charles.
Chuckey, Chuckie, Chucky

CHUI (Swahili) leopard.

CHUL (Korean) firm.

CHUMA (Ibo) having many beads, wealthy. (Swahili) iron.

CHUMINGA (Spanish) a familiar form of Dominic.
Chumin

CHUMO (Spanish) a familiar form of Thomas.

CHUN (Chinese) spring.

CHUNG (Chinese) intelligent.
Chungo, Chuong

CHURCHILL (English) church on the hill. History: Sir Winston Churchill served as British prime minister and won a Nobel Prize for literature.

CIAN (Irish) ancient.
Céin, Cianán, Kian

CICERO (Latin) chickpea. History: a famous Roman orator and statesman.
Cicerón

CID (Spanish) lord. History: an eleventh-century Spanish soldier and national hero.
Cyd

CIQALA (Dakota) little.

CIRRILLO (Italian) a form of Cyril.
Cirilio, Cirillo, Cirilo, Ciro

CISCO (Spanish) a short form of Francisco.

CLANCY (Irish) red-headed fighter.
Clancey, Claney

CLARE (Latin) a short form of Clarence.
Clair, Clarey, Clary

CLARENCE (Latin) clear; victorious.
Clarance, Clare, Clarrance, Clarrence, Clearence

CLARK (French) cleric; scholar.
Clarke, Clerc, Clerk

CLAUDE (Latin, French) lame.
Claud, Claudan, Claudel, Claudell, Claudey, Claudi, Claudian, Claudianus, Claudie, Claudien, Claudin, Claudio, Claudis, Claudius, Claudy

CLAUDIO (Italian) a form of Claude.

CLAUS (German) a short form of Nicholas. See also Klaus.
Claas, Claes, Clause

CLAY (English) clay pit. A short form of Clayborne, Clayton.
Klay

CLAYBORNE (English) brook near the clay pit.
Claibern, Claiborn, Claiborne, Claibrone, Clay, Claybon, Clayborn, Claybourn, Claybourne, Clayburn, Clebourn

CLAYTON (English) town built on clay.
Clay, Clayten, Cleighton, Cleyton, Clyton, Klayton

CLEARY (Irish) learned.

CLEAVON (English) cliff.
Clavin, Clavion, Clavon, Clavone, Clayvon, Claywon, Clévon, Clevonn, Clyvon

CLEM (Latin) a short form of Clement.
Cleme, Clemmy, Clim

CLEMENT (Latin) merciful. Bible: a disciple of Paul. See also Klement, Menz.
Clem, Clemens, Clément, Clemente, Clementius, Clemmons

CLEMENTE (Italian, Spanish) a form of Clement.
Clemento, Clemenza

CLEON (Greek) famous.
Kleon

CLETUS (Greek) illustrious. History: a Roman pope and martyr.
Cleatus, Cledis, Cleotis, Clete, Cletis

CLEVELAND (English) land of cliffs.
Cleaveland, Cleavland, Cleavon, Cleve, Clevelend, Clevelynn, Clevey, Clevie, Clevon

CLIFF (English) a short form of Clifford, Clifton.
Clif, Clift, Clive, Clyff, Clyph, Kliff

CLIFFORD (English) cliff at the river crossing.
Cliff, Cliford, Clyfford, Klifford

CLIFTON (English) cliff town.
Cliff, Cliffton, Clift, Cliften, Clyfton

CLINT (English) a short form of Clinton.
Klint

CLINTON (English) hill town.
Clenten, Clint, Clinten, Clintion, Clintton, Clynton, Klinton

CLIVE (English) an alternate form of Cliff.
Cleve, Clivans, Clivens, Clyve, Klyve

CLOVIS (German) famous soldier. See also Louis.

CLUNY (Irish) meadow.

CLYDE (Welsh) warm. (Scottish) Geography: a river in Scotland.
Cly, Clywd, Klyde

COBY (Hebrew) a familiar form of Jacob.
Cob, Cobby, Cobe, Cobey, Cobi, Cobia, Cobie

COCHISE (Apache) hardwood. History: a famous Apache warrior and chief.

COCO (French) a familiar form of Jacques.
Coko, Koko

CODEY (English) an alternate form of Cody.
Coday

CODI, Codie (English) alternate forms of Cody.
Coadi, Codea

CODY (English) cushion. History: William Cody (Buffalo Bill) was a sharpshooter and showman in the American "Wild" West. See also Kody.
Coady, Coddy, Code, Codee, Codell, Codey, Codi, Codiak, Codie, Coedy

COFFIE (Ewe) born on Friday.

COLA (Italian) a familiar form of Nicholas, Nicola.
Colas

COLAR (French) a form of Nicholas.

COLBERT (English) famous seafarer.
Cole, Colt, Colvert, Culbert

COLBY (English) dark; dark haired.
Colbey, Colbi, Colbie, Colbin, Colebee, Coleby, Collby, Kolby

COLE (Greek) a short form of Nicholas. (Latin) cabbage farmer. (English) a short form of Coleman.
Colet, Coley, Colie, Kole

COLEMAN (Latin) cabbage farmer. (English) coal miner.
Cole, Colemann, Colm, Colman, Koleman

COLIN (Greek) a short form of Nicholas. (Irish) young cub.
Cailean, Colan, Cole, Colen, Coleon, Colinn, Collin, Colyn, Kolin

COLLEY (English) black haired; swarthy.
Colee, Collie, Collis

COLLIER (English) miner.
Colier, Collayer, Collie, Collyer, Colyer

COLLIN (Scottish) a form of Colin, Collins.
Collan, Collen, Collian, Collon, Collyn

COLLINS (Greek) son of Colin. (Irish) holly.
Collin, Collis

COLSON (Greek, English) son of Nicholas.
Colsen, Coulson

COLT (English) young horse; frisky. A short form of Colter, Colton.
Colte

COLTEN (English) an alternate form of Colton.

COLTER (English) herd of colts.
Colt

COLTON (English) coal town.
Colt, Coltan, Colten, Coltin, Coltinn, Coltn, Coltrane, Colttan, Coltton, Coltun, Coltyn, Coltyne, Kolton

COLUMBA (Latin) dove.
Coim, Colum, Columbia, Columbus

COLWYN (Welsh) Geography: a river in Wales.
Colwin, Colwinn

COMAN (Arabic) noble. (Irish) bent.
Comán

CONALL (Irish) high, mighty.
Conal, Connal, Connel, Connell, Connelly, Connolly

CONAN (Irish) praised; exalted. (Scottish) wise.
Conant, Conary, Connen, Connie, Connon, Connor, Conon

CONARY (Irish) an alternate form of Conan.
Conaire

CONLAN (Irish) hero.
Conlen, Conley, Conlin, Conlyn

CONNER (Irish) an alternate form of Connor.
Connar, Connary, Conneer, Connery, Konner

CONNIE (English, Irish) a familiar form of Conan, Conrad, Constantine, Conway.
Con, Conn, Conney, Conny

CONNOR (Scottish) wise. (Irish) an alternate form of Conan.
Conner, Connoer, Connory, Connyr, Conor, Konner, Konnor

CONOR (Irish) an alternate form of Connor.
Conar, Coner, Conour, Konner

CONRAD (German) brave counselor.
Connie, Conrade, Conrado, Corrado, Konrad

CONROY (Irish) wise.
Conry, Roy

CONSTANT (Latin) a short form of Constantine.

CONSTANTINE (Latin) firm, constant. History: Constantine the Great was one of the most famous Roman emperors. See also Dinos, Konstantin, Stancio.
Connie, Constadine, Constandine, Constandios, Constanstine, Constant, Constantin, Constantino, Constantinos, Constantios, Costa

CONWAY (Irish) hound of the plain.
Connie, Conwy

COOK (English) cook.
Cooke

COOPER (English) barrel maker. See also Keiffer.
Coop, Couper

CORBETT (Latin) raven.
Corbbitt, Corbet, Corbette, Corbit, Corbitt

CORBIN (Latin) raven.
Corban, Corben, Corbey, Corbie, Corbon, Corby, Corbyn, Korbin

CORCORAN (Irish) ruddy.

CORDARO (Spanish) an alternate form of Cordero.
Coradaro, Cordairo, Cordara, Cordarel, Cordarell, Cordarelle, Cordareo, Cordarin, Cordario, Cordarion, Cordarious, Cordarius, Cordarrel, Cordarrell, Cordarris, Cordarrius, Cordarro, Cordarrol, Cordarus, Cordarryl, Cordaryal, Corddarro, Corrdarl

CORDELL (French) rope maker.
Cord, Cordae, Cordale, Corday, Cordeal, Cordeil, Cordel, Cordele, Cordelle, Cordie, Cordy, Kordell

CORDERO (Spanish) little lamb.
Cordaro, Cordeal, Cordeara, Cordearo, Cordeiro, Cordelro, Corder, Cordera, Corderall, Corderias, Corderious, Corderral, Corderro, Corderryn, Corderun, Corderus, Cordiaro, Cordierre, Cordy, Corrderio

COREY (Irish) hollow. See also Korey, Kory.
Core, Coreaa, Coree, Cori, Corian, Corie, Corio, Correy, Corria, Corrie, Corry, Corrye, Cory

CORMAC (Irish) raven's son. History: a third-century king of Ireland who founded schools.
Cormack, Cormick

CORNELIUS (Greek) cornel tree. (Latin) horn colored. See also Kornel, Kornelius, Nelek.
Carnelius, Conny, Cornealous, Corneili, Corneilius, Corneilus, Corneliaus, Cornelious, Cornelias, Cornelis, Corneliu, Cornell, Cornellious, Cornellis, Cornellius, Cornelous, Corneluis, Cornelus, Corney, Cornie, Cornielius, Corniellus, Corny, Cournelius, Cournelyous, Nelius, Nellie

CORNELL (French) a form of Cornelius.
Carnell, Cornall, Corneil, Cornel, Cornelio, Corney, Cornie, Corny, Nellie

CORNWALLIS (English) from Cornwall.

CORRADO (Italian) a form of Conrad.
Carrado

CORRIGAN (Irish) spearman.
Carrigan, Carrigen, Corrigon, Corrigun, Korrigan

CORRIN (Irish) spear carrier.
Corin, Corion

CORRY (Latin) a form of Corey.

CORT (German) bold. (Scandinavian) short. (English) a short form of Courtney.
Corte, Cortie, Corty, Kort

CORTEZ (Spanish) conqueror. History: Hernando Cortez was an explorer who conquered the Aztecs in Mexico.
Cartez, Cortes, Cortis, Cortize, Courtes, Courtez, Curtez, Kortez

CORWIN (English) heart's companion; heart's delight.
Corwinn, Corwyn, Corwynn, Corwynne

CORY (Latin) a form of Corey. (French) a familiar form of Cornell.
Corye

CORYDON (Greek) helmet, crest.
Coridon, Corradino, Cory, Coryden, Coryell

COSGROVE (Irish) victor, champion.

COSMO (Greek) orderly; harmonious; universe.
Cos, Cosimo, Cosme, Cosmé, Cozmo, Kosmo

COSTA (Greek) a short form of Constantine.
Costandinos, Costantinos, Costas, Costes

COTY (French) slope, hillside.
Cote, Cotee, Cotey, Coti, Cotie, Cotty, Cotye

COURTLAND (English) court's land.
Court, Courtlan, Courtlana, Courtlandt, Courtlin, Courtlind, Courtlon, Courtlyn, Kourtland

COURTNEY (English) court.
Cort, Cortnay, Cortne, Cortney, Court, Courten, Courtenay, Courteney, Courtnay, Courtnee, Curt, Kortney

COWAN (Irish) hillside hollow.
Coe, Coven, Covin, Cowen, Cowey, Cowie

COY (English) woods.
Coye, Coyie, Coyt

COYLE (Irish) leader in battle.

COYNE (French) modest.
Coyan

CRADDOCK (Welsh) love.
Caradoc, Caradog

CRAIG (Irish, Scottish) crag; steep rock.
Crag, Craige, Craigen, Craigery, Craigh, Craigon, Creag, Creg, Cregan, Cregg, Creig, Creigh, Criag, Kraig

CRANDALL (English) crane's valley.
Cran, Crandal, Crandel, Crandell, Crendal

CRAWFORD (English) ford where crows fly.
Craw, Crow, Ford

CREED (Latin) belief.
Creedon

CREIGHTON (English) town near the rocks.
Cray, Crayton, Creighm, Creight, Creighto, Crichton

CREPIN (French) a form of Crispin.

CRISPIN (Latin) curly haired.
Crepin, Cris, Crispian, Crispien, Crispino, Crispo, Krispin

CRISTIAN (Greek) an alternate form of Christian.
Crétien, Cristean, Cristhian, Cristiano, Cristien, Cristino, Cristle, Criston, Cristos, Cristy, Cristyan, Crystek, Crystian

CRISTOBAL (Greek) an alternate form of Christopher.
Cristóbal, Cristoval, Cristovao

CRISTOFORO (Italian) a form of Christopher.
Cristofor

CRISTOPHER (Greek) an alternate form of Christopher.
Cristaph, Cristhofer, Cristifer, Cristofer, Cristoph, Cristophe, Crystapher, Crystifer

CROFTON (Irish) town with cottages.

CROMWELL (English) crooked spring, winding spring.

CROSBY (Scandinavian) shrine of the cross.
Crosbey, Crosbie, Cross

CROSLEY (English) meadow of the cross.
Cross

CROWTHER (English) fiddler.

CRUZ (Portuguese, Spanish) cross.
Cruze, Kruz

CRYSTEK (Polish) a form of Christian.

CSABA (Hungarian) Geography: a city in southwestern Hungary.

CULLEN (Irish) handsome.
Cull, Cullan, Cullie, Cullin

CULLEY (Irish) woods.
Cullie, Cully

CULVER (English) dove.
Colver, Cull, Cullie, Cully

CUNNINGHAM (Irish) village of the milk pail.

CURRAN (Irish) hero.
Curan, Curon, Curr, Curren, Currey, Curri, Currie, Currin, Curry

CURRITO (Spanish) a form of Curtis.
Curcio

CURT (Latin) a short form of Courtney, Curtis. See also Kurt.

CURTIS (Latin) enclosure. (French) courteous. See also Kurtis.
Curio, Currito, Curt, Curtice, Curtiss, Curtus

CUTHBERT (English) brilliant.

CUTLER (English) knife maker.
Cut, Cuttie, Cutty

CY (Persian) a short form of Cyrus.

CYLE (Irish) an alternate form of Kyle.

CYPRIAN (Latin) from the island of Cyprus.
Ciprian, Cipriano, Ciprien, Cyprien

CYRANO (Greek) from Cyrene, an ancient Greek city. Literature: *Cyrano de Bergerac* is a play by Edmond Rostand about a

Cyrano *(cont.)*
great swordsman whose large nose prevented him from pursuing the woman he loved.

CYRIL (Greek) lordly. See also Kiril.
Cerek, Cerel, Cyrell, Ceril, Ciril, Cirillo, Cirrillo, Cyra, Cyrel, Cyrell, Cyrelle, Cyrill, Cyrille, Cyrillus, Syrell, Syril

CYRUS (Persian) sun. Historial: Cyrus the Great was a king in ancient Persia. See also Kir.
Ciro, Cy, Cyress, Cyris, Cyriss, Cyruss, Syris, Syrus

DABI (Basque) a form of David.

DABIR (Arabic) tutor.

DACEY (Latin) from Dacia, an area now in Romania. (Irish) southerner.
Dace, Dache, Dacian, Dacias, Dacio, Dacy, Daicey, Daicy

DADA (Yoruba) curly haired.
Dadi

DAEGEL (English) from Daegel, England.

DAELEN (English) an alternate form of Dale.
Daelan, Daelin, Daelon, Daelyn, Daelyne

DAEMON (Greek) an alternate form of Damian.
Daemean, Daemeon, Daemien, Daemin, Daemion, Daemyen

DAEQUAN (American) an alternate form of Daquan.
Daequane, Daequon, Daequone, Daeqwan

DAESHAWN (American) a combination of the prefix Da + Shawn.
Daesean, Daeshaun, Daeshon, Daeshun, Daisean, Daishaun, Daishawn, Daishon, Daishoun

DAEVON (American) an alternate form of Davon.
Daevion, Daevohn, Daevonne, Daevonte, Daevontey

DAFYDD (Welsh) a form of David.
Dafyd

DAG (Scandinavian) day; bright.
Daeg, Daegan, Dagen, Dagny, Deegan

DAGAN (Hebrew) corn; grain.
Daegan, Daegon, Dagen, Dageon, Dagon

DAGWOOD (English) shining forest.

DAI (Japanese) big.

DAIMIAN (Greek) an alternate form of Damian.
Daiman, Daimean, Daimen, Daimeon, Daimeyon, Daimien, Daimin, Daimion, Daimyan

DAIMON (Greek, Latin) an alternate form of Damon.
Daimone

DAIQUAN (American) an alternate form of Dajuan.

Daekwaun, Daekwon, Daiqone, Daiqua, Daiquane, Daiquawn, Daiquon, Daiqwan, Daiqwon

DAIVON (American) an alternate form of Davon.
Daivain, Daivion, Daivonn, Daivonte, Daiwan

DAJON (American) an alternate form of Dajuan.
Dajean, Dajiawn, Dajin, Dajion, Dajn, Dajohn, Dajonae

DAJUAN (American) a combination of the prefix Da + Juan. See also Dejuan.
Daejon, Daejuan, Daiquan, Dajon, Da Jon, Da-Juan, Dajwan, Dajwoun, Dakuan, Dakwan, Dawan, Dawaun, Dawawn, Dawon, Dawoyan, Dijuan, Diuan, Dujuan, D'Juan, D'juan, Dwaun

DAKARAI (Shona) happy.
Dakairi, Dakar, Dakaraia, Dakari, Dakarri

DAKODA (Dakota) an alternate form of Dakota.
Dacoda, Dacodah, Dakodah, Dakodas

DAKOTA (Dakota) friend; partner; tribal name.
Dac, Dack, Dackota, Dacota, DaCota, Dak, Dakcota, Dakkota, Dakoata, Dakoda, Dakotah, Dakotha, Dakotta, Dekota

DAKOTAH (Dakota) an alternate form of Dakota.
Dakottah

DAKSH (Hindi) efficient.

DALAL (Sanskrit) broker.

DALBERT (English) bright, shining. See also Delbert.

DALE (English) dale, valley.
Dael, Daelen, Dal, Dalen, Daley, Dalibor, Dallan, Dallin, Dallyn, Daly, Dayl, Dayle

DALEN (English) an alternate form of Dale.
Dailin, Dalaan, Dalan, Dalane, Daleon, Dalian, Dalibor, Dalione, Dallan, Dalon, Daylan, Daylen, Daylin, Daylon

DALEY (Irish) assembly. (English) a familiar form of Dale.
Daily, Daly, Dawley

DALLAN (English) an alternate form of Dale.
Dallen, Dallon

DALLAS (Scottish) Geography: a town in Scotland; a city in Texas.
Dal, Dalieass, Dall, Dalles, Dallis, Dalys, Dellis

DALLIN, Dallyn (English) alternate forms of Dale.
Dalin, Dalyn

DALSTON (English) Daegel's place.
Dalis, Dallon

DALTON (English) town in the valley.
Dal, Dalaton, Dallton, Dalt, Daltan, Dalten, Daltin, Daltyn, Daulton, Delton

DALVIN (English) an alternate form of Delvin.
Dalven, Dalvon, Dalvyn

DALZIEL (Scottish) small field.

DAMAR (American) a short form of Damarcus, Damario.
Damare, Damari, Damarre, Damauri

DAMARCUS (American) a combination of the prefix Da + Marcus.
Damacus, Damar, Damarco, Damarcue, Damarick, Damark, Damarkco, Damarkis, Damarko, Damarkus, Damarques, Damarquez, Damarquis, Damarrco

DAMARIO (American) a combination of the prefix Da + Mario.
Damar, Damarea, Damareus, Damaria, Damarie, Damarino, Damarion, Damarious, Damaris, Damarius, Damarrea, Damarrion, Damarrious, Damarrius, Damaryo, Dameris, Damerius

DAMEK (Slavic) a form of Adam.
Damick, Damicke

DAMEON (Greek) an alternate form of Damian.
Damein, Dameion, Dameone

DAMETRIUS (Greek) an alternate form of Demetrius.
Dametri, Dametries, Dametrious, Damitri, Damitric, Damitrie, Damitrious, Damitrius

DAMIAN (Greek) tamer; soother.
Daemon, Daimian, Damaiaon, Damaian, Damaien, Damain, Damaine, Damaion, Damani, Damanni, Damaun, Damayon, Dame, Damean, Dameon, Damián, Damiane, Damiann, Damiano, Damianos, Damien, Damion, Damiyan, Damján, Damyan, Daymian, Dema, Demyan

DAMIEN (Greek) an alternate form of Damian. Religion: Father Damien spent his life serving the leper colony on Molokai island, Hawaii.
Daemien, Daimien, Damie, Damienne, Damyen

DAMION (Greek) an alternate form of Damian.
Damieon, Damiion, Damin, Damine, Damionne, Damiyon, Dammion, Damyon

DAMON (Greek) constant, loyal. (Latin) spirit, demon.
Daemen, Daemon, Daemond, Daimon, Daman, Damen, Damond, Damone, Damoni, Damonn, Damonni, Damonta, Damontae, Damonte, Damontez, Damontis, Damyn, Daymon, Daymond

DAN (Hebrew) a short form of Daniel. (Vietnamese) yes.
Dahn, Danh, Danne

DANA (Scandinavian) from Denmark.
Dain, Daina, Dayna

DANDIN (Hindi) holy man.

DANDRÉ (French) a combination of the prefix De + André.
D'André, Dandrae, D'andrea, Dandras, Dandray, Dandre, Dondrea

DANE (English) from Denmark. See also Halden.
Dain, Daine, Danie, Dayne, Dhane

DANEK (Polish) a form of Daniel.

DANFORTH (English) a form of Daniel.

DANIAL (Hebrew) an alternate form of Daniel.
Danal, Daneal, Danieal, Daniyal, Dannial

DANICK, Dannick (Slavic) familiar forms of Daniel.
Danek, Danieko, Danik, Danika, Danyck

DANIEL (Hebrew) God is my judge. Bible: a great Hebrew prophet. See also Danno, Kanaiela.
Dacso, Dainel, Dan, Daneel, Daneil, Danek, Danel, Danforth, Danial, Danick, Dániel, Daniël, Daniele, Danielius, Daniell, Daniels, Danielson, Danilo, Daniyel, Dan'l, Dannel, Dannick, Danniel, Dannil, Danno, Danny, Dano, Danukas, Dany, Danyel, Danyell, Daoud, Dasco, Dayne, Deniel, Doneal, Doniel, Donois, Dusan, Nelo

DANIELE (Hebrew) an alternate form of Daniel.
Danile, Danniele

DANILO (Slavic) a form of Daniel.
Danielo, Danil, Danila, Danilka, Danylo

DANIOR (Gypsy) born with teeth.

DANLADI (Hausa) born on Sunday.

DANNO (Hebrew) a familiar form of Daniel. (Japanese) gathering in the meadow.
Dannon, Dano

DANNON (American) a form of Danno.
Daenan, Daenen, Dainon, Danaan, Danen, Danon

DANNY, Dany (Hebrew) familiar forms of Daniel.
Daney, Dani, Dannee, Danney, Danni, Dannie, Dannye

DANO (Czech) a form of Daniel.
Danko, Danno

DANTE, Danté (Latin) lasting, enduring.
Danatay, Danaté, Dant, Dantae, Dantay, Dantee, Dauntay, Dauntaye, Daunté, Dauntrae, Deante, Dontae, Donté

DANTRELL (American) a combination of Dante + Darell.
Dantrel, Dantrey, Dantril, Dantyrell, Dontrell

DANYEL (Hebrew) an alternate form of Daniel.
Danya, Danyal, Danyale, Danyele, Danyell, Danyiel, Danyl, Danyle, Danylets, Danylo, Donyell

DAOUD (Arabic) a form of David.
Daudi, Daudy, Dauod, Dawud

DAQUAN (American) a combination of the prefix Da + Quan.
Daequan, Daqon, Daquain, Daquaine, Da'quan, Daquandre, Daquandrey, Daquane, Daquann, Daquantae, Daquante, Daquarius, Daquaun, Daquawn, Daquin, Daquon, Daquone, Daquwon, Daqwain, Daqwan, Daqwane, Daqwann, Daqwon, Daqwone, Dayquan, Dequain, Dequan, Dequann, Dequaun

DAR (Hebrew) pearl.

DARA (Cambodian) stars.

DARAN (Irish) an alternate form of Darren.
Darann, Darawn, Darian, Darran, Dayran, Deran

DARBY (Irish) free. (English) deer park.
Dar, Darb, Darbee, Darbey, Darbie, Derby

DARCY (Irish) dark. (French) from Arcy.
Dar, Daray, D'Aray, Darce, Darcee, Darcel, Darcey, Darcio, D'Arcy, Darsey, Darsy

DAREH (Persian) wealthy.

DARELL (English) a form of Darrell.
Darall, Daralle, Dareal, Darel, Darelle, Darral, Darrall

DAREN (Irish) an alternate form of Darren. (Hausa) born at night.
Dare, Dayren, Dheren

DARIAN, Darrian (Irish) alternative forms of Darren.
Daryan

DARICK (German) an alternate form of Derek.
Darek, Daric, Darico, Darieck, Dariek, Darik, Daryk

DARIEN, Darrien (Irish) alternative forms of Darren.

DARIN (Irish) an alternate form of Darren.
Daryn, Darynn, Dayrin, Dearin, Dharin

DARIO (Spanish) affluent.

DARION, Darrion (Irish) alternative forms of Darren.
Daryeon, Daryon

DARIUS (Greek) wealthy.
Dairus, Dare, Darieus, Darioush, Dariuse, Dariush, Dariuss, Dariusz, Darrius

DARNELL (English) hidden place.
Dar, Darn, Darnall, Darneal, Darneil, Darnel, Darnelle, Darnyell, Darnyll

DARON (Irish) an alternate form of Darren.
Daeron, Dairon, Darone, Daronn, Darroun, Dayron, Dearon, Dharon, Diron

DARRELL (French) darling, beloved; grove of oak trees.
Dare, Darel, Darell, Darral, Darrel, Darrill, Darrol, Darryl, Derrell

DARREN (Irish) great. (English) small; rocky hill.
Daran, Dare, Daren, Darian, Darien, Darin, Darion, Daron, Darran, Darrian, Darrien, Darrience, Darrin, Darrion, Darron, Darryn, Darun, Daryn, Dearron, Deren, Dereon, Derren, Derron

DARRICK (German) an alternate form of Derek.
Darrec, Darrek, Darric, Darrik, Darryk

DARRIN (Irish) an alternate form of Darren.

DARRION (Irish) an alternate form of Darren.
Dairean, Dairion, Darian, Darien, Darion, Darrian, Darrien, Darrione, Darriyun, Derrian, Derrion

DARRIUS (Greek) an alternate form of Darius.
Darreus, Darrias, Darrious, Darris, Darriuss, Darrus, Darryus, Derrious, Derris, Derrius

DARRON (Irish) an alternate form of Darren.
Darriun, Darroun

DARRYL (French) darling, beloved; grove of oak trees. An alternate form of Darrell.
Dahrll, Darryle, Darryll, Daryl, Daryle, Daryll, Derryl

DARSHAN (Hindi) god; godlike. Religion: another name for the Hindu god Shiva.
Darshaun, Darshon

DARTON (English) deer town.
Dartel, Dartrel

DARWIN (English) dear friend. History: Charles Darwin was the naturalist who established the theory of evolution.
Darvin, Darvon, Darwyn, Derwin, Derwynn, Durwin

DARYL (French) an alternate form of Darryl.
Darel, Daril, Darl, Darly, Daryell, Daryle, Daryll, Darylle, Daroyl

DASAN (Pomo) leader of the bird clan.
Dassan

DASHAWN (American) a combination of the prefix Da + Shawn.
Dasean, Dashan, Dashane, Dashante, Dashaun, Dashaunte, Dashean, Dashon, Dashonnie, Dashonte, Dashuan, Dashun, Dashwan, Dayshawn

DAUID (Swahili) a form of David.

DAULTON (English) an alternate form of Dalton.

DAVANTE (American) an alternate form of Davonte.
Davanta, Davantay, Davinte

DAVARIS (American) a combination of Dave + Darius.
Davario, Davarious, Davarius, Davarrius, Davarus

DAVE (Hebrew) a short form of David, Davis.

DAVEY (Hebrew) a familiar form of David.
Davee, Davi, Davie, Davy

DAVID (Hebrew) beloved. Bible: the first king of Israel. See also Dov, Havika, Kawika, Taaveti, Taffy, Tevel.
Dabi, Daevid, Dafydd, Dai, Daivid, Daoud, Dauid, Dav, Dave, Daved, Daveed, Daven, Davey, Davidde, Davide, Davidek, Davido, Davon, Davoud, Davyd, Dawid, Dawit, Dawud, Dayvid, Dodya, Dov

DAVIN (Scandinavian) brilliant Finn.
Daevin, Davion, Davon, Davyn, Dawan, Dawin, Dawine, Dayvon, Deavan, Deaven

DAVION (American) a form of Davin.
Davione, Davionne, Daviyon, Davyon, Deaveon

DAVIS (Welsh) son of David.
Dave, Davidson, Davies, Davison

DAVON (American) a form of Davin.
Daevon, Daivon, Davon, Davone, Davonn, Davonne, Deavon, Deavone, Devon

DAVONTE (American) a combination of Davon + the suffix -te.
Davante, Davonnte, Davonta, Davontae, Davontah, Davontai, Davontay, Davontaye, Davontea, Davontee, Davonti

DAWAN (American) a form of Davin.
Dawann, Dawante, Dawaun, Dawayne, Dawon, Dawone, Dawoon, Dawyne, Dawyun

DAWIT (Ethiopian) a form of David.

DAWSON (English) son of David.
Dawsyn

DAX (French, English) water.

DAYLON (American) a form of Dillon.
Daylan, Daylen, Daylin, Daylun, Daylyn

DAYMIAN (Greek) an alternate form of Damian.
Daymayne, Daymen, Daymeon, Daymiane, Daymien, Daymin, Dayminn, Daymion, Daymn

DAYNE (Scandinavian) a form of Dane.
Dayn

DAYQUAN (American) an alternate form of of Daquan.
Dayquain, Dayquawane, Dayquin, Dayqwan

DAYSHAWN (American) an alternate form of of Dashawn.
Daysean, Daysen, Dayshaun, Dayshon, Dayson

DAYTON (English) day town; bright, sunny town.
Daeton, Daiton, Daythan, Daython, Daytona, Daytonn, Deyton

DAYVON (American) a form of Davin.
Dayven, Dayveon, Dayvin, Dayvion, Dayvonn

DE (Chinese) virtuous.

DEACON (Greek) one who serves.
Deke

DEAN (French) leader. (English) valley. See also Dino.
Deane, Deen, Dene, Deyn, Deyne

DEANDRE (French) a combination of the prefix De + André.
D'andre, D'andré, D'André, D'andrea, Deandra, Deandrae, Déandre, Deandré, De André, Deandrea, De Andrea, Deandres, Deandrey, Deaundera, Deaundra, Deaundray, Deaundre, De Aundre, Deaundrey, Deaundry, Deondre, Diandre, Dondre

DEANGELO (Italian) a combination of the prefix De + Angelo.
Dang, Dangelo, D'Angelo, Danglo, Deaengelo, Deangelio, Deangello, Déangelo, De Angelo, Deangilio, Deangleo, Deanglo, Deangulo, Diangelo, Di'angelo

DEANTE (Latin) an alternate form of Dante.
Deanta, Deantai, Deantay, Deanté, De Anté, Deanteé, Deaunta, Diantae, Diante, Diantey

DEANTHONY (Italian) a combination of the prefix De + Anthony.
D'anthony, Danton, Dianthony

DEARBORN (English) deer brook.
Dearbourn, Dearburne, Deaurburn, Deerborn

DECARLOS (Spanish) a combination of the prefix De + Carlos.
Dacarlos, Decarlo, Di'carlos

DECHA (Tai) strong.

DECIMUS (Latin) tenth.

DECLAN (Irish) man of prayer. Religion: Saint Declan was a fifth-century Irish bishop.
Deklan

DEDRICK (German) ruler of the people. See also Derek, Theodoric.
Deadrick, Deddrick, Dederick, Dedrek, Dedreko, Dedric, Dedrix, Dedrrick, Deedrick, Diedrich, Diedrick, Dietrich, Detrick

DEEMS (English) judge's child.

DEION (Greek) an alternate form of Dion.
Deione, Deionta, Deionte

DEJUAN (American) a combination of the prefix De + Juan. See also Dajuan.
Dejan, Dejon, Dejuane, Dejun, Dewan, Dewaun, Dewon, Dijaun, Djuan, D'Juan, Dujuan, Dujuane, D'Won

DEKEL (Hebrew, Arabic) palm tree, date tree.

DEKOTA (Dakota) an alternate form of Dakota.
Decoda, Dekoda, Dekodda, Dekotes

DEL (English) a short form of Delbert, Delvin, Delwin.

DELANEY (Irish) descendant of the challenger.
Delaine, Delainey, Delainy, Delan, Delane, Delanny, Delany

DELANO (French) nut tree. (Irish) dark.
Delanio, Delayno, Dellano

DELBERT (English) bright as day. See also Dalbert.
Bert, Del, Dilbert

DELFINO (Latin) dolphin.
Delfine

DÉLÌ (Chinese) virtuous.

DELL (English) small valley. A short form of Udell.

DELLING (Scandinavian) scintillating.

DELMAR (Latin) sea.
Dalmar, Dalmer, Delmare, Delmario, Delmarr, Delmer, Delmor, Delmore

DELON (American) a form of Dillon.
Deloin, Delone, Deloni, Delonne

DELROY (French) belonging to the king. See also Elroy, Leroy.
Delray, Delree, Delroi

DELSHAWN (American) a combination of Del + Shawn.
Delsean, Delshon, Delsin, Delson

DELSIN (Native American) he is so.
Delsy

DELTON (English) an alternate form of Dalton.
Delten, Deltyn

DELVIN (English) proud friend; friend from the valley.
Dalvin, Del, Delavan, Delvian, Delvon, Delvyn, Delwin

DELWIN (English) an alternate form of Delvin.
Dalwin, Dalwyn, Del, Dellwin, Dellwyn, Delwyn, Delwynn

DEMAN (Dutch) man.

DEMARCO (Italian) a combination of the prefix De + Marco.
Damarco, Demarcco, Demarceo, Demarcio, Demarkco, Demarkeo, Demarko, Demarquo, D'Marco

DEMARCUS (American) a combination of the prefix De + Marcus.
Damarcius, Damarcus, Demarces, Demarcis, Demarcius, Demarcos, Demarcuse, Demarkes, Demarkis, Demarkos, Demarkus, Demarqus, D'Marcus

DEMARIO (Italian) a combination of the prefix De + Mario.
Demarea, Demaree, Demareo, Demari, Demaria, Demariea, Demarion, Demarreio, Demariez, Demarious, Demaris, Demariuz, Demarrio, Demerio, Demerrio

DEMARIUS (American) a combination of the prefix De + Marius.

DEMARQUIS (American) a combination of the prefix De + Marquis.
Demarques, Demarquez, Demarqui

DEMBE (Luganda) peaceful.
Damba

DEMETRI, Demitri (Greek) short forms of Demetrius.
Dametri, Damitré, Demeter, Demetre, Demetrea, Demetriel, Demitre, Demitrie, Domotor

DEMETRIS (Greek) a short form of Demetrius.
Demeatric, Demeatrice, Demeatris, Demetres, Demetress, Demetric, Demetrice, Demetrick, Demetrics, Demetricus, Demetrik, Demitrez, Demitries, Demitris

DEMETRIUS (Greek) lover of the earth. Mythology: a follower of Demeter, the goddess of the harvest and fertility. See also Dimitri, Mimis, Mitsos.
Dametrius, Demeitrius, Demeterious, Demetreus, Demetri, Demetrias, Demetrio, Demetrios, Demetrious, Demetris, Demetriu, Demetrium, Demetrois, Demetruis, Demetrus, Demitirus, Demitri, Demitrias, Demitriu, Demitrius, Demitrus, Demtrius, Demtrus, Dimitri, Dimitrios, Dimitrius, Dmetrius, Dymek

DEMICHAEL (American) a combination of the prefix De + Michael.
Dumichael

DEMOND (Irish) a short form of Desmond.
Demonde, Demonds, Demone, Dumonde

DEMONT (French) mountain.
Démont, Demonta, Demontae, Demontay, Demontaz, Demonte, Demontez, Demontre

DEMORRIS (American) a combination of the prefix De + Morris.
Demoris, DeMorris, Demorus

DEMOS (Greek) people.
Demas, Demosthenes

DEMOTHI (Native American) talks while walking.

DEMPSEY (Irish) proud.
Demp, Demps, Dempsie, Dempsy

DEMPSTER (English) one who judges.
Demster

DENBY (Scandinavian) Geography: a Danish village.
Danby, Den, Denbey, Denney, Dennie, Denny

DENHAM (English) village in the valley.

DENHOLM (Scottish)
Geography: a town in
Scotland.

DENIS (Greek) an alternate
form of Dennis.
Denise, Deniz

DENLEY (English) meadow;
valley.
Denlie, Denly

DENMAN (English) man from
the valley.

DENNIS (Greek) Mythology: a
follower of Dionysius, the god
of wine. See also Dion, Nicho.
*Den, Dénes, Denies, Denis,
Deniz, Dennes, Dennet, Dennez,
Denny, Dennys, Denya, Denys,
Deon, Dinis*

DENNISON (English) son of
Dennis. See also Dyson,
Tennyson.
*Den, Denison, Denisson,
Dennyson*

DENNY (Greek) a familiar form
of Dennis.
Den, Denney, Dennie, Deny

DENTON (English) happy home.
Dent, Denten, Dentin

DENVER (English) green valley.
Geography: the capital of
Colorado.

DENZEL (Cornish) an alternate
form of Denzil.
*Danzel, Danzell, Dennzel,
Denzal, Denzale, Denzall,
Denzell, Denzelle, Denzle,
Denzsel*

DENZIL (Cornish) Geography: a
location in Cornwall, England.
*Dennzil, Dennzyl, Denzel,
Denzial, Denziel, Denzill,
Denzyel, Denzyl, Donzell*

DEON (Greek) an alternate form
of Dennis. See also Dion.
Deion, Deone, Deonn, Deonno

DEONDRE (French) an alter-
nate form of Deandre.
*Deiondray, Deiondre, Deondra,
Deondrae, Deondray, Deondré,
Deondrea, Deondree, Deondrei,
Deondrey, Diondra, Diondrae,
Diondre, Diondrey*

DEONTAE (American) a combi-
nation of the prefix De +
Dontae.
*Deonta, Deontai, Deontay,
Deontaye, Deonte, Deonté,
Deontea, Deonteya, Deonteye,
Deontia, Deontre, Dionte*

DEONTE, Deonté (American)
alternate forms of Deontae.
*D'Ante, Deante, Deontée,
Deontie*

DEONTRE (American) alternate
forms of Deontae.
*Deontrae, Deontrais, Deontray,
Deontrea, Deontrey, Deontrez,
Deontreze, Deontrus*

DEQUAN (American) a combi-
nation of the prefix De +
Quan.
*Dequain, Dequane, Dequann,
Dequante, Dequantez,
Dequantis, Dequaun,
Dequavius, Dequawn, Dequian,
Dequin, Dequine, Dequinn,
Dequion, Dequoin, Dequon,
Deqwan, Deqwon, Deqwone*

DERECK, Derick (German)
alternate forms of Derek.
*Derekk, Dericka, Derico, Deriek,
Derique, Deryck, Deryk, Deryke,
Detrek*

DEREK (German) ruler of the
people. A short form of
Theodoric. See also Dedrick,
Dirk.
*Darek, Darick, Darrick, Derak,
Dereck, Derecke, Derele, Deric,
Derick, Derik, Derk, Derke,
Derrek, Derrick, Deryek*

DERIC, Derik (German) alternate forms of Derek.
Deriek, Derikk

DERMOT (Hebrew) a short
form of Jeremiah. (Irish) free
from envy. (English) free. See
also Kermit.
*Der, Dermod, Dermott, Diarmid,
Diarmuid*

DERON (Hebrew) bird; free-
dom. (American) a combina-
tion of the prefix De + Ron.
*Daaron, Daron, Da-Ron, Darone,
Darron, Dayron, Dereon,
Deronn, Deronne, Derrin,
Derrion, Derron, Derronn,
Derronne, Derryn, Diron, Duron,
Durron, Dyron*

DEROR (Hebrew) lover of
freedom.
Derori, Derorie

DERREK (German) an alternate
form of Derek.
Derrec, Derreck

DERRELL (French) an alternate
form of Darrell.
*Derel, Derele, Derell, Derelle,
Derrel, Dérrell, Derriel, Derril,
Derrill, Deryl, Deryll*

DERREN (Irish) great. An alter-
nate form of Darren.
*Deren, Derran, Derraun,
Derreon, Derrian, Derrien,
Derrin, Derrion, Derron, Derryn,
Deryan, Deryn, Deryon*

DERRICK (German) ruler of the
people. An alternate form of
Derek.
Derric, Derrik, Derryck, Derryk

DERRY (Irish) redhead. Geography: a city in Northern Ireland.
Darrie, Darry, Derri, Derrie, Derrye, Dery

DERRYL (French) an alternate form of Darryl.
Deryl, Deryll

DERWARD (English) deer keeper.

DERWIN (English) an alternate form of Darwin.
Derwyn

DESEAN (American) a combination of the prefix De + Sean.
Dasean, D'Sean, Dusean

DESHANE (American) a combination of the prefix De + Shane.
Deshan, Deshayne

DESHAUN (American) a combination of the prefix De + Shaun.
Deshan, Deshane, Deshann, Deshaon, Deshaune, D'shaun, D'Shaun, Dushaun

DESHAWN (American) a combination of the prefix De + Shawn.
Dashaun, Dashawn, Deshauwn, Deshawan, Deshawon, Deshon, D'shawn, D'Shawn, Dushan, Dushawn

DESHEA (American) a combination of the prefix De + Shea.
Deshay

DÉSHÌ (Chinese) virtuous.

DESHON (American) an alternate form of Deshawn.
Deshondre, Deshone, Deshonn, Deshonte, Deshun, Deshunn

DESIDERIO (Spanish) desired.

DESMOND (Irish) from south Munster.
Demond, Des, Desi, Desimon, Desman, Desmand, Desmane, Desmen, Desmine, Desmon, Desmound, Desmund, Desmyn, Dezmon, Dezmond

DESTIN (French) destiny, fate.
Destan, Desten, Destine, Deston, Destry, Destyn

DESTRY (American) a form of Destin.
Destrey, Destrie

DETRICK (German) an alternate form of Dedrick.
Detrek, Detric, Detrich, Detrik, Detrix

DEVAN (Irish) an alternate form of Devin.
Devaan, Devain, Devane, Devann, Devean, Devun, Diwan

DEVANTE (American) a combination of Devan + the suffix -te.
Devanta, Devantae, Devantay, Devanté, Devantée, Devantez, Devanty, Devaughntae, Devaughnte, Devaunte, Deventae, Deventay, Devente, Divante

DEVAUGHN (American) a form of Devin.
Devaugh, Devaun

DEVAYNE (American) an alternate form of Dewayne.
Devain, Devaine, Devan, Devane, Devayn, Devein, Deveion

DEVEN (Hindi) for God. (Irish) an alternate form of Devin.
Deaven, Deiven, Devein, Devenn, Devven, Diven

DEVERELL (English) riverbank.

DEVIN (Irish) poet.
Deavin, Deivin, Dev, Devan, Devaughn, Deven, Devlyn, Devon, Devvin, Devy, Devyn, Dyvon

DEVINE (Latin) divine. (Irish) ox.
Davon, Devinn, Devon, Devyn, Devyne, Dewine

DEVLIN (Irish) brave, fierce.
Dev, Devlan, Devland, Devlen, Devlon, Devlyn

DEVON (Irish) an alternate form of Devin.
Deavon, Deivon, Deivone, Deivonne, Deveon, Deveone, Devion, Devoen, Devohn, Devonae, Devone, Devoni, Devonio, Devonn, Devonne, Devontaine, Devvon, Devvonne, Dewon, Dewone, Divon, Diwon

DEVONTA (American) a combination of Devon + the suffix -ta.
Deveonta, Devonnta, Devonntae, Devontae, Devontai, Devontay, Devontaye

DEVONTE (American) a combination of Devon + the suffix -te.
Deveonte, Devionte, Devonté, Devontea, Devontee, Devonti, Devontia, Devontre

DEVYN (Irish) an alternate form of Devin.
Devyin, Devynn, Devynne

DEWAYNE (Irish) an alternate form of Dwayne. (American) a combination of the prefix De + Wayne.
Deuwayne, Devayne, Dewain, Dewaine, Dewan, Dewane, Dewaun, Dewaune, Dewayen, Dewean, Dewon, Dewune

DEWEI (Chinese) highly virtuous.

DEWEY (Welsh) prized.
Dew, Dewi, Dewie

DEWITT (Flemish) blond.
Dewitt, Dwight, Wit

DEXTER (Latin) dexterous, adroit. (English) fabric dyer.
Daxter, Decca, Deck, Decka, Dekka, Dex, Dextar, Dextor, Dextrel, Dextron

DEZMON, Dezmond (Irish) alternate forms of Desmond.
Dezman, Dezmand, Dezmen, Dezmin

DIAMOND (English) brilliant gem; bright guardian.
Diaman, Diamanta, Diamante, Diamend, Diamenn, Diamont, Diamonta, Diamonte, Diamund, Dimond, Dimonta, Dimontae, Dimonte

DICK (German) a short form of Frederick, Richard.
Dic, Dicken, Dickens, Dickie, Dickon, Dicky, Dik

DICKRAN (Armenian) History: an ancient Armenian king.
Dicran, Dikran

DICKSON (English) son of Dick.
Dickenson, Dickerson, Dikerson, Diksan

DIDI (Hebrew) a familiar form of Jedidiah, Yedidyah.

DIDIER (French) desired, longed for. A masculine form of Desiree.

DIEDRICH (German) an alternate form of Dedrick, Dietrich.
Didrich, Didrick, Didrik, Diederick

DIEGO (Spanish) a form of Jacob, James.
Iago, Diaz, Jago

DIETBALD (German) an alternate form of Theobald.
Dietbalt, Dietbolt

DIETER (German) army of the people.
Deiter

DIETRICH (German) an alternate form of Dedrick.
Deitrich, Deitrick, Deke, Diedrich, Dietrick, Dierck, Dieter, Dieterich, Dieterick, Dietz

DIGBY (Irish) ditch town; dike town.

DILLAN (Irish) an alternate form of Dillon.
Dilan, Dillian, Dilun, Dilyan

DILLON (Irish) loyal, faithful. See also Dylan.
Daylon, Delon, Dil, Dill, Dillan, Dillen, Dillie, Dillin, Dillion, Dilly, Dillyn, Dilon, Dilyn, Dilynn

DILWYN (Welsh) shady place.
Dillwyn

DIMA (Russian) a familiar form of Vladimir.
Dimka

DIMITRI (Russian) a form of Demetrius.
Dimetra, Dimetri, Dimetric, Dimetrie, Dimitr, Dimitric, Dimitrie, Dimitrik, Dimitris, Dimitry, Dimmy, Dmitri, Dymitr, Dymitry

DIMITRIOS (Greek) an alternate form of Demetrius.
Dhimitrios, Dimitrius, Dimos, Dmitrios

DIMITRIUS (Greek) an alternate form of Demetrius.
Dimetrius, Dimitricus, Dimitrius, Dimetrus, Dmitrius

DINGBANG (Chinese) protector of the country.

DINH (Vietnamese) calm, peaceful.
Din

DINO (German) little sword. (Italian) a form of Dean.
Deano

DINOS (Greek) a familiar form of Constantine, Konstantin.

DINSMORE (Irish) fortified hill.
Dinnie, Dinny, Dinse

DIOGENES (Greek) honest. History: an ancient philosopher who searched the streets for an honest man.
Diogenese

DION (Greek) a short form of Dennis, Dionysus.
Deion, Deon, Dio, Dione, Dionigi, Dionis, Dionn, Dionne, Diontae, Dionte, Diontray

DIONTE (American) an alternate form of Deontae.
Diante, Dionta, Diontae, Diontay, Diontaye, Dionté, Diontea

DIONYSUS (Greek) celebration. Mythology: the god of wine.
Dion, Dionesios, Dionicio, Dionisio, Dionisios, Dionusios, Dionysios, Dionysius, Dunixi

DIQUAN (American) a combination of the prefix Di + Quan.
Diqawan, Diqawn, Diquane

DIRK (German) a short form of Derek, Theodoric.
Derk, Dirck, Dirke, Durc, Durk, Dyrk

DIXON (English) son of Dick.
Dickson, Dix

DMITRI (Russian) an alternate form of Dimitri.
Dmetriy, Dmitiri, Dmitri, Dmitrik, Dmitriy

DOANE (English) low, rolling hills.
Doan

DOB (English) a familiar form of Robert.
Dobie

DOBRY (Polish) good.

DOHERTY (Irish) harmful.
Docherty, Dougherty, Douherty

DOLAN (Irish) dark haired.
Dolin, Dolyn

DOLF, Dolph (German) short forms of Adolf, Adolph, Rudolf, Rudolph.
Dolfe, Dolfi, Dolphe, Dolphus

DOM (Latin) a short form of Dominic.
Dome, Domó

DOMENIC (Latin) an alternte form of Dominic.
Domanick, Domenick

DOMENICO (Italian) a form of Dominic.
Domenic, Domicio, Dominico, Menico

DOMINGO (Spanish) born on Sunday. See also Mingo.
Demingo, Domingos

DOMINIC (Latin) belonging to the Lord. See also Chuminga.
Deco, Demenico, Dom, Domanic, Domeka, Domenic, Domenico, Domini, Dominie, Dominik, Dominique, Dominitric, Dominy, Domminic, Domnenique, Domokos, Domonic, Nick

DOMINICK (Latin) an alternate form of Dominic.
Domiku, Domineck, Dominick, Dominicke, Dominiek, Dominik, Dominnick, Dominyck, Domminick, Dommonick, Domnick, Domokos, Domonick, Donek, Dumin

DOMINIK (Latin) an alternte form of Dominic.
Domenik, Dominiko, Dominyk, Domonik

DOMINIQUE (French) a form of Dominic.
Domeniq, Domeniqu, Domenique, Domenque, Dominiqu, Dominque, Dominiqueia, Domnenique, Domnique, Domoniqu, Domonique, Domunique

DOMOKOS (Hungarian) a form of Dominic.
Dedo, Dome, Domek, Domok, Domonkos

DON (Scottish) a short form of Donald. See also Kona.
Donn

DONAHUE (Irish) dark warrior.
Donohoe, Donohue

DONAL (Irish) a form of Donald.

DONALD (Scottish) world leader; proud ruler. See also Bohdan, Tauno.
Don, Donal, Dónal, Donaldo, Donall, Donalt, Donát, Donaugh, Donnie

DONATIEN (French) gift.
Donathan, Donathon

DONATO (Italian) gift.
Dodek, Donatello, Donati, Donatien, Donatus

DONAVAN (Irish) an alternate form of Donovan.

Donaven, Donavin, Donavon, Donavyn

DONDRE (French) an alternate form of Deandre.
Dondra, Dondrae, Dondray, Dondré, Dondrea

DONG (Vietnamese) easterner.
Duong

DONKOR (Akan) humble.

DONNELL (Irish) brave; dark.
Doneal, Donel, Donele, Donell, Donelle, Donnel, Donnele, Donnelly, Doniel, Donielle, Donnel, Donnelle, Donniel, Donyel, Donyell

DONNELLY (Irish) an alternate form of Donnell.
Donelly, Donlee, Donley

DONNIE, Donny (Irish) familiar forms of Donald.

DONOVAN (Irish) dark warrior.
Dohnovan, Donavan, Donevan, Donevon, Donivan, Donnivan, Donnovan, Donnoven, Donoven, Donovin, Donovon, Donvan

DONTAE, Donté (American) forms of Dante.
Donta, Dontai, Dontao, Dontate, Dontavious, Dontavius, Dontay, Dontaye, Dontea, Dontee, Dontez

DONTRELL (American) an alternate form of Dantrell.
Dontral, Dontrall, Dontray, Dontre, Dontreal, Dontrel, Dontrelle, Dontriel, Dontriell

DONZELL (Cornish) an alternate form of Denzil.
Donzeil, Donzel, Donzelle, Donzello

DOOLEY (Irish) dark hero.
Dooly

DOR (Hebrew) generation.

DORAN (Greek, Hebrew) gift. (Irish) stranger; exile.
Dore, Dorin, Dorran, Doron, Dorren, Dory

DORIAN (Greek) from Doris, Greece. See also Isidore.
Dore, Dorey, Dorie, Dorien, Dorin, Dorion, Dorján, Doron, Dorrian, Dorrien, Dorrin, Dorrion, Dorron, Dorryen, Dory

DORRELL (Scottish) king's doorkeeper. See also Durell.
Dorrel, Dorrelle

DOTAN (Hebrew) law.
Dothan

DOUG (Scottish) a short form of Dougal, Douglas.
Dougie, Dougy, Dugey, Dugie, Dugy

DOUGAL (Scottish) dark stranger. See also Doyle.
Doug, Dougall, Dugal, Dugald, Dugall, Dughall

DOUGLAS (Scottish) dark river, dark stream. See also Koukalaka.
Doug, Douglass, Dougles, Dugaid, Dughlas

DOV (Hebrew) a familiar form of David. (Yiddish) bear.
Dovid, Dovidas, Dowid

DOVEV (Hebrew) whisper.

DOW (Irish) dark haired.

DOYLE (Irish) a form of Dougal.
Doy, Doyal, Doyel

DRAGO (Italian) a form of Drake.

DRAKE (English) dragon; owner of the inn with the dragon trademark.
Drago

DRAPER (English) fabric maker.
Dray, Draypr

DRAVEN (American) a combination of the letter D + Raven.
Dravian, Dravin, Dravion, Dravon, Dravone, Dravyn, Drayven, Drevon

DRENG (Norwegian) hired hand; brave.

DRESHAWN (American) a combination of Drew + Shawn.
Dreshaun, Dreshon, Dreshown

DREVON (American) an alternate form of Draven.
Drevan, Drevaun, Dreven, Drevin, Drevion, Drevone

DREW (Welsh) wise. (English) a short form of Andrew.
Drewe, Dru

DRU (English) an alternate form of Drew.
Druan, Drud, Drue, Drugi, Drui

DRUMMOND (Scottish) druid's mountain.
Drummund, Drumond, Drumund

DRURY (French) loving. Geography: Drury Lane is a street in London's theater district. Literature: according to a nursery rhyme, Drury Lane is where the Muffin Man lives.

DRYDEN (English) dry valley.
Dry

DUANE (Irish) an alternate form of Dwayne.
Deune, Duain, Duaine, Duana

DUARTE (Portuguese) rich guard. See also Edward.

DUC (Vietnamese) moral.
Duoc, Duy

DUDD (English) a short form of Dudley.
Dud, Dudde, Duddy

DUDLEY (English) common field.
Dudd, Dudly

DUER (Scottish) heroic.

DUFF (Scottish) dark.
Duffey, Duffie, Duffy

DUGAN (Irish) dark.
Doogan, Dougan, Douggan, Duggan

DUKE (French) leader; duke.
Dukey, Dukie, Duky

DUKKER (Gypsy) fortuneteller.

DULANI (Ngoni) cutting.

DUMAKA (Ibo) helping hand.

DUMAN (Turkish) misty, smoky.

DUNCAN (Scottish) brown warrior. Literature: King Duncan was MacBeth's victim in Shakespeare's play *MacBeth*.
Dunc, Dunn

DUNHAM (Scottish) brown.

DUNIXI (Basque) a form of Dionysus.

DUNLEY (English) hilly meadow.

DUNLOP (Scottish) muddy hill.

DUNMORE (Scottish) fortress on the hill.

DUNN (Scottish) a short form of Duncan.
Dun, Dune, Dunne

DUNSTAN (English) brownstone fortress.
Dun, Dunston

DUNTON (English) hill town.

DUR (Hebrew) stacked up.

DURAND (Latin) an alternate form of Durant.

DURANT (Latin) enduring.
Duran, Durance, Durand, Durante, Durontae, Durrant

DURELL (Scottish, English) king's doorkeeper. See also Dorrell.
Durel, Durial, Durreil, Durrell, Durrelle

DURKO (Czech) a form of George.

DURRIKEN (Gypsy) fortuneteller.

DURRIL (Gypsy) gooseberry.
Durrel, Durrell

DURWARD (English) gatekeeper.
Dur, Ward

DURWIN (English) an alternate form of Darwin.

DUSHAWN (American) a combination of the prefix Du + Shawn.
Dusan, Dusean, Dushan, Dushane, Dushaun, Dushon, Dushun

DUSTIN (German) valiant fighter. (English) brown rock quarry.
Dust, Dustain, Dustan, Dusten, Dustie, Dustine, Dustion, Duston, Dusty, Dustyn, Dustynn

DUSTY (English) a familiar form of Dustin.

DUSTYN (English) an alternate form of Dustin.

DUTCH (Dutch) from the Netherlands; from Germany.

DUVAL (French) a combination of the prefix Du + Val.
Duvall, Duveuil

DWAUN (American) an alternate form of Dajuan.
Dwan, Dwaunn, Dwawn, Dwon, Dwuann

DWAYNE (Irish) dark. See also Dewayne.
Dawayne, Dawyne, Duane, Duwain, Duwan, Duwane, Duwayn, Duwayne, Dwain, Dwaine, Dwan, Dwane, Dwyane, Dywan, Dywane, Dywayne, Dywone

DWIGHT (English) a form of DeWitt.

DYAMI (Native American) soaring eagle.

DYER (English) fabric dyer.

DYKE (English) dike; ditch.
Dike

DYLAN (Welsh) sea. See also Dillon.
Dylane, Dylann, Dylen, Dylian, Dylin, Dyllan, Dyllen, Dyllian, Dyllin, Dyllyn, Dylon, Dylyn

DYLON (Welsh) an alternate form of Dylan.
Dyllion, Dyllon

DYRE (Norwegian) dear heart.

DYSON (English) a short form of Dennison.
Dysen, Dysonn

EA (Irish) a form of Hugh.

EACHAN (Irish) horseman.

EAGAN (Irish) very mighty.
Egan, Egon

EAMON (Irish) a form of Edmond, Edmund.
Aimon, Eammon, Eamonn

EAN (English) a form of Ian.
Eaen, Eann, Eayon, Eion, Eon, Eyan, Eyon

EARL (Irish) pledge. (English) nobleman.
Airle, Earld, Earle, Earlie, Earlson, Early, Eorl, Erl, Erle, Errol

EARNEST (English) an alternate form of Ernest.
Earn, Earnesto, Earnie, Eranest

EASTON (English) eastern town.
Eason, Easten, Eastin, Eastton

EATON (English) estate on the river.
Eatton, Eton, Eyton

EB (Hebrew) a short form of Ebenezer.
Ebb, Ebbie, Ebby

EBEN (Hebrew) rock.
Eban, Ebin, Ebon

EBENEZER (Hebrew) foundation stone. Literature: Ebenezer Scrooge is a

Ebenezer (cont.)
character in Charles
Dickens's *A Christmas Carol.*
*Eb, Ebbaneza, Eben, Ebeneezer,
Ebeneser, Ebenezar, Eveneser*

EBERHARD (German) coura-
geous as a boar. See also
Everett.
*Eber, Ebere, Eberardo,
Eberhardt, Evard, Everard,
Everardo, Everhardt, Everhart*

EBNER (English) a form of
Abner.

EBO (Fante) born on Tuesday.

ED (English) a short form of
Edgar, Edsel, Edward.
Edd

EDAN (Scottish) fire.
Edain

EDBERT (English) wealthy;
bright.
Ediberto

EDDIE (English) a familiar form
of Edgar, Edsel, Edward.
Eddee, Eddy, Edi, Edie

EDDY (English) an alternate
form of Eddie.
Eddye, Edy

EDEL (German) noble.
Adel, Edell, Edelmar, Edelweiss

EDEN (Hebrew) delightful.
Bible: the earthly paradise.
*Eaden, Eadin, Edan, Edenson,
Edin, Edyn, Eiden*

EDER (Hebrew) flock.
Ederick, Edir

EDGAR (English) successful
spearman. See also Garek,
Gerik, Medgar.
*Ed, Eddie, Edek, Edgard,
Edgardo, Edgars*

EDGARDO (Spanish) a form of
Edgar.

EDISON (English) son of
Edward.
Eddison, Edisen, Edson

EDMOND (English) an alternate
form of Edmund.
*Eamon, Edmon, Edmonde,
Edmondo, Edmondson, Esmond*

EDMUND (English) prosperous
protector.
*Eadmund, Eamon, Edmand,
Edmaund, Edmond, Edmun,
Edmundo, Edmunds*

EDMUNDO (Spanish) a form of
Edmund.
Edmando, Mundo

EDO (Czech) a form of Edward.

EDOARDO (Italian) a form of
Edward.

EDORTA (Basque) a form of
Edward.

EDOUARD (French) a form of
Edward.
Édoard, Édouard

EDRIC (English) prosperous
ruler.
*Eddric, Eddrick, Ederick, Edrek,
Edrice, Edrick, Edrico*

EDSEL (English) rich man's
house.
Ed, Eddie, Edsell

EDSON (English) a short form
of Edison.
Eddson, Edsen

EDUARDO (Spanish) a form of
Edward.
Estuardo, Estvardo

EDUR (Basque) snow.

EDWARD (English) prosperous
guardian. See also Audie,
Duarte, Ekewaka, Ned, Ted,
Teddy.
*Ed, Eddie, Edik, Edko, Edo,
Edoardo, Edorta, Édouard,
Eduard, Eduardo, Edus, Edvard,
Edvardo, Edwardo, Edwards,
Edwy, Edzio, Ekewaka, Etzio,
Ewart*

EDWIN (English) prosperous
friend. See also Ned, Ted.
*Eadwinn, Edik, Edlin, Eduino,
Edwan, Edwen, Edwon, Edwyn*

EFRAIN (Hebrew) fruitful.
*Efran, Efrane, Efrayin, Efren,
Efrian, Eifraine*

EFRAT (Hebrew) honored.

EFREM (Hebrew) a short form
of Ephraim.
Efe, Efraim, Efrim, Efrum

EFREN (Hebrew) an alternate
form of Efrain.

EGAN (Irish) ardent, fiery.
Egann, Egen, Egon

EGBERT (English) bright sword.
See also Bert, Bertie.

EGERTON (English) Edgar's
town.
*Edgarton, Edgartown, Edgerton,
Egeton*

EGIL (Norwegian) awe inspiring.
Eigil

EGINHARD (German) power of
the sword.
*Eginhardt, Einhard, Einhardt,
Enno*

EGON (German) formidable.

EGOR (Russian) a form of
George. See also Igor, Yegor.

EHREN (German) honorable.

EIKKI (Finnish) ever-powerful.

EINAR (Scandinavian) individualist.
Ejnar, Inar

EION (Irish) a form of Ean, Ian.
Eann, Eian, Ein, Eine, Einn

EITAN (Hebrew) an alternate form of Ethan.
Eita, Eithan, Eiton

EJAU (Ateso) we have received.

EKEWAKA (Hawaiian) a form of Edward.

EKON (Nigerian) strong.

ELAM (Hebrew) highlands.

ELAN (Hebrew) tree. (Native American) friendly.
Elann

ELBERT (English) a form of Albert.
Elberto

ELCHANAN (Hebrew) an alternate form of John.
Elchan, Elchonon, Elhanan, Elhannan

ELDEN (English) an alternate form of Alden, Aldous.
Eldan, Eldin

ELDER (English) dweller near the elder trees.

ELDON (English) holy hill.

ELDRED (English) an alternate form of Aldred.
Eldrid

ELDRIDGE (English) an alternate form of Aldrich.
El, Eldred, Eldredge, Eldrege, Eldrid, Eldrige, Elric

ELDWIN (English) an alternate form of Aldwin.
Eldwinn, Eldwyn, Eldwynn

ELEAZAR (Hebrew) God has helped. See also Lazarus.
Elazar, Elazaro, Eleasar, Eléazar, Eliazar, Eliezer

ELEK (Hungarian) a form of Alec, Alex.
Elec, Elic, Elik

ELGER (German) an alternate form of Alger.
Elger, Ellgar, Ellger

ELGIN (English) noble; white.
Elgan, Elgen

ELI (Hebrew) uplifted. A short form of Elijah, Elisha. Bible: the high priest who trained the prophet Samuel. See also Elliot.
Elie, Elier, Ellie, Eloi, Eloy, Ely

ELIA (Zuni) a short form of Elijah.
Eliah, Elio, Eliya, Elya

ELIAN (English) a form of Elijah. See also Trevelyan.
Elion

ELIAS (Greek) a form of Elijah.
Elia, Eliasz, Elice, Eliyas, Ellias, Ellice, Ellis, Elyas, Elyes

ELIAZAR (Hebrew) an alternate form of Eleazar.
Eliasar, Eliazer, Elizar, Elizardo

ELIE (Hebrew) an alternate form of Eli.

ELIEZER (Hebrew) an alternate form of Eleazar.
Elieser

ELIHU (Hebrew) a short form of Eliyahu.
Elih, Eliu, Ellihu

ELIJAH (Hebrew) the Lord is my God. An alternate form of Eliyahu. Bible: a great Hebrew prophet. See also Eli, Elliot, Elisha, Ilias, Ilya.
El, Elia, Elian, Elias, Elija, Elijha, Elijiah, Elijio, Elijuah, Elijuo, Elisjsha, Eliya, Eliyah, Ellis

ELIKA (Hawaiian) a form of Eric.

ELISEO (Hebrew) an alternate form of Elisha.
Elisee, Elisée, Elisei, Elisiah, Elisio

ELISHA (Hebrew) God is my salvation. Bible: a great Hebrew prophet, successor to Elijah. See also Eli, Elijah.
Elijsha, Eliseo, Elish, Elishah, Elisher, Elishia, Elishua, Elysha, Lisha

ELIYAHU (Hebrew) the Lord is my God. The original form of Elijah.
Eliyahou, Elihu

ELKAN (Hebrew) God is jealous.
Elkana, Elkanah, Elkin, Elkins

ELKI (Moquelumnan) hanging over the top.

ELLARD (German) sacred; brave.
Allard, Ellerd

ELLERY (English) elder tree island.
Ellary, Ellerey

ELLIOT, Elliott (English) forms of Eli, Elijah.
Elio, Eliot, Eliott, Eliud, Eliut, Elliotte, Elyot, Elyott

ELLIS (English) a form of Elias.
Elis

ELLISON (English) son of Ellis.
Elison, Ellson, Ellyson, Elson

ELLSWORTH (English) noble-man's estate.
Ellswerth, Elsworth

ELMAN (German) like an elm tree.
Elmen

ELMER (English) noble; famous.
Aylmer, Elemér, Ellmer, Elmir, Elmo

ELMO (Latin) a familiar form of Anselm. (Greek) lovable, friendly. (Italian) guardian. (English) an alternate form of Elmer.

ELMORE (English) moor where the elm trees grow.

ELONZO (Spanish) an alternate form of Alonzo.
Elon, Élon, Elonso

ELOY (Latin) chosen.
Eloi

ELRAD (Hebrew) God rules.
Rad, Radd

ELROY (French) an alternate form of Delroy, Leroy.
Elroi

ELSDON (English) nobleman's hill.

ELSTON (English) noble's town.
Ellston

ELSU (Native American) swooping, soaring falcon.

ELSWORTH (English) noble's estate.

ELTON (English) old town.
Alton, Eldon, Ellton, Elthon, Eltonia

ELVERN (Latin) an alternate form of Alvern.
Elver, Elverne

ELVIN (English) a form of Alvin.
El, Elvyn, Elwin, Elwyn, Elwynn

ELVIO (Spanish) light skinned; blond.

ELVIS (Scandinavian) wise.
El, Elviz, Elvys

ELVY (English) elfin warrior.

ELWELL (English) old well.

ELWOOD (English) old forest. See also Wood, Woody.

ELY (Hebrew) an alternate form of Eli. Geography: a river in Wales.
Elya, Elyie

EMAN (Czech) a form of Emmanuel.
Emaney, Emani

EMANUEL (Hebrew) an alternate form of Emmanuel.
Emaniel, Emannual, Emannuel, Emanual, Emanueal, Emanuele, Emanuell, Emanuell, Emanuelle

EMERSON (German, English) son of Emery.
Emmerson, Emreson

EMERY (German) industrious leader.
Aimery, Emari, Emarri, Emeri, Emerich, Emerio, Emmerich, Emmerie, Emmery, Emmo, Emory, Emrick, Emry, Inre, Imrich

EMIL (Latin) flatterer. (German) industrious. See also Milko, Milo.
Aymil, Emiel, Émile, Emilek, Emiliano, Emilio, Emill, Emils, Emilyan, Emlyn

ÉMILE (French) a form of Emil.
Emiel, Emile, Emille

EMILIANO (Italian) a form of Emil.
Emilian, Emilion

EMILIEN (Latin) friendly; industrious.

EMILIO (Italian, Spanish) a form of Emil.
Emielio, Emileo, Emilio, Emilios, Emillio, Emilo

EMLYN (Welsh) a form of Emil.
Emelen, Emlen, Emlin

EMMANUEL (Hebrew) God is with us. See also Immanuel, Maco, Mango, Manuel.
Eman, Emanuel, Emanuell, Emek, Emmahnuel, Emmanel, Emmaneuol, Emmanle, Emmanual, Emmanueal, Emmanuele, Emmanuell, Emmanuelle, Emmanuil, Enmanuel

EMMETT (German) industrious; strong. (English) ant. History: Robert Emmett was an Irish patriot.
Em, Emet, Emett, Emitt, Emmet, Emmette, Emmitt, Emmot, Emmott, Emmy

EMMITT (German, English) an alternate form of Emmett.
Emmit

EMORY (German) an alternate form of Emery.
Amory, Emmory, Emorye

EMRE (Turkish) brother.
Emra, Emrah, Emreson

EMRICK (German) an alternate form of Emery.
Emeric, Emerick, Emric, Emrique, Emryk

ENAPAY (Sioux) brave appearance; he appears.

ENDRE (Hungarian) a form of Andrew.
Ender

ENEAS (Greek) an alternate form of Aeneas.
Eneias, Enné

ENGELBERT (German) bright as an angel. See also Ingelbert.
Bert, Englebert

ENLI (Dene) that dog over there.

ENNIS (Greek) mine. (Scottish) an alternate form of Angus.
Eni, Enni

ENOCH (Hebrew) dedicated, consecrated. Bible: the father of Methuselah.
Enoc, Enock, Enok

ENOS (Hebrew) man.
Enosh

ENRIC (Romanian) a form of Henry.
Enrica

ENRICK (Spanish) a form of Henry.
Enricky

ENRICO (Italian) a form of Henry.
Enzio, Enzo, Rico

ENRIKOS (Greek) a form of Henry.

ENRIQUE (Spanish) a form of Henry. See also Quiqui.
Enrigué, Enriqué, Enriquez, Enrrique

ENVER (Turkish) bright; handsome.

ENYETO (Native American) walks like a bear.

ENZI (Swahili) powerful.

EOIN (Welsh) a form of Evan.

EPHRAIM (Hebrew) fruitful. Bible: the second son of Joseph.
Efraim, Efrayim, Efrem, Efren, Ephraen, Ephrain, Ephram, Ephrem, Ephriam

ERASMUS (Greek) lovable.
Érasme, Erasmo, Rasmus

ERASTUS (Greek) beloved.
Éraste, Erastious, Ras, Rastus

ERBERT (German) a short form of Herbert.
Ebert, Erberto

ERCOLE (Italian) splendid gift.

EREK (Scandinavian) an alternate form of Eric.
Erec

ERHARD (German) strong; resolute.
Erhardt, Erhart

ERIBERTO (Italian) a form of Herbert.
Erberto, Heriberto

ERIC (German) a short form of Frederick. (Scandinavian) ruler of all. (English) brave ruler. History: Eric the Red was a Norse hero and explorer.
Aric, Ehrich, Elika, Erek, Éric, Erica, Ericc, Erich, Erick, Erico, Erik, Erikur, Erric, Eryc, Rick

ERICH (Czech, German) a form of Eric.

ERICK (English) an alternate form of Eric.
Errick, Eryck

ERICKSON (English) son of Eric.
Erickzon, Erics, Ericson, Ericsson, Erikson, Erikzzon, Eriqson

ERIK (Scandinavian) an alternate form of Eric.
Erek, Erike, Eriks, Erikur, Errick, Errik, Eryk

ERIKUR (Icelandic) a form of Eric, Erik.

ERIN (Irish) peaceful. History: another name for Ireland.
Erine, Erinn, Erino, Eron, Errin, Eryn, Erynn

ERLAND (English) nobleman's land.
Erlend

ERLING (English) nobleman's son.

ERMANNO (Italian) a form of Herman.
Erman

ERMANO (Spanish) a form of Herman.
Ermin, Ermine, Erminio, Ermon

ERNEST (English) earnest, sincere. See also Arno.
Earnest, Ernestino, Ernesto, Ernestus, Ernie, Erno, Ernst

ERNESTO (Spanish) a form of Ernest.
Ernester, Neto

ERNIE (English) a familiar form of Ernest.
Earnie, Erney, Erny

ERNO (Hungarian) a form of Ernest.
Ernö

ERNST (German) a form of Ernest.
Erns

EROL (Turkish) strong, courageous.
Eroll

ERON (Irish) an alternate form of Erin.
Erran, Erren, Errion, Erron

ERRANDO (Basque) bold.

ERROL (Latin) wanderer. (English) an alternate form of Earl.
Erol, Erold, Erroll, Erryl

ERROMAN (Basque) from Rome.

ERSKINE (Scottish) high cliff. (English) from Ireland.
Ersin, Erskin, Kinny

ERVIN, Erwin (English) sea friend. Alternate forms of Irving, Irwin.
Earvin, Erv, Erven, Ervyn, Erwan, Erwinek, Erwinn, Erwyn, Erwynn

ERVINE (English) a form of Irving.
Erv, Ervin, Ervince, Erving, Ervins

ESAU (Hebrew) rough; hairy. Bible: Jacob's twin brother.
Esaw

ESEQUIEL (Hebrew) an alternate form of Ezekiel.

ESHKOL (Hebrew) grape clusters.

ESKIL (Norwegian) god vessel.

ESMOND (English) rich protector.

ESPEN (Danish) god-bear.

ESSIEN (Ochi) sixth-born son.

ESTE (Italian) east.
Estes

ESTÉBAN (Spanish) a form of Stephen.
Estabon, Esteben, Estefan, Estefano, Estefen, Estephan, Estephen

ESTEBE (Basque) a form of Stephen.

ESTEVAN (Spanish) a form of Stephen.
Esteven, Estevon, Estiven

ESTEVAO (Spanish) a form of Stephen.
Estevez

ETHAN (Hebrew) strong; firm.
Eathan, Eathen, Eathon, Eeathen, Eitan, Etan, Ethaen, Ethe, Ethen, Ethian

ÉTIENNE (French) a form of Stephen.
Etian, Etien, Étienn, Ettien

ETTORE (Italian) steadfast.
Etor, Etore

ETU (Native American) sunny.

EUCLID (Greek) intelligent. History: the founder of Euclidean geometry.

EUGEN (German) a form of Eugene.

EUGENE (Greek) born to nobility. See also Ewan, Gene, Gino, Iukini, Jenö, Yevgenyi, Zenda.
Eoghan, Eugen, Eugéne, Eugeni, Eugenio, Eugenius, Evgeny, Ezven

EUGENIO (Spanish) a form of Eugene.

EULISES (Latin) an alternate form of Ulysses.

EUSTACE (Greek) productive. (Latin) stable, calm. See also Stacey.

Eustache, Eustachius, Eustachy, Eustashe, Eustasius, Eustatius, Eustazio, Eustis, Eustiss

EVAN (Irish) young warrior. (English) a form of John. See also Bevan, Owen.
Eavan, Eoin, Ev, Evaine, Evann, Evans, Even, Evens, Evin, Evon, Evyn, Ewan, Ewen

EVANGELOS (Greek) an alternate form of Andrew.
Evagelos, Evaggelos, Evangelo

EVELYN (English) hazelnut.
Evelin

EVERARDO (German) strong as a boar.
Everado

EVERETT (English) a form of Eberhard.
Ev, Evered, Everet, Everette, Everhett, Everit, Everitt, Everrett, Evert, Evrett

EVERLEY (English) boar meadow.
Everlea, Everlee

EVERTON (English) boar town.

EVGENY (Russian) a form of Eugene. See also Zhek.
Evgeni, Evgenij, Evgenyi

EVIN (Irish) an alternate form of Evan.
Evian, Evinn, Evins

EWALD (German) always powerful. (English) powerful lawman.

EWAN (Scottish) a form of Eugene, Evan. See also Keon.
Euan, Euann, Euen, Ewen, Ewhen

EWERT (English) ewe herder, shepherd.
Ewart

EWING (English) friend of the law.
Ewin, Ewynn

EXAVIER (Basque) an alternate form of Xavier.
Exaviar, Exavior, Ezavier

EYOTA (Native American) great.

EZEKIEL (Hebrew) strength of God. Bible: a Hebrew prophet. See also Haskel, Zeke.
Esequiel, Ezakeil, Ezéchiel, Ezeck, Ezeckiel, Ezeeckel, Ezekeial, Ezekeil, Ezekeyial, Ezekial, Ezekielle, Ezell, Ezequiel, Eziakah, Eziechiele

EZEQUIEL (Hebrew) an alternate form of Ezekiel.
Esequiel, Eziequel

EZER (Hebrew) an alternate form of Ezra.

EZRA (Hebrew) helper; strong. Bible: a prophet and leader of the Israelites.
Esdras, Esra, Ezer, Ezera, Ezrah, Ezri, Ezry

EZVEN (Czech) a form of Eugene.
Esven, Esvin, Ezavin, Ezavine

FABER (German) a form of Fabian.

FABIAN (Latin) bean grower.
Fabain, Fabayan, Fabe, Fabein, Fabek, Fabeon, Faber, Fabert,

Fabi, Fabiano, Fabien, Fabin, Fabio, Fabion, Fabius, Fabiyan, Fabiyus, Fabyan, Fabyen, Faybian, Faybien

FABIANO (Italian) a form of Fabian.
Fabianno, Fabio

FABIO (Latin) an alternate form of Fabian. (Italian) a short form of Fabiano.
Fabbio

FABRIZIO (Italian) craftsman.
Fabrice, Fabricio, Fabrizius

FABRON (French) little blacksmith; apprentice.
Fabre, Fabroni

FADEY (Ukrainian) a form of Thaddeus.
Faday, Faddei, Faddey, Faddy, Fade, Fadeyka, Fadie, Fady

FADI (Arabic) redeemer.
Fadhi

FADIL (Arabic) generous.
Fadeel, Fadel

FAGAN (Irish) little fiery one.
Fagin

FAHD (Arabic) lynx.
Fahaad, Fahad

FAI (Chinese) beginning.

FAIRFAX (English) blond.
Fair, Fax

FAISAL (Arabic) decisive.
Faisel, Faisil, Faisl, Faiyaz, Faiz, Faizal, Faize, Faizel, Faizi, Fasel, Fasil, Faysal, Fayzal, Fayzel

FAKHIR (Arabic) excellent.
Fahkry, Fakher

FAKIH (Arabic) thinker; reader of the Koran.

FALCO (Latin) falconer.
Falcon, Falk, Falke, Falken

FALITO (Italian) a familiar form of Rafael, Raphael.

FALKNER (English) trainer of falcons. See also Falco.
Falconer, Falconner, Faulconer, Faulconner, Faulkner

FANE (English) joyful, glad.
Fanes, Faniel

FARAJI (Swahili) consolation.

FARID (Arabic) unique.

FARIS (Arabic) horseman.
Faraz, Fares, Farhaz, Farice, Fariez, Farris

FARLEY (English) bull meadow; sheep meadow. See also Lee.
Fairlay, Fairlee, Fairleigh, Fairley, Fairlie, Far, Farlay, Farlee, Farleigh, Farlie, Farly, Farrleigh, Farrley

FARNELL (English) fern-covered hill.
Farnall, Fernald, Fernall, Furnald

FARNHAM (English) field of ferns.
Farnam, Farnum, Fernham

FARNLEY (English) fern meadow.
Farnlea, Farnlee, Farnleigh, Farnly, Fernlea, Fernlee, Fernleigh, Fernley

FAROH (Latin) an alternate form of Pharaoh.

FAROLD (English) mighty traveler.

FARQUHAR (Scottish) dear.
Fark, Farq, Farquar, Farquarson, Farque, Farquharson, Farquy, Farqy

FARR (English) traveler.
Faer, Farran, Farren, Farrin, Farrington, Farron

FARRELL (Irish) heroic.
Farrel, Farrill, Farryll, Ferrell

FARROW (English) piglet.

FARRUCO (Spanish) a form of Francis, Francisco.
Frascuelo

FARUQ (Arabic) honest.
Farook, Farooq, Faroque, Farouk, Faruqh

FASTE (Norwegian) firm.

FATH (Arabic) victor.

FATIN (Arabic) clever.

FAUST (Latin) lucky, fortunate. History: the sixteenth-century German doctor who inspired many legends.
Faustino, Faustis, Fausto, Faustus

FAUSTINO (Italian) a form of Faust.

FAUSTO (Italian) a form of Faust.

FAVIAN (Latin) understanding.
Favain, Favio, Favyen

FAXON (German) long haired.

FEDERICO (Italian, Spanish) a form of Frederick.
Federic, Federigo, Federoquito

FEIVEL (Yiddish) God aids.

FELIKS (Russian) a form of Felix.

FELIPE (Spanish) a form of Philip.
Feeleep, Felipino, Felo, Filip, Filippo, Filips, Fillip, Flip

FELIPPO (Italian) a form of Philip.
Felip, Filippo, Lipp, Lippo, Pip, Pippo

FELIX (Latin) fortunate; happy. See also Pitin.
Fee, Felic, Félice, Feliciano, Felicio, Felike, Feliks, Felo, Félix, Felizio, Phelix

FELTON (English) field town.
Felten, Feltin

FENTON (English) marshland farm.
Fen, Fennie, Fenny, Fintan, Finton

FEODOR (Slavic) a form of Theodore.
Dorek, Fedar, Fedinka, Fedor, Fedya, Fyodor

FEORAS (Greek) smooth rock.

FERDINAND (German) daring, adventurous. See also Hernando.
Feranado, Ferd, Ferda, Ferdie, Ferdinánd, Ferdy, Ferdynand, Fernando, Nando

FERENC (Hungarian) a form of Francis.
Feri, Ferke, Ferko

FERGUS (Irish) strong; manly.
Fearghas, Fearghus, Feargus, Ferghus, Fergie, Ferguson, Fergusson

FERMIN (French, Spanish) firm, strong.
Ferman, Firmin, Furman

FERNANDO (Spanish) a form of Ferdinand.
Ferando, Ferdinando, Ferdnando, Ferdo, Fernand, Fernandez, Fernendo

FEROZ (Persian) fortunate.

FERRAN (Arabic) baker.
Feran, Feron, Ferrin, Ferron

FERRAND (French) iron gray hair.
Farand, Farrand, Farrant, Ferrant

FERRELL (Irish) an alternate form of Farrell.
Ferrel, Ferrill, Ferryl

FERRIS (Irish) a form of Peter.
Fares, Faris, Fariz, Farris, Farrish, Feris, Ferriss

FICO (Spanish) a familiar form of Frederick.

FIDEL (Latin) faithful.
Fidele, Fidèle, Fidelio, Fidelis, Fidell, Fido

FIELD (English) a short form of Fielding.
Fields

FIELDING (English) field; field worker.
Field

FIFE (Scottish) from Fife, Scotland.
Fyfe

FIFI (Fante) born on Friday.

FIL (Polish) a form of Phil.
Filipek

FILBERT (English) brilliant. See also Bert.
Filberte, Filberto, Filiberto, Philbert

FILIBERTO (Spanish) a form of Filbert.

FILIP (Greek) an alternate form of Philip.
Filip, Filippo

FILLIPP (Russian) a form of Philip.
Filip, Filipe, Filipek, Filips, Fill, Fillip, Filya

FILMORE (English) famous.
Fillmore, Filmer, Fyllmer, Fylmer, Philmore

FILYA (Russian) a form of Philip.

FINEAS (Irish) a form of Phineas.
Finneas

FINIAN (Irish) light skinned; white.
Finnen, Finnian, Fionan, Fionn, Phinean

FINLAY (Irish) blond-haired soldier.
Findlay, Findley, Finlea, Finlee, Finley, Finn, Finnlea, Finnley

FINN (German) from Finland. (Irish) blond haired; light skinned. A short form of Finlay. (Norwegian) from the Lapland.
Fin, Finnie, Finnis, Finny

FINNEGAN (Irish) light skinned; white.
Finegan

FIORELLO (Italian) little flower.
Fiore

FIRAS (Arabic) persistent.

FIRMAN (French) firm; strong.
Ferman, Firmin

FIRTH (English) woodland.

FISCHEL (Yiddish) a form of Phillip.

FISKE (English) fisherman.
Fisk

FITCH (English) weasel, ermine.
Fitche

FITZ (English) son.
Filz

FITZGERALD (English) son of Gerald.

FITZHUGH (English) son of Hugh.
Hugh

FITZPATRICK (English) son of Patrick.

FITZROY (Irish) son of Roy.

FLAMINIO (Spanish) Religion: a Roman priest.

FLANN (Irish) redhead.
Flainn, Flannan, Flannery

FLAVIAN (Latin) blond, yellow haired.
Flavel, Flavelle, Flavien, Flavio, Flawiusz

FLAVIO (Italian) a form of Flavian.
Flabio, Flavious, Flavius

FLEMING (English) from Denmark; from Flanders.
Flemming, Flemmyng, Flemyng

FLETCHER (English) arrow featherer, arrow maker.
Flecher, Fletch

FLINT (English) stream; flint-stone.
Flynt

FLIP (Spanish) a short form of Felipe. (American) a short form of Philip.

FLORENCIO (Italian) a form of Florent.

FLORENT (French) flowering.
Florenci, Florencio, Florentin, Florentino, Florentyn, Florentz, Florinio, Florino

FLORIAN (Latin) flowering, blooming.
Florien, Florrian, Flory, Floryan

FLOYD (English) a form of Lloyd.

FLURRY (English) flourishing, blooming.

FLYNN (Irish) son of the red-haired man.
Flin, Flinn, Flyn

FOLKE (German) an alternate form of Volker.
Folker

FOLUKE (Yoruba) given to God.

FOMA (Bulgarian, Russian) a form of Thomas.
Fomka

FONSO (German, Italian) a short form of Alphonso.
Fonzo

FONTAINE (French) fountain.

FONZIE (German) a familiar form of Alphonse.
Fons, Fonsie, Fonsy, Fonz

FORBES (Irish) prosperous.
Forbe

FORD (English) a short form of names ending in "ford."

FORDEL (Gypsy) forgiving.

FOREST (French) an alternate form of Forrest.
Forestt, Foryst

FORESTER (English) forest guardian.
Forrester, Forrie, Forry, Forster, Foss, Foster

FORREST (French) forest; woodsman.
Forest, Forester, Forrestar, Forrester, Forrestt, Forrie

FORTINO (Italian) fortunate, lucky.

FORTUNE (French) fortunate, lucky.
Fortun, Fortunato, Fortuné, Fortunio

FOSTER (Latin) a short form of Forester.

FOWLER (English) trapper of wild fowl.

FRAN (Latin) a short form of Francis.
Franh

FRANCESCO (Italian) a form of Francis.

FRANCHOT (French) a form of Francis.

FRANCIS (Latin) free; from France. Religion: Saint Francis of Assisi was the founder of the Franciscan order. See also Farruco, Ferenc.
Fran, France, Frances, Francesco, Franchot, Francisco, Franciskus, Franco, François, Frang, Frank, Frannie, Franny, Frans, Franscis, Fransis, Franta, Frantisek, Frants, Franus, Frantisek, Franz, Frencis

FRANCISCO (Portuguese, Spanish) a form of Francis. See also Chilo, Cisco, Farruco, Paco, Pancho.

Franco, Fransisco, Fransysco, Frasco, Frisco

FRANCO (Latin) a short form of Francis.
Franko

FRANÇOIS (French) a form of Francis.
Francoise

FRANK (English) a short form of Francis, Franklin. See also Palani, Pancho.
Franc, Franck, Franek, Frang, Franio, Franke, Frankie, Franko

FRANKIE (English) a familiar form of Frank.
Francky, Franke, Frankey, Franki, Franky, Franqui

FRANKLIN (English) free landowner.
Fran, Francklen, Francklin, Francklyn, Francylen, Frank, Frankin, Franklen, Franklinn, Franklyn, Franquelin

FRANKLYN (English) an alternate form of Franklin.
Franklynn

FRANS (Swedish) a form of Francis.
Frants

FRANTISEK (Czech) a form of Francis.
Franta

FRANZ (German) a form of Francis.
Fransz, Frantz, Franzen, Franzie, Franzin, Franzl, Franzy

FRASER (French) strawberry. (English) curly haired.
Fraizer, Frasier, Fraze, Frazer, Frazier

FRAYNE (French) dweller at the ash tree. (English) stranger.

Fraine, Frayn, Frean, Freen, Freyne

FRED (German) a short form of Alfred, Frederick, Manfred.
Fredd, Fredde, Fredo, Fredson

FREDDIE (German) a familiar form of Frederick.
Freddi, Freddy, Fredi, Fredy

FREDDY, Fredy (German) familiar forms of Frederick.

FREDERIC (German) an alternate form of Frederick.
Frédéric, Frederich, Frederric, Fredric, Fredrich

FREDERICK (German) peaceful ruler. See also Dick, Eric, Fico, Peleke, Rick.
Federico, Fico, Fred, Fredderick, Freddie, Freddrick, Freddy, Fredek, Frederic, Frédérick, Frédérick, Frederik, Frederique, Frederrick, Fredo, Fredrick, Fredwick, Fredwyck, Fredy, Friedrich, Fritz

FREDERICO (Spanish) a form of Frederick.
Fredrico, Frederigo

FREDERIK (German) an alternate form of Frederick.
Frédérik, Frederrik, Fredrik

FREDERIQUE (French) a form of Frederick.

FREDO (Spanish) a form of Fred.

FREDRICK (German) an alternate form of Frederick.
Fredric, Fredricka, Fredricks

FREEBORN (English) child of freedom.
Free

FREEMAN (English) free.
Free, Freedman, Freemin, Freemon, Friedman, Friedmann

FREMONT (German) free; noble protector.

FREWIN (English) free; noble friend.
Frewen

FREY (English) lord. (Scandinavian) Mythology: god of prosperity.

FRICK (English) bold.

FRIDOLF (English) peaceful wolf.
Freydolf, Freydulf, Fridulf

FRIEDRICH (German) a form of Frederick.
Friedel, Friedrick, Fridrich, Fridrick, Friedrike, Friedryk, Fryderyk

FRISCO (Spanish) a short form of Francisco.

FRITZ (German) a familiar form of Frederick.
Fritson, Fritts, Fritzchen, Fritzl

FRODE (Norwegian) wise.

FULBRIGHT (German) very bright.
Fulbert

FULLER (English) cloth thickener.

FULTON (English) field near town.

FUNSONI (Ngoni) requested.

FYFE (Scottish) an alternate form of Fife.
Fyffe

FYNN (Ghanian) Geography: another name for the Offin river.

FYODOR (Russian) an alternate form of Theodore.

GABBY (American) a familiar form of Gabriel.
Gabbi, Gabbie, Gabi, Gabie, Gaby

GABE (Hebrew) a short form of Gabriel.

GABINO (American) a form of Gabriel.
Gabin, Gabrino

GÁBOR (Hungarian) God is my strength.
Gabbo, Gabko, Gabo

GABRIAL (Hebrew) an alternate form of Gabriel.
Gaberial, Gabrael, Gabraiel, Gabrail, Gabreal, Gabriael, Gabrieal, Gabryalle

GABRIEL (Hebrew) devoted to God. Bible: the Archangel of Annunciation.
Gab, Gabe, Gabby, Gabino, Gabis, Gábor, Gabreil, Gabrel, Gabrell, Gabrial, Gabriël, Gabriele, Gabriell, Gabrielle, Gabrielli, Gabrile, Gabris, Gabryel, Gabys, Gavril, Gebereal, Ghabriel, Riel

GABRIELLI (Italian) a form of Gabriel.
Gabriello

GADI (Arabic) God is my fortune.
Gad, Gaddy, Gadiel

GAETAN (Italian) from Gaeta, a region in southern Italy.
Gaetano, Gaetono

GAGE (French) pledge.
Gager, Gaige, Gaje

GAIGE (French) an alternate form of Gage.

GAIR (Irish) small.
Gaer, Gearr, Geir

GAIUS (Latin) rejoicer. See also Cai.

GALBRAITH (Irish) Scotsman in Ireland.
Galbrait, Galbreath

GALE (Greek) a short form of Galen.
Gael, Gail, Gaile, Gayle

GALEN (Greek) healer; calm. (Irish) little and lively.
Gaelan, Gaelen, Gaelin, Gaelyn, Gailen, Galan, Gale, Galeno, Galin, Galyn, Gaylen

GALENO (Spanish) illuminated child.

GALLAGHER (Irish) eager helper.

GALLOWAY (Irish) Scotsman in Ireland.
Gallway, Galway

GALT (Norwegian) high ground.

GALTON (English) owner of a rented estate.
Gallton

GALVIN (Irish) sparrow.
Gal, Gall, Gallven, Gallvin, Galvan, Galven

GAMAL (Arabic) camel. See also Jamal.
Gamall, Gamel, Gamil

GAMBLE (Scandinavian) old.

GAN (Chinese) daring, adventurous. (Vietnamese) near.

GANNON (Irish) light skinned, white.
Gannan, Gannen, Gannie, Ganny

GANYA (Zulu) clever.

GAR (English) a short form of Gareth, Garnett, Garrett, Garvin.
Garr

GARCIA (Spanish) mighty with a spear.

GARDNER (English) gardener.
Gard, Gardener, Gardie, Gardiner, Gardy

GAREK (Polish) a form of Edgar.

GAREN (English) an alternate form of Garry.
Garan, Garen, Garin, Garion, Garon, Garyn, Garyon

GARETH (Welsh) gentle.
Gar, Garith, Garreth, Garrith, Garth, Garyth

GARETT (Irish) an alternate form of Garrett.
Gared, Garet, Garette, Garhett, Garit, Garitt, Garritt

GARFIELD (English) field of spears; battlefield.

GARLAND (French) wreath of flowers; prize. (English) land of spears; battleground.
Garlan, Garlen, Garllan, Garlund, Garlyn

GARMAN (English) spearman.
Garmann, Garrman

GARNER (French) army guard, sentry.
Garnier

GARNETT (Latin) pomegranate seed; garnet stone. (English) armed with a spear.
Gar, Garnet, Garnie, Garrnett

GARNOCK (Welsh) dweller by the alder river.

GARRAD (English) a form of Garrett.
Gared, Garrard, Garred, Garrod, Gerred, Gerrid, Gerrod, Garrode, Jared

GARRET (Irish) an alternate form of Garrett.
Garrit, Garyt, Gerret, Garrid, Gerrit, Gerrot

GARRETT (Irish) brave spearman. See also Jarrett.
Gar, Gareth, Garett, Garrad, Garret, Garrette, Gerrett, Gerritt, Gerrott

GARRICK (English) oak spear.
Gaerick, Garek, Garick, Garik, Garreck, Garrek, Garric, Garrik, Garryck, Garryk, Gerreck, Gerrick

GARREN, Garrin (English) alternate forms of Garry.
Garran, Garrion, Garron, Garyn, Gerren, Gerron, Gerryn

GARRISON (French) troops stationed at a fort; garrison.
Garison, Garisson, Garris

GARROWAY (English) spear fighter.
Garraway

GARRY (English) an alternate form of Gary.

Garen, Garrey, Garri, Garrie, Garren, Garrin

GARSON (English) son of Gar.

GARTH (Scandinavian) garden, gardener. (Welsh) a short form of Gareth.

GARVEY (Irish) rough peace.
Garbhán, Garrvey, Garrvie, Garv, Garvan, Garvie, Garvy

GARVIN (English) comrade in battle.
Gar, Garvan, Garven, Garvyn, Garwen, Garwin, Garwyn, Garwynn

GARWOOD (English) evergreen forest. See also Wood, Woody.
Garrwood

GARY (German) mighty spearman. (English) a familiar form of Gerald. See also Kali.
Gare, Garey, Gari, Garry

GASPAR (French) a form of Casper.
Gáspár, Gaspard, Gaspare, Gaspari, Gasparo, Gasper, Gazsi

GASTON (French) from Gascony, France.
Gascon, Gastaun

GAUTE (Norwegian) great.

GAUTIER (French) a form of Walter.
Galtero, Gaulterio, Gaultier, Gaultiero, Gauthier

GAVIN (Welsh) white hawk.
Gav, Gavan, Gaven, Gavinn, Gavino, Gavn, Gavohn, Gavon, Gavyn, Gavynn, Gawain

GAVRIEL (Hebrew) man of God.
Gav, Gavi, Gavrel, Gavril, Gavy

GAVRIL (Russian) a form of Gavriel.
Ganya, Gavrilo, Gavrilushka

GAWAIN (Welsh) an alternate form of Gavin.
Gawaine, Gawayn, Gawayne, Gawen, Gwayne

GAYLEN (Greek) an alternate form of Galen.
Gaylin, Gaylinn, Gaylon, Gaylyn

GAYLORD (French) merry lord; jailer.
Gaillard, Gallard, Gay, Gayelord, Gayler, Gaylor

GAYNOR (Irish) son of the fair-skinned man.
Gainer, Gainor, Gay, Gayner, Gaynnor

GEARY (English) variable, changeable.
Gearey, Gery

GEDEON (Bulgarian, French) a form of Gideon.

GEFFREY (English) an alternate form of Geoffrey. See also Jeffrey.
Gefery, Geff, Geffery, Geffrard

GELLERT (Hungarian) a form of Gerald.

GENA (Russian) a short form of Yevgenyi.
Genka, Genya, Gine

GENARO (Latin) consecrated to God.
Genereo, Genero, Gennaro

GENE (Greek) born to nobility. A short form of Eugene.
Genek

GENEK (Polish) a form of Gene.

GENO (Italian) a form of John. A short form of Genovese.
Genio, Jeno

GENOVESE (Italian) from Genoa, Italy.
Geno, Genovis

GENT (English) gentleman.
Gentle, Gentry

GENTY (Irish, English) snow.

GEOFF (English) a short form of Geoffrey.

GEOFFERY (English) an alternate form of Geoffrey.
Geofery

GEOFFREY (English) divinely peaceful. A form of Jeffrey. See also Giotto, Godfrey, Gottfried, Jeff.
Geffrey, Geoff, Geoffery, Geoffre, Geoffrie, Geoffroi, Geoffroy, Geoffry, Geofrey, Geofri, Gofery

GEORDAN (Scottish) a form of Gordon.
Geordann, Geordian, Geordin, Geordon

GEORDIE (Scottish) a form of George.
Geordi, Geordy

GEORG (Scandinavian) a form of George.

GEORGE (Greek) farmer. See also Durko, Egor, Iorgos, Jerzy, Jiri, Joji, Jörg, Jorge, Jorgen, Joris, Jorrín, Jur, Jurgis, Keoki, Mahiái, Semer, Yegor, Yorgos, Yoyi, Yrjo, Yuri, Zhora.
Geordie, Georg, Georgas, Georges, Georget, Georgi, Georgii, Georgio, Georgios, Georgiy, Georgy, Gevork,

Gheorghe, Giorgio, Giorgos, Goerge, Goran, Gordios, Gorge, Gorje, Gorya, Grzegorz, Gyorgy

GEORGES (French) a form of George.
Geórges

GEORGIO (Italian) a form of George.

GEORGIOS (Greek) an alternate form of George.
Georgious, Georgius

GEORGY (Greek) a familiar form of George.
Georgie

GEOVANNI, Geovanny (Italian) alternate forms of Giovanni.
Geovan, Geovani, Geovanne, Geovannee, Geovannhi, Geovany

GERAINT (English) old.

GERALD (German) mighty spearman. See also Fitzgerald, Jarell, Jarrell, Jerald, Jerry, Kharald.
Garald, Garold, Garolds, Gary, Gearalt, Gellert, Gérald, Geralde, Geraldo, Gerale, Geraud, Gerek, Gerick, Gerik, Gerold, Gerrald, Gerrell, Gérrick, Gerrild, Gerrin, Gerrit, Gerrold, Gerry, Geryld, Giraldo, Giraud, Girauld

GERALDO (Italian, Spanish) a form of Gerald.

GERARD (English) brave spearman. See also Jerard, Jerry.
Garrard, Garrat, Garratt, Gearard, Gerad, Gerar, Gérard, Gerardo, Geraro, Géraud, Gerd, Gerek, Gerhard, Gerrard, Gerrit, Gerry, Girard

GERARDO (Spanish) a form of Gerard.
Gherardo

GÉRAUD (French) a form of Gerard.
Gerrad, Gerraud

GEREK (Polish) a form of Gerard.

GEREMIA (Hebrew) exalted by God. (Italian) a form of Jeremiah.

GEREMIAH (Italian) a form of Jeremiah.
Geremia, Gerimiah, Geromiah

GERHARD (German) a form of Gerard.
Garhard, Gerhardi, Gerhardt, Gerhart, Gerhort

GERIK (Polish) a form of Edgar.
Geric, Gerick

GERMAIN (French) from Germany. (English) sprout, bud. See also Jermaine.
Germaine, German, Germane, Germano, Germayn, Germayne

GEROME (English) a form of Jerome.

GERONIMO (Greek, Italian) a form of Jerome. History: a famous Apache chief.
Geronemo

GERRIT (Dutch) a form of Gerald.

GERRY (English) a familiar form of Gerald, Gerard. See also Jerry.
Geri, Gerre, Gerri, Gerrie, Gerryson

GERSHOM (Hebrew) exiled. (Yiddish) stranger in exile.
Gersham, Gersho, Gershon, Gerson, Geurson, Gursham, Gurshan

GERSON (English) son of Gar.
Gersan, Gershawn

GERT (German, Danish) fighter.

GERVAISE (French) honorable. See also Jervis.
Garvais, Garvaise, Garvey, Gervais, Gervase, Gervasio, Gervaso, Gervayse, Gervis, Gerwazy

GERWIN (Welsh) fair love.

GETHIN (Welsh) dusky.
Geth

GHAZI (Arabic) conqueror.

GHILCHRIST (Irish) servant of Christ. See also Gil.
Gilchrist, Gilcrist, Gilie, Gill, Gilley, Gilly

GHISLAIN (French) pledge.

GI (Korean) brave.

GIA (Vietnamese) family.

GIACINTO (Portuguese, Spanish) an alternate form of Jacinto.
Giacintho

GIACOMO (Italian) a form of Jacob.
Gaimo, Giacamo, Giaco, Giacobbe, Giacobo, Giacopo

GIAN (Italian) a form of Giovanni, John.
Gianetto, Giann, Gianne, Giannes, Gianni, Giannis, Giannos, Ghian

GIANCARLO (Italian) a combination of John + Charles.
Giancarlos, Gianncarlo

GIANLUCA (Italian) a combination of John + Lucas.

GIANNI (Italian) a form of Johnny.
Giani, Gionni

GIANPAOLO (Italian) a combination of John + Paul.
Gianpaulo

GIB (English) a short form of Gilbert.
Gibb, Gibbie, Gibby

GIBOR (Hebrew) powerful.

GIBSON (English) son of Gilbert.
Gibbon, Gibbons, Gibbs, Gillson, Gilson

GIDEON (Hebrew) tree cutter. Bible: the judge who delivered the Israelites from captivity.
Gedeon, Gideone, Gidon, Hedeon

GIDON (Hebrew) an alternate form of Gideon.

GIFFORD (English) bold giver.
Giff, Giffard, Gifferd, Giffie, Giffy

GIG (English) horse-drawn carriage.

GIL (Greek) shield bearer. (Hebrew) happy. (English) a short form of Ghilchrist, Gilbert.
Gili, Gill, Gilli, Gillie, Gillis, Gilly

GILAD (Arabic) camel hump; from Giladi, Saudi Arabia.
Giladi, Gilead

GILAMU (Basque) a form of William.
Gillen

GILBERT (English) brilliant pledge; trustworthy. See also Gil, Gillett.
Gib, Gilberto, Gilburt, Giselbert, Giselberto, Giselbertus, Guilbert

GILBERTO (Spanish) a form of Gilbert.

GILBY (Scandinavian) hostage's estate. (Irish) blond boy.
Gilbey, Gillbey, Gillbie, Gillby

GILCHRIST (Irish) an alternate form of Ghilchrist.

GILEN (Basque, German) illustrious pledge.

GILES (French) goatskin shield.
Gide, Gilles, Gyles

GILLEAN (Irish) Bible: Saint John's servant.
Gillan, Gillen, Gillian

GILLESPIE (Irish) son of the bishop's servant.
Gillis

GILLETT (French) young Gilbert.
Gelett, Gelette, Gillette

GILMER (English) famous hostage.
Gilmar

GILMORE (Irish) devoted to the Virgin Mary.
Gillmore, Gillmour, Gilmour

GILON (Hebrew) circle.

GILROY (Irish) devoted to the king.
Gilderoy, Gildray, Gildroy, Gillroy, Roy

GINO (Greek) a familiar form of Eugene. (Italian) a short form of names ending in "gene," "gino."
Ghino

GIONA (Italian) a form of Jonah.

GIORDANO (Italian) a form of Jordan.
Giordan, Giordana, Giordin, Guordan

GIORGIO (Italian) a form of George.

GIORGOS (Greek) an alternate form of George.
Georgos, Giorgios

GIOSIA (Italian) a form of Joshua.

GIOTTO (Italian) a form of Geoffrey.

GIOVANI (Italian) an alternate form of Giovanni.
Giavani, Giovan, Giovane, Giovanie, Giovon

GIOVANNI (Italian) a form of John. See also Jeovanni, Jiovanni.
Geovanni, Geovanny, Gian, Gianni, Giannino, Giovani, Giovann, Giovannie, Giovanno, Giovanny, Giovonathon, Giovonni, Giovonnia, Giovonnie, Givonni

GIOVANNY (Italian) an alternate form of Giovanni.
Giovany

GIPSY (English) wanderer.
Gipson, Gypsy

GIRVIN (Irish) small; tough.
Girvan, Girven, Girvon

GITANO (Spanish) gypsy.

GIULIANO (Italian) a form of Julius.
Giulano, Giulino, Giulliano

GIULIO (Italian) a form of Julius.
Guilano

GIUSEPPE (Italian) a form of Joseph.
Giuseppi, Giuseppino, Giusseppe, Guiseppe, Guiseppi, Guiseppie, Guisseppe

GIUSTINO (Italian) a form of Justin.
Giusto

GIVON (Hebrew) hill; heights.
Givan, Givawn, Givyn

GLADWIN (English) cheerful. See also Win.
Glad, Gladdie, Gladdy, Gladwinn, Gladwyn, Gladwynne

GLANVILLE (English) village with oak trees.

GLEN (Irish) an alternate form of Glenn.
Glyn

GLENDON (Scottish) fortress in the glen.
Glenden, Glendin, Glenn, Glennden, Glennton, Glenton

GLENDOWER (Welsh) from Glyndwer, England.

GLENN (Irish) a short form of Glendon.
Gleann, Glen, Glennie, Glennis, Glennon, Glenny, Glynn

GLENTWORTH (English) from Glenton, England.

GLENVILLE (Irish) village in the glen.

GLYN (Welsh) a form of Glen.
Glin, Glynn

GODDARD (German) divinely firm.
Godard, Godart, Goddart, Godhardt, Godhart, Gothart, Gotthard, Gotthardt, Gotthart

GODFREY (German) a form of Jeffrey. (Irish) God's peace. See also Geoffrey, Gottfried.
Giotto, Godefroi, Godfree, Godfry, Godofredo, Godoired,

Godfrey *(cont.)*
Godrey, Goffredo, Gofraidh, Gofredo, Gorry

GODWIN (English) friend of God. See also Win.
Godewyn, Godwinn, Godwyn, Goodwin, Goodwyn, Goodwynn, Goodwynne

GOEL (Hebrew) redeemer.

GOLDWIN (English) golden friend. See also Win.
Golden, Goldewin, Goldewinn, Goldewyn, Goldwyn, Goldwynn

GOLIATH (Hebrew) exiled. Bible: the giant Phillistine whom David slew with a slingshot.
Golliath

GOMDA (Kiowa) wind.

GOMER (Hebrew) completed, finished. (English) famous battle.

GONZA (Rutooro) love.

GONZALO (Spanish) wolf.
Goncalve, Gonsalo, Gonsalve, Gonzales, Gonzelee, Gonzolo

GORDON (English) triangular hill.
Geordan, Gord, Gordain, Gordan, Gorden, Gordonn, Gordy

GORDY (English) a familiar form of Gordon.
Gordie

GORE (English) triangular-shaped land; wedge-shaped land.

GORMAN (Irish) small; blue eyed.

GORO (Japanese) fifth.

GOSHEVEN (Native American) great leaper.

GOTTFRIED (German) a form of Geoffrey, Godfrey.
Gotfrid, Gotfrids, Gottfrid

GOTZON (German) a form of Angel.

GOVERT (Dutch) heavenly peace.

GOWER (Welsh) pure.

GOWON (Tiv) rainmaker.
Gowan

GOZOL (Hebrew) soaring bird.
Gozal

GRADY (Irish) noble; illustrious.
Gradea, Gradee, Gradey, Gradleigh, Graidey, Graidy

GRAEME (Scottish) a form of Graham.
Graem

GRAHAM (English) grand home.
Graeham, Graehame, Graehme, Graeme, Grahamme, Grahm, Grahame, Grahme, Gram, Grame, Gramm, Grayeme, Grayham

GRANGER (French) farmer.
Grainger, Grange

GRANT (English) a short form of Grantland.
Grand, Grantham, Granthem, Grantley

GRANTLAND (English) great plains.
Grant

GRANVILLE (French) large village.
Gran, Granvel, Granvil, Granvile, Granvill, Grenville, Greville

GRAY (English) gray haired.
Graye, Grey, Greye

GRAYDEN (English) gray haired.
Graden, Graydan, Graydyn, Greyden

GRAYDON (English) gray hill.
Gradon, Grayton, Greydon

GRAYSON (English) bailiff's son. See also Sonny.
Graysen, Greyson

GREELEY (English) gray meadow.
Greelea, Greeleigh, Greely

GREENWOOD (English) green forest.
Green, Greener

GREG, Gregg (Latin) short forms of Gregory.
Graig, Greig, Gregson

GREGGORY (Latin) an alternate form of Gregory.
Greggery

GREGOR (Scottish) a form of Gregory.
Gregoor, Grégor, Gregore

GREGORIO (Italian, Portuguese) a form of Gregory.
Gregorios

GREGORY (Latin) vigilant watchman. See also Jörn, Krikor.
Gergely, Gergo, Greagoir, Greagory, Greer, Greg, Gregary, Greger, Gregery, Greggory, Grégoire, Gregor, Gregorey, Gregori, Grégorie, Gregorio, Gregorius, Gregors, Gregos, Gregrey, Gregroy, Gregry, Greogry, Gries, Grisha, Grzegorz

GRESHAM (English) village in the pasture.

GREYSON (English) an alternate form of Grayson.
Greysen, Greysten, Greyston

GRIFFIN (Latin) hooked nose.
Griff, Griffen, Griffie, Griffon, Griffy, Gryphon

GRIFFITH (Welsh) fierce chief; ruddy.
Grifen, Griff, Griffeth, Griffie, Griffy, Griffyn, Griffynn, Gryphon

GRIGORI (Bulgarian) a form of Gregory.
Grigoi, Grigor, Grigore, Grigorios, Grigorov, Grigory

GRIMSHAW (English) dark woods.

GRISHA (Russian) a form of Gregory.

GRISWOLD (German, French) gray forest.
Gris, Griz, Grizwald

GROSVENER (French) big hunter.

GROVER (English) grove.
Grove

GUADALUPE (Arabic) river of black stones.
Guadalope

GUALBERTO (Spanish) a form of Walter.
Gualterio

GUALTIERO (Italian) a form of Walter.
Gualterio

GUGLIELMO (Italian) a form of William.

GUIDO (Italian) a form of Guy.

GUILFORD (English) ford with yellow flowers.
Guildford

GUILHERME (Portuguese) a form of William.

GUILLAUME (French) a form of William.
Guillaums, Guilleaume, Guilem, Guyllaume

GUILLERMO (Spanish) a form of William.
Guillerrmo

GUNNAR (Scandinavian) an alternate form of Gunther.
Guner, Gunner

GUNTHER (Scandinavian) battle army; warrior.
Guenter, Guenther, Gun, Gunnar, Guntar, Gunter, Guntero, Gunthar, Günther

GUOTIN (Chinese) polite; strong leader.

GURION (Hebrew) young lion.
Gur, Guri, Guriel

GURPREET (Punjabi) devoted to the guru; devoted to the Prophet.
Gurjeet, Gurmeet, Guruprit

GURVIR (Sikh) guru's warrior.
Gurveer

GUS (Scandinavian) a short form of Angus, Augustine, Gustave.
Guss, Gussie, Gussy, Gusti, Gustry, Gusty

GUSTAF (Swedish) a form of Gustave.
Gustaaf, Gustaff

GUSTAVE (Scandinavian) staff of the Goths. History: Gustavus Adolphus was a king of Sweden. See also Kosti, Tabo, Tavo.
Gus, Gustaf, Gustaff, Gustaof, Gustav, Gustáv, Gustava, Gustaves, Gustavo, Gustavs, Gustavus, Gustik, Gustus, Gusztav

GUSTAVO (Italian, Spanish) a form of Gustave.
Gustabo

GUTHRIE (German) war hero. (Irish) windy place.
Guthrey, Guthry

GUTIERRE (Spanish) a form of Walter.

GUY (Hebrew) valley. (German) warrior. (French) guide. See also Guido.
Guyon

GUYAPI (Native American) candid.

GWAYNE (Welsh) an alternate form of Gawain.
Gwaine, Gwayn

GWIDON (Polish) life.

GWILYM (Welsh) a form of William.
Gwillym

GWYN (Welsh) fair; blessed.
Gwynn, Gwynne

GYASI (Akan) marvelous baby.

GYORGY (Russian) a form of George.
Gyoergy, György, Gyuri, Gyurka

GYULA (Hungarian) youth.
Gyala, Gyuszi

HABIB (Arabic) beloved.

HACKETT (German, French) little woodcutter.
Hacket, Hackit, Hackitt

HACKMAN (German, French) woodcutter.

HADAR (Hebrew) glory.

HADDAD (Arabic) blacksmith.

HADDEN (English) heather-covered hill.
Haddan, Haddon, Haden

HADEN (English) an alternate form of Hadden.
Hadin, Hadon, Hadyn, Haeden

HADI (Arabic) guiding to the right.
Hadee, Hady

HADLEY (English) heather-covered meadow.
Had, Hadlea, Hadlee, Hadleigh, Hadly, Lee, Leigh

HADRIAN (Latin, Swedish) dark.
Adrian, Hadrien

HADWIN (English) friend in a time of war.
Hadwinn, Hadwyn, Hadwynn, Hadwynne

HAGAN (German) strong defense.
Haggan

HAGEN (Irish) young, youthful.

HAGLEY (English) enclosed meadow.

HAGOS (Ethiopian) happy.

HAHNEE (Native American) beggar.

HAI (Vietnamese) sea.

HAIDAR (Arabic) lion.
Haider

HAIDEN (English) an alternate form of Hayden.
Haidyn

HAIG (English) enclosed with hedges.

HAILEY (Irish) an alternate form of Haley.
Haile, Haille, Haily, Halee

HAJI (Swahili) born during the pilgrimage to Mecca.

HAKAN (Native American) fiery.

HAKEEM (Arabic) an alternate form of Hakim.
Hakam, Hakem

HAKIM (Arabic) wise. (Ethiopian) doctor.
Hakeem, Hakiem

HAKON (Scandinavian) of Nordic ancestry.
Haaken, Haakin, Haakon, Haeo, Hak, Hakan, Hako

HAL (English) a short form of Halden, Hall, Harold.

HALBERT (English) shining hero.
Bert, Halburt

HALDEN (Scandinavian) half-Danish. See also Dane.
Hal, Haldan, Haldane, Halfdan, Halvdan

HALE (English) a short form of Haley. (Hawaiian) a form of Harry.
Hayle, Heall

HALEN (Swedish) hall.
Hale, Hallen, Haylan, Haylen

HALEY (Irish) ingenious.
Hailey, Hale, Haleigh, Halley, Hayleigh, Hayley, Hayli

HALFORD (English) valley ford.

HALI (Greek) sea.

HALIAN (Zuni) young.

HALIL (Turkish) dear friend.
Halill

HALIM (Arabic) mild, gentle.
Haleem

HALL (English) manor, hall.
Hal, Halstead, Halsted

HALLAM (English) valley.

HALLAN (Engish) dweller at the hall; dweller at the manor.
Halin, Hallene, Hallin

HALLEY (English) meadow near the hall; holy.
Hallie

HALLIWELL (English) holy well.
Hallewell, Hellewell, Helliwell

HALLWARD (English) hall guard.

HALSEY (English) Hal's island.

HALSTEAD (English) manor grounds.
Halsted

HALTON (English) estate on the hill.

HALVOR (Norwegian) rock; protector.
Halvard

HAM (Hebrew) hot. Bible: one of Noah's sons.

HAMAL (Arabic) lamb. Astronomy: a bright star in the constellation of Aries.

HAMAR (Scandinavian) hammer.

HAMID (Arabic) praised. See also Muhammad.
Haamid, Hamaad, Hamadi, Hamd, Hamdrem, Hamed, Hamedo, Hameed, Hamidi, Hammad, Hammed, Humayd

HAMILL (English) scarred.
Hamel, Hamell, Hammill

HAMILTON (English) proud estate.
Hamel, Hamelton, Hamil, Hamill, Tony

HAMISH (Scottish) a form of Jacob, James.

HAMISI (Swahili) born on Thursday.

HAMLET (German, French) little village; home. Literature: one of Shakespeare's tragic heroes.

HAMLIN (German, French) loves his home.
Hamblin, Hamelen, Hamelin, Hamlen, Hamlyn, Lin

HAMMET (English, Scandinavian) village.
Hammett, Hamnet, Hamnett

HAMMOND (English) village.
Hamond

HAMPTON (English) Geography: a town in England.
Hamp

HAMZA (Arabic) powerful.
Hamzah, Hamze, Hamzeh, Hamzia

HANALE (Hawaiian) a form of Henry.
Haneke

HANAN (Hebrew) grace.
Hananel, Hananiah, Johanan

HANBAL (Arabic) pure. History: founder of an Islamic school of thought.

HANDEL (German, English) a form of John.

HANFORD (English) high ford.

HANIF (Arabic) true believer.
Haneef, Hanef

HANK (American) a familiar form of Henry.

HANLEY (English) high meadow.
Handlea, Handleigh, Handley, Hanlea, Hanlee, Hanleigh, Hanly, Henlea, Henlee, Henleigh, Henley

HANNES (Finnish) a form of John.

HANNIBAL (Phoenician) grace of God. History: a famous Carthaginian general who fought the Romans.
Anibal

HANNO (German) a short form of Johan.
Hanna, Hannah, Hannon, Hannu, Hanon

HANS (Scanadinavian) a form of John.
Hanschen, Hansel, Hants, Hanz

HANSEL (Scandinavian) an alternate form of Hans.
Haensel, Hansell, Hansl, Hanzel

HANSEN (Scandinavian) son of Hans.
Hanson

HANSH (Hindi) god; godlike. Religion: another name for the Hindu god Shiva.

HANSON (Scandinavian) an alternate form of Hansen.
Hansen, Hanssen, Hansson

HANUS (Czech) a form of John.

HAOA (Hawaiian) a form of Howard.

HARA (Hindi) seizer. Religion: another name for the Hindu god Shiva.

HARALD (Scandinavian) an alternate form of Harold.
Haraldo, Haralds, Haralpos

HARB (Arabic) warrior.

HARBIN (German, French) little bright warrior.
Harben, Harbyn

HARCOURT (French) fortified dwelling.
Court, Harcort

HARDEEP (Punjabi) an alternate form of Harpreet.

HARDEN (English) valley of the hares.
Hardian, Hardin

HARDING (English) brave man's son.
Hardin

HARDWIN (English) brave friend.

HARDY (German) bold, daring.
Hardie

HAREL (Hebrew) mountain of God.
Harell, Hariel, Harrell

HARFORD (English) ford of the hares.

HARGROVE (English) grove of the hares.
Hargreave, Hargreaves

HARI (Hindi) tawny. Religion: another name for the Hindu god Vishnu.
Hariel, Harin

HARITH (Arabic) cultivator.

HARJOT (Sikh) light of God.
Harjeet, Harjit, Harjodh

HARKIN (Irish) dark red.
Harkan, Harken

HARLAN (English) hare's land; army land.
Harland, Harlen, Harlenn, Harlin, Harlon, Harlyn, Harlynn

HARLAND (English) an alternate form of Harlan.
Harlend

HARLEY (English) hare's meadow; army meadow.
Arley, Harlea, Harlee, Harleigh, Harly

HARLOW (English) hare's hill; army hill. See also Arlo.

HARMAN, Harmon (English) forms of Herman.
Harm, Harmen, Harmond, Harms

HAROLD (Scandinavian) army ruler. See also Jindra.
Araldo, Garald, Garold, Hal, Harald, Haraldas, Haraldo,

Haralds, Harry, Heraldo, Herold, Heronim, Herrick, Herryck

HAROUN (Arabic) lofty; exalted.
Haarun, Harin, Haron, Haroon, Harron, Harun

HARPER (English) harp player.
Harp, Harpo

HARPREET (Punjabi) loves God, devoted to God.
Hardeep

HARRIS (English) a short form of Harrison.
Haris, Hariss

HARRISON (English) son of Harry.
Harison, Harreson, Harris, Harrisen, Harrisson

HARROD (Hebrew) hero; conqueror.

HARRY (English) a familiar form of Harold. See also Arrigo, Hale, Parry.
Harm, Harray, Harrey, Harri, Harrie

HART (English) a short form of Hartley.

HARTLEY (English) deer meadow.
Hart, Hartlea, Hartlee, Hartleigh, Hartly

HARTMAN (German) hard; strong.

HARTWELL (English) deer well.
Harwell, Harwill

HARTWIG (German) strong advisor.

HARTWOOD (English) deer forest.
Harwood

HARVEY (German) army warrior.
Harv, Hervé, Hervey, Hervie, Hervy

HARVIR (Sikh) God's warrior.
Harvier

HASAD (Turkish) reaper, harvester.

HASAN (Arabic) an alternate form of Hassan.
Hasaan, Hasain, Hasaun, Hashaan, Hason

HASANI (Swahili) handsome.
Hasan, Hasanni, Hassani, Heseny, Hassen, Hassian, Husani

HASHIM (Arabic) destroyer of evil.
Haashim, Hasham, Hasheem, Hashem

HASIN (Hindi) laughing.
Haseen, Hasen, Hassin, Hazen, Hesen

HASKEL (Hebrew) an alternate form of Ezekiel.
Haskell

HASLETT (English) hazel-tree land.
Haze, Hazel, Hazlett, Hazlitt

HASSAN (Arabic) handsome.
Hasan, Hassen, Hasson

HASSEL (German, English) witches' corner.
Hassal, Hassall, Hassell, Hazael, Hazell

HASTIN (Hindi) elephant.

HASTINGS (Latin) spear. (English) house council.
Hastie, Hasty

HATIM (Arabic) judge.
Hateem, Hatem

HAUK (Norwegian) hawk.
Haukeye

HAVELOCK (Norwegian) sea battler.

HAVEN (Dutch, English) harbor, port; safe place.
Haeven, Havin, Hevin, Hevon, Hovan

HAVIKA (Hawaiian) a form of David.

HAWK (English) hawk.
Hawke, Hawkin, Hawkins

HAWLEY (English) hedged meadow.
Hawleigh, Hawly

HAWTHORNE (English) hawthorn tree.

HAYDEN (English) hedged valley.
Haiden, Haydan, Haydenn, Haydn, Haydon

HAYES (English) hedged valley.
Hayse

HAYWARD (English) guardian of the hedged area.
Haward, Heyvard, Heyward

HAYWOOD (English) hedged forest.
Heywood, Woody

HEARN (Scottish, English) a short form of Ahearn.
Hearne, Herin, Hern

HEATH (English) heath.
Heathe, Heith

HEATHCLIFF (English) cliff near the heath. Literature: the hero of Emily Brontë's novel *Wuthering Heights*.

HEATON (English) high place.

HEBER (Hebrew) ally, partner.

HECTOR (Greek) steadfast. Mythology: the greatest hero of the Trojan war.

HEDLEY (English) heather-filled meadow.
Headley, Headly, Hedly

HEINRICH (German) an alternate form of Henry.
Heindrick, Heiner, Heinreich, Heinrick, Heinrik, Hinrich

HEINZ (German) a familiar form of Henry.

HELAKU (Native American) sunny day.

HELGE (Russian) holy.

HELKI (Moquelumnan) touching.

HELMER (German) warrior's wrath.

HELMUT (German) courageous.
Helmuth

HEMAN (Hebrew) faithful.

HENDERSON (Scottish, English) son of Henry.
Hendrie, Hendries, Hendron, Henryson

HENDRICK (Dutch) a form of Henry.
Hendricks, Hendrickson, Hendrik, Hendriks, Hendrikus, Hendrix, Henning

HENIEK (Polish) a form of Henry.
Henier

HENLEY (English) high meadow.

HENNING (German) an alternate form of Hendrick, Henry.

HENOCH (Yiddish) initiator.
Enoch, Henock, Henok

HENRI (French) a form of Henry.
Henrico, Henrri

HENRICK (Dutch) a form of Henry.
Heinrick, Henerik, Henrich, Henrik, Henryk

HENRIQUE (Portuguese) a form of Henry.

HENRY (German) ruler of the household. See also Arrigo, Enric, Enrick, Enrico, Enrikos, Enrique, Hanale, Honok, Kiki.
Hagan, Hank, Harro, Harry, Heike, Heinrich, Heinz, Hendrick, Henery, Heniek, Henning, Henraoi, Henri, Henrick, Henrim, Henrique, Henrry, Heromin, Hersz

HERALDO (Spanish) a form of Harold.
Herald, Hiraldo

HERB (German) a short form of Herbert.
Herbie, Herby

HERBERT (German) glorious soldier.
Bert, Erbert, Eriberto, Harbert, Hebert, Hébert, Heberto, Herb, Heriberto, Hurbert

HERCULES (Greek) glorious gift. Mythology: a famous Greek hero renowned for his twelve labors.
Herakles, Herc, Hercule, Herculie

HERIBERTO (Spanish) a form of Herbert.
Heribert

HERMAN (Latin) noble. (German) soldier. See also Armand, Ermanno, Ermano, Mandek.

Herman *(cont.)*
Harmon, Hermaan, Hermann, Hermie, Herminio, Hermino, Hermon, Hermy, Heromin

HERMES (Greek) messenger. Mythology: the messenger for the Greek gods.

HERNAN (German) peacemaker.

HERNANDO (Spanish) a form of Ferdinand.
Hernandes, Hernandez

HERRICK (German) war ruler.
Herrik, Herryck

HERSCHEL (Hebrew) an alternate form of Hershel.
Herchel, Hersch, Herschel, Herschell

HERSH (Hebrew) a short form of Hershel.
Hersch, Hirsch

HERSHEL (Hebrew) deer.
Herschel, Hersh, Hershal, Hershall, Hershell, Herzl, Hirschel, Hirshel

HERTZ (Yiddish) my strife.
Herzel

HERVÉ (French) a form of Harvey.

HESPEROS (Greek) evening star.
Hespero

HESUTU (Moquelumnan) picking up a yellow jacket's nest.

HEW (Welsh) a form of Hugh.
Hewe, Huw

HEWITT (German, French) little smart one.
Hewe, Hewet, Hewett, Hewie, Hewit, Hewlett, Hewlitt, Hugh

HEWSON (English) son of Hugh.

HEZEKIAH (Hebrew) God gives strength.
Hezekyah, Hazikiah, Hezikyah

HIAMOVI (Cheyenne) high chief.

HIBAH (Arabic) gift.

HIDEAKI (Japanese) smart, clever.
Hideo

HIEREMIAS (Greek) God will uplift.

HIERONYMOS (Greek) a form of Jerome.
Hierome, Hieronim, Hieronimo, Hieronimos, Hieronymo, Hieronymus

HIEU (Vietnamese) respectful.

HILARIO (Spanish) a form of Hilary.

HILARY (Latin) cheerful. See also Ilari.
Hi, Hilair, Hilaire, Hilarie, Hilario, Hilarion, Hilarius, Hil, Hill, Hillary, Hillery, Hilliary, Hillie, Hilly

HILDEBRAND (German) battle sword.
Hildebrando, Hildo

HILEL (Arabic) new moon.

HILLEL (Hebrew) greatly praised. Religion: Rabbi Hillel originated the Talmud.

HILLIARD (German) brave warrior.
Hillard, Hiller, Hillier, Hillierd, Hillyard, Hillyer, Hillyerd

HILMAR (Swedish) famous noble.

HILTON (English) town on a hill
Hylton

HINTO (Dakota) blue.

HINUN (Native American) spirit of the storm.

HIPPOLYTE (Greek) horseman.
Hipolito, Hippolit, Hippolitos, Hippolytus, Ippolito

HIRAM (Hebrew) noblest; exalted.
Hi, Hirom, Huram, Hyrum

HIROMASA (Japanese) fair, just.

HIROSHI (Japanese) generous.

HISOKA (Japanese) secretive, reserved.

HIU (Hawaiian) a form of Hugh.

HO (Chinese) good.

HOANG (Vietnamese) finished.

HOBART (German) Bart's hill.
Hobard, Hobbie, Hobby, Hobie, Hoebart

HOBERT (German) Bert's hill.
Hobey

HOBSON (English) son of Robert.
Hobbs, Hobs

HOC (Vietnamese) studious.

HOD (Hebrew) a short form of Hodgson.

HODGSON (English) son of Roger.
Hod

HOGAN (Irish) youth.
Hogin

HOLBROOK (English) brook in the hollow.
Brook, Holbrooke

HOLDEN (English) hollow in the valley.
Holdan, Holdin, Holdon, Holdun, Holdyn

HOLIC (Czech) barber.

HOLLAND (French) Geography: A country in the Netherlands.

HOLLEB (Polish) dove.
Hollub, Holub

HOLLIS (English) grove of holly trees.
Hollie, Holly

HOLMES (English) river islands.

HOLT (English) forest.
Holten, Holton

HOMER (Greek) hostage; pledge; security. Literature: a renowned Greek poet.
Homar, Homere, Homère, Homero, Homeros, Homerus

HONDO (Shona) warrior.

HONESTO (Filipino) honest.

HONI (Hebrew) gracious.
Choni

HONOK (Polish) a form of Henry.

HONON (Moquelumnan) bear.

HONORATO (Spanish) honorable.

HONORÉ (Latin) honored.
Honor, Honoratus, Honoray, Honorio, Honorius

HONOVI (Native American) strong.

HONZA (Czech) a form of John.

HOP (Chinese) agreeable.

HORACE (Latin) keeper of the hours. Literature: a famous Latin poet.
Horacio, Horaz

HORACIO (Latin) an alternate form of Horace.

HORATIO (Latin) clan name. See also Orris.
Horatius, Oratio

HORST (German) dense grove; thicket.
Hurst

HORTON (English) garden estate.
Hort, Horten, Orton

HOSA (Arapaho) young crow.

HOSEA (Hebrew) salvation. Bible: a Hebrew prophet.
Hose, Hoseia, Hoshea, Hosheah

HOTAH (Lakota) white.

HOTOTO (Native American) whistler.

HOUGHTON (English) settlement on the headland.

HOUSTON (English) hill town. Geography: a city in Texas.
Housten, Houstin, Hustin, Huston

HOWARD (English) watchman. See also Haoa.
Howie, Ward

HOWE (German) high.
Howey, Howie

HOWELL (Welsh) remarkable.
Howel

HOWI (Moquelumnan) turtle dove.

HOWIE (English) a familiar form of Howard, Howland.
Howey

HOWIN (Chinese) loyal swallow.

HOWLAND (English) hilly land.
Howie, Howlan, Howlen

HOYT (Irish) mind; spirit.

HU (Chinese) tiger.

HUBBARD (German) an alternate form of Hubert.

HUBERT (German) bright mind; bright spirit. See also Beredei, Uberto.
Bert, Hobart, Hubbard, Hubbert, Huber, Hubertek, Huberto, Hubertson, Hubie, Huey, Hugh, Hugibert, Huibert, Humberto

HUBERTO (Spanish) a form of Hubert.
Humberto

HUBIE (English) a familiar form of Hubert.
Hube, Hubi

HUD (Arabic) Religion: a Muslim prophet.

HUDSON (English) son of Hud.

HUEY (English) a familiar form of Hugh.
Hughey, Hughie, Hughy, Hui

HUGH (English) a short form of Hubert. See also Ea, Hewitt, Huxley, Maccoy, Ugo.
Fitzhugh, Hew, Hiu, Hue, Huey, Hughes, Hugo, Hugues

HUGO (Latin) a form of Hugh.
Ugo

HULBERT (German) brilliant grace.

Hulbert *(cont.)*
Bert, Hulbard, Hulburd, Hulburt, Hull

HUMBERT (German) brilliant strength. See also Umberto.
Hum, Humberto

HUMBERTO (Portuguese) a form of Humbert.

HUMPHREY (German) peaceful strength. See also Onofrio, Onufry.
Hum, Humfredo, Humfrey, Humfrid, Humfried, Humfry, Hump, Humph, Humphery, Humphry, Humphrys, Hunfredo

HUNG (Vietnamese) brave.

HUNT (English) a short form of names beginning with "Hunt."

HUNTER (English) hunter.
Hunt, Huntur

HUNTINGTON (English) hunting estate.
Hunt, Huntingdon

HUNTLEY (English) hunter's meadow.
Hunt, Huntlea, Huntlee, Huntleigh, Huntly

HURLEY (Irish) sea tide.
Hurlee, Hurleigh

HURST (English) a form of Horst.
Hearst, Hirst

HUSAM (Arabic) sword.

HUSAMETTIN (Turkish) sharp sword.

HUSLU (Native American) hairy bear.

HUSSAIN (Arabic) an alternate form of Hussein.

Hossain, Husain, Husani, Husayn, Hussan, Hussayn

HUSSEIN (Arabic) little; handsome.
Hossein, Houssein, Houssin, Huissien, Huossein, Husein, Husien, Hussain, Hussien

HUSSIEN (Arabic) an alternate form of Hussein.
Husian, Hussin

HUTCHINSON (English) son of the hutch dweller.
Hutcheson

HUTE (Native American) star. Astronomy: a star in the Big Dipper.

HUTTON (English) house on the jutting ledge.
Hut, Hutt, Huttan

HUXLEY (English) Hugh's meadow.
Hux, Huxlea, Huxlee, Huxleigh, Lee

HUY (Vietnamese) glorious.

HY (Vietnamese) hopeful. (English) a short form of Hyman.

HYACINTHE (French) hyacinth.

HYATT (English) high gate.
Hyat

HYDE (English) measure of land equal to 120 acres.

HYDER (English) tanner, preparer of animal hides for tanning.

HYMAN (English) a form of Chaim.
Haim, Hayim, Hayvim, Hayyim, Hy, Hyam, Hymie

HYUN-KI (Korean) wise.

HYUN-SHIK (Korean) clever.

IAGO (Spanish, Welsh) a form of Jacob, James. Literature: the villain in Shakespeare's *Othello*.
Jago

IAIN (Scottish) an alternate form of Ian.

IAKOBOS (Greek) a form of Jacob.
Iakov, Iakovos, Iakovs

IAN (Scottish) a form of John. See also Ean, Eion.
Iain, Iane, Iann

IANOS (Czech) a form of John.
Iannis

IB (Phoenician, Danish) oath of Baal.

IBAN (Basque) a form of John.

IBON (Basque) a form of Ivor.

IBRAHIM (Arabic) a form of Abraham. (Hausa) my father is exalted.
Ibrahaim, Ibraham, Ibraheem, Ibrahem, Ibrahiem, Ibrahiim, Ibrahmim

ICHABOD (Hebrew) glory is gone. Literature: Ichabod Crane was the main character of Washington Irving's story "The Legend of Sleepy Hollow."

IDI (Swahili) born during the Idd festival.

IDRIS (Welsh) eager lord. Religion: a Muslim prophet.
Idrease, Idrees, Idres, Idress, Idreus, Idriece, Idriss, Idrissa, Idriys

IESTYN (Welsh) a form of Justin.

IGASHU (Native American) wanderer; seeker.
Igasho

IGGY (Latin) a familiar form of Ignatius.

IGNACIO (Italian) a form of Ignatius.
Ignazio

IGNATIUS (Latin) fiery, ardent. Religion: Saint Ignatious of Loyola was the founder of the Jesuit order. See also Inigo, Neci.
Iggie, Iggy, Ignac, Ignác, Ignace, Ignacio, Ignacius, Ignatios, Ignatious, Ignatz, Ignaz, Ignazio

IGOR (Russian) a form of Inger, Ingvar. See also Egor, Yegor.
Igoryok

IHSAN (Turkish) compassionate.

IKE (Hebrew) a familiar form of Isaac. History: the nickname of the thirty-fourth U.S. president Dwight D. Eisenhower.
Ikee, Ikey

IKER (Basque) visitation.

ILAN (Hebrew) tree. (Basque) youth.

ILARI (Basque) a form of Hilary.
Ilario

ILIAS (Greek) a form of Elijah.
Illias, Illyas, Ilyas, Ilyes

ILLAN (Basque, Latin) youth.

ILOM (Ibo) my enemies are many.

ILYA (Russian) a form of Elijah.
Ilia, Ilie, Ilija, Iliya, Ilja, Illia, Illya

IMAD (Arabic) supportive; mainstay.

IMAN (Hebrew) a short form of Immanuel.
Imani, Imanni

IMMANUEL (Hebrew) an alternate form of Emmanuel.
Iman, Imanol, Imanuel, Immanual, Immanuele, Immuneal

IMRAN (Arabic) host. Bible: a character in the Old Testament.
Imraan

IMRE (Hungarian) a form of Emery.
Imri

IMRICH (Czech) a form of Emery.
Imrus

INAY (Hindi) god; godlike. Religion: another name for the Hindu god Shiva.

INCE (Hungarian) innocent.

INDER (Hindi) god; godlike. Religion: another name for the Hindu god Shiva.
Inderbir, Inderdeep, Inderjeet, Inderjit, Inderpal, Inderpreet, Inderveer, Indervir, Indra, Indrajit

INDIANA (Hindi) from India.
Indi, Indy

INEK (Welsh) an alternate form of Irvin.

ING (Scandinavian) a short form of Ingmar.
Inge

INGELBERT (German) an alternate form of Engelbert.
Inglebert

INGER (Scandinavian) son's army.
Igor, Ingemar, Ingmar

INGMAR (Scandinavian) famous son.
Ing, Ingamar, Ingamur, Ingemar

INGRAM (English) angel.
Inglis, Ingra, Ingraham, Ingrim

INGVAR (Scandinavian) Ing's soldier.
Igor, Ingevar

INIGO (Basque) a form of Ignatius.
Iñaki, Iniego, Iñigo

INIKO (Ibo) born during bad times.

INNIS (Irish) island.
Innes, Inness, Inniss

INNOCENZIO (Italian) innocent.
Innocenty, Inocenci, Inocencio, Inocente, Inosente

INTEUS (Native American) proud; unashamed.

IOAKIM (Russian) a form of Joachim.
Ioachime, Ioakimo, Iov

IOAN (Greek, Bulgarian, Romanian) a form of John.
Ioane, Ioann, Ioannes, Ioannikios, Ioannis, Ionel

IOKEPA (Hawaiian) a form of Joseph.
Keo

IOLO (Welsh) the Lord is worthy.
Iorwerth

IONAKANA (Hawaiian) a form of Jonathan.

IORGOS (Greek) an alternate form of George.

IOSIF (Greek, Russian) a form of Joseph.

IOSUA (Romanian) a form of Joshua.

IPYANA (Nyakusa) graceful.

IRA (Hebrew) watchful.

IRAM (English) bright.

IRUMBA (Rutooro) born after twins.

IRV (Irish, Welsh, English) a short form of Irvin, Irving.

IRVIN (Irish, Welsh, English) a short form of Irving. See also Ervine.
Inek, Irv, Irven, Irvine, Irvinn, Irvon

IRVING (Irish) handsome. (Welsh) white river. (English) sea friend. See also Ervin, Ervine.
Irv, Irvin, Irvington, Irwin, Irwing

IRWIN (English) an alternate form of Irving. See also Ervin.
Irwinn, Irwyn

ISA (Arabic) a form of Jesus.
Isaah

ISAAC (Hebrew) he will laugh. Bible: the son of Abraham

and Sarah. See also Itzak, Izak, Yitzchak.
Aizik, Icek, Ike, Ikey, Ikie, Isaak, Isaakios, Isac, Isacc, Isacco, Isack, Isaic, Ishaq, Isiac, Isiacc, Issac, Issca, Itzak, Izak, Izzy

ISAAK (Hebrew) an alternate form of Isaac.
Isack, Isak, Isik, Issak

ISAIAH (Hebrew) God is my salvation. Bible: an influential Hebrew prophet.
Isa, Isai, Isaia, Isaias, Isaid, Isaih, Isaish, Ishaq, Isia, Isiah, Isiash, Issia, Issiah, Izaiah, Izaiha, Izaya, Izayah, Izayaih, Izayiah, Izeyah, Izeyha

ISAIAS (Hebrew) an alternate form of Isaiah.
Isaiahs, Isais, Izayus

ISAM (Arabic) safeguard.

ISAS (Japanese) meritorious.

ISEKEMU (Native American) slow-moving creek.

ISHAM (English) home of the iron one.

ISHAN (Hindi) direction.
Ishaan, Ishaun

ISHAQ (Arabic) a form of Isaac.
Ishaac, Ishak

ISHMAEL (Hebrew) God will hear. Literature: the narrator of Melville's novel *Moby Dick*.
Isamael, Isamail, Ishma, Ishmail, Ishmale, Ishmeal, Ishmeil, Ishmel, Ishmil, Ismael, Ismail

ISIDORE (Greek) gift of Isis. See also Dorian, Ysidro.
Isador, Isadore, Isadorios, Isidor, Isidro, Issy, Ixidor, Izadore, Izidor, Izidore, Izydor, Izzy

ISIDRO (Greek) an alternate form of Isidore.
Isidoro, Isidoros

ISKANDER (Afghani) a form of Alexander.

ISMAEL (Arabic) a form of Ishmael.

ISMAIL (Arabic) a form of Ishmael.
Ismeil, Ismiel

ISRAEL (Hebrew) prince of God; wrestled with God. History: the nation of Israel took its name from the name given Jacob after he wrestled with the Angel of the Lord.
Iser, Isreal, Israhel, Isrell, Isrrael, Isser, Izrael, Izzy, Yisrael

ISREAL (Hebrew) an alternate form of Israel.
Isrieal

ISSA (Swahili) God is our salvation.

ISSAC (Hebrew) an alternate form of Isaac.
Issacc, Issaic, Issiac

ISSIAH (Hebrew) an alternate form of Isaiah.
Issaiah, Issia

ISTU (Native American) sugar pine.

ISTVÁN (Hungarian) a form of Stephen.
Isti, Istvan, Pista

ITHEL (Welsh) generous lord.

ITTAMAR (Hebrew) island of palms.
Itamar

ITZAK (Hebrew) an alternate form of Isaac, Yitzchak.
Itzik

IUKINI (Hawaiian) a form of Eugene.
Kini

IUSTIN (Bulgarian, Russian) a form of Justin.

IVAN (Russian) a form of John.
Iván, Ivanchik, Ivanichek, Ivann, Ivano, Ivas, Iven, Ivin, Ivon, Ivyn, Vanya

IVAR (Scandinavian) an alternate form of Ivor. See also Yves, Yvon.
Iv, Iva

IVES (English) young archer.
Ive, Iven, Ivey, Yves

IVO (German) yew wood; bow wood.
Ibon, Ivar, Ives, Ivon, Ivonnie, Ivor, Yvo

IVOR (Scandinavian) a form of Ivo.
Ibon, Ifor, Ivar, Iver, Ivory, Ivry

IWAN (Polish) a form of John.

IYAPO (Yoruba) many trials; many obstacles.

IYE (Native American) smoke.

IZAK (Czech) a form of Isaac.
Itzhak, Ixaka, Izaac, Izaak, Izac, Izaic, Izak, Izec, Izeke, Izick, Izik, Izsak, Izsák, Izzak

IZZY (Hebrew) a familiar form of Isaac, Isidore, Israel.
Issy

J (American) an initial used as a first name.
J.

JA (Korean) attractive, magnetic.

JAALI (Swahili) powerful.

JAAN (Estonian) a form of Christian.

JAAP (Dutch) a form of Jim.

JABARI (Swahili) fearless.
Jabaar, Jabahri, Jabar, Jabarae, Jabare, Jabaree, Jabarei, Jabarie, Jabarri, Jabarrie, Jabary, Jabbar, Jabbaree, Jabbari, Jaber, Jabiari, Jabier, Jabori, Jaborie

JABEZ (Hebrew) born in pain.
Jabe, Jabes, Jabesh

JABIN (Hebrew) God has created.
Jabain, Jabien, Jabon

JABIR (Arabic) consoler, comforter.
Jabiri, Jabori

JABRIL (Arabic) an alternate form of Jibril.
Jabrail, Jabree, Jabreel, Jabrel, Jabrell, Jabrelle, Jabri, Jabrial, Jabrie, Jabriel, Jabrielle, Jabrille

JABULANI (Shona) happy.

JACAN (Hebrew) trouble.
Jachin

JACARI (American) an alternate form of Jacorey.
Jacarey, Jacaris, Jacarius, Jacarre, Jacarri, Jacarrus, Jacarus, Jacary, Jacaure, Jacauri, Jaccar, Jaccari

JACE (American) a combination of the initials J. + C.
JC, J.C., Jacee, Jacek, Jacey, Jacie, Jaice, Jaicee

JACEN (Greek) an alternate form of Jason.
Jaceon

JACINTO (Portuguese, Spanish) hyacinth. See also Giacinto.
Jacindo, Jacint, Jacinta

JACK (American) a familiar form of Jacob, John. See also Keaka.
Jackie, Jacko, Jackub, Jak, Jax, Jock, Jocko

JACKIE, Jacky (American) familiar forms of Jack.
Jackey

JACKSON (English) son of Jack.
Jacksen, Jacksin, Jacson, Jakson, Jaxon

JACO (Portuguese) a form of Jacob.

JACOB (Hebrew) supplanter, substitute. Bible: son of Isaac, brother of Esau. See also Akiva, Chago, Checha, Coby, Diego, Giacomo, Hamish, Iago, Iakobos, James, Kiva, Koby, Kuba, Tiago, Yakov, Yasha, Yoakim.

Jacob (cont.)
Jaap, Jachob, Jack, Jackob,
Jackub, Jaco, Jacobb, Jacobe,
Jacobi, Jacobo, Jacoby, Jacolbi,
Jacolby, Jacque, Jacques, Jacub,
Jaecob, Jago, Jaicob, Jaime,
Jake, Jakob, Jalu, Jasha,
Jaycob, Jecis, Jeks, Jeska, Jim,
Jocek, Jock, Jocob, Jocobb,
Jocoby, Jocolby, Jokubas

JACOBI, Jacoby (Hebrew) alternate forms of Jacob.
Jachobi, Jacobbe, Jacobee,
Jacobey, Jacobie, Jacobii,
Jacobis

JACOBO (Hebrew) an alternate form of Jacob.

JACOBSON (English) son of Jacob.
Jacobs, Jacobsen, Jacobsin,
Jacobus

JACOREY (American) a combination of Jacob + Corey.
Jacari, Jacori, Jacoria, Jacorie,
Jacoris, Jacorius, Jacorrey,
Jacorrien, Jacorry, Jacory,
Jacouri, Jacourie, Jakari

JACQUE (French) a familiar form of Jacob.
Jacquay, Jacqui, Jocque, Jocqui

JACQUES (French) a form of Jacob, James. See also Coco.
Jackque, Jackques, Jackquise,
Jacot, Jacquan, Jacquees,
Jacquese, Jacquess, Jacquet,
Jacquett, Jacquez, Jacquis,
Jacquise, Jaquez, Jarques,
Jarquis

JACQUEZ, Jaquez (French) alternate forms of Jacques.
Jaques, Jaquese, Jaqueus,
Jaqueze, Jaquis, Jaquise,
Jaquze, Jocquez

JACY (Tupi-Guarani) moon.
Jaicy, Jaycee

JADE (Spanish) jade, precious stone.
Jaeid, Jaid, Jaide

JADEN (Hebrew) an alternate form of Jadon.
Jadee, Jadeen, Jadenn, Jadeon,
Jadin, Jaeden

JADON (Hebrew) God has heard.
Jaden, Jadyn, Jaedon, Jaiden,
Jaydon

JADRIEN (American) a combination of Jay + Adrien.
Jad, Jada, Jadd, Jader, Jadrian

JADYN (Hebrew) an alternate form of Jadon.
Jadyne, Jaedyn

JAEGAR (German) hunter.
Jaager, Jaeger, Jagur

JAE-HWA (Korean) rich, prosperous.

JAEL (Hebrew) mountain goat.
Yael

JAELEN (American) an alternate form of Jalen.
Jaelan, Jaelaun, Jaelin, Jaelon,
Jaelyn

JA'FAR (Sanskrit) little stream.
Jafar, Jafari, Jaffar, Jaffer, Jafur

JAGGER (English) carter.
Jagar, Jager, Jaggar

JAGO (English) an alternate form of James.

JAGUAR (Spanish) jaguar.
Jagguar

JAHI (Swahili) dignified.

JAHLIL (Hindi) an alternate form of Jalil.
Jahlal, Jahlee, Jahleel, Jahliel

JAHMAR (American) an alternate form of Jamar.
Jahmare, Jahmari, Jahmarr,
Jahmer

JAHVON (Hebrew) an alternate form of Javan.
Jahvan, Jahvine, Jahwaan,
Jahwon

JAI (Tai) heart.
Jaie, Jaii

JAIDEN (Hebrew) an alternate form of Jadon.
Jaidan, Jaidon, Jaidyn

JAILEN (American) an alternate form of Jalen.
Jailan, Jailani, Jaileen Jailen,
Jailon, Jailyn, Jailynn

JAIME (Spanish) a form of Jacob, James.
Jaimee, Jaimey, Jaimie, Jaimito,
Jaimy, Jayme, Jaymie

JAIRO (Spanish) God enlightens.
Jair, Jairay, Jaire, Jairus, Jarius

JAISON (Greek) an alternate form of Jason.
Jaisan, Jaisen, Jaishon, Jaishun

JAIVON (Hebrew) an alternate form of Javan.
Jaiven, Jaivion, Jaiwon

JAJA (Ibo) honored.

JAJUAN (American) a combination of the prefix Ja + Juan.
Ja Juan, Jauan, Jawaun, Jejuan,
Jujuan, Juwan

JAKARI (American) an alternate form of Jacorey.
Jakaire, Jakar, Jakaray, Jakarie,
Jakarious, Jakarius, Jakarre,
Jakarri, Jakarus

JAKE (Hebrew) a short form of Jacob.
Jakie, Jayk, Jayke

JAKEEM (Arabic) uplifted.

JAKOB (Hebrew) an alternate form of Jacob.
Jaekob, Jaikab, Jaikob, Jakab, Jakeb, Jakeob, Jakeub, Jakib, Jakiv, Jakobe, Jakobi, Jakobus, Jakoby, Jakov, Jakovian, Jakub, Jakubek, Jekebs

JAKOME (Basque) a form of James. Bible: another name for Saint James.
Xanti

JAL (Gypsy) wanderer.

JALAN (American) an alternate form of Jalen.
Jalaan, Jalaen, Jalain, Jaland, Jalane, Jalani, Jalanie, Jalann, Jalaun, Jalean, Jallan

JALEEL (Hindi) an alternate form of Jalil.
Jaleell, Jaleil, Jalel

JALEN (American) a combination of the prefix Ja + Len.
Jaelen, Jailen, Jalan, Jaleen, Jalend, Jalene, Jalin, Jallen, Jalon, Jalyn

JALIL (Hindi) god; godlike. Religion: another name for the Hindu god Shiva.
Jahlil, Jalaal, Jalal

JALIN, Jalyn (American) alternate forms of Jalen.
Jalian, Jaline, Jalynn, Jalynne

JALON (American) an alternate form of Jalen.
Jalone, Jaloni, Jalun

JAM (American) a short form of Jamal, Jamar.
Jama

JAMAAL (Arabic) an alternate form of Jamal.

JAMAINE (Arabic) a form of Germain.

JAMAL (Arabic) handsome. See also Gamal.
Jahmal, Jahmall, Jahmalle, Jahmeal, Jahmeel, Jahmeil, Jahmel, Jahmelle, Jahmil, Jahmile, Jaimal, Jam, Jamaal, Jamael, Jamahl, Jamail, Jamaile, Jamala, Jamale, Jamall, Jamalle, Jamar, Jamaul, Jamel, Jamil, Jammal, Jamor, Jamual, Jarmal, Jaumal, Jemal, Jermal, Jomal, Jomall

JAMAR (American) a form of Jamal.
Jam, Jamaar, Jamaari, Jamahrae, Jamair, Jamara, Jamaras, Jamaraus, Jamarl, Jamarr, Jamarre, Jamarrea, Jamarree, Jamarri, Jamarvis, Jamaur, Jamir, Jamire, Jamiree, Jammar, Jarmar, Jarmarr, Jaumar, Jemaar, Jemar, Jimar, Jomar

JAMARCUS (American) a combination of the prefix Ja + Marcus.
Jamarco, Jamarkus, Jemarcus, Jimarcus

JAMARI (American) an alternate form of Jamario.
Jamare, Jamarea, Jamaree, Jamareh, Jamaria, Jamarie, Jamaul

JAMARIO (American) a combination of the prefix Ja + Mario.
Jamareo, Jamari, Jamariel, Jamarious, Jamaris, Jamarius, Jamariya, Jemario, Jemarus

JAMARQUIS (American) a combination of the prefix Ja + Marquis.

Jamarkees, Jamarkeus, Jamarkis, Jamarqese, Jamarqueis, Jamarques, Jamarquez, Jamarquios, Jamarqus

JAMEL (Arabic) an alternate form of Jamal.
Jameel, Jamele, Jamell, Jamelle, Iammel, Jamuel, Jamul, Jarmel, Jaumal, Jaumell, Je-Mell, Jimell

JAMES (Hebrew) supplanter, substitute. (English) a form of Jacob. Bible: James the Great and James the Lesser were two of the Twelve Apostles. See also Diego, Hamish Iago, Kimo, Santiago, Seamus, Seumas, Yago, Yasha.
Jacques Jago, Jaime, Jaimes, Jakome, Jamesie, Jamesy, Jamez, Jameze, Jamie, Jamies, Jamse, Jamyes, Jamze, Jas, Jasha, Jay, Jaymes, Jem, Jemes, Jim

JAMESON (English) son of James.
Jamerson, Jamesian, Jamison, Jaymeson

JAMIE (English) a familiar form of James.
Jaime, Jaimey, Jaimie, Jame, Jamee, Jamey, Jameyel, Jami, Jamia, Jamiah, Jamian, Jamme, Jammie Jamiee, Iammy, Jamy, Jamye, Jayme, Jaymee, Jaymie

JAMIL (Arabic) an alternate form of Iamal
Jamiel, Jamiell, Iamielle, Jamile, Jamill, Jamille, Jamyl, Jarmil

JAMIN (Hebrew) favored.
Jamen, Jamian, Jamien, Jamion, Jamionn Jamon, Jamun, Jamyn, Jarmin, Jarmon, Jaymin

JAMISON (English) son of James.
Jamiesen, Jamieson, Jamis, Jamisen, Jamyson, Jaymison

JAMON (Hebrew) an alternate form of Jamin.
Jamohn, Jamone, Jamoni

JAMOND (American) a combination of James + Raymond.
Jamod, Jamont, Jamonta, Jamontae, Jamontay, Jamonte, Jarmond

JAMOR (American) a form of Jamal.
Jamoree, Jamori, Jamorie, Jamorius, Jamorrio, Jamorris, Jamory, Jamour

JAMSHEED (Persian) from Persia.
Jamshaid, Jamshed

JAN (Dutch, Slavic) a form of John.
Jaan, Jana, Janae, Jann, Janne, Jano, Janson, Jenda, Yan

JANCO (Czech) a form of John.
Jancsi, Janke, Janko

JANDO (Spanish) a form of Alexander.
Jandino

JANEIL (American) a combination of the prefix Ja + Neil.
Janal, Janel, Janell, Janelle, Janiel, Janielle, Janile, Janille, Jarnail, Jarneil, Jarnell

JANEK (Polish) a form of John.
Janak, Janik, Janika, Janka, Jankiel, Janko

JANIS (Latvian) a form of John.
Ansis, Jancis, Zanis

JANNE (Finnish) a form of John.
Jann, Jannes

JÁNOS (Hungarian) a form of John.
Jancsi, Jani, Jankia, Jano

JANSON (Scandinavian) son of Jan.
Janse, Jansen, Jansin, Janssen, Jansun, Jantzen, Janzen, Jensen, Jenson

JANTZEN (Scandinavian) an alternate form of Janson.
Janten, Jantsen, Jantson

JANUS (Latin) gate, passageway; born in January. Mythology: the Roman god of beginnings.
Jannese, Jannus, Januario, Janusz

JAPHETH (Hebrew) handsome. (Arabic) abundant. Bible: a son of Noah. See also Yaphet.
Japeth, Japhet

JAQUAN (American) a combination of the prefix Ja + Quan.
Jaequan, Jaiqaun, Jaiquan, Jaqaun, Jaqawan, Jaquaan, Jaquain, Ja'quan, Jaquane, Jaquann, Jaquanne, Jaquavius, Jaquawn, Jaquin, Jaquon, Jaqwan

JAQUARIUS (American) a combination of Jaquan + Darius.
Jaquari, Jaquarious, Jaquaris

JAQUAVIUS (American) an alternate form of Jaquan.
Jaquavas, Jaquaveis, Jaquaveius, Jaquaveon, Jaquaveous, Jaquavias, Jaquavious, Jaquavis, Jaquavus

JAQUON (American) an alternate form of Jaquan.
Jaequon, Jaqoun, Jaquinn, Jaqune, Jaquoin, Jaquone, Jaqwon

JARAD (Hebrew) an alternate form of Jared.
Jaraad, Jaraed

JARAH (Hebrew) sweet as honey.
Jerah

JARDAN (Hebrew) an alternate form of Jordan.
Jarden, Jardin, Jardon

JAREB (Hebrew) contending.
Jarib

JARED (Hebrew) descendant.
Jahred, Jaired, Jarad, Jaredd, Jareid, Jarid, Jarod, Jarred, Jarrett, Jarrod, Jarryd, Jerad, Jered, Jerod, Jerrad, Jerred, Jerrod, Jerryd, Jordan

JAREK (Slavic) born in January.
Janiuszck, Januarius, Januisz, Jarec, Jarrek, Jarric, Jarrick

JARELL (Scandinavian) a form of Gerald.
Jairell, Jarael, Jareil, Jarel, Jarelle, Jariel, Jarrell, Jarryl, Jayryl, Jerel, Jerell, Jerrell, Jharell

JAREN (Hebrew) an alternate form of Jaron.
Jarian, Jarien, Jarin, Jarion

JARETH (American) a combination of Jared + Gareth.
Jarreth, Jereth, Jarreth

JARETT (English) an alternate form of Jarrett.
Jaret, Jarette

JARL (Scandinavian) earl, nobleman.

JARLATH (Latin) in control.
Jarl, Jarlen

JARMAN (German) from Germany.
Jerman

JAROD (Hebrew) an alternate form of Jared.
Jarodd, Jaroid

JARON (Hebrew) he will sing; he will cry out.
Jaaron, Jairon, Jaren, Jarone, Jarren, Jarron, Jaryn, Jayron, Jayronn, Je Ronn, J'ron

JAROSLAV (Czech) glory of spring.
Jarda

JARRED (Hebrew) an alternate form of Jared.
Ja'red, Jarrad, Jarrayd, Jarrid, Jarrod, Jarryd, Jerrid

JARRELL (English) a form of Gerald.
Jarel, Jarell, Jarrel, Jerall, Jerel, Jerell

JARREN (Hebrew) an alternate form of Jaron.
Jarrain, Jarran, Jarrian, Jarrin

JARRETT (English) a form of Garrett, Jared.
Jairett, Jareth, Jarett, Jaretté, Jarhett, Jarratt, Jarret, Jarrette, Jarrot, Jarrott, Jerrett

JARROD (Hebrew) an alternate form of Jared.
Jarod, Jerod, Jerrod

JARRYD (Hebrew) an alternate form of Jared.
Jarrayd, Jaryd

JARVIS (German) skilled with a spear.
Jaravis, Jarv, Jarvaris, Jarvas, Jarvaska, Jarvey, Jarvez, Jarvie, Jarvios, Jarvious, Jarvius, Jarvorice, Jarvoris, Jarvous, Jarvus, Javaris, Jervey, Jervis

JARYN (Hebrew) an alternate form of Jaron.
Jarryn, Jarynn, Jaryon

JAS (Polish) a form of John. (English) a familiar form of James.
Jasio

JASHA (Russian) a familiar form of Jacob, James.
Jascha

JASHAWN (American) a combination of the prefix Ja + Shawn.
Jasean, Jashan, Jashaun, Jashion, Jashon

JASKARAN (Sikh) sings praises to the Lord.
Jaskaren, Jaskarn, Jaskiran

JASMIN (Persian) jasmine flower.
Jasman, Jasmanie, Jasmine, Jasmon, Jasmond

JASON (Greek) healer. Mythology: the hero who led the Argonauts in search of the Golden Fleece.
Jacen, Jaeson, Jahson, Jaison, Jasan, Jasaun, Jase, Jasen, Jasin, Jasson, Jasten, Jasun, Jasyn, Jathan, Jathon, Jay, Jayson

JASPAL (Punjabi) living a virtuous lifestyle.

JASPER (French) green ornamental stone. (English) a form of Casper. See also Kasper.
Jaspar, Jazper, Jespar, Jesper

JASSON (Greek) an alternate form of Jason.
Jassen, Jassin

JATINRA (Hindi) great Brahmin sage.

JAVAN (Hebrew) Bible: son of Japheth.
Jaewan, Jahvaughan, Jahvon, laivon, Javante, Javaon,
JaVaughn, Javen, Javian, Javien, Javin, Javine, Javoanta, Javon, Javona, Javone, Javonte, Jayvin, Jayvion, Jayvon, Jevan, Jevon

JAVANTE (American) a form of Javan.
Javantae, Javantai, Javantée, Javanti

JAVARIS (English) a form of Jarvis.
Javaor, Javar, Javaras, Javare, Javares, Javari, Javarias, Javaries, Javario, Javarius, Javaro, Javaron, Javarous, Javarre, Javarreis, Javarri, Javarrious, Javarris, Javarro, Javarous, Javarte, Javarus, Javorious, Javoris, Javorius, Javouris

JAVAS (Sanskrit) quick, swift.
Jayvas, Jayvis

JAVIER (Spanish) owner of a new house. See also Xavier.
Jabier, Javer, Javere, Javiar

JAVON (Hebrew) an alternate form of Javan.
Jaavon, Jaevin, Jaevon, Jaewon, Javeon, Javion, Javionne, Javohn, Javona, Javone, Javoney, Javoni, Javonn, Javonne, Javonni, Javonnie, Javonnte, Javoun, Jayvon

JAVONTE (American) a form of Javan.
Javona, Javontae, Javontai, Javontay, Javontaye, Javonté, Javontee, Javonteh, Javontey

JAWAUN (American) an alternate form of Jajuan.
Jawaan, Jawan, Jawann, Jawn, Jawon, Jawuan

JAWHAR (Arabic) jewel; essence.

JAXON (English) an alternate form of Jackson.

Jaxon *(cont.)*
Jaxen, Jaxsen, Jaxson, Jaxsun, Jaxun

JAY (French) blue jay. (English) a short form of James, Jason.
Jae, Jai, Jave, Jaye, Jeays, Jeyes

JAYCE (American) a combination of the initials J. + C.
JC, J.C., Jayc, Jaycee, Jay Cee, Jaycey, Jecie

JAYCOB (Hebrew) an alternate form of Jacob.
Jaycub, Jaykob

JAYDE (American) a combination of the initials J. + D.
JD, J.D., Jayd, Jaydee, Jayden

JAYDEN (American) an alternate form of Jayde.
Jaydan, Jaydin, Jaydn, Jaydon

JAYLEE (American) a combination of Jay + Lee.
Jayla, Jayle, Jaylen

JAYLEN (American) a combination of Jay + Len.
Jaylaan, Jaylan, Jayland, Jayleen, Jaylend, Jaylin, Jayln, Jaylon, Jaylun, Jaylund, Jaylyn

JAYLIN (American) an alternate form of Jaylen.
Jaylian, Jayline

JAYLON (American) an alternate form of Jaylen.
Jayleon

JAYLYN (American) an alternate form of Jaylen.
Jaylynd, Jaylynn, Jaylynne

JAYME (English) an alternate form of Jamie.
Jaymie

JAYMES (English) an alternate form of James.
Jaymis, Jayms, Jaymz

JAYQUAN (American) a combination of Jay + Quan.
Jaykwan, Jaykwon, Jayqon, Jayquawn, Jayqunn

JAYSON (Greek) an alternate form of Jason.
Jaycent, Jaysean, Jaysen, Jayshaun, Jayshawn, Jayshon, Jayshun, Jaysin, Jaysn, Jayssen, Jaysson, Jaysun

JAYVON (American) a form of Javon.
Jayvion, Jayvohn, Jayvone, Jayvonn, Jayvontay, Jayvonte, Jaywan, Jaywaun, Jaywin

JAZZ (American) jazz.
Jaz, Jazze, Jazzlee, Jazzman, Jazzmen, Jazzmin, Jazzmon, Jazztin, Jazzton, Jazzy

JEAN (French) a form of John.
Jéan, Jeane, Jeannah, Jeannie, Jeannot, Jeano, Jeanot, Jeanty, Jene

JEB (Hebrew) a short form of Jebediah.
Jebb, Jebi, Jeby

JEBEDIAH (Hebrew) an alternate form of Jedidiah.
Jeb, Jebadia, Jebadiah, Jebadieh, Jebidiah

JED (Hebrew) a short form of Jedidiah. (Arabic) hand.
Jedd, Jeddy, Jedi

JEDIAH (Hebrew) hand of God.
Jedaia, Jedaiah, Jedeiah, Jedi, Yedaya

JEDIDIAH (Hebrew) friend of God, beloved of God. See also Didi.
Jebediah, Jed, Jedadiah, Jeddediah, Jedediah, Jedediha, Jedidia, Jedidiah, Jedidiyah, Yedidya

JEDREK (Polish) strong; manly.
Jedric, Jedrik, Jedrus

JEFF (English) a short form of Jefferson, Jeffrey. A familiar form of Geoffrey.
Jef, Jefe, Jeffe, Jeffey, Jeffie, Jeffy, Jhef

JEFFERSON (English) son of Jeff. History: Thomas Jefferson was the third U.S. president.
Jeferson, Jeff, Jeffers

JEFFERY (English) an alternate form of Jeffrey.
Jefery, Jeffari, Jeffary, Jeffeory, Jefferay, Jeffereoy, Jefferey, Jefferie, Jeffory

JEFFORD (English) Jeff's ford.

JEFFREY (English) divinely peaceful. See also Geffrey, Geoffrey, Godfrey.
Jeff, Jefferies, Jeffery, Jeffre, Jeffree, Jeffrie, Jeffrery, Jeffrie, Jeffries, Jeffry, Jefre, Jefri, Jefry, Jeoffroi, Joffre, Joffrey

JEFFRY (English) an alternate form of Jeffrey.

JEHAN (French) a form of John.
Jehann

JEHU (Hebrew) God lives. Bible: a military commander and king of Israel.
Yehu

JELANI (Swahili) mighty.
Jel, Jelan, Jelanie, Jelaun

JEM (English) a short form of James, Jeremiah.
Jemmie, Jemmy

JEMAL (Arabic) an alternate form of Jamal.
Jemaal, Jemael, Jemale, Jemel

JEMEL (Arabic) an alternate form of Jemal.
Jemeal, Jemehl, Jemehyl, Jemell, Jemelle, Jemello, Jemeyle, Jemile, Jemmy

JEMOND (French) worldly.
Jemon, Jémond, Jemonde, Jemone

JENKIN (Flemish) little John.
Jenkins, Jenkyn, Jenkyns, Jennings

JENÖ (Hungarian) a form of Eugene.
Jenci, Jency, Jenoe, Jensi, Jensy

JENS (Danish) a form of John.
Jense, Jensen, Jenson, Jenssen, Jensy, Jentz

JEOVANNI (Italian) an alternate form of Giovanni.
Jeovahny, Jeovan, Jeovani, Jeovany

JEQUAN (American) a combination of the prefix Je + Quan.
Jeqaun, Jequann, Jequon

JERAD, Jerrad (Hebrew) alternate forms of Jared.
Jeread, Jeredd

JERAHMY (Hebrew) a form of Jeremy.
Jerahmeel, Jerahmeil, Jerahmey

JERALD (English) a form of Gerald.
Jeraldo, Jerold, Jerral, Jerrald, Jerrold, Jerry

JERALL (English) an alternate form of Jarrell.
Jerael, Jerai, Jerail, Jeraile, Jeral, Jerale, Jerall, Jerrail, Jerral, Jerrel, Jerrell, Jerrelle

JERAMIE, Jeramy (Hebrew) alternate forms of Jeremy.
Jerame, Jeramee, Jeramey, Jerami, Jerammie

JERARD (French) a form of Gerard.
Jarard, Jarrard, Jerardo, Jeraude, Jerrard

JERE (Hebrew) a short form of Jeremiah, Jeremy.
Jeré, Jeree

JERED, Jerred (Hebrew) alternate forms of Jared.
Jereed, Jerid, Jerryd, Jeryd

JEREL, Jerell, Jerrell (English) forms of Jarell.
Jerelle, Jeriel, Jeril, Jerrail, Jerral, Jerrall, Jerrel, Jerrill, Jerrol, Jerroll, Jerryl, Jerryll, Jeryl, Jeryle

JEREME, Jeremey (Hebrew) alternate forms of Jeremy.
Jarame

JEREMIAH (Hebrew) God will uplift. Bible: a great Hebrew prophet. See also Dermot, Yeremey, Yirmaya.
Geremiah, Jaramia, Jem, Jemeriah, Jemiah, Jeramiah, Jeramiha, Jere, Jereias, Jeremaya, Jeremi, Jeremia, Jeremial, Jeremias, Jeremija, Jeremy, Jerimiah, Jerimiha, Jerimya, Jermiah, Jermija, Jerry

JEREMIE, Jérémie (Hebrew) alternate forms of Jeremy.
Jeremi, Jérémie, Jeremii

JEREMY (English) a form of Jeremiah.
Jaremay, Jaremi, Jaremy, Jem, Jemmy, Jerahmy, Jeramie, Jeramy, Jere, Jereamy, Jereme, Jeremee, Jeremey, Jeremie, Jérémie, Jeremry, Jérémy, Jeremye, Jereomy, Jeriemy, Jerime, Jerimy, Jermey, Jeromy, Jerremy

JERIAH (Hebrew) Jehovah has seen.

JERICHO (Arabic) city of the moon. Bible: a city conquered by Joshua.
Jeric, Jerick, Jerico, Jerik, Jerric, Jerrick, Jerrico, Jerricoh, Jerryco

JERMAINE (French) an alternate form of Germain. (English) sprout, bud.
Jarman, Jeremaine, Jeremane, Jerimane, Jermain, Jerman, Jermane, Jermanie, Jermanne, Jermany, Jermayn, Jermayne, Jermiane, Jermine, Jer-Mon, Jermone, Jermoney, Jhirmaine

JERMAL (Arabic) an alternate form of Jamal.
Jermael, Jermail, Jermall, Jermaul, Jermel, Jermell, Jermil, Jermol, Jermyll

JERMEY (English) an alternate form of Jeremy.
Jerme, Jermee, Jermere, Jermery, Jermie, Jermy, Jhermie

JERMIAH (Hebrew) an alternate form of Jeremiah.
Jermiha, Jermiya

JERNEY (Slavic) a form of Bartholomew.

JEROD, Jerrod (Hebrew) alternate forms of Jarrod.
Jerode, Jeroid

JEROLIN (Basque, Latin) holy.

JEROME (Latin) holy. See also Geronimo, Hieronymos.
Gerome, Jere, Jeroen, Jerom, Jérome, Jérôme, Jeromo, Jeromy, Jeron, Jerónimo, Jerrome, Jerromy

JEROMY (Latin) an alternate form of Jerome.
Jeromee, Jeromey, Jeromie

JERON (English) a form of Jerome.
Jéron, Jerone, Jeronimo, Jerrin, Jerrion, Jerron, Jerrone, J'ron

JERRETT (Hebrew) a form of Jarrett.
Jeret, Jerett, Jeritt, Jerret, Jerrette, Jerriot, Jerritt, Jerrot, Jerrott

JERRICK (American) a combination of Jerry + Derrick.
Jaric, Jarrick, Jerick, Jerrik

JERRY (German) mighty spearman. (English) a familiar form of Gerald, Gerard. See also Gerry, Kele.
Jehri, Jere, Jeree, Jeris, Jerison, Jerri, Jerrie, Jery

JERVIS (English) a form of Gervaise, Jarvis.

JERZY (Polish) a form of George.
Jersey, Jerzey, Jurek

JESHUA (Hebrew) an alternate form of Joshua.
Jeshuah

JESS (Hebrew) a short form of Jesse.

JESSE (Hebrew) wealthy. Bible: the father of David. See also Yishai.
Jese, Jesee, Jesi, Jess, Jessé, Jessee, Jessie, Jessy

JESSIE (Hebrew) an alternate form of Jesse.
Jesie, Jessi, Jessi

JESSY (Hebrew) an alternate form of Jesse.

Jescey, Jessey, Jessye, Jessyie, Jesy

JESTIN (Welsh) a form of Justin.
Jessten, Jesten, Jeston, Jesstin, Jesston

JESUS (Hebrew) God is my salvation. An alternate form of Joshua. Bible: son of Mary and Joseph, believed by Christians to be the Son of God. See also Chucho, Isa, Yosu.
Jecho, Jessus, Jesu, Jesús, Josu

JESÚS (Hispanic) a form of Jesus.

JETHRO (Hebrew) abundant. Bible: the father-in-law of Moses. See also Yitro.
Jeth, Jethroe, Jetro, Jett

JETT (Hebrew) a short form of Jethro. (English) hard, black mineral.
Jet, Jetson, Jetter, Jetty

JEVAN (Hebrew) an alternate form of Javan.
Jevaun, Jeven, Jevin

JEVON (Hebrew) an alternate form of Javan.
Jevion, Jevohn, Jevone, Jevonn, Jevonne, Jevonnie

JEVONTE (American) a form of Jevon.
Jevonta, Jevontae, Jevontaye, Jevonté

JIBADE (Yoruba) born close to royalty.

JIBBEN (Gypsy) life.
Jibin

JIBRIL (Arabic) archangel of Allah.
Jabril, Jibreel, Jibriel

JILT (Dutch) money.

JIM (Hebrew) supplanter, substitute. (English) a short form of James. See also Jaap.
Jimbo, Jimm, Jimmy

JIMBO (American) a familiar form of Jim.
Jimboo

JIMELL (Arabic) an alternate form of Jamel.
Jimel, Jimelle, Jimill, Jimmell, Jimmelle, Jimmiel, Jimmil

JIMIYU (Abaluhya) born in the dry season.

JIMMIE (English) an alternate form of Jimmy.
Jimi, Jimie, Jimmee, Jimmi

JIMMY (English) a familiar form of Jim.
Jimmey, Jimmie, Jimmye, Jimmyjo, Jimy

JIMOH (Swahili) born on Friday.

JIN (Chinese) gold.
Jinn

JINDRA (Czech) a form of Harold.

JING-QUO (Chinese) ruler of the country.

JIOVANNI (Italian) an alternate form of Giovanni.
Jio, Jiovani, Jiovanie, Jiovann, Jiovannie, Jiovanny, Jiovany, Jiovoni, Jivan

JIRAIR (Armenian) strong; hard working.

JIRI (Czech) a form of George.
Jirka

JIRO (Japanese) second son.

JIVIN (Hindi) life giver.
Jivanta

JO (Hebrew, Japanese) a form of Joe.

JOAB (Hebrew) God is father. See also Yoav.
Joabe, Joaby

JOACHIM (Hebrew) God will establish. See also Akeem, Ioakim, Yehoyakem.
Joacheim, Joakim, Joaquim, Joaquín, Jokin, Jov

JOÃO (Portuguese) a form of John.

JOAQUIM (Portuguese) a form of Joachim.

JOAQUÍN (Spanish) a form of Joachim, Yehoyakem.
Jehoichin, Joaquin, Jocquin, Jocquinn, Joquin, Juaquin

JOB (Hebrew) afflicted. Bible: a righteous man who endured many afflictions.
Jobe, Jobert, Jobey, Jobie, Joby

JOBEN (Japanese) enjoys cleanliness.
Joban, Jobin

JOBO (Spanish) a familiar form of Joseph.

JOBY (Hebrew) a familiar form of Job.
Jobie

JOCK (American) a familiar form of Jacob.
Jocko, Joco, Jocoby, Jocolby

JOCQUEZ (French) an alternate form of Jacquez.
Jocques, Jocquis, Jocquise

JODAN (Hebrew) a combination of Jo + Dan.
Jodahn, Joden, Jodhan, Jodian, Jodin, Jodon, Jodonnis

JODY (Hebrew) a familiar form of Joseph.
Jodey, Jodi, Jodie, Jodiha, Joedy

JOE (Hebrew) a short form of Joseph.
Jo, Joely, Joey

JOEL (Hebrew) God is willing. Bible: an Old Testament Hebrew prophet.
Jôel, Joël, Joell, Joelle, Joely, Jole, Yoel

JOESEPH (Hebrew) an alternate form of Joseph.
Joesph

JOEY (Hebrew) a familiar form of Joe, Joseph.

JOHAN, Johann (German) forms of John. See also Anno, Hanno, Yoan, Yohan.
Joahan, Joan, Joannes, Johahn, Johan, Johanan, Johane, Johannan, Johannes, Johanthan, Johatan, Johathan, Johathon, Johaun, Johon

JOHANNES (German) an alternate form of Johan, Johann.
Johanes, Johannas, Johannus, Johansen, Johanson, Johonson

JOHN (Hebrew) God is gracious. Bible: name honoring John the Baptist and John the Evangelist. See also Elchanan, Evan, Geno, Gian, Giovanni, Handel, Hannes, Hans, Hanus, Honza, Ian, Ianos, Iban, Ioan, Ivan, Iwan, Keoni, Kwam, Ohannes, Sean, Ugutz, Yan, Yanka, Yanni, Yochanan, Yohance, Zane.
Jack, Jacsi, Jaenda, Jahn, Jan, Janak, Janco, Janek, Janis, Janne, János, Jansen, Jantje, Jantzen, Jas, Jean, Jehan, Jen, Jenkin, Jenkyn, Jens, Jhan, Jhanick, Jhon, Jian, João, João, Jock, Joen, Johan, Johann, Johne, Johnl, Johnlee, Johnnie, Johnny, Johnson, Jon, Jonam, Jonas, Jone, Jones, Jonny, Jonté, Jovan, Juan, Juhana

JOHNATHAN (Hebrew) an alternate form of Jonathan.
Jhonathan, Johathe, Johnatan, Johnathann, Johnathaon, Johnathen, Johnathyne, Johnatten, Johniathin, Johnothan, Johnthan

JOHNATHON (Hebrew) an alternate form of Jonathon. See also Yanton.
Johnaton

JOHNNIE (Hebrew) a familiar form of John.
Johnie, Johnier, Johnni, Johnsie, Jonni, Jonnie

JOHNNY (Hebrew) a familiar form of John. See also Gianni.
Jantje, Jhonny, Johney, Johnney, Johny, Jonny

JOHNSON (English) son of John.
Johnston, Jonson

JOJI (Japanese) a form of George.

JOJO (Fante) born on Monday.

JOKIN (Basque) a form of Joachim.

JOLON (Native American) valley of the dead oaks.
Jolyon

JOMAR (American) an alternate form of Jamar.
Jomari, Jomarie, Jomarri

JOMEI (Japanese) spreads light.

JON (Hebrew) an alternate form of John. A short form of Jonathan.
J'on, Joni, Jonn, Jonnie, Jonny, Jony

JONAH (Hebrew) dove. Bible: an Old Testament prophet who was swallowed by a large fish.
Giona, Jona, Yonah, Yunus

JONAS (Lithuanian) a form of John. (Hebrew) he accomplishes.
Jonahs, Jonass, Jonaus, Jonelis, Jonukas, Jonus, Jonutis, Joonas

JONATAN (Hebrew) an alternate form of Jonathan.
Jonatane, Jonate, Jonattan, Jonnattan

JONATHAN (Hebrew) gift of God. Bible: the son of King Saul who became a loyal friend of David. See also Ionakana, Yanton, Yonatan.
Janathan, Johnathan, Johnathon, Jon, Jonatan, Jonatha, Jonathen, Jonathin, Jonathon, Jonathun, Jonathyn, Jonethen, Jonnatha, Jonnathan, Jonnathun, Jonothan, Jonthan

JONATHON (Hebrew) an alternate form of Jonathan.
Joanathon, Johnathon, Jonnathon, Jonothon, Jonthon, Jounathon, Yanaton

JONES (Welsh) son of John.
Joenns, Joness, Jonesy

JONNY (Hebrew) a familiar form of John.
Jonhy, Joni, Jonnee, Jony

JONTAE (French) a combination of Jon + the suffix -tae.
Johntae, Jontay, Jontea, Jonteau, Jontez

JONTAY (American) a form of Jontae.
Johntay, Johnte, Johntez, Jontai, Jonte, Jonté, Jontez

JOOP (Dutch) a familiar form of Joseph.
Jopie

JOOST (Dutch) just.

JOQUIN (Spanish) an alternate form of Joaquin.
Joquan, Joquawn, Joqunn, Joquon

JORA (Hebrew) teacher.
Yora, Jorah

JORAM (Hebrew) Jehovah is exalted.
Joran, Jorim

JORDAN (Hebrew) descending. See also Giordano, Yarden.
Jardan, Jared, Jordaan, Jordae, Jordain, Jordaine, Jordane, Jordani, Jordanio, Jordann, Jordanny, Jordano, Jordany, Jordão, Jordayne, Jorden, Jordian, Jordin, Jordon, Jordun, Jordy, Jordyn, Jorrdan, Jory, Jourdan

JORDEN (Hebrew) an alternate form of Jordan.
Jordenn

JORDON (Hebrew) an alternate form of Jordan.
Jeordon, Johordan

JORDY (Hebrew) a familiar form of Jordan.
Jordi, Jordie

JORDYN (Hebrew) an alternate form of Jordan.

JORELL (American) he saves. Literature: a name inspired by the fictional character Jor-el, Superman's father.
Jorel, Jor-El, Jorelle, Jorl, Jorrel, Jorrell

JÖRG (German) a form of George.
Jeorg, Juergen, Jungen, Jürgen

JORGE (Spanish) a form of George.
Jorrín

JORGEN (Danish) a form of George.
Joergen, Jorgan, Jörgen

JORIS (Dutch) a form of George

JÖRN (German) a familiar form of Gregory.

JORRÍN (Spanish) a form of George.
Jorian, Jorje

JORY (Hebrew) a familiar form of Jordan.
Joar, Joary, Jorey, Jori, Jorie, Jorrie

JOSÉ (Spanish) a form of Joseph. See also Ché, Pepe.
Josean, Josecito, Josee, Joseito, Joselito, Josey

JOSEF (German, Portuguese, Czech, Scandinavian) a form of Joseph.
Joosef, Joseff, Josif, Jozef, József, Juzef

JOSELUIS (Spanish) a combination of Jose + Luis.

JOSEPH (Hebrew) God will add, God will increase. Bible: in the Old Testament, the son of Jesse who came to rule Egypt; in the New Testament, the husband of Mary. See also Beppe, Cheche, Chepe, Giuseppe, Iokepa, Iosif, Osip, Pepa, Peppe, Pino, Sepp, Yeska, Yosef, Yousef, Youssel, Yusif, Yusuf, Zeusef.
Jazeps, Jo, Jobo, Jody, Joe, Joeseph, Joey, Jojo, Joop, Joos, Jooseppi, Jopie, José, Joseba, Josef, Josep, Josephat, Josephe, Josephie, Josephus, Josheph, Josip, Jóska, Joza, Joze, Jozef, Jozeph, Jozhe, Jozio, Jozka, Jozsi, Jozzepi, Jupp, Juziu

JOSH (Hebrew) a short form of Joshua.
Joshe

JOSHA (Hindi) satisfied.

JOSHI (Swahili) galloping.

JOSHUA (Hebrew) God is my salvation. Bible: led the Israelites into the Promised Land. See also Giosia, Iosua, Jesus, Yehoshua.
Jeshua, Johsua, Johusa, Josh, Joshau, Joshaua, Joshauh, Joshawa, Joshawah, Joshia, Joshu, Joshuaa, Joshuah, Joshuea, Joshuia, Joshula, Joshus, Joshusa, Joshuwa, Joshwa, Josue, Jousha, Jozshua, Jozsua, Jozua, Jushua

JOSIAH (Hebrew) fire of the Lord. See also Yoshiyahu.
Joshiah, Josia, Josiahs, Josian, Josias, Josie

JOSS (Chinese) luck; fate.
Josse, Jossy

JOSUE (Hebrew) an alternate form of Joshua.
Joshue, Jossue, Josu, Josua, Josuha, Jozus

JOTHAM (Hebrew) may God complete. Bible: a king of Judah.

JOURDAN (Hebrew) an alternate form of Jordan.
Jourdain, Jourden, Jourdin, Jourdon, Jourdyn

JOVAN (Latin) Jove-like, majestic. (Slavic) a form of John. Mythology: Jove, also known as Jupiter, was the supreme Roman god.
Johvan, Johvon, Jovaan, Jovane, Jovani, Jovanic, Jovann, Jovanni, Jovannis, Jovanny, Jovany, Jovaughn, Jovaun, Joven, Jovenal, Jovenel, Jovi, Jovian, Jovin, Jovito, Jovoan, Jovon, Jovone, Jovonn, Jovonne, Jowan, Jowaun, Yovan, Yovani

JOVANI, Jovanni (Latin) alternate forms of Jovan.
Jovanie, Jovannie, Jovoni, Jovonie, Jovonni

JOVANNY, Jovany (Latin) alternate forms of Jovan.
Jovony

JR (Latin) a short form of Junior.
Jr.

JUAN (Spanish) a form of John. See also Chan.
Juanch, Juanchito, Juane, Juanito, Juann, Juaun

JUANCARLOS (Spanish) a combination of Juan + Carlos.

JUAQUIN (Spanish) an alternate form of Joaquín.
Juaqin, Juaqine, Juquan, Juaquine

JUBAL (Hebrew) ram's horn. Bible: a musician and a descendant of Cain.

JUDAH (Hebrew) praised. Bible: the fourth of Jacob's sons. See also Yehudi.
Juda, Judas, Judd, Jude

JUDAS (Latin) a form of Judah. Bible: Judas Iscariot was the disciple who betrayed Jesus.
Jude

JUDD (Hebrew) a short form of Judah.
Jud, Judson

JUDE (Latin) a short form of Judah, Judas. Bible: one of the Christian apostles, author of the New Testament book, "The Epistle of Saint Jude."

JUDSON (English) son of Judd.

JUHANA (Finnish) a form of John.
Juha, Juho

JUKU (Estonian) a form of Richard.
Jukka

JULES (French) a form of Julius.
Joles, Jule

JULIAN (Greek, Latin) an alternate form of Julius.
Jolyon, Julean, Juliaan, Julianne, Juliano, Julien, Jullian, Julyan

JULIEN (Latin) an alternate form of Julian.
Juliene, Julienn, Julienne, Jullien, Jullin

JULIO (Hispanic) a form of Julius.

JULIUS (Greek, Latin) youthful, downy bearded. History:

Julius (cont.)
Julius Caesar was a great Roman emperor. See also Giuliano.
Jolyon, Julas, Jule, Jules, Julen, Jules, Julian, Julias, Julie, Julio, Juliusz, Jullius, Juluis

JUMAANE (Swahili) born on Tuesday.

JUMAH (Arabic, Swahili) born on Friday, a holy day in the Islamic religion.
Jimoh, Juma

JUMOKE (Yoruba) loved by everyone.

JUN (Chinese) truthful. (Japanese) obedient; pure.
Junnie

JUNIOR (Latin) young.
Jr, Junious, Junius, Junor

JUPP (German) a form of Joseph.

JUR (Czech) a form of George.
Juraz, Jurek, Jurik, Jurko, Juro

JURGIS (Lithuanian) a form of George.
Jurgi, Juri

JURO (Japanese) best wishes; long life.

JURRIEN (Dutch) God will uplift.
Jore, Jurian, Jurre

JUSTEN (Latin) an alternate form of Justin.
Jasten

JUSTICE (Latin) an alternate form of Justis.
Justic, Justiz, Justyc, Justyce

JUSTIN (Latin) just, righteous. See also Giustino, Iestyn, Iustin, Tutu, Ustin, Yustyn.
Jastin, Jaston, Jestin, Jobst, Joost, Jost, Jusa, Just, Justain, Justan, Justas, Justek, Justen, Justian, Justinas, Justine, Justinian, Justinius, Justinn, Justino, Justins, Justinus, Justo, Juston, Justton, Justukas, Justun, Justyn

JUSTIS (French) just.
Justice, Justs, Justus, Justyse

JUSTYN (Latin) an alternate form of Justin.
Justn, Justyne, Justynn

JUVENAL (Latin) young. Literature: a Roman satiric poet.
Juvon, Juvone

JUWAN (American) an alternate form of Jajuan.
Juvon, Juvone, Juvaun, Juwaan, Juwain, Juwane, Juwann, Juwaun, Juwon, Juwonn, Juwuan, Juwuane, Juwvan, Jwan, Jwon

KABIITO (Rutooro) born while foreigners are visiting.

KABIL (Turkish) a form of Cain.
Kabel

KABIR (Hindi) History: a Hindu mystic.
Kabar, Kabeer, Kabier

KABONERO (Runyankore) sign.

KABONESA (Rutooro) difficult birth.

KACEY (Irish) an alternate form of Casey. (American) a combination of the initials K. + C. See also KC.
Kace, Kacee, Kaci, Kacy, Kaesy, Kase, Kasey, Kasie, Kasy, Kaycee

KADAR (Arabic) powerful.
Kader

KADARIUS (American) a combination of Kade + Darius.
Kadairious, Kadarious, Kadaris, Kadarrius, Kadarus, Kaddarrius, Kaderious, Kaderius

KADE (Scottish) wetlands. (American) a combination of the initials K. + D.
Kadee, Kady, Kaid, Kaide, Kaydee

KADEEM (Arabic) servant.
Kadim, Khadeem

KADEN (Arabic) an alternate form of Kadin.
Kadeen, Kadein, Kaidan, Kaiden

KADIN (Arabic) friend, companion.
Caden, Kaden, Kadyn, Kaeden, Kayden

KADIR (Arabic) spring greening.
Kadeer

KADO (Japanese) gateway.

KAEDEN (Arabic) an alternate form of Kadin.
Kaedin, Kaedon, Kaedyn

KAELAN, Kaelin (Irish) alternate forms of Kellen.
Kael, Kaelen, Kaelon, Kaelyn

KAELEB (Hebrew) an alternate form of Kaleb.
Kaelib, Kaelob, Kaelyb, Kailab, Kaileb

KAEMON (Japanese) joyful; right handed.
Kaeman, Kaemen, Kaemin

KAENAN (Irish) an alternate form of Keenan.
Kaenen, Kaenin, Kaenyn

KA'EO (Hawaiian) victorious.

KAFELE (Ngoni) worth dying for.

KAGA (Native American) writer.

KAGAN (Irish) an alternate form of Keegan.
Kage, Kagen, Kaghen, Kaigan

KAHALE (Hawaiian) home.

KAHIL (Turkish) young; inexperienced; naive.
Cahil, Kaheel, Kale, Kayle

KAHLIL (Arabic) an alternate form of Khalîl.
Kahleal, Kahlee, Kahleel, Kahleil, Kahli, Kahliel, Kahlill, Kalel, Kalil

KAHOLO (Hawaiian) runner.

KAHRAMAN (Turkish) hero.

KAI (Welsh) keeper of the keys. (German) an alternate form of Kay. (Hawaiian) sea.
Kae, Kaie, Kaii

KAIKARA (Runyoro) Religion: a Banyoro deity.

KAILEN (Irish) an alternate form of Kellen.

Kail, Kailan, Kailey, Kailin, Kailon, Kailyn

KAILI (Hawaiian) Religion: a Hawaiian deity.
Kailli

KAIN (Welsh, Irish) an alternate form of Kane.
Kainan, Kaine, Kainen, Kainin, Kainon

KAINOA (Hawaiian) name.

KAIPO (Hawaiian) sweetheart.

KAIRO (Arabic) an alternate form of Cairo.
Kaire, Kairee, Kairi

KAISER (German) a form of Caesar.
Kaesar, Kaisar, Kaizer

KAIVEN (American) a form of Kevin.
Kaivan, Kaiven, Kaivon, Kaiwan

KAJ (Danish) earth.
Kai, Kaje

KAKAR (Hindi) grass.

KALA (Hindi) black; time. (Hawaiian) sun. Religion: another name for the Hindu god Shiva.

KALAMA (Hawaiian) torch.
Kalam

KALAN (Irish) an alternate form of Kalen.
Kalane, Kallan

KALANI (Hawaiian) heaven; chief.
Kalan

KALE (Arabic) a short form of Kahlil. (Hawaiian) a familiar form of Carl.

Kalee, Kalen, Kaleu, Kaley, Kali, Kalin, Kalle, Kayle

KALEB (Hebrew) an alternate form of Caleb.
Kaeleb, Kal, Kalab, Kalabe, Kalb, Kale, Kaleob, Kalev, Kalib, Kalieb, Kallb, Kalleb, Kalob, Kaloeb, Kalub, Kalyb, Kilab

KALEN, Kalin (Arabic) alternate forms of Kale. (Irish) alternate forms of Kellen.
Kalan

KALEVI (Finnish) hero.

KALI (Arabic) a short form of Kalil. (Hawaiian) a form of Gary.

KALIL (Arabic) an alternate form of Khalîl.
Kaleel, Kalell, Kali, Kaliel, Kaliil

KALIQ (Arabic) an alternate form of Khaliq.
Kalic, Kalique

KALKIN (Hindi) tenth. Religion: the tenth incarnation of the Hindu god Vishnu.
Kalki

KALLE (Scandinavian) a form of Carl.

KALLEN (Irish) an alternate form of Kellen.
Kallan, Kallin, Kallion, Kallon, Kallun, Kalun

KALON, Kalyn (Irish) alternate forms of Kellen
Kalone, Kalonn, Kalyen, Kalyne, Kalynn

KALOOSH (Armenian) blessed event.

KALVIN (Latin) an alternate form of Calvin.

Kalvin *(cont.)*
Kal, Kalv, Kalvan, Kalven, Kalvon, Kalvyn, Vinny

KAMAKA (Hawaiian) face.

KAMAKANI (Hawaiian) wind.

KAMAL (Hindi) lotus. Religion: a Hindu god. (Arabic) perfect, perfection.
Kamaal, Kamel, Kamil

KAMAU (Kikuyu) quiet warrior.

KAMDEN (Scottish) an alternate form of Camden.
Kamdon

KAMERON (Scottish) an alternate form of Cameron.
Kam, Kamaren, Kamaron, Kameran, Kameren, Kamerin, Kamerion, Kamerron, Kamerun, Kameryn, Kamey, Kammeren, Kammeron, Kammy, Kamoryn, Kamran, Kamron

KAMI (Hindi) loving.

KAMIL (Arabic) an alternate form of Kamal.
Kameel

KAMOGA (Luganda) name of a royal Baganda family.

KAMRAN, Kamron (Scottish) alternate forms of Kameron.
Kammron, Kamrein, Kamren, Kamrin, Kamrun, Kamryn

KAMUELA (Hawaiian) a form of Samuel.

KAMUHANDA (Runyankore) born on the way to the hospital.

KAMUKAMA (Runyankore) protected by God.

KAMUZU (Ngoni) medicine.

KAMYA (Luganda) born after twin brothers.

KANA (Japanese) powerful; capable. (Hawaiian) Mythology: a god who took the form of a rope extending from Molokai to Hawaii.

KANAIELA (Hawaiian) a form of Daniel.
Kana, Kaneii

KANE (Welsh) beautiful. (Irish) tribute. (Japanese) golden. (Hawaiian) eastern sky. (English) an alternate form of Keene. See also Cain.
Kahan, Kain, Kaney, Kayne

KANGE (Lakota) raven.
Kang, Kanga

KANIEL (Hebrew) stalk, reed.
Kan, Kani, Kannie, Kanny

KANNAN (Hindi) Religion: another name for the Hindu god Krishna.
Kanaan, Kanan, Kanen, Kanin, Kanine, Kannen

KANNON (Polynesian) free. An alternate form of Cannon.
Kanon

KANOA (Hawaiian) free. (Chinese) Religion: the Chinese god of mercy.

KANTU (Hindi) happy.

KANU (Swahili) wildcat.

KAORI (Japanese) strong.

KAPILA (Hindi) ancient prophet.
Kapil

KAPONO (Hawaiian) righteous.
Kapena

KARDAL (Arabic) mustard seed.
Karandal, Kardell

KARE (Norwegian) enormous.
Karee

KAREEM (Arabic) noble; distinguished.
Karee, Karem, Kareme, Karim, Karriem

KAREL (Czech) a form of Carl.
Karell, Karil, Karrell

KAREY (Greek) an alternate form of Carey.
Karee, Kari, Karry, Kary

KARIF (Arabic) born in autumn.
Kareef

KARIISA (Runyankore) herdsman.

KARIM (Arabic) an alternate form of Kareem.

KARL (German) an alternate form of Carl.
Kaarle, Kaarlo, Kale, Kalle, Kalman, Kálmán, Karcsi, Karel, Kari, Karlen, Karlitis, Karlo, Karlos, Karlton, Karlus, Karol, Kjell

KARLEN (Latvian, Russian) a form of Carl.
Karlan, Karlens, Karlik, Karlin, Karlis, Karlon

KARMEL (Hebrew) an alternate form of Carmel.

KARNEY (Irish) an alternate form of Carney.

KAROL (Czech, Polish) a form of Carl.
Karal, Karolek, Karolis, Karalos, Károly, Karrel, Karrol

KARR (Scandinavian) an alternate form of Carr.

KARSON (English) an alternate form of Carson.
Karrson, Karsen

KARSTEN (Greek) anointed.
Carsten, Karstan, Karston

KARU (Hindi) cousin. Bible: the cousin of Moses.
Karun

KARUTUNDA (Runyankore) little.

KARWANA (Rutooro) born during wartime.

KASEEM (Arabic) divided.
Kasceem, Kaseam, Kaseym, Kasim, Kasseem, Kassem, Kazeem

KASEKO (Rhodesian) mocked, ridiculed.

KASEM (Tai) happiness.

KASEN (Basque) protected with a helmet.
Kasean, Kasene, Kaseon, Kasin, Kason, Kassen

KASEY (Irish) an alternate form of Casey.
Kaese, Kaesy, Kasay, Kassey

KASHAWN (American) a combination of the prefix Ka + Shawn.
Kashain, Kashan, Kashaun, Kashen, Kashon

KASIB (Arabic) fertile.

KASIM (Arabic) an alternate form of Kaseem.
Kassim

KASIMIR (Arabic) peace. (Slavic) an alternate form of Casimir.
Kasim, Kazimierz, Kazimir, Kazio, Kazmer, Kazmér, Kázmér

KASIYA (Ngoni) separate.

KASPER (Persian) treasurer. (German) an alternate form of Casper.
Jasper, Kaspar, Kaspero

KASS (German) blackbird.
Kaese, Kasch, Kase

KASSIDY (Irish) an alternate form of Cassidy.
Kassady, Kassie, Kassy

KATEB (Arabic) writer.

KATO (Runyankore) second of twins.

KATUNGI (Runyankore) rich.

KAVAN (Irish) handsome.
Cavan, Kavanagh, Kavaugn, Kaven, Kavenaugh, Kavin, Kavon, Kayvan

KAVEH (Persian) ancient hero.

KAVI (Hindi) poet.

KAVIN, Kavon (Irish) alternate forms of Kavan.
Kaveon, Kavion, Kavone, Kayvon, Kaywon

KAWIKA (Hawaiian) a form of David.

KAY (Greek) rejoicing. (German) fortified place. Literature: one of the knights of King Arthur's Round Table.
Kai, Kaycee, Kaye, Kayson

KAYDEN (Arabic) an alternate form of Kadin.
Kayde, Kaydee, Kaydin, Kaydn, Kaydon

KAYIN (Nigerian) celebrated. (Yoruba) long-hoped-for child.

KAYLE (Hebrew) faithful dog. (Arabic) a short form of Kahlil.
Kayl, Kayla, Kaylee

KAYLEB (Hebrew) an alternate form of Caleb.
Kaylib, Kaylob, Kaylub

KAYLEN (Irish) an alternate form of Kellen.
Kaylan, Kaylin, Kaylon, Kaylyn, Kaylynn

KAYNE (Hebrew) an alternate form of Cain.
Kaynan, Kaynen, Kaynon

KAYODE (Yoruba) he brought joy.

KAYONGA (Runyankore) ash. History: a great Ankole warrior.

KAZIO (Polish) a form of Casimir, Kasimir. See also Cassidy.

KAZUO (Japanese) man of peace.

KC (American) a combination of the initials K. + C. See also Kacey.
Kc, K.C., Kcee, Kcey

KEAGAN (Irish) an alternate form of Keegan.
Keagean, Keagen, Keaghan, Keagyn

KEAHI (Hawaiian) flames.

KEAKA (Hawaiian) a form of Jack.

KEALOHA (Hawaiian) fragrant.
Ke'ala

KEANAN (Irish) an alternate form of Keenan.
Keanen, Keanna, Keannan, Keanon

KEANDRE (American) a combination of the prefix Ke + Andre.

Keandre *(cont.)*
Keandra, Keandray, Keandré, Keandree, Keandrell, Keondre

KEANE (German) bold; sharp. (Irish) handsome. (English) an alternate form of Keene.
Kean

KEANU (Irish) an alternate form of Keenan.
Keaneu, Keani, Keanno, Keano, Keanue, Keeno, Keenu, Kianu

KEARN (Irish) a short form of Kearney.
Kearne

KEARNEY (Irish) an alternate form of Carney.
Kar, Karney, Karny, Kearn, Kearny

KEARY (Irish) an alternate form of Kerry.
Kearie

KEATON (English) where hawks fly.
Keatan, Keaten, Keatin, Keatton, Keatyn, Keeton, Keetun

KEAVEN (Irish) an alternate form of Kevin.
Keavan, Keavon

KEAWE (Hawaiian) strand.

KEB (Egyptian) earth. Mythology: an ancient earth god, also known as Geb.

KEDAR (Hindi) mountain lord. (Arabic) powerful. Religion: another name for the Hindu god Shiva.
Kadar, Kedaar, Keder

KEDDY (Scottish) a form of Adam.
Keddie

KEDEM (Hebrew) ancient.

KEDRICK (English) an alternate form of Cedric.
Keddrick, Kederick, Kedrek, Kedric, Kiedric, Kiedrick

KEEFE (Irish) handsome; loved.

KEEGAN (Irish) little; fiery.
Kaegan, Kagan, Keagan, Keagen, Keeghan, Keegon, Keegun, Kegan, Keigan

KEELAN (Irish) little; slender.
Keelen, Keelin, Keelyn, Keilan, Kelan

KEELEY (Irish) handsome.
Kealey, Kealy, Keeli, Keelian, Keelie, Keely

KEENAN (Irish) little Keene.
Kaenan, Keanan, Keanu, Keenen, Keennan, Keenon, Kenan, Keynan, Kienan, Kienon

KEENE (German) bold; sharp. (English) smart. See also Kane.
Kaene, Keane, Keen, Keenan

KEENEN (Irish) an alternate form of Keenan.
Keenin, Kienen

KEES (Dutch) a form of Kornelius.
Keese, Keesee, Keyes

KEEVON (Irish) an alternate form of Kevin.
Keevan, Keeven, Keevin, Keewan, Keewin

KEGAN (Irish) an alternate form of Keegan.
Kegen, Keghan, Kegon, Kegun

KEHIND (Yoruba) second-born twin.
Kehinde

KEIFFER (German) a form of Cooper.
Keefer, Keifer, Kiefer

KEIGAN (Irish) an alternate form of Keegan.
Keighan, Keighen

KEIJI (Japanese) cautious ruler.

KEILAN (Irish) an alternate form of Keelan.
Keilen, Keilin, Keillene, Keillyn, Keilon, Keilynn

KEIR (Irish) a short form of Kieran.

KEITARO (Japanese) blessed.
Keita

KEITH (Welsh) forest. (Scottish) battle place. See also Kika.
Keath, Keeth, Keithen

KEITHEN (Welsh, Scottish) an alternate form of Keith.
Keithan, Keitheon, Keithon

KEIVAN (Irish) an alternate form of Kevin.
Keiven, Keivn, Keivon, Keivone

KEKAPA (Hawaiian) tapa cloth.

KEKIPI (Hawaiian) rebel.

KEKOA (Hawaiian) bold, courageous.

KELBY (German) farm by the spring.
Keelby, Kelbee, Kelbey, Kelbi, Kellby

KELE (Hawaiian) a form of Jerry. (Hopi) sparrow hawk.
Kelle

KELEMEN (Hungarian) gentle; kind.
Kellman

KELEVI (Finnish) hero.

KELI (Hawaiian) a form of Terry.

KELI'I (Hawaiian) chief.

KELILE (Ethiopian) protected.

KELL (Scandinavian) spring.

KELLAN (Irish) an alternate form of Kellen.
Keillan

KELLEN (Irish) mighty warrior.
Kaelan, Kailen, Kalan, Kalen, Kalin, Kallen, Kalon, Kalyn, Kaylen, Keelan, Kelden, Kelin, Kellan, Kelle, Kellin, Kellyn, Kelyn, Kelynn

KELLER (Irish) little companion.

KELLY (Irish) warrior.
Kelle, Kellen, Kelley, Kelli, Kellie, Kely

KELMEN (Basque) merciful.
Kelmin

KELSEY (Scandinavian) island of ships.
Kelcy, Kelse, Kelsea, Kelsi, Kelsie, Kelso, Kelsy, Kesley, Kesly

KELTON (English) keel town; port.
Kelden, Keldon, Kelson, Kelston, Kelten, Keltin, Keltonn, Keltyn

KELVIN (Irish, English) narrow river. Geography: a river in Scotland.
Kelvan, Kelven, Kelvon, Kelvyn, Kelwin, Kelwyn

KEMAL (Turkish) highest honor.

KEMEN (Basque) strong.

KEMP (English) fighter; champion.

KEMPTON (English) military town.

KEN (Japanese) one's own kind. (Scottish) a short form of Kendall, Kendrick, Kenneth.
Kena, Kenn, Keno

KENAN (Irish) an alternate form of Keenan.

KENAZ (Hebrew) bright.

KENDAL (English) an alternate form of Kendall.
Kendale, Kendali, Kendel, Kendul, Kendyl

KENDALL (English) valley of the river Kent.
Ken, Kendal, Kendell, Kendrall, Kendryll, Kendyll, Kyndall

KENDARIUS (American) a combination of Ken + Darius.
Kendarious, Kendarrious, Kendarrius, Kenderious, Kenderius, Kenderyious

KENDELL (English) an alternate form of Kendall.
Kendelle, Kendrel, Kendrell

KENDREW (Scottish) a form of Andrew.

KENDRICK (Irish) son of Henry. (Scottish) royal chieftain.
Ken, Kenderrick, Kendric, Kendrich, Kenedrick, Kendricks, Kendrik, Kendrix, Kendryck, Kenndrick, Keondric, Keondrick

KENLEY (English) royal meadow.
Kenlea, Kenlee, Kenleigh, Kenlie, Kenly

KENN (Scottish) an alternate form of Ken.

KENNAN (Scottish) little Ken.
Kenna, Kenan, Kenen, Kennen, Kennon

KENNARD (Irish) brave chieftain.
Kenner

KENNEDY (Irish) helmeted chief. History: John F. Kennedy was the thirty-fifth U.S. president.
Kenedy, Kenidy, Kennady, Kennedey

KENNETH (Irish) handsome. (English) royal oath.
Ken, Keneth, Kenneith, Kennet, Kennethen, Kennett, Kennieth, Kennith, Kennth, Kenny, Kennyth, Kenya

KENNY (Scottish) a familiar form of Kenneth.
Keni, Kenney, Kenni, Kennie, Kinnie

KENRICK (English) bold ruler; royal ruler.
Kenric, Kenricks, Kenrik

KENT (Welsh) white; bright. (English) a short form of Kenton. Geography: a county in England.

KENTARO (Japanese) big boy.

KENTON (English) from Kent, England.
Kent, Kenten, Kentin, Kentonn

KENTRELL (English) king's estate.
Kenreal, Kentrel, Kentrelle

KENWARD (English) brave; royal guardian.

KENYA (Hebrew) animal horn. (Russian) a form of Kenneth. Geography: a country in Africa.
Kenyatta

KENYATTA (American) a form of Kenya.
Kenyata, Kenyatae, Kenyatee, Kenyatter, Kenyatti, Kenyotta

KENYON (Irish) white haired, blond.
Kenyan, Kenynn, Keonyon

KENZIE (Scottish) wise leader. See also Mackenzie.
Kensie

KEOKI (Hawaiian) a form of George.

KEOLA (Hawaiian) life.

KEON (Irish) a form of Ewan.
Keeon, Keion, Keionne, Keondre, Keone, Keonne, Keonte, Keony, Keyon, Kian, Kion

KEONI (Hawaiian) a form of John.

KEONTE (American) a form of Keon.
Keonntay, Keonta, Keontae, Keontay, Keontaye, Keontez, Keontia, Keontis, Keontrae, Keontre, Keontrey, Keontrye

KERBASI (Basque) warrior.

KEREL (Afrikaans) young.
Kerell

KEREM (Turkish) noble; kind.
Kereem

KEREY (Gypsy) homeward-bound.
Ker

KERMAN (Basque) from Germany.

KERMIT (Irish) an alternate form of Dermot.
Kermey, Kermie, Kermitt, Kermy

KERN (Irish) a short form of Kieran.
Kearn, Kerne

KERR (Scandinavian) an alternate form of Carr.
Karr

KERRICK (English) king's rule.

KERRY (Irish) dark, dark haired.
Keary, Keri, Kerrey, Kerri, Kerrie

KERS (Todas) Botany: an Indian plant.

KERSEN (Indonesian) cherry.

KERSTAN (Dutch) a form of Christian.

KERWIN (Irish) little; dark. (English) friend of the marshlands.
Kervin, Kervyn, Kerwinn, Kerwyn, Kerwynn, Kirwin, Kirwyn

KESAR (Russian) a form of Caesar.
Kesare

KESHAWN (American) a combination of the prefix Ke + Shawn.
Keeshaun, Keeshawn, Keeshon, Kesean, Keshan, Keshane, Keshaun, Keshayne, Keshion, Keshon, Keshone, Keshun, Kishan

KESIN (Hindi) long-haired beggar.

KESSE (Ashanti, Fante) chubby baby.
Kessie

KESTER (English) a form of Christopher.

KESTREL (English) falcon.
Kes

KEUNG (Chinese) universe.

KEVAN (Irish) an alternate form of Kevin.
Kavan, Kewan, Kewane, Kewaun, Keyvan, Kiwan, Kiwane

KEVEN (Irish) an alternate form of Kevin.
Keve, Keveen, Kiven

KEVIN (Irish) handsome. See also Cavan.
Kaiven, Keaven, Keevon, Keivan, Kev, Kevan, Keven, Keverne, Kevian, Kevien, Kévin, Kevinn, Kevins, Kevis, Kevn, Kevon, Kevvy, Kevyn, Kyven

KEVON (Irish) an alternate form of Kevin.
Keveon, Kevion, Kevone, Kevonne, Kevontae, Kevonte, Kevoyn, Kevron, Kewon, Kewone, Keyvon, Kivon

KEVYN (Irish) an alternate form of Kevin.
Kevyon

KEY (English) key; protected.

KEYON (Irish) an alternate form of Keon.
Keyan, Keyen, Keyin, Keyion

KEYSHAWN (American) a combination of Key + Shawn.
Keyshan, Keyshaun, Keyshon, Keyshun

KHACHIG (Armenian) small cross.
Khachik

KHAIM (Russian) a form of Chaim.

KHALDUN (Arabic) forever.
Khaldoon, Khaldoun

KHALFANI (Swahili) born to lead.
Khalfan

KHÄLID (Arabic) eternal.
Khaled, Khallid, Khalyd

KHALÍL (Arabic) friend.
Kahlil, Kaleel, Kalil, Khahlil, Khailil, Khailyl, Khalee, Khaleel, Khaleil, Khali, Khalial, Khaliel, Khalihl, Khalill, Khaliyl

KHALIQ (Arabic) creative.
Kaliq, Khalique

KHAMISI (Swahili) born on Thursday.
Kham

KHAN (Turkish) prince.
Khanh

KHARALD (Russian) a form of Gerald.

KHAYRU (Arabic) benevolent.
Khiri, Khiry, Kiry

KHOURY (Arabic) priest.
Khory

KHRISTIAN (Greek) an alternate form of Christian, Kristian.
Khris, Khristan, Khristin, Khriston, Khrystian

KHRISTOPHER (Greek) an alternate form of Kristopher.
Khristofer, Khristophar, Khrystopher

KHRISTOS (Greek) an alternate form of Christos.
Khris, Khristophe, Kristo, Kristos

KIBO (Uset) worldly; wise.

KIBUUKA (Luganda) brave warrior. History: a brave Buganda warrior.

KIDD (English) child; young goat.

KIEFER (German) an alternate form of Keifer.
Kief, Kieffer, Kiefor, Kiffer, Kiiefer

KIEL (Irish) an alternate form of Kyle.
Kiell

KIELE (Hawaiian) gardenia.

KIERAN (Irish) little and dark; little Keir.
Keiran, Keiren, Keiron, Kiaron, Kiarron, Kier, Kieren, Kierian, Kierien, Kierin, Kiernan, Kieron, Kierr, Kierre, Kierron, Kyran

KIERNAN (Irish) an alternate form of Kieran.
Kern, Kernan, Kiernen

KIET (Tai) honor.

KIFEDA (Luo) only boy among girls.

KIHO (Dutooro) born on a foggy day.

KIJIKA (Native American) quiet walker.

KIKA (Hawaiian) a form of Keith.

KIKI (Spanish) a form of Henry.

KILE (Irish) an alternate form of Kyle.
Kilee, Kilen, Kiley, Kiyl, Kiyle

KILLIAN (Irish) little Kelly.
Kilean, Kilian, Kilien, Killie, Killien, Killiean, Killion, Killy

KIM (English) a short form of Kimball.
Kimie, Kimmy

KIMBALL (Greek) hollow vessel (English) warrior chief.
Kim, Kimbal, Kimbel, Kimbell, Kimble

KIMO (Hawaiian) a form of James.

KIMOKEO (Hawaiian) a form of Timothy

KIN (Japanese) golden.

KINCAID (Scottish) battle chief.
Kincade, Kinkaid

KINDIN (Basque) fifth.

KING (English) king. A short form of names beginning with "King."

KINGSLEY (English) king's meadow
King, Kings, Kingslea, Kingslie, Kingsly, Kingzlee, Kinslea, Kinslee, Kinsley, Kinslie, Kinsly

KINGSTON (English) king's estate.
King, Kinston

KINGSWELL (English) king's well.
King

KINI (Hawaiian) a short form of Iukini.

KINNARD (Irish) tall slope.

KINSEY (English) victorious royalty.
Kinze, Kinzie

KINTON (Hindi) crowned.

KION (Irish) an alternate form of Keon.
Kione, Kionie, Kionne

KIOSHI (Japanese) quiet.

KIPP (English) pointed hill.
Kip, Kippar, Kipper, Kippie, Kippy

KIR (Bulgarian) a familiar form of Cyrus.

KIRAL (Turkish) king; supreme leader.

KIRAN (Sanskrit) beam of light.
Kyran

KIRBY (Scandinavian) church village. (English) cottage by the water.
Kerbey, Kerbie, Kerby, Kirbey, Kirbie, Kirkby

KIRI (Cambodian) mountain.

KIRIL (Slavic) a form of Cyril.
Kirill, Kiryl, Kyrillos

KIRITAN (Hindi) wearing a crown.

KIRK (Scandinavian) church.
Kerk

KIRKLAND (English) church land.
Kirklin, Kirklind, Kirklynd

KIRKLEY (English) church meadow.

KIRKLIN (English) an alternate form of Kirkland.
Kirklan, Kirklen, Kirkline, Kirkloun, Kirklun, Kirklyn, Kirklynn

KIRKWELL (English) church well; church spring.

KIRKWOOD (English) church forest.

KIRTON (English) church town.

KISHAN (American) an alternate form of Keshawn.

Kishaun, Kishawn, Kishen, Kishon, Kyshon, Kyshun

KISTNA (Hindi) sacred, holy. Geography: a sacred river in India.

KISTUR (Gypsy) skillful rider.

KIT (Greek) a familiar form of Christian, Christopher, Kristopher.
Kitt, Kitts

KITO (Swahili) jewel; precious child.

KITWANA (Swahili) pledged to live.

KIVA (Hebrew) a short form of Akiva, Jacob.
Kiba, Kivi, Kiwa

KIYOSHI (Japanese) quiet; peaceful.

KIZZA (Luganda) born after twins.
Kizzy

KJELL (Swedish) a form of Karl.
Kjel

KLAUS (German) a short form of Nicholas. An alternate form of Claus.
Klaas, Klaes, Klas, Klause

KLAY (English) an alternate form of Clay.

KLAYTON (English) an alternate form of Clayton.

KLEEF (Dutch) cliff.

KLEMENT (Czech) a form of Clement.
Klema, Klemenis, Klemens, Klemet, Klemo, Klim, Klimek, Kliment, Klimka

KLENG (Norwegian) claw.

KNIGHT (English) armored knight.
Knightly

KNOTON (Native American) an alternate form of Nodin.

KNOWLES (English) grassy slope.
Knolls, Nowles

KNOX (English) hill.

KNUTE (Scandinavian) an alternate form of Canute.
Knud, Knut

KOBY (Polish) a familiar form of Jacob.
Kobby, Kobe, Kobey, Kobi, Kobia, Kobie

KODI (English) an alternate form of Kody.
Kode, Kodee, Kodie

KODY (English) an alternate form of Cody.
Kodey, Kodi, Kodye, Koty

KOFI (Twi) born on Friday.

KOHANA (Lakota) swift.

KOI (Hawaiian) a form of Troy. (Choctaw) panther.

KOJO (Akan) born on Monday.

KOKA (Hawaiian) Scotsman.

KOKAYI (Shona) gathered together.

KOLBY (English) an alternate form of Colby.
Kelby, Koalby, Koelby, Kohlbe, Kohlby, Kolbe, Kolbey, Kolbi, Kolbie, Kolebe, Koleby, Kollby

KOLE (English) an alternate form of Cole.
Kohl, Kohle

KOLEMAN (English) an alternate form of Coleman.
Kolemann, Kolemen

KOLIN (English) an alternate form of Colin.
Kolen, Kollen, Kollin, Kollyn, Kolyn

KOLTON (English) an alternate form of Colton.
Kolt, Koltan, Kolte, Kolten, Koltin, Koltn, Koltyn

KOLYA (Russian) a familiar form of Nikolai, Nikolos.
Kola, Kolenka, Kolia, Kolja

KONA (Hawaiian) a form of Don.
Konala

KONANE (Hawaiian) bright moonlight.

KONDO (Swahili) war.

KONG (Chinese) glorious; sky.

KONNER (Irish) an alternate form of Conner, Connor.
Konar, Koner

KONNOR (Irish) an alternate form of Connor.
Kohner, Kohnor, Konor

KONO (Moquelumnan) squirrel eating a pine nut.

KONRAD (German) a form of Conrad.
Khonrad, Koen, Koenraad, Kon, Konn, Konney, Konni, Konnie, Konny, Konrád, Konrade, Konrado, Kord, Kort, Kunz

KONSTANTIN (German, Russian) a form of Constantine. See also Dinos.
Konstancji, Konstadine, Konstadino, Konstandinos, Konstantinas, Konstantine, Konstantinos, Konstantio, Konstanty, Konstantyn, Konstanz, Konstatino, Kostadino, Kostadinos, Kostandino, Kostandinos, Kostantin, Kostantino, Kostas, Kostenka, Kostya, Kotsos

KONTAR (Akan) only child.

KORB (German) basket.

KORBIN (English) a form of Corbin.
Korban, Korben, Korbyn

KORDELL (English) a form of Cordell.
Kordel

KOREY (Irish) an alternate form of Corey, Kory.
Kore, Koree, Korei, Korio, Korre, Korria, Korrye

KORNEL (Latin) a form of Cornelius, Kornelius.
Kees, Korneil, Kornél, Korneli, Kornelisz, Kornell, Krelis, Soma

KORNELIUS (Latin) an alternate form of Cornelius. See also Kees, Kornel.
Karnelius, Korneilius, Korneliaus, Kornelious, Kornellius

KORRIGAN (Irish) an alternate form of Corrigan.
Korigan, Korigan, Korrigon, Korrigun

KORT (German, Dutch) an alternate form of Cort, Kurt.
Kourt

KORTNEY (English) an alternate form of Courtney.
Kortni, Kourtney

KORUDON (Greek) helmeted one.

KORY (Irish) an alternate form of Corey.
Korey, Kori, Korie, Korrey, Korri, Korrie, Korry

KOSEY (African) lion.
Kosse

KOSMO (Greek) an alternate form of Cosmo.
Kosmy, Kozmo

KOSTAS (Greek) a short form of Konstantin.

KOSTI (Finnish) a form of Gustave.

KOSUMI (Moquelumnan) spear fisher.

KOUKALAKA (Hawaiian) a form of Douglas.

KOURTLAND (English) an alternate form of Courtland.
Kortlan, Kortland, Kortlend, Kortlon, Kourtlin

KOVIT (Tai) expert.

KRAIG (Irish, Scottish) an alternate form of Craig.
Kraggie, Kraggy, Krayg, Kreg, Kreig, Kreigh

KRIKOR (Armenian) a form of Gregory.

KRIS (Greek) an alternate form of Chris. A short form of Kristian, Kristofer, Kristopher.
Kriss, Krys

KRISCHAN (German) a form of Christian.
Krishan, Krishaun, Krishawn, Krishon, Krishun

KRISHNA (Hindi) delightful, pleasurable. Religion: one of the human incarnations of the Hindu god.

Krishna *(cont.)*
Kistna, Kistnah, Krisha, Krishnah

KRISPIN (Latin) an alternate form of Crispin.
Krispian, Krispino, Krispo

KRISTER (Swedish) a form of Christian.
Krist, Kristar

KRISTIAN (Greek) an alternate form of Christian, Khristian.
Kerstan, Khristos, Kit, Kris, Krischan, Krist, Kristan, Kristar, Kristek, Kristen, Krister, Kristien, Kristin, Kristine, Kristinn, Kristion, Kristjan, Kristo, Kristos, Krists, Krystek, Krystian, Khrystiyan

KRISTO (Greek) a short form of Khristos.

KRISTOFER (Swedish) a form of Kristopher.
Kris, Kristafer, Kristef, Kristifer, Kristoff, Kristoffer, Kristofo, Kristofor, Kristofyr, Kristufer, Kristus, Krystofer

KRISTOFF (Greek) a short form of Kristofer, Kristopher.
Kristof, Kristóf

KRISTOPHE (French) a form of Kristopher.

KRISTOPHER (Greek) Christ-bearer. An alternate form of Christopher. See also Topher.
Khristopher, Kit, Kris, Krisstopher, Kristapher, Kristepher, Kristfer, Kristfor, Kristo, Kristofer, Kristoff, Kristoforo, Kristoph, Kristophe, Kristophor, Kristos, Krists, Krisus, Krystopher, Krystupas, Krzysztof

KRUZ (Spanish) an alternate form of Cruz.
Kruise, Kruize, Kruse, Kruze

KRYSTIAN (Polish) a form of Christian.
Krys, Krystek, Krystien, Krystin

KUBA (Czech) a form of Jacob.
Kubo, Kubus

KUENG (Chinese) universe.

KUGONZA (Dutooro) love.

KUIRIL (Basque) lord.

KUMAR (Sanskrit) prince.

KUNLE (Yoruba) home filled with honors.

KUPER (Yiddish) copper.

KURT (Latin, German, French) courteous; enclosure. A short form of Kurtis. An alternate form of Curt.
Kirt, Kort, Kuno, Kurtt

KURTIS (Latin, French) an alternate form of Curtis.
Kirtis, Kirtus, Kurt, Kurtes, Kurtez, Kurtice, Kurties, Kurtiss, Kurtus, Kurtys

KURUK (Pawnee) bear.

KUZIH (Carrier) good speaker.

KWABENA (Akan) born on Tuesday.

KWACHA (Ngoni) morning.

KWAKO (Akan) born on Wednesday.
Kwaka, Kwaku

KWAM (Zuni) a form of John.

KWAME (Akan) born on Saturday.
Kwamen, Kwami, Kwamin

KWAN (Korean) strong.
Kwane

KWASI (Akan) born on Sunday. (Swahili) wealthy.
Kwasie, Kwazzi, Kwesi

KWAYERA (Ngoni) dawn.

KWENDE (Ngoni) let's go.

KYELE (Irish) an alternate form of Kyle.

KYLAN (Irish) an alternate form of Kyle.
Kyelen, Kyleen, Kylen, Kylin, Kyline, Kylon, Kylun

KYLE (Irish) narrow piece of land; place where cattle graze. (Yiddish) crowned with laurels.
Cyle, Kiel, Kilan, Kile, Kilen, Kiley, Ky, Kye, Kyel, Kyele, Kylan, Kylee, Kyler, Kyley, Kylie, Kyll, Kylle, Kyrell

KYLER (English) a form of Kyle.
Kylar, Kylor

KYNAN (Welsh) chief.

KYNDALL (English) an alternate form of Kendall.
Kyndal, Kyndel, Kyndell, Kyndle

KYNE (English) royal.

KYRAN (Sanskrit) an alternate form of Kiran.
Kyren, Kyron, Kyrone

KYROS (Greek) master.

KYVEN (American) a form of Kevin.
Kyvan, Kyvaun, Kyvon, Kywon, Kywynn

LABAN (Hawaiian) white.
Labon, Lebaan, Leban, Liban

LABARON (American) a combination of the prefix La + Baron.
Labaren, Labarren, Labarron, Labearon, Labron

LABIB (Arabic) sensible; intelligent.

LABRENTSIS (Russian) a form of Lawrence.
Labhras, Labhruinn, Labrencis

LACHLAN (Scottish) land of lakes.
Lache, Lachlann, Lachunn, Lakelan, Lakeland

LADARIAN (American) a combination of the prefix La + Darian.
Ladarien, Ladarin, Ladarion, Ladarren, Ladarrian, Ladarrien, Ladarrin, Ladarrion, Laderion, Laderrian, Laderrion

LADARIUS (American) a combination of the prefix La + Darius.
Ladarious, Ladaris, Ladarrius, Ladauris, Laderius, Ladirus

LADARRIUS (American) an alternate form of Ladarius.
Ladarrias, Ladarries, Ladarrious, Laderrious, Laderris

LADD (English) attendant.
Lad, Laddey, Laddie, Laddy

LADERRICK (American) a combination of the prefix La + Derrick.
Ladarrick, Ladereck, Laderic, Laderricks

LADISLAV (Czech) a form of Walter.
Laco, Lada, Ladislaus

LADO (Fante) second-born son.

LAFAYETTE (French) History: Marquis de Lafayette was a French soldier and politician who aided the American Revolution.
Lafaiete, Lafayett, Lafette, Laffyette

LAINE (English) an alternate form of Lane.
Lain

LAIRD (Scottish) wealthy landowner.

LAIS (Arabic) lion.

LAJOS (Hungarian) famous; holy.
Lajcsi, Laji, Lali

LAKE (English) lake.
Lakan, Lakane, Lakee, Laken, Lakin

LAKOTA (Dakota) a tribal name.
Lakoda

LAL (Hindi) beloved.

LAMAR (German) famous throughout the land. (French) sea, ocean.
Lamair, Lamario, Lamaris, Lamarr, Lamarre, Larmar, Lemar

LAMBERT (German) bright land.
Bert, Lambard, Lamberto, Lambirt, Lampard, Landbert

LAMOND (French) world.
Lammond, Lamon, Lamonde, Lamondo, Lamondre, Lamund, Lemond

LAMONT (Scandinavian) lawyer.
Lamaunt, Lamonta, Lamonte, Lamontie, Lamonto, Lamount, Lemont

LANCE (German) a short form of Lancelot.
Lancy, Lantz, Lanz, Launce

LANCELOT (French) attendant. Literature: the knight who loved King Arthur's wife, Queen Guinevere.
Lance, Lancelott, Launcelet, Launcelot

LANDEN (English) an alternate form of Landon.
Landenn

LANDER (Basque) lion man. (English) landowner.
Landers, Landor

LANDO (Portuguese, Spanish) a short form of Orlando, Rolando.

LANDON (English) open, grassy meadow.
Landan, Landen, Landin, Landyn

LANDRY (French, English) ruler.
Landre, Landré, Landrue

LANE (English) narrow road.
Laine, Laney, Lanie, Layne

LANG (Scandinavian) tall man.
Lange

LANGDON (English) long hill.
Landon, Langsdon, Langston

LANGFORD (English) long ford.
Lanford, Lankford

LANGLEY (English) long meadow.
Langlea, Langlee, Langleigh, Langly

LANGSTON (English) long, narrow town.
Langsden, Langsdon

LANGUNDO (Native American) peaceful.

LANI (Hawaiian) heaven.

LANNY (American) a familiar form of Lawrence, Laurence.
Lanney, Lannie, Lennie

LANU (Moquelumnan) running around the pole.

LANZ (Italian) a form of Lance.
Lanzo, Lonzo

LAO (Spanish) a short form of Stanislaus.

LAP (Vietnamese) independent.

LAPIDOS (Hebrew) torches.
Lapidoth

LAQUAN (American) a combination of the prefix La + Quan.
Laquain, Laquann, Laquanta, Laquantae, Laquante, Laquawn, Laquawne, Laquin, Laquinn, Laqun, Laquon, Laquone, Laqwan, Laqwon

LAQUINTIN (American) a combination of the prefix La + Quintin.
Laquentin, Laquenton, Laquintas, Laquinten, Laquintiss, Laquinton

LARAMIE (French) tears of love. Geography: a town in Wyoming on the Overland Trail.
Larami, Laramy, Laremy

LARENZO (Italian, Spanish) an alternate form of Lorenzo.
Larenz, Larenza, Larinzo, Laurenzo

LARKIN (Irish) rough; fierce.
Larklin

LARNELL (American) a combination of Larry + Darnell.

LARON (French) thief.
Laran, La'ron, La Ron, Larone, Laronn, Larron, La Ruan

LARRIMORE (French) armorer.
Larimore, Larmer, Larmor

LARRY (Latin) a familiar form of Lawrence.
Larrie, Lary

LARS (Scandinavian) a form of Lawrence.
Laris, Larris, Larse, Larsen, Larson, Larsson, Larz, Lasse, Laurans, Laurits, Lavrans, Lorens

LASALLE (French) hall.
Lasal, Lasalle, Lascell, Lascelles

LASH (Gypsy) a form of Louis.
Lashi, Lasho

LASHAWN (American) a combination of the prefix La + Shawn.
Lasaun, Lasean, Lashajaun, Lashan, Lashane, Lashaun, Lashon, Lashun

LASHON (American) an alternate form of Lashawn.
Lashone, Lashonne

LASSE (Finnish) a form of Nicholas.

LÁSZLÓ (Hungarian) famous ruler.
Laci, Lacko. Laslo, Lazlo

LATEEF (Arabic) gentle; pleasant.
Latif, Letif

LATHAM (Scandinavian) barn. (English) district.
Laith, Lathe, Lay

LATHAN (American) a combination of the prefix La + Nathan.
Lathaniel, Lathen, Lathyn, Leathan

LATHROP (English) barn, farmstead.
Lathe, Lathrope, Lay

LATIMER (English) interpreter.
Lat, Latimor, Lattie, Latty, Latymer

LATRAVIS (American) a combination of the prefix La + Travis.
Latavious, Latavius, Latraveus, Latraviaus, Latravious, Latravius, Latrayvious, Latrayvous, Latrivis

LATRELL (American) a combination of the prefix La + Kentrell.
Latreal, Latreil, Latrel, Latrelle, Letreal, Letrel, Letrell, Letrelle

LAUDALINO (Portuguese) praised.
Lino

LAUGHLIN (Irish) servant of Saint Secundinus.
Lanty, Lauchlin, Leachlainn

LAURENCE (Latin) crowned with laurel. An alternate form of Lawrence. See also Rance, Raulas, Raulo, Renzo.
Lanny, Lauran, Laurance, Laureano, Lauren, Laurencho,

Laurencio, Laurens, Laurent, Laurentij, Laurentios, Laurentiu, Laurentius, Laurentz, Laurentzi, Laurie, Laurin, Lauris, Laurits, Lauritz, Laurnet, Lauro, Laurus, Lavrenti, Lurance

LAURENCIO (Spanish) a form of Laurence.

LAURENS (Dutch) a form of Laurence.
Laurenz

LAURENT (French) a form of Laurence.
Laurente

LAURIE (English) a familiar form of Laurence.
Lauri, Laury, Lorry

LAURIS (Swedish) a form of Laurence.

LAURO (Filipino) a form of Laurence.

LAVALLE (French) valley.
Lavail, Laval, Lavalei, Lavalle, Lavell

LAVAN (Hebrew) white.
Lavane, Lavaughan, Laven, Lavon, Levan

LAVAUGHAN (American) a form of Lavan.
Lavaughn, Levaughan, Levaughn

LAVE (Italian) lava. (English) lord.

LAVELL (French) an alternate form of LaValle.
Lavel, Lavele, Lavelle, Levele, Levell, Levelle

LAVI (Hebrew) lion.

LAVON (American) a form of Lavan.

Lavion, Lavone, Lavonn, Lavonne, Lavont, Lavonte

LAVRENTI (Russian) a form of Lawrence.
Larenti, Lavrentij, Lavrusha, Lavrik, Lavro

LAWERENCE (Latin) an alternate form of Lawrence.
Lawerance

LAWFORD (English) ford on the hill.
Ford, Law

LAWLER (Irish) mutterer.
Lawlor, Lollar, Loller

LAWRENCE (Latin) crowned with laurel. See also Brencis, Chencho.
Labrentsis, Laiurenty, Lanny, Lanty, Larance, Laren, Larian, Larien, Laris, Larka, Larrance, Larrence, Larry, Lars, Larya, Laurence, Lavrenti, Law, Lawerence, Lawrance, Lawren, Lawrey, Lawrie, Lawron, Lawry, Lencho, Lon, Lóránt, Loreca, Loren, Loretto, Lorenzo, Lorne, Lourenco, Lowrance

LAWSON (English) son of Lawrence.
Lawsen, Layson

LAWTON (English) town on the hill.
Laughton, Law

LAYNE (English) an alternate form of Lane.
Layn, Laynee

LAYTON (English) an alternate form of Leighton.
Laydon, Layten, Layth, Laythan, Laython

LAZARO (Italian) a form of Lazarus.
Lazarillo, Lazarito, Lazzaro

LAZARUS (Greek) a form of Eleazar. Bible: Lazarus was raised from the dead.
Lazar, Lázár, Lazare, Lazarius, Lazaro, Lazaros, Lazorus

LEANDER (Greek) lion-man; brave as a lion.
Ander, Leandro

LEANDRO (Spanish) a form of Leander.
Leandra, Léandre, Leandrew, Leandros

LEBEN (Yiddish) life.
Laben, Lebon

LEBNA (Ethiopian) spirit; heart.

LEDARIUS (American) a combination of the prefix Le + Darius.
Ledarrious, Ledarrius, Lederious, Lederris

LEE (English) a short form of Farley, Leonard, and names containing "lee."
Leigh

LEGGETT (French) one who is sent; delegate.
Legate, Legette, Leggitt, Liggett

LEI (Chinese) thunder. (Hawaiian) a form of Ray.

LEIB (Yiddish) roaring lion.
Leibel

LEIF (Scandinavian) beloved.
Laif, Leife, Lief

LEIGH (English) an alternate form of Lee.

LEIGHTON (English) meadow farm.
Lay, Layton, Leigh, Leyton

LEITH (Scottish) broad river.

LEK (Tai) small.

LEKEKE (Hawaiian) powerful ruler.

LEKS (Estonian) a familiar form of Alexander.
Leksik, Lekso

LEL (Gypsy) taker.

LELAND (English) meadowland; protected land.
Lealand, Lee, Leeland, Leigh, Leighland, Lelan, Lelann, Lelend, Lelund, Leyland

LEMAR (French) an alternate form of Lamar.
Lemario, Lemarr

LEMUEL (Hebrew) devoted to God.
Lem, Lemmie, Lemmy

LEN (German) a short form of Leonard. (Hopi) flute.

LENARD (German) an alternate form of Leonard.
Lennard

LENCHO (Spanish) a form of Lawrence.
Lenci, Lenzy

LENNART (Swedish) a form of Leonard.
Lennerd

LENNO (Native American) man.

LENNON (Irish) small cloak; cape.
Lenon

LENNOR (Gypsy) spring; summer.

LENNOX (Scottish) with many elms.
Lennix, Lenox

LENNY (German) a familiar form of Leonard.
Leni, Lennie, Leny

LEO (Latin) lion. (German) a short form of Leopold, Leon.
Lavi, Leão, Lee, Leib, Leibel, Leos, Leosko, Léo, Léocadie, Leos, Leosoko, Lev, Lio, Lion, Liutas, Lyon, Nardek

LEOBARDO (Italian) a form of Leonard.

LEON (Greek, German) a short form of Leonard, Napoleon.
Leo, Léon, Leonas, Léonce, Leoncio, Leondris, Leone, Leonek, Leonetti, Leoni, Leonid, Leonidas, Leonirez, Leonizio, Leonon, Leons, Leontes, Leontios, Leontrae, Liutas

LEONARD (German) brave as a lion.
Leanard, Lee, Len, Lena, Lenard, Lennart, Lenny, Leno, Leobardo, Leon, Léonard, Leonardis, Leonardo, Leonart, Leonerd, Leonhard, Leonidas, Leonnard, Leontes, Lernard, Lienard, Linek, Lnard, Lon, Londard, Lonnard, Lonya, Lynnard

LEONARDO (Italian) a form of Leonard.
Leonaldo, Lionardo

LEONEL (English) little lion. See also Lionel.
Leonell

LEONHARD (German) an alternate form of Leonard.
Leonhards

LEONID (Russian) a form of Leonard.
Leonide, Lyonechka, Lyonya

LEONIDAS (Greek) a form of Leonard.
Leonida, Leonides

LEOPOLD (German) brave people.
Leo, Leopoldo, Leorad, Lipót, Lopolda, Luepold, Luitpold, Poldi

LEOPOLDO (Italian) a form of Leopold.

LEOR (Hebrew) my light.
Leory, Lior

LEQUINTON (American) a combination of the prefix Le + Quinton.
Lequentin, Lequenton, Lequinn

LERON (French) round, circle. (American) a combination of the prefix Le + Ron.
Leeron, Le Ron, Lerone, Liron, Lyron

LEROY (French) king. See also Delroy, Elroy.
Lee, Leeroy, LeeRoy, Leigh, Lerai, Leroi, LeRoi, LeRoy, Roy

LES (Scottish, English) a short form of Leslie, Lester.
Lessie

LESHARO (Pawnee) chief

LESHAWN (American) a combination of the prefix Le + Shawn.
Lashan, Lesean, Leshaun, Leshon, Leshun

LESLIE (Scottish) gray fortress.
Lee, Leigh, Les, Leslea, Leslee, Lesley, Lesli, Lesly, Lezlie, Lezly

LESTER (Latin) chosen camp. (English) from Leicester, England.
Leicester, Les

LEV (Hebrew) heart. (Russian) a form of Leo. A short form of Leverett, Levi.
Leb, Leva, Levka, Levko, Levushka

LEVERETT (French) young hare.
Lev, Leveret, Leverit, Leveritt

LEVI (Hebrew) joined in harmony. Bible: the son of Jacob; the priestly tribe of Israel.
Leavi, Leevi, Leevie, Lev, Levey, Levie, Levin, Levitis, Levy, Lewi, Leyvi

LEVIN (Hebrew) an alternate form of Levi.
Levine, Levion

LEVON (American) an alternate form of Lavon.
Leevon, Levone, Levonn, Levonne, Levonte, Lyvonne

LEW (English) a short form of Lewis.

LEWIN (English) beloved friend.

LEWIS (English) a form of Louis. (Welsh) an alternate form of Llewellyn.
Lew, Lewes, Lewie, Lewy

LEX (English) a short form of Alexander.
Lexi, Lexie, Lexin

LEXUS (Greek) a short form of Alexander.
Lexis, Lexius, Lexxus

LEYATI (Moquelumnan) shape of an abalone shell.

LÍ (Chinese) strong.

LIAM (Irish) a form of William.
Liem, Lliam, Lyam

LIANG (Chinese) good, excellent.

LIBAN (Hawaiian) an alternate form of Laban.
Libaan, Lieban

LIBERIO (Portuguese) liberation.
Liberaratore, Liborio

LIDIO (Greek, Portuguese) ancient. Geography: an ancient province in Asia Minor.

LIGONGO (Yao) means "who is this?"

LIKEKE (Hawaiian) a form of Richard.

LIKO (Chinese) protected by Buddha. (Hawaiian) bud.
Like

LIN (Burmese) bright. (English) a short form of Lyndon.
Linh, Linn, Linny, Lyn, Lynn

LINC (English) a short form of Lincoln.
Link

LINCOLN (English) settlement by the pool. History: Abraham Lincoln was the sixteenth U.S. president.
Linc, Lincon, Lyncoln

LINDBERG (German) mountain where linden trees grow.
Lindbergh, Lindburg, Lindy

LINDELL (English) valley of the linden trees.
Lendall, Lendel, Lendell, Lindall, Lindel, Lyndale, Lyndall, Lyndel, Lyndell

LINDEN (English) an alternate form of Lyndon.

LINDLEY (English) linden field.
Lindlea, Lindlee, Lindleigh, Lindly

LINDON (English) an alternate form of Lyndon.
Lin, Lindan

LINDSAY (English) an alternate form of Lindsey.
Linsay

LINDSEY (English) linden-tree island.
Lind, Lindsay, Lindsee, Lindsie, Lindsy, Lindzy, Linsey, Linzie, Linzy, Lyndsay, Lyndsey, Lyndsie, Lynzie

LINFORD (English) linden-tree ford.
Lynford

LINFRED (German) peaceful, calm.

LINLEY (English) flax meadow.
Linlea, Linlee, Linleigh, Linly

LINTON (English) flax town.
Lintonn, Lynton, Lyntonn

LINU (Hindi) lily.

LINUS (Greek) flaxen haired.
Linas, Linux

LINWOOD (English) flax wood.

LIO (Hawaiian) a form of Leo.

LIONEL (French) lion cub. See also Leonel.
Lional, Lionell, Lionello, Lynel, Lynell, Lyonel

LIRON (Hebrew) my song.
Lyron

LISE (Moquelumnan) salmon's head coming out of the water.

LISIMBA (Yao) lion.
Simba

LISTER (English) dyer.

LITTON (English) town on the hill.
Liton

LIU (African) voice.

LIUZ (Polish) light.
Lius

LIVINGSTON (English) Leif's
town.
Livingstone

LIWANU (Moquelumnan) growl-
ing bear.

LLEWELLYN (Welsh) lionlike.
*Lewis, Llewelin, Llewellen,
Llewelleyn, Llewellin, Llewlyn,
Llywellyn, Llywellynn, Llywelyn*

LLOYD (Welsh) gray haired;
holy. See also Floyd.
Loy, Loyd, Loyde, Loydie

LOBO (Spanish) wolf.

LOCHLAIN (Irish, Scottish) land
of lakes.
*Laughlin, Lochlan, Lochlann,
Lochlin, Locklynn*

LOCKE (English) forest.
Lock, Lockwood

LOE (Hawaiian) a form of Roy.

LOGAN (Irish) meadow.
*Llogan, Loagan, Loagen,
Loagon, Logann, Logen, Loggan,
Loghan, Logon, Logn, Logun,
Logunn, Logyn*

LOK (Chinese) happy.

LOKELA (Hawaiian) a form of
Roger.

LOKNI (Moquelumnan) raining
through the roof.

LOMÁN (Irish) bare. (Slavic)
sensitive.

LOMBARD (Latin) long bearded.
Bard, Barr

LON (Spanish) a short form of
Alonso, Alonzo, Leonard,
Lonnie. (Irish) fierce.
Lonn

LONAN (Zuni) cloud.

LONATO (Native American) flint
stone.

LONDON (English) fortress of
the moon. Geography: the
capital of Great Britain.
*Londen, Londyn, Lunden,
Lundon*

LONG (Chinese) dragon.
(Vietnamese) hair.

LONNIE (German, Spanish) a
familiar form of Alonso,
Alonzo.
*Lon, Loni, Lonie, Lonnell,
Lonney, Lonni, Lonniel, Lonny*

LONO (Hawaiian) Mythology: a
god of peace and farming.

LONZO (German, Spanish) a
short form of Alonso, Alonzo.
Lonso

LOOTAH (Lakota) red.

LOPAKA (Hawaiian) a form of
Robert.

LORÁND (Hungarian) a form of
Roland.

LÓRÁNT (Hungarian) a form of
Lawrence.
Lorant

LORCAN (Irish) little; fierce.

LORD (English) noble title.

LOREN (Latin) a short form of
Lawrence.
Lorin, Lorren, Lorrin, Loryn

LORENZO (Italian, Spanish) a
form of Lawrence.
*Larenzo, Lerenzo, Lewrenzo,
Lorenc, Lorence, Lorenco,
Lorencz, Lorens, Lorenso,
Lorentz, Lorenz, Lorenza,
Loretto, Lorinc, Lörinc, Lorinzo,
Loritz, Lorrenzo, Lorrie, Lorry,
Lourenza, Lourenzo, Lowrenzo,
Renzo, Zo*

LORETTO (Italian) a form of
Lawrence.
Loreto

LORIMER (Latin) harness
maker.
Lorrie, Lorrimer, Lorry

LORING (German) son of the
famous warrior.
Lorrie, Lorring, Lorry

LORIS (Dutch) clown.

LORITZ (Latin, Danish) laurel.
Lauritz

LORNE (Latin) a short form of
Lawrence.
Lorn, Lornie

LORRY (English) an alternate
form of Laurie.
Lori, Lorri, Lory

LOT (Hebrew) hidden, covered.
Bible: Lot fled from Sodom,
but his wife glanced back
upon its destruction and was
transformed into a pillar of
salt.
Lott

LOTHAR (German) an alternate
form of Luther.
*Lotaire, Lotarrio, Lothair,
Lothaire, Lothario, Lotharrio*

LOU (German) a short form of
Louis.

LOUDON (German) low valley.
Loudan, Louden, Loudin, Lowden

LOUIE (German) a familiar form of Louis.

LOUIS (German) famous warrior. See also Aloisio, Aloysius, Clovis, Luigi.
Lash, Lashi, Lasho, Lewis, Lou, Loudovicus, Louie, Louies, Louise, Lucho, Lude, Ludek, Ludirk, Ludis, Ludko, Ludwig, Lughaidh, Lui, Luigi, Luis, Luiz, Luki, Lutek

LOURDES (French) from Lourdes, France. Geography: a town in France. Religion: a place where the Virgin Mary was said to have appeared.

LOUVAIN (English) Lou's vanity. Geography: a city in Belgium.
Louvin

LOVELL (English) an alternate form of Lowell.
Louvell, Lovel, Lovelle, Lovey

LOWELL (French) young wolf. (English) beloved.
Lovell, Lowe, Lowel

LOYAL (English) faithful, loyal.
Loy, Loyall, Loye, Lyall, Lyell

LUBOMIR (Polish) lover of peace.

LUBOSLAW (Polish) lover of glory.
Lubs, Lubz

LUC (French) a form of Luke.
Luce

LUCA (Italian) a form of Lucius.
Lucca, Luka

LUCAS (German, Irish, Danish, Dutch) a form of Lucius.
Lucais, Lucassie, Lucaus, Luccas, Luccus, Luckas, Lucus

LUCIAN (Latin) an alternate form of Lucius.
Liuz, Lucan, Lucanus, Luciano, Lucianus, Lucias, Lucjan, Lukianos, Lukyan

LUCIANO (Italian) a form of Lucian.
Luca, Lucca, Lucino, Lucio

LUCIEN (French) a form of Lucius.

LUCIO (Italian) a form of Lucius.

LUCIUS (Latin) light; bringer of light.
Loukas, Luc, Luca, Lucais, Lucanus, Lucas, Luce, Lucian, Lucien, Lucio, Lucious, Lucis, Luke, Lusio

LUCKY (American) fortunate.
Luckee, Luckie, Luckson, Lucson

LUDLOW (English) prince's hill.

LUDOVIC (German) an alternate form of Ludwig.
Ludovick, Ludovico

LUDWIG (German) an alternate form of Louis. Music: Ludwig Van Beethoven was a famous nineteenth-century German composer.
Ludovic, Ludvig, Ludvik, Ludwik, Lutz

LUI (Hawaiian) a form of Louis.

LUIGI (Italian) a form of Louis.
Lui, Luiggi, Luigino, Luigy

LUIS, Luiz (Spanish) forms of Louis.
Luise

LUKAS, Lukus (Greek, Czech, Swedish) forms of Luke.
Loukas, Lukais, Lukash, Lukasha, Lukass, Lukasz, Lukaus, Lukkas

LUKE (Latin) a form of Lucius. Bible: author of the "Gospel of Saint Luke" and "Acts of the Apostles"—two New Testament books.
Luc, Luchok, Luck, Lucky, Luk, Luka, Lúkács, Lukas, Luken, Lukes, Lukus, Lukyan, Lusio

LUKELA (Hawaiian) a form of Russel.

LUKEN (Basque) bringer of light.
Lucan, Lucane, Lucano, Luk

LUKI (Basque) famous warrior.

LUKMAN (Arabic) prophet.
Luqman

LULANI (Hawaiian) highest point in heaven.

LUMO (Ewe) born face-downward.

LUNDY (Scottish) grove by the island.

LUNN (Irish) warlike.
Lon, Lonn

LUNT (Swedish) grove.

LUSILA (Hindi) leader.

LUSIO (Zuni) a form of Lucius.

LUTALO (Luganda) warrior.

LUTFI (Arabic) kind, friendly.

LUTHER (German) famous warrior. History: the Protestant reformer Martin Luther was

Luther *(cont.)*
one of the central figures of
the Reformation.
Lothar, Lutero, Luthor

LUTHERUM (Gypsy) slumber.

LUYU (Moquelumnan) head
shaker.

LYALL, Lyell (Scottish) loyal.

LYLE (French) island.
Lisle, Ly, Lysle

LYMAN (English) meadow.
Leaman, Leeman, Lymon

LYNCH (Irish) mariner.
Linch

LYNDAL (English) valley of lime
trees.
Lyndale, Lyndall, Lyndel, Lyndell

LYNDON (English) linden-tree
hill. History: Lyndon B.
Johnson was the thirty-sixth
U.S. president.
*Lin, Linden, Lindon, Lyden,
Lydon, Lyn, Lyndan, Lynden, Lynn*

LYNN (English) waterfall; brook.
*Lyn, Lynell, Lynette, Lynnard,
Lynoll*

LYRON (Hebrew) an alternate
form of Leron, Liron.

LYSANDER (Greek) liberator.
Lyzander, Sander

MAALIK (Punjabi) an alternate
form of Malik.
Maalek, Maaliek

MAC (Scottish) son.
Macs

MACADAM (Scottish) son of
Adam.
MacAdam, McAdam

MACALLISTER (Irish) son of
Alistair.
*Macalaster, Macalister,
MacAlister, McAlister, McAllister*

MACARIO (Spanish) happy;
blessed.

MACARTHUR (Irish) son of
Arthur.
MacArthur, McArthur

MACAULAY (Scottish) son of
righteousness.
*Macaulee, Macauley, Macaully,
Macauly, Maccauley, Mackauly,
Macualay, McCauley*

MACBRIDE (Scottish) son of a
follower of Saint Brigid.
Macbryde, Mcbride, McBride

MACCOY (Irish) son of Hugh,
Coy.
MacCoy, Mccoy, McCoy

MACCREA (Irish) son of grace.
*MacCrae, MacCray, MacCrea,
Macrae, Macray, Makray,
Mccrea, McCrea*

MACDONALD (Scottish) son of
Donald.
*MacDonald, Mcdonald,
McDonald, Mcdonna,
Mcdonnell, McDonnell*

MACDOUGAL (Scottish) son of
Dougal.
*MacDougal, Mcdougal,
McDougal, McDougall, Dougal*

MACE (French) club. (English) a
short form of Macy, Mason.
*Macean, Maceo, Macer, Macey,
Macie, Macy*

MACGREGOR (Scottish) son of
Gregor.
Macgreggor

Machas (Polish) a form of
Michael.

MACK (Scottish) a short form
of names beginning with
"Mac" and "Mc."
*Macke, Mackey, Mackie,
Macklin, Macks, Macky*

MACKENZIE (Irish) son of
Kenzie.
*Mackensy, Mackenxo, Mackenze,
Mackenzey, Mackenzi,
MacKenzie, Mackenzly,
Mackenzy, Mackienzie,
Mackinsey, Mackinzie, Makenzie,
McKenzie, Mickenzie*

MACKINNLEY (Irish) son of the
learned ruler.
*Mackinley, MacKinnley,
Mackinnly, Mckinley*

MACKLAIN (Irish) an alternate
form of Maclean.
Macklaine, Macklane

MACLEAN (Irish) son of
Leander.
*Machlin, Macklain, MacLain,
MacLean, Maclin, Maclyn,
Makleen, McLaine, McLean*

MACMAHON (Irish) son of Mahon.
MacMahon, McMahon

MACMURRAY (Irish) son of Murray.
McMurray

MACNAIR (Scottish) son of the heir.
Macknair

MACO (Hungarian) a form of Emmanuel.

MACON (German, English) maker.

MACY (French) Matthew's estate.
Mace, Macey

MADDOCK (Welsh) generous.
Madoc, Madock, Madog

MADDOX (Welsh, English) benefactor's son.
Maddux, Madox

MADHAR (Hindi) god; godlike. Religion: another name for the Hindu god Shiva.

MADISON (English) son of Maude; good son.
Maddie, Maddison, Maddy, Madisen, Madisson, Madisyn, Madsen, Son, Sonny

MADONGO (Luganda) uncircumcised.

MADU (Ibo) people.

MAGAR (Armenian) groom's attendant.
Magarious

MAGEE (Irish) son of Hugh.
MacGee, MacGhee, McGee

MAGEN (Hebrew) protector.

MAGNAR (Norwegian) strong; warrior.
Magne

MAGNUS (Latin) great.
Maghnus, Magnes, Manius, Mayer

MAGOMU (Luganda) younger of twins.

MAGUIRE (Irish) son of the beige one.
MacGuire, McGuire, McGwire

MAHAMMED (Arabic) an alternate form of Muhammad.
Mahamad, Mahamed

MAHDI (Arabic) guided to the right path.
Mahde, Mahdee, Mahdy

MAHESA (Hindi) great lord. Religion: another name for the Hindu god Shiva.

MAHI'AI (Hawaiian) a form of George.

MAHIR (Arabic, Hebrew) excellent; industrious.
Maher

MAHKAH (Lakota) earth.

MAHMOUD (Arabic) an alternate form of Muhammad.
Mahamoud, Mahmmoud, Mahmuod

MAHMÚD (Arabic) an alternate form of Muhammad.
Mahmed, Mahmood, Mahmut

MAHOMET (Arabic) an alternate form of Muhammad.
Mehemet, Mehmet

MAHON (Irish) bear.

MAHPEE (Lakota) sky.

MAIMUN (Arabic) lucky.
Maimon

MAIRTIN (Irish) a form of Martin.
Martain, Martainn

MAITIAS (Irish) a form of Mathias.
Maithias

MAITIÚ (Irish) a form of Matthew.

MAITLAND (English) meadowland.

MAJID (Arabic) great, glorious.
Majd, Majde, Majdi, Majdy, Majed, Majeed

MAJOR (Latin) greater; military rank.
Majar, Maje, Majer, Mayer, Mayor

MAKAIO (Hawaiian) a form of Matthew.

MAKALANI (Mwera) writer.

MAKANI (Hawaiian) wind.

MAKARIOS (Greek) happy; blessed.
Macario, Macarios, Maccario, Maccarios

MAKENZIE (Irish) an alternate form of Mackenzie.
Makensie, Makenzy

MAKIN (Arabic) strong.
Makeen

MAKIS (Greek) a form of Michael.

MAKOTO (Japanese) sincere.

MAKS (Hungarian) a form of Max.
Makszi

MAKSIM (Russian) a form of Maximilian.
Maksimka, Maksym, Maxim

MAKSYM (Polish) a form of Maximilian.
Makimus, Maksim, Maksymilian

MAKYAH (Hopi) eagle hunter.

MAL (Irish) a short form of names beginning with "Mal."

MALACHI (Hebrew) angel of God. Bible: the last canonical Hebrew prophet.
Maeleachlainn, Mal, Malachai, Malachia, Malachie, Malachy, Malakai, Malake, Malaki, Malchija, Malechy, Málik

MALACHY (Irish) a form of Malachi.

MALAJITM (Sanskrit) garland of victory.

MALCOLM (Scottish) follower of Saint Columba, an early Scottish saint. (Arabic) dove.
Mal, Malcalm, Malcohm, Malcolum, Malcom, Malkolm

MALCOM (Scottish) an alternate form of Malcolm.
Malcome, Malcum, Malkom, Malkum

MALDEN (English) meeting place in a pasture.
Mal, Maldon

MALEK (Arabic) an alternate form of Malik.
Maleak, Maleek, Maleik, Maleka, Maleke, Mallek

MALEKO (Hawaiian) a form of Mark.

MÁLIK (Arabic) a form of Malachi. (Punjabi) lord, master.

Maalik, Mailik, Malak, Malic, Malick, Malicke, Maliek, Maliik, Malik, Malike, Malikh, Maliq, Malique, Mallik, Malyk, Malyq

MALIN (English) strong, little warrior.
Mal, Mallin, Mallon

MALLORY (German) army counselor. (French) wild duck.
Lory, Mal, Mallery, Mallori, Mallorie, Malory

MALONEY (Irish) church going.
Malone, Malony

MALVERN (Welsh) bare hill.
Malverne

MALVIN (Irish, English) an alternate form of Melvin.
Mal, Malvinn, Malvyn, Malvynn

MAMO (Hawaiian) yellow flower; yellow bird.

MANCHU (Chinese) pure.

MANCO (Peruvian) supreme leader. History: a thirteenth-century Incan king.

MANDALA (Yao) flowers.
Manda, Mandela

MANDEEP (Punjabi) mind full of light.
Mandieep

MANDEL (German) almond.
Mandell

MANDEK (Polish) a form of Armand, Herman.
Mandie

MANDER (Gypsy) from me.

MANFORD (English) small ford.

MANFRED (English) man of peace. See also Fred.

Manfret, Manfrid, Manfried, Maniferd, Mannfred, Mannfryd

MANGER (French) stable.

MANGO (Spanish) a familiar form of Emmanuel, Manuel.

MANHEIM (German) servant's home.

MANIPI (Native American) living marvel.

MANIUS (Scottish) a form of Magnus.
Manus, Manyus

MANLEY (English) hero's meadow.
Manlea, Manleigh, Manly

MANN (German) man.
Manin

MANNING (English) son of the hero.

MANNIX (Irish) monk.
Mainchin

MANNY (German, Spanish) a familiar form of Manuel.
Mani, Manni, Mannie, Many

MANO (Hawaiian) shark. (Spanish) a short form of Manuel.
Manno, Manolo

MANOJ (Sanskrit) cupid.

MANSA (Swahili) king. History: a fourteenth-century emperor of Mali.

MANSEL (English) manse; house occupied by a clergyman.
Mansell

MANSFIELD (English) field by the river; hero's field.

MAN-SHIK (Korean) deeply rooted.

MANSÜR (Arabic) divinely aided.
Mansoor, Mansour

MANTON (English) man's town; hero's town.
Mannton, Manten

MANU (Hindi) lawmaker. History: the writer of the Hindi code of conduct. (Hawaiian) bird. (Ghanian) second-born son.

MANUEL (Hebrew) a short form of Emmanuel.
Maco, Mango, Mannuel, Manny, Mano, Manolón, Manual, Manuale, Manue, Manuelli, Manuelo, Manuil, Manyuil, Minel

MANVILLE (French) worker's village. (English) hero's village.
Mandeville, Manvel, Manvil

MAN-YOUNG (Korean) ten thousand years of prosperity.

MANZO (Japanese) third son.

MAONA (Winnebago) creator, earth maker.

MAPIRA (Yao) millet.

MARAR (Watamare) mud; dust.

MARC (French) a form of Mark.

MARCEL (French) a form of Marcellus.
Marcell, Marsale, Marsel

MARCELINO (Italian) a form of Marcellus.
Marceleno, Marcelin, Marcellin, Marcellino

MARCELO, Marcello (Italian) forms of Marcellus.
Marchello, Marsello, Marselo

MARCELLUS (Latin) a familiar form of Marcus.
Marceau, Marcel, Marceles, Marcelias, Marcelino, Marcelis, Marcelius, Marcellas, Marcelleous, Marcellis, Marcellous, Marcelluas, Marcelo, Marcelus, Marcely, Marciano, Marcilka, Marcsseau, Marquel, Marsalis

MARCH (English) dweller by a boundary.

MARCIANO (Italian) a form of Martin.
Marci, Marcio

MARCILKA (Hungarian) a form of Marcellus.
Marci, Marcilki

MARCIN (Polish) a form of Martin.

MARCO (Italian) a form of Marcus. History: Marco Polo was the thirteenth-century Venetian traveler who explored Asia.
Marcko, Marko

MARCOS (Spanish) a form of Marcus.
Marckos, Marcous, Markos, Markose

MARCUS (Latin) martial, war-like.
Marc, Marcas, Marcellus, Marcio, Marckus, Marco, Marcos, Marcous, Marcuss, Marcuus, Marcux, Marek, Mark, Markov, Markus

MAREK (Slavic) a form of Marcus.

MAREN (Basque) sea.

MAREO (Japanese) uncommon.

MARIAN (Polish) a form of Mark.

MARIANO (Italian) a form of Mark.

MARID (Arabic) rebellious.

MARIN (French) sailor.
Marine, Mariner, Marino, Marius, Marriner

MARINO (Italian) a form of Marin.
Marinos, Marinus, Mario, Mariono

MARIO (Italian) an alternate form of Marino.
Marios, Marrio

MARION (French) bitter; sea of bitterness. A masculine form of Mary.
Mareon, Mariano

MARIUS (Latin) a form of Marin. History: a Roman clan name.
Marious

MARK (Latin) an alternate form of Marcus. Bible: author of the New Testament book, "The Gospel According to Saint Mark." See also Maleko.
Marc, Marek, Marian, Mariano, Marke, Markee, Markel, Markell, Markey, Marko, Markos, Márkus, Markusha, Marque, Martial, Marx

MARKANTHONY (Italian) a combination of Mark + Anthony.

MARKE (Polish) a form of Mark.

MARKEL, Markell (Latin) alternate forms of Mark.
Markelle, Markelo

MARKES (Portuguese) an alternate form of Marques.
Markess, Markest

MARKESE (French) an alternate form of Marquis.
Markease, Markeece, Markees, Markeese, Markei, Markeice, Markeis, Markeise, Markes, Markez, Markeze, Markice

MARKHAM (English) homestead on the boundary.

MARKIS (French) an alternate form of Marquis.
Markies, Markiese, Markise, Markiss, Markist

MARKO (Latin) an alternate form of Marco, Mark.
Markco

MARKUS (Latin) an alternate form of Marcus.
Markas, Markcus, Markcuss, Markys, Marqus

MARLAND (English) lake land.

MARLEY (English) lake meadow.
Marlea, Marleigh, Marly, Marrley

MARLIN (English) deep-sea fish.
Marlen, Marlion, Marlyn

MARLON (French) a form of Merlin.

MARLOW (English) hill by the lake.
Mar, Marlo, Marlowe

MARMION (French) small.
Marmyon

MARNIN (Hebrew) singer; bringer of joy.

MARO (Japanese) myself.

MARQUAN (American) a combination of Mark + Quan.
Marquane, Marquante

MARQUEL (American) a form of Marcellus.
Marqueal, Marquelis, Marquell, Marquelle, Marquellis, Marquiel, Marquil, Marquiles, Marquill, Marquille, Marquillus, Marqwel, Marqwell

MARQUES (Portuguese) nobleman.
Markes, Markqes, Markques, Markquese, Marqese, Marqesse, Marqez, Marqeze, Marquees, Marquese, Marquess, Marquesse, Marquest, Markqueus, Marquez, Marqus

MARQUEZ (Portuguese) an alternate form of Marques.
Marqueze, Marquiez

MARQUICE (American) a form of Marquis.
Marquaice, Marquece

MARQUIS, Marquise (French) nobleman.
Marcquis, Marcuis, Markis, Markquis, Markquise, Markuis, Marqise, Marquee, Marqui, Marquice, Marquie, Marquies, Marquiss, Marquist, Marquiz, Marquize

MARQUON (American) a combination of Mark + Quon.
Marquin, Marquinn, Marqwan, Marqwon, Marqwyn

MARR (Spanish) divine. (Arabic) forbidden.

MARS (Latin) bold warrior. Mythology: the Roman god of war.

MARSALIS (Italian) a form of Marcellus.
Marsalius, Marsallis, Marsellis, Marsellius, Marsellus

MARSDEN (English) marsh valley.
Marsdon

MARSH (French) a short form of Marshall. (English) swamp land.

MARSHAL (French) an alternate form of Marshall.
Marschal, Marshel

MARSHALL (French) caretaker of the horses; military title.
Marsh, Marshal, Marshell

MARSHAWN (American) a combination of Mark + Shawn.
Marshaine, Marshaun, Marshauwn, Marshean, Marshon, Marshun

MARSTON (English) town by the marsh.

MARTELL (English) hammerer.
Martel, Martele, Martellis

MARTEN (Dutch) a form of Martin.
Maarten, Martein

MARTEZ (Spanish) a form of Martin.
Martaz, Martaze, Martes, Martese, Marteze, Martice, Martiece, Marties, Martiese, Martiez, Martis, Martise, Martize

MARTI (Spanish) a form of Martin.
Martee, Martie

MARTIAL (French) a form of Mark.

MARTIN (Latin) martial, warlike. (French) a form of Martinus. History: Martin Luther King, Jr. led the civic rights movement and won the Nobel Peace Prize. See also Tynek.
Maartin, Mairtin, Marciano, Marcin, Marinos, Marius, Mart, Martan, Marten, Martez, Marti, Martijn, Martinas, Martine, Martinez, Martinho, Martiniano, Martinien, Martinka, Martino, Martins, Marto, Marton, Márton, Marts, Marty, Martyn, Mattin, Mertin, Morten, Moss

MARTINEZ (Spanish) a form of Martin.
Martines

MARTINHO (Portuguese) a form of Martin.

MARTINO (Italian) a form of Martin.
Martinos

MARTINS (Latvian) a form of Martin.

MARTINUS (Latin) martial, warlike.
Martin

MARTY (Latin) a familiar form of Martin.
Martey, Marti, Martie

MARUT (Hindi) Religion: the Hindu god of the wind.

MARV (English) a short form of Marvin.
Marve, Marvi, Marvis

MARVIN (English) lover of the sea.
Marv, Marvein, Marven, Marvion, Marvn, Marvon, Marvyn, Marwin, Marwynn, Mervin

MARWAN (Arabic) history personage.

MARWOOD (English) forest pond.

MASACCIO (Italian) twin.
Masaki

MASAHIRO (Japanese) broad minded.

MASAMBA (Yao) leaves.

MASAO (Japanese) righteous.

MASATO (Japanese) just.

MASHAMA (Shona) surprising.

MASKA (Native American) powerful.

MASLIN (French) little Thomas.
Maslen, Masling

MASON (French) stone worker.
Mace, Maison, Masson, Masun, Masyn, Sonny

MASOU (Native American) fire god.

MASSEY (English) twin.
Massi

MASSIMO (Italian) greatest.
Massimiliano

MASUD (Arabic, Swahili) fortunate.
Masood, Masoud, Mhasood

MATAI (Basque, Bulgarian) a form of Matthew.
Máté, Matei

MATALINO (Filipino) bright.

MATEO (Spanish) a form of Matthew.
Matías, Matteo

MATEUSZ (Polish) a form of Matthew.
Matejs, Mateus

MATHE (German) a short form of Matthew.

MATHER (English) powerful army.

MATHEU (German) a form of Matthew.
Matheau, Matheus, Mathu

MATHEW (Hebrew) an alternate form of Matthew.

MATHIAS, Matthias (German, Swedish) forms of Matthew.
Maitias, Mathi, Mathia, Mathis, Matías, Matthia, Matthieus, Mattia, Mattias, Matus

MATHIEU, Matthieu (French) forms of Matthew.
Mathie, Mathieux, Mathiew, Matthiew, Mattieu, Mattieux

MATÍAS (Spanish) a form of Mathias.
Mattias

MATO (Native American) brave.

MATOPE (Rhodesian) our last child.

MATOSKAH (Lakota) white bear.

MATS (Swedish) a familiar form of Matthew.
Matts, Matz

MATSON (Hebrew) son of Matt.
Matison, Matsen, Mattison, Mattson

MATT (Hebrew) a short form of Matthew.
Mat

MATTEEN (Afghani) disciplined; polite.

MATTEUS (Scandinavian) a form of Matthew.

MATTHEW (Hebrew) gift of God. Bible: author of the New Testament book, "The Gospel According to Saint Matthew."
Mads, Makaio, Maitiú, Mata, Matai, Matek, Mateo, Mateusz, Matfei, Mathe, Matheson, Matheu, Mathew, Mathian, Mathias, Mathieson, Mathieu, Matro, Mats, Matt, Matteus, Matthaeus, Matthaios, Matthaus, Matthäus, Mattheus, Matthews, Mattmias, Matty, Matvey, Matyas, Mayhew

MATTY (Hebrew) a familiar form of Matthew.
Mattie

MATUS (Czech) a form of Mathias.

MATVEY (Russian) a form of Matthew.
Matviy, Matviyko, Matyash, Motka, Motya

MATYAS (Polish) a form of Matthew.
Mátyás

MAULI (Hawaiian) a form of Maurice.

MAURICE (Latin) dark skinned; moor; marshland. See also Seymour.
Mauli, Maur, Maurance, Maureo, Mauricio, Maurids, Mauriece, Maurikas, Maurin, Maurino, Maurise, Mauritz, Maurius, Maurizio, Mauro, Maurrel, Maurtel, Maury, Maurycy, Meurig, Moore, Morice, Moritz, Morrel, Morrice, Morrie, Morrill, Morris

MAURICIO (Spanish) a form of Maurice.

Mauriccio, Mauriceo, Maurico, Maurisio

MAURITZ (German) a form of Maurice.

MAURIZIO (Italian) a form of Maurice.

MAURO (Latin) a short form of Maurice.
Maur, Maurio

MAURY (Latin) a familiar form of Maurice.
Maurey, Maurie, Morrie

MAVERICK (American) independent.
Maverik, Maveryke, Mavric, Mavrick

MAWULI (Ewe) there is a God.

MAX (Latin) a short form of Maximilian, Maxwell.
Mac, Mack, Maks, Maxe, Maxx, Maxy, Miksa

MAXFIELD (English) Mack's field.

MAXI (Czech, Hungarian, Spanish) a familiar form of Maximilian, Máximo.
Makszi, Maxey, Maxie, Maxis, Maxy

MAXIM (Russian) a form of Maxime.

MAXIME (French) most excellent.
Maxim, Maxyme

MAXIMILIAN (Latin) greatest.
Mac, Mack, Maixim, Maksim, Maksym, Max, Maxamillion, Maxemilian, Maxemilion, Maxi, Maximalian, Maximili, Maximilia, Maximiliano, Maximilianus, Maximilien, Maximillian, Máximo, Maximos, Maxmilian,

Maxmillion, Maxon, Maxymilian, Maxymillian, Mayhew, Miksa

MAXIMILIANO (Italian) a form of Maximilian.
Massimiliano, Maximiano, Maximino

MAXIMILLIAN (Latin) an alternate form of Maximilian.
Maximillan, Maximillano, Maximillien, Maximillion, Maxmillian, Maxximillian, Maxximillion

MÁXIMO (Spanish) a form of Maximilian.
Massimo, Maxi, Maximiano, Maximiliano, Maximino, Máximo

MAXIMOS (Greek) a form of Maximilian.

MAXWELL (English) great spring.
Max, Maxwel, Maxwill, Maxxwell, Maxy

MAXY (English) a familiar form of Max, Maxwell.
Maxi

MAYER (Hebrew) an alternate form of Meir. (Latin) an alternate form of Magnus, Major.
Mahyar, Mayeer, Mayor, Mayur

MAYES (English) field.
Mayo, Mays

MAYHEW (English) a form of Matthew.

MAYNARD (English) powerful; brave. See also Meinhard.
May, Mayne, Maynhard, Maynor, Ménard

MAYO (Irish) yew-tree plain. (English) an alternate form of Mayes. Geography: a county in Ireland.

MAYON (Hindi) god. Religion: ancient name for the Hindu god Krishna.

MAYONGA (Luganda) lake sailor.

MAZI (Ibo) sir.
Mazzi

MAZIN (Arabic) proper.
Mazen, Mazinn, Mazzin

MBITA (Swahili) born on a cold night.

MBWANA (Swahili) master.

MCGEORGE (Scottish) son of George.
MacGeorge

MCKADE (Scottish) son of Kade.
Mccade

MCKAY (Scottish) son of Kay.
Mackay, MacKay, Mckae, Mckai, McKay

MCKENZIE (Irish) an alternate form of Mackenzie.
Mccenzie, Mckennzie, Mckensey, Mckensie, Mckenson, Mckensson, Mckenzi, Mckenzy, Mckinzie

MCKINLEY (Irish) an alternate form of Mackinnley.
Mckinely, Mckinnely, Mckinnlee, Mckinnley, McKinnley

MEAD (English) meadow.
Meade, Meed

MEDGAR (German) a form of Edgar.

MEDWIN (German) faithful friend.

MEHETABEL (Hebrew) who God benefits.

MEHRDAD (Persian) gift of the sun.

MEHTAR (Sanskrit) prince.
Mehta

MEINHARD (German) strong, firm. See also Maynard.
Meinhardt, Meinke, Meino, Mendar

MEINRAD (German) strong counsel.

MEIR (Hebrew) one who brightens, shines; enlightener. History: a leading second-century scholar.
Mayer, Meyer, Muki, Myer

MEKA (Hawaiian) eyes.

MEL (English, Irish) a familiar form of Melvin.

MELBOURNE (English) mill stream.
Melborn, Melburn, Melby, Milborn, Milbourn, Milbourne, Milburn, Millburn, Millburne

MELCHIOR (Hebrew) king.
Meilseoir, Melchor, Melker, Melkior

MELDON (English) mill hill.
Melden

MELRONE (Irish) servant of Saint Ruadhan.

MELVERN (Native American) great chief.

MELVILLE (French) mill town. Literature: Herman Melville was a well-known nineteenth-century American writer.
Milville

MELVIN (Irish) armored chief. (English) mill friend; council friend. See also Vinny.
Malvin, Mel, Melvino, Melvon, Melvyn, Melwin, Melwyn, Melwynn

MENACHEM (Hebrew) comforter.
Menahem, Nachman

MENASSAH (Hebrew) cause to forget.
Menashe, Menashi, Menashia, Menashiah, Menashya, Manasseh

MENDEL (English) repairman.
Mendeley, Mendell, Mendie, Mendy

MENGESHA (Ethiopian) kingdom.

MENICO (Spanish) a short form of Domenico.

MENSAH (Ewe) third son.

MENZ (German) a short form of Clement.

MERCER (English) storekeeper.
Merce

MERED (Hebrew) revolter.

MEREDITH (Welsh) guardian from the sea.
Meredyth, Merideth, Meridith, Merry

MERION (Welsh) from Merion, England.
Merrion

MERLE (French) a short form of Merlin, Merrill.
Meryl

MERLIN (English) falcon. Literature: the wizard in King Arthur's court.

Merlin *(cont.)*
Marlon, Merle, Merlen, Merlinn, Merlyn, Merlynn

MERRICK (English) ruler of the sea.
Merek, Meric, Merick, Merik, Merric, Merrik, Meryk, Meyrick, Myrucj

MERRILL (Irish) bright sea. (French) famous.
Meril, Merill, Merle, Merrel, Merrell, Merril, Meryl

MERRITT (Latin, Irish) valuable; deserving.
Merit, Meritt, Merrett

MERTON (English) sea town.
Murton

MERV (Irish) a short form of Mervin.

MERVILLE (French) sea village.

MERVIN (Irish) a form of Marvin.
Merv, Mervyn, Mervynn, Merwin, Merwinn, Merwyn, Murvin, Murvyn, Myrvyn, Myrvynn, Myrwyn

MESHACH (Hebrew) artist. Bible: one of Daniel's three friends who were rescued from a fiery furnace by an angel.

MESUT (Turkish) happy.

METIKLA (Moquelumnan) reaching a hand under water to catch a fish.

METTE (Greek, Danish) pearl.
Almeta, Mete

MEURIG (Welsh) a form of Maurice.

MEYER (Hebrew) an alternate form of Meir. (German) farmer.
Mayer, Meier, Myer

MHINA (Swahili) delightful.

MICAH (Hebrew) an alternate form of Michael. Bible: a Hebrew prophet.
Mic, Micaiah, Michiah, Mika, Mikah, Myca, Mycah

MICHA (Hebrew) a short form of Michael.
Mica, Micha, Michah

MICHAEL (Hebrew) who is like God? See also Micah, Miguel, Mika, Miles.
Machael, Machas, Mahail, Maichail, Maikal, Makael, Makal, Makel, Makell, Makis, Meikel, Mekal, Mekhail, Mhichael, Micael, Micah, Micahel, Mical, Micha, Michaele, Michaell, Michail, Michak, Michal, Michale, Michalek, Michalel, Michau, Micheal, Micheil, Michel, Michele, Michelet, Michiel, Micho, Michoel, Mick, Mickael, Mickey, Mihail, Mihalje, Mihkel, Mika, Mikael, Mikáele, Mikal, Mike, Mikeal, Mikel, Mikelis, Mikell, Mikhail, Mikkel, Mikko, Miksa, Milko, Miquel, Misael, Misi, Miska, Mitchell, Mychael, Mychajlo, Mychal, Mykal, Mykhas

MICHAIL (Russian) a form of Michael.
Mihas, Mikail, Mikale, Misha

MICHAL (Polish) a form of Michael.
Michak, Michalek, Michall

MICHEAL (Irish) a form of Michael.

MICHEL (French) a form of Michael.
Michaud, Miche, Michee, Michell, Michelle, Michon

MICHELANGELO (Italian) a combination of Michael + Angelo. Art: Michelangelo Buonarroti was one of the greatest Italian Renaissance painters.
Michelange, Miguelangelo

MICHELE (Italian) a form of Michael.

MICHIO (Japanese) man with the strength of three thousand.

MICK (English) a short form of Michael, Mickey.
Mickerson

MICKAEL (English) a form of Michael.
Mickaele, Mickal, Mickale, Mickeal, Mickel, Mickell, Mickelle, Mickle

MICKENZIE (Irish) an alternate form of Mackenzie.
Mickenze, Mickenzy, Mikenzie

MICKEY (Irish) a familiar form of Michael.
Mick, Micki, Mickie, Micky, Miki, Mique

MICU (Hungarian) a form of Nick.

MIGUEL (Portuguese, Spanish) a form of Michael.
Migeel, Migel, Miguelly, Migui

MIGUELANGEL (Spanish) a combination of Miguel + Angel.

MIHAIL (Greek, Bulgarian, Romanian) a form of Michael.
Mihailo, Mihal, Mihalis, Mikail

MIKA (Hebrew) an alternate form of Micah. (Russian) a familiar form of Michael. (Ponca) raccoon.
Miika, Mikah

MIKAEL (Swedish) a form of Michael.
Mikaeel, Mikaele

MIKÁELE (Hawaiian) a form of Michael.
Mikele

MIKAL (Hebrew) an alternate form of Michael.
Mekal, Mikahl, Mikale

MIKASI (Omaha) coyote.

MIKE (Hebrew) a short form of Michael.
Mikey, Myk

MIKEAL (Irish) a form of Michael.

MIKEL (Basque) a form of Michael.
Mekel, Mikele, Mekell, Mikell, Mikelle

MIKELIS (Latvian) a form of Michael.
Mikus, Milkins

MIKHAIL (Greek, Russian) a form of Michael.
Mekhail, Mihály, Mikhael, Mikhale, Mikhalis, Mikhalka, Mikhall, Mikhel, Mikhial, Mikhos

MIKI (Japanese) tree.
Mikio

MIKKEL (Norwegian) a form of Michael.
Mikkael, Mikle

MIKKO (Finnish) a form of Michael.
Mikk, Mikka, Mikkohl, Mikkol, Miko, Mikol

MIKOLAJ (Polish) a form of Nicholas.
Mikolai

MIKOLAS (Greek) an alternate form of Nicholas.
Miklós, Milek

MIKSA (Hungarian) a form of Max.
Miks

MILAN (Italian) northerner. Geography: a city in northern Italy.
Milaan, Milano, Milen, Millan, Millen, Mylan, Mylen, Mylon, Mylynn

MILAP (Native American) giving.

MILBOROUGH (English) middle borough.
Milbrough

MILEK (Polish) a familiar form of Nicholas.

MILES (Greek) millstone. (Latin) soldier. (German) merciful. (English) a short form of Michael.
Milas, Milles, Milo, Milson, Myles

MILFORD (English) mill by the ford.

MILILANI (Hawaiian) heavenly caress.

MILKO (Czech) a form of Michael. (German) a familiar form of Emil.
Milkins

MILLARD (Latin) caretaker of the mill.
Mill, Millar, Miller, Millward, Milward, Myller

MILLER (English) miller, grain grinder.
Mellar, Millard, Millen

MILLS (English) mills.

MILO (German) an alternate form of Miles. A familiar form of Emil.
Millo, Mylo

MILOS (Greek, Slavic) pleasant.

MILOSLAV (Czech) lover of glory.
Milda

MILT (English) a short form of Milton.

MILTON (English) mill town.
Milt, Miltie, Milty, Mylton

MIMIS (Greek) a familiar form of Demetrius.

MIN (Burmese) king.
Mina

MINCHO (Spanish) a form of Benjamin.

MINEL (Spanish) a form of Manuel.

MINER (English) miner.

MINGAN (Native American) gray wolf.

MINGO (Spanish) a short form of Domingo.

MINH (Vietnamese) bright.
Minhao, Minhduc, Minhkhan, Minhtong, Minhy

MINKAH (Akan) just, fair.

MINOR (Latin) junior; younger.
Mynor

MINORU (Japanese) fruitful.

MIQUE (Spanish) a form of Mickey.
Mequel, Mequelin, Miquel

MIRON (Polish) peace.

MIROSLAV (Czech) peace; glory.
Mirek, Miroslaw, Miroslawy

MIRWAIS (Afghani) noble ruler. History: a famous king who lived in 900 A.D.

MISAEL (Hebrew) an alternate form of Michael.
Mischael, Mishael, Missael

MISHA (Russian) a short form of Michail.
Misa, Mischa, Mishael, Mishal, Mishe, Mishenka, Mishka

MISKA (Hungarian) a form of Michael.
Misi, Misik, Misko, Miso

MISTER (English) mister.
Mistur

MISU (Moquelumnan) rippling water.

MITCH (English) a short form of Mitchell.

MITCHEL (English) an alternate form of Mitchell.
Mitchael, Mitchal, Mitcheal, Mitchele, Mitchil, Mytchel

MITCHELL (English) a form of Michael.
Mitch, Mitchall, Mitchel, Mitchelle, Mitchem, Mytch, Mytchell

MITSOS (Greek) a familiar form of Demetrius.

MODESTO (Latin) modest.

MOE (English) a short form of Moses.
Mo

MOGENS (Dutch) powerful.

MOHAMAD (Arabic) an alternate form of Muhammad.
Mohamid

MOHAMED (Arabic) an alternate form of Muhammad.
Mohamd, Mohameed

MOHAMET (Arabic) an alternate form of Muhammad.
Mahomet, Mehemet, Mehmet

MOHAMMAD (Arabic) an alternate form of Muhammad.
Mahammad, Mohammadi, Mohammd, Mohammid, Mohanad, Mohmad

MOHAMMED (Arabic) an alternate form of Muhammad.
Mahammed, Mahomet, Mohammad, Mohaned, Mouhamed, Muhammad

MOHAMUD (Arabic) an alternate form of Muhammad.
Mohammud, Mohamoud

MOHAN (Hindi) delightful. Religion: another name for the Hindu god Krishna.

MOISES (Portuguese, Spanish) a form of Moses.
Moices, Moise, Moisés, Moisey, Moisis

MOISHE (Yiddish) a form of Moses.
Moshe

MOJAG (Native American) crying baby.

MOLIMO (Moquelumnan) bear going under shady trees.

MOMUSO (Moquelumnan) yellow jackets crowded in their nests for the winter.

MONA (Moquelumnan) gathering jimsonweed seed.

MONAHAN (Irish) monk.
Monaghan, Monoghan

MONGO (Yoruba) famous.

MONROE (Irish) Geography: the mouth of the Roe River.
Monro, Munro, Munroe

MONTAGUE (French) pointed mountain.
Montagne, Montagu, Monte

MONTANA (Spanish) mountain. Geography: a U.S. state. Culture: name popularized by football player Joe Montana.
Montaine, Montanna

MONTARO (Japanese) big boy.
Montario, Monterio, Montero

MONTE (Spanish) a short form of Montgomery.
Montae, Montaé, Montay, Montea, Montee, Monti, Montoya, Monty

MONTEL (American) a form of Montreal.
Montele, Montell, Montelle

MONTEZ (Spanish) dweller in the mountains.
Monteiz, Monteze, Montezz, Montisze

MONTGOMERY (English) rich man's mountain.
Monte, Montgomerie, Monty

MONTRE (French) show.
Montra, Montrae, Montray, Montraz, Montres, Montrey, Montrez, Montreze

MONTREAL (French) royal mountain. Geography: a city in Quebec.
Montel, Monterial, Monterrell, Montrail, Montrale, Montrall, Montreall, Montrell, Montrial

MONTRELL (French) an alternate form of Montreal.
Montral, Montrel, Montrele, Montrelle

MONTSHO (Tswana) black.

MONTY (English) a familiar form of Montgomery.

MOORE (French) dark; moor; marshland. See also Maurice.
Moor, Mooro, More

MORDECAI (Hebrew) martial, warlike. Mythology: Marduk was the Babylonian god of war.
Mord, Mordachai, Mordechai, Mordie, Mordy, Mort

MORDRED (Latin) painful. Literature: the nephew of King Arthur.
Modred

MOREL (French) an edible mushroom.
Morrel

MORELAND (English) moor; marshland.
Moorland, Morland

MORELL (French) dark; from Morocco.
Moor, Moore, Morelle, Morelli, Morill, Morrell, Morrill, Murrel, Murrell

MOREY (Greek) a familiar form of Moris. (Latin) an alternate form of Morrie.
Morrey, Morry

MORGAN (Scottish) sea warrior.
Morgen, Morghan, Morgin, Morgon, Morgun, Morgunn, Morgwn, Morgyn, Morrgan

MORIO (Japanese) forest.

MORIS (Greek) son of the dark one. (English) an alternate form of Morris.
Morey, Morisz, Moriz

MORITZ (German) a form of Maurice, Morris.
Morisz

MORLEY (English) meadow by the moor.
Moorley, Moorly, Morlee, Morleigh, Morlon, Morly, Morlyn, Morrley

MORRIE (Latin) a familiar form of Maurice, Morse.
Maury, Morey, Mori, Morie, Morry, Mory, Morye

MORRIS (Latin) dark skinned; moor; marshland. (English) a form of Maurice.
Moris, Moriss, Moritz, Morrese, Morrise, Morriss, Morry, Moss

MORSE (English) son of Maurice.
Morresse, Morrie, Morrison, Morrisson

MORT (French, English) a short form of Morten, Mortimer, Morton.
Morte, Mortey, Mortie, Mortty, Morty

MORTEN (Norwegian) a form of Martin.
Mort

MORTIMER (French) still water.
Mort, Mortymer

MORTON (English) town near the moor.
Mort

MORVEN (Scottish) mariner.
Morvien, Morvin

MOSE (Hebrew) a short form of Moses.

MOSES (Hebrew) drawn out of the water. (Egyptian) son, child. Bible: the Hebrew leader who brought the Ten Commandments down from Mount Sinai.
Moe, Moise, Moïse, Moisei, Moises, Moishe, Mose, Mosese, Moshe, Mosiah, Mosie, Moss, Mosses, Mosya, Mosze, Moszek, Mousa, Moyses, Moze

MOSHE (Hebrew, Polish) an alternate form of Moses.
Mosheh

MOSI (Swahili) first-born.

MOSS (Irish) a short form of Maurice, Morris. (English) a short form of Moses.

MOSWEN (African) light in color.

MOTEGA (Native American) new arrow.

MOUHAMED (Arabic) an alternate form of Muhammad.
Mouhamad, Mouhamadou, Mouhammed, Mouhamoin

MOUSA (Arabic) a form of Moses.
Moussa

MOZE (Lithuanian) a form of Moses.
Mozes, Mózes

MPASA (Ngoni) mat.

MPOSI (Nyakusa) blacksmith.

MPOZA (Luganda) tax collector.

MSRAH (Akan) sixth-born.

MTIMA (Ngoni) heart.

MUATA (Moquelumnan) yellow jackets in their nest.

MUGAMBA (Runyoro) talks too much.

MUGISA (Rutooro) lucky.
Mugisha, Mukisa

MUHAMMAD (Arabic) praised. History: the founder of the Islamic religion. See also Ahmad, Hamid, Yasin.
Mahmoud, Mahmúd, Mohamad, Mohamed, Mohamet, Mohamud, Mohammed, Mouhamed, Muhamad, Muhamed, Muhamet, Muhammadali, Muhammed

MUHANNAD (Arabic) sword.
Muhanad

MUHSIN (Arabic) beneficent; charitable.

MUHTADI (Arabic) rightly guided.

MUIR (Scottish) moor; marshland.

MUJAHID (Arabic) fighter in the way of Allah.

MUKASA (Luganda) God's chief administrator.

MUKHTAR (Arabic) chosen.
Mukhtaar

MUKUL (Sanskrit) bud, blossom; soul.

MULOGO (Musoga) wizard.

MUNDAN (Rhodesian) garden.

MUNDO (Spanish) a short form of Edmundo.

MUNDY (Irish) from Reamonn, Ireland.

MUNGO (Scottish) amiable.

MUN-HEE (Korean) literate; shiny.

MUNIR (Arabic) brilliant; shining.

MUNNY (Cambodian) wise.

MURACO (Native American) white moon.

MURALI (Hindi) god. Religion: another name for the Hindu god Krishna.

MURAT (Turkish) wish come true.

MURDOCK (Scottish) wealthy sailor.
Murdo, Murdoch, Murtagh

MURPHY (Irish) sea-warrior.
Murfey, Murfy

MURRAY (Scottish) sailor.
Macmurray, Moray, Murrey, Murry

MURTAGH (Irish) a form of Murdock.
Murtaugh

MUSA (Swahili) child.

MUSÁD (Arabic) untied camel.

MUSOKE (Rukonjo) born while a rainbow was in the sky.

MUSTAFA (Arabic) chosen; royal.
Mostafa, Mostaffa, Moustafa, Mustafaa, Mustafah, Mustafe, Mustaffa, Mustafo, Mustapha, Mustoffa, Mustofo

MUSTAPHA (Arabic) an alternate form of Mustafa.
Mostapha, Moustapha

MUTI (Arabic) obedient.

MWAKA (Luganda) born on New Year's Eve.

MWAMBA (Nyakusa) strong.

MWANJE (Luganda) leopard.

MWINYI (Swahili) king.

MWITA (Swahili) summoner.

MYCHAJLO (Latvian) a form of Michael.
Mykhaltso, Mykhas

MYCHAL (American) a form of Michael.
Mychall, Mychalo, Mycheal

MYER (English) a form of Meir.
Myers, Myur

MYKAL, Mykel (American) a form of Michael.
Mykael, Mikele, Mykell

MYLES (Latin) soldier. (German) an alternate form of Miles.
Myels, Mylez, Mylles, Mylz

MYNOR (Latin) an alternate form of Minor.

MYO (Burmese) city.

MYRON (Greek) fragrant ointment.
Mehran, Mehrayan, My, Myran, Myrone, Ron

MYUNG-DAE (Korean) right; great.

MZUZI (Swahili) inventive.

NAAMAN (Hebrew) pleasant.

NABIHA (Arabic) intelligent.

NABIL (Arabic) noble.
Nabeel, Nabiel

NACHMAN (Hebrew) a short form of Menachem.
Nachum, Nahum

NADA (Arabic) generous.

NADAV (Hebrew) generous; noble.
Nadiv

NADIDAH (Arabic) equal to anyone else.

NADIM (Arabic) friend.
Nadeem

NADIR (Afghani, Arabic) dear, rare.
Nader

NADISU (Hindi) beautiful river.

NAEEM (Arabic) benevolent.
Naem, Naim, Naiym, Nieem

NAFTALI (Hebrew) wreath.
Naftalie

NAGID (Hebrew) ruler, prince.

NAHELE (Hawaiian) forest.

NAHMA (Native American) sturgeon.

NAILAH (Arabic) successful.

NAIRN (Scottish) river with alder trees.
Nairne

NAJEE (Arabic) an alternate form of Naji.
Najae, Najée, Najei, Najiee

NAJI (Arabic) safe.
Najee, Najih

NAJÍB (Arabic) born to nobility.
Najib, Nejeeb

NAJJI (Muganda) second child.

NAKIA (Arabic) pure.
Nakai, Nakee, Nakeia, Naki, Nakiah, Nakii

NAKOS (Arapaho) sage, wise.

NALDO (Spanish) a familiar form of Reginald.

NALREN (Dene) thawed out.

NAM (Vietnamese) scrape off

NAMAKA (Hawaiian) eyes.

NAMID (Chippewa) star dancer.

NAMIR (Hebrew) leopard.
Namer

NANDIN (Hindi) god; destroyer Religion: another name for the Hindu god Shiva.
Nandan

NANDO (German) a familiar form of Ferdinand.
Nandor

NANGILA (Abaluhya) born while parents traveled.

NANGWAYA (Mwera) don't mess with me.

NANSEN (Swedish) son of Nancy.

NANTAI (Navajo) chief.

NANTAN (Apache) spokesman.

NAOKO (Japanese) straight, honest.

NAPAYSHNI (Lakota) he does not flee; courageous.

NAPIER (Spanish) new city.
Neper

NAPOLEON (Greek) lion of the woodland. (Italian) from Naples, Italy. History: Napoleon Bonaparte was a famous nineteenth-century French emperor.
Leon, Nap, Napolean, Napoléon, Napoleone, Nappie, Nappy

NAQUAN (American) a combination of the prefix Na + Quan.
Naqawn, Naquain, Naquen, Naquon

NARAIN (Hindi) protector. Religion: another name for the Hindu god Vishnu.
Narayan

NARCISSE (French) a form of Narcissus.
Narcis, Narciso, Narkis, Narkissos

NARCISSUS (Greek) daffodil. Mythology: the youth who fell in love with his own reflection.
Narcisse

NARD (Persian) chess player.

NARDO (German) strong, hardy. (Spanish) a short form of Bernardo.

NARVE (Dutch) healthy, strong.

NASHASHUK (Fox, Sauk) loud thunder.

NASHOBA (Choctaw) wolf.

NASIM (Persian) breeze, fresh air.
Naseem, Nassim

NASSER (Arabic) victorious.
Naseer, Naser, Nasier, Nasir, Nasr, Nassir, Nassor

NAT (English) a short form of Nathan, Nathaniel.
Natt, Natty

NATAL (Spanish) a form of Noël.
Natale, Natalie, Natalino, Natalio, Nataly

NATAN (Hebrew, Hungarian, Polish, Russian, Spanish) God has given.
Naten

NATANAEL (Hebrew) an alternate form of Nathaniel.
Natanel, Nataniel

NATE (Hebrew) a short form of Nathan, Nathaniel.

NATESH (Hindi) destroyer. Religion: another name for the Hindu god Shiva.

NATHAN (Hebrew) a short form of Nathaniel. Bible: an Old Testament prophet who saved Solomon's kingdom.
Naethan, Nat, Nate, Nathann, Nathean, Nathen, Nathian, Nathin, Nathon, Nathyn, Natthan, Naythan, Nethan

NATHANAEL (Hebrew) an alternate form of Nathaniel.
Nathanae, Nathanal, Nathaneal, Nathaneil, Nathanel, Nathaneol

NATHANIAL (Hebrew) an alternate form of Nathaniel.
Nathanyal, Nathanual

NATHANIE (Hebrew) a familiar form of Nathaniel.
Nathania, Nathanni

NATHANIEL (Hebrew) gift of God. Bible: one of the Twelve Apostles.
Nat, Natanael, Nate, Nathan, Nathanael, Nathanial, Nathanie, Nathanielle, Nathanil, Nathanile, Nathanuel, Nathanyel, Nathanyl, Natheal, Nathel, Nathinel, Nethaniel, Thaniel

NATHEN (Hebrew) an alternate form of Nathan.

NAV (Gypsy) name.

NAVARRO (Spanish) plains.
Navarre

NAVDEEP (Sikh) new light.
Navdip

NAVIN (Hindi) new, novel.
Naveen, Naven

NAWAT (Native American) left-handed.

NAWKAW (Winnebago) wood.

NAYATI (Native American) wrestler.

NAYLAND (English) island dweller.

NAZARETH (Hebrew) born in Nazareth, Israel.
Nazaire, Nazaret, Nazarie, Nazario, Nazerene, Nazerine

NAZIH (Arabic) pure, chaste.
Nazeeh, Nazeem, Nazeer, Nazieh, Nazim, Nazir, Nazz

NDALE (Ngoni) trick.

NEAL (Irish) an alternate form of Neil.
Neale, Neall, Nealle, Nealon, Nealy

NECI (Latin) a familiar form of Ignatius.

NECTARIOS (Greek) saint. Religion: a recent saint in the Greek Orthodox church.

NED (English) a familiar form of Edward, Edwin.
Neddie, Neddym, Nedrick

NEHEMIAH (Hebrew) compassion of Jehovah. Bible: a Hebrew prophet.
Nahemiah, Nechemya, Nehemias, Nehemie, Nehemyah, Nehimiah, Nehmia, Nehmiah, Nemo, Neyamia

NEHRU (Hindi) canal.

NEIL (Irish) champion.
Neal, Neel, Neihl, Neile, Neill, Neille, Nels, Niall, Niele, Niels, Nigel, Nil, Niles, Nilo, Nils, Nyle

NEKA (Native American) wild goose.

NELEK (Polish) a form of Cornelius.

NELLIE (English) a familiar form of Cornelius, Cornell, Nelson.
Nell, Nelly

NELIUS (Latin) a short form of Cornelius.

NELO (Spanish) a form of Daniel.
Nello, Nilo

NELS (Scandinavian) a form of Neil, Nelson.
Nelse, Nelson, Nils

NELSON (English) son of Neil.
Nealson, Neilsen, Neilson, Nellie, Nels, Nelsen, Nilson, Nilsson

NEMESIO (Spanish) just.
Nemi

NEMO (Greek) glen, glade. (Hebrew) a short form of Nehemiah.

NEN (Egyptian) ancient waters.

NEPTUNE (Latin) sea ruler. Mythology: the Roman god of the sea.

NERO (Latin, Spanish) stern.
Neron, Nerone, Nerron

NESBIT (English) nose-shaped bend in a river.
Naisbit, Naisbitt, Nesbitt, Nisbet, Nisbett

NESTOR (Greek) traveler; wise.
Nester

NETHANIEL (Hebrew) an alternate form of Nathaniel.
Netanel, Netania, Netaniah, Netaniel, Netanya, Nethanel, Nethanial, Nethaniel, Nethanyal, Nethanyel

NETO (Spanish) a short form of Ernesto.

NEVADA (Spanish) covered in snow. Geography: a U.S. state.
Navada, Nevade

NEVAN (Irish) holy.
Nevean

NEVILLE (French) new town.
Nev, Nevil, Nevile, Nevill, Nevyle

NEVIN (Irish) worshiper of the saint. (English) middle; herb.
Nefen, Nev, Nevan, Neven, Nevins, Nevyn, Niven

NEWBOLD (English) new tree.

NEWELL (English) new hall.
Newall, Newel, Newyle

NEWLAND (English) new land.
Newlan

NEWLIN (Welsh) new lake.
Newlyn

NEWMAN (English) newcomer.
Neiman, Neimann, Neimon, Neuman, Numan, Numen

NEWTON (English) new town.
Newt

NGAI (Vietnamese) herb.

NGHIA (Vietnamese) forever.

NGOZI (Ibo) blessing.

NGU (Vietnamese) sleep.
Nguyen

NHEAN (Cambodian) self-knowledge.

NIALL (Irish) an alternate form of Neil. History: Niall of the Nine Hostages was a famous Irish ruler who founded the clan O'Neill.
Nial, Nialle

NIBAL (Arabic) arrows.
Nibel

NIBAW (Native American) standing tall.

NICABAR (Gypsy) stealthly.

NICHO (Spanish) a form of Dennis.

NICHOLAS (Greek) victorious people. Religion: the patron saint of children. See also Caelan, Claus, Cola, Colar, Cole, Colin, Colson, Klaus, Lasse, Mikolaj, Mikolas, Milek.
Niccolas, Nichalas, Nichelas, Nichele, Nichlas, Nichlos, Nichola, Nicholaas, Nicholaes, Nicholase, Nicholaus, Nichole, Nicholias, Nicholl, Nichollas, Nicholos, Nichols, Nicholus, Nick, Nickalus, Nicklaus, Nickolas, Nicky, Niclas, Niclasse, Nico, Nicola, Nicolai, Nicolas, Nicoles, Nicolis, Nicoll, Nicolo, Nikhil, Niki, Nikili, Nikita, Nikko, Niklas, Niko, Nikolai, Nikolas, Nikolaus, Nikolos, Nils, Nioclás, Niocol, Nycholas

NICHOLAUS (Greek) an alternate form of Nicholas.
Nichalaus, Nichalous, Nichaolas, Nichlaus, Nichloas, Nichlous, Nicholaos, Nicholous

NICHOLS, Nicholson (English) son of Nicholas.
Nicholes, Nicholis, Nicolls, Nickelson, Nickoles

NICK (English) a short form of Dominic, Nicholas. See also Micu.
Nic, Nik

NICKALUS (Greek) an alternate form of Nicholas.
Nickalas, Nickalis, Nickalos, Nickelas, Nickelus

NICKLAUS, Nicklas (Greek) an alternate form of Nicholas.
Nickalaus, Nickalous, Nickelous, Nicklauss, Nicklos, Nicklous, Nicklus, Nickolau, Nickolaus, Nicolaus, Niklaus, Nikolaus

NICKOLAS (Greek) an alternate form of Nicholas.
Nickolaos, Nickolis, Nickolos, Nickolus, Nickolys, Nickoulas

NICKY (Greek) a familiar form of Nicholas.
Nickey, Nicki, Nickie, Niki, Nikki

NICO (Greek) a short form of Nicholas.
Nicco

NICODEMUS (Greek) conqueror of the people.
Nicodem, Nicodemius, Nikodem, Nikodema, Nikodemious, Nikodim

NICOLA (Italian) a form of Nicholas. See also Cola.
Nicolá, Nikolah

NICOLAI (Norwegian, Russian) a form of Nicholas.
Nicholai, Nickolai, Nicolaj, Nicolau, Nicolay, Nicoly, Nikalai

NICOLAS (Italian) a form of Nicholas.
Nico, Nicolaas, Nicolás, Nicolaus, Nicoles, Nicolis, Nicolus

NICOLO (Italian) a form of Nicholas.
Niccolo, Niccolò, Nicol, Nicolao, Nicollo

NIELS (Danish) a form of Neil.
Niel, Nielsen, Nielson, Niles, Nils

NIEN (Vietnamese) year.

NIGAN (Native American) ahead.
Nigen

NIGEL (Latin) dark night.
Niegel, Nigal, Nigale, Nigele, Nigell, Nigiel, Nigil, Nigle, Nijel, Nye, Nygel, Nyigel, Nyjil

NIKA (Yoruba) ferocious.

NIKE (Greek) victorious.
Nikka

NIKI (Hungarian) a familiar form of Nicholas.

Nikia, Nikiah, Nikki, Nikkie, Nykei, Nykey

NIKITA (Russian) a form of Nicholas.
Nakita, Nakitas, Nikula

NIKITI (Native American) round and smooth like an abalone shell.

NIKKO, Niko (Hungarian) forms of Nicholas.
Nikoe, Nyko

NIKLAS (Latvian, Swedish) a form of Nicholas.
Niklaas, Niklaus

NIKOLA (Greek) a short form of Nicholas.
Nikolao, Nikolay, Nykola

NIKOLAI (Estonian, Russian) a form of Nicholas.
Kolya, Nikolais, Nikolaj, Nikolajs, Nikolay, Nikoli, Nikolia, Nikula, Nikulas

NIKOLAS (Greek) an alternate form on Nicholas.
Nicanor, Nikalas, Nikalis, Nikalus, Nikholas, Nikolaas, Nikolaos, Nikolis, Nikolos, Nikos, Nilos, Nykolas, Nykolus

NIKOLAUS (Greek) an alternate form of Nicholas.
Nikalous, Nikolaos

NIKOLOS (Greek) an alternate form of Nicholas. See also Kolya.
Niklos, Nikolaos, Nikolò, Nikolous, Nikolus, Nikos, Nilos

NIL (Russian) a form of Neil.
Nilya

NILA (Hindi) blue.

NILES (English) son of Neil.
Nilesh, Nyles

NILO (Finnish) a form of Neil.

NILS (Swedish) a short form of Nicholas.

NIMROD (Hebrew) rebel. Bible: a great-grandson of Noah.

NIÑO (Spanish) young child.

NIRAN (Tai) eternal.

NISHAN (Armenian) cross, sign, mark.
Nishon

NISSAN (Hebrew) sign, omen; miracle.
Nisan, Nissim, Nissin, Nisson

NITIS (Native American) friend.
Netis

NIXON (English) son of Nick.
Nixan, Nixson

NIZAM (Arabic) leader.

NKUNDA (Runyankore) loves those who hate him.

N'NAMDI (Ibo) his father's name lives on.

NOACH (Hebrew) an alternate form of Noah.

NOAH (Hebrew) peaceful, restful. Bible: the patriarch who built the ark to survive the Great Flood.
Noach, Noak, Noe, Noé, Noi

NOAM (Hebrew) sweet; friend.

NOBLE (Latin) born to nobility.
Nobe, Nobie, Noby

NODIN (Native American) wind.
Knoton, Noton

NOE (Czech, French) a form of Noah.

NOÉ (Hebrew, Spanish) quiet, peaceful. See also Noah.

NOËL (French) day of Christ's birth. See also Natal.
Noel, Noél, Noell, Nole, Noli, Nowel, Nowell

NOHEA (Hawaiian) handsome.
Noha, Nohe

NOKONYU (Native American) katydid's nose.
Noko, Nokoni

NOLAN (Irish) famous; noble.
Noland, Nolande, Nolane, Nolen, Nolin, Nollan, Nolyn

NOLLIE (Latin, Scandinavian) a familiar form of Oliver.
Noll, Nolly

NORBERT (Scandinavian) brilliant hero.
Bert, Norberto, Norbie, Norby

NORBERTO (Spanish) a form of Norbert.

NORMAN (French) norseman. History: a name for the Scandinavians who conquered Normandy in the tenth century, and who later conquered England in 1066.
Norm, Normand, Normen, Normie, Normy

NORRIS (French) northerner. (English) Norman's horse.
Norice, Norie, Noris, Norreys, Norrie, Norry, Norrys

NORTHCLIFF (English) northern cliff.
Northcliffe, Northclyff, Northclyffe

NORTHROP (English) north farm.
North, Northup

NORTON (English) northern town.

NORVILLE (French, English) northern town.
Norval, Norvel, Norvell, Norvil, Norvill, Norvylle

NORVIN (English) northern friend.
Norvyn, Norwin, Norwinn, Norwyn, Norwynn

NORWARD (English) protector of the north.
Norwerd

NORWOOD (English) northern woods.

NOTAKU (Moquelumnan) growing bear.

NOWLES (English) a short form of Knowles.

NSOAH (Akan) seventh-born.

NUMA (Arabic) pleasant.

NUMAIR (Arabic) panther.

NUNCIO (Italian) messenger.
Nunzi, Nunzio

NURI (Hebrew, Arabic) my fire.
Nery, Noori, Nur, Nuris, Nurism, Nury

NURIEL (Hebrew, Arabic) fire of the Lord.
Nuria, Nuriah, Nuriya

NURU (Swahili) born in daylight.

NUSAIR (Arabic) bird of prey.

NWA (Nigerian) son.

NWAKE (Nigerian) born on market day.

NYE (English) a familiar form of Aneurin, Nigel.

NYLE (Irish) an alternate form of Neil. (English) island.
Nyal, Nyll

OAKES (English) oak trees.
Oak, Oakie, Oaks, Ochs

OAKLEY (English) oak-tree field.
Oak, Oakes, Oakie, Oaklee, Oakleigh, Oakly, Oaks

OALO (Spanish) a form of Paul.

OBA (Yoruba) king.

OBADELE (Yoruba) king arrives at the house.

OBADIAH (Hebrew) servant of God.
Obadias, Obed, Obediah, Obie, Ovadiach, Ovadiah, Ovadya

OBED (English) a short form of Obadiah.

OBERON (German) noble; bearlike. Literature: the king of the fairies in the Shakespearean play *A Midsummer Night's Dream*. See also Auberon, Aubrey.
Oberen, Oberron, Oeberon

OBERT (German) wealthy; bright.

OBIE (English) a familiar form of Obadiah.
Obbie, Obe, Obey, Obi, Oby

OCAN (Luo) hard times.

OCTAVIO (Latin) eighth. See also Tavey, Tavian.
Octave, Octavia, Octavian, Octaviano, Octavien, Octavious, Octavius, Octavo, Octavous, Octavus, Ottavio

OCTAVIOUS, Octavius (Latin) alternate forms of Octavio.
Octavaius, Octaveous, Octaveus, Octavias, Octaviaus, Octavis, Octavous, Octavus

ODAKOTA (Lakota) friendly.
Oda

ODD (Norwegian) point.
Oddvar

ODE (Benin) born along the road. (Irish, English) a short form of Odell.
Odey, Odie, Ody

ODED (Hebrew) encouraging.

ODELL (Greek) ode, melody. (Irish) otter. (English) forest-ed hill.
Dell, Odall, Ode

ODIN (Scandinavian) ruler. Mythology: the chief Norse god.
Oden

ODION (Benin) first of twins.

ODO (Norwegian) a form of Otto.

ODOLF (German) prosperous wolf.
Odolff

ODOM (Ghanian) oak tree.

ODON (Hungarian) wealthy protector.
Odi

ODRAN (Irish) pale green.
Odhrán, Oran, Oren, Orin, Orran, Orren, Orrin

ODYSSEUS (Greek) wrathful. Literature: the hero of Homer's epic *The Odyssey*.

OFER (Hebrew) young deer.

OG (Aramaic) king. Bible: the king of Basham.

OGALEESHA (Lakota) red shirt.

OGBAY (Ethiopian) don't take him from me.

OGBONNA (Ibo) image of his father.
Ogbonnia

OGDEN (English) oak valley. Literature: Ogden Nash was a twentieth-century American writer.
Ogdan, Ogdon

OGIMA (Chippewa) chief.

OGUN (Nigerian) Mythology: the god of war.
Ogunkeye, Ogunsanwo, Ogunsheye

OHANKO (Native American) restless.

OHANNES (Turkish) a form of John.

OHANZEE (Lakota) comforting shadow.

OHIN (African) chief.
Ohan

OHITEKAH (Lakota) brave.

OISTIN (Irish) a form of Austin.
Osten, Ostyn, Ostynn

OJ (American) a combination of the initials O. + J.
O.J., Ojay

OJO (Yoruba) difficult delivery.

OKAPI (Swahili) giraffe-like animal with a long neck.

OKE (Hawaiian) a form of Oscar.

OKECHUKU (Ibo) God's gift.

OKEKE (Ibo) born on market day.
Okorie

OKIE (American) from Oklahoma.
Okee, Okey

OKO (Ga) older twin. (Yoruba) god of war.

OKORIE (Ibo) an alternate form of Okeke.

OKPARA (Ibo) first son.

OKUTH (Luo) born in a rain shower.

OLA (Yoruba) wealthy, rich.

OLAF (Scandinavian) ancestor. History: a patron saint and king of Norway.
Olaff, Olafur, Olav, Ole, Olef, Olof, Oluf

OLAJUWON (Yoruba) wealth and honor are God's gifts.
Olajawon, Olajawun, Olajowuan, Olajuan, Olajuanne, Olajuawon, Olajuwa, Olajuwan, Olaujawon, Oljuwoun

OLAMINA (Yoruba) this is my wealth.

OLATUNJI (Yoruba) honor reawakens.

OLAV (Scandinavian) an alternate form of Olaf.
Ola, Olave, Olavus, Ole, Olen, Olin, Olle, Olov, Olyn

OLE (Scandinavian) a familiar form of Olaf, Olav.
Olay, Oleh, Olle

OLEG (Latvian, Russian) holy.
Olezka

OLEKSANDR (Russian) a form of Alexander.
Olek, Olesandr, Olesko

OLÉS (Polish) a familiar form of Alexander.

OLIN (English) holly.
Olen, Olney, Olyn

OLINDO (Italian) from Olinthos, Italy.

OLIVER (Latin) olive tree. (Scandinavian) kind; affectionate.
Nollie, Oilibhéar, Oliverio, Oliverios, Olivero, Olivier, Oliviero, Oliwa, Ollie, Olliver, Ollivor, Olvan

OLIVIER (French) a form of Oliver.

OLIWA (Hawaiian) a form of Oliver.

OLLIE (English) a familiar form of Oliver.
Olie, Olle, Olley, Olly

OLO (Spanish) a short form of Orlando, Rolando.

OLUBAYO (Yoruba) highest joy.

OLUFEMI (Yoruba) wealth and honor favors me.

OLUJIMI (Yoruba) God gave me this.

OLUSHOLA (Yoruba) God has blessed me.

OMAR (Arabic) highest; follower of the Prophet. (Hebrew) reverent.
Omair, Omari, Omarr, Omer, Umar

OMARI (Swahili) a form of Omar.
Omare, Omaree, Omarey

OMER (Arabic) an alternate form of Omar.
Omeer, Omero

OMOLARA (Benin) child born at the right time.

ON (Burmese) coconut. (Chinese) peace.

ONAN (Turkish) prosperous.

ONAONA (Hawaiian) pleasant fragrance.

ONDRO (Czech) a form of Andrew.
Ondra, Ondre, Ondrea, Ondrey

O'NEIL (Irish) son of Neil.
Oneal, O'neal, Oneil, O'neill, Onel, Oniel, Onil

ONKAR (Hindi) pure being. Religion: another name for the Hindu god Shiva.

ONOFRIO (German) an alternate form of Humphrey.
Oinfre, Onfre, Onfrio, Onofre, Onofredo

ONSLOW (English) enthusiast's hill.
Ounslow

ONUFRY (Polish) a form of Humphrey.

ONUR (Turkish) honor.

OPHIR (Hebrew) faithful. Bible: an Old Testament character.

OPIO (Ateso) first of twin boys.

ORAL (Latin) verbal, speaker.

ORAN (Irish) green.
Odhran, Odran, Ora, Orane, Orran

ORATIO (Latin) an alternate form of Horatio.
Orazio

ORBÁN (Hungarian) born in the city.

ORDELL (Latin) beginning.
Orde

OREN (Hebrew) pine tree. (Irish) light skinned, white.
Oran, Orin, Oris, Orono, Orren, Orrin

ORESTES (Greek) mountain man. Mythology: the son of the Greek leader Agamemnon.
Aresty, Oreste

ORI (Hebrew) my light.
Oree, Orie, Orri, Ory

ORIEN (Latin) visitor from the east.
Orian, Orie, Orin, Oris, Oron, Orono, Orrin, Oryan

ORION (Greek) son of fire. Mythology: a hunter who became a constellation. See also Zorion.

ORJI (Ibo) mighty tree.

ORLANDO (German) famous throughout the land. (Spanish) a form of Roland.
Lando, Olando, Olo, Orlan, Orland, Orlanda, Orlandas,

Orlando (cont.)
Orlandes, Orlandis, Orlandos, Orlandus, Orlo, Orlondo, Orlondon

ORLEANS (Latin) golden.
Orlean, Orlin

ORMAN (German) mariner, seaman. (Scandinavian) serpent, worm.
Ormand

ORMOND (English) bear mountain; spear protector.
Ormande, Ormon, Ormonde

ORO (Spanish) golden.

ORONO (Latin) a form of Oren.
Oron

ORRICK (English) old oak tree.
Orric

ORRIN (English) river. Geography: a river in England.
Orin, Oryn, Orynn

ORRIS (Latin) an alternate form of Horatio.
Oris, Orriss

ORRY (Latin) from the Orient.
Oarrie, Orrey, Orrie

ORSINO (Italian) a form of Orson.

ORSON (Latin) bearlike.
Orscino, Orsen, Orsin, Orsini, Orsino, Son, Sonny, Urson

ORTON (English) shore town.

ORTZI (Basque) sky.

ORUNJAN (Yoruba) born under the midday sun.

ORVAL (English) an alternate form of Orville.
Orvel

ORVILLE (French) golden village. History: Orville Wright and his brother Wilbur were the first men to fly an airplane.
Orv, Orval, Orvell, Orvie, Orvil

ORVIN (English) spear friend.
Orwin, Owynn

OSAHAR (Benin) God hears.

OSAYABA (Benin) God forgives.

OSAZE (Benin) whom God likes.

OSBERT (English) divine; bright.

OSBORN (Scandinavian) divine bear. (English) warrior of God.
Osbern, Osbon, Osborne, Osbourn, Osbourne, Osburn, Osburne, Oz, Ozzie

OSCAR (Scandinavian) divine spearman.
Oke, Oskar, Osker, Oszkar

OSEI (Fante) noble.
Osee

OSGOOD (English) divinely good.

O'SHEA (Irish) son of Shea.
Oshae, Oshai, Oshane, O'Shane, Oshaun, Oshay, Oshaye, Oshe, Oshea, Osheon

OSIP (Russian, Ukrainian) a form of Joseph, Yosef. See also Osya.

OSKAR (Scandinavian) an alternate form of Oscar.
Osker, Ozker

OSMAN (Turkish) ruler. (English) servant of God.
Osmanek, Osmen, Osmin, Otthmor, Ottmar

OSMAR (English) divine; wonderful.

OSMOND (English) divine protector.
Osmand, Osmonde, Osmont, Osmund, Osmunde, Osmundo

OSRIC (English) divine ruler.
Osrick

OSTIN (Latin) an alternate form of Austin.
Ostan, Osten, Ostyn

OSVALDO (Spanish) a form of Oswald.
Osbaldo, Osbalto, Osvald, Osvalda

OSWALD (English) God's power; God's crest. See also Waldo.
Osvaldo, Oswaldo, Oswall, Oswell, Oswold, Oz, Ozzie

OSWALDO (Spanish) a form of Oswald.

OSWIN (English) divine friend.
Osvin, Oswinn, Oswyn, Oswynn

OSYA (Russian) a familiar form of Osip.

OTA (Czech) prosperous.
Otik

OTADAN (Native American) plentiful.

OTAKTAY (Lakota) kills many; strikes many.

OTEK (Polish) a form of Otto.

OTELLO (Italian) a form of Othello.

OTEM (Luo) born away from home.

OTHELLO (Spanish) a form of Otto. Literature: the title character in the Shakespearean tragedy *Othello*.
Otello

OTHMAN (German) wealthy.
Ottoman

OTIS (Greek) keen of hearing. (German) son of Otto.
Oates, Odis, Otes, Otess, Otez, Otise, Ottis, Otys

OTTAH (Nigerian) thin baby.

OTTAR (Norwegian) point warrior; fright warrior.

OTTMAR (Turkish) an alternate form of Osman. History: the founder of the Ottoman Empire.
Otomars, Ottomar

OTTO (German) rich.
Odo, Otek, Otello, Otfried, Othello, Otho, Othon, Otik, Otilio, Otman, Oto, Otón, Otton, Ottone

OTTOKAR (German) happy warrior.
Otokars, Ottocar

OTU (Native American) collecting seashells in a basket.

OURAY (Ute) arrow. Astrology: born under the sign of Sagittarius.

OVED (Hebrew) worshiper, follower.

OWEN (Irish) born to nobility; young warrior. (Welsh) a form of Evan.
Owain, Owens, Owin, Uaine

OWNEY (Irish) elderly.
Oney

OXFORD (English) place where oxen cross the river.
Ford

OYA (Moquelumnan) speaking of the jacksnipe.

OYSTEIN (Norwegian) rock of happiness.
Ostein, Osten, Ostin, Øystein

OZ (Hebrew) a short form of Osborn, Oswald.

OZTURK (Turkish) pure; genuine Turk.

OZZIE (English) a familiar form of Osborn, Oswald.
Ossie, Ossy, Ozee, Ozi, Ozzi, Ozzy

PAAVO (Finnish) a form of Paul.
Paaveli

PABLO (Spanish) a form of Paul.
Pable, Paublo

PACE (English) a form of Pascal.
Payce

PACIFICO (Filipino) peaceful.

PACO (Italian) pack. (Spanish) a familiar form of Francisco. (Native American) bald eagle. See also Quico.
Pacorro, Panchito, Pancho, Paquito

PADDY (Irish) a familiar form of Padraic, Patrick.
Paddey, Paddi, Paddie

PADEN (English) an altenate form of Patton.

PADGET (English) a form of Page.
Padgett, Paget, Pagett

PADRAIC (Irish) a form of Patrick.
Paddrick, Paddy, Padhraig, Padrai, Pádraig, Padraigh, Padreic, Padriac, Padric, Padron, Padruig

PAGE (French) youthful assistant.
Padget, Paggio, Paige, Payge

PAIGE (English) a form of Page.

PAKELIKA (Hawaiian) a form of Patrick.

PAKI (African) witness.

PAL (Swedish) a form of Paul.

PÁL (Hungarian) a form of Paul.
Pali, Palika

PALAINA (Hawaiian) a form of Brian.

PALANI (Hawaiian) a form of Frank.

PALASH (Hindi) flowery tree.

PALBEN (Basque) blond.

PALLADIN (Native American) fighter.
Pallaton, Palleten

PALMER (English) palm-bearing pilgrim.
Pallmer, Palmar

PALTI (Hebrew) God liberates.
Palti-el

PANAS (Russian) immortal.

PANAYIOTIS (Greek) an alternate form of Peter.
Panagiotis, Panajotis, Panayioti, Panayoti, Panayotis

PANCHO (Spanish) a familiar form of Francisco, Frank.
Panchito

PANOS (Greek) an alternate form of Peter.
Petros

PAOLO (Italian) a form of Paul.

PAQUITO (Spanish) a familiar form of Paco.

PARAMESH (Hindi) greatest. Religion: another name for the Hindu god Shiva.

PARDEEP (Sikh) mystic light.
Pardip

PARIS (Greek) lover. Geography: the capital of France. Mythology: the prince of Troy who started the Trojan War by abducting Helen.
Paras, Paree, Pares, Parese, Parie, Parris, Parys

PARK (Chinese) cypress tree. (English) a short form of Parker.
Parke, Parkes, Parkey, Parks

PARKER (English) park keeper.
Park

PARKIN (English) little Peter.
Perkin

PARLAN (Scottish) a form of Bartholomew. See also Parthalán.

PARNELL (French) little Peter. History: Charles Stewart Parnell was a famous Irish politician.
Nell, Parle, Parnel, Parrnell, Pernell

PARR (English) cattle enclosure, barn.

PARRISH (English) church district.
Parish, Parrie, Parrisch, Parrysh

PARRY (Welsh) son of Harry.
Parrey, Parrie, Pary

PARTH (Irish) a short form of Parthalán.
Partha, Parthey

PARTHALÁN (Irish) plow-man. See also Bartholomew.
Parlan, Parth

PARTHENIOS (Greek) virgin. Religion: a Greek Orthodox saint.

PASCAL (French) born on Easter or Passover.
Pace, Pascale, Pascalle, Paschal, Paschalis, Pascoe, Pascow, Pascual, Pasquale

PASCUAL (Spanish) a form of Pascal.
Pascul

PASHA (Russian) a form of Paul.
Pashenka, Pashka

PASQUALE (Italian) a form of Pascal.
Pascuale, Pasqual, Pasquali, Pasquel

PASTOR (Latin) spiritual leader.

PAT (English) a short form of Patrick. (Native American) fish.
Pattie, Patty

PATAKUSU (Moquelumnan) ant biting a person.

PATAMON (Native American) raging.

PATEK (Polish) a form of Patrick.
Patick

PATRIC (Latin) an alternate form of Patrick.

PATRICE (French) a form of Patrick.

PATRICIO (Spanish) a form of Patrick.
Patricius, Patrizio

PATRICK (Latin) nobleman. Religion: the patron saint of Ireland. See also Fitzpatrick, Ticho.
Paddy, Padraic, Pakelika, Pat, Patek, Patric, Patrice, Patricio, Patrickk, Patrik, Patrique, Patrizius, Patryk, Pats, Patsy, Pattrick

PATRIN (Gypsy) leaf trail.

PATRYK (Latin) an alternate form of Patrick.
Patryck

PATTERSON (Irish) son of Pat.
Patteson

PATTIN (Gypsy) leaf.

PATTON (English) warrior's town.
Paden, Paten, Patin, Paton, Patten, Pattin, Patty, Payton, Peyton

PATWIN (Native American) man.

PATXI (Basque, Teutonic) free.

PAUL (Latin) small. Bible: Saul, later renamed Paul, was the first to bring the teachings of Christ to the Gentiles.
Oalo, Paavo, Pablo, Pal, Pál, Pall, Paolo, Pasha, Pasko, Pauli, Paulia, Paulin, Paulino, Paulis, Paulo, Pauls, Paulus, Pavel, Pavlos, Pawel, Pol, Poul

PAULI (Latin) a familiar form of Paul.
Pauley, Paulie, Pauly

PAULIN (German, Polish) a form of Paul.

PAULINO (Spanish) a form of Paul.

PAULO (Portuguese, Swedish, Hawaiian) a form of Paul.

PAVEL (Russian) a form of Paul.
Paavel, Pasha, Pavils, Pavlik, Pavlo, Pavlusha, Pavlushenka, Pawl

PAVIT (Hindi) pious, pure.

PAWEL (Polish) a form of Paul.
Pawelek, Pawl

PAX (Latin) peaceful.
Paz

PAXTON (Latin) peaceful town.
Packston, Pax, Paxon, Paxten, Paxtun

PAYAT (Native American) he is on his way.
Pay, Payatt

PAYDEN (English) an alternate form of Payton.
Paydon

PAYNE (Latin) man from the country.
Paine, Paynn

PAYTAH (Lakota) fire.
Pay, Payta

PAYTON (English) an alternate form of Patton.
Paiton, Pate, Payden, Peaton, Peighton, Peyton

PAZ (Spanish) a form of Pax.

PEARCE (English) an alternate form of Pierce.
Pears, Pearse

PEARSON (English) son of Peter. See also Pierson.
Pearsson, Pehrson, Peirson, Peterson

PEDER (Scandinavian) a form of Peter.
Peadar, Pedey

PEDRO (Spanish) a form of Peter.
Pedrin, Pedrín, Petronio

PEERS (English) a form of Peter.
Peerus, Piers

PEETER (Estonian) a form of Peter.
Peet

PEIRCE (English) a form of Peter.
Peirs

PEKELO (Hawaiian) a form of Peter.
Pekka

PELEKE (Hawaiian) a form of Frederick.

PELHAM (English) tannery town.

PELÍ (Latin, Basque) happy.

PELL (English) parchment.
Pall

PELLO (Greek, Basque) stone.
Peru, Piarres

PELTON (English) town by a pool.

PEMBROKE (Welsh) headland. (French) wine dealer. (English) broken fence.
Pembrook

PENIAMINA (Hawaiian) a form of Benjamin.
Peni

PENLEY (English) enclosed meadow.

PENN (Latin) pen, quill. (German) a short form of Penrod. (English) enclosure.
Pen, Penna, Penney, Pennie, Penny

PENROD (German) famous commander.
Penn, Pennrod, Rod

PEPA (Czech) a familiar form of Joseph.
Pepek, Pepik

PEPE (Spanish) a familiar form of José.
Pepillo, Pepito, Pequin, Pipo

PEPIN (German) determined; petitioner. History: Pepin the short, an eighth-century king of the Franks, was the father of Charlemagne.
Pepi, Peppie, Peppy

PEPPE (Italian) a familiar form of Joseph.
Peppi, Peppo, Pino

PER (Swedish) a form of Peter.

PERBEN (Greek, Danish) stone.

PERCIVAL (French) pierce the valley; pierce the veil of religion mystery. Literature: a name invented by Chrétien de Troyes for the knight-hero of his epic about the Holy Grail.
Parsafal, Parsefal, Parsifal, Parzival, Perc, Perce, Perceval, Percevall, Percivall, Percy, Peredur, Purcell

PERCY (French) a familiar form of Percival.
Pearcey, Pearcy, Percey, Percie, Piercey, Piercy

PEREGRINE (Latin) traveler; pilgrim; falcon.
Peregrin, Peregryne, Perine, Perry

PERICLES (Greek) just leader. History: an Athenian statesman and general.

PERICO (Spanish) a form of Peter.
Pequin, Perequin

PERINE (Latin) a short form of Peregrine.
Perino, Perion, Perrin, Perryn

PERKIN (English) little Peter.
Perka, Perkins, Perkyn, Perrin

PERNELL (French) an alternate form of Parnell.
Perren, Perrnall

PERRY (English) a familiar form of Peregrine, Peter.
Parry, Perrie, Perrye

PERTH (Scottish) thornbush thicket. Geography: a county in Scotland; a city in Australia.

PERVIS (Latin) passage.
Pervez

PESACH (Hebrew) spared. Religion: another name for the Jewish holiday Passover.
Pessach

PETAR (Greek) an alternate form of Peter.

PETE (English) a short form of Peter.
Peat, Peet, Petey, Peti, Petie, Piet, Pit

PETER (Greek, Latin) small rock. Bible: Simon, renamed Peter, was the leader of the Twelve Apostles. See also Boutros, Ferris, Takis.

Panayiotos, Panos, Peadair, Peder, Pedro, Peers, Peeter, Peirce, Pekelo, Per, Perico, Perion, Perkin, Perry, Petar, Pete, Péter, Peterke, Peterus, Petr, Petras, Petros, Petru, Petruno, Petter, Peyo, Piaras, Pierce, Piero, Pierre, Pieter, Pietrek, Pietro, Piotr, Piter, Piti, Pjeter, Pyotr

PETERSON (English) son of Peter.
Peteris, Petersen

PETIRI (Shona) where we are.
Petri

PETR (Bulgarian) a form of Peter.

PETRAS (Lithuanian) a form of Peter.
Petra, Petrelis

PETROS (Greek) an alternate form of Peter.
Petro

PETRU (Romanian) a form of Peter.
Petrukas, Petrus, Petruso

PETTER (Norwegian) a form of Peter.

PEVERELL (French) piper.
Peverall, Peverel, Peveril

PEYO (Spanish) a form of Peter.

PEYTON (English) an alternate form of Patton, Payton.
Peyt, Peyten, Peython, Peytonn

PHARAOH (Latin) ruler. History: a title for the ancient rulers of Egypt.
Faroh, Pharo, Pharoah, Pharoh

PHELAN (Irish) wolf.

PHELIPE (Spanish) a form of Philip.

PHELIX (Latin) an alternate form of Felix.

PHELPS (English) son of Phillip.

PHIL (Greek) a short form of Philip, Phillip.
Fil, Phill

PHILANDER (Greek) lover of mankind.

PHILBERT (English) an alternate form of Filbert.
Philibert, Phillbert

PHILEMON (Greek) kiss.
Phila, Philamina, Phileman, Philémon, Philmon

PHILIP (Greek) lover of horses. Bible: one of the Twelve Apostles. See also Felipe, Felippo, Filip, Fillipp, Filya, Fischel, Flip.
Phelps, Phelipe, Phil, Philipp, Philippe, Philippo, Phillip, Phillipos, Phillp, Philly, Philp, Phylip, Piers, Pilib, Pilipo, Pippo

PHILIPP (German) a form of Philip.
Phillipp

PHILIPPE (French) a form of Philip.
Philipe, Phillepe, Phillipe, Phillippe, Phillippee, Phyllipe

PHILLIP (Greek) an alternate form of Philip.
Phil, Phillipos, Phillipp, Phillips, Philly, Phyllip

PHILLIPOS (Greek) an alternate form of Phillip.

PHILLY (American) a familiar form of Philip, Phillip.
Phillie

PHILO (Greek) love.

PHINEAN (Irish) an alternate form of Finian.
Phinian

PHINEAS (English) a form of Pinchas.
Fineas, Phinehas, Phinny

PHIRUN (Cambodian) rain.

PHOENIX (Latin) phoenix, a legendary bird.
Phenix, Pheonix, Phynix

PHUOK (Vietnamese) good.
Phuoc

PIAS (Gypsy) fun.

PICKFORD (English) ford at the peak.

PICKWORTH (English) woodcutter's estate.

PIERCE (English) a form of Peter.
Pearce, Peerce, Peers, Peirce, Piercy, Piers

PIERO (Italian) a form of Peter.
Pero, Pierro

PIERRE (French) a form of Peter.
Peirre, Piere, Pierrot

PIERRE-LUC (French) a combination of Pierre + Luc.
Piere Luc

PIERS (English) a form of Philip.

PIERSON (English) son of Peter. See also Pearson.
Pierrson, Piersen, Piersson, Piersun

PIETER (Dutch) a form of Peter.
Pietr

PIETRO (Italian) a form of Peter.

PILAR (Spanish) pillar.

PILI (Swahili) second born.

PILIPO (Hawaiian) a form of Philip.

PILLAN (Native American) supreme essence.
Pilan

PIN (Vietnamese) faithful boy.

PINCHAS (Hebrew) oracle. (Egyptian) dark skinned.
Phineas, Pincas, Pinchos, Pincus, Pinkas, Pinkus, Pinky

PINKY (American) a familiar form of Pinchas.
Pink

PINO (Italian) a form of Joseph.

PIÑON (Tupi-Guarani) Mythology: the hunter who became the constellation Orion.

PIO (Latin) pious.

PIOTR (Bulgarian) a form of Peter.
Piotrek

PIPPIN (German) father.

PIRAN (Irish) prayer. Religion: the patron saint of miners.
Peran, Pieran

PIRRO (Greek, Spanish) flaming hair.

PISTA (Hungarian) a familiar form of István.
Pisti

PITI (Spanish) a form of Peter.

PITIN (Spanish) a form of Felix.
Pito

PITNEY (English) island of the strong-willed man.
Pittney

PITT (English) pit, ditch.

PLACIDO (Spanish) serene.
Placide, Placidus, Placyd, Placydo

PLATO (Greek) broad shouldered. History: a famous Greek philosopher.
Platon

PLATT (French) flat land.
Platte

POL (Swedish) a form of Paul.
Pól, Pola, Poul

POLDI (German) a familiar form of Leopold.
Poldo

POLLARD (German) close-cropped head.
Poll, Pollerd, Pollyrd

POLLOCK (English) a form of Pollux.
Pollack, Polloch

POLLUX (Greek) crown. Astronomy: one of the twins in the Gemini constellation.
Pollock

POLO (Greek) a short form of Apollo. (Tibetan) brave wanderer. Culture: a game played on horseback. History: Marco Polo was a Venetian explorer who traveled throughout Asia in the thirteenth and fourteenth centuries.

POMEROY (French) apple orchard.
Pommeray, Pommeroy

PONCE (Spanish) fifth. History: Juan Ponce de León of Spain searched for the fountain of youth in Florida.

PONY (Scottish) small horse.
Poni

PORFIRIO (Greek, Spanish) purple stone.
Porphirios, Prophyrios

PORTER (Latin) gatekeeper.
Port, Portie, Porty

POSHITA (Sanskrit) cherished.

PO SIN (Chinese) grand-father elephant.

POUL (Danish) a form of Paul.
Poulos, Poulus

POV (Gypsy) earth.

POWA (Native American) wealthy.

POWELL (English) alert.
Powel

PRAMAD (Hindi) rejoicing.

PRAVAT (Tai) history.

PREM (Hindi) love.

PRENTICE (English) apprentice.
Prent, Prentis, Prentiss, Printes, Printiss

PRESCOTT (English) priest's cottage. See also Scott.
Prescot, Prestcot, Prestcott

PRESLEY (English) priest's meadow.
Presleigh, Presly, Presslee, Pressley, Prestley, Priestley, Priestly

PRESTON (English) priest's estate.
Prestan, Presten, Prestin, Prestyn

PREWITT (French) brave little one.
Preuet, Prewet, Prewett, Prewit, Pruit, Pruitt

PRICE (Welsh) son of the ardent one.
Brice, Bryce, Pryce

PRICHA (Tai) clever.

PRIMO (Italian) first; premier quality.
Preemo, Premo

PRINCE (Latin) chief; prince.
Prence, Prinz, Prinze

PRINCETON (English) princely town.
Prenston, Princeston, Princton

PROCTOR (Latin) official, administrator.
Prockter, Procter

PROKOPIOS (Greek) declared leader.

PROSPER (Latin) fortunate.
Prospero, Próspero

PRYOR (Latin) head of the monastery; prior.
Prior, Pry

PUMEET (Sanskrit) pure.

PURDY (Hindi) recluse.

PURVIS (French, English) providing food.
Pervis, Purves, Purviss

PUTNAM (English) dweller by the pond.
Putnem

PYOTR (Russian) a form of Peter.
Petenka, Petinka, Petrusha, Petya, Pyatr

QABIL (Arabic) able.

QADIM (Arabic) ancient.

QADIR (Arabic) powerful.
Qaadir, Qadeer, Quaadir, Quadeer, Quadir

QAMAR (Arabic) moon.
Quamar, Quamir

QASIM (Arabic) divider.
Quasim

QIMAT (Hindi) valuable.

QUAASHIE (Ewe) born on Sunday.

QUADARIUS (American) a combination of Quan + Darius.
Quadara, Quadarious, Quadaris, Quandarious, Quandarius, Quandarrius, Qudarius, Qudaruis

QUADE (Latin) fourth.
Quadell, Quaden, Quadon, Quadre, Quadrie, Quadrine, Quadrion, Quaid, Quayd, Quayde, Qwade

QUAMAINE (American) a combination of Quan + Jermaine.
Quamain, Quaman, Quamane, Quamayne, Quarmaine

QUAN (Comanche) a short form of Quanah.

QUANAH (Comanche) fragrant.
Quan

QUANDRE (American) a combination of Quan + Andre.
Quandrae, Quandré

QUANT (Greek) means "how much?"
Quanta, Quantae, Quantai, Quantas, Quantay, Quante, Quantea, Quantey, Quantez, Quantu

QUANTAVIUS (American) a combination of Quan + Octavius.
Quantavian, Quantavin, Quantavion, Quantavious, Quantavis, Quantavous, Quatavious, Quatavius

QUASHAWN (American) a combination of Quan + Shawn.
Quasean, Quashaan, Quashan, Quashaun, Quashaunn, Quashon, Quashone, Quashun, Queshan, Queshon, Qweshawn, Qyshawn

QUDAMAH (Arabic) courage.

QUENBY (Scandinavian) an alternate form of Quimby.

QUENNELL (French) small oak.
Quenell, Quennel

QUENTEN (Latin) an alternate form of Quentin.
Quienten

QUENTIN (Latin) fifth. (English) Queen's town.
Qeuntin, Quantin, Quent, Quentan, Quenten, Quentine, Quenton, Quentyn, Quentynn, Quientin, Quinten, Quintin, Quinton, Qwentin

QUENTON (Latin) an alternate form of Quentin.
Quienton

QUICO (Spanish) a familiar form of many names.
Paco

QUIGLEY (Irish) maternal side.
Quigly

QUILLAN (Irish) cub.
Quill, Quillen, Quillin, Quillon

QUIMBY (Scandinavian) woman's estate.
Quenby, Quinby

QUINCY (French) fifth son's estate.
Quenci, Quency, Quince, Quincee, Quincey, Quinci, Quinn, Quinncy, Quinnsy, Quinsey, Quinzy

QUINDARIUS (American) a combination of Quinn + Darius.
Quindarious, Quindarrius, Quinderious, Quinderus, Quindrius

QUINLAN (Irish) strong; well shaped.
Quindlen, Quinlen, Quinlin, Quinn, Quinnlan, Quinnlin

QUINN (Irish) a short form of Quincy, Quinlan, Quinton.
Quin

QUINTAVIUS (American) a combination of Quinn + Octavius.
Quintavious, Quintavis, Quintavus, Quintayvious

QUINTEN (Latin) an alternate form of Quentin.
Quinnten

QUINTIN (Latin) an alternate form of Quentin.
Quinntin, Quintine, Quintyn

QUINTON (Latin) an alternate form of Quentin.
Quinn, Quinneton, Quinnton, Quint, Quintan, Quintann, Quintin, Quintion, Quintus, Quitin, Quito, Quiton, Qunton, Qwinton

QUIQUI (Spanish) a familiar form of Enrique.
Quinto, Quiquin

QUITIN (Latin) a short form of Quinton.
Quiten, Quito, Quiton

QUITO (Spanish) a short form of Quinton.

QUON (Chinese) bright.

RAANAN (Hebrew) fresh; luxuriant.

RABI (Arabic) breeze.
Rabbi, Rabee, Rabeeh, Rabiah, Rabie, Rabih

RACE (English) race.
Racel, Rayce

RACHAM (Hebrew) compassionate.
Rachaman, Rachamim, Rachim, Rachman, Rachmiel, Rachum, Raham, Rahamim

RAD (English) advisor. (Slavic) happy.
Raad, Radd, Raddie, Raddy, Rade, Radee, Radell, Radey, Radi

RADBERT (English) brilliant advisor.

RADBURN (English) red brook; brook with reeds.
Radborn, Radborne, Radbourn, Radbourne, Radburne

RADCLIFF (English) red cliff; cliff with reeds.
Radcliffe, Radclyffe

RADFORD (English) red ford; ford with reeds.

RADLEY (English) red meadow; meadow of reeds.
Radlea, Radlee, Radleigh, Radly

RADMAN (Slavic) joyful.
Radmen, Radusha

RADNOR (English) red shore; shore with reeds.

RADOMIL (Slavic) happy peace.

RADOSLAW (Polish) happy glory.
Radik, Rado, Radzmir, Slawek

RAEKWON (American) an alternate form of Raquan.
Raekwan, Raikwan, Rakwane, Rakwon

RAEQUAN (American) an alternate form of Raquan.
Raequon, Raeqwon, Raiquan, Raiquen, Raiqoun

RAESHAWN (American) an alternate form of Rashawn.
Raesean, Raeshaun, Raeshon, Raeshun

RAFAEL (Spanish) a form of Raphael. See also Falito.
Rafaelle, Rafaello, Rafaelo, Rafal, Rafeal, Rafeé, Rafel, Rafello, Raffael, Raffaelo, Raffeal, Raffel, Raffiel, Rafiel

RAFAELE (Italian) a form of Raphael.
Raffaele

RAFAL (Polish) a form of Raphael.

RAFE (English) a short form of Rafferty, Ralph.
Raff

RAFER (Irish) a short form of Rafferty.
Raffer

RAFFERTY (Irish) rich, prosperous.
Rafe, Rafer, Raferty, Raffarty, Raffer

RAFI (Hebrew) a familiar form of Raphael. (Arabic) exalted.
Raffe, Raffee, Raffi, Raffy, Rafi

RAFIQ (Arabic) friend.
Raafiq, Rafeeq, Rafic, Rafique

RAGHIB (Arabic) desirous.
Raquib

RAGHNALL (Irish) wise power.

RAGNAR (Norwegian) powerful army.
Ragnor, Rainer, Rainier, Ranieri, Rayner, Raynor, Reinhold

RAGO (Hausa) ram.

RAHEEM (Punjabi) compassionate God.
Rakeem

RAHIM (Arabic) merciful.
Raaheim, Rahaeim, Raheam, Raheim, Rahiem, Rahiim, Rahime, Rahium, Rakim

RAHMAN (Arabic) compassionate.
Rahmatt, Rahmet

RAHUL (Arabic) traveler.

RAÍD (Arabic) leader.

RAIDEN (Japanese) Mythology: the thunder god.
Raidan, Rayden

RAIMONDO (Italian) a form of Raymond.
Raymondo, Reimundo

RAIMUND (German) a form of Raymond.
Rajmund

RAIMUNDO (Portuguese, Spanish) a form of Raymond.
Mundo, Raimon, Raimond, Raimonds, Raymundo

RAINE (English) lord; wise.
Rain, Raines, Rayne

RAINER (German) counselor.
Rainar, Rainey, Rainier, Rainor, Raynier, Reinier

RAINEY (German) a familiar form of Rainer.
Raine, Rainee, Rainie, Rainney, Rainy, Reiny

RAINI (Tupi-Guarani) Religion: the Native American god who created the world.

RAISHAWN (American) an alternate form of Rashawn.
Raishon, Raishun

RAJABU (Swahili) born in the seventh month of the Islamic calendar.

RAJAH (Hindi) prince, chief.
Raj, Raja, Rajaah, Rajae, Rajahe, Rajan, Raje, Rajeh, Raji

RAJAK (Hindi) cleansing.

RAJAN (Hindi) an alternate form of Rajah.
Rajaahn, Rajain, Rajen, Rajin

RAKEEM (Punjabi) an alternate form of Raheem.
Rakeeme, Rakeim, Rakem

RAKIM (Arabic) an alternate form of Rahim.
Rakiim

RAKIN (Arabic) respectable.
Rakeen

RAKTIM (Hindi) bright red.

RALEIGH (English) an alternate form of Rawleigh.
Ralegh

RALPH (English) wolf counselor.
Radolphus, Rafe, Ralf, Ralpheal, Ralphel, Ralphie, Ralston, Raoul, Raul, Rolf

RALPHIE (English) a familiar form of Ralph.
Ralphy

RALSTON (English) Ralph's settlement.

RAM (Hindi) god; godlike. Religion: another name for the Hindu god Shiva. (English) male sheep.
Rami, Ramie, Ramy

RAMADAN (Arabic) ninth month of the Arabic year.
Rama

RAMANAN (Hindi) god; godlike. Religion: another name for the Hindu god Shiva.
Raman, Ramandeep, Ramanjit, Ramanjot

RAMI (Spanish) a short form of Ramiro.
Rame, Ramee, Ramey, Ramih

RAMIRO (Portuguese, Spanish) supreme judge.
Ramario, Rameer, Rameir, Ramere, Rameriz, Ramero, Rami, Ramires, Ramirez, Ramos

RAMÓN (Spanish) a form of Raymond.
Ramon, Remon, Remone, Romone

RAMONE (Dutch) a form of Raymond.
Raemon, Raemonn, Ramond, Ramonte, Remone

RAMSDEN (English) valley of rams.

RAMSEY (English) ram's island.
Ram, Ramsay, Ramsee, Ramsie, Ramsy, Ramzee, Ramzey, Ramzi, Ramzy

RANCE (English) a short form of Laurence, Ransom. (American) a familiar form of Laurence.
Rancel, Rancell, Rances, Rancey, Rancie, Rancy, Ransel, Ransell

RAND (English) shield; warrior.
Randy

RANDAL (English) an alternate form of Randall.
Randahl, Randale, Randel, Randl, Randle

RANDALL (English) an alternate form of Randolph.
Randal, Randell, Randy, Randyll

RANDOLPH (English) shield-wolf.
Randall, Randol, Randolf, Randolfo, Randolpho, Randy, Ranolph

RANDY (English) a familiar form of Rand, Randall, Randolph.
Randdy, Randee, Randey, Randi, Randie, Ranndy

RANGER (French) forest keeper.
Rainger, Range

RANGLE (American) cowboy.
Rangler, Wrangle

RANGSEY (Cambodian) seven kinds of colors.

RANI (Hebrew) my song; my joy.
Ranen, Ranie, Ranon, Roni

RANIERI (Italian) a form of Ragnar.
Raneir, Ranier, Rannier

RANJAN (Hindi) delighted; gladdened.

RANKIN (English) small shield.
Randkin

RANSFORD (English) raven's ford.

RANSLEY (English) raven's field.

RANSOM (Latin) redeemer. (English) son of the shield.
Rance, Ransome, Ranson

RAOUL (French) a form of Ralph, Rudolph.
Raol, Raul, Raúl, Reuel

RAPHAEL (Hebrew) God has healed. Bible: one of the archangels. Art: a prominent painter of the Italian Renaissance. See also Falito, Rafi.
Rafael, Rafaele, Rafal, Rafel, Raphaél, Raphale, Raphaello, Rapheal, Raphel, Raphello, Raphiel, Ray, Rephael

RAPHEAL (Hebrew) an alternate form of Raphael.
Rafel, Raphiel

RAPIER (French) blade-sharp.

RAQUAN (American) a combination of the prefix Ra + Quan.

Raquan *(cont.)*
Raaquan, Rackwon, Racquan, Raekwon, Raequan, Rahquan, Raquané, Raquon, Raquwan, Raquwn, Raquwon, Raqwan, Raqwann

RASHAAD (Arabic) an alternate form of Rashad.

RASHAAN (American) an alternate form of Rashawn.
Rasaan, Rashan, Rashann

RASHAD (Arabic) wise counselor.
Raashad, Rachad, Rachard, Raeshad, Raishard, Rashaad, Rashadd, Rashade, Rashaud, Rasheed, Rashid, Rashod, Reshad, Rhashad, Rishad, Roshad

RASHARD (American) a form of Richard.
Rasharrd

RASHAUD (Arabic) an alternate form of Rashad.
Rachaud, Rashaude

RASHAUN (American) an alternate form of Rashawn.

RASHAWN (American) a combination of the prefix Ra + Shawn.
Raashawn, Raashen, Raeshawn, Rahshawn, Raishawn, Rasaun, Rasawn, Rashaan, Rashaun, Rashaw, Rashon, Rashun, Raushan, Raushawn, Rhashan, Rhashaun, Rhashawn

RASHEAN (American) a combination of the prefix Ra + Sean.
Rahsaan, Rahsean, Rahseen, Rasean, Rashane, Rasheen, Rashien, Rashiena

RASHEED (Arabic) an alternate form of Rashad.

Rashead, Rashed, Rasheid, Rhasheed

RASHID (Arabic) an alternate form of Rashad.
Rasheyd, Rashida, Rashidah, Rashied, Rashieda, Raushaid

RASHIDA (Swahili) righteous.

RASHIDI (Swahili) wise counselor.

RASHOD (Arabic) an alternate form of Rashad.
Rashoda, Rashodd, Rashoud, Rayshod, Rhashod

RASHON (American) an alternate form of Rashawn.
Rashion, Rashone, Rashonn, Rashuan, Rashun, Rashunn

RASMUS (Greek, Danish) a short form of Erasmus.

RAUL (French) a form of Ralph.

RAULAS (Lithuanian) a form of Laurence.

RAULO (Lithuanian) a form of Laurence.
Raulas

RAVEN (English) a short form of Ravenel.
Ravan, Ravean, Raveen, Ravin, Ravine, Ravon, Ravyn, Reven, Rhaven

RAVENEL (English) raven.
Raven, Ravenell, Revenel

RAVI (Hindi) sun. Religion: another name for the Hindu sun god Surya.
Ravee, Ravijot

RAVID (Hebrew) an alternate form of Arvid.

RAVIV (Hebrew) rain, dew.

RAVON (English) an alternate form of Raven.
Raveon, Ravion, Ravone, Ravonn, Ravonne, Rayvon, Revon

RAWDON (English) rough hill.

RAWLEIGH (English) deer meadow.
Raleigh, Rawle, Rawley, Rawling, Rawly, Rawylyn

RAWLINS (French) a form of Roland.
Rawlings, Rawlinson, Rawson

RAY (French) kingly, royal. (English) a short form of Rayburn, Raymond. See also Lei.
Rae, Raye

RAYAN (Irish) an alternate form of Ryan.
Rayaun

RAYBURN (English) deer brook.
Burney, Raeborn, Raeborne, Raebourn, Ray, Raybourn, Raybourne, Rayburne

RAYCE (English) an alternate form of Race.

RAYDEN (Japanese) an alternate form of Raiden.
Raidin, Raydun, Rayedon

RAYHAN (Arabic) favored by God.
Rayhaan

RAYI (Hebrew) my friend, my companion.

RAYMON (English) an alternate form of Raymond.
Rayman, Raymann, Raymen, Raymone, Raymun, Reamonn

RAYMOND (English) mighty; wise protector. See also Aymon.

Radmond, Raemond, Raimondo, Raimund, Raimundo, Ramón, Ramond, Ramonde, Ramone, Ray, Raymand, Rayment, Raymon, Raymont, Raymund, Raymunde, Raymundo, Redmond, Reymond, Reymundo

RAYMUNDO (Spanish) a form of Raymond.
Raemondo, Raimondo, Raimundo, Raymondo

RAYNALDO (Spanish) an alternate form of Renaldo, Reynold.
Raynal, Raynald, Raynold

RAYNARD (French) an alternate form of Renard, Reynard.
Raynarde

RAYNE (English) an alternate form of Raine.
Raynee, Rayno

RAYNOR (Scandinavian) a form of Ragnar.
Rainer, Rainor, Ranier, Ranieri, Raynar, Rayner

RAYSHAWN (American) a combination of Ray + Shawn.
Raysean, Rayshaan, Rayshan, Rayshaun, Raysheen, Rayshon, Rayshone, Rayshonn, Rayshun, Rayshunn

RAYSHOD (American) a form of Rashad.
Raychard, Rayshad, Rayshard, Rayshaud

RAYVON (American) a form of Ravon.
Rayvan, Rayvaun, Rayven, Rayvone, Reyven, Reyvon

RAZI (Aramaic) my secret.
Raz, Raziel, Raziq

READ (English) an alternate form of Reed, Reid.

Raed, Raede, Raeed, Reaad, Reade

READING (English) son of the red wanderer. Geography: a city in Pennsylvania.
Redding, Reeding, Reiding

REAGAN (Irish) little king. History: Ronald Wilson Reagan was the fortieth U.S. president.
Raegan, Reagen, Reaghan, Reegan, Reegen, Regan, Reigan, Reighan, Reign, Rheagan

REBEL (American) rebel.
Reb

RED (American) red, redhead.
Redd

REDA (Arabic) satisfied.
Ridha

REDFORD (English) red river crossing.
Ford, Radford, Reaford, Red, Redd

REDLEY (English) red meadow; meadow with reeds.
Radley, Redlea, Redleigh, Redly

REDMOND (German) protecting counselor. (English) an alternate form of Raymond.
Radmond, Radmund, Reddin, Redmund

REDPATH (English) red path.

REECE (Welsh) enthusiastic; stream.
Reace, Rece, Reese, Reice, Reyes, Rhys, Rice, Ryese

REED (English) an alternate form of Reid.
Raeed, Read, Reyde, Rheed

REESE (Welsh) an alternate form of Reece.
Rease, Rees, Reis, Reise, Reiss, Rhys, Riese, Riess

REEVE (English) steward.
Reave, Reaves, Reeves

REG (English) a short form of Reginald.

REGAN (Irish) an alternate form of Reagan.
Regen

REGGIE (English) a familiar form of Reginald.
Regi, Regie

REGINAL (English) a form of Reginald.
Reginale, Reginel

REGINALD (English) king's advisor. An alternate form of Reynold. See also Naldo.
Reg, Reggie, Regginald, Reggis, Reginal, Reginaldo, Reginalt, Reginauld, Reginault, Reginold, Reginuld, Regnauld, Ronald

REGIS (Latin) regal.

REHEMA (Kiswahili) second-born.

REI (Japanese) rule, law.

REID (English) redhead.
Read, Reed, Reide, Reyd, Ried

REIDAR (Norwegian) nest warrior.

REILLY (Irish) an alternate form of Riley.
Reiley, Reilley, Reily, Rielly

REINALDO (Spanish) a form of Reynold.

REINHART (German) a form of Reynard.

Reinhart (cont.)
Rainart, Rainhard, Rainhardt,
Rainhart, Reinart, Reinhard,
Reinhardt, Renke

REINHOLD (Swedish) a form of
Ragnar.
Reinold

REKU (Finnish) a form of
Richard.

REMI, Rémi (French) alternate
forms of Remy.
Remie, Remmie

REMINGTON (English) raven
estate.
Rem, Reminton, Tony

REMUS (Latin) speedy, quick.
Mythology: Remus and his
twin brother Romulus founded Rome.

REMY (French) from Rheims,
France.
Ramey, Remee, Remi, Rémi,
Remmy

RENALDO (Spanish) a form of
Reynold.
Raynaldo, Reynaldo, Rinaldo

RENARD (French) an alternate
form of Reynard.
Ranard, Raynard, Reinard,
Rennard

RENARDO (Italian) a form of
Reynard.

RENATO (Italian) reborn.

RENAUD (French) a form of
Reynard, Reynold.
Renauld, Renauldo, Renault,
Renould

RENDOR (Hungarian) policeman.

RENÉ (French) reborn.
Renat, Renato, Renatus,
Renault, Renay, Renee, Renny

RENFRED (English) lasting
peace.

RENFREW (Welsh) raven woods.

RENJIRO (Japanese) virtuous.

RENNY (Irish) small but strong.
(French) a familiar form of
René.
Ren, Renn, Renne, Rennie

RENO (American) gambler.
Geography: a gambling town
in Nevada.
Renos, Rino

RENSHAW (English) raven
woods.
Renishaw

RENTON (English) settlement
of the roe deer.

RENZO (Latin) a familiar form
of Laurence. (Italian) a short
form of Lorenzo.
Renz, Renzy, Renzzo

RESHAD (American) a form of
Rashad.
Reshade, Reshard, Resharrd,
Reshaud, Reshawd, Reshead,
Reshod

RESHAWN (American) a combi-
nation of the prefix Re +
Shawn.
Reshaun, Reshaw, Reshon,
Reshun

RESHEAN (American) a combi-
nation of the prefix Re +
Sean.
Resean, Reshae, Reshane,
Reshay, Reshayne, Reshea,
Resheen, Reshey

REUBEN (Hebrew) behold a son.
Reuban, Reubin, Reuven,
Rheuben, Rhuben, Rube, Ruben,
Rubey, Rubin, Ruby, Rueben

REUVEN (Hebrew) an alternate
form of Reuben.
Reuvin, Rouvin, Ruvim

REX (Latin) king.
Rexx

REXFORD (English) king's ford.

REXTON (English) king's town.

REY (Spanish) a short form of
Reynaldo, Reynard, Reynold.

REYES (English) an alternate
form of Reece.
Reyce

REYHAN (Arabic) favored by
God.
Reyham

REYMOND (English) an alternate form of Raymond.
Reymon. Reymound, Reymund

REYMUNDO (Spanish) a form
of Raymond.
Reimond, Reimonde, Reimundo,
Reymon

REYNALDO (Spanish) a form of
Reynold.
Renaldo, Rey, Reynauldo

REYNARD (French) wise; bold,
courageous.
Raynard, Reinhard, Reinhardt,
Reinhart, Renard, Renardo,
Renaud, Rennard, Rey,
Reynardo, Reynaud

REYNOLD (English) king's
advisor. See also Reginald.
Rainault, Rainhold, Ranald,
Raynald, Raynaldo, Reinald,
Reinaldo, Reinaldos, Reinhart,
Reinhold, Reinold, Reinwald,

*Renald, Renaldi, Renaldo,
Renaud, Renauld, Rennold,
Renold, Rey, Reynald, Reynaldo,
Reynaldos, Reynol, Reynolds,
Rinaldo, Ronald*

RÉZ (Hungarian) copper;
redhead.
Rezsö

RHETT (Welsh) an alternate
form of Rhys. Literature:
Rhett Butler was the hero of
Margaret Mitchell's novel
Gone with the Wind.
Rhet

RHODES (Greek) where roses
grow. Geography: an island
off the coast of Greece.
Rhoads, Rhodas, Rodas

RHYAN (Irish) an alternate
form of Rian.
Rhian

RHYS (Welsh) an alternate
form of Reece, Reese.
Rhett, Rhyce, Rhyse, Rice

RIAN (Irish) little king.
Rhyan

RIC (Italian, Spanish) a short
form of Rico.
Ricca, Ricci, Ricco

RICARDO (Portuguese,
Spanish) a form of Richard.
*Racardo, Recard, Ricaldo,
Ricard, Ricardoe, Ricardos,
Riccardo, Riccarrdo, Ricciardo,
Richardo*

RICE (Welsh) an alternate form
of Reece. (English) rich, noble.
Ryce

RICH (English) a short form of
Richard.
Ritch

RICHARD (English) rich and
powerful ruler. See also Aric,
Dick, Juku, Likeke.
*Rashard, Reku, Ricardo, Rich,
Richar, Richards, Richardson,
Richart, Richaud, Richer,
Richerd, Richie, Richird,
Richshard, Rick, Rickard,
Rickert, Rickey, Ricky, Rico,
Rihardos, Rihards, Rikard,
Riocard, Riócard, Risa,
Risardas, Rishard, Ristéard,
Ritchard, Rostik, Rye, Rysio,
Ryszard*

RICHART (German) rich and
powerful ruler. The original
form of Richard.

RICHIE (English) a familiar
form of Richard.
*Richey, Richi, Richy, Rishi,
Ritchie*

RICHMAN (English) powerful.

RICHMOND (German) powerful
protector.
Richmon, Richmound

RICK (German, English) a
short form of Cedric,
Frederick, Richard.
*Ric, Ricke, Rickey, Ricks, Ricky,
Rik, Riki, Rykk*

RICKARD (Swedish) a form of
Richard.

RICKER (English) powerful
army.

RICKEY (English) a familiar
form of Richard, Rick, Riqui.

RICKIE (English) an alternate
form of Ricky.
Rickee, Ricki

RICKWARD (English) mighty
guardian.
Rickwerd, Rickwood

RICKY (English) a familiar form
of Richard, Rick.
*Ricci, Rickie, Riczi, Riki, Rikki,
Rikky, Riqui*

RICO (Spanish) a familiar form
of Richard. (Italian) a short
form of Enrico.
Ric, Ricco

RIDA (Arabic) favor.

RIDDOCK (Irish) smooth field.
Riddick

RIDER (English) horseman.
Ridder, Ryder

RIDGE (English) ridge of a cliff.
Ridgy, Rig, Rigg

RIDGELEY (English) meadow
near the ridge.
*Ridgeleigh, Ridglea, Ridglee,
Ridgleigh, Ridgley*

RIDGEWAY (English) path along
the ridge.

RIDLEY (English) meadow of
reeds.
*Rhidley, Riddley, Ridlea,
Ridleigh, Ridly*

RIEL (Spanish) a short form of
Gabriel.

RIGBY (English) ruler's valley.

RIGEL (Arabic) foot. Astronomy:
one of the stars in the Orion
constellation.

RIGG (English) ridge.
Rigo

RIGOBERTO (German) splendid; wealthy.
Rigobert

RIKARD (Scandinavian) a form
of Richard.
Rikárd

RIKI (Estonian) a form of Rick.
Rikkey, Rikki, Riks, Riky

RILEY (Irish) valiant.
Reilly, Rhiley, Rhylee, Rhyley, Rieley, Rielly, Riely, Rilee, Rilley, Rily, Rilye, Rylee, Ryley

RINALDO (Italian) a form of Reynold.
Rinald, Rinaldi

RING (English) ring.
Ringo

RINGO (Japanese) apple. (English) a familiar form of Ring.

RIO (Spanish) river. Geography: Rio de Janeiro is a seaport in Brazil.

RIORDAN (Irish) bard, royal poet.
Rearden, Reardin, Reardon

RIP (Dutch) ripe, full-grown. (English) a short form of Ripley.
Ripp

RIPLEY (English) meadow near the river.
Rip, Ripleigh, Ripply

RIQUI (Spanish) a form of Rickey.

RISHAD (American) a form of Rashad.
Rishaad

RISHAWN (American) a combination of the prefix Ri + Shawn.
Rishan, Rishaun, Rishon, Rishone

RISHI (Hindi) sage.

RISLEY (English) meadow with shrubs.

Rislea, Rislee, Risleigh, Risly, Wrisley

RISTO (Finnish) a short form of Christopher.

RISTON (English) settlement near the shrubs.
Wriston

RITCHARD (English) an alternate form of Richard.
Ritcherd, Ritchyrd, Ritshard, Ritsherd

RITCHIE (English) an alternate form of Richie.
Ritchy

RITHISAK (Cambodian) powerful.

RITTER (German) knight; chivalrous.
Rittner

RIVER (English) river; river bank.
Rivers, Riviera, Rivor

RIYAD (Arabic) gardens.
Riad, Riyaad, Riyadh, Riyaz, Riyod

ROALD (Norwegian) famous ruler.

ROAN (English) a short form of Rowan.
Rhoan

ROAR (Norwegian) praised warrior.
Roary

ROARKE (Irish) famous ruler.
Roark, Rorke, Rourke, Ruark

ROB (English) a short form of Robert.
Robb, Robe

ROBBIE (English) a familiar form of Robert.
Robie, Robbi

ROBBY (English) a familiar form of Robert.
Rhobbie, Robbey, Robhy, Roby

ROBERT (English) famous brilliance. See also Bobek, Dob, Lopaka.
Bob, Bobby, Rab, Rabbie, Raby, Riobard, Riobart, Rob, Robars, Robart, Robbie, Robby, Rober, Roberd, Robers, Roberte, Roberto, Roberts, Robin, Robinson, Roibeárd, Rosertas, Rubert, Ruberto, Rudbert, Rupert

ROBERTO (Portuguese, Spanish) a form of Robert.

ROBERTS, Robertson (English) son of Robert.
Roberson, Robertson, Robeson, Robinson, Robson

ROBIN (English) a short form of Robert.
Robben, Robbin, Robbins, Robbyn, Roben, Robinet, Robinn, Robins, Robyn, Roibín

ROBINSON (English) son of Robert. An alternate form of Roberts, Robertson.
Robbinson, Robens, Robenson, Robson, Robynson

ROBYN (English) an alternate form of Robin.

ROCCO (Italian) rock.
Rocca, Rocio, Rocko, Rocky, Roko, Roque

ROCHESTER (English) rocky fortress.
Chester, Chet

ROCK (English) a short form of Rockwell.
Roch, Rocky

ROCKFORD (English) rocky ford.

ROCKLAND (English) rocky land.

ROCKLEDGE (English) rocky ledge.

ROCKLEY (English) rocky field.
Rockle

ROCKWELL (English) rocky spring. Art: Norman Rockwell was a well-known twentieth-century American illustrator.
Rock

ROCKY (American) a familiar form of Rocco, Rock.
Rockey, Rockie

ROD (English) a short form of Penrod, Roderick, Rodney.
Rodd

RODAS (Greek, Spanish) an alternate form of Rhodes.

RODDY (English) a familiar form of Roderick.
Roddie, Rody

RODEN (English) red valley.
Rodin

RODERICH (German) an alternate form of Roderick.

RODERICK (German) famous ruler. See also Broderick.
Rhoderick, Rod, Rodderick, Roddy, Roderic, Roderich, Roderigo, Roderik, Roderrick, Roderyck, Rodgrick, Rodrick, Rodricki, Rodrigo, Rodrigue, Rodrugue, Roodney, Rory, Rurik, Ruy

RODGER (German) an alternate form of Roger.
Rodge, Rodgy

RODMAN (German) famous man, hero.
Rodmond

RODNEY (English) island clearing.
Rhodney, Rod, Rodnee, Rodnei, Rodni, Rodnie, Rodnne, Rodny

RODOLFO (Spanish) a form of Rudolph.
Rodolpho, Rodulfo

RODRICK (German) an alternate form of Roderick.
Roddrick, Rodric, Rodrich, Rodrik, Rodrique, Rodryck, Rodryk

RODRIGO (Italian, Spanish) a form of Roderick.

RODRIGUEZ (Spanish) son of Rodrigo.
Roddrigues, Rodrigues, Rodriquez

RODRIK (German) famous ruler.

RODRIQUEZ (Spanish) an alternate form of Rodriguez.
Rodrigquez, Rodriques, Rodriquiez

ROE (English) roe deer.
Row, Rowe

ROGAN (Irish) redhead.
Rogein, Rogen

ROGELIO (Spanish) famous warrior.
Rojelio

ROGER (German) famous spearman. See also Lokela.
Rodger, Rog, Rogelio, Rogerick, Rogerio, Rogers, Rogiero, Rojelio, Rüdiger, Ruggerio, Rutger

ROGERIO (Portuguese, Spanish) a form of Roger.
Rogerios

ROHAN (Hindi) sandalwood.

ROHIN (Hindi) upward path.

ROHIT (Hindi) big and beautiful fish.

ROI (French) an alternate form of Roy.

ROJA (Spanish) red.
Rojay

ROLAND (German) famous throughout the land.
Loránd, Orlando, Rawlins, Rolan, Rolanda, Rolando, Rolek, Rolland, Rolle, Rollie, Rollin, Rollo, Rowe, Rowland, Ruland

ROLANDO (Portuguese, Spanish) a form of Roland.
Lando, Olo, Roldan, Roldán, Rolondo

ROLF (German) a form of Ralph. A short form of Rudolph.
Rolfe, Rolle, Rolph, Rolphe

ROLLE (Swedish) a familiar form of Roland, Rolf.

ROLLIE (English) a familiar form of Roland.
Roley, Rolle, Rolli, Rolly

ROLLIN (English) a form of Roland.
Rolin, Rollins

ROLLO (English) a familiar form of Roland.
Rolla, Rolo

ROLON (Spanish) famous wolf.

ROMAIN (French) a form of Roman.
Romaine, Romane, Romanne

ROMAN (Latin) from Rome, Italy.
Roma, Romain, Romann, Romanos, Romman, Romochka, Romy

ROMANOS (Greek) a form of Roman.
Romano

ROMARIO (Italian) a form of Romeo.
Romar, Romarius, Romaro, Romarrio

ROMEL (Latin) a short form of Romulus.
Romele, Romell, Romello, Rommel

ROMELLO (Italian) an alternate form of Romel.
Romelo, Rommello

ROMEO (Italian) pilgrim to Rome; Roman. Literature: the title character of the Shakespearean play *Romeo and Juliet*.
Romario, Roméo, Romero

ROMERO (Latin) an alternate form of Romeo.
Romario, Romeiro, Romer, Romere, Romerio, Romeris, Romeryo

ROMNEY (Welsh) winding river.
Romoney

ROMULUS (Latin) citizen of Rome. Mythology: Romulus and his twin brother Remus founded Rome.
Romel, Romolo, Romono, Romulo

ROMY (Italian) a familiar form Roman.
Rommie, Rommy

RON (Hebrew) a short form of Aaron, Ronald.
Ronn

RONALD (Scottish) a form of Reginald.
Ranald, Ron, Ronal, Ronaldo, Ronnald, Ronney, Ronnie, Ronnold, Ronoldo

RONALDO (Portuguese) a form of Ronald.

RÓNÁN (Irish) seal.
Renan, Ronan, Ronat

RONDEL (French) short poem.
Rondal, Rondale, Rondall, Rondeal, Rondell, Rondey, Rondie, Rondrell, Rondy, Ronel

RONEL (American) a form of Rondel.
Ronell, Ronelle, Ronnel, Ronnell, Ronyell

RONI (Hebrew) my song; my joy.
Rani, Roneet, Roney, Ronit, Ronli, Rony

RONNIE (Scottish) a familiar form of Ronald.
Roni, Ronie, Ronnie, Ronny

RONNY (Scottish) an alternate form of Ronnie.
Ronney

RONSON (Scottish) son of Ronald.
Ronaldson

RONTÉ (American) a combination of Ron + the suffix -te.
Rontae, Rontay, Ronte, Rontez

ROONEY (Irish) redhead.

ROOSEVELT (Dutch) rose field. History: Theodore and Franklin D. Roosevelt were the twenty-sixth and thirty-second U.S. presidents, respectively.
Roosvelt, Rosevelt

ROPER (English) rope maker.

RORY (German) a familiar form of Roderick. (Irish) red king.
Rorey, Rori, Rorrie, Rorry

ROSALIO (Spanish) rose.
Rosalino

ROSARIO (Portuguese) rosary.

ROSCOE (Scandinavian) deer forest.
Rosco

ROSHAD (American) a form of Rashad.
Roshard

ROSHEAN (American) a combination of the prefix Ro + Sean.
Roshain, Roshan, Roshane, Roshaun, Roshawn, Roshay, Rosheen, Roshene

ROSITO (Filipino) rose.

ROSS (Latin) rose. (Scottish) peninsula. (French) red.
Rosse, Rossell, Rossi, Rossie, Rossy

ROSSWELL (English) springtime of roses.
Rosvel

ROSTISLAV (Czech) growing glory.
Rosta, Rostya

ROSWALD (English) field of roses.
Ross, Roswell

ROTH (German) redhead.

ROTHWELL (Scandinavian) red spring.

ROVER (English) traveler.

ROWAN (English) tree with red berries.
Roan, Rowe, Rowen, Rowney, Rowyn

ROWELL (English) roe deer well.

ROWLAND (German) an alternate form of Roland. (English) rough land.
Rowlando, Rowlands, Rowlandson

ROWLEY (English) rough meadow.
Rowlea, Rowlee, Rowleigh, Rowly

ROWSON (English) son of the redhead.

ROXBURY (English) rook's town or fortress.
Roxburghe

ROY (French) king. A short form of Royal, Royce. See also Conroy, Delroy, Fitzroy, Leroy, Loe.
Rey, Roi, Roye, Ruy

ROYAL (French) kingly, royal.
Roy, Royale, Royall, Royell

ROYCE (English) son of Roy.
Roice, Roy, Royz

ROYDEN (English) rye hill.
Royd, Roydan

RUBEN (Hebrew) an alternate form of Reuben.
Ruban, Rube, Rubean, Rubens, Rubin, Ruby

RUBERT (Czech) a form of Robert.

RUBY (Hebrew) a familiar form of Reuben, Ruben.

RUDD (English) a short form of Rudyard.

RUDA (Czech) a form of Rudolph.
Rude, Rudek

RUDI (Spanish) a familiar form of Rudolph.
Ruedi

RUDO (Shona) love.

RUDOLF (German) an alternate form of Rudolph.
Rodolf, Rodolfo, Rudolfo

RUDOLPH (German) famous wolf. See also Dolf.
Raoul, Rezsó, Rodolfo, Rodolph, Rodolphe, Rolf, Ruda, Rudek, Rudi, Rudolf, Rudolpho, Rudolphus, Rudy

RUDOLPHO (Italian) a form of Rudolph.

RUDY (English) a familiar form of Rudolph.
Roody, Ruddy, Ruddie, Rudey, Rudi, Rudie

RUDYARD (English) red enclosure.
Rudd

RUEBEN (Hebrew) an alternate form of Reuben.
Rueban, Ruebin

RUFF (French) redhead.

RUFIN (Polish) redhead.
Rufino

RUFORD (English) red ford; ford with reeds.
Rufford

RUFUS (Latin) redhead.
Rayfus, Rufe, Ruffis, Ruffus, Rufino, Rufo, Rufous

RUGBY (English) rook fortress. History: a famous British school after which the sport of rugby was named.

RUGGERIO (Italian) a form of Roger.
Rogero, Ruggero, Ruggiero

RUHAKANA (Rukiga) argumentative.

RULAND (German) an alternate form of Roland.
Rulan, Rulon, Rulondo

RUMFORD (English) wide river crossing.

RUNAKO (Shona) handsome.

RUNE (German, Swedish) secret.

RUNROT (Tai) prosperous.

RUPERT (German) a form of Robert.
Ruperth, Ruperto, Ruprecht

RUPERTO (Italian) a form of Rupert.

RUPRECHT (German) an alternate form of Rupert.

RUSH (French) redhead. (English) a short form of Russell.
Rushi

RUSHFORD (English) ford with rushes.

RUSK (Spanish) twisted bread

RUSKIN (French) redhead.
Rush, Russ

RUSS (French) a short form of Russell.

RUSSEL (French) an alternate form of Russell.

RUSSELL (French) redhead; fox colored. See also Lukela.
Roussell, Rush, Russ, Russel, Russelle, Rusty

RUSTY (French) a familiar form of Russell.
Ruste, Rusten, Rustie, Rustin, Ruston, Rustyn

RUTGER (Scandinavian) a form of Roger.
Ruttger

RUTHERFORD (English) cattle ford.
Rutherfurd

RUTLAND (Scandinavian) red land.

RUTLEDGE (English) red ledge.

RUTLEY (English) red meadow.

RUY (Spanish) a short form of Roderick.
Rui

RYAN (Irish) little king.
Rayan, Rhyan, Rhyne, Ryane, Ryann, Ryen, Ryian, Ryiann, Ryin, Ryne, Ryon, Ryuan, Ryun, Ryyan

RYCROFT (English) rye field.
Ryecroft

RYDER (English) an alternate form of Rider.
Rydder, Rye

RYE (English) a short form of Ryder. A grain used in cereal and whiskey. (Gypsy) gentleman.
Ry.

RYEN (Irish) an alternate form of Ryan.
Ryein, Ryien

RYERSON (English) son of Rider, Ryder.

RYESE (English) an alternate form of Reece.
Reyse, Ryez, Ryse

RYKER (American) a surname used as a first name.
Riker, Ryk

RYLAN (English) land where rye is grown.
Ryland, Rylean, Rylen, Rylin, Rylon, Rylyn, Rylynn

RYLAND (English) an alternate form of Rylan.
Ryeland, Rylund

RYLE (English) rye hill.
Ryal, Ryel

RYLEE (Irish) an alternate form of Riley.
Ryeleigh, Ryleigh, Rylie, Rillie

RYLEY (Irish) an alternate form of Riley.
Ryely

RYMAN (English) rye seller.

RYNE (Irish) an alternate form of Ryan.
Rynn

RYON (Irish) an alternate form of Ryan.

SABASTIAN (Greek) an alternate form of Sebastian.
Sabastain, Sabastiano, Sabastien, Sabastin, Sabastion, Sabaston, Sabbastiun, Sabestian

SABER (French) sword.
Sabir, Sabre

SABIN (Basque) ancient tribe of central Italy.
Saban, Saben, Sabian, Sabien, Sabino

SABITI (Rutooro) born on Sunday.

SABOLA (Ngoni) pepper.

SABURO (Japanese) third-born son.

SACHA (Russian) an alternate form of Sasha.
Sascha

SACHAR (Russian) a form of Zachary.

SADDAM (Arabic) powerful ruler.

SADIKI (Swahili) faithful.
Saadiq, Sadeek, Sadek, Sadik, Sadiq, Sadique

SADLER (English) saddle maker.
Saddler

SAFARI (Swahili) born while traveling.
Safa, Safarian

SAFFORD (English) willow-river crossing.

SAGE (English) wise. Botany: an herb with healing powers.
Sagen, Sager, Saige, Saje

SAHALE (Native American) falcon.
Sael, Sahal, Sahel, Sahil

SAHEN (Hindi) above.
Sahan

SAHIL (Native American) an alternate form of Sahale.
Saheel, Sahel

SAHIR (Hindi) friend.

SA'ID (Arabic) happy.
Sa'ad, Saaid, Saed, Sa'eed, Saeed, Sahid, Saide, Sa'ied, Saied, Saiyed, Saiyeed, Sajid, Sajjid, Sayed, Sayeed, Sayid, Seyed, Shahid

SAJAG (Hindi) watchful.

SAKA (Swahili) hunter.

SAKERI (Danish) a form of Zachary.
Sakarai, Sakari

SAKIMA (Native American) king.

SAKURUTA (Pawnee) coming sun.

SAL (Italian) a short form of Salvatore.

SALAM (Arabic) lamb.
Salaam

SALAMON (Spanish) a form of Solomon.
Saloman, Salomón

SALAUN (French) a form of Solomon.

SÁLIH (Arabic) right, good.
Saleeh, Saleh, Salehe

SALIM (Swahili) peaceful.

SALÍM (Arabic) peaceful, safe.
Saleem, Salem, Saliym, Salman

SALMALIN (Hindi) taloned.

SALMAN (Czech) a form of Salím, Solomon.
Salmaan, Salmaine, Salmon

SALOMON (Hebrew) an alternate form of Solomon.
Salomone

SALTON (English) manor town; willow town.

SALVADOR (Spanish) savior.
Salvadore

SALVATORE (Italian) savior. See also Xavier.
Sal, Salbatore, Sallie, Sally, Salvator, Salvattore, Salvidor, Sauveur

SAM (Hebrew) a short form of Samuel.
Samm, Sammy, Sem, Shem, Shmuel

SAMBO (American) a familiar form of Samuel.
Sambou

SAMEER (Arabic) an alternate form of Samír.

SAMI, Samy (Hebrew) alternate forms of Sammy.
Sameeh, Sameh, Samie, Samih, Sammi

SAMÍR (Arabic) entertaining companion.
Sameer

SAMMAN (Arabic) grocer.
Saman, Sammon

SAMMY (Hebrew) a familiar form of Samuel.
Saamy, Samey, Sami, Sammee, Sammey, Sammie, Samy

SAMO (Czech) a form of Samuel.
Samho, Samko

SAMSON (Hebrew) like the sun. Bible: a strong man betrayed by Delilah.
Sampson, Sansao, Sansom, Sansón, Shem, Shimshon

SAMUAL (Hebrew) an alternate form of Samuel.
Samuael, Samuail

SAMUEL (Hebrew) heard God; asked of God. Bible: a famous Old Testament prophet and judge. See also Kamuela, Zamiel, Zanvil.
Sam, Samael, Samaru, Samauel, Samaul, Sambo, Sameul, Samiel, Sammail, Sammel, Sammuel, Sammy, Samo, Samouel, Samu, Samual, Samuele, Samuelis, Samuell, Samuello, Samuil, Samuka, Samule, Samuru, Samvel, Sanko, Saumel, Schmuel, Shem, Shmuel, Simão, Simuel, Somhairle, Zamuel

SAMUELE (Italian) a form of Samuel.
Samulle

SAMURU (Japanese) a form of Samuel.

SANAT (Hindi) ancient.

SANBORN (English) sandy brook.
Sanborne, Sanbourn, Sanbourne, Sanburn, Sanburne, Sandborn, Sandbourne

SANCHEZ (Latin) an alternate form of Sancho.
Sanchaz, Sancheze

SANCHO (Latin) sanctified; sincere. Literature: Sancho Panza was Don Quixote's faithful companion.
Sanchez, Sauncho

SANDEEP (Punjabi) enlightened.
Sandip

SANDER (English) a short form of Alexander, Lysander.
Sandor, Sándor, Saunder

SANDERS (English) son of Sander.
Sanderson, Saunders, Saunderson

SÁNDOR (Hungarian) a short form of Alexander.
Sanyi

SANDRO (Greek, Italian) a short form of Alexander.
Sandero, Sandor, Sandre, Saundro, Shandro

SANDY (English) a familiar form of Alexander.
Sande, Sandey, Sandi, Sandie

SANFORD (English) sandy river crossing.
Sandford

SANI (Hindi) Saturn. (Navajo) old.

SANJAY (American) a combination of Sanford + Jay.
Sanjaya, Sanje, Sanjey, Sanjo

SANJIV (Hindi) long lived.
Sanjeev

SANKAR (Hindi) god. Religion: another name for the Hindu god Shiva.

SANSÓN (Spanish) a form of Samson.
Sanson, Sansone, Sansun

SANTANA (Spanish) History: Antonio Santa Ana was a revolutionary general and president of Mexico.
Santanna

SANTIAGO (Spanish) a form of James.

SANTINO (Spanish) an alternate form of Santonio.
Santion

SANTO (Italian, Spanish) holy.
Santos

SANTON (English) sandy town.

SANTONIO (Spanish) Geography: a short form of San Antonio, a town in Texas.
Santino, Santon, Santoni

SANTOS (Spanish) saint.
Santo

SANTOSH (Hindi) satisfied.

SANYU (Luganda) happy.

SAQR (Arabic) falcon.

SAQUAN (American) a combination of the predix Sa + Quan.
Saquané, Saquin, Saquon, Saqwan, Saqwone

SARAD (Hindi) born in the autumn.

SARGENT (French) army officer.
Sargant, Sarge, Sarjant, Sergeant, Sergent, Serjeant

SARITO (Spanish) a form of Caesar.
Sarit

SARIYAH (Arabic) clouds at night.

SARNGIN (Hindi) archer; protector.

SAROJIN (Hindi) like a lotus.
Sarojun

SASHA (Russian) a short form of Alexander.
Sacha, Sash, Sashenka, Sashka, Sashok, Sausha

SASSON (Hebrew) joyful.
Sason

SATCHEL (French) small bag.
Satch

SATORDI (French) Saturn.
Satori

SAUL (Hebrew) asked for, borrowed. Bible: in the Old Testament, a king of Israel and the father of Jonathan; in the New Testament, Saint Paul's original name was Saul.
Saül, Shaul, Sol, Solly

SAVERIO (Italian) a form of Xavier.

SAVILLE (French) willow town.
Savelle, Savil, Savile, Savill, Savylle, Seville, Siville

SAVON (American) a masculine form of Savannah. (Spanish) a treeless plain.
Savan, Savaughn, Saveion, Saveon, Savhon, Saviahn, Savian, Savino, Savion, Savo, Savone, Sayvon, Sayvone

SAW (Burmese) early.

SAWYER (English) wood worker.
Sawyere

SAX (English) a short form of Saxon.
Saxe

SAXON (English) swordsman. History: the Roman name for Germanic people who fought with short swords.
Sax, Saxen, Saxsin, Saxxon

SAYER (Welsh) carpenter.
Say, Saye, Sayers, Sayr, Sayre, Sayres

SAYYID (Arabic) master.
Sayed, Sayid, Sayyad, Sayyed

SCANLON (Irish) little trapper.
Scanlan, Scanlen

SCHAFER (German) shepherd.
Schaefer, Schaffer, Schiffer, Shaffar, Shäffer

SCHMIDT (German) blacksmith.
Schmid, Schmit, Schmitt, Schmydt

SCHNEIDER (German) tailor.
Schnieder, Snider, Snyder

SCHÖN (German) handsome.
Schoen, Schönn, Shon

SCHUYLER (Dutch) sheltering.
Schuylar, Schyler, Scoy, Scy, Skuyler, Sky, Skylar, Skyler, Skylor

SCHYLER (Dutch) an alternate form of Schuyler.
Schylar, Schylre, Schylur

SCORPIO (Latin) dangerous, deadly. Astronomy: a southern constellation between Libra and Sagittarius resembling a scorpion. Astrology: the eighth sign of the zodiac.
Scorpeo

SCOTT (English) from Scotland. A familiar form of Prescott.
Scot, Scottie, Scotto, Scotty

SCOTTIE (English) a familiar form of Scott.
Scotie, Scotti

SCOTTY (English) a familiar form of Scott.
Scottey

SCOVILLE (French) Scott's town.

SCULLY (Irish) town crier.

SEABERT (English) shining sea.
Seabright, Sebert, Seibert

SEABROOK (English) brook near the sea.

SEAMUS (Irish) a form of James.
Seamas, Seumas, Shamus

SEAN (Hebrew) God is gracious. (Irish) a form of John.
Seaghan, Séan, Seán, Seanán, Seane, Seann, Shaan, Shaine, Shane, Shaun, Shawn, Shayne, Shon, Siôn

SEARLAS (Irish, French) a form of Charles.
Séarlas, Searles, Searlus

SEARLE (English) armor.

SEASAR (Latin) an alternate form of Caesar.
Seasare, Seazar, Sesar, Sesear, Sezar

SEATON (English) town near the sea.
Seeton, Seton

SEBASTIAN (Greek) venerable. (Latin) revered.
Bastian, Sabastian, Sabastien, Sebashtian, Sebastain, Sebastiane, Sebastiano, Sebastien, Sébastien, Sebastin, Sebastine, Sebastion, Sebbie, Sebestyén, Sebo, Sepasetiano

SEBASTIEN, Sébastien (French) forms of Sebastian.
Sebasten, Sebastyen

SEBASTION (Greek) an alternate form of Sebastian.

SEDGELY (English) sword meadow.
Sedgeley, Sedgly

SEDRIC (Irish) a form of Cedric.
Seddrick, Sederick, Sedrick, Sedrik, Sedriq

SEELEY (English) blessed.
Sealey, Seely, Selig

SEF (Egyptian) yesterday. Literature: an Egyption lion god in *The Book of the Dead*.

SEFTON (English) village of rushes.

SEFU (Swahili) sword.

SEGER (English) sea spear; sea warrior.
Seager, Seeger, Segar

SEGUN (Yoruba) conqueror.

SEGUNDO (Spanish) second.

SEIBERT (English) bright sea.
Seabert, Sebert

SEIF (Arabic) religion's sword.

SEIFERT (German) an alternate form of Siegfried.

SEIN (Basque) innocent.

SEKAYE (Shona) laughter.

SELBY (English) village by the mansion.
Selbey, Shelby

SELDON (English) willow tree valley.
Selden, Seliden

SELIG (German) a form of Seeley.
Seligman, Seligmann, Zelig

SELWYN (English) friend from the palace.
Selvin, Selwin, Selwinn, Selwynn, Selwynne, Wyn

SEMANDA (Luganda) cow clan.

SEMER (Ethiopian) a form of George.
Semere, Semier

SEMON (Greek) a form of Simon.
Semion

SEMPALA (Luganda) born in prosperous times.

SEN (Japanese) wood fairy.
Senh

SENER (Turkish) bringer of joy.

SENIOR (French) lord.

SENNETT (French) elderly.
Sennet

SENON (Spanish) living.

SENWE (African) dry as a grain stalk.

SEPP (German) a form of Joseph.
Seppi

SEPTIMUS (Latin) seventh.

SERAFINO (Portuguese) a form of Seraphim.

SERAPHIM (Hebrew) fiery, burning. Bible: the fiery angels who guard the throne of God.
Saraf, Saraph, Serafim, Serafin, Serafino, Seraphimus, Seraphin

SERENO (Latin) calm, tranquil.

SERGE (Latin) attendant.
Seargeoh, Serg, Sergei, Sergio, Sergios, Sergius, Sergiusz, Serguel, Sirgio, Sirgios

SERGEI (Russian) a form of Serge.
Sergey, Sergeyuk, Serghey, Sergi, Sergie, Sergo, Sergunya, Serhiy, Serhiyko, Serjiro, Serzh

SERGIO (Italian) a form of Serge.
Serginio, Serigo, Serjio

SERVANDO (Spanish) to serve.
Servan, Servio

SETH (Hebrew) appointed. Bible: the third son of Adam.
Set, Sethan, Sethe, Shet

SETIMBA (Luganda) river dweller. Geography: a river in Uganda.

SEUMAS (Scottish) a form of James.
Seaumus

SEVERIANO (Italian) a form of Séverin.

SÉVERIN (French) severe.
Seve, Sevé, Severan, Severian, Severiano, Severo, Sevien, Sevrin, Sevryn

SEVERN (English) boundary. Geography: a river in southern England.
Sevearn, Sevren, Sevrnn

SEVILEN (Turkish) beloved.

SEWARD (English) sea guardian.
Sewerd, Siward

SEWATI (Moquelumnan) curved bear claws.

SEXTON (English) church offical, sexton.

SEXTUS (Latin) sixth.
Sixtus

SEYMOUR (French) prayer. Religion: name honoring Saint Maur. See also Maurice.
Seamor, Seamore, Seamour, See

SHABOUH (Armenian) king, noble. History: a Persian king.

SHAD (Punjabi) happy-go-lucky.
Shadd

SHADI (Arabic) singer.
Shadde, Shaddi, Shaddy, Shade, Shadee, Shadeed, Shadey, Shadie, Shady, Shydee, Shydi

SHADRACH (Babylonian) god; godlike. Religion: another name for Aku, the sun god. Bible: one of Daniel's three companions in captivity.
Shad, Shadrack, Shadrick, Sheddrach, Shedrach, Shedrick

SHADWELL (English) shed by a well.

SHAH (Persian) king. History: a title for rulers of Iran.

SHAHEEM (American) a combination of Shah + Raheem.
Shaheim, Shahiem, Shahm

SHAHID (Arabic) an alternate form of Sa'id.
Shahed, Shaheed

SHAI (Hebrew) a short form of Yeshaya.
Shaie

SHAIMING (Chinese) life; sunshine.

SHAINE (Irish) an alternate form of Sean.
Shain

SHAKA (Zulu) founder, first. History: Shaka Zulu was the founder of the Zulu empire.

SHAKEEL (Arabic) an alternate form of Shaquille.
Shakeil, Shakel, Shakell, Shakiel, Shakil, Shakille, Shakyle

SHAKIR (Arabic) thankful.
Shaakir, Shakeer, Shakeir, Shakur

SHAKUR (Arabic) an alternate form of Shakir.
Shakuur

SHALOM (Hebrew) peace.
Shalum, Shlomo, Sholem, Sholom

SHALYA (Hindi) throne.

SHAMAN (Sanskrit) holy man, mystic, medicine man.
Shamaine, Shamaun, Shamin, Shamine, Shammon, Shamon, Shamone

SHAMAR (Hebrew) an alternate form of Shamir.
Shamaar, Shamare, Shamari

SHAMIR (Hebrew) precious stone. Bible: a hard, precious stone used to build Solomon's temple.
Shahmeer, Shahmir, Shamar, Shameer, Shamyr

SHAMUS (Irish) an alternate form of Seamus. (American) slang for detective.
Shamas, Shames, Shamos, Shemus

SHAN (Irish) an alternate form of Shane.
Shann, Shanne

SHANAHAN (Irish) wise, clever.

SHANDY (English) rambunctious.
Shandey, Shandie

SHANE (Irish) an alternate form of Sean.
Shan, Shayn, Shayne

SHANGOBUNNI (Yoruba) gift from Shango.

SHANLEY (Irish) small; ancient.
Shaneley, Shannley

SHANNON (Irish) small and wise.
Shanan, Shannan, Shannen, Shannin, Shannone, Shanon

SHANTAE (French) an alternate form of Chante.
Shant, Shanta, Shantai, Shante, Shantell, Shantelle, Shanti, Shantia, Shantie, Shanton, Shanty

SHAP (English) an alternate form of Shep.

SHAQUAN (American) a combination of the prefix Sha + Quan.
Shaqaun, Shaquand, Shaquane, Shaquann, Shaquaunn, Shaquawn, Shaquen, Shaquian, Shaquin, Shaqwan

SHAQUELL (American) a form of Shaquille.
Shaqueal, Shaqueil, Shaquel, Shaquelle, Shaquiel, Shaquiell, Shaquielle

SHAQUILLE (Arabic) handsome.
Shakeel, Shaquell, Shaquil, Shaquile, Shaquill, Shaqul

SHAQUON (American) a combination of the prefix Sha + Quon.
Shaikwon, Shaqon, Shaquoin, Shaquoné

SHARAD (Pakistani) autumn.
Sharod

SHARÍF (Arabic) honest; noble.
Shareef, Sharef, Shareff, Shareif, Sharief, Sharife, Shariff, Shariyf, Sharrif, Sharyif

SHAROD (Pakistani) an alternate form of Sharad.
Sharrod

SHARRON (Hebrew) flat area, plain. Bible: the area from Mount Carmel south to Jaffa, covered with oak trees.
Sharon, Sharone, Sharonn, Sharonne

SHATTUCK (English) little shad fish.

SHAUN (Irish) an alternate form of Sean.
Shaughan, Shaughn, Shaugn, Shauna, Shaunahan, Shaune, Shaunn, Shaunne

SHAVAR (Hebrew) comet.
Shavit

SHAVON (American) a combination of the prefix Sha + Yvon.
Shauvan, Shauvon, Shavan, Shavaughn, Shaven, Shavin, Shavone, Shawan, Shawon, Shawun

SHAW (English) grove.

SHAWN (Irish) an alternate form of Sean.
Shawen, Shawne, Shawnee, Shawnn, Shawon

SHAWNTA (American) a combination of Shawn + suffixes beginning with a "t."
Shawntae, Shawntel, Shawnti

SHAY (Irish) an alternate form of Shea.
Shae, Shai, Shaya, Shaye, Shey

SHAYAN (Cheyenne) an alternate form of Cheyenne.
Shayaan, Shayann, Shayon

SHAYNE (Hebrew) an alternate form of Sean.
Shayn, Shaynne, Shean

SHEA (Irish) courteous.
Shay

SHEDRICK (Babylonian) an alternate form of Shadrach.
Shadriq, Shederick, Shedric, Shedrique

SHEEHAN (Irish) little; peaceful.
Shean

SHEFFIELD (English) crooked field.
Field, Shef, Sheff, Sheffie, Sheffy

SHEL (English) a short form of Shelby, Sheldon, Shelton.

SHELBY (English) ledge estate.
Shel, Shelbe, Shelbey, Shelbie, Shell, Shellby, Shelley, Shelly

SHELDON (English) farm on the ledge.
Shel, Sheldan, Shelden, Sheldin, Sheldyn, Shell, Shelley, Shelly, Shelton

SHELLEY (English) a familiar form of Shelby, Sheldon, Shelton. Literature: Percy Bysshe Shelly was a British poet.
Shell, Shelly

SHELTON (English) town on a ledge.
Shel, Shelley, Shelten

SHEM (Hebrew) name; reputation. (English) a short form of Samuel. Bible: Noah's oldest son.

SHEN (Egyptian) sacred amulet. (Chinese) meditation.

SHEP (English) a short form of Shepherd.
Shap, Ship, Shipp

SHEPHERD (English) shepherd.
Shep, Shepard, Shephard, Shepp, Sheppard, Shepperd

SHEPLEY (English) sheep meadow.
Sheplea, Sheplee, Shepply, Shipley

SHERBORN (English) clear brook.
Sherborne, Sherbourn, Sherburn, Sherburne

SHERIDAN (Irish) wild.
Dan, Sheredan, Sheriden, Sheridon, Sherridan

SHERILL (English) shire on a hill.
Sheril, Sherril, Sherrill

SHERLOCK (English) light haired. Literature: Sherlock Holmes was Sir Arthur Conan Doyle's famous British detective character.
Sherlocke, Shurlock, Shurlocke

SHERMAN (English) sheep shearer; resident of a shire.
Scherman, Schermann, Sherm, Shermain, Shermaine, Shermann, Shermie, Shermon, Shermy

SHERROD (English) clearer of the land.
Sherod, Sherrad, Sherrard, Sherrodd

SHERWIN (English) swift runner, one who cuts the wind.
Sherveen, Shervin, Sherwan, Sherwind, Sherwinn, Sherwyn, Sherwynd, Sherwynne, Win

SHERWOOD (English) bright forest.
Sherwoode, Shurwood, Woody

SHIHAB (Arabic) blaze.

SHÌLÍN (Chinese) intellectual.
Shilan

SHILOH (Hebrew) God's gift.
Shi, Shile, Shiley, Shilo, Shiloe, Shy, Shyle, Shylo, Shyloh

SHIMON (Hebrew) an alternate form of Simon.
Shymon

SHIMSHON (Hebrew) an alternate form of Samson.
Shimson

SHING (Chinese) victory.
Shingae, Shingo

SHIPTON (English) sheep village; ship village.

SHIQUAN (American) a combination of the prefix Shi + Quan.
Shiquane, Shiquann, Shiquawn, Shiquoin, Shiqwan

SHIRO (Japanese) fourth-born son.

SHIVA (Hindi) life and death. Religion: the most common name for the god of destruction and reproduction.
Shiv, Shivan, Siva

SHLOMO (Hebrew) an alternate form of Solomon.
Shelmu, Shelomo, Shelomoh, Shlomi, Shlomot

SHMUEL (Hebrew) an alternate form of Samuel.
Shem, Shemuel, Shmelke, Shmiel, Shmulka

SHNEUR (Yiddish) senior.
Shneiur

SHON (German) an alternate form of Schön. (American) a form of Sean.
Shoan, Shoen, Shondae, Shondale, Shondel, Shone, Shonn, Shonntay, Shontae, Shontarious, Shouan, Shoun

SHUNNAR (Arabic) pheasant.

SI (Hebrew) a short form of Silas, Simon.
Sy

SID (French) a short form of Sidney.
Cyd, Siddie, Siddy, Sidey, Syd

SIDDEL (English) wide valley.
Siddell

SIDDHARTHA (Hindi) History: the original name of Buddha, an Indian mystic and founder of Buddhism.
Sida, Siddartha, Siddhaarth, Siddhart, Siddharth, Sidh, Sidharth, Sidhartha, Sidhdharth

SIDNEY (French) from Saint Denis, France.
Cydney, Sid, Sidnee, Sidny, Sidon, Sidonio, Sydney, Sydny

SIDONIO (Spanish) a form of Sidney.

SIDWELL (English) wide stream.

SIEGFRIED (German) victorious peace. Literature: a dragon-slaying hero. See also Zigfrid, Ziggy.
Seifert, Seifried, Siegfred, Siffre, Sig, Sigfrid, Sigfried, Sigfroi, Sigfryd, Siggy, Sigifredo, Sigvard, Singefrid, Sygfried, Szygfrid

SIERRA (Irish) black. (Spanish) saw toothed. Geography: a range of mountains with a sawtooth appearance.
Siera

SIG (German) a short form of Siegfried, Sigmund.

SIGIFREDO (German) an alternate form of Siegfried.
Sigefriedo, Sigfrido, Siguefredo

SIGGY (German) a familiar form of Siegfried, Sigmund.

SIGMUND (German) victorious protector. See also Ziggy, Zsigmond, Zygmunt.
Siegmund, Sig, Siggy, Sigismond, Sigismondo, Sigismund, Sigismundo, Sigismundus, Sigmond, Sigsmond, Szygmond

SIGURD (German, Scandinavian) victorious guardian.
Sigord, Sjure, Syver

SIGWALD (German) victorious leader.

SILAS (Latin) a short form of Silvan.
Si, Sias, Sylas

SILVAN (Latin) forest dweller.
Silas, Silvain, Silvano, Silvaon, Silvie, Silvio, Sylvain, Sylvan, Sylvanus, Sylvio

SILVANO (Italian) a form of Silvan.
Silvanos, Silvanus, Silvino

SILVESTER (Latin) an alternate form of Sylvester.
Silvestr, Silvestre, Silvestro, Silvy

SILVESTRO (Italian) a form of Sylvester.

SILVIO (Italian) a form of Silvan.

SIMÃO (Portuguese) a form of Samuel.

SIMBA (Swahili) lion. (Yao) a short form of Lisimba.
Sim

SIMCHA (Hebrew) joyful.
Simmy

SIMEON (French) a form of Simon.
Simione, Simone

SIMMS (Hebrew) son of Simon.
Simm, Sims

SIMMY (Hebrew) a familiar form of Simcha, Simon.
Simmey, Simmi, Simmie, Symmy

SIMON (Hebrew) he heard. Bible: in the Old Testament, the second son of Jacob and Leah; in the New Testament, one of the Twelve Disciples. See also Symington, Ximenes.
Saimon, Samien, Semon, Shimon, Si, Sim, Simao, Simen, Simeon, Simion, Simm, Simmon, Simmonds, Simmons, Simms, Simmy, Simonas, Simone, Simson, Simyon, Síomón, Symon, Szymon

SIMPSON (Hebrew) son of Simon.
Simonson, Simson

SINCLAIR (French) prayer. Religion: name honoring Saint Clair.
Sinclare, Synclair

SINGH (Hindi) lion.
Sing

SINJON (English) saint, holy man. Religion: name honoring Saint John.

Sinjon (cont.)
Sinjin, Sinjun, Sjohn, Syngen,
Synjen, Synjon

SIPATU (Moquelumnan) pulled
out.

SIPHO (Zulu) present.

SIRAJ (Arabic) lamp, light.

SISEAL (Irish) a form of Cecil.

SISI (Fante) born on Sunday.

SIVA (Hindi) an alternate form
of Shiva.
Siv

SIVAN (Hebrew) ninth month of
the Jewish year.

SIWATU (Swahili) born during a
time of conflict.
Siwazuri

SIWILI (Native American) long
fox's tail.

SKAH (Lakota) white.
Skai

SKEE (Scandinavian) projectile.
Ski, Skie

SKEETER (English) swift.
Skeat, Skeet, Skeets

SKELLY (Irish) storyteller.
Shell, Skelley, Skellie

SKELTON (Dutch) shell town.

SKERRY (Scandinavian) stony
island.

SKIP (Scandinavian) a short
form of Skipper.

SKIPPER (Scandinavian) ship-
master.
Skip, Skipp, Skippie, Skipton

SKIRIKI (Pawnee) coyote.

SKULE (Norwegian) hidden.

SKYE (Dutch) a short form of
Skylar, Skyler, Skylor.
Sky

SKYLAR (Dutch) an alternate
form of Schuyler.
Skilar, Skkylar, Skye, Skyelar,
Skylaar, Skylare, Skylarr, Skylayr

SKYLER (Dutch) an alternate
form of Schuyler.
Skieler, Skiler, Skye, Skyeler,
Skylee, Skyller

SKYLOR (Dutch) an alternate
form of Schuyler.
Skye, Skyelor, Skyloer, Skylore,
Skylour, Skylur, Skylyr

SLADE (English) child of the
valley.
Slaide, Slayde

SLANE (Czech) salty.
Slan

SLATER (English) roof slater.
Slader, Slate, Slayter

SLAVA (Russian) a short form
of Stanislav, Vladislav,
Vyacheslav.
Slavik, Slavoshka

SLAWEK (Polish) a short form
of Radoslaw.

SLEVIN (Irish) mountaineer.
Slaven, Slavin, Slawin

SLOAN (Irish) warrior.
Sloane, Slone

SMEDLEY (English) flat meadow.
Smedleigh, Smedly

SMITH (English) blacksmith.
Schmidt, Smid, Smidt, Smitt,
Smitty, Smyth, Smythe

SNOWDEN (English) snowy hill.
Snowdon

SOCRATES (Greek) wise,
learned. History: a famous
ancient Greek philosopher.
Socratis, Sokrates, Sokratis

SOFIAN (Arabic) devoted.

SOHRAB (Persian) ancient hero.

SOJA (Yoruba) soldier.

SOL (Hebrew) a short form of
Saul, Solomon.
Soll, Sollie, Solly

SOLLY (Hebrew) a familiar form
of Saul, Solomon.
Sollie, Zollie, Zolly

SOLOMON (Hebrew) peaceful.
Bible: a king of Israel famous
for his wisdom. See also
Zalman.
Salamen, Salamon, Salamun,
Salaun, Salman, Salomo,
Salomon, Selim, Shelomah,
Shlomo, Sol, Solamh, Solaman,
Solly, Solmon, Soloman,
Solomonas, Sulaiman

SOLON (Greek) wise. History: a
sixth-century Athenian lawmaker noted for his wisdom.

SOMERSET (English) place of
the summer settlers.
Literature: William Somerset
Maugham was a well-known
British writer.
Sommerset, Sumerset,
Summerset

SOMERVILLE (English) summer
town.
Somerton, Summerton,
Summerville

SON (Vietnamese) mountain.
(Native American) star.
(English) son, boy. A short
form of Madison, Orson.
Sonny

SONGAN (Native American) strong.
Song

SONNY (English) a familiar form of Grayson, Madison, Orson, Son.
Soni, Sonnie, Sony

SONO (Akan) elephant.

SÖREN (Danish) thunder; war. Mythology: Thor was the Norse god of thunder and war.
Sorren

SORREL (French) reddish brown.
Sorel, Sorell, Sorrell

SOROUSH (Persian) happy.

SOTERIOS (Greek) savior.
Soteris, Sotero

SOUTHWELL (English) south well.

SOVANN (Cambodian) gold.

SOWANDE (Yoruba) wise healer sought me out.

SPALDING (English) divided field.
Spaulding

SPANGLER (German) tinsmith.
Spengler

SPARK (English) happy.
Sparke, Sparkie, Sparky

SPEAR (English) spear carrier.
Speare, Spears, Speer, Speers, Spiers

SPEEDY (English) quick; successful.
Speed

SPENCE (English) a short form of Spencer.
Spense

SPENCER (English) dispenser of provisions.
Spence, Spencre, Spenser

SPENSER (English) an alternate form of Spencer. Literature: Edmund Spenser was the British poet who wrote *The Faerie Queene*.
Spanser, Spense

SPIKE (English) ear of grain; long nail.
Spyke

SPIRO (Greek) round basket; breath.
Spiridion, Spiridon, Spiros, Spyridon, Spyros

SPOOR (English) spur maker.
Spoors

SPROULE (English) energetic.
Sprowle

SPURGEON (English) shrub.

SPYROS (Greek) an alternate form of Spiro.

SQUIRE (English) knight's assistant; large landholder.

STACEY, Stacy (English) familiar forms of Eustace.
Stace, Stacee

STAFFORD (English) riverbank landing.
Staffard, Stafforde, Staford

STAMFORD (English) an alternate form of Stanford.

STAMOS (Greek) an alternate form of Stephen.
Stamatis, Stamatos

STAN (Latin, English) a short form of Stanley.

STANBURY (English) stone fortification.
Stanberry, Stanbery, Stanburghe, Stansbury

STANCIO (Spanish) a form of Constantine.
Stancy

STANCLIFF (English) stony cliff.
Stanclife, Stancliffe

STANDISH (English) stony parkland. History: Miles Standish was a prominent pilgrim in colonial America.

STANE (Slavic) a short form of Stanislaus.

STANFIELD (English) stony field.
Stansfield

STANFORD (English) rocky ford.
Sandy, Stamford, Stan, Standford, Stanfield

STANISLAUS (Latin) stand of glory. See also Lao, Tano.
Slavik, Stana, Standa, Stane, Stanislao, Stanislas, Stanislau, Stanislav, Stanislus, Stannes, Stano, Stasik, Stasio

STANISLAV (Slavic) a form of Stanislaus. See also Slava.
Stanislaw

STANLEY (English) stony meadow.
Stan, Stanely, Stanlea, Stanlee, Stanleigh, Stanly

STANMORE (English) stony lake.

STANNARD (English) hard as stone.

STANTON (English) stony farm.
Stan, Stanten, Staunton

STANWAY (English) stony road.

STANWICK (English) stony village.
Stanwicke, Stanwyck

STANWOOD (English) stony woods.

STARBUCK (English) challenger of fate. Literature: a character in Herman Melville's novel *Moby Dick*.

STARK (German) strong, vigorous.
Starke, Stärke, Starkie

STARLING (English) bird.
Sterling

STARR (English) star.
Star, Staret, Starlight, Starlon, Starwin

STASIK (Russian) a familiar form of Stanislaus.
Stas, Stash, Stashka, Stashko, Stasiek

STASIO (Polish) a form of Stanislaus.
Stas, Stasiek, Stasiu, Staska, Stasko

STAVROS (Greek) an alternate form of Stephen.

STEADMAN (English) owner of a farmstead.
Steadmann, Stedman, Stedmen, Steed

STEEL (English) like steel.
Steele

STEEN (German, Danish) stone.
Steenn, Stein

STEEVE (Greek) a short form of Steeven.

STEEVEN (Greek) an alternate form of Steven.
Steaven, Steavin, Steavon, Steevan, Steeve, Steevn

STEFAN (German, Polish, Swedish) a form of Stephen.
Steafan, Steafeán, Stefaan, Stefane, Stefanson, Stefaun, Stefawn, Steffan

STEFANO (Italian) an alternate form of Stephen.
Stefanos, Steffano

STEFANOS (Greek) a form of Stephen.
Stefans, Stefos, Stephano, Stephanos

STEFEN (Norwegian) a form of Stephen.
Steffen, Steffin, Stefin

STEFFAN (Swedish) an alternate form of Stefan.
Staffan

STEFON (Polish) a form of Stephon.
Staffon, Steffon, Steffone, Stefone, Stefonne

STEIN (German) an alternate form of Steen.
Steine, Steiner

STEINAR (Norwegian) rock warrior.

STEPAN (Russian) a form of Stephen.
Stepa, Stepane, Stepanya, Stepka, Stipan

STEPH (English) a short form of Stephen.

STEPHAN (Greek) an alternate form of Stephen.
Stepfan, Stephanas, Stephano, Stephanos, Stephanus, Stephaun

STÉPHANE (French) a form of Stephen.
Stefane, Stepháne, Stephanne

STEPHEN (Greek) crowned. See also Estéban, Estebe, Estevan, Estevao, Étienne, István, Szczepan, Tapani, Teb, Teppo, Tiennot.
Stamos, Stavros, Stefan, Stefano, Stefanos, Stefen, Stenya, Stepan, Stepanos, Steph, Stephan, Stephanas, Stéphane, Stephens, Stephenson, Stephfan, Stephin, Stephon, Stepven, Steve, Steven, Stevie

STEPHON (Greek) an alternate form of Stephen.
Stefon, Stepfon, Stepfone, Stephfon, Stephion, Stephone, Stephonne

STERLING (English) valuable; silver penny. An alternate form of Starling.
Sterlen, Sterlin, Stirling

STERN (German) star.

STERNE (English) austere.
Stearn, Stearne, Stearns

STETSON (Danish) stepson.
Steston, Steton, Stetsen, Stetzon

STEVAN (Greek) an alternate form of Steven.
Stevano, Stevanoe, Stevaughn, Stevean

STEVE (Greek) a short form of Stephen, Steven.
Steave, Stevie, Stevy

STEVEN (Greek) crowned. An alternate form of Stephen.
Steeven, Steiven, Stevan, Steve, Stevens, Stevie, Stevin, Stevon, Stiven

STEVENS (Greek) son of Steven.
Stevenson, Stevinson

STEVIE (English) a familiar form of Stephen, Steven.
Stevey, Stevy

STEVIN, Stevon (Greek) alternate forms of Steven.
Stevieon, Stevion, Stevyn

STEWART (English) an alternate form of Stuart.
Steward, Stu

STIAN (Norwegian) quick on his feet.

STIG (Swedish) mount.

STIGGUR (Gypsy) gate.

STILLMAN (English) quiet.
Stillmann, Stillmon

STING (English) spike of grain.

STOCKMAN (English) tree-stump remover.

STOCKTON (English) tree-stump town.

STOCKWELL (English) tree-stump well.

STODDARD (English) horse keeper.

STOFFEL (German) a short form of Christopher.

STOKER (English) furnace tender.
Stoke, Stokes, Stroker

STONE (English) stone.
Stoen, Stoner, Stoney, Stonie, Stonie, Stoniy, Stony

STORM (English) tempest, storm.
Storme, Stormey, Stormi, Stormmie, Stormy

STORR (Norwegian) great.
Story

STOVER (English) stove tender.

STOWE (English) hidden, packed away.

STRAHAN (Irish) minstrel.
Strachan

STRATFORD (English) bridge over the river. Literature: Stratford-upon-Avon was Shakespeare's birthplace.
Stradford

STRATTON (Scottish) river valley town.
Straten, Straton

STREPHON (Greek) one who turns. Literature: a character in Gilbert and Sullivan's play *Iolanthe*.

STROM (Greek) bed, mattress. (German) stream.

STRONG (English) powerful.

STROUD (English) thicket.

STRUTHERS (Irish) brook.

STU (English) a short form of Stewart, Stuart.
Stew

STUART (English) caretaker, steward. History: the Scottish and English royal dynasty.
Stewart, Stu, Stuarrt

STUDS (English) rounded nail heads; shirt ornaments; male horses used for breeding. History: Studs Terkel, a famous American radio journalist.
Stud, Studd

STYLES (English) stairs put over a wall to help cross it.
Stiles, Style, Stylz

SUBHI (Arabic) early morning.

SUCK CHIN (Korean) unshakable rock.

SUDI (Swahili) lucky.
Su'ud

SUED (Arabic) master, chief.
Suede

SUFFIELD (English) southern field.

SUGDEN (English) valley of sows.

SUHAIL (Arabic) gentle.
Sohail, Sohayl, Souhail, Suhael, Sujal

SUHUBA (Swahili) friend.

SUKRU (Turkish) grateful.

SULAIMAN (Arabic) a form of Solomon.
Sulaman, Sulay, Sulaymaan, Sulayman, Suleiman, Suleman, Suleyman, Sulieman, Sulman, Sulomon, Sulyman

SULLIVAN (Irish) black eyed.
Sullavan, Sullevan, Sully

SULLY (Irish) a familiar form of Sullivan. (French) stain, tarnish. (English) south meadow.
Sulleigh, Sulley

SULTAN (Swahili) ruler.
Sultaan

SUM (Tai) appropriate.

SUMMIT (English) peak, top.
Sumeet, Sumit, Summet, Summitt

SUMNER (English) church officer, summoner.
Summer

SUNDEEP (Punjabi) light; enlightened.
Sundip

SUNNY (English) sunny, sunshine.
Sun, Sunni

SUNREEP (Hindi) pure.
Sunrip

SUTCLIFF (English) southern cliff.
Sutcliffe

SUTHERLAND (Scandinavian) southern land.
Southerland, Sutherlan

SUTTON (English) southern town.

SVEN (Scandinavian) youth.
Svein, Svend, Svenn, Swen, Swenson

SWAGGART (English) one who sways and staggers.
Swaggert

SWAIN (English) herdsman; knight's attendant.
Swaine, Swane, Swanson, Swayne

SWALEY (English) winding stream.
Swail, Swailey, Swale, Swales

SWEENEY (Irish) small hero.
Sweeny

SWINBOURNE (English) stream used by swine.
Swinborn, Swinborne, Swinburn, Swinburne, Swinbyrn, Swynborn

SWINDEL (English) valley of the swine.
Swindell

SWINFEN (English) swine's mud.

SWINFORD (English) swine's crossing.
Swynford

SWINTON (English) swine town.

SY (Latin) a short form of Sylas, Symon.
Si

SYDNEY (French) an alternate form of Sidney.
Syd, Sydne, Sydnee, Syndey

SYED (Arabic) happy.
Syeed, Syid

SYING (Chinese) star.

SYLAS (Latin) an alternate form of Silas.
Sy, Syles, Sylus

SYLVAIN (French) a form of Silvan, Sylvester.
Sylvan, Sylvian

SYLVESTER (Latin) forest dweller.
Silvester, Silvestro, Sly, Syl, Sylvain, Sylverster, Sylvestre

SYMINGTON (English) Simon's town, Simon's estate.

SYMON (Greek) a form of Simon.
Sy, Syman, Symeon, Symion, Symms, Symon, Symone

SZCZEPAN (Polish) a form of Stephen.

SZYGFRID (Hungarian) a form of Siegfried.
Szigfrid

SZYMON (Polish) a form of Simon.

TAAVETI (Finnish) a form of David.
Taavi, Taavo

TAB (German) shining, brilliant. (English) drummer.
Tabb, Tabbie, Tabby

TABARI (Arabic) he remembers. History: a Muslim historian.
Tabahri, Tabares, Tabarious, Tabarius, Tabarus, Tabur

TABIB (Turkish) physician.
Tabeeb

TABO (Spanish) a short form of Gustave.

TABOR (Persian) drummer. (Hungarian) encampment.
Tabber, Taber, Taboras, Taibor, Tayber, Taybor, Taver

TAD (Greek, Latin) a short form of Thaddeus. (Welsh) father.
Tadd, Taddy, Tade, Tadek, Tadey

TADAN (Native American) plentiful.
Taden

TADARIUS (American) a combination of the prefix Ta + Darius.
Tadar, Tadarious, Tadaris, Tadarrius

TADDEO (Italian) a form of Thaddeus.
Tadeo

TADDEUS (Greek, Latin) an alternate form of Thaddeus.
Taddeous, Taddeusz, Taddius, Tadeas, Tades, Tadeusz, Tadio, Tadious

TADI (Omaha) wind.

TADZI (Carrier) loon.

TADZIO (Polish, Spanish) a form of Thaddeus.
Taddeusz

TAFFY (Welsh) a form of David. (English) a familiar form of Taft.

TAFT (English) river.
Taffy, Tafton

TAGE (Danish) day.
Tag

TAGGART (Irish) son of the priest.
Tagart, Taggert

TAHÍR (Arabic) innocent, pure.
Taheer

TAI (Vietnamese) weather; prosperous; talented.

TAIMA (Native American) born during a storm.

TAISHAWN (American) a combination of Tai + Shawn.
Taisen, Taishaun, Taishon

TAIT (Scandinavian) an alternate form of Tate.
Taite, Taitt

TAIWAN (Chinese) island; island dweller. Geography: a country off the coast of mainland China.

Taewon, Tahwan, Taivon, Taiwain, Tawain, Tawan, Tawann, Tawaun, Tawon, Taywan, Tywan

TAIWO (Yoruba) first-born of twins.

TAJ (Urdu) crown.
Taje, Tajee, Tajeh, Tajh, Taji

TAJO (Spanish) day.
Taio

TAJUAN (American) a combination of the prefix Ta + Juan.
Taijuan, Taijun, Taijuon, Tájuan, Tajwan, Taquan, Tyjuan

TAKEO (Japanese) strong as bamboo.
Takeyo

TAKIS (Greek) a familiar form of Peter.
Takias, Takius

TAKODA (Lakota) friend to everyone.

TAL (Hebrew) dew; rain.
Tali, Talia, Talley, Talor, Talya

TALBERT (German) bright valley.

TALBOT (French) boot maker.
Talbott, Tallbot, Tallbott, Tallie, Tally

TALCOTT (English) cottage near the lake.

TALE (Tswana) green.

TALEN (English) an alternate form of Talon.
Talin, Tallen

TALIB (Arabic) seeker.

TALIESIN (Welsh) radiant brow.
Tallas, Tallis

TALIKI (Hausa) fellow.

TALLI (Lenape) legendary hero.

TALMADGE (English) lake between two towns.
Talmage

TALMAI (Aramaic) mound; furrow. Bible: a king of Geshur and father-in-law of King David.
Telem

TALMAN (Aramaic) injured; oppressed.
Talmon

TALON (French, English) claw, nail.
Taelon, Taelyn, Talen, Tallin, Tallon, Talyn

TALOR (English) a form of Tal. An alternate form of Taylor.
Taelor, Taelur

TAM (Hebrew) honest. (English) a short form of Thomas. (Vietnamese) number eight.
Tama, Tamas, Tamás, Tameas, Tamlane, Tammany, Tammas, Tammen, Tammy

TAMAN (Slavic) dark, black.
Tama, Tamann, Tamin, Tamon, Tamone

TAMAR (Hebrew) date; palm tree.
Tamarie, Tamario, Tamarr, Timur

TAMBO (Swahili) vigorous.

TAMIR (Arabic) tall as a palm tree.
Tameer

TAMMY (English) a familiar form of Thomas.
Tammie

TAMSON (Scandinavian) son of Thomas.
Tamsen

TAN (Burmese) million. (Vietnamese) new.
Than

TANEK (Greek) immortal. See also Atek.

TANELI (Finnish) God is my judge.
Taneil, Tanell, Tanella

TANER (English) an alternate form of Tanner.
Tanar

TANGUY (French) warrior.

TANI (Japanese) valley.

TANMAY (Sanskrit) engrossed.

TANNER (English) leather worker, tanner.
Tan, Taner, Tanery, Tann, Tannar, Tannir, Tannor, Tanny

TANNIN (English) tan-colored, dark.
Tanin, Tannen, Tannon, Tanyen, Tanyon

TANNY (English) a familiar form of Tanner.
Tana, Tannee, Tanney, Tannie, Tany

TANO (Spanish) camp glory. (Russian) a short form of Stanislaus. (Ghanian) Geography: a river in Ghana.
Tanno

TANTON (English) town by the still river.

TAPAN (Sanskrit) sun; summer.

TAPANI (Finnish) a form of Stephen.
Tapamn, Teppo

TÄPKO (Kiowa) antelope.

TAQUAN (American) a combination of the prefix Ta + Quan.
Taquann, Taquawn, Taquon, Taqwan

TARAK (Sanskrit) star; protector.

TARAN (Sanskrit) heaven.
Tarran

TAREK (Arabic) an alternate form of Táriq.
Tareek, Tareke

TARELL (German) an alternate form of Terrell.
Tarelle, Tarrel, Tarrell, Taryl

TAREN (American) an alternate form of Taron.
Tarren, Tarrin

TARIF (Arabic) uncommon.
Tareef

TARIK (Arabic) an alternate form of Táriq.
Taric, Tarick, Tariek, Tarikh, Tarrick, Tarrik, Taryk

TÁRIQ (Arabic) conqueror. History: Tarik was the Muslim general who conquered Spain.
Tareck, Tarek, Tarik, Tarique, Tarreq, Tereik

TARLETON (English) Thor's settlement.
Tarlton

TARO (Japanese) first-born male.

TARON (American) a combination of Tad + Ron.
Taeron, Tahron, Taren, Tarone, Tarrion, Tarron, Taryn

TARRANT (Welsh) thunder.
Terrant

TARUN (Sanskrit) young, youth.
Taran

TARVER (English) tower; hill; leader.
Terver

TARYN (American) an alternate form of Taron.
Tarryn, Taryon

TAS (Gypsy) bird's nest.

TASHAWN (American) a combination of the prefix Ta + Shawn.
Tashaan, Tashan, Tashaun, Tashon, Tashun

TASS (Hungarian) ancient mythology name.

TASUNKE (Dakota) horse.

TATE (Scandinavian, English) cheerful. (Native American) long-winded talker.
Tait, Tayte

TATIUS (Latin) king, ruler. History: a Sabine king.
Tatianus, Tazio, Titus

TATUM (English) cheerful.

TAU (Tswana) lion.

TAUNO (Finnish) a form of Donald.

TAUREAN (Latin) strong; forceful. Astrology: born under the sign of Taurus.
Tauraun, Taurein, Taurin, Taurion, Taurone, Taurus

TAURUS (Latin) an alternate form of Taurean.
Taurice, Tauris

TAVARES (Aramaic) an alternate form of Tavor.
Tarvarres, Tavarres, Taveress

TAVARIS (Aramaic) an alternate form of Tavor.
Tarvaris, Tavar, Tavaras, Tavari, Tavarian, Tavarious, Tavarius, Tavarous, Tavarri, Tavarris, Tavars, Tavarse, Tavarus, Tevaris, Tevarius, Tevarus

TAVEY (Latin) a familiar form of Octavio.

TAVI (Aramaic) good.

TAVIAN (Latin) a short form of Octavio.
Taveon, Taviann, Tavien, Tavieon, Tavin, Tavio, Tavion, Tavionne, Tavon, Tayvon

TAVISH (Scottish) a form of Thomas.
Tav, Tavi, Tavis

TAVO (Slavic) a short form of Gustave.

TAVON (American) a form of Tavian.
Tavonn, Tavonne, Tavonni

TAVOR (Aramaic) misfortune.
Tarvoris, Tavares, Tavaris, Tavores, Tavorious, Tavoris, Tavorise, Tavorres, Tavorris, Tavuris

TAWNO (Gypsy) little one.
Tawn

TAYIB (Hindi) good; delicate.

TAYLER (English) an alternate form of Taylor.
Tailer, Taylar, Tayller, Teyler

TAYLOR (English) tailor.
Tailor, Talor, Tayler, Tayllor, Taylour, Taylr, Teylor

TAYSHAWN (American) a combination of Taylor + Shawn.
Taysean, Tayshan, Tayshun, Tayson

TAYVON (American) a form of Tavian.
Tayvan, Tayvaughn, Tayven, Tayveon, Tayvin, Tayvohn, Taywon

TAZ (Arabic) shallow ornamental cup.
Tazz

TAZIO (Italian) a form of Tatius.

TEAGAN (Irish) an alternate form of Teague.
Teagen, Teagun, Teegan

TEAGUE (Irish) bard, poet.
Teag, Teagan, Teage, Teak, Tegan, Teige

TEARENCE (Latin) an alternate form of Terrence.
Tearance, Tearnce, Tearrance

TEARLACH (Scottish) a form of Charles.

TEARLE (English) stern, severe.

TEASDALE (English) river dweller. Geography: a river in England.

TEB (Spanish) a short form of Stephen.

TED (English) a short form of Edward, Edwin, Theodore.
Tedd, Tedek, Tedik, Tedson

TEDDY (English) a familiar form of Edward, Theodore.
Teddey, Teddie, Tedy

TEDMUND (English) protector of the land.
Tedman, Tedmond

TEDORIK (Polish) a form of Theodore.
Teodoor, Teodor, Teodorek

TEDRICK (American) a combination of Ted + Rick.
Teddrick, Tederick, Tedric

TEETONKA (Lakota) big lodge.

TEFERE (Ethiopian) seed.

TEGAN (Irish) an alternate form of Teague.
Teghan, Teigan, Tiegan

TEJ (Sanskrit) light; lustrous.

TEJAS (Sanskrit) sharp.

TEKLE (Ethiopian) plant.

TELEK (Polish) a form of Telford.

TELEM (Hebrew) mound; furrow.
Talmai, Tel

TELFORD (French) iron cutter.
Telek, Telfer, Telfor, Telfour

TELLER (English) storyteller.
Tell, Telly

TELLY (Greek) a familiar form of Teller, Theodore.

TELMO (English) tiller, cultivator.

TELUTCI (Moquelumnan) bear making dust as it runs.

TELVIN (American) a combination of the prefix Te + Melvin.
Tellvin, Telvan

TEM (Gypsy) country.

TEMAN (Hebrew) on the right side; southward.

TEMBO (Swahili) elephant.

TEMPEST (French) storm.

TEMPLE (Latin) sanctuary.

TEMPLETON (English) town near the temple.
Temp, Templeten

TENNANT (English) tenant, renter.
Tenant, Tennent

TENNESSEE (Cherokee) mighty warrior. Geography: a state in the American south.
Tennessee, Tennesy, Tennysee

TENNYSON (English) an alternate form of Dennison.
Tenney, Tenneyson, Tennie, Tennis, Tennison, Tenny, Tenson

TEO (Vietnamese) a form of Tom.

TEOBALDO (Italian, Spanish) a form of Theobald.

TEODORO (Italian, Spanish) a form of Theodore.
Teodore, Teodorico

TEPPO (French) a familiar form of Stephen.

TEQUAN (American) a combination of the prefix Te + Quan.
Tequinn, Tequon

TERANCE (Latin) an alternate form of Terrence.
Terriance

TERELL (German) an alternate form of Terrell.
Tarell, Tereall, Terel, Terelle, Tyrel

TEREMUN (Tiv) father's acceptance.

TERENCE (Latin) an alternate form of Terrence.
Teren, Teryn

TERENCIO (Spanish) a form of Terrence.

TERRAN (Latin) a short form of Terrance.
Teran, Teren, Terran, Terren

TERRANCE (Latin) an alternate form of Terrence.
Tarrance, Terran

TERRELL (German) thunder ruler.
Terell, Terrail, Terral, Terrale, Terrall, Terreal, Terrel, Terrelle, Terrill, Terryal, Terryel, Tirel, Tirrel, Tirrell, Turrell, Tyrel, Tyrell

TERRENCE (Latin) smooth.
Tarrance, Tearence, Terance, Terence, Terencio, Terrance, Terren, Terrin, Terry, Torrence, Tyreese

TERRICK (American) a combination of the prefix Te + Derrick.
Teric, Terick, Terik, Teriq, Terric, Terrik, Tirek, Tirik

TERRILL (German) an alternate form of Terrell.
Teriel, Teriell, Terril, Terryl, Terryll, Teryll, Teryl, Tyrill

TERRIN (Latin) a short form of Terrence.
Terin, Terrien, Terryn, Teryn, Tiren

TERRIS (Latin) son of Terry.

TERRON (American) a form of Tyrone.
Tereon, Terion, Terione, Teron, Terone, Terrion, Terrione, Terriyon, Terrone, Terronn, Terryon, Tiron

TERRY (English) a familiar form of Terrence. See also Keli.
Tarry, Terrey, Terri, Terrie, Tery

TERTIUS (Latin) third.

TESHAWN (American) a combination of the prefix Te + Shawn.
Tesean, Teshaun, Teshon

TEVA (Hebrew) nature.

TEVAN (American) an alternate form of Tevin.
Tevaughan, Tevaughn, Teven, Tevvan

TEVEL (Yiddish) a form of David.

TEVIN (American) a combination of the prefix Te + Kevin.
Teavin, Teivon, Tevan, Tevien, Tevinn, Tevon, Tevvin, Tevyn

TEVIS (Scottish) a form of Thomas.
Tevish

TEVON (American) an alternate form of Tevin.
Tevion, Tevohn, Tevone, Tevonne, Tevoun, Teyvon

TEWDOR (German) a form of Theodore.

TEX (American) from Texas.
Tejas

THABIT (Arabic) firm, strong.

THAD (Greek, Latin) a short form of Thaddeus.
Thadd, Thade, Thadee, Thady

THADDEUS (Greek) courageous. (Latin) praiser. Bible: one of the Twelve Apostles. See also Fadey.
Tad, Taddeo, Taddeus, Thaddis, Thadeaus, Tadzio, Thad, Thaddaeus, Thaddaus, Thaddeau, Thaddeaus, Thaddeo, Thaddeous, Thaddiaus, Thaddius, Thadeaou, Thadeous,

Thadeus, Thadieus, Thadious, Thadius, Thadus

THADY (Irish) praise.
Thaddy

THAI (Vietnamese) many, multiple.

THAMAN (Hindi) god; godlike. Religion: another name for the Hindu god Shiva.

THAN (Burma) million.
Tan, Thanh

THANE (English) attendant warrior.
Thain, Thaine, Thayne

THANG (Vietnamese) victorious.

THANH (Vietnamese) finished.

THANIEL (Hebrew) a short form of Nathaniel.

THANOS (Greek) nobleman; bear-man.
Athanasios, Thanasis

THATCHER (English) roof thatcher, repairer of roofs.
Thacher, Thatch, Thaxter

THAW (English) melting ice.

THAYER (French) nation's army.
Thay

THEL (English) upper story.

THENGA (Yao) bring him.

THEO (English) a short form of Theodore.

THEOBALD (German) people's prince. See also Dietbald.
Teobaldo, Thebault, Theòbault, Thibault, Tibalt, Tibold, Tiebold, Tiebout, Toiboid, Typald, Tybalt, Tvbault

THEODORE (Greek) gift of God. See also Feodor, Fyodor.
Téadóir, Teador, Ted, Teddy, Tedor, Tedorek, Tedorik, Telly, Teodomiro, Teodoro, Teodus, Teos, Tewdor, Theo, Theodor, Theódor, Theodors, Theodorus, Theodosios, Theodrekr, Tivadar, Todor, Tolek, Tudor

THEODORIC (German) ruler of the people. See also Dedrick, Derek, Dirk.
Teodorico, Thedric, Thedrick, Thierry, Till

THEOPHILUS (Greek) loved by God.
Teofil, Théophile, Theophlous, Theopolis

THERON (Greek) hunter.
Theran, Theren, Thereon, Therin, Therion, Therrin, Therron, Theryn, Theryon

THIAN (Vietnamese) smooth.
Thien

THIBAULT (French) a form of Theobald.
Thibaud, Thibaut

THIERRY (French) a form of Theodoric.
Theirry, Theory

THOM (English) a short form of Thomas.
Thomy

THOMA (German) a form of Thomas.

THOMAS (Greek, Aramaic) twin. Bible: one of the Twelve Apostles. See also Chuma, Foma, Maslin.
Tam, Tammy, Tavish, Tevis, Thom, Thoma, Thomason, Thomaz, Thomeson, Thomison, Thommas, Thompson, Thomson,

Tom, Toma, Tomas, Tomás, Tomasso, Tomcy, Tomey, Tomey, Tomi, Tommy, Toomas

THOMPSON (English) son of Thomas.
Thomason, Thomison, Thomsen, Thomson

THOR (Scandinavian) thunder. Mythology: the Norse god of thunder and war.
Thorin, Tor, Tyrus

THORALD (Scandinavian) Thor's follower.
Terrell, Terrill, Thorold, Torald

THORBERT (Scandinavian) Thor's brightness.
Torbert

THORBJORN (Scandinavian) Thor's bear.
Thorburn, Thurborn, Thurburn

THORGOOD (English) Thor is good.

THORLEIF (Scandinavian) Thor's beloved.
Thorlief

THORLEY (English) Thor's meadow.
Thorlea, Thorlee, Thorleigh, Thorly, Torley

THORNDIKE (English) thorny embankment.
Thorn, Thorndyck, Thorndyke, Thorne

THORNE (English) a short form of names beginning with "Thorn."
Thorn, Thornie, Thorny

THORNLEY (English) thorny meadow.
Thorley, Thorne, Thornlea, Thornleigh, Thornly

THORNTON (English) thorny
town.
Thorne

THORPE (English) village.
Thorp

THORWALD (Scandinavian)
Thor's forest.
Thorvald

THUC (Vietnamese) aware.

THURLOW (English) Thor's hill.
Thurlo

THURMOND (English) defended
by Thor.
Thormond, Thurmund

THURSTON (Scandinavian)
Thor's stone.
*Thorstan, Thorstein, Thorsten,
Thurstain, Thurstan, Thursten,
Torsten, Torston*

TIAGO (Spanish) a form of
Jacob.

TIBERIO (Italian) from the Tibor
River region.
*Tiberias, Tiberious, Tiberiu,
Tiberius, Tibius, Tyberious,
Tyberius, Tyberrius*

TIBOR (Hungarian) holy place.
Tiburcio

TICHAWANNA (Shona) we shall
see.

TICHO (Spanish) a short form
of Patrick.

TIELER (English) an alternate
form of Tyler.
Tielar, Tielor, Tielyr

TIENNOT (French) a form of
Stephen.
Tien

TIERNAN (Irish) lord.

TIERNEY (Irish) lordly.
Tiarnach, Tiernan

TIGE (English) a short form of
Tiger.
*Ti, Tig, Tighe, Ty, Tyg, Tyge,
Tygh, Tyghe*

TIGER (American) tiger; powerful and energetic.
Tige, Tigger, Tyger

TIIMU (Moquelumnan) cater-
piller coming out of the
ground.

TILDEN (English) tilled valley.
Tildon

TIKTU (Moquelumnan) bird
digging up potatoes.

TILFORD (English) prosperous
ford.

TILL (German) a short form of
Theodoric.
*Thilo, Til, Tillman, Tilman,
Tillmann, Tilson*

TILTON (English) prosperous
town.

TIM (Greek) a short form of
Timothy.
Timmie, Timmy

TIMIN (Arabic) born near the
sea. Mythology: sea serpent.

TIMMOTHY (Greek) an alter-
nate form of Timothy.
*Timmathy, Timmithy, Timmoty,
Timmthy*

TIMMY (Greek) a familiar form
of Timothy.
Timmie

TIMO (Finnish) a form of
Timothy.
Timio

TIMOFEY (Russian) a form of
Timothy.
Timofei, Timofej, Timofeo

TIMON (Greek) honorable.
History: a famous Greek
philosopher.

TIMOTEO (Portuguese,
Spanish) a form of Timothy.

TIMOTHY (Greek) honoring
God. See also Kimokeo.
*Tadhg, Taidgh, Tiege, Tim, Tima,
Timithy, Timka, Timkin,
Timmothy, Timmy, Timo,
Timofey, Timok, Timon,
Timontheo, Timonthy, Timót,
Timote, Timotei, Timoteo,
Timoteus, Timothé, Timothée,
Timotheo, Timotheos,
Timotheus, Timothey, Timothie,
Timthie, Tiomóid, Tisha,
Tomothy, Tymon, Tymothy*

TIMUR (Hebrew) an alternate
form of Tamar. (Russian)
conqueror.
Timour

TIN (Vietnamese) thinker.

TINO (Greek) a short form of
Augustine. (Spanish) venera-
ble, majestic. (Italian) small.
A familiar form of Antonio.
Tion

TINSLEY (English) fortified field.

TIQUAN (American) a combina-
tion of the prefix Ti + Quan.
*Tiquawn, Tiquine, Tiquon,
Tiquwan, Tiqwan*

TISHA (Russian) a form of
Timothy.
Tishka

TISHAWN (American) a combina-
tion of the prefix Ti + Shawn.
*Tishaan, Tishaun, Tishean,
Tishon, Tishun*

TITO (Italian) a form of Titus.
Titas, Titis, Titos

TITUS (Greek) giant. (Latin) hero. Bible: a recipient of one of Paul's New Testament letters.
Tite, Titek, Tito, Tytus

TIVON (Hebrew) nature lover.

TJ (American) a combination of the initials T. + J.
Teejay, Tj, T.J., T Jae, Tjayda

TOBAL (Spanish) a short form of Christopher.
Tabalito

TOBAR (Gypsy) road.

TOBI (Yoruba) great.

TOBIAS (Hebrew) God is good.
Tobia, Tobiah, Tobiás, Tobiath, Tobin, Tobit, Toby, Tobyas, Tuvya

TOBIN (Hebrew) an alternate form of Tobias.
Toben, Tobian, Tobyn, Tovin

TOBY (Hebrew) a familiar form of Tobias.
Tobbie, Tobby, Tobe, Tobee, Tobey, Tobie

TODD (English) fox.
Tod, Toddie, Toddy

TODOR (Basque, Russian) a form of Theodore.
Teodor, Todar, Todas, Todos

TOFT (English) small farm.

TOHON (Native American) cougar.

TOKALA (Dakota) fox.

TOLAND (English) owner of taxed land.
Tolan

TOLBERT (English) bright tax collector.

TOLLER (English) tax collector.

TOM (English) a short form of Tomas, Thomas.
Teo, Thom, Tommey, Tommie, Tommy

TOMA (Romanian) a form of Thomas.
Tomah

TOMAS (German) a form of Thomas.
Tom, Tomaisin, Tomaz, Tomcio, Tome, Tomek, Tomelis, Tomico, Tomik, Tomislaw, Tommas, Tomo, Tomson

TOMÁS (Irish, Spanish) a form of Thomas.
Tomas, Tómas, Tomasz

TOMASSO (Italian) a form of Thomas.
Tomaso, Tommaso

TOMBE (Kakwa) northerners. Geography: a village in northern Uganda.

TOMEY (Irish) a familiar form of Thomas.
Tome, Tomi, Tomie, Tomy

TOMI (Japanese) rich. (Hungarian) a form of Thomas.

TOMLIN (English) little Tom.
Tomkin, Tomlinson

TOMMIE (Hebrew) an alternate form of Tommy
Tommi

TOMMY (Hebrew) a familiar form of Thomas.
Tommie, Tomy

TONDA (Czech) a form of Tony.
Tonek

TONG (Vietnamese) fragrant.

TONI (Greek, German, Slavic) a form of Tony.
Tonee, Tonie, Tonio, Tonis, Tonnie

TONIO (Portuguese) a form of Tony. (Italian) a short form of Antonio.
Tono, Tonyo

TONY (Greek) flourishing. (Latin) praiseworthy. (English) a short form of Anthony. A familiar form of Remington.
Tonda, Tonek, Toney, Toni, Tonik, Tonio, Tonny

TOOANTUH (Cherokee) spring frog.

TOOMAS (Estonian) a form of Thomas.
Toomis, Tuomas, Tuomo

TOPHER (Greek) a short form of Christopher, Kristopher.
Tofer, Tophor

TOPO (Spanish) gopher.

TOPPER (English) hill.

TOR (Norwegian) thunder. (Tiv) royalty, king.
Thor

TORIAN (Irish) an alternate form of Torin.
Toran, Torean, Toriano, Toriaun, Torien, Torrian, Torrien, Torryan

TORIN (Irish) chief.
Thorfin, Thorstein, Torian, Iorion, Torrin, Toryn

TORKEL (Swedish) Thor's cauldron.

TORMEY (Irish) thunder spirit.
Tormé, Tormee

TORMOD (Scottish) north.

TORN (Irish) a short form of Torrence.
Toran

TORQUIL (Danish) Thor's kettle.
Torkel

TORR (English) tower.
Tory

TORRANCE (Irish) an alternate form of Torrence.
Torance

TORREN (Irish) a short form of Torrence.
Torehn, Toren

TORRENCE (Latin) an alternate form of Terrence. (Irish) knolls.
Tawrence, Toreence, Torence, Torenze, Torey, Torin, Torn, Torr, Torrance, Torren, Torreon, Torrin, Torry, Tory, Torynce, Tuarence, Turance

TORREY (English) an alternate form of Tory.
Toreey, Torie, Torre, Torri, Torrie, Torry

TORU (Japanese) sea.

TORY (English) familiar form of Torr, Torrence.
Torey, Tori, Torrey

TOSHI-SHITA (Japanese) junior.

TOVI (Hebrew) good.
Tov

TOWNLEY (English) town meadow.
Townlea, Townlee, Townleigh, Townlie, Townly

TOWNSEND (English) town's end.
Town, Townes, Towney, Townie, Townsen, Townshend, Towny

TRACE (Irish) an alternate form of Tracy.
Trayce

TRACEY (Irish) an alternate form of Tracy.
Traci

TRACY (Greek) harvester. (Latin) courageous. (Irish) battler.
Trace, Tracey, Tracie, Treacy

TRADER (English) well-trodden path; skilled worker.

TRAE (English) an alternate form of Trey.
Trai, Traie, Tre, Trea

TRAHERN (Welsh) strong as iron.
Traherne, Tray

TRAMAINE (Scottish) an alternate form of Tremaine, Tremayne.
Tramain, Traman, Tramane, Tramayne, Traymain, Traymon

TRAQUAN (American) a combination of Travis + Quan.
Traequan, Traqon, Traquon, Traqwan, Traqwaun, Trayquan, Trayquane, Trayqwon

TRASHAWN (American) a combination of Travis + Shawn.
Trasen, Trashaun, Trasean, Trashon, Trashone, Trashun, Trayshaun, Trayshawn

TRAUGOTT (German) God's truth.

TRAVARIS (French) an alternate form of Travers.
Travares, Travaress, Travarious, Travarius, Travarous, Travarus, Travauris, Traveress, Traverez, Traverus, Travoris, Travorus

TRAVELL (English) traveler.
Travail, Travale, Travel, Travelis, Travelle, Trevel, Trevell, Trevelle

TRAVEN (American) an alternate form of Trevon.
Travin, Travine, Trayven

TRAVERS (French) crossroads.
Travaris, Traver, Travis

TRAVION (American) an alternate form of Trevon.
Traveon, Travian, Travien, Travione, Travioun

TRAVIS (English) a form of Travers.
Travais, Travees, Traves, Traveus, Travious, Traviss, Travius, Travous, Travus, Travys, Trayvis, Trevais, Trevis

TRAVON (American) an alternate form of Trevon.
Traevon, Traivon, Travone, Travonn, Travonne

TRAY (English) an alternate form of Trey.
Traye

TRAYTON (English) town full of trees.
Trayten

TRAYVON (American) a combination of Tray + Von.
Trayveon, Trayvin, Trayvion, Trayvond, Trayvone, Trayvonne, Trayvyon

TREAVON (American) an alternate form of Trevon.
Treavan, Treavin, Treavion

TREDWAY (English) well-worn road.
Treadway

TREMAINE, Tremayne (Scottish) house of stone.

*Tramaine, Tremain, Tremane,
Treymaine, Trimaine*

TRENT (Latin) torrent, rapid
stream. (French) thirty. Geography: a city in northern Italy.
*Trente, Trentino, Trento,
Trentonio*

TRENTON (Latin) town by the
rapid stream. Geography: a
city in New Jersey.
*Trendon, Trendun, Trenten,
Trentin, Trentton, Trentyn,
Trinten, Trintin, Trinton*

TREQUAN (American) a combi-
nation of Trey + Quan.
*Trequanne, Trequaun, Trequian,
Trequon, Treqwon, Treyquane*

TRESHAWN (American) a com-
bination of Trey + Shawn.
*Treshaun, Treshon, Treshun,
Treysean, Treyshawn, Treyshon*

TRESTON (Welsh) an alternate
form of Tristan.
Trestan, Trestin, Trestton, Trestyn

TREV (Irish, Welsh) a short
form of Trevor.

TREVAUGHN (American) a com-
bination of Trey + Vaughn.
*Trevaughan, Trevaugn, Trevaun,
Trevaune, Trevaunn, Treyvaughn*

TREVELYAN (English) Elian's
homestead.

TREVIN (American) an alter-
nate form of Trevon.
*Trevian, Trevien, Trevine,
Trevinne, Trevyn, Treyvin*

TREVION (American) an alter-
nate form of Trevon.
*Trevione, Trevionne, Trevyon,
Treyveon, Treyvion*

TREVIS (English) an alternate
form of Travis.
Treves, Trevez, Treveze, Trevius

TREVON (American) a combina-
tion of Trey + Von.
*Traven, Travion, Travon, Tre,
Treavon, Trévan, Treveyon,
Trevin, Trevion, Trevohn,
Trevoine, Trévon, Trevone,
Trevonn, Trevonne, Treyvon*

TREVOR (Irish) prudent.
(Welsh) homestead.
*Travor, Treavor, Trebor, Trefor,
Trev, Trevar, Trevares,
Trevarious, Trevaris, Trevarius,
Trevaros, Trevarus, Trever,
Trevore, Trevores, Trevoris,
Trevorus, Trevour, Trevyr, Treyvor*

TREY (English) three; third.
Trae, Trai, Tray, Treye, Tri, Trie

TREYVON (American) an alter-
nate form of Trevon.
*Treyvan, Treyven, Treyvenn,
Treyvone, Treyvonn, Treyvun*

TRIGG (Scandinavian) trusty.

TRINI (Latin) a short form of
Trinity.

TRINITY (Latin) holy trinity.
Trenedy, Trini, Trinidy

TRIP, Tripp (English) traveler.

TRISTAN (Welsh) bold.
Literature: a knight in the
Arthurian legends who fell in
love with his uncle's wife.
*Treston, Tris, Trisan, Tristain,
Tristano, Tristen, Tristian,
Tristin, Triston, Tristyn, Trystan*

TRISTANO (Italian) a form of
Tristan.

TRISTEN (Welsh) an alternate
form of Tristan.
Trisden, Trissten

TRISTIN (Welsh) an alternate
form of Tristan.
Tristian, Tristinn

TRISTON (Welsh) an alternate
form of Tristan.

TRISTRAM (Welsh) sorrowful.
Literature: the title character
in Laurence Sterne's eigh-
teenth-century novel *Tristram
Shandy.*
Tristam

TRISTYN (Welsh) an alternate
form of Tristan.
Tristynne

TROT (English) trickling stream.

TROWBRIDGE (English) bridge
by the tree.

TROY (Irish) foot soldier.
(French) curly haired.
(English) water. See also Koi.
Troi, Troye, Troyton

TRUE (English) faithful, loyal.
Tru

TRUESDALE (English) faithful
one's homestead.

TRUITT (English) little and
honest.
Truett

TRUMAN (English) honest.
History: Harry S Truman was
the thirty-third U.S. president.
*Trueman, Trumain, Trumaine,
Trumann*

TRUMBLE (English) strong; bold.
Trumball, Trumbell, Trumbull

TRUSTIN (English) trustworthy.
Trustan, Trusten, Truston

TRYGVE (Norwegian) brave
victor.

TRYSTAN (Welsh) an alternate form of Tristan.
Tryistan, Trysten, Trystian, Trystin, Trystn, Tryston, Trystyn

TSALANI (Ngoni) good-bye.

TSE (Ewe) younger of twins.

TU (Vietnamese) tree.

TUACO (Ghanian) eleventh-born.

TUAN (Vietnamese) goes smoothly.

TUCKER (English) fuller, tucker of cloth.
Tuck, Tuckie, Tucky, Tuckyr

TUDOR (Welsh) a form of Theodore. History: an English dynasty.
Todor

TUG (Scandinavian) draw, pull.
Tugg

TUKETU (Moquelumnan) bear making dust as it runs.

TUKULI (Moquelumnan) caterpillar crawling down a tree.

TULIO (Italian, Spanish) lively.
Tullio

TULLIS (Latin) title, rank.
Tullius, Tullos, Tully

TULLY (Latin) a familiar form of Tullis. (Irish) at peace with God.
Tull, Tulley, Tullie, Tullio

TUMAINI (Mwera) hope.

TUMU (Moquelumnan) deer thinking about eating wild onions

TUNG (Vietnamese) stately, dignified. (Chinese) everyone.

TUNGAR (Sanskrit) high; lofty.

TUPI (Moquelumnan) pulled up.

TUPPER (English) ram raiser.

TURI (Spanish) a short form of Arthur.
Ture

TURK (English) from Turkey.

TURNER (Latin) lathe worker; woodworker.

TURPIN (Scandinavian) Finn named after Thor.

TUT (Arabic) strong and courageous. History: a short form of Tutankhamen, an Egyptian pharoah.
Tutt

TUTU (Spanish) a familiar form of Justin.

TUVYA (Hebrew) an alternate form of Tobias.
Tevya, Tuvia, Tuviah

TUWILE (Mwera) death is inevitable.

TUYEN (Vietnamese) angel.

TWAIN (English) divided in two. Literature: Mark Twain (whose real name was Samuel Clemens) was one of the most prominent nineteenth-century American writers.
Tawine, Twaine, Twan, Twane, Tway, Twayn, Twayne

TWIA (Fante) born after twins.

TWITCHELL (English) narrow passage.
Twytchell

TWYFORD (English) double river crossing.

TXOMIN (Basque) like the Lord.

TY (English) a short form of Tyler, Tyrone, Tyrus.
Tye

TYEE (Native American) chief.

TYGER (English) a form of Tiger.
Tige, Tyg, Tygar

TYLAR (English) an alternate form of Tyler.
Tyelar, Tylarr

TYLER (English) tile maker.
Tieler, Tiler, Ty, Tyel, Tyeler, Tyelor, Tyhler, Tylar, Tyle, Tylee, Tylere, Tyller, Tylor, Tylyr

TYLOR (English) an alternate form of Tyler.
Tylour

TYMON (Polish) a form of Timothy.
Tymain, Tymaine, Tymane, Tymeik, Tymek, Tymen

TYMOTHY (English) a form of Timothy.
Tymithy, Tymmothy, Tymoteusz, Tymothee, Timothi

TYNAN (Irish) dark.
Ty

TYNEK (Czech) a form of Martin.
Tynko

TYQUAN (American) a combination of Ty + Quan.
Tykwan, Tykwane, Tykwon, Tyquaan, Tyquane, Tyquann, Tyquine, Tyquinn, Tyquon, Tyquone, Tyquwon, Tyqwan

TYRAN (American) a form of Tyrone.
Tyraine, Tyrane

TYREE (Scottish) island dweller. Geography: Tiree is an island

off the west coast of
Scotland.
*Tyra, Tyrae, Tyrai, Tyray, Tyre,
Tyrea, Tyrée*

TYREESE (American) a form of
Terrence.
*Tyreas, Tyrease, Tyrece,
Tyreece, Tyreice, Tyres, Tyrese,
Tyresse, Tyrez, Tyreze, Tyrice,
Tyriece, Tyriese*

TYREL, Tyrell (American) forms
of Terrell.
Tyrelle, Tyrrel, Tyrrell

TYRICK (American) a combina-
tion of Ty + Rick.
*Tyreck, Tyreek, Tyreik, Tyrek,
Tyreke, Tyric, Tyriek, Tyrik, Tyriq,
Tyrique*

TYRIN (American) a form of
Tyrone.
Tyrinn, Tyrion, Tyrrin, Tyryn

TYRON (American) a form of
Tyrone.
Tyrohn, Tyronn, Tyronna, Tyronne

TYRONE (Greek) sovereign.
(Irish) land of Owen
*Tayron, Tayrone, Teirone, Terron,
Ty, Tyerone, Tyhrone, Tyran,
Tyrin, Tyron, Tyroney, Tyronne,
Tyroon, Tyroun*

TYRUS (English) a form of Thor.
Ty, Tyruss, Tyryss

TYSHAWN (American) a combi-
nation of Ty + Shawn.
*Tyshan, Tyshaun, Tyshauwn,
Tyshian, Tyshinn, Tyshion,
Tyshon, Tyshone, Tyshonne,
Tyshun, Tyshunn, Tyshyn*

TYSON (French) son of Ty.
*Tison, Tiszon, Tyce, Tycen,
Tyesn, Tyeson, Tysen, Tysie,
Tysin, Tysne, Tysone*

TYTUS (Polish) a form of Titus.
Tyus

TYVON (American) a combina-
tion of Ty + Von.
*Tyvan, Tyvin, Tyvinn, Tyvone,
Tyvonne*

TYWAN (Chinese) an alternate
form of Taiwan.
*Tywain, Tywaine, Tywane,
Tywann, Tywaun, Tywen, Tywon,
Tywone, Tywonne*

TZADOK (Hebrew) righteous.
Tzadik, Zadok

TZION (Hebrew) sign from God.
Zion

TZURIEL (Hebrew) God is my
rock.
Tzuriya

TZVI (Hebrew) deer.
Tzevi, Zevi

UAINE (Irish) a form of Owen.

UBADAH (Arabic) serves God.

UBAID (Arabic) faithful.

UBERTO (Italian) a form of
Hubert.

UCHE (Ibo) thought.

UDAY (Sanskrit) to rise.

UDELL (English) yew-tree valley.
Dell, Eudel, Udale, Udall, Yudell

UDIT (Sanskrit) grown; shining.

UDO (Japanese) ginseng plant.
(German) a short form of
Udolf.

UDOLF (English) prosperous
wolf.
Udo, Udolfo, Udolph

UGO (Italian) an alternate form
of Hugh, Hugo.

UGUTZ (Basque) a form of
John. Religion: name honoring John the Baptist.

UILLIAM (Irish) a form of
William.
Uileog, Uilleam, Ulick

UINSEANN (Irish) a form of
Vincent.

UISTEAN (Irish) intelligent.
Uisdean

UJA (Sanskrit) growing.

UKU (Hawaiian) flea, insect;
skilled ukulele player.

ULAN (African) first-born twin.

ULBRECHT (German) an alternate form of Albert.

ULF (German) wolf.

ULFRED (German) peaceful wolf.

ULGER (German) warring wolf.

ULISES (Latin) an alternate
form of Ulysses.
Ulishes, Ulisse, Ulisses

ULLOCK (German) sporting wolf.

ULMER (English) famous wolf.
Ullmar, Ulmar

ULMO (German) from Ulm,
Germany.

ULRIC (German) an alternate form of Ulrich.
Ullric

ULRICH (German) wolf ruler; ruler of all. See also Alaric.
Uli, Ull, Ulric, Ulrick, Ulrik, Ulrike, Ulu, Ulz, Uwe

ULTMAN (Hindi) god; godlike. Religion: another name for the Hindu god Shiva.

ULYSES (Latin) an alternate form of Ulysses.
Ulysee, Ulysees

ULYSSES (Latin) wrathful. A form of Odysseus.
Eulises, Ulick, Ulises, Ulyses, Ulysse, Ulyssees, Ulysses, Ulyssius

UMANG (Sanskrit) enthusiastic.
Umanga

UMAR (Arabic) an alternate form of Omar.
Umair, Umarr, Umayr, Umer

UMBERTO (Italian) a form of Humbert.
Uberto

UMI (Yao) life.

UMIT (Turkish) hope.

UNAI (Basque) shepherd.
Una

UNER (Turkish) famous.

UNIKA (Lomwe) brighten.

UNIQUE (Latin) only, unique.
Uneek, Unek, Unikque, Uniqué, Unyque

UNWIN (English) nonfriend.
Unwinn, Unwyn

UPSHAW (English) upper wooded area.

UPTON (English) upper town.

UPWOOD (English) upper forest.

URBAN (Latin) city dweller; courteous.
Urbain, Urbaine, Urbane, Urbano, Urbanus, Urvan, Urvane

URBANE (English) a form of Urban.

URBANO (Italian) a form of Urban.

URI (Hebrew) a short form of Uriah.
Urie

URIAH (Hebrew) my light. Bible: the husband of Bathsheba and a captain in David's army. See also Yuri.
Uri, Uria, Urias, Urijah

URIAN (Greek) heaven.
Urihaan

URIEL (Hebrew) God is my light.
Urie

URSON (French) a form of Orson.
Ursan, Ursus

URTZI (Basque) sky.

USAMAH (Arabic) like a lion.
Usama

USENI (Yao) tell me.
Usene, Usenet

USI (Yao) smoke.

USTIN (Russian) a form of Justin.

UTATCI (Moquelumnan) bear scratching itself.

UTHMAN (Arabic) companion of the Prophet.
Usman, Uthmaan

UTTAM (Sanskrit) best.

UWE (German) a familiar form of Ulrich.

UZI (Hebrew) my strength.
Uzzia

UZIEL (Hebrew) God is my strength; mighty force.
Uzie, Uzziah, Uzziel

UZOMA (Nigerian) born during a journey.

UZUMATI (Moquelumnan) grizzly bear.

VACHEL (French) small cow.
Vache, Vachell

VACLAV (Czech) wreath of glory.
Vasek

VADIN (Hindi) speaker.
Vaden

VAIL (English) valley.
Vaile, Vaill, Vale, Valle

VAL (Latin) a short form of Valentin.

VALBORG (Swedish) mighty mountain.

VALDEMAR (Swedish) famous ruler.

VALENTIN (Latin) strong; healthy.
Val, Valencio, Valenté, Valentijn, Valentine, Valentino, Valenton, Valentyn, Velentino

VALENTINO (Italian) a form of Valentin.

VALERIAN (Latin) strong; healthy.
Valeriano, Valerii, Valerio, Valeryn

VALERII (Russian) a form of Valerian.
Valera, Valerie, Valerij, Valerik, Valeriy, Valery

VALFRID (Swedish) strong peace.

VALIN (Hindi) an alternate form of Balin. Mythology: a tyrannical monkey king.

VALLIS (French) from Wales, England.
Valis

VALTER (Lithuanian, Swedish) a form of Walter.
Valters, Valther, Valtr, Vanda

VAN (Dutch) a short form of Vandyke.
Vander, Vane, Vann, Vanno

VANCE (English) thresher.

VANDA (Lithuanian) a form of Walter.
Vander

VANDYKE (Dutch) dyke.
Van

VANYA (Russian) a familiar form of Ivan.
Vanechka, Vanek, Vanja, Vanka, Vanusha, Wanya

VARDON (French) green knoll.
Vardaan, Varden, Verdan, Verdon, Verdun

VARIAN (Latin) variable.

VARICK (German) protecting ruler.
Varak, Varek, Warrick

VARTAN (Armenian) rose producer; rose giver.

VARUN (Hindi) rain god.
Varron

VASANT (Sanskrit) spring.
Vasanth

VASHAWN (American) a combination of the prefix Va + Shawn.
Vashae, Vashan, Vashann, Vashaun, Vashawnn, Vashon, Vashun, Vishon

VASILIS (Greek) an alternate form of Basil.
Vas, Vasaya, Vaselios, Vashon, Vasil, Vasile, Vasileior, Vasileios, Vasilios, Vasilius, Vasilos, Vasilus, Vasily, Vassilios, Vasylko, Vasyltso, Vazul

VASILY (Russian) a form of Vasilis.
Vasilek, Vasili, Vasilii, Vasilije, Vasilik, Vasiliy, Vassili, Vassilij, Vasya, Vasyenka

VASIN (Hindi) ruler, lord.

VASU (Sanskrit) wealth.

VASYL (German, Slavic) a form of William.
Vasos, Vassily, Vassos, Vasya, Vasyuta, VaVaska, Wassily

VAUGHN (Welsh) small.
Vaughan, Vaughen, Vaun, Vaune, Von, Voughn

VEASNA (Cambodian) lucky.

VED (Sanskrit) sacred knowledge.

VEDIE (Latin) sight.

VEER (Sanskrit) brave.

VEGARD (Norwegian) sanctuary; protection.

VELVEL (Yiddish) wolf.

VENCEL (Hungarian) a short form of Wenceslaus.
Venci, Vencie

VENEDICTOS (Greek) a form of Benedict.
Venedict, Venediktos, Venka, Venya

VENIAMIN (Bulgarian) a form of Benjamin.
Venyamin, Verniamin

VENKAT (Hindi) god; godlike. Religion: another name for the Hindu god Shiva.

VENYA (Russian) a familiar form of Benedict.
Venedict, Venka

VERE (Latin, French) true.

VERED (Hebrew) rose.

VERGIL (Latin) an alternate form of Virgil.
Verge

VERN (Latin) a short form of Vernon.
Verna, Vernal, Verne, Verneal, Vernel, Vernell, Vernelle, Vernial, Vernine, Vernis, Vernol

VERNADOS (German) courage of the bear.

VERNER (German) defending army.
Varner

VERNEY (French) alder grove.
Vernie

VERNON (Latin) springlike; youthful.
Vern, Varnan, Vernen, Verney, Vernin

VERRILL (German) masculine. (French) loyal.
Verill, Verrall, Verrell, Verroll, Veryl

VIAN (English) full of life. A masculine short form of Vivian.

VIC (Latin) a short form of Victor.
Vick, Vicken, Vickenson

VICENTE (Spanish) a form of Vincent.
Vicent, Visente

VICENZO (Italian) a form of Vincent.

VICTOIR (French) a form of Victor.

VICTOR (Latin) victor, conqueror.
Vic, Victa, Victer, Victoir, Victoriano, Victorien, Victorin, Victorio, Viktor, Vitin, Vittorio, Vitya, Wikoli, Wiktor, Witek

VICTORIO (Spanish) a form of Victor.
Victorino

VIDAL (Spanish) a form of Vitas.
Vida, Vidale, Vidall, Videll

VIDAR (Norwegian) tree warrior.

VIDOR (Hungarian) cheerful.

VIDUR (Hindi) wise.

VIHO (Cheyenne) chief.

VIJAY (Hindi) victorious. Religion: another name for the Hindu god Shiva.

VIKAS (Hindi) growing.
Vikash, Vikesh

VIKRAM (Hindi) valorous.
Vikrum

VIKRANT (Hindi) powerful.
Vikran

VIKTOR (German, Hungarian, Russian) a form of Victor.
Viktoras, Viktors

VILHELM (German) a form of William.
Vilhelms, Vilho, Vilis, Viljo, Villem

VILI (Hungarian) a short form of William.
Villy, Vilmos

VILIAM (Czech) a form of William.
Vila, Vilek, Vilém, Viliami, Viliamu, Vilko, Vilous

VILJO (Finnish) a form of William.

VILLE (Swedish) a short form of William.

VIMAL (Hindi) pure.

VIN (Latin) a short form of Vincent.
Vinn

VINAY (Hindi) polite.

VINCE (English) a short form of Vincent.
Vence, Vint

VINCENT (Latin) victor, conqueror. See also Binkentios, Binky.
Uinseann, Vencent, Vicente, Vicenzo, Vikent, Vikenti, Vikesha, Vin, Vince, Vincence, Vincens, Vincente, Vincentius, Vincents, Vincenty, Vincenzo,

Vinci, Vinclen, Vinclent, Vinciente, Vincint, Vinny, Vinsent, Vinsint, Wincent

VINCENTE (Spanish) a form of Vincent.
Vencente

VINCENZO (Italian) a form of Vincent.
Vincenz, Vincenza, Vincenzio, Vinchenzo, Vinzenz

VINCI (Hungarian, Italian) a familiar form of Vincent.
Vinci, Vinco, Vincze

VINNY (English) a familiar form of Calvin, Melvin, Vincent.
Vinnee, Vinney, Vinni, Vinnie

VINOD (Hindi) happy, joyful.
Vinodh, Vinood

VINSON (English) son of Vincent.
Vinnis

VIPUL (Hindi) plentiful.

VIRAJ (Hindi) resplendent.

VIRAT (Hindi) very big.

VIRGIL (Latin) rod bearer, staff bearer. Literature: a Roman poet best known for his epic *Aenid*.
Vergil, Virge, Virgial, Virgie, Virgilio

VIRGILIO (Spanish) a form of Virgil.
Virjilio

VIROTE (Tai) strong, powerful.

VISHAL (Hindi) huge; great.
Vishaal

VISHNU (Hindi) protector.

VITAS (Latin) alive, vital.
Vidal, Vitus

VITO (Latin) a short form of Vittorio.
Veit, Vidal, Vital, Vitale, Vitalis, Vitas, Vitin, Vitis, Vitus, Vitya, Vytas

VITTORIO (Italian) a form of Victor.
Vito, Vitor, Vitorio, Vittore, Vittorios

VITYA (Russian) a form of Victor.
Vitenka, Vitka

VIVEK (Hindi) wisdom.
Vivekinan

VLADIMIR (Russian) famous prince. See also Dima, Waldemar, Walter.
Bladimir, Vimka, Vlad, Vladamir, Vladik, Vladimar, Vladimeer, Vladimer, Vladimere, Vladimire, Vladimyr, Vladjimir, Vladka, Vladko, Vladlen, Vladmir, Volodimir, Volodya, Volya, Vova, Wladimir

VLADISLAV (Slavic) glorious ruler. See also Slava.
Vladik, Vladya, Vlas, Vlasislava, Vyacheslav, Wladislav

VLAS (Russian) a short form of Vladislav.

VOLKER (German) people's guard.
Folke

VOLNEY (German) national spirit.

VON (German) a short form of many German names.

VOVA (Russian) a form of Walter.
Vovka

VUAI (Swahili) savior.

VYACHESLAV (Russian) a form of Vladislav. See also Slava.

WABAN (Chippewa) white.
Wabon

WADE (English) ford; river crossing.
Wad, Wadesworth, Wadi, Wadie, Waed, Waid, Waide, Wayde, Waydell, Whaid

WADLEY (English) ford meadow.
Wadleigh, Wadly

WADSWORTH (English) village near the ford.
Waddsworth

WAGNER (German) wagoner, wagon maker. Music: Richard Wagner was a famous German composer.
Waggoner

WAHID (Arabic) single; exclusively unequaled.
Waheed

WAHKAN (Lakota) sacred.

WAHKOOWAH (Lakota) charging.

WAIN (English) a short form of Wainwright. An alternate form of Wayne.

WAINWRIGHT (English) wagon maker.
Wain, Wainright, Wayne, Wayneright, Waynewright, Waynright, Wright

WAITE (English) watchman.
Waitman, Waiton, Waits, Wayte

WAKEFIELD (English) wet field.
Field, Wake

WAKELY (English) wet meadow.

WAKEMAN (English) watchman
Wake

WAKIZA (Native American) determined warrior.

WALCOTT (English) cottage by the wall.
Wallcot, Wallcott, Wolcott

WALDEMAR (German) powerful; famous. See also Vladimir.
Valdemar, Waldermar, Waldo

WALDEN (English) wooded valley. Literature: Henry David Thoreau made Walden Pond famous with his book *Walden*.
Waldi, Waldo, Waldon, Welti

WALDO (German) a familiar form of Oswald, Waldemar, Walden.
Wald, Waldy

WALDRON (English) ruler.

WALEED (Arabic) newborn.
Waled, Walid

WALERIAN (Polish) strong; brave.

WALES (English) from Wales, England.
Wael, Wail, Wali, Walie, Waly

WALFORD (English) Welshman's ford.

WALFRED (German) peaceful ruler.
Walfredo, Walfried

WALI (Arabic) all-governing.

WALKER (English) cloth walker; cloth cleaner.
Wallie, Wally

WALLACE (English) from Wales.
Wallach, Wallas, Wallie, Wallis, Wally, Walsh, Welsh

WALLACH (German) a form of Wallace.
Wallache

WALLER (German) powerful. (English) wall maker.

WALLY (English) a familiar form of Walter.
Walli, Wallie

WALMOND (German) mighty ruler.

WALSH (English) an alternate form of Wallace.
Welch, Welsh

WALT (English) a short form of Walter, Walton.
Waltey, Waltli, Walty

WALTER (German) army ruler, general. (English) woodsman. See also Gautier, Gualberto, Gualtiero, Gutierre, Ladislav, Vladimir.
Valter, Vanda, Vova, Walder, Wally, Walt, Waltli, Walther, Waltr, Wat, Waterio, Watkins, Watson, Wualter

WALTHER (German) an alternate form of Walter.

WALTON (English) walled town.
Walt

WALTR (Czech) a form of Walter.

WALWORTH (English) fenced-in farm.

WALWYN (English) Welsh friend.
Walwin, Walwinn, Walwynn, Walwynne, Welwyn

WAMBLEE (Lakota) eagle.

WANG (Chinese) hope; wish.

WANIKIYA (Lakota) savior.

WANYA (Russian) an alternate form of Vanya.
Wanyai

WAPI (Native American) lucky.

WARBURTON (English) fortified town.

WARD (English) watchman, guardian.
Warde, Warden, Worden

WARDELL (English) watchman's hill.

WARDLEY (English) watchman's meadow.
Wardlea, Wardleigh

WARE (English) wary, cautious.

WARFIELD (English) field near the weir; fishtrap.

WARFORD (English) ford near the weir; fishtrap.

WARLEY (English) meadow near the weir; fishtrap.

WARNER (German) armed defender. (French) park keeper.
Werner

WARREN (German) general; warden; rabbit hutch.
Ware, Waring, Warrenson, Warrin, Warriner, Worrin

WARTON (English) town near the weir; fishtrap.

WARWICK (English) buildings near the weir; fishtrap.
Warick, Warrick

WASHBURN (English) overflowing river.

WASHINGTON (English) town near water. History: George Washington was the first U.S. president.
Wash

WASILI (Russian) a form of Basil.
Wasyl

WASIM (Arabic) graceful; good looking.
Waseem, Wasseem, Wassim

WATENDE (Nyakyusa) there will be revenge.

WATERIO (Spanish) a form of Walter.
Gualtiero

WATFORD (English) wattle ford; dam made of twigs and sticks.

WATKINS (English) son of Walter.
Watkin

WATSON (English) son of Walter.
Wathson, Whatson

WAVERLY (English) quaking aspen-tree meadow.
Waverlee, Waverley

WAYLAND (English) an alternate form of Waylon.
Weiland, Weyland

WAYLON (English) land by the road.
Wallen, Walon, Way, Waylan, Wayland, Waylen, Waylin, Weylin

WAYMAN (English) road man; traveler.
Waymon

WAYNE (English) wagon maker. A short form of Wainwright.
Wain, Wanye, Wayn, Waynell, Waynne, Wene, Whayne

WAZIR (Arabic) minister.

WEBB (English) weaver.
Web, Weeb

WEBER (German) weaver.
Webber, Webner

WEBLEY (English) weaver's meadow.
Webbley, Webbly, Webly

WEBSTER (English) weaver.

WEDDEL (English) valley near the ford.

WEI-QUO (Chinese) ruler of the country.
Wei

WELBORNE (English) spring-fed stream.
Welborn, Welbourne, Welburn, Wellborn, Wellborne, Wellbourn, Wellburn

WELBY (German) farm near the well.
Welbey, Welbie, Wellbey, Wellby

WELDON (English) hill near the well.
Weldan

WELFEL (Yiddish) a form of William.
Welvel

WELFORD (English) ford near the well.

WELLS (English) springs.
Welles

WELSH (English) an alternate form of Wallace, Walsh.
Welch

WELTON (English) town near the well.

WEMILAT (Native American) all give to him.

WEMILO (Native American) all speak to him.

WEN (Gypsy) born in winter.

WENCESLAUS (Slavic) wreath of honor. Music: "Good King Wenceslaus" is a popular Christmas carol.
Vencel, Wenceslao, Wenceslas, Wenzel, Wenzell, Wiencyslaw

WENDELL (German) wanderer. (English) good dale, good valley.
Wandale, Wendall, Wendel, Wendle, Wendy

WENE (Hawaiian) a form of Wayne.

WENFORD (English) white ford.
Wynford

WENTWORTH (English) pale man's settlement.

WENUTU (Native American) clear sky.

WERNER (English) a form of Warner.
Wernhar, Wernher

WES (English) a short form of Wesley.
Wess

WESH (Gypsy) woods.

WESLEY (English) western meadow.
Wes, Weseley, Wesle, Weslee, Wesleyan, Weslie, Wesly, Wessley, Westleigh, Westley, Wezley

WEST (English) west.

WESTBROOK (English) western brook.
Brook, West, Westbrooke

WESTBY (English) western farmstead.

WESTCOTT (English) western cottage.
Wescot, Wescott, Westcot

WESTLEY (English) an alternate form of Wesley.
Westlee, Westly

WESTON (English) western town.
West, Westen, Westin

WETHERBY (English) wether-sheep farm.
Weatherbey, Weatherbie, Weatherby, Wetherbey, Wetherbie

WETHERELL (English) wether-sheep corner.

WETHERLY (English) wether-sheep meadow.

WEYLIN (English) an alternate form of Waylon.
Weylan, Weylyn

WHALLEY (English) woods near a hill.
Whaley

WHARTON (English) town on the bank of a lake.
Warton

WHEATLEY (English) wheat field.
Whatley, Wheatlea, Wheatleigh, Wheatly

WHEATON (English) wheat town.

WHEELER (English) wheel maker; wagon driver.

WHISTLER (English) whistler, piper.

WHIT (English) a short form of Whitman, Whitney.
Whitt, Whyt, Whyte, Wit, Witt

WHITBY (English) white house.

WHITCOMB (English) white valley.
Whitcombe, Whitcumb

WHITELAW (English) small hill.
Whitlaw

WHITEY (English) white skinned; white haired.

WHITFIELD (English) white field.

WHITFORD (English) white ford.

WHITLEY (English) white meadow.
Whitlea, Whitlee, Whitleigh

WHITMAN (English) white-haired man.
Whit

WHITMORE (English) white moor.
Whitmoor, Whittemore, Witmore, Wittemore

WHITNEY (English) white island; white water.
Whit, Whittney, Widney, Widny

WHITTAKER (English) white field.
Whitacker, Whitaker, Whitmaker

WICASA (Dakota) man.

WICENT (Polish) a form of Vincent.
Wicek, Wicus

WICHADO (Native American) willing.

WICKHAM (English) village enclosure.
Wick

WICKLEY (English) village meadow.
Wilcley

WID (English) wide.

WIES (German) renowned warrior.

WIKOLI (Hawaiian) a form of Victor.

WIKTOR (Polish) a form of Victor.

WILANU (Moquelumnan) pouring water on flour.

WILBERT (German) brilliant; resolute.
Wilberto, Wilburt

WILBUR (English) wall fortification; bright willows.
Wilber, Wilburn, Wilburt, Willbur, Wilver

WILDER (English) wilderness, wild.
Wylder

WILDON (English) wooded hill.
Wilden, Willdon

WILE (Hawaiian) a form of Willie.

WILEY (English) willow meadow; Will's meadow.
Whiley, Wildy, Willey, Wylie

WILFORD (English) willow-tree ford.
Wilferd

WILFRED (German) determined peacemaker.
Wilferd, Wilfredo, Wilfrid, Wilfride, Wilfried, Wilfryd, Will, Willfred, Willfried, Willie, Willy

WILFREDO (Spanish) a form of Wilfred.
Fredo, Wifredo, Wilfrido, Willfredo

WILHELM (German) determined guardian. The original form of William.
Wilhelmus, Willem

WILIAMA (Hawaiian) a form of William.
Pila, Wile

WILKIE (English) a familiar form of Wilkins.
Wikie, Wilke

WILKINS (English) William's kin.
Wilkens, Wilkes, Wilkie, Wilkin, Wilks, Willkes, Willkins

WILKINSON (English) son of little William.
Wilkenson, Willkinson

WILL (English) a short form of William.
Wil, Wilm, Wim

WILLARD (German) determined and brave.
Williard

WILLEM (German) a form of William.
Willim

WILLIAM (English) determined guardian. See also Gilamu, Guglielmo, Guilherme, Guillaume, Guillermo, Gwilym, Liam, Uilliam, Wilhelm.
Bill, Billy, Vasyl, Vilhelm, Vili, Viliam, Viljo, Ville, Villiam, Welfel, Wilek, Wiliam, Wiliama, Wiliame, Wiliame, Will, Willaim, Willam, Willeam, Willem, Williams, Willie, Willil, Willis, Willium, Williw, Willyam, Wim

WILLIAMS (German) son of William.
Wilams, Willaims, Williamson, Wuliams

WILLIE (German) a familiar form of William.
Wile, Wille, Willi, Willia, Willy

WILLIS (German) son of Willie.
Willice, Wills, Willus, Wyllis

WILLOUGHBY (English) willow farm.
Willoughbey, Willoughbie

WILLS (English) son of Will.

WILLY (German) an alternate form of Willie.
Wilkey, Wily

WILMER (German) determined and famous.
Willimar, Willmer, Wilm, Wilmar, Wylmar, Wylmer

WILMOT (Teutonic) resolute spirit.
Willmont, Willmot, Wilm, Wilmont

WILNY (Native American) eagle singing while flying.

WILSON (English) son of Will.
Wilkinson, Willson, Wilsen, Wolson

WILT (English) a short form of Wilton.

WILTON (English) farm by the spring.
Will, Wilt

WILU (Moquelumnan) chicken hawk squawking.

WIN (Cambodian) bright. (English) a short form of Winston and names ending in "win."
Winn, Winnie, Winny

WINCENT (Polish) a form of Vincent.
Wicek, Wicenty, Wicus, Wince, Wincenty

WINCHELL (English) bend in the road; bend in the land.

WINDSOR (English) riverbank with a winch. History: the surname of the British royal family.
Wincer, Winsor, Wyndsor

WINFIELD (English) friendly field.
Field, Winfred, Winfrey, Winifield, Winnfield, Wynfield, Wynnfield

WINFRIED (German) friend of peace.

WING (Chinese) glory.
Wing-Chiu, Wing-Kit

WINGATE (English) winding gate.

WINGI (Native American) willing.

WINSLOW (English) friend's hill.

WINSTON (English) friendly town; victory town.
Win, Winsten, Winstin, Winstonn, Winton, Wynstan, Wynston

WINTER (English) born in winter.
Winterford, Wynter

WINTHROP (English) victory at the crossroads.

WINTON (English) an alternate form of Winston.
Wynten, Wynton

WINWARD (English) friend's guardian; friend's forest.

WIT (Polish) life. (English) an alternate form of Whit. (Flemish) a short form of DeWitt.
Witt, Wittie, Witty

WITEK (Polish) a form of Victor.

WITHA (Arabic) handsome.

WITTER (English) wise warrior.

WITTON (English) wise man's estate.

WLADISLAV (Polish) a form of Vladislav.
Wladislaw

WOLCOTT (English) cottage in the woods.

WOLF (German, English) a short form of Wolfe, Wolfgang.
Wolff, Wolfie, Wolfy

WOLFE (English) wolf.
Wolf, Woolf

WOLFGANG (German) wolf quarrel. Music: Wolfgang Amadeus Mozart was a famous eighteenth-century Austrian composer.
Wolf, Wolfegang, Wolfgans

WOOD (English) a short form of Elwood, Garwood, Woodrow.
Woody

WOODFIELD (English) forest meadow.

WOODFORD (English) ford through the forest.

WOODROW (English) passage in the woods. History: Thomas Woodrow Wilson was the twenty-eighth U.S. president.
Wood, Woodman, Woodroe, Woody

WOODRUFF (English) forest ranger.

WOODSON (English) son of Wood.
Woods, Woodsen

WOODWARD (English) forest warden.
Woodard

WOODVILLE (English) town at the edge of the woods.

WOODY (American) a familiar form of Elwood, Garwood, Woodrow.
Wooddy, Woodie

WOOLSEY (English) victorious wolf.

WORCESTER (English) forest army camp.

WORDSWORTH (English) wolf-guardian's farm. Literature: William Wordsworth was a famous English poet.
Worth

WORIE (Ibo) born on market day.

WORTH (English) a short form of Woodsworth.
Worthey, Worthington, Worthy

WORTON (English) farm town.

WOUTER (German) powerful warrior.

WRANGLE (American) an alternate form of Rangle.
Wrangler

WRAY (Scandinavian) corner property. (English) crooked.
Wreh

WREN (Welsh) chief, ruler. (English) wren.

WRIGHT (English) a short form of Wainwright.

WRISLEY (English) an alternate form of Risley.
Wrisee, Wrislie, Wrisly

WRISTON (English) an alternate form of Riston.
Wryston

WULITON (Native American) will do well.

WUNAND (Native American) God is good.

WUYI (Moquelumnan) turkey vulture flying.

WYATT (French) little warrior.
Wiatt, Wyat, Wyatte, Wye, Wyeth, Wyett, Wyitt, Wytt

WYBERT (English) battle-bright.

WYBORN (Scandinavian) war bear.

WYCK (Scandinavian) village.

WYCLIFF (English) white cliff; village near the cliff.
Wyckliffe, Wycliffe

WYLIE (English) charming.
Wiley, Wye, Wyley, Wyllie, Wyly

WYMAN (English) fighter, warrior.

WYMER (English) famous in battle.

WYN (Welsh) light skinned, white. (English) friend. A short form of Selwyn.
Win, Wyne, Wynn, Wynne

WYNDHAM (Scottish) village near the winding road.
Windham, Wynndham

WYNONO (Native American) first-born son.

WYTHE (English) willow tree.

XABAT (Basque) savior.

XAIVER (Basque) an alternate form of Xavier.
Xajavier, Xzaiver

XAN (Greek) a short form of Alexander.
Xane

XANDER (Greek) a short form of Alexander.
Xande, Xzander

XANTHUS (Latin) golden haired.
Xanthos

XARLES (Basque) a form of Charles

XAVIER (Arabic) bright. (Basque) owner of the new house. See also Exavier, Javier, Salvatore, Saverio. *Xabier, Xaiver, Xavaeir, Xaver, Xavian, Xaviar, Xavior, Xavon, Xavyer, Xever, Xizavier, Xxavier, Xzavier, Zavier*

XENOPHON (Greek) strange voice. *Xeno, Zennie*

XENOS (Greek) stranger; guest. *Zenos*

XERXES (Persian) ruler. History: a name used by many Persian emperors. *Zerk*

XIMENES (Spanish) a form of Simon. *Ximenez, Ximon, Ximun, Xymenes*

XYLON (Greek) forest.

XZAVIER (Basque) an alternate form of Xavier. *Xzavaier, Xzaver, Xzavion, Xzavior, Xzvaier*

YADID (Hebrew) friend; beloved. *Yedid*

YADON (Hebrew) he will judge. *Yadean, Yadin, Yadun*

YAEL (Hebrew) an alternate form of Jael.

YAFEU (Ibo) bold.

YAGIL (Hebrew) he will rejoice.

YAGO (Spanish) a form of James.

YAHTO (Lakota) blue.

YAHYA (Arabic) living. *Yahye*

YAIR (Hebrew) he will enlighten. *Yahir*

YAKECEN (Dene) sky song.

YAKEZ (Carrier) heaven.

YAKOV (Russian) a form of Jacob. *Yaacob, Yaacov, Yaakov, Yachov, Yacoub, Yacov, Yakob, Yashko*

YALE (German) productive. (English) old.

YAN, Yann (Russian) forms of John. *Yanichek, Yanick, Yanka, Yannick*

YANA (Native American) bear.

YANCY (Native American) Englishman, Yankee. *Yan, Yance, Yancey, Yanci, Yansey, Yansy, Yantsey, Yauncey, Yauncy, Yency*

YANICK, Yannick (Russian) familiar forms of Yan. *Yanic, Yanik, Yannic, Yannik, Yonic, Yonnik*

YANKA (Russian) a familiar form of John. *Yanikm*

YANNI (Greek) a form of John. *Ioannis, Yani, Yannakis, Yannis, Yanny, Yiannis, Yoni*

YANTON (Hebrew) an alternate form of Johnathon, Jonathon.

YAO (Ewe) born on Thursday.

YAPHET (Hebrew) an alternate form of Japheth. *Yapheth, Yefat, Yephat*

YARB (Gypsy) herb.

YARDAN (Arabic) king.

YARDEN (Hebrew) an alternate form of Jordan. Geography: another name for the Jordan River, which flows through Israel.

YARDLEY (English) enclosed meadow. *Lee, Yard, Yardlea, Yardlee, Yardleigh, Yardly*

YAROM (Hebrew) he will raise up. *Yarum*

YARON (Hebrew) he will sing; he will cry out. *Jaron, Yairon*

YASASHIKU (Japanese) gentle; polite.

YASH (Hindi) victorious; glory.

YASHA (Russian) a form of Jacob, James. *Yascha, Yashka, Yashko*

YASHWANT (Hindi) glorious.

YASIN (Arabic) prophet. Religion: another name for Muhammad. *Yasine, Yasseen, Yassin, Yassine, Yazen*

YASIR (Afghani) humble; takes it easy. (Arabic) wealthy. *Yasar, Yaser, Yashar, Yasser*

YASUO (Japanese) restful.

YATES (English) gates.
Yeats

YATIN (Hindi) ascetic.

YAVIN (Hebrew) he will understand.
Jabin

YAWO (Akan) born on Thursday.

YAZID (Arabic) his power will increase.
Yazeed, Yazide

YECHIEL (Hebrew) God lives.

YEDIDYA (Hebrew) an alternate form of Jedidiah. See also Didi.
Yadai, Yedidia, Yedidiah, Yido

YEGOR (Russian) a form of George. See also Egor, Igor.
Ygor

YEHOSHUA (Hebrew) an alternate form of Joshua.
Yeshua, Yeshuah, Yoshua, Y'shua, Yushua

YEHOYAKEM (Hebrew) an alternate form of Joachim, Joaquín.
Yakim, Yehayakim, Yokim, Yoyakim

YEHUDI (Hebrew) an alternate form of Judah.
Yechudi, Yechudit, Yehuda, Yehudah, Yehudit

YELUTCI (Moquelumnan) bear walking silently.

YEOMAN (English) attendent; retainer.
Yoeman, Youman

YEREMEY (Russian) a form of Jeremiah.
Yarema, Yaremka, Yeremy, Yerik

YERVANT (Armenian) king, ruler. History: an Armenian king.

YESHAYA (Hebrew) gift. See also Shai.

YESHURUN (Hebrew) right way.

YESKA (Russian) a form of Joseph.
Yesya

YESTIN (Welsh) just.

YEVGENYI (Russian) a form of Eugene.
Gena, Yevgeni, Yevgenij, Yevgeniy

YIGAL (Hebrew) he will redeem.
Yagel, Yigael

YIRMAYA (Hebrew) an alternate form of Jeremiah.
Yirmayahu

YISHAI (Hebrew) an alternate form of Jesse.

YISRAEL (Hebrew) an alternate form of Israel.
Yesarel, Yisroel

YITRO (Hebrew) an alternate form of Jethro.

YITZCHAK (Hebrew) an alternate form of Isaac. See also Itzak.
Yitzak, Yitzchok, Yitzhak

YNGVE (Swedish) ancestor; lord, master.

YO (Cambodian) honest.

YOAKIM (Slavic) a form of Jacob.
Yoackim

YOAN (German) an alternate form of Johan, Johann.
Yoann

YOAV (Hebrew) an alternate form of Joab.

YOCHANAN (Hebrew) an alternate form of John.
Yohanan

YOEL (Hebrew) an alternate form of Joel.

YOGESH (Hindi) ascetic. Religion: another name for the Hindu god Shiva.

YOHANCE (Hausa) a form of John.

YOHAN, Yohann (German) forms of Johan, Johann.
Yohane, Yohanes, Yohanne, Yohannes, Yohans, Yohn

YONAH (Hebrew) an alternate form of Jonah.
Yona, Yonas

YONATAN (Hebrew) an alternate form of Jonathan.
Yonathan, Yonathon, Yonaton, Yonattan

YONG (Chinese) courageous.
Yonge

YONG-SUN (Korean) dragon in the first position; courageous.

YONI (Greek) an alternate form of Yanni.
Yonis, Yonnas, Yonny, Yony

YOOFI (Akan) born on Friday.

YOOKU (Fante) born on Wednesday.

YORAM (Hebrew) high God.
Joram

YORGOS (Greek) an alternate form of George.
Yiorgos, Yorgo

YORK (English) boar estate; yew-tree estate.
Yorick, Yorke, Yorker, Yorkie, Yorrick

YORKOO (Fante) born on Thursday.

YOSEF (Hebrew) an alternate form of Joseph. See also Osip.
Yoceph, Yoosuf, Yoseff, Yoseph, Yosief, Yosif, Yosuf, Yosyf, Yousef, Yusif

YÓSHI (Japanese) adopted son.
Yoshiki, Yoshiuki

YOSHIYAHU (Hebrew) an alternate form of Josiah.
Yoshia, Yoshiah, Yoshiya, Yoshiyah, Yosiah

YOSKOLO (Moquelumnan) breaking off pinecones.

YOSU (Hebrew) an alternate form of Jesus.

YOTIMO (Moquelumnan) yellow jacket carrying food to its hive.

YOTTOKO (Native American) mud at the water's edge.

YOUNG (English) young.
Yung

YOUNG-JAE (Korean) pile of prosperity.

YOUNG-SOO (Korean) keeping the prosperity.

YOURI (Russian) an alternate form of Yuri.

YOUSEF (Yiddish) a form of Joseph.
Yousaf, Youseef, Yousef, Youseph, Yousif, Youssef, Yousseff, Yousuf

YOUSSEL (Yiddish) a familiar form of Joseph.
Yussel

YOV (Russian) a short form of Yoakim.

YOVANI (Slavic) an alternate form of Jovan.
Yovan, Yovanni, Yovanny, Yovany, Yovni

YOYI (Hebrew) a form of George.

YRJO (Finnish) a form of George.

YSIDRO (Greek) a short form of Isidore.

YU (Chinese) universe.
Yue

YUDELL (English) an alternate form of Udell.
Yudale, Yudel

YUKI (Japanese) snow.
Yukiko, Yukio, Yuuki

YUL (Mongolian) beyond the horizon.

YULE (English) born at Christmas.

YULI (Basque) youthful.

YUMA (Native American) son of a chief.

YUNUS (Turkish) a form of Jonah.

YURCEL (Turkish) sublime.

YURI (Russian, Ukrainian) a form of George. (Hebrew) a familiar form of Uriah.
Yehor, Youri, Yura, Yure, Yuric, Yurii, Yurij, Yurik, Yurko, Yurri, Yury, Yusha

YUSIF (Russian) a form of Joseph.
Yuseph, Yusof, Yussof, Yusup, Yuzef, Yuzep

YUSTYN (Russian) a form of Justin.
Yusts

YUSUF (Arabic, Swahili) a form of Joseph.
Yusef, Yusuff

YUTU (Moquelumnan) coyote out hunting.

YUVAL (Hebrew) rejoicing.

YVES (French) a form of Ivar, Ives.
Yvens, Yvon, Yyves

YVON (French) an alternate form of Ivar, Yves.
Ivon, Yuvon, Yvan, Yvonne

ZAC (Hebrew) a short form of Zachariah, Zachary.
Zacc

ZACARIAS (Portuguese, Spanish) a form of Zachariah.
Zacaria, Zacariah

ZACARY (Hebrew) an alternate form of Zachary.
Zac, Zacaras, Zacari, Zacariah, Zacarias, Zacarie, Zacarious, Zacery, Zacory, Zacrye

ZACCARY (Hebrew) an alternate form of Zachary.
Zac, Zaccaeus, Zaccari, Zaccaria, Zaccariah, Zaccary, Zaccea, Zaccharie, Zacchary, Zacchery, Zaccury

ZACCHEUS (Hebrew) innocent, pure.
Zacceus, Zacchaeus, Zacchious

ZACH (Hebrew) a short form of Zachariah, Zachary.

ZACHARI (Hebrew) an alternate form of Zachary.
Zacheri

ZACHARIA (Hebrew) an alternate form of Zachary.
Zacharya

ZACHARIAH (Hebrew) God remembered.
Zac, Zacarias, Zacarius, Zacary, Zaccary, Zach, Zacharias, Zachary, Zacharyah, Zachory, Zachury, Zack, Zakaria, Zako, Zaquero, Zecharia, Zechariah, Zecharya, Zeggery, Zeke, Zhachory

ZACHARIAS (German) a form of Zachariah.
Zacarías, Zacharais, Zachariaus, Zacharius, Zackarias, Zakarias, Zecharias, Zekarias

ZACHARIE (Hebrew) an alternate form of Zachary.
Zachare, Zacharee, Zachurie, Zecharie

ZACHARY (Hebrew) God remembered. A familiar form of Zachariah. History: Zachary Taylor was the twelfth U.S. president. See also Sachar, Sakeri.
Xachary, Zac, Zacary, Zaccary, Zach, Zacha, Zachaery, Zachaios, Zacharay, Zacharey,

Zachari, Zacharia, Zacharias, Zacharie, Zacharry, Zachaury, Zachery, Zachory, Zachrey, Zachry, Zachuery, Zachury, Zack, Zackary, Zackery, Zackory, Zakaria, Zakary, Zakery, Zakkary, Zechary, Zechery, Zeke

ZACHERY (Hebrew) an alternate form of Zachary.
Zacheray, Zacherey, Zacheria, Zacherias, Zacheriah, Zacherie, Zacherius, Zackery

ZACHORY (Hebrew) an alternate form of Zachary.

ZACHRY (Hebrew) an alternate form of Zachary.
Zachre, Zachrey, Zachri

ZACK (Hebrew) a short form of Zachariah, Zachary.
Zach, Zak, Zaks

ZACKARY (Hebrew) an alternate form of Zachary.
Zack, Zackari, Zacharia, Zackare, Zackaree, Zackariah, Zackarie, Zackery, Zackhary, Zackie, Zackree, Zackrey, Zackry

ZACKERY (Hebrew) an alternate form of Zachery.
Zackere, Zackeree, Zackerey, Zackeri, Zackeria, Zackeriah, Zackerie, Zackerry

ZACKORY (Hebrew) an alternate form of Zachary.
Zackoriah, Zackorie, Zacorey, Zacori, Zacory, Zacry, Zakory

ZADOK (Hebrew) a short form of Tzadok.
Zaddik, Zadik, Zadoc, Zaydok

ZADORNIN (Basque) Saturn.

ZAFIR (Arabic) victorious.
Zafar, Zafeer, Zafer, Zaffar

ZAHID (Arabic) self-denying, ascetic.
Zaheed

ZAHIR (Arabic) shining, bright.
Zahair, Zahar, Zaheer, Zahi, Zair, Zaire, Zayyir

ZAHUR (Swahili) flower.

ZAID (Arabic) increase, growth.
Zaied, Zaiid, Zayd

ZAIDE (Hebrew) older.

ZAIM (Arabic) brigadier general.

ZAIN (English) an alternate form of Zane.
Zaine

ZAKARIA (Hebrew) an alternate form of Zachariah.
Zakaraiya, Zakareeya, Zakareeyah, Zakariah, Zakariya, Zakeria, Zakeriah

ZAKARIYYA (Arabic) prophet. Religion: an Islamic prophet.

ZAKARY (Hebrew) an alternate form of Zachery.
Zak, Zakarai, Zakare, Zakaree, Zakari, Zakarias, Zakarie, Zakarius, Zakariye, Zake, Zakhar, Zaki, Zakir, Zakkai, Zako, Zakqary, Zakree, Zakri, Zakris, Zakry

ZAKERY (Hebrew) an alternate form of Zachary.
Zakeri, Zakerie, Zakiry

ZAKI (Arabic) bright; pure. (Hausa) lion.
Zakee, Zakia, Zakie, Zakiy, Zakki

ZAKIA (Swahili) intelligent.

ZAKKARY (Hebrew) an alternate form of Zachary.
Zakk, Zakkari, Zakkery, Zakkyre

ZAKO (Hungarian) a form of Zachariah.

ZALE (Greek) sea-strength.
Zayle

ZALMAI (Afghani) young.

ZALMAN (Yiddish) a form of Solomon.
Zaloman

ZAMIEL (German) a form of Samuel.
Zamal, Zamuel

ZAMIR (Hebrew) song; bird.
Zameer

ZAN (Italian) clown.
Zann, Zanni, Zannie, Zanny, Zhan

ZANDER (Greek) a short form of Alexander.
Zandore, Zandra, Zandrae, Zandy

ZANE (English) a form of John.
Zain, Zayne, Zhane

ZANIS (Latvian) an alternate form of Janis.
Zannis

ZANVIL (Hebrew) an alternate form of Samuel.
Zanwill

ZAQUAN (American) a combination of the prefix Za + Quan.
Zaquain, Zaquon, Zaqwan

ZAREB (African) protector.

ZARED (Hebrew) ambush.
Zaryd

ZAREK (Polish) may God protect the king.
Zarik, Zarrick, Zerek, Zerick, Zerric, Zerrick

ZAVIER (Arabic) an alternate form of Xavier.

Zavair, Zaverie, Zavery, Zavierre, Zavior, Zavyr, Zayvius, Zxavian

ZAYIT (Hebrew) olive.

ZAYNE (English) an alternate form of Zane.
Zayan, Zayin, Zayn

ZDENEK (Czech) follower of Saint Denis.

ZEB (Hebrew) a short form of Zebediah, Zebulon.
Zev

ZEBEDIAH (Hebrew) God's gift.
Zeb, Zebadia, Zebadiah, Zebedee, Zebedia, Zebidiah, Zedidiah

ZEBEDEE (Hebrew) a familiar form of Zebediah.
Zebadee

ZEBULON (Hebrew) exalted, honored; lofty house.
Zabulan, Zeb, Zebulan, Zebulen, Zebulin, Zebulun, Zebulyn, Zev, Zevulon, Zevulun, Zhebulen, Zubin

ZECHARIAH (Hebrew) an alternate form of Zachariah.
Zecharia, Zecharian, Zecheriah, Zechuriah, Zekariah, Zekarias, Zeke, Zekeria, Zekeriah, Zekerya

ZED (Hebrew) a short form of Zedekiah.

ZEDEKIAH (Hebrew) God is mighty and just.
Zed, Zedechiah, Zedekias, Zedikiah

ZEDIDIAH (Hebrew) an alternate form of Zebediah.

ZEEMAN (Dutch) seaman.

ZEÉV (Hebrew) wolf.
Zeévi, Zeff, Zif

ZEHEB (Turkish) gold.

ZEKE (Hebrew) a short form of Ezekiel, Zachariah, Zachary, Zechariah.

ZEKI (Turkish) clever, intelligent.
Zeky

ZELGAI (Afghani) heart.

ZELIG (Yiddish) a form of Selig.
Zeligman, Zelik

ZELIMIR (Slavic) wishes for peace.

ZEMAR (Afghani) lion.

ZEN (Japanese) religious. Religion: a form of Buddhism.

ZENDA (Czech) a form of Eugene.
Zhek

ZENO (Greek) cart; harness. History: a Greek philosopher.
Zenan, Zenas, Zenon, Zino, Zinon

ZEPHANIAH (Hebrew) treasured by God.
Zaph, Zaphania, Zeph, Zephan

ZEPHYR (Greek) west wind.
Zeferino, Zeffrey, Zephery, Zephire, Zephram, Zephran, Zephrin

ZERO (Arabic) empty, void.

ZEROUN (Armenian) wise and respected.

ZESHAWN (American) a combination of the prefix Ze + Shawn.
Zeshan, Zeshaun, Zeshon, Zishaan, Zishan, Zshawn

ZESIRO (Luganda) older of twins.

ZEUS (Greek) living. Mythology: chief god in the Greek pantheon who ruled from Mount Olympus.

ZEUSEF (Portuguese) a form of Joseph.

ZEV (Hebrew) a short form of Zebulon.

ZEVI (Hebrew) an alternate form of Tzvi.
Zhvie, Zhvy, Zvi

ZHEK (Russian) a short form of Evgeny.
Zhenechka, Zhenka, Zhenya

ZHÌXIN (Chinese) ambitious.
Zhi, Zhìhuán, Zhipeng, Zhi-yang, Zhìyuan

ZHUÀNG (Chinese) strong.

ZHORA (Russian) a form of George.
Zhorik, Zhorka, Zhorz, Zhurka

ZIA (Hebrew) trembling; moving.
Ziah

ZIGFRID (Latvian, Russian) a form of Siegfried.
Zegfrido, Zigfrids, Ziggy, Zygfryd, Zygi

ZIGGY (American) a familiar form of Siegfried, Sigmund.
Ziggie

ZIGOR (Basque) punishment.

ZILABA (Luganda) born while sick.
Zilabamuzale

ZIKOMO (Ngoni) thank you.

ZIMRA (Hebrew) song of praise.
Zemora, Zimrat, Zimri, Zimria, Zimriah, Zimriya

ZIMRAAN (Arabic) praise.

ZINAN (Japanese) second son.

ZINDEL (Yiddish) a form of Alexander.
Zindil, Zunde

ZION (Hebrew) sign, omen; excellent. Bible: name used to refer to the land of Israel and to the Hebrew people.
Tzion, Zyon

ZISKIND (Yiddish) sweet child.

ZIV (Hebrew) shining brightly. (Slavic) a short form of Ziven.

ZIVEN (Slavic) vigorous, lively.
Zev, Ziv, Zivka, Zivon

ZIYAD (Arabic) increase.
Zayd, Ziyaad

ZLATAN (Czech) gold.
Zlatek, Zlatko

ZOHAR (Hebrew) bright light.
Zohair

ZOLLIE, Zolly (Hebrew) alternate forms of Solly.
Zoilo

ZOLTÁN (Hungarian) life.

ZORBA (Greek) live each day.

ZORION (Basque) a form of Orion.
Zoran, Zoren, Zorian, Zoron, Zorrine, Zorrion

ZORYA (Slavic) star; dawn.

ZOTIKOS (Greek) saintly, holy. Religion: a recent saint in the Greek Orthodox church.

ZOTOM (Kiowa) a biter.

ZSIGMOND (Hungarian) a form of Sigmund.
Ziggy, Zigmund, Zsiga

ZUBERI (Swahili) strong.

ZUBIN (Hebrew) a short form of Zebulon.
Zubeen

ZUHAYR (Arabic) brilliant, shining.
Zyhair, Zuheer

ZUKA (Shona) sixpence.

ZURIEL (Hebrew) God is my rock.

ZYGMUNT (Polish) a form of Sigmund.